The First Tractate

The Second Tractate: On The Division Of The Orb Of The Signs, And Their Nature, And How They Are Ordered And Disposed, And Why There Are Exactly Twelve, And Not More, Or Less, And How They Got Their Names, And Things Connected To These Matters

GUIDO BONATTI'S

BOOK OF ASTRONOMY

PART ONE

I

On The Utility Of Astronomy In General

The soul, which is the most noble thing which is found in man, for it gives the body essence and perfection, and its food is the most noble in respect of the body's food, just as it is most noble in respect of the body. She rejoices in the intellectual wealth, which relies on knowledge (namely philosophy), and this delights the soul and it rejoices in it. That in which she delights is its food, since with this food (knowledge) there is a part of truth, and the mind loves truth. And it is not possible to grasp this truth in a more vigorous and plentiful manner than through astronomy.

And there is nothing else besides the first philosophy in which the mind delights to the same extent as it does with astronomy, or astrology. Through it we know and recognise impassable, unalterable and immutable creatures of another essence, which are the supercelestial bodies. And through these creatures we can approach an understanding of The Creator, and know as much about Him as the human mind can attain to, and we can perceive His being as impassable and unalterable. And since the aforementioned bodies are from what is most noble and perfect (which nobody will deny), their forms are also the most noble and perfect forms (namely spheres), from which will not be found a beginning, a middle (excluding the centre) or an end. And in such a manner so too are their operations the most noble and perfect of all the operations in this world; even if the professions of physicians is one of the more noble, in fact the most noble of all the professions on this terrestrial world, nevertheless the works and duties of the stars are the most noble, surpassing all other professions and operations. For a perfect cause induces a perfect effect.

The doctor concerns himself with the inferior bodies, corruptible things, alterable things and the like; the astrologer however, concerns himself with the operations of the supercelestial bodies which are not corrupted or changed; for they themselves act on the inferior corruptible bodies, which the doctor concerns himself with). But in these supercelestial bodies there is nothing corporeal which acts, and they and do not suffer, and will not suffer, up until the day that God wills it (from which it is said that neither the angels or the Son but the Father alone…).

And so all inferior bodies (namely those made of elements) consist of four elements, all of which are corruptible: and of this truth there is no doubt. The celestial bodies however consist of another essence, which is different to these four elements, namely a fifth essence which is incorruptible and impassable. For if they were of the other four elements they would undergo alterations and suffering(namely increase and diminution), just as happens to the inferior corruptible bodies. And from this it is said that the super celestial bodies are of a fifth essence, or material. And (just as it is seemed to certain men) these bodies are moved by a natural motion, and it is also seemed to certain men that they are moved by a voluntary motion: since they are moveable but not changeable by an altering motion; and they are bright, and round, and spherical, which is the foremost and noblest of all shapes.

And the changes, alterations and conversions, are those which are made by the motions of the stars surrounding, moving, and corrupting the elements from their borders, and their unrelenting revolution (which has not ended and will never end, except in the manner which has been said above). In philosophy it is said that the motions of the earth are joined to the world of heaven - however this is to be understood metaphorically, not in an absolute sense; and from this mutations, changes, and alterations are made in this corruptible world. Because the solidity of the celestial world reaches the elements and surrounds them (namely surrounding fire; and fire surrounds air, and the air the water and the manifest earth, and water the earth); and from this comes the corruption of the elements and also that of the individuals of the elements.

II

What The Stars Impress Upon The Inferior Bodies And What Changes Are Made In This World, Made By Their Motions

First principles ought not to be proven, but supposed, since all other beginnings can be traced back to the first principle which is before all things. I certainly do not believe that there is any doubt that the movements of the surrounding heavens change fire and air, and these change the other elements (water and earth) and all animal and vegetable life and so on which have their being under the circle of the Moon (and existing in them), and all things which are susceptible to change or alteration. Because the Sun and air operate on all terrestrial individuals and their individual parts, wherefore the changes of the earth do not happen without the changes of the Sun through the signs - namely the four seasons (which are spring, summer, autumn and winter), which appear manifestly in the fruits and foliage of the trees and also in the animals, which, according to the seasons of the year are moved to generate their individual species, especially so in spring more so than in any other time of the year; and also in the fig trees and shrubbery of vegetable things, on which fruits appear.

And we also see the earth heated, chilled, dried, and moistened from the daily rotations of the heavens. And we also see in certain times of the year an excess of water and other changes, which come to be according to the circular revolutions of the acting heavens; from which occur the alterations of all things placed on the earth, and especially in the waxing and waning of the Moons light, since she is closer to the earth than all the other stars, and her impressions are felt more. And similarly from the heat of the Sun, which is sensed above all the others; even if other planets sometimes increase his efficacy, other times decrease it in accordance with their nature and their applications to him and his to them. The impressions of the other stars are not felt as much, but their effects appear in longer spans of time. The effects of the Sun appear more manifestly in the fruits and foliage of the trees and plants, and also in those things which are sown and planted; even if they operate in other things, they cannot appear openly to the masses, but are only known to those skilled in this science. Other stars act with the planets on the inferior things by means of motion and generation.

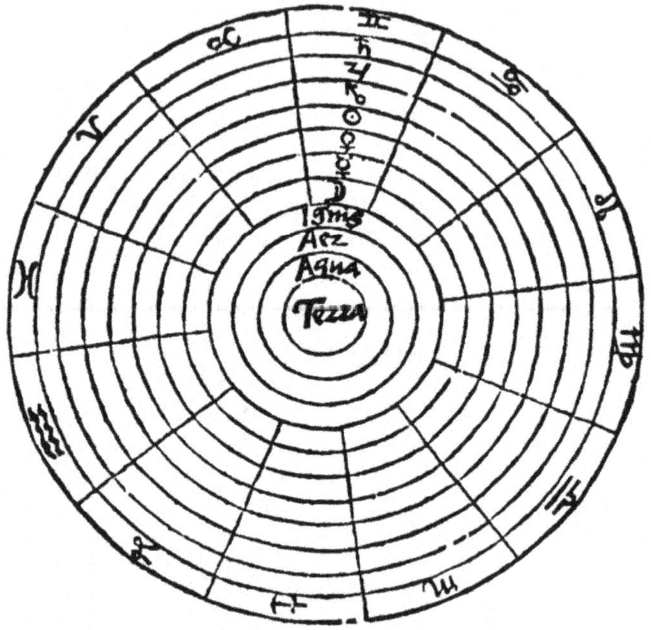

III

How Knowledge Of The Judgments Of The Stars Is Reached And How It Can Be Excused

Concerning this science it is certain that not only can we have cognition of the present, but we can also recollect the past and look into the future, both of kinds and individuals and even of the two parts of the world. For through the subject of this science their benefits and effects can be known, even if certain begrudgers might say that astronomy is nothing. It is certain that astronomy is one of the four mathematical sciences, in fact it is the more noble of them; and if it is more noble, it has more noble effects, and greater utility, and (just as will be said in its own place in what follows) the subject of the other mathematical sciences are under the subject of astronomy. The subject of arithmetic is numbers, geometry measure, music harmony, and (just as it is said by others) these are more noble because of their demonstrations. The subject of astrology however is the qualities of the motions of the supercelestial bodies. And the astrologer knows the qualities of every motion of every supercelestial body. And if he knows the qualities of the motions, he knows the quality of the impressions, and what are their significations, and everything which comes to be on earth in accordance with the natural order, and in the other elements by the motions of the super celestial bodies - which no one seems to doubt, unless he is an idiot or a fool! And this is known by the astrologer due to the aforementioned reason. Therefore all which is present, and which has been up until now, and which will be, can be known by the astrologer when he knows the qualities of the motions which were, which are, and which will be, and in which times they will be, and what will occur as a result of them.

IV

Against Those Who Say That Knowledge Of The Stars Cannot Be Known By Anyone

Those who say this science is to be scorned, have stumbled upon some reasons (frivolous ones) to deem it worthy of condemnation.

Their first point is that the knowledge of the stars cannot be completely known. They say that the empyrean heaven is entirely a star, and that it imprints and influences just as the other stars influence (just as certain fools in tunics affirm); and the astrologer does not care to mention this star. It appears therefore that the knowledge of the stars cannot be known in full.

It appears to me that there is one way to briefly respond to these arguments, namely that they do not prove it is so, and therefore their contradiction means nothing. Even if, however, we grant them their point, it appears that we can respond again in this manner: that although their arguments may have the appearance of truth, they do not have the reality of truth. For if the ninth heaven is entirely a star (as they say it is), it is not in motion (as has been said). Moreover, all of its parts are of equal power, and one part cannot have more ability to effect things than another, and so it is necessary that it imprints or influences equally and everywhere with all of its parts, because its parts are individually and all coequal and equally powerful, not differing at all in light, number, nor virtue, nor moving from place to place, nor to any place. However the parts of the other heavens differ in light, virtue, and number, since the greater virtue of each one is gathered in different parts. The splendour or light of each heaven of the seven planets is gathered in one sensible body. The light or splendour of the eighth heaven is gathered in diverse places, or sensible bodies to different parts of it; for diverse operations were assigned to them from the first cause: and so they can imprint many and diverse significations, following from how the First Architect constituted them from their formation. In impressions the ninth heaven is one and the same, the other heavens are not the same, but diverse (just as I will to you in its own place and time). And without them generation and corruption could not be made. The impressions of the sensible heavens are perceived according to their diversity. And even if impressions or influences (different or the same) were received from the ninth heaven, they still could not influence or imprint on the inferior things in one uniform manner, but in diverse ways and differently. It is not possible for the ninth heaven to influence or imprint on the inferior things, unless it is mediated by the sensible heavens, whose impressions are manifest. Indeed the impressions of the ninth heaven are hidden, and cannot be made manifest unless they are diversified - like water or wind, when it enters through the straits and narrows and it becomes more powerful, and its virtue is more apparent and perceptible; and like water which runs through narrow channels of mills operates more strongly, and has more strength than that water which flows through a wide riverbed. And just as the light, or the splendour of the Moon, when it enters through a narrow passage and meets with a horse with a suture on his back; and should it pierce the suture completely, the horse would die; however if he stands out in the light of the Moon in such a way that he is covered by it completely (whereby the light strikes the suture and the rest of his body equally), neither the horse, nor his suture shall be harmed by the Moon, and the horse will not die from this - to which the physicians will testify.

Moreover, there is nobody who condemns astrology, only certain individuals who proclaim themselves to be Theologians (if that is what they are). These men say that astrologers do not know the whole of astronomy, therefore they cannot make judgements from it nor predict the future, since the stars are almost innumerable and astrologers do not care to mention them all, except for 1022 of them (besides the planets).

To which we can respond, that astrologers are permitted not to name all of the stars, as this would be extremely long winded, however they still use them all, since they use the twelve signs, under which practically all stars are comprehended. It is also possible to say to them that they do not know the whole of theology, but nevertheless they preach it every day: and so if they can preach based on their small knowledge of theology, much more strongly can astrologers be permitted to judge based on their vast knowledge of astronomy. It is not possible to know so little about astronomy that it will not appear great when compared to that which can be known about theology. The First Cause is greater with respect to the heavens than the heavens are with respect to a mustard seed; and astrologers know much more about the heavens than they do about a mustard seed; and the theologians know less about God with respect to Himself than they do about a mustard seed. It stands therefore that astrologers know more about astronomy than theologians know about theology; therefore it is all the more possible for an astrologer to judge, than it is for a theologian to preach.

For astrologers can know as much about astronomy as is possible for the stars and sensible heavens to imprint and signify. The empyrean heaven (or the imperceptible heaven), is of no concern to the astrologer, nor to judgements, nor to the movements of the stars, nor what comes to pass from them. This heaven, since it is immutable and immobile, is not an agent; since the stars do not act on the inferior corruptible bodies because they are stars, or because they are supercelestial, they act because they have motion and are moved.

V

Against Those Who Say That The Planets Or Other Stars Do Not Signify Anything Regarding Generation Or Corruption, Or Regarding Anything That Is On This Side Of The Moon

It is another occasion regarding those who say that the planets or other stars do not signify anything over generation or corruption, or over anything which comes to be by generation or corruption on this side of the Moon. The response to these individuals is that all philosophers agree with this point: which is that inferiors are ruled by superiors. Not that the stars rule men, or horses, or chariots, or ships, or other corruptible instruments in the same manner in which these things are ruled by corruptible men (as the effect is not fitting of the dignity of its cause), but the stars rule these things by the movement, corruption and alteration of the elements, and from this is effected generation and corruption, and individuals are made out of corrupted elements; until these individual things are corrupted and returned to elements, and so they are annihilated, as they say.

VI

Against Those Who Say That The Planets Only Have Signification Over Universal Things

It is another occasion to respond to those who say that the planets only have signification over universal things, and not particular ones. These individuals can be responded to in the following manner: that all individual things consisting of elements are composed of the four elements, and they are constituted of elements. Nor can they constitute something else, unless they are corrupted by the planets (not excluding the other stars moving themselves around with incessant and whirling motion). And if the planets signify species universally (as they say they do, and which is the truth) it is necessary that they signify individuals constituting the species; and not only individuals, but also parts of individuals, like the hands, feet, head and so on. And the planets through the conversion of elements, their change, and their alteration, make individuals grow, increase, age, become ill etc. on account of the corruption and conversion of the elements; and again to be corrupted and return to elements.

VII

Against Those Who Say That The Stars Only Signify Two Things: The Necessary And The Impossible, But Not The Possible

It is another occasion to respond to those who say that the stars only signify two things: the necessary and the possible; but not the possible. The necessary, like fire being hot; the impossible, like a flying horse; but not the possible, such as a man moving or writing. To whom we can respond to in the following manner. Evidently there are necessary things, and there are impossible things. For certain things are necessary, such as the heavens turning through their own nature; certain things are impossible, such as fire being cold through its own nature; and certain things are possible, such as water being hot by accident, and not through its own nature. And it is possible for a man to speak through his own nature, or to speak now, to have spoken up until now, and to speak in the future. However, even if he has spoken at two times, the present and the past, it is not necessary that he will speak in the future.

For what is necessary or natural for a given species is what belongs to every individual of that species. For example, if it is necessary and natural for a species to fly, the possibility of being able to fly will be found in each individual of that species. What is possible for a species is possible for every individual of that species.

From this it appears that while it is possible for a man to swim, it is not necessary for a man to swim, nor is it impossible for a man to swim. From which we will see that certain men swim, while others do not swim. It is possible for this man when he is born, to be a king, and it is possible that this same man will not be a king. However, if he was not a king, it would be impossible for him to be a king. But between necessary and impossible, the middle is possible; and between the necessary and the possible, the middle is judgement. Therefore the possible exists, and the judgments of the stars are true and useful; and therefore they are natural: whereby they are not caused by accident, but from that which is natural to themselves. From this, judgements are not to be held as being worthless, as the begrudgers say; and so they have spoken badly who said that the possible does not exist: since we see clearly that the possible does exist. And so too do the works and judgements of the stars.

It is also necessary that when it rains, there are some clouds. It is impossible that when there are no clouds, it rains perceptibly. However it is not necessary that it always rains when there are clouds, nor is it impossible that rain can come from any cloud; but it is possible that from this cloud it might rain, and it is possible that from this cloud there might not be rain. Therefore the possible exists, and so do the judgements of the stars. Wherefore through the motions and dispositions of the supercelestial bodies, and the variations of the air, you can know from which cloud there ought to be rain and from which cloud there ought not to be rain, just as will be said in the Tractate on the Mutations of the Air.

Similarly when someone has something in their mouth, it is possible that they will eat it and swallow it, and it is possible that they will not eat and not swallow it: and this possible thing has regards to both the necessary and the impossible. Because if it is possible that he will eat it, and he eats it, the possible has now been made necessary; because it has come into act, and the possibility is been taken away from him, and effected, and arrives at the definition of necessary. Similarly if something is possible, but does not pass into action, it becomes impossible, and arrives at the definition of the impossible, and possibility is taken. And so the stars and the elements signify the possible, and not just the necessary and the impossible. It is fitting therefore, for the astrologer to know the truth, and to predict the future.

VIII

Against Those Who Speak Against The Judgements Of Astronomy And Who Condemn It; Due To Not Knowing Its Dignity, And Because It Is Not Lucrative

It is another occasion to respond to those who say that the judgements of astronomy (if they exist) are of no worth because they are not monetarily useful; and themselves knowing how to figure out when and how to make money, proclaim the science to be nothing. The appropriate response to this, in my opinion, is that they do not care about the wheat, but only the chaff: for knowledge is to money as the wheat is to the chaff. Those who say that money is to be preferred to the knowledge of the judgments of the stars, appear to show that nothing has as much nobility amongst them as the accumulation of wealth does (which can very easily be lost), saying that he who abounds in wealth, lacks nothing, and that it does him no harm if he is not wise. They say that wealth suffers stupidity and the fortunate fool stands in no need of knowledge; not considering their own error, and not recognising their own false (or rather void) proofs. All matters which are subject to proof are proven by things similar to them in every way, just as knowledge is proven by knowledge, and substance by substance. And I most often see that the masses do not commend anything except the accumulation of money; which is not surprising, considering they sometimes see certain men (both religious and others who believe), wise in astrology and medicine and other sciences, give heed to this - whose opinions, if they are well considered, in my opinion could very well be checked. Knowledge, with respect to money, is most noble, while money, with respect to knowledge, is most base. For money can be given to the wise, the foolish, the good, the bad, the base, and others who are considered worthless; and as it were, are worthless. Nor is there any base or foolish man who has such a quantity of money that it can make him anything other than a guardian of money for someone else. He was not given money on account of his strength, as we see many strong men in need of money, and other strong men who abound in wealth; and some weak men in need of money and other weak men who abound in wealth. The reason for this will be stated below in the section about judgements, or possibly the Tractate on Nativities.

There is nothing which can ennoble man without the support of others, except for wisdom. Magnanimity cannot completely ennoble man without money, as the magnanimous man is not able to perfectly demonstrate his magnanimity unless he has what he can give to others. The wealthy man cannot show his riches without magnanimity and the will to do good, as his heart will not allow him to perform good deeds, and so his money will be a buried treasure. Knowledge is the only thing which can ennoble man without the support of another, and so knowledge prevails over all other accidents of fortune.

And if there is no other reason for a man to be praised, he will be praised on account of his knowledge; for all other accidents may be deprived of him, apart from his knowledge. And this knowledge cannot be adopted by someone on account of strength, nor on account of weakness, nor on account of birth, nor on account of wealth. However riches can be adapted on account of knowledge, although the true sage does not care for such temporal things, since he can take nothing from these things, besides the corruption of being subjected to them. And this is the reason why the wise man does not care for these things, as he is not praised on account of wisdom, intellect, discernment, or the understanding of things which make man deserving of nobility. For man is more worthy than the other animals, and this would not have been so if it were not for his wisdom, philosophy, and understanding of those things which are not understood by other animals; and through the instrument of reason and the rationality which are in man. And this is wisdom and the understanding of things; and this consists more in the understanding of what was, what is, and what will be.

Knowledge is an accident of such a nature, that the more it increased in man, the further it removes him from the other animals; and makes man more dignified and nobler than the beasts on account of this - which is the soul of knowledge, and discernment, and the understanding of things which were, which are, and which will be. And the less wisdom a man has, the more remote he is from rationality, and the closer he is to the beasts.

This (becoming more noble and dignified than the other animals), cannot happen to man, save through wisdom and philosophy; and these things will only be allotted to him through literature. They cannot be attained through accumulation of wealth, although from wealth it is possible for him to live in peace, however this is not living in the sense of true living, as Seneca says

"Leisure without literature is death; a tomb for a living man".

Whence, unless a man is wise, he is not more worthy than the rest of the animals. This is so because all the animals participate with man in everything, except for wisdom. They all live, they all eat, some drink, some eat and drink, they generate, are born, grow, are increased, grow old, and die - just as men do. And so through wisdom, understanding, and intellect, man is made more worthy than all other animals. And if wisdom is what makes men deserving of nobility, it is necessary that wisdom which is more noble, more worthy, and higher, will make man more noble, more deserving, loftier, and more intelligent. And this wisdom is knowledge of the future, which cannot be known except through the science of the stars; therefore the science of the stars is more noble than the other sciences, apart from the first philosophy; and even this cannot be known, nor perfectly attained, only though the science of the stars.

IX

Against Those Who Say That Knowledge Of The Stars Is Not Useful, But Rather Damning, As It Induces Sadness And Anxiety In Those Who Have Foreknowledge Of Future Events, Whence They Suffer Before These Impediments Take Place

It is another occasion to respond to those who say that the judgements of the stars are not valuable or useful, but rather are harmful. Even if this science is true, and that the judgements are true, still it is more harmful than useful. For if some grave event is to befall someone is foreseen from afar, it will send forth fear and sorrow before the time of suffering, up until the evil itself occurs; and nevertheless afterwards it will be necessary for him to suffer, grieve and lament. Nor can the astrologer avert this grave event which is set to happen according to the stars, and even if he could, it would not lessen the anger and anxiety which arises in him whom the evil is set to befall until the hour of its occurrence.

To whom we can respond in our familiar way - that they do not know what they are saying, for it seems that they are ignorant of how worthy and how useful this wisdom is: because if they knew, they would not say the things that they say. For if some evil (which is going to happen, according to the stars) were to threaten a man, and he sees this evil in advance, he would see how evil it is, and what kind of evil it is, and he would oppose himself to it. Ptolemy says in his Centiloquium ,

"The best astrologer will be able to avert many evil things which are going to come about according to the stars".

Accidents which are yet to take place are either universal, or particular. Universals such as winter, summer, heat, cold, distempeances of the air (such as rain, snow, and hail), and pestilences such as mortality, hunger, sterility; an abundance of earthborn things, and so on. Of these universals, certain things are known only by the wise, other things are not only known by the wise, but also by the masses. The wise know these things through their own efforts, specifically through this science of the stars. Laymen however, and others who are inexperienced in this science, know that certain universal things are set to occur, through long standing experiences which they have seen in their own time, and heard from those who went before them, and who saw such things in their own time.

For in the climes where the horizon is turned to the north, they saw that it becomes colder when the Sun enters Gemini, and that this lasts until he enters Virgo; even if the time or effect may vary somewhat. Whence in summer when they feel the heat, they say that in such a time there it will be cold, there will be snow, rain, winds, and so on. They then secure themselves grain, wine, wood, clothes, and other necessities which they can ward off adversity in those times; and those who do not have houses, apply themselves to building them so that they can flee from rain, snows, and other adverse events to come; which if they had not foreseen them, they wouldn't have secured the aforementioned necessities, and this could have been the cause of their demise. Therefore it stands that foreknowledge of the future has value.

Likewise, they knew from the above-mentioned experiences in which times they ought to sow seeds, so that they could harvest them in the future; whence they could lead their lives according to the diverse kinds of different things. They also planted trees in such times that they were accustomed to seeing them live, according to the diverse kinds of plants. For every kind of seed or plant is not planted in every season of the year equally, nor in every region according to the same seasons of that year.

Things are planted one way in Spain, another in England, another in Lombardy, another in

Romania, another in Apulia, another in Asia, another in Aethiopia, another in the Alps, another in the plains, another in winter, another in summer; and other things are planted in one season rather than another, each one in whichever season which is suitable for it, and in which it is hoped future utility will be gained from them: and all this according to the diverse regions and diverse positions of locations. All this is foreseen by those experienced in locations in such a manner that they are rarely wrong. Therefore foreknowledge of the future is useful.

However another tunic clad fool may rise up and say that these things did not occur from the impressions of the planets - whence there is no arguing with them, because they do not consider that every region and every site in a region grows warm according to the approach of the Sun, and grows cold according to the receding of the Sun, and on account of it being too close, a region dries up, and on account of it being too far away, a region becomes too cold. From which they know that they cannot sow whatever seeds they want, nor plant whatever crops they want, on account of the excessive heat or cold. And they do these things since they know in advance that things will happen this way, and because they have seen these things through long experience and practice. And if they did not know these things, they would not know in which seasons they ought to do the aforementioned things; and thus they would lose their money and waste their labour.

Regarding other universal things, which occur universally, in all regions, and in all climes, some are possible to avoid, others are not. However the ones which cannot be avoided, can be changed or lessened in such a way that it is useful for one to know of them beforehand. These things cannot be known in any way other than by experience in this science, although certain things may be known by experienced doctors. Hippocrates says in his Aphorisms

"*Those things which are foreknown by astrologers, cannot be foreseen by the commoners*".

There are many of these, such as pestilence, famine, penury, infirmity, mortality (as much for the rational men as the brutes), rain, snow, hail, and excessive cold or heat. He with foreknowledge can guard himself against all of these things, and so foreknowledge is useful and not harmful. An unknown evil cannot be avoided, while a known evil can be avoided, if it is foreseen, especially from far off. For if someone foresees that grain will be expensive in the future, he can buy it when it is cheap, and reserve it up until a time when it will be useful to him. This method can also be employed for wine, oil, and so on.

If he sees that there will be mortality in a certain climate or region, he can remove himself, withdrawing from that region and travelling to another which is not threatened by plague in that year. If he foresees illness in a certain region, he can oppose himself to the cause threatening the illness, or similarly he may travel to a region where he can live safely. And so the foreknowledge of these matters is the reason for the evasion of these matters, and also the health of him who foresees it.

Similarly if one foresees rain in the future, it will be possible for him to flee to shelter and to a place where the rain won't drench him. Similarly if someone is going to make a journey by sea and foresees wind in the future, or a storm of some kind, he will be able to enter port before the advent of the storm, where he will be safe and not suffer a shipwreck; or he could postpone his departure until the time of doubt had passed. Similarly if a question concerning an ill person should be made, or if the astrologer knew the time of the beginning of the illness, he would be able to foresee if the ill person ought to escape the illness, or if he will die. For if he foresees death, he will be able to predict death, and even if the ill person did not believe he would die, he could confess his sins, and Our Lord Jesus Christ would provide for him in the life to come, that is the imperceptible life. He could also make a will, set his house and affairs in order, and settle with his creditors and debtors, which if he fails to do, may lead to danger for those he leaves behind, and those who ought to inherit his goods. His goods may also fall into the hands of those who he did not want to inherit them, rather than coming into the possession of those who he had intended, which may lead to him being reproached and spoken ill of after death: for sometimes men esteem one heir more than another; sometimes a male heir more than a female heir; sometimes his natural hair more than his lawful heir. And similarly for him who was setting out to sea, if he had not received a prediction from an astrologer, a future storm may have been the cause of his danger, and so it is good and useful to know the future in advance, and evil and harmful to remain ignorant. Therefore these (and many more) reasons can be assigned, as to why it is most useful to know matters of the future in advance.

Similarly, foreknowledge is very useful for certain particular matters: such as if someone's nativity is known, or if he has a general question, or one on a particular matter which he wishes to know about, you (or any other astrologer) can see what ought to happen to him regarding the matter in question. Whence if evil threatens, he will be able to evade it; or if wealth is promised, he will be able to capture it - and so it would be useful to him. And if you were to see in one of his revolutions of the year that he is threatened by a certain danger, he will be able to avoid it; and if he is to fall ill, you may predict this, and also the cause of the illness, and he can oppose himself to it, and convert his nature to the contrary of the cause. Furthermore you could see what type of illness ought to arise; and whence if it did come (or if it doesn't approach) or if it does approach, it won't be as harmful as it would have been. Whereas if precautions were not taken, he might have been overcome by such an illness, so that it might have been the cause of his death. The illness also might have become chronic, and he might have died in the end. If there is to be death, the astrologer can predict the man's death for him in that year, and he may set his affairs in order, as has been said above; and he couldn't be seized by a sudden death unexpectedly without having both his spiritual and temporal affairs in order. Should there be an illness, or a death of a brother, or of children, or of a father, or a mother, whichever person it is will be able to oppose themselves to this. Should there be a death of an animal, either big or small, he will be able to remove them before the onset of the plague, whence he will not suffer any damage from them: and understand similarly concerning the significations of every house.

Similarly, should anyone ask of you, fearing lest his enemy inflict an injury on him, you will be able to predict for him regarding whether his enemy will make an attack against him or not, and then he will be able to fortify himself with his friends, arms, and so on, so that he may drive his enemy away from him. In this case, if he did not take precautions, he might have been killed by his enemy or otherwise treated evilly.

These, and many other particular things can be assigned which can befall men, and are useful to know in advance; and which are not harmful to know in advance (as some wish to claim foreknowledge of such things is). Likewise skilled doctors, when they see a corruption of the air in one season of the year (through any mutation of the air from one condition to another, through some notable winds, or through a great deal of rain, or on any other occasion), they predict a plague in the future, such as a quartan fever, acute fevers, headaches, earaches, eye inflammation, and similar things. From these predictions men can prepare themselves to drive out these future illnesses by means of drugs, diet, and contrary causes for expelling the above mentioned illnesses. If they did not take precautions however, they might have fallen ill or contracted the plague, or similar things. For this reason physicians (and even the commoners), since they have seen in their time that the heat increases in the summer, they oppose themselves to the hot humours in the spring by drawing them out by using medicines to purge them, so that the heat of the summer does not increase the sharpness of the hot humours, lest it be a cause of a fatal illness. And so the foreknowledge of future accidents is most useful.

And so, just as a skilled doctor can preserve the body against the threat of the aforementioned illnesses, so can the astrologer avert many horrible future events which are signified to occur by the stars; which if they were not foreseen, would cause many harmful things to befall men. And so it is made manifestly clear that that the knowledge of the future is supremely useful and in no way harmful. Whence those who wish to pretend that they don't see the truth, can know manifestly that just as astrologers can foresee future accidents, so too can they know how these dangers may be avoided.

For, foreknowledge is useful in two ways. One is that since a man knows he is set to meet with some adversity, he may either avoid it completely (or in part), or effectively diminish it. The second is if it were a useful event which caused joy and elation for the one who it was set to occur to, he would rejoice from the hour he knew he was to achieve a matter which he strives for, right up until the time of its achievement. And if he did not foresee that he was set to achieve this, the matter in question would have caused him sorrow, anxiety, and fatigue; and he would have fatigued his friends, and expended his goods in order to achieve the matter in question until he had achieved that which he desired.

However some will object to this, saying that foreknowledge of a matter will induce sorrow or lamentation after the attainment of the matter, due to not being able to hope for more once it is attained. To whom it is to be said that this is far removed from the truth. For if this is true, that after someone obtains an object of their desire, upon the fulfilment of his desire he is overcome with grief - it is not appropriate for anyone to enjoy delightful things: because these things which delight man do not last forever. Still man is not saddened after the attainment of such things, but rather his mind is at peace because he has attained the thing which he sought. For if it was true (that man was saddened after attaining what he wished for), delightful things should not be enjoyed by anyone. Man would not rejoice in the embrace of a beautiful woman, nor in conviviality, nor in beautiful objects, nor in beautiful clothes, nor in music, nor in dignities, nor in anything in which his nature delights - since he will not delight in these things forever. The perfection of joy however is when the mind is at peace and satiated with what it has attained; however before attaining it, there is no joy, only the hope of fulfilling the desire for the matter in question. Hope and joy differ, just as fear and sorrow, since fear and hope come from that which is potential, while sorrow and joy come from that which is in act.

X

Against Those Who Say The Judgements Of The Stars Are Of No Worth, Nor Elections, Saying That It Can Be Elected For An Enemy Just As It Can Be For Him For Whom It Is Elected

It is another occasion for those who say that the judgements of the stars are of no worth, nor are elections which are made by astrologers according to astronomy of any worth. It is not surprising that they say these things, since they do not see the truth, and in a certain way, what they say seems similar to the truth (and this condemnation appears to as it were, comprehend the others, and prevail over all said previously), and it doesn't seem, and neither do they believe, that it can be contradicted or resisted; but rather it appears that it is almost impossible that things could be otherwise than they say.

For they say that if you make an election for one army you will say to them "If you set out at such an hour and such a sign is rising, you will prevail". However if the enemy moves his army at the same hour, under the same Ascendant, who will prevail? You can say to him "He who is stronger and has more men" He will respond "both of them are equally strong, and have an equal number of men, and their knights and infantry are equally capable. Who will prevail?" You will say "Whoever leads his army more wisely" They respond "Both lead their armies with equal wisdom, who will prevail?" You say "He who was born at night". They respond "Both were born at night, who will prevail?" You will say "The army that goes into battle first" They respond "Both enter battle simultaneously, who will prevail?". You say "Whoever moves his men from the east facing west, or he who moves his men from the north facing the south". And he will then say, which is almost an impossibility "If both armies move themselves from the east towards the west, or from the north towards the south, who will prevail?" You will then say that he is a fool and you ought not to speak to him, for it is impossible for two opposing armies to move themselves from one and the same place at one and the same time; that there will be some difference of orientality, occidentality, or one will be further north or south than the other.

However he will, in the manner of a fool or critic, posit that both armies move themselves from the east, or the west, or the north, or the south, (this does not however seem possible). And it should be said to them that they posit something unseen and unheard of, that two opposing armies will hold fast in one place when one begins to move against the other. This is as impossible as it is for the heavens to fall. However posit to them that if the heavens will fall, where will the stars remain? And if the heavens fell, would the earth not be submerged? If it is posited that asses can fly, the vulture doesn't lose his ability to fly.

However, in order that they cannot say that you failed in your response, you can respond to them in such a manner that they will not have anything else to ask, and that you will cut off all ways of questioning, condemning, and reproaching. And you will be able to respond to them in this manner by saying that whoever has the Part of Fortune in his direction will prevail; and whoever has his back to the west or the parts more closely adjacent to it, and his face to the east will succumb; or he who has his back to the south or the parts more closely adjacent to it, and his face to the north. And he will prevail who has his back to the east or the parts more closely adjacent to it and his face to the west; or his back to the north and his face to the south, or the parts adjacent to it. And in this manner all ways of the reproachers and maledictors have been cut off and removed. Should it be said again that the Part of Fortune will be on the side of he who holds his back to the south or the west, say that whoever has the Part of Fortune on their side will emerge victorious, and so will their objections (which only have appearance and not reality) cease.

Some fool may rise up speaking irrationally asking why you, an astrologer who ought to know all future events, allow anything bad to happen to yourself. To which we will respond that such people count among their judgements all chance events which occur in near imperceptible spaces of time, such as a man getting a thorn in his foot, or tripping over, and other such things. Of such things, there is no art, as judgements are only concerned with matters which can be deliberated before they occur. These events, which due to the swiftness of fortune one is not permitted to deliberate on, are left to the industry or caution of the wise; and are not to be considered by art, nor by nature; which come about by accident, according to these foolish men.

XI

Against Those Who Say Generally That Astrology Is Nothing; To Demonstrate That It Has Existence, And To Demonstrate What It Does

I said that I was going to speak about the judgements of astronomy and about those things which seem to pertain to judgements, and about certain things which I said to you in the beginning of this work. It now seems fitting for me to tell you what astrology is, according to how the philosophers defined it ;and to demonstrate to those men who say that it is nothing, and to make manifestly clear that astrology is something, and that it is useful, true, natural and good. For nothing natural can be found which can lawfully said to be bad, useless, false or deceitful. Astronomy, as certain philosophers define it, is the rule of the stars. A rule is rightly ordered, and manifestly declares that which is true according to its own truth. It is not from a rule that we take truth, but from truth that the rule is born. A lawyer however, even if he doesn't change his opinion, says "The rule is the matter that is". Briefly he says that it is not that justice is taken from the rule, but that the law which is the rule, is taken from justice.

Certain men, not far removed from these opinions, define the matter as such: "Astronomy is the science by which understanding is given not only of the present but also of the past and the future". It is also defined in another way, according to its two parts, or species: the contemplative and the active - which are Astrology and Astronomy.

I will tell you how these two parts differ: Astrology, which is its contemplative part, or species, is the science of moveable magnitudes which inquires by a certain method into the course of the stars, and their figures around each other and around the earth. This part (namely Astrology), itself has three parts.

The first of which is concerned with the number and the figure of the celestial bodies; their order in the universe, their quantities, positions and proportions and the quantities of their distances between each other.

The second part is concerned with the motions of the supercelestials; how many there are, and that all of their motions are circular, and which of them are common to all stars, and which of them are particular, and how many kinds of motions each of them have, and toward which directions they are moved - which are six, namely forwards, backwards, (these are called direct and retrograde) then there is upwards, downwards, rightwards and leftwards. There are also another six, however these might seem to be of consideration in astrology; they are generation and corruption, increase and decrease, alteration, and change according to place. Certain men have said that alteration is not a motion - since it (and changes like it) happens according to aspects and conjunctions.

The third part inquires as to what parts of the earth are inhabited and uninhabited, and as to the dispositions of the seven climes, and the differences of the lengths of day and night in different regions.

XII

What Astronomy Is (Which Is The Active Part Of The Science)

Astronomy is the second part of this science, namely the active part; even if once in a while (in fact, oftentimes) the names of the two parts are used interchangeably. Following from this, the question may be asked, "What is Astronomy? What are its species? What are its duties? What is its end? What are its instruments? Who is its artisan? Why is it called by such a name? And what order should it be taught in?"

Its definition is given above, others however define it in a different way, saying "Astronomy is the science in which the courses of the stars and their dispositions are described according to those who utilise them, and describes the times according to the above mentioned method".

Moreover, what each one of the parts is, is understood with its definition or its quiddity. For the genus is that according to which one makes a fitting response to a question posed to him by judging according to the position of the planets and the signs, and the nature of these things. There are however many other sciences of judging questions posed to them, such as geomancy which is practiced in the earth, and in several other ways which are suited to it. Hydromancy in water, Aeromancy in air, Pryomancy in fire, Chiromancy in the hands, as is testified by Aristotle in his book "*History of Animals*". Also Spatulamancy, which is practiced on the shoulder blades of certain animals. And there are many other sciences of augury besides these, such as the voice of certain animals, or the songs of certain birds, or the wailing, chattering, or encountering of other thing, and many more which could be listed, on which we will say no more for the time being.

But his art, namely Astronomy, with all its parts and kinds, is more worthy than the rest, since it announces from the dispositions of the most noble supercelestial bodies on the past, present and future of all things on the earth, to which all philosophers will agree. Whence Alphabarius says in reference to this science

"*Astronomy is the science of the significations of the stars, namely what the stars signify regarding things past, present and future*".

Its material, or subject, is magnitude, as has been said.

The parts of this part, or species, are four. The first part deals with the position and form of the world and the celestial circles. The second part deals with the courses or motions of the planets and other stars. The third deals with the rising and setting of the signs. The fourth part then deals with the eclipses of the Sun and the Moon and the other planets.

In these, or regarding these parts almost the whole virtue of Astronomy is to be found. Its species are generally two; the first of those being number or computation, insofar as it depends on the first science of mathematics (namely arithmetic), which is prior to all other theoretical sciences, since all other mathematical sciences stand in need of it, but it does not stand in need of them.

The second species of Astronomy is judgement. Computation or number revolves around the definitions or cognitions of tables. Judgements however revolve around the understanding of times, places, signs, planets, and the positions and aspects of planets, and similar things which arise from these.

Its duty is to observe the courses of the planets and other stars, their conjunctions and aspects, the angles, the succeedents, and the signs cadent from the angles, and their effects following the above method.

Its end, or its utility is to determine the truth regarding the present, past and future, by inspecting the aforementioned matters and the inquiry discussed.

The instruments of this science are many, namely the astrolabe, quadrant, the armilla suspensoria, the other armillae, the planisphere, the curvisphericum, the statua plosica, and other such instruments.

The artist of this science is known as an Astronomer, who practices this art named

Astronomy, and who observes the law of the stars by means of the interpretation above.

I will now tell you why astronomy is called by such a name. It is because this name is composed of "*astris*" (stars) and "*norma*" (which is a rule) - from which Astronomy is the rule of the stars, or the practice of the stars, or the working of the stars. The difference between Astronomy and Astrology is this: astrology is (according to the truth of the matter) for intellectual or theoretical knowledge. Astronomy however (according to those who utilise it), is pursued for the purpose of its effects, or practical knowledge.

In regards to what order this science should be taught, certain men say that it ought to be taught before the other mathematical sciences because it is more noble. Others say that it should be taught after Arithmetic, because it is in need of calculation. Others say that it should be taught after arithmetic and geometry, because it is in need of calculation and measure. However to me it seems that it ought to be taught after all other mathematical sciences. It is to be taught after music just as much as it is to be taught after arithmetic and geometry, since it is in need of harmony as well as calculation and measurement.

XIII

That This Science Ought Not To Be Condemned, Due To Its Use By The Holy Fathers

This art ought not to be condemned, but rather it is deserving of commendation, since the Holy Fathers from antiquity utilised it. From this we can say that those who condemn this science do evil, especially those who follow in the footsteps of Abraham, or are his followers. For Abraham instructed the Egyptians (and others of that time who wished to utilise astronomy) how to use it exceptionally: especially Atalanta, who was superior to all others in this science to such an extent that he was almost seen as a god. And from this it is said that "Atlas held up the heavens", on account of him knowing more than anyone else of his time about the supercelestial bodies. Indeed even the Lord Himself said to His Apostles "*Let us go back to Judaea*" and they said to Him, "Now the Jews sought to stone you, and again you go there?" and He, responding, said "Are there not 12 hours in a day?". And so it is as if He said that one hour is good, and another hour is bad: that in the bad hour they would have ill will towards Him, however when this hour had passed, and the good hour had arrived, then He knew that their ill will had gone from their hearts - He wanted to elect himself an hour in which they would not harm Him.

And from this we see that He utilised elections, and did not condemn astrology, as certain prejudiced men and detractors do today. Even if the above example manifestly demonstrated that much utility and good things can follow from the science and judgements of the stars, as much in foreknowledge of things as in other matters; nevertheless there are still some stupid fools, among whose ranks is that hypocrite John of Vicenza (of the Order of Preachers) to be counted, who said that astrology is not an art or a science, but a sort of application discovered by those who applied it. To which I think the best response is to say that there are fools, they err, and they will perish in their foolishness and errors. For it is clear to all that Astrology is a science and one of the seven liberal arts. And even if our response to these men is brief, it does not seem right to me to omit proving that astrology is an art and a theoretical science, using sufficient and clear reasons, although the order may seem inverted.

XIV

To Demonstrate That Astronomy Is An Art And One Of The Four Mathematical Ones, And A Theoretical Science

That astrology is a science is proven by evident reason in this way. It is a science of moveable magnitudes, which through an investigation by reason, defines the motion of the celestial bodies according to the threefold course of time. Or, astrology is the science which investigates the courses of the stars and their figures and their arrangements with regard to themselves, and with regard to the earth by calculation. Therefore from this, astrology is, by definition, a science. Moreover the word "*astrology*" is said to be from "*astron*", which is a star and "*logos*", which is a statement, knowledge, or computation of the stars. And so, by this etymology or interpretation of the name, astrology is a science. The same thing can be proven by another method: everything which is of such a kind that it is from true, first, prior things, and so on, is a science; however Astrology has a substantial genus, both accidental and essential, which differentiates it from other sciences: therefore it is a science.

Moreover, anything which is a collection of precepts tended towards one end is an art or a science: and astrology is one such thing. Therefore it is an art, or a science, which St. Augustine proves clearly enough, saying "an art is the precepts which give a certain way and method to speaking and acting". For all precepts of astronomy tend to one end, that is to knowing, or considering past, present, and future things; and it is in these precepts which the whole purpose of astrology consists. Whence Seneca:

"To remember the past, consider the present, foresee the future".

None of these things can be rightly observed unless by the astrologer, who considers all of these things, and who alone can know them.

Moreover, if astrology (or astronomy), was not an art or a science, that famous phrase which is universally proclaimed - that there are seven liberal arts, would be destroyed. It is not that there would only be six remaining, but rather that there would be none: for by the same reasoning that astronomy is not considered an art, the remaining six must also be stripped of their status, something which is most inappropriate and truly horrible. And since it is said to be one fourth of the quadrivium, if astronomy is not an art or science, the whole quadrivium will be destroyed. And if the quadrivium is destroyed so is mathematics, and if mathematics is destroyed so is theory; since mathematics is, (as the philosopher attests), one-third of theory. And if there is no theory, there is no philosophy: which is an impudent, ill-tempered, and absolutely preposterous thing to say. Therefore astronomy is by necessity a science, and whoever destroys astronomy, destroys science, just as whoever destroys first principles would destroy wisdom, as Aristotle testifies in the second book of his *"Metaphysics"*. Such people who wish to destroy science are not to be disputed with, as they are worse than the beasts.

Besides Aristotle, Ptolemy, Japhar, Ahaydimon, Albumasar, Messala, Almetus, Alfraganus, Thebit, Irgis, Ahomar, Dorotheus, Alkindi, Albenait, Astaphaz, Almansor, Haly, Alboali and many other sages have written on this science and taught that astrology is a science. It does not have similarity to truth if it is not a science, as so many great men have called it. Moreover, everything which posits something though a cause or through an effect, posits science - as Aristotle affirms in "Posterior Analytics". The astrologer demonstrates the eclipse by a cause, namely by interposition, and the interposition by the eclipse; on account of this, and many other reasons, it is clearly proven that astrology is a Science.

THE SECOND TRACTATE

On The Division Of The Orb Of The Signs, And Their Nature, And How They Are Ordered And Disposed, And Why There Are Exactly Twelve, And Not More, Or Less, And How They Got Their Names, And Things Connected To These Matters

I shall speak following in the footsteps of our venerable predecessors about things which seem to be useful for this work, remembering their opinions, namely those of: Ptolemy, Hermes, Japhar, Thebit, Alchabitius, Alcaiat, Alchindi, Alenzedegoz, Messala, Adila, Jergis, Albenait, Aardimon, Arestali, and others who studied this science: and in addition to these what I myself deem useful, according to God granting me grace in composition and restoring these things to my memory.

I

On The Division Of The Orb Of Signs, And That The Signs Are Only Twelve, And That They Are Not More Or Less

You should know that the circle of signs is divided in twelve equal divisions, which can be called signs; the first of which is Aries, the second Taurus, the third Gemini, the fourth Cancer, the fifth Leo, the sixth Virgo, the seventh Libra, the eighth Scorpio, the ninth Sagittarius, the tenth Capricorn, the eleventh Aquarius, the twelfth Pisces.

However, someone may ask why there are only twelve signs. There are many reasons which can be assigned as to why there are only twelve signs, and not more, or less. One of which (although it is not very efficacious) is that the duodenary is more perfect than practically all of the other number-unities which do not exceed it; and the multiplications out of which the duodenary arises are multiplied in its own parts. For it receives in itself more ordered divisions than any other number. This arises out of the multiplication of the ternary by the quaternary, the quaternary by the ternary, the binary by the senary and the senary by the binary. And by the same parts it is divided in as many ways.

And there is another reason, no less efficacious than the one above, according from what was said by Arastellus, Albumasar, and Aaydimon, which no other philosophers have dared to contradict: namely that all elemental things are composed out of the four elements - namely from fire, air, water and earth: and the individual elemental things and the parts of these individuals, all consist of the above four elements. And in each of these individuals there are three things: namely, the beginning, the middle, and the end - whence four multiplied by three gives us twelve.

The signs are not corrupted, but they corrupt the elements. And there are four elements which are corrupted by the signs and the planets, namely from their ceaseless whirling circular motions. Wherefore the elements could not be otherwise corrupted (as much as they are in themselves), were they not corrupted by the whirling circular motion of the stars. For the whirling circular motion of the stars around the elements corrupts them, and they mutually corrupt one another; and the more noble ones (or the more active) corrupts the less noble (or the more passive). On account of which they are complected with each other, which is the cause of the generation of the individuals of every species.

The signs were divided according to the number of the four elements, since through the four elements (which are of four diverse natures, or qualities), the number of the signs is perceived to be twelve. For one of the elements is hot and dry - this beng fire, another is hot and moist - this being air, another is cold and moist - this being water, and another is cold and dry - this being air.

And even if it may be said that the elements are complected, nevertheless each one of them still has only one peculiar property. For the property of fire is heat, the property of air is moistness; the property of water is coldness; and the property of earth is dryness. Whence it is necessary that the signs should be in accordance with the four diversities imprinted on the inferiors (namely hot and dry, hot and moist, cold and moist, and cold and dry), and so three of the signs are said to be fiery, namely Aries, Leo and Sagittarius. Another three of these are said to be earthy, these are Taurus, Virgo and Capricorn. Another three of these are said to be airy, these being Gemini, Libra and Aquarius. And another three are then said to be watery, these are Cancer, Scorpio and Pisces.

And so it is found that there are twelve signs, not more and not less. It is not possible for there to be more, as each of them acts in the four elements, and each one of them acts in the element assigned to it according to the three states of being mentioned above (namely the beginning, middle, and end). From which, the signs act on the elements according to the three states of being the signs in the elements, and there are four elements, and so it is necessary that there are only twelve signs, not more, and not less. Wherefore since Aries, Leo and Sagittarius are fiery; Taurus, Virgo and Capricorn are earthy; Gemini Libra and Aquarius are airy; and Cancer, Scorpio and Pisces are watery

II

How The Signs Act On The Elements And In Which Element Each Of The Signs Act

It was said in the previous chapter that the signs act in the elements. Now in this chapter it will be stated in which element each sign acts, and in what way. For Aries, Leo and Sagittarius, since they are all fiery, act in the fire element, but in diverse ways.

On Aries

Aries acts in the fire element by imprinting temperate heat and dryness in it, from which is caused the beginning of the natural motion of the individual each species. Namely to cause one animal to join with another to generate an individual of the species from individuals of the same species, so that the species may be preserved by succession. Wherefore the species is not preserved by individuals over a long space of time, as individuals are deficient in respect of duration of time. And so the species will be destroyed and lost, unless it is saved by succession. And so Aries is the beginning of the natural motion similar to that which makes seeds germinate, and which makes trees flower, and make foliage and produce fruit, and which makes herbs and germinated seeds be born, to increase, and multiply; and all invigorating things to be increased and to grow. And this is the first state of being through which the fiery signs are said to act, and they even act in the fire element.

On Leo

Leo acts in fire by inserting intemperate heat and dryness into it, in such a way that from this intemperance it makes the beginning of the natural motion to impede the fruits and foliage of trees and herbs, and to make these things decline towards destruction, wherefore they mature, and maturation is a form of destruction; and so that there are few seeds with germinate at this time, and few animating things which grow or increase, and few animals lacking free will are moved towards the augmentation of their own species or towards its preservation, but rather certain animals begin to be hidden, and appear almost to be destroyed. When Leo performs its work in the fire element, the fall of seeds and their devastation is effected, many fruits of the trees mature and rot, and other similar things are done from the impressions of Leo in the fire element. And this is according to the state of being through which the fiery signs act on the fire element.

On Sagittarius

Sagittarius acts in the fire element by imprinting an intemperate level of heat and dryness into it; in fact he acts towards the destruction of seeds and herbs, and towards the completion of the falling and destruction of the foliage of the trees which fall to the ground in winter; and to the harm of many animals, and the concealing and destruction of many species, with them not daring to appear above the ground. And this is the third state of being through which the fiery signs act on the fire element.

And these are the three states of being through which the signs act on the elements. Everything comes to be according to this order insofar as it is through the natural significations of the signs and planets; and for the reason that the superior bodies act in the elements, all changes take place, allowing for some variance considering different times and places, and even if natural consideration may appear otherwise than this. Nevertheless if rightly considered, each will be the same as described.

On Earth Signs, And First ,On Taurus

Taurus, Virgo, and Capricorn, which are the earth signs, act in the earth element, albeit in diverse ways. Taurus acts in the earth element by imprinting coldness and dryness into it, in such a manner that it only is a slight, or sometimes non-existent impediment; so that in this temperateness the generation of many sensible things happens, both of species, and of the growth and increase of animating things and the like.

On Virgo

Virgo acts on the earth element by imprinting a less temperate coldness and dryness which is closer to destruction into it; so that from its action comes a natural motion that makes animating things suffer detriment and diminution, and retards herbs, and so that the leaves fall from the trees and dry out. Still it is not so intemperately cold that even if some things dry out and are destroyed, other things are still generated, and certain seeds germinate, and certain herbs are newly born and grow, and the like.

On Capricorn

Capricorn acts in the earth element by imprinting a distemperate, destructive, and mortifying coldness and dryness into it. Things are not generated easily at this time, and animals, if they are generated at this time, are few in number, and most of these are domestic animals, on account of their domesticated nourishment and way of life.

Nor is nature moved so that herbs are born, or trees flower or bring forth foliage (unless it happens fortuitously), nor do seeds germinate, and similar things.

On Air Signs, And First, On Gemini

Gemini, Libra, and Aquarius act in the air element, albeit in diverse ways. For Gemini acts in the air element by imprinting temperate heat and moisture into it, strengthening nature and all odours and odiferous breezes, and strengthening natural heat and the temperateness of the air in which individuals of species rejoice, and causing certain seeds to germinate, and the like.

On Libra

Libra acts on the air element by inserting intempe rate heat and moistur e into it, condens ing and thickeni ng it, and causing it to be mixed and

harmful to the individual species, seeds, herbs and the foliage of trees and their fruits, and making it vaporous with dense and harmful vapours and similar things.

On Aquarius

Aquarius acts on the air element by inserting distemperate, harmful, and impeding heat and moisture into it, and making it extinguished, and destroying individuals of species, so that much of the harm which animals, seeds and other vegetables receive from the air, and these situations and these impressions come about from the impressions of Aquarius on the air, and the like.

On Water Signs, And First, On Cancer

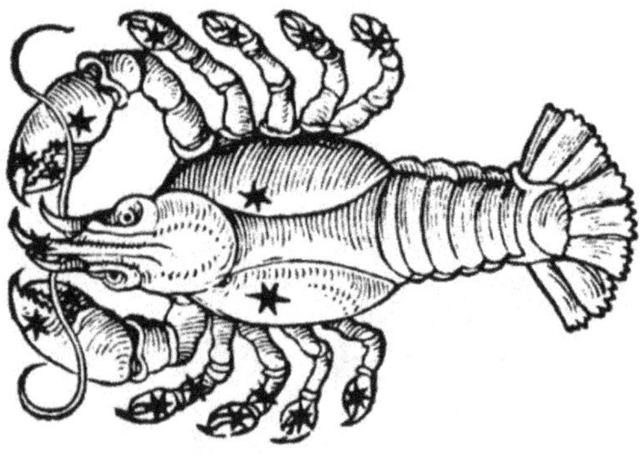

Cancer, Scorpio and Pisces, which are the water signs, act in the water element, albeit in diverse ways; with Cancer acting on the water element by imprinting a temperate coldness and moisture into it, through which is made a motion of nature that gives a sweetness and nourishment by which animals live and are nourished, and all invigorating things are nourished, and the like.

On Scorpio

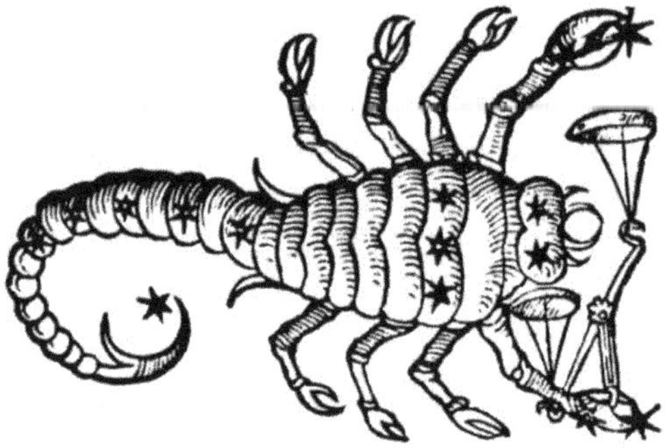

Scorpio acts on the water element by inserting an intemperate moisture and coldness in it, through which is made a motion of nature more apt for corruption than for nourishment or preservation, on account of the corruption and saltiness which the action of Scorpio inserts into the water, only able to strengthen very few things, and providing little in the way of nourishment.

On Pisces

Pisces acts on the water element by inserting an intemperate and harmful coldness in it, through which is made a motion of nature which causes the extinguishing and destruction of animals, seeds, and almost all animating things; on account of the corruption, bitterness and foulness which the action of Pisces inserts into the water.

Summary

This the reason why there are twelve signs and not more or less, since there are four elements, and the signs act on the elements in three ways: with nourishment and augmentation according to the first state of being; then being neither wholly nourishing nor wholly destructive according to the second state of being; while destruction follows from the third state of being. And these three contain the beginning, the middle, and the end in themselves.

And every three signs act in one of the four elements, but the three fire signs act in fire according to the three ways mentioned above, the three air signs act in air according to the three ways mentioned above, and the three earth signs act in earth according to the three ways mentioned above.

And due to this Ptolemy, Aaydimon, Astaphan, Arastellus, Albumasar, and the other philosophers agreed that there were four triplicities of the signs, since every three signs of the same nature act in the element assigned to that nature (namely fire on fire, air on air, water on water, and earth on earth); and from this it is not possible for there to be more or less.

There is another reason why there were only twelve signs; namely that the Zodiac consists of four quarters. Of which two are northern and two are southern; and from which one quarter is given to fire signs, one to air signs, one to water signs, and one to earth signs; of which quarters each contains three signs, in accordance with the natures of the four elements outlined above.

III

Why The Elements Are Disposed And Ordered As They Are

It has been stated in the preceding chapter in which element every sign acts, and in what way. Now in this chapter it will be explained why the elements were ordered and disposed in the manner in which they are: namely that fire is above (immediately bordering the Moon in the concavity of the globe), with air immediately under it, then water, then earth.

IV

To Demonstrate Why There Are Four Elements, And Not More, And Not Less

It was stated in the previous chapter how the elements are ordered or disposed. In this chapter it will be explained why there are only four elements, and not more, or less: even if there is more on this to be said, and that more on this has been said, all of which may not seem to be relevant to the astrologer. Nevertheless it is fitting for us to mention these things due to the relevance of the elements in our work.

The elements can only be four, not more, and not less, since all elemental bodies consist of four elements, and have in them four qualities (those being heat, dryness, coldness, and moisture), and four accidents happen to them (namely generation, durability or conservation, corruption, and destruction). Along these lines through heat something is generated most effectively, through dryness it endures most effectively, through moisture it is corrupted most effectively, and through coldness it is destroyed most effectively. Understand this well. These four states of being are in every, and around every elemental thing. For they get heat from fire, moisture from the air, coldness from water, and dryness from earth. Whence, since the accidents of elemental things cannot be found, and do not exist, other than as being four, and are drawn from the elements, it is necessary that the elements are four in number not more, and not less.

The elements, insofar as they are simple and pure in their spheres, have simple qualities ruling in them; with heat ruling in fire, humidity in air, coldness in water and dryness in earth. However, according to them being connected and mixed together, they have composite qualities between each other: namely fire having heat and dryness, air having heat and moisture, water having coldness and moisture, and earth having coldness and dryness.

V

Why The Signs Were Ordered Or Disposed In The Manner In Which They Are

It has been said in preceding chapters why the signs are twelve in number, and not more or less, and why the elements are four in number. However it remains to be said in this chapter why the signs are ordered, or disposed, in the manner in which they are. The order, or disposition, of the signs begins from the fire signs (as has been said by Aaydimon and Albumasar). And fire signs were put at the beginning, then earth signs, then air signs, then water signs. However you might ask why didn't the sages order the signs according to the order of the elements, beginning from fire, followed by air, then water, then earth, just as the elements are successively placed in their own order? The reasons which moved the sages to order the signs in this manner were numerous. One of which was that the elements (as was said) receive corruption and alteration from the motions and continual, ceaseless revolutions of the signs and the heavens; and from this corruption and alteration come the four accidental qualities which befall the elemental bodies: namely generation, preservation, corruption and destruction.

And since generation is more noble than the other qualities of the elemental things, the sages began the order of signs from those by which generation (or the movement of nature towards generation) happens - those being fire signs.

And the quality which is most noble after generation is durability, or conservation, and this comes to be from the signs through which a motion of nature to conservation or durability comes to be (insofar as corruptible things may receive durability) - and these signs are the earth signs.

And the quality which is ignoble, and follows from durability, is corruption; and this comes to be from the signs through which nature is moved towards corruption - and these are air signs.

And an even more ignoble, in fact the worst quality, which comes after corruption, is destruction; and this comes to be through the signs by which nature is moved towards destruction - and these are water signs.

There is another reason why the order begins from fire signs and finishes with water signs; which is that heat and cold are agents, while dryness and moisture are patients; and since heat is the stronger agent (signifying generation), it was more deserving of being placed first before the other agents. Similarly since dryness is the stronger of the patients, it was justifiably placed before the other passive qualities. And since generation precedes duration, the signs signifying generation were placed before the signs signifying duration. And since corruption precedes destruction, the signs signifying corruption were placed before the signs signifying destruction. And just as generation is the beginning of everything which can be generated and ended, the signs signifying destruction were posited last (these being water signs).

Moreover, fire signs were placed in the beginning due to heat predominating in fire, through which (heat) vivification (which is the most noble of all things) comes to be.

And earth signs were posited as following immediately from fire signs on account of the affinity they have with fire signs based on the dryness which predominates in them.

And the water signs were placed last, as they would be placed directly opposite the fire signs, just as they are directly opposite to them in nature.

And air signs were placed before water signs (immediately before them) on account of the affinity which they have on account of their moistness, and so that the two active qualities would be posited in the extremes, with the two passive qualities in between.

These are the reasons which moved the wise men of this profession to order the signs in the manner in which they did, namely placing the fire signs first, followed by earth, then air, then finally water. And from the fire signs they placed Aries first, from the earth signs they placed Taurus first, from the air signs they placed Gemini first, and from the water signs they placed Cancer first, on account of the reasons assigned above.

VI

Why The Denomination Of The Signs Begins From Aries, And Not From Any Other Sign

It has been said in the preceding chapter why the signs were ordered in the way they are. In this chapter it will be explained why the denomination of the signs begins from Aries and not from any other sign, when the heaven is a spherical body, and all spheres lack a beginning, and anything that lacks a beginning lacks an end. And since it lacks a beginning and an end, it also lacks a middle centre (this being excluded in bodily things).

There are many reasons, one of which was that the denomination of the signs began from Aries because the circle of the signs intersects the circle of the equator of the day at the beginning of Aries and at its opposite point, not at a right angle, but obliquely. From this six signs are northern and six are southern, as will be discussed more broadly elsewhere. And that part which is northern is stronger than that part which is southern, since when the Sun leaves Pisces it enters into Aries, Aries being the first northern sign; and the northern part is stronger and more noble than the southern. And that this is true, does not need to be proven (even though it can be proven completely), since all proclaim this, and none contradict it.. And therefore the denomination of the signs begins from Aries, since the stronger part of the Zodiac begins from Aries.

Another Reason Why The Denomination Of The Signs Begins From Aries

Another reason is that when the Sun enters Aries the days begin to get longer than the nights; and since increase is a noble thing, it seemed concordant to the wise men of this art that the beginning of the denomination of the signs was from the sign which this increase begins.

Another Reason Why The Denomination Of The Signs Begins From Aries

Another reason is that since the four qualities (which are hotness and coldness, dryness and humidity) are simple, and since they are simple they do not increase or decrease; but when they are composite (that is hot and moist, cold and dry, hot and dry, and cold and moist), then certain ones signify an effect and increase, while others signify corruption and diminution. Whence it was more apt to begin from Aries than from any other sign: since when the Sun enters Aries things begin to be effected and increase; and since effect and increase are noble things, and friendly to nature; and defect and diminution are ignoble and inimical to nature, it merited beginning the denomination of the signs from Aries, because at this time things grow tender, and this is similar to youth, which is the most potent part of life, and so this is the most potent time of year, when the above mentioned things take place. Since the Sun then recedes from the equator of the day and approaches the northern regions, and causes heat to act on the moisture which had existed from the preceding winter. And then nature is moved to the generation and increase of things, and the herbs grow, and the trees bring forth branches which flower, and produce fruit, and many seeds germinate; and these things do not happen in other times of the year, unless fortuitously. Therefore it merited beginning the denomination of the signs from Aries more so than any other sign.

VII

Why The Signs Were Named These Names

It has been stated above why the denomination of the signs begins from Aries. Now it is to be explained why the signs were named as they are. The reasons are numerous, one of which is that in these places which are called signs, there are stars so disposed and ordered that if a line is drawn from one to another, such a figure will result that is in accordance with the sign in question. And it is said that Ptolemy travelled so far south that he was under the equator, and stood there long enough to see all of these things.

There is another reason as to why the signs are called such names, that is because when the Sun enters Aries the heat is increased, due to the Sun beginning to move away from the equinoctial line and approaches the zenith of the northern regions; and is fortified, in accordance with how "The Ram" (Aries) is said to have power with respect to the strength of the other animals.

From here the heat is increased and it is made stronger, more so than when the Sun was in Aries, and it is then likened to the nature of "The Bull" (Taurus), since the bull is a stronger animal than the ram, and the declination of the Sun is further from the equator than it was in Aries, and so too is it closer to the zenith of the northern regions than it was in Aries.

Then the Sun enters Gemini, and that sign is called "The Twins" since the heat is now doubled and duplicated beyond what it was at first, and now the Sun's declination is at its furthest from the equator, and its closest point to the highest summit.

Then the Sun begins to return towards the equator, and it is the said to have entered "The Crab" (Cancer), since the crab is an animal which moves backwards; whence just as a crab is said to sometimes move backwards, and other times move forwards, so too when the Sun is at its point of furthest elongation from the equinoctial line, and begins to move back towards the equinoctial line; he too is said to move backwards like the crab.

Then when the Sun leaves Cancer it enters Leo, and is said to be in "*The Lion*" because the heat increases, and is made stronger, sharper, and more unyielding on account of the impurity of the air, and since it now lacks moisture; just as the lion is a strong, harsh, and unyielding animal. And so it was very apt to name the sign after this animal.

Then there is a remission of heat, and there is no longer an increase of things, nor an ordained generation (besides the germination of certain seeds), and this sign is called Virgo, since "The Virgin" is a humble and sterile animal, from which everything tends to diminution, and almost to sterility.

Then the Sun enters "The Scales" (Libra), where the days are equal to the nights, and there is a remission of heat, and an equality between heat and cold is brought into effect, from which now the cold somewhat begins to gain power, and all things are in a state of equality at this time.

Then the Sun enters "The Scorpion" (Scorpio), and the cold increases beyond the heat, and things become cold at one time, warm at another; he air is made distemperate, rain falls, and vicious illnesses are generated, and pestilences, and death bearing things in the manner of poisons and the like. And from this, the sign was named after the poisonous animal, the Scorpion.

Then the cold increases so that it is manifestly greater than the heat, and the Sun is now said to have entered "The Archer" (Sagittarius), where mutations of the air occur, and the air declines in temperature significantly, sending forth winds carrying hard frost, snow and ice, almost like an arrow wounding animal and vegetable life.

Then the coldness increases further over the heat, as if the hotness was put to sleep; and the air becomes frigidly distemperate and melancholic, and a great amount of snow, ice coldness and so on is brought forth. From this, since "The Goat" (Capricorn) is a cold, dry, and melancholic animal, the sign is named after this creature. And at this point the Sun is at its furthest southerly declination from the equator.

Then the Sun begins to return towards the equator, and now the coldness begins to diminish somewhat, with rain sometimes arriving in place of the snow, and the air is made more moist, from which the sign of "*The Water-Bearer*" (Aquarius) is named; after the disposition of the air which thrives at this time.

Then the Sun enters Pisces, and this sign is named after the fish, which is an aquatic animal; since at this time rain abounds more so than at any other time of the year, lest a greater amount should occur at some other time by accident. And if there is snow, frost or ice at this time, it is more rapidly changed into water than at any other time of the winter.

THE SECOND PART OF THE SECOND TRACTATE

On The Nature Of The Essential Circle

I

On The Division Of The Orb Of Signs Into Twelve Signs And Of Every Sign Into Thirty Degrees, And Every Degree Into Sixty Minutes, And Every Minute Into Sixty Seconds

Of the things which have been said previously in this tractate, much has been demonstrated to both appear useful, and are useful for this work, especially on the number of signs and their order, and their division.

What will be said in this chapter relates to the division of the orb of signs, following in the footsteps of our most reverent predecessor Ptolemy, and off those who must be honoured, namely Hermes, Albumasar, Alezdegoz, Messala, Alchabitius, Adila, Alhayat, Thebit, Astaphan, Arastellus, and other prudent men who studied this science and adding those things which seem useful to me, according to God granting me the grace to arrange these things and to return them to my memory

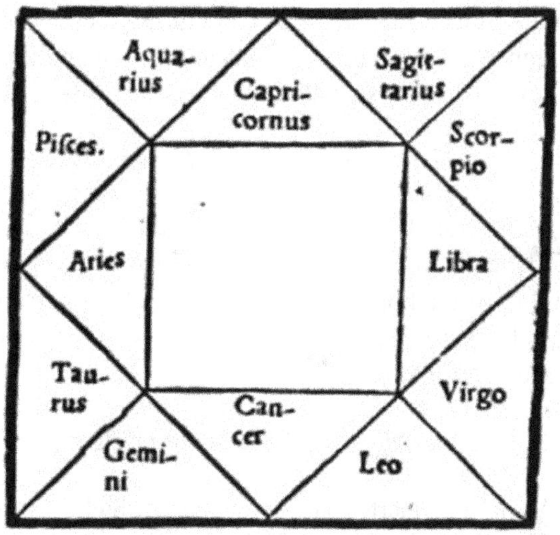

You ought to know that the circle of signs (which is called the Zodiac or Zodial) is divided into twelve equal divisions, each of which is called a sign; which are (as said above) said to be in the likeness of certain animals, in whose shapes the signs are formed, just as I said above. The first sign therefore is called Aries (The Ram), the second Taurus (The Bull), the third Gemini (The Twins), the fourth Cancer (The Crab), the fifth Leo (The Lion), the sixth Virgo (The Virgin), the seventh Libra (The Scales), the eighth Scorpio (The Scorpion), the ninth Sagittarius (The Archer), the tenth Capricorn (The Goat), the eleventh Aquarius (The Water-Bearer), and the twelfth Pisces (The Fishes).

And each one of these signs is divided into thirty equal parts, each one of which is called a degree. And each degree is divided into sixty equal parts, which are called minutes. And each minute is divided into sixty equal parts which are called seconds. And each second is divided into sixty equal parts which are called thirds. And each third is divided into sixty equal parts which are called fourths, and so on until the end of numbers - however these will be dispensed with in your work, and especially in any equations of some numbers beyond these, even if certain men of the order of Order of Preachers divided up to fifths and sixths, not so that they could philosophise, but that they could appear to philosophise!

II

To Demonstrate Which Signs Are Northern And Which Are Southern

It has been stated above that there are twelve signs, and in how many parts each sign is divided into. Now it is to be explained which, and how many of the signs are northern, and which, and how many, of the signs are southern. The northern signs are six in number, namely those from the beginning of Aries to the end of Virgo: these being Aries, Taurus, Gemini, Cancer, Leo, and Virgo. And they are said to be northern, because they are on the northern side of the equator. The remaining six, those which are from the beginning of Libra up to the end of Pisces, are said to be southern, because they are on the southern side of the equator.

III

Which Signs Are Of Direct Ascension And Which Are Of Crooked Ascension

It has been stated which signs are northern and which are southern. Now it is to be explained which signs are of direct ascension and which are of crooked ascension. Those of direct ascension are six in number, namely those from the beginning of Cancer up until the end of Sagittarius. And these are said to be of direct ascension as they ascend directly, and in a longer time than those opposite to them. The remaining six, namely those from the beginning of Capricorn to the end of Gemini, are said to be of crooked ascension: since they do not ascend as directly as those signs opposite to them. And they are said to be of crooked ascension because they ascend crookedly, and in a shorter time than those signs opposite to them. These signs of crooked ascension are Capricorn, Aquarius, Pisces, Aries, Taurus, and Gemini. Each sign ought to ascend in two hours; however the signs of direct ascension rise in more than two hours, and the signs of crooked ascension rise in less than two hours.

Which Signs Are Obeying

Alchabitius said that the signs of crooked ascension obey the signs of direct ascension. Namely that from two signs which are of the same longitude from the beginning of Cancer, the one of crooked ascension will obey the one of direct ascension. So Gemini obeys Cancer, because the end of Gemini and the beginning of Cancer are the same distance from the equator (as are the beginning of Gemini and the end of Cancer). Taurus can also be said to obey Leo for the same reason, and the same can be said of Aries obeying Virgo, Pisces: Libra, Aquarius: Scorpio, and Capricorn: Sagittarius.

Which Signs Are Concordant In Journeys

And that same philosopher said that two signs which are the same longitude from the beginning of Aries are said to be "*concordant in journeys*", as with Aries and Pisces. For the beginning of Aries is the same distance from the equator as the end of Pisces; and Taurus is as far from the equator as Aquarius; Gemini is as far from the equator as Capricorn; Cancer is as far from the equator as Sagittarius; Leo is as far from the equator as Scorpio; and Virgo is as far from the equator as Libra.

The Greater Or Solar Half, And The Lesser Or Lunar Half

There is another method of dividing between the ascensions of signs: and that is according to the two halves of the circle of signs. And it is said that certain signs are greater than their opposites, not that one sign is greater or longer than another in its circle, but that one takes more time in ascending than its opposite, and sets in less time, and these begin from Leo, which is the sign of the Sun, and this is said to be the greater half. And this is also called the half of the Sun, from the beginning of Leo up to end of Capricorn. In this half the Sun has as much strength as the other five planets have in their own terms.

The remaining half (namely that which is from the beginning of Aquarius up to the end of Cancer), is called the lesser half; not that it is lesser than the other half, but because it ascends in less time than its opposite half, and sets in a greater time, according to the diverse climes and regions. And this is called the half of the Moon, since the Moon has as much strength in this half as the other planets have in their own terms, on account of the many impressions and many effects she has on us, more so than any of the other planets.

And this is the reason why terms were not assigned to the Sun or the Moon in the signs, as they were assigned to the other five planets, as will be said below when we discuss the terms of the planets.

The Hot And Cold Halves

And that half of the circle, that is from the beginning of Aries up to the end of Virgo is said to be the hot half, while the other half, namely that from the beginning of Libra to the end of Pisces is said to be the cold half.

The Quarters Of The Circle Of Signs

And that quarter part of the circle which is from the beginning of Aries up to the end of Gemini is called the hot, humid, vernal, childish, and sanguine quarter; and it signifies childhood up to youth. And the next quarter of the circle, which is from the beginning of Cancer up to the end of

Virgo is called the hot, dry, summery, choleric, and youthful quarter; and it signifies youth up until middle age. The next quarter of the circle, which is from the beginning of Libra up until the end of Sagittarius is called the cold, dry, autumnal and melancholic quarter; and it signifies middle age up until the beginning of old age. The remaining quarter, namely from the beginning of Capricorn to the end of Pisces, is called the cold, humid, wintry, phlegmatic, senile, and defective quarter; and it signifies old age and senility up to the end of natural life.

IV

On The Order Of The Circles Of The Seven Planets, And The Dispositions Of These Seven Planets, And Their Courses, And In What Times They Complete Their Courses

In this chapter I will speak to you in accordance with what has been said by the philosophers, and what is true, about the order of the circles of the seven planets. Of which the first, highest, most superior, and closest to the orb of the signs is the circle of Saturn; followed by the circle of Jupiter; third is the circle of Mars; fourth is the circle of the Sun; fifth is the circle of Venus; sixth is the circle of Mercury; and seventh is the circle of the Moon - which is lower than all others and closer to the earth.

Of the courses of the seven planets, the highest, most superior, and slowest is that of Saturn, who completes his course in approximately thirty years. Then comes Jupiter, who completes his course in approximately 12 years. Then comes Mars, who completes his course in approximately 2 years. Then the Sun, who completes his course in one year. Then Venus, who completes her course in one year, like the Sun. Then Mercury, who similarly completes his course in one year. Then comes the Moon (who is faster, more inferior, and closer to the earth than all the others), who completes her course in 27 days and almost a third of a day.

There are also two places in the sky besides the planets, understood to be in the circle of the signs, one of which is called the Caput Draconis, and the other of which is called the Cauda Draconis. They are two opposite crossing points which the circle of the Moon makes through the circle of the Sun, and they signify certain things, which will be said below, when we deal with the Caput and the Cauda.

V

What Powers The Planets Have In The Signs

Every planet has powers in the signs, some of which are by nature, others which are by accident. Those which are by nature are domicile, exaltation, term, triplicity, and face. Those which are by accident are the joys of the planets, their placement in strong places and houses, and when they have reception, (that is, when one planet receives another), like the other strengths, which will be spoken of in their own time and place.

VI

On The Domiciles Of The Planets

The signs (as has been demonstrated) are twelve in number, and are assigned as domiciles to the seven planets. Whereby Leo is the domicile of the Sun (as the philosophers will attest); Cancer is the domicile of the Moon; Gemini and Virgo are the domiciles houses of Mercury; Taurus and Libra are the domiciles of Venus; Aries and Scorpio are the domiciles of Mars; Pisces and Sagittarius are the domiciles of Jupiter; and Aquarius and Capricorn are the domiciles of Saturn.

However you might say "Why are the are the houses of the planets ordered in this way, and why do the Sun and Moon only have one house each, while the other planets have two, when the luminaries appear more likely to have two houses than any of the other planets, on account of their strength, and on account of many other reasons which could be assigned, especially since Albumasar says that the Sun and Moon are stronger and greater than the other benefics.

To which we can respond that among the ancients there were diverse ways of ordering the houses of the planets, with some of them beginning from the houses of the luminaries, others beginning from the houses of Saturn, others beginning from the houses of Mars, others beginning from the houses of Jupiter, others beginning from the houses of Mercury, and others still beginning from the houses of Venus, and each of them provided their own reasons according to how it seemed to him. Nevertheless, I do not see much force in their differences. For there are many reasons which could be assigned, however I do not wish to list them all, nor do I want to recite all of the opinions of the ancients, which would be extremely long winded, and not useful to you. However I will give you one reason, and that will suffice for you. One reason why Leo, and no other sign, was assigned to the Sun as its domicile, is that the Sun is the greater luminary, the diurnal luminary, and is bright, and judged to be hot and dry, and his heat is intense, and the virtue of his heat appears stronger when it is in Leo more so than in any other sign, and the nature of summer appears stronger at this time than at any other. And the Sun is a masculine, diurnal planet signifying heat and dryness through its own nature. And Leo is a masculine, hot and dry fire sign; and when the Sun is in it, then it is the culmination of the summer, and the completion of the increase in heat. And no other sign is closer to the nature of the Sun than Leo, even even if Aries and Sagittarius are fire signs, the virtue of the Sun's heat is not as manifestly apparent in them, nor is its light as bright, or as fine, as it is in Leo. And Albumasar says that the Sun and Leo concord in this: that the Sun is in the middle of the planets, and Leo is in the middle of the summer, and so that time when the Sun is in Leo is when the greatest heat of the summer occurs.

Why Cancer Is The Domicile Of The Moon

Cancer was the only sign assigned as the domicile of the Moon (which is the nocturnal luminary), according to Cancer being the first mobile sign from the beginning of the signs, which concords with the Moon in its femininity, mobility, frigidity, and moistness. And it is closer to the domicile of the luminary from which the Moon receives her light than any other mobile sign, or cold sign, or moist sign which concords with the nature of the Moon. It is also said that the Moon is the "*lamp of the sun*", as she receives light from him, and these two signs are brighter and more splendid, and more in concordance with the nature of the luminaries than any of the other signs in all climes and in all regions of the world.

Why Capricorn And Aquarius Are The Domiciles Of Saturn

And just as the Sun and Moon are brighter, more splendid, and more luminous than the other supercelestial bodies, and their light is more perceptible and manifest than the light of any of the others, and more increasing of fortune, so is Saturn's darkness and obscurity perceived to be darker and more obscure than all other supercelestial bodies, and he is destructive, and he is worse than all other malefics. And since light and splendour are directly contrary to darkness and obscurity (and vice versa) and the luminaries signify light, splendour, and clarity, while Saturn signifies obscurity and darkness: the domiciles of the luminaries and the domiciles of Saturn are directly opposite to one another. And this is the reason why Capricorn and Aquarius were assigned to Saturn for his two domiciles. And similarly Capricorn and Aquarius are dark signs, so that when the Sun is in them, the air is more obscure and further removed from purity, especially when he is in Aquarius, at which time the coldness of winter is at its peak.

Why Sagittarius And Pisces Are The Domiciles Of Jupiter

Sagittarius and Pisces were assigned to Jupiter as domiciles because they are next to the domiciles of Saturn just as Jupiter immediately succeeds Saturn in the order of the planetary circles, and is the greater benefic which shatters the evil of Saturn, and these two signs aspect the domiciles of the luminaries by trine, which is an aspect of whole and perfect friendship, just as the opposition is an aspect of ultimate enmity. And therefore, since Jupiter is the most fortunate benefic aside from the luminaries, it is appropriate that his domiciles are in such a location that they aspect the domiciles of the luminaries by the aspect more loving than the rest of the aspects. Pisces aspects Cancer (which is the domicile of the nocturnal luminary), by a trine aspect, and is of the same triplicity, which increases the good of the aspect. And similarly, Sagittarius aspects Leo (which is the domicile of the diurnal luminary) from a trine aspect, and is of the same triplicity.

Why Aries And Scorpio Are The Domiciles Of Mars

Aries and Scorpio were assigned to Mars as his domiciles, because they are next to the houses of Jupiter, just as Mars succeeds Jupiter in the order of the circles of the planets. And he is unfortunate and malefic, but his malice and his evil are less than the malice and evil of Saturn. And these two signs aspect the domiciles of the luminaries by a square aspect, which is an aspect of moderate enmity. And therefore, since Mars is less evil than Saturn, who signifies the ultimate evil, it is fitting that Mars' domiciles are assigned in such a location that they aspect the domiciles of the luminaries through an aspect of moderate enmity. Aries aspects Cancer (which is the domicile of the nocturnal luminary) by a square aspect, and is not of its triplicity, which worsens the aspect. Similarly, Scorpio aspects Leo (which is the domicile of the diurnal luminary) from a square aspect.

Why Taurus And Libra Are The Domiciles Of Venus

Taurus and Libra were assigned to Venus as her domiciles next to the domiciles of Mars, since Venus succeeds the Sun in the order of the circles of the planets, but the Sun has his own domicile, so because of this the domiciles of Venus succeed those of Mars. And Venus is a good benefic, but not a perfect benefic like Jupiter, as Jupiter is so strongly benefic that it shatters all the evil of malefics, which Venus cannot do. Still, even if she can't shatter evil like Jupiter, she can still diminish it, and through herself confers fortune and good. And her fortune and goodness are below the fortune and goodness of Jupiter. And these two signs aspect the domiciles of the luminaries by a sextile aspect, which is an aspect of moderate friendship. And therefore, since her good fortune is below that of Jupiter (who signifies the perfect and ultimate good and friendship), it is appropriate that her domiciles are assigned such locations that they aspect the domiciles of the luminaries by an aspect of moderate friendship. Taurus aspects Cancer (which is the domicile of the nocturnal luminary) by a sextile aspect, which is an aspect of moderate friendship, even if they are not of the same triplicity. And Libra aspects Leo (which is the domicile of the diurnal luminary) by a sextile aspect.

Why Gemini And Virgo Were Assigned As The Domiciles Of Mercury

Gemini and Virgo were assigned to Mercury as his domiciles since they are next to the domiciles of Venus, and Mercury succeeds Venus in the order of the circles of the planets. And is mixed, yet in his own nature is more benefic than malefic; although he converts to the nature of any planet with which he is joined. And this is the reason why he is said to be of mixed nature, namely that his domiciles do not aspect the domiciles of the luminaries by any aspect, since they are contiguous with them. And since Mercury is never far enough away from the Sun that he can be in any aspect with him. But you might say that Gemini aspects Leo, and Virgo aspects Cancer; however this has no place in such a case: since according to this consideration no sign could be said to aspect the domiciles of the luminaries by any aspect, such that the domicile of the other luminary falls within these limits. Whence Gemini cannot be said to aspect Leo, since Cancer (the domicile of the Moon) falls between these limits; nor can Virgo be said to aspect Cancer, since Leo (the domicile of the Sun) falls between these limits. And understand thusly for the other signs; since Aries does not aspect Leo by trine on account of Cancer (the domicile of the Moon, which Aries aspects by square) falling between these limits. Scorpio does not aspect Cancer by trine, since Leo (the domicile of the Sun, which Scorpio aspects by square) falls between these limits. Taurus does not aspect Leo by square on account of it aspecting Cancer (the domicile of the Moon, which falls between these limits) by a sextile aspect. Libra does not aspect Cancer by a square aspect, on account of it aspecting Leo (the domicile of the Sun, which falls between these limits) by a sextile aspect.

You will consider all these things according to the consideration as to why the signs were assigned to the planets as domiciles. It is different however when the planets are placed in these signs, as will be discussed at length in the chapter on the aspects of the planets. We can assign many other reasons, and many more opinions of philosophers, however to avoid prolixity, let the reason above be sufficient for you.

VII

On The Detriments Of The Planets

The detriment of any given planet is said to be the seventh sign from its domicile, namely its opposite one, and this can also be called a planet's fall.

And so just as Libra is opposite Aries and Aries is opposite Libra, the detriment of Mars is Libra, and the detriment of Venus is Aries. And Scorpio is opposite Taurus, and is the detriment of Venus, and Taurus is opposite Scorpio and is the detriment of Mars.

And Sagittarius is opposite Gemini and is the detriment of Mercury, and Gemini is opposite Sagittarius and is the detriment of Jupiter.

Capricorn is opposite Cancer, and is the detriment of the Moon, and Cancer is opposite Capricorn and is the detriment of Saturn.

Aquarius is opposite Leo and is the detriment of the Sun. Leo is opposite Aquarius and is the detriment of Saturn.

Pisces is opposite Virgo and is the detriment of Mercury. Virgo is opposite Pisces and is the detriment of Jupiter.

And Alchabitius said that if two signs are the domicile of one planet, they are said to be concordant in almanticam, that is in a circle which is sewn in the middle and tied together with a ligature - namely in a zodiac which appears in a handmade sphere: since where the zodiac crosses the equator, there the circle is said to be tied, and where it declines from the equator to the south or to the north, there it is said to be wide. Albumasar said that two signs which are the domicile of one planet are said to be in "*concordant in journey*", as are Aries and Scorpio, either of which are a domicile of Mars, and as are Taurus and Libra, which are both domiciles of Venus; Gemini and Virgo, which are both domiciles of Mercury; Sagittarius and Pisces, which are both domiciles of Jupiter; Capricorn and Aquarius, which are both domiciles of Saturn; and Leo and Cancer, which are both domiciles of the luminaries.

On The Joys Of The Planets According To Dorotheus

Dorotheus says that Saturn rejoices in Aquarius, Jupiter rejoices in Sagittarius, Mars rejoices in Scorpio, Venus rejoices in Taurus, and Mercury rejoices in Virgo.

VIII

On The Exaltations Of The Planets

Albumashar and Alchabicius said that the Sun is exalted in Aries, namely in the nineteenth degree. The Moon is exalted in Taurus, namely in the third degree. Saturn is exalted in Libra, namely in the twenty-first degree. Jupiter is exalted in Cancer, namely in the fifteenth degree. Mars is exalted in Capricorn, namely in the twenty-eighth degree. Venus is exalted in Pisces, namely in the twenty-seventh degree. Mercury is exalted in Virgo, namely in the fifteenth degree. The Caput Draconis is exalted in Gemini, namely in the third degree. The Cauda Draconis is exalted in Sagittarius, namely in the third degree. And Albumasar said that the planets are exalted in the degrees mentioned above because they were in these degrees when they were formed.

IX

Why Aries Is The Exaltation Of The Sun, And Libra Its Descension, And Why Other Signs Are The Exaltations Of The Planets

Albumashar said that Ptolemy (author of a book of judgements) said that when the Sun enters Aries he begins to ascend towards the north, that is the zenith above our heads, and then the days increase in length above the nights, and the Suns nature begins to increase in heat, maximally when the Sun reaches the nineteenth degree of Aries. However when he is in Libra he begins descending to the south, receding and elongating from the zenith above our heads, and the days are diminished, and the night is increased in length over the day, and the Suns nature begins to decrease in heat, and his noble and useful operations begin to diminish, maximally when he reaches the nineteenth degree of Libra.

Albumasar also said that he discovered in a certain book of the ancients that Taurus was posited as the exaltation of the Moon, since when the Sun is in

Aries (his exaltation) and the Moon is in Taurus, then there will be an appearance of the Moons light. Taurus is also the first sign of the triplicity of the Moon, since it immediately follows the sign of the Sun's exaltation, and the Moon herself is joined to the Sun in her operations. And they posited Scorpio as the descension of the Moon, since it is opposite the sign of her exaltation.

And they posited Libra as the exaltation of Saturn and Aries as his fall, on account of Saturn being opposed to the Sun in both his nature and his operations, and so their exaltations are similarly opposed, as is said above.

And they posited Cancer as the exaltation of Jupiter, as Jupiter by nature signifies northern winds, and when he is in Cancer, nourishing northern winds arise, providing growth to animating things, and strengthening the nature of Jupiter. And they posited Capricorn as his descension since it is opposite his exaltation

They also posited Capricorn as being the exaltation of Mars, since Capricorn is southerly, and in opposition to the exaltation of Jupiter (Jupiter and Mars being inimical to one another), and since Mars is southern and burning by nature, and his heat is strengthened when he is in Capricorn. And they posited Cancer as his descension, as it is opposite to its exaltation.

And they posited Pisces as the exaltation of Venus, since the nature of Pisces is moist, and in concordance with Venus, and since at that time the moisture of the season begins to thrive, and the moisture of Venus is strengthened in this. And they posited Virgo as her descension because it is opposite to her exaltation.

Gemini was posited as the exaltation of the Caput Draconis, on account of Gemini being the first bicorporeal and common sign after Aries, and the Caput himself is similarly bicorporeal, being composed of two natures (those of Venus and Jupiter, which are two benefics). Sagittarius is posited as the exaltation of the Cauda, as Sagittarius is opposite to Gemini just as the Cauda is opposite to the Caput.

X

On The Falls Or Descensions Of The Planets

Albuumashar and Alchabicius said that the seventh sign from the exaltation of any planet is its descension or fall.

For the Sun falls in the nineteenth degree of Libra, just as he is exalted in the like degree of Aries.

The Moon has her fall or descension in the third degree of Scorpio, just as she is exalted in the like degree of Taurus.

Saturn has his fall or descension in the twenty-first degree of Aries, just as he is exalted in a like degree of Libra

Jupiter has his fall or descension in the fifteenth degree of Capricorn, and his exaltation in Cancer in a like degree.

Mars has its fall or descension in the twenty-eighth degree of Cancer, and his exaltation in Capricorn in a like degree.

Venus has her fall or descension in the twenty-seventh degree of Virgo, and her exaltation in Pisces in the like degree.

Mercury has his fall or descension in the fifteenth degree of Pisces, and his exaltation in Virgo in a like degree.

The Caput has his fall in Sagittarius, the Cauda in Gemini, both at three degrees.

There is a difference between descension and fall, even if one term is often used in place of the other. And the difference is that descension is opposite to the exaltation of a planet, while fall is opposite to the domicile of a planet. Dignity relating to domicile is dignity from essential or individual sources, while dignity by exaltation is similar to extrinsic honours or dignity, rather than inherited honour or dignity.

XI

On The Four Triplicities Of The Seven Planets

It was said by the aforementioned philosophers that the number of triplicities are four, and are distinguished in this manner: namely, when three signs all concord in one nature, and in one complexion, they form a triplicity; and triplicities are so called because they are "*trina plicitas*" or "*three fold*".

On The First Triplicity

Aries, Leo, and Sagittarius make up the first triplicity. For Aries is a hot and dry fire sign, and so is the first hot and dry sign. Leo is similarly a hot and dry sign, and so there are two hot and dry signs. And Sagittarius is a hot and dry sign, and so we have a triplicity of hot and dry signs. And so the three signs are agreeing in one complexion. And this triplicity is said to be hot and dry, since each one of these signs is a fiery, hot, dry, masculine, oriental, diurnal, choleric, and of bitter taste. And the triplicity is said to be eastern; and its triplicity Lord in the day is the Sun, at night Jupiter, and its participating ruler in both day and night is Saturn

On The Second Triplicity

Taurus, Virgo and Capricorn make up the second triplicity: since each of these signs are earthy, cold and dry, feminine, nocturnal, melancholic, southern, and harsh or sour tasting. And this triplicity is said to be southern; and its triplicity Lord in the day is Venus, at night the Moon, and its participating ruler in both day and night is Mars

On The Third Triplicity

Gemini, Libra, and Aquarius make up the third triplicity, since each of these are air signs, hot and moist, masculine, diurnal, sanguine, occidental, and sweet tasting. And this triplicity is said to be western; and its triplicity Lord in day is Saturn, at night Mercury, and its participating ruler in both day and night is Jupiter.

On The Fourth Triplicity

Cancer, Scorpio and Pisces make up the fourth triplicity, since each of these are water signs, cold and humid, feminine, nocturnal, phlegmatic, salty tasting, and (according to some) weak. And this triplicity is said to be northern; and its triplicity Lord in day is Venus, at night Mars, and its participating ruler in both day and night is Jupiter

XII

On The Mobile, Fixed, And Common Signs

Know that of the twelve signs, four are mobile signs, namely Aries, Cancer, Libra, and Capricorn. And four are fixed, namely Taurus, Leo, Scorpio and Aquarius. And the remaining four are common, namely Gemini, Virgo, Sagittarius and Pisces.

They are called mobile signs, not because they are moved (no more than any other signs), but are said to be mobile because when the Sun enters one of these signs, the disposition of the air changes, and it no longer remains in the state which it was in previously.

The fixed signs are so called, as when the Sun enters any of them, the disposition of the air remains fixed, and perseveres and remains fixed and firm in the same state, even if now and then it may change by accident, it still remains fixed by nature.

The common signs are so called, as when the Sun enters any of these signs, the weather becomes common, so that it can neither be said to be fixed nor mobile, but is partly fixed and partly mobile. And so part of the weather is fixed, while another part is mobile.

For when the Sun enters Aries (which is a mobile sign), then the weather changes (namely the disposition of the air), since the winter turns to spring. And when the Sun leaves Aries and enters Taurus, then the weather becomes fixed: namely, it remains in the state of spring. And when the Sun leaves Taurus and enters Gemini, then the spring weather changes, and becomes partly vernal, partly summery. And when the Sun leaves Gemini and enters Cancer, then the weather changes and becomes summery. And when the Sun leaves Cancer and enters Leo, then the summer weather is fixed, and perseveres in the same state. And when the Sun leaves Leo and enters Virgo, then the summer weather changes, and becomes partly summery and partly autumnal. And when the Sun leaves Virgo and enters Libra, the weather changes and becomes autumnal. And when the Sun leaves Libra and enters Scorpio, the autumnal weather becomes fixed, and perseveres in the same state. And when the Sun leaves Scorpio and enters Sagittarius, the weather becomes common, being partly autumnal and partly wintry. And when the Sun leaves Sagittarius and enters Capricorn, the weather changes, and autumn turns to winter. And when the Sun leaves Capricorn and enters Aquarius, then the winter weather becomes fixed, and perseveres in the same state. And finally when the Sun leaves Aquarius and enters Pisces, the weather is made common, since it is partly wintry, and partly vernal.

XIII

On The Aspects Of The Planets

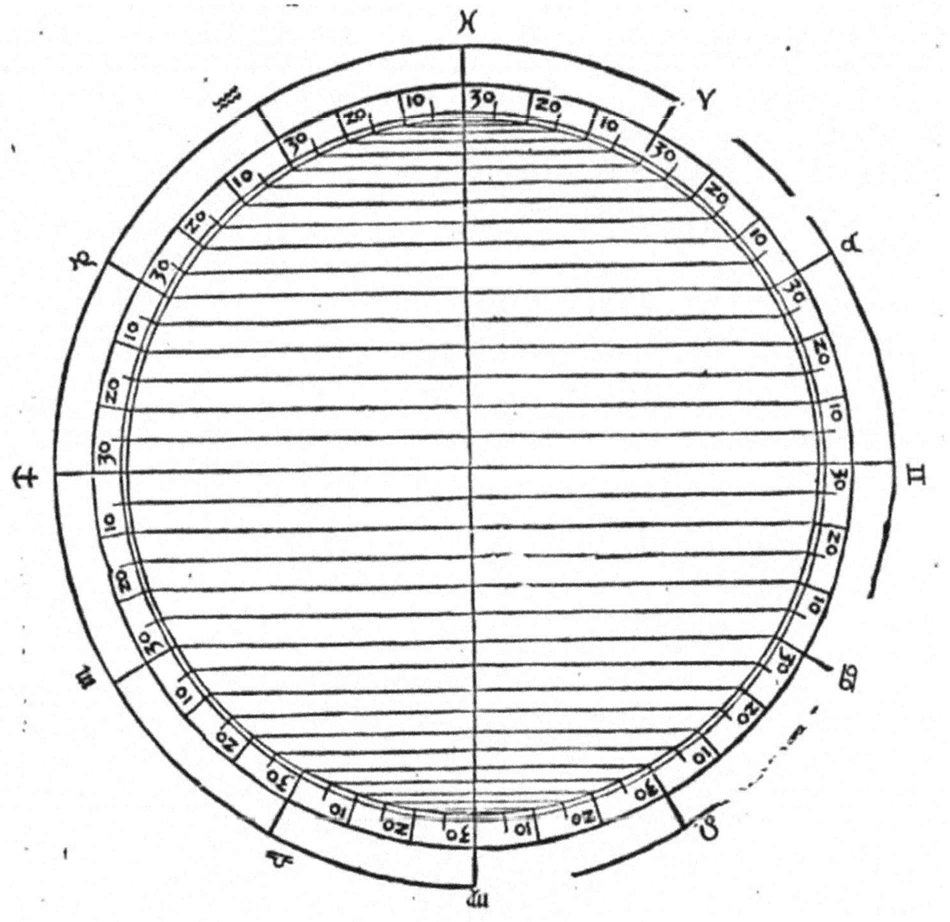

Messala, Alchabicius, and many other philosophers said that the signs are said to look at each other by different aspects, namely the sextile, square, trine, and opposition.

The sextile aspect is that which has one sixth of the heavens, namely sixty degrees forwards or backwards.

The square aspect is that which has a quarter of the heavens, namely ninety degrees forwards or backwards.

The trine aspect is that which has one third of the heavens, namely one hundred and twenty degrees forwards or backwards.

And the opposition aspect is that which has one half of the heavens, namely one hundred and eighty degrees.

And it is said that the sextile is a good aspect, and of moderate friendship and concordance, but not perfect. And it is said to be an aspect of moderate friendship since it is drawn from Venus and the luminaries; namely the aspect of the domiciles of Venus to the domiciles of the luminaries, as was explained previously. And it is said to be an aspect of moderate friendship since Venus is a moderately strong benefic, but not a perfect one.

And the square aspect is said to be moderately evil, and it is an aspect of moderate enmity and discord, but not perfect. And it is said to be an aspect of moderate enmity since it is drawn from Mars and the luminaries, and the domiciles of Mars aspect the domiciles of the luminaries by square, as was explained previously. And it is also said to be an aspect of moderate enmity since Mars is less malefic than Saturn, just as Venus is less benefic than Jupiter.

The trine aspect is said to be a good aspect, and it is an aspect of perfect friendship and concordance, in fact it is the perfection of goodness. And it is said to be an aspect of perfect friendship and concordance because it is drawn from Jupiter and the luminaries, and the domiciles of Jupiter aspect the domiciles of the luminaries by trine. And it is said to be an aspect of perfect friendship since Jupiter is a strong and perfect benefic, beyond all other benefics; and lacks nothing in terms of goodness.

But the opposition is said to be an evil aspect, and the aspect of ultimate enmity, ultimate malice, and ultimate discord. And it is said to be an aspect of such enmity since it is drawn from Saturn and the luminaries: since the domiciles of Saturn aspect the domiciles of the luminaries by opposition. And it is also said to be the aspect of ultimate enmity because Saturn is the greater malefic, and stronger than all other malefics.

To give an example of all the above mentioned aspects, take a planet that is in the first degree of Aries. He will aspect a planet in the first degree of Gemini ahead of him, and this aspect is called an anterior sextile, or a sextile "from the face". And he will aspect the planet in the first degree of Aquarius behind him, and this aspect is called a posterior sextile, or a sextile "from the back". And such an aspect is said to be a hexagonal ray, since it radiates or aspects from one sixth of the heavens.

And he will aspect the planet in the first degree of Cancer ahead of him, and this aspect is called an anterior square, or a square "from the face", and he will aspect the planet in the first degree of Capricorn behind him, and this aspect is called an anterior square, or a square "from the back". And this aspect is said to be a tetragonal ray, as it radiates or aspects from a quarter of the heavens.

And he will aspect the planet in the first degree of Leo ahead of him, and this aspect is called an anterior trine, or a trine "from the face". Similarly he will aspect the planet in the first degree of Sagittarius behind him, and this is called a posterior trine, or a trine "from the back". And such an aspect is said to be a trigonal ray, as it radiates or aspects from a third of the heavens.

And he will aspect the planet in the first degree of Libra, and this aspect is called an opposition. Certain men say that the opposition is not an aspect, however I do not agree with them.

Whence, if some planet were in these signs aspecting each other in this way, he would be said to aspect another planet which was in the other signs mentioned above, and this second planets would aspect him in a similar fashion.

And a planet which is in Taurus aspects the planet ahead of him in Cancer, and the planet behind him in Pisces by a sextile aspect. And aspects the planet ahead of him in Leo, and behind him in Aquarius by a square aspect. And aspects the planet ahead of him in Virgo, and the planet behind him in Capricorn by a trine aspect. And aspects the planet in Scorpio by opposition. And understand the same for all signs.

And just as the first degree of one sign aspects the first degree of another sign, so the second degree of one sign aspects the second degree of another sign, and the third the third, and the fourth the fourth. And so it is to be understood for all the degrees.

XIV

On The Terms Of The Five Planets Besides The Luminaries

It is said that five planets, namely Saturn, Jupiter, Mars, Venus, and Mercury, have defined and determined terms in each of the signs, defined according to what I will tell you below. They are called terms or bounds, as when a planet is in these degrees it is said to have a certain power, which is called "strength". And the terms were found by philosophers by long experience that when a planet was in the degrees which were assigned as its terms in a given sign, it imprinted more strongly on the inferior things than it did in the other degrees of the same sign. And from this they were called terms, just as boundaries placed in a field impose limits, and divide one field from another, so too do the degrees assigned to the planets as their terms impose boundaries to the strength of each planet, and divide the place of strength of one planet from that of another. And there were diverse methods of dividing the terms among the ancients; since Ptolemy assigned two different terms following two different opinions, those being the opinion of the Egyptians and that of the Chaldeans, and afterwards posited his own opinion, which was different to the aforementioned opinions of the ancients, which he discovered in a certain very ancient book (as he reported it), and he approved of these sayings.

Albumasar listed five ancient opinions on the terms, those being of the Egyptians, Ptolemy, Chaldeans, that of a certain philosopher named Asthoatol, and that of the Indians. All of these opinions would take a long time to list here, so I will dismiss them and only give you the reasons which Ptolemy claimed that he said he found in an ancient book. Not wanting to boast, he did not attribute the discovery of these terms to himself, but only to those who he believed to have composed this ancient book. And Albumasar and himself said that the degrees of the terms written below (which are noted in the following Table), were so divided, and so attributed to the five planets, that through them we are given understanding of the greater years of each of the five planets, regarding which, collected together give fifty seven for Saturn, seventy nine for Jupiter, sixty six for Mars, eighty-two for Venus, and seventy-six for Mercury: which added together make three hundred and sixty degrees. And this is the reason why the greater years of the planets are such, not more, and not less; so that each of the five planets has as many degrees for its terms, as it has for its greater years. And this is the table demonstrating these terms: (*Bonattis table had errors which I amended; he makes reference to his own table in the explanation below*)

Aries	Jupiter	6	Venus	8	Mercury	7	Mars	5	Saturn	4
Taurus	Venus	8	Mercury	7	Jupiter	7	Saturn	4	Mars	4
Gemini	Mercury	7	Jupiter	6	Venus	7	Mars	6	Saturn	4
Cancer	Mars	6	Jupiter	7	Mercury	7	Venus	7	Saturn	3
Leo	Saturn	6	Mercury	7	Mars	6	Venus	6	Mars	5
Virgo	Mercury	7	Venus	6	Jupiter	5	Saturn	6	Mars	6
Libra	Saturn	6	Venus	5	Mercury	8	Jupiter	5	Mars	6
Scorpio	Mars	6	Venus	8	Jupiter	7	Mercury	6	Saturn	3
Sagittarius	Jupiter	8	Venus	6	Mercury	5	Saturn	6	Mars	5
Capricorn	Venus	6	Mercury	6	Jupiter	7	Saturn	6	Mars	5
Aquarius	Saturn	6	Mercury	6	Venus	8	Jupiter	5	Mars	5
Pisces	Venus	8	Jupiter	6	Mercury	6	Mars	6	Saturn	4

And certain people may ask, why have the philosophers ordered the terms in this manner. And this question can be responded to like so; even though the reason for it has been assigned above, there is another reason which can be given, even if it is more lengthy than the previous one. The philosophers first considered the exaltation Lords, then the triplicity Lords, then the sign Lords. And if one of the planets had two of these dignities (be it a benefic or a malefic), he was placed first, and they gave him the first terms. And if a malefic didn't have two of these dignities, he was given the last terms of the sign, and the Lord of exaltation was preferred, and he was given the first terms. Then the second terms were given to the triplicity Lord, the third to the sign Lord. And thus everywhere the planet who had two of these dignities was preferred over the planet who only had one; Cancer and Leo excepted, since they are the domiciles of the luminaries, which are not assigned terms in the signs like the other planets; and they are the domiciles opposite the domiciles of Saturn, who is a malefic. And since Cancer is opposite the exaltation of Mars, Mars is given the first terms; while the first terms of Leo are assigned to Saturn; and so these two are placed first in these signs, whereas in all other signs they are usually placed last (apart from Leo, where Jupiter is placed last). And the aforementioned terms are divided in this manner, because since Jupiter or Venus do not have two of the aforementioned dignities in the same sign, nor in the second, nor in the third, nor in the fourth, they are given seven degrees for their terms. Saturn is given five degrees for his terms, Mars is given five degrees for his terms, and Mercury, since he is of a mixed nature, is given six degrees. And similarly if any planet has two of the aforementioned dignities in any sign, he is given another degree; such as Venus in Taurus, who has dignity by domicile and triplicity, and so is given eight degrees for her terms at the beginning of Taurus, and this extra degree is taken from those of Saturn. And in other cases the degrees are also taken from the planet with only one, or even none, of the aforementioned dignities, especially for Saturn and Jupiter, due to the slowness of their movement, as Ptolemy says. And from these terms the planets can gain strength, from which is said that when a planet is in its own terms, it is similar to a man who is amongst his parents, and the people who he is related to and who love him, like his relatives, or kin.

XV

When The Terms Are To Be Preferred To The Triplicities, And When The Triplicities Are To Be Preferred To The Terms

There were certain philosophers who preferred the term Lords to the triplicity Lords, (and to the triplicities themselves). And there were others who preferred the triplicity Lords (and the triplicities) to the term Lords. And all of these men had a reason for doing so, since the terms and term Lords preferred in directing, while the triplicities and the triplicity Lords are preferred in nourishing. What directing is and what nourishing is, will be explained below, but I will also say something on them here.

Some might say that directing and nourishing are the same, but this is not so: since directing comes to be through the triplicity Lords of the Ascendant of both a nativity and a question, and generally disposes the life of the native or querent, according to the three divisions from the beginning of the natives life up to his natural end. For the first triplicity Lord of the nativities Ascendant disposes the first third of the natives life, the second triplicity Lord disposes the second third of the natives life, while the third triplicity Lord disposes the final third, up until the end of life. I said "natural life" because death often takes people early, so that they do not reach the natural end of life, but rather they die accidentally before the time they were supposed to die naturally; sometimes through fire, iron, a fall, a collapse of a building, drowning, sometimes by being hanged, sometimes through suffocation, sometimes by an acute illness, or a very acute illness (which often occurs due to an inordinate diet, or inordinate way of life), and many other ways besides. And you will judge for the native or querent on each one-third of their life, according to the condition of the Lord of each one-third of life.

To give an example, a certain native asked a universal question about his own being, or his fortune in life, or in that year. The Ascendant was Taurus, whose triplicity Lords are Venus, Moon, and Mars. And Venus disposes the first third of the natives life (since she is the first Lord of this triplicity); the Moon disposes the second third (since she is the second Lord of this triplicity), and Mars disposes the last third (since he is the third triplicity Lord). Whence if Venus were well disposeed, things would be good for the native in the first part of his life (that is, in adolescence, which is almost up until thirty years of age). And if Venus were badly disposeed, things would be bad for him in this part of life. And if the Moon was well disposeed, things would be good for him in his youth (that is in the second third of his life, practically from thirty years old up to sixty years old; and if she were badly disposeed, things would be bad for him during this time. And if Mars were well disposeed, things would be good for him in the final third of his life (that is in old age); and if Mars were badly disposeed, things would be bad for him during that same time. And if any of the above were averagely disposeed, things would be average for the native in the age governed by that significator. And this is to be understood for all the triplicities and their Lords.

But should someone say "this has a place in nativities, but not in questions, since it is given in a nativity what ought to happen to the native" - the response to this is that we might not always have nativities, however we can always have questions: whence it is fitting for us to take the barley for the grain, and the question after the nativity, just as an appeal after the sentence.

XVI

On Direction, Which Is Made Through The Term Lords

Ddirection is made through the term Lords in this manner. Posit that the Ascendant is in the first degree of Gemini, which is in the terms of Mercury (which are up until the seventh degree of the same sign). Then Mercury will dispose the life of the native or querent for as many years as there are degrees of the terms. And from the seventh degree of the same sign, up until the thirteenth degree are the terms of Jupiter: and so Jupiter will dispose the life of the native or querant for as many years as there are degrees of these terms. And from the thirteenth up to the twentieth are the terms of Venus: and then Venus will dispose the life of the native for as many years as her terms have degrees. And from the twentieth up to the twenty-sixth are the terms of Mars: then Mars will then dispose the life of the native for as many years as his terms have degrees. And from the twenty-sixth degree up until the end of the sign are the terms of Saturn: and then Saturn will dispose the life of the native for as many years as his terms have degrees. And this should be understood for all of the signs and all of the term Lords. And I will speak to you about it in greater detail (so that it is better understood), when the direction of the degrees through the right circle and the oblique circle is discussed in the ninth tractate.

XVII

The Faces Of The Signs

The faces of the signs are distinguished in this manner: that is, each sign is divided into three equal parts, which are called "faces"; and each of them consists of ten degrees. The first face, which begins from the start of Aries and lasts up until the tenth full degree, and belongs to Mars. And the second begins from the start of the eleventh degree of Aries and lasts until the twentieth full degree, and belongs to the Sun. And the third face begins from the start of the twenty-first degree of Aries and lasts up to the end of the sign, and belongs to Venus. Similarly the first face of Taurus begins from the start of the first degree of the sign and lasts up to the end of the tenth degree, and belongs to Mercury. The second begins from the beginning of the eleventh degree and lasts up until the end of the twentieth, and belongs to the Moon. The third begins from the start of the twenty-first degree and lasts up to the end of the sign, and belongs to Saturn. The first face of Cancer belongs to Venus, the second to Mercury, and the third to the Moon. The first face of Leo belongs to Saturn, the second to Jupiter, and the third to Mars. The first face of Virgo belongs to the Sun, the second to Venus, the third to Mercury. The first face of Libra belongs to the Moon, the second to Saturn, the third to Jupiter. The first face of Scorpio belongs to Mars, the second to the Sun, the third to Venus. The first face of Sagittarius belongs to Mercury, the second to the Moon, the third to Saturn. The first face of Capricorn belongs to Jupiter, the second to Mars, the third to the Sun. The first face of Aquarius belongs to Venus, the second to Mercury, the third to the Moon. The first face of Pisces belongs to Saturn, the second to Jupiter, the third Mars. And to make this more readily apparent to you, that is what planet owns a given face of a given sign, I present you with this table on the faces of the signs

Aries	Mars	10	Sun	10	Venus	10
Taurus	Mercury	10	Moon	10	Saturn	10
Gemini	Jupiter	10	Mars	10	Sun	10
Cancer	Venus	10	Mercury	10	Moon	10
Leo	Saturn	10	Jupiter	10	Mars	10
Virgo	Sun	10	Venus	10	Mercury	10
Libra	Moon	10	Saturn	10	Jupiter	10
Scorpio	Mars	10	Sun	10	Venus	10
Sagittarius	Mercury	10	Moon	10	Saturn	10
Capricorn	Jupiter	10	Mars	10	Sun	10
Aquarius	Venus	10	Mercury	10	Moon	10
Pisces	Saturn	10	Jupiter	10	Mars	10

XVIII

To Discover The Face Of Any Given Degree Of Any Given Sign

If you were ever given some degree of some sign in a question, or any other matter which came into your hands, and you wish to know which planets face the degree is in: take all the complete signs that there are from the beginning of Aries up to the sign of the degree in question; multiply the number of signs by three, and divide the sum by seven, and subtract the remainder from seven: and that will be the number of faces which have been passed over. Therefore begin to project according to this number from Mars (who is the planet to whom the first face is assigned), and add the number of faces already passed over (up as far as this sign in which the degree in question is), and give each planet one of the number of faces which remained after you subtracted from seven (namely the first to Mars, the second to the Sun, the third to Venus, the fourth to Mercury, the fifth to Moon, the sixth to Saturn, and the seventh to Jupiter) and see where the number finishes, and over what planets it falls - this planet owns the face you are looking for.

To give an example: posit that you are given the eleventh degree of Leo, and wish to know the face of this degree. Count the number of complete signs between the beginning of Aries and Leo - which is four (namely Aries, Taurus, Gemini, and Cancer): then multiply four by three - giving you twelve; and now divide twelve by seven, giving you a remainder of five; then you ought to add two to five - that is, the first and second faces of Leo, since the eleventh degree of Leo is his second face, the first on account of the initial ten degrees which were passed over in Leo, which made one face; and the second because you have one degree of the second face, namely the eleventh degree of Leo (which touches the second face). Thus from the five (remaining from seven) and the addition of these two, you will make seven. Therefore begin to project from Mars, and give one to Mars, one to the Sun, one to Venus, one to Mercury, one to the Moon, one to Saturn, and so the number (seven) will fall over the seventh planet from Mars, which is Jupiter: therefore Jupiter must be the Lord of the second face of Leo.

And understand the same for all other signs and of all the faces, so that if you meet with any degree you can know which planets face it is in. For example if you take any degree of Virgo, and posit that this degree is between the twentieth and thirtieth degree of the sign, and you wish to know whose face it is: count the number of complete signs between Virgo and the beginning of Aries - which is five; multiply this by three and you have fifteen; now divide by seven and you have a remainder of one; add on three to this (since your degree falls in the third face of Virgo), which makes four. Then begin to count from Mars, and give one of these four to him, one to the Sun, one to Venus; then one remains, (the fourth of this four), which is given to Mercury - it is necessary then that the third face of Virgo belongs to Mercury (who is the fourth planet from Mars). And so it will be for all the other faces.

XIX

On The Strength Of Each Planet In Each Of Its Dignities

Since it has been said above concerning the power of each planet in each sign, now it seems fitting to deal with the strength of each planet in each sign. Alchabicius says that the Lord of a domicile has five fortitudes, the Lord of the exaltation has four, the triplicity Lord has three, the term Lord has two, and the face Lord has one. And according to this method, you will be able to know the strength of the planets in the signs - whence, whichever planet has more fortitudes in a sign will be said to be stronger in this place, and more powerful, and having greater authority.

Whence Messala preferred the term Lords to the triplicity Lords, and Alezdegoz preferred the triplicity Lords to the term Lords - which appears to be contradictory, but is not so. For Messala was speaking about direction, whereas Alezdegoz was speaking about nourishment; and so both of them spoke well, and spoke correctly, and both of their statements stand. As to what direction and nourishment are, I think I made that sufficiently clear to you above. And he gave the following analogy on this matter:

That when a planet is in its own domicile, it is like a man who is in his own home: for he is stronger here by law, than he is in another house, and is often stronger than another person who would otherwise be stronger than him; whence Trutanus,

"*Every vassal stands a cock before his own gate*".

And when a planet is in its exaltation, it is like a man who is in his own kingdom, and in glory, like kingship, a position of power, or other lay dignities, which can be lost before his own qualities.

And when a planet is in its own terms, it is like a man who is amongst his kin, blood relatives, his relatives on his fathers' side, his relatives on his mothers' side, his allies, and relatives by marriage, and those who are otherwise closely related to him.

And when a planet is in its own triplicity, it is like a man among his allies and his people, his aides, and his followers, who obey and follow him, who are not related to him by blood.

And when a planet is in its own face it is like a man who is among people who he does not know very well, as sometimes happens to foreigners and similar people, yet he lives amongst them due to a shared profession, art, or other trade, or lay profession.

XX

Which Signs Are Said To Be Rational, And Which Have Beautiful Voices, And Which Are Domesticated, And Which Have Wings, And Which Are Four-footed

Alchabicius says that four completely signs are said to be rational, those being Gemini, Virgo, Libra, Aquarius; and the first half of Sagittarius is also said to be rational - whose images are formed in the image of man. And they are said to have beautiful voices, and are said to thrive when they are in the east, where their virtue will appear somewhat better, and they thrive when they are in the oriental quarter more so than any other quarter.

And three of the signs are said to have wings, those being Gemini, Virgo, and Pisces.

And four complete signs are said to be four-footed, those being Aries, Taurus, Leo, and Capricorn - and the latter half of Sagittarius.

And three of the signs are said to be domesticated, since they are formed in the image of domestic animals; namely Aries, Taurus and Capricorn.

And two of the signs, namely Aries and Taurus, are said to thrive in the south, for their strength appears somewhat greater and more fit in the southern quarter than in any other quarter.

And two of the signs are said to thrive in the north, these being Virgo and Aquarius. And certain men said that Virgo thrives in the east and the north.

Capricorn thrives in the south and in the north. As Alchabicius said, Aries and Taurus thrive in the south. Virgo, Capricorn and Aquarius are said to thrive in the north.

And the signs which are said to be wicked and crooked are Aries, Taurus, Cancer, Scorpio, and Capricorn.

And those which are said to have many offspring are Cancer, Scorpio and Pisces.

Whence if you were asked a question regarding children, and the Ascendant, or the Lord of the Ascendant, or the house of children, or the Lord of the house of children, or the Moon, were in one of these signs (of many offspring): it would signify many children, lest something else impedes things, (as will be discussed in the chapter on children). And these three signs thrive in the west.

And three signs are said to be sterile: namely Gemini, Leo, and Virgo. Whence if you were asked a question about children, and any of the aforementioned significators were found in these signs, it would signify sterility, unless something else assists (as will be discussed in the chapter on children below).

And six signs are said to have few children: namely Aries, Taurus, Libra, Sagittarius, Capricorn, and Aquarius. Whence if you are asked a question about children, and any of the aforementioned significators were in any of these signs, it would indicate a small number of children.

And four signs are said to be very wicked, these being Aries, Taurus, Leo, and Capricorn.

And certain signs are said to be half-voiced namely those which are formed in the image of bleating, braying or roaring animals: which are Aries, Taurus, Leo, Capricorn, and the last part of Sagittarius. Whence if the Ascendant or the Lord of the Ascendant, or the Moon, are in one of these signs in a nativity, there will not be much talk out of the native, unless something assists (as will be said in the tractate on nativities).

And certain signs are said to be voiceless: namely those which are formed in the image of animals which themselves lack a voice; which are Scorpio, Cancer and Pisces. Whence if the Ascendant, the Lord of the Ascendant, or the Moon are in these signs, it signifies that the native lacks a voice, unless something assists (as I will explain to you in the tractate on nativities, God willing).

And two signs are said to be dark: namely Libra and Capricorn. Whence if the Ascendant, the Ascendant Lord, or the Moon are impeded in either of these signs in any nativity, it signifies that the native will be dull and of a dark countenance.

And there is a certain place in the signs which is said to be combust: namely the *via combusta*, which is from the middle of Libra up to the middle of Scorpio.

However you may ask what use are these things which Alchabicius says: that certain signs are said to thrive in the east, or the south, or the west, or the north, or that certain signs are rational, certain ones are four-footed, others are domesticated, others have beautiful voices, others are half-voiced, while others are voiceless. To which the response is, that the aim of the philosophers in this was that whenever someone is born and their significator (or the Moon) was in these signs: that the nature and being of the native would be in accordance with what was indicated by the significator being in the sign. So that if the significator, the Moon, and the Ascendant were all in one of the signs formed in the image of man, the native will be more rational, and will speak more, and better, than someone who has his significators placed in other signs.

And if someone was born with his significator, Moon, and Ascendant in one of the signs formed in the image of bleating, braying, or roaring animals: then this native would be less talkative and less knowledgeable on how to order his words. And if someone was born with their Moon, significator, and Ascendant in any of the voiceless signs, or those signs which bray, bleat or roar: then the native will have a stutter and speak little. And if the significator or the Moon (namely only one of them) were impeded in a nativity then the native will be less talkative in accordance with the severity of the impediment. And if both are impeded, the native will be an even poorer speaker, and even less talkative, so much so that he is barely able to utter word without struggle and fatigue. If the significator of the nativity and the Moon were impeded in any of the voiceless signs, then the native will be mute; and this even more so if the Ascendant is in such a sign.

And it is said that the signs thrive in certain quarters (as was said) since their virtue appears greater when they are in these quarters. Not that they have any different significations in one quarter or another; but rather they are similar to certain trees, which are the same tree in winter as they are in summer and spring, but still in the beginning of the spring they begin to bloom, as their foliage and flowers are expanded, while still remaining the same tree they were before. And Leo, which thrives in all quarters, is similar to evergreen trees which are full of life at all times of the year, like olive trees, pines, juniper trees and so on.

XXI

Which Parts Of The Body Each Sign Is Said To Have, And What Signification In Each Limb, And What Character Traits, And What They Signify Of Seeds, And Regions, And Similar Things

The body of man is divided into twelve parts, in the likeness of the twelve signs; and each sign has one of these parts.

On Aries

Of the body of man, Aries has the head and the whole face, whence it is said "*And since The Rams power is greater at the head*", and so it deservedly has the head. Of regions, Babylonia, Babyl, Persia, Azerbaijan, and Palestine. And Aries is said to have the head since the virtue or power of the ram thrives more greatly in the head than any other part of it. And Aries is said to have these regions since its significations appear more in these regions than anywhere else.

On Taurus

Of the body of man, Taurus has the neck up to the beginning of the shoulders, whence it is said "*From this they gave the Bull the neck: since his place follows the Ram, so should his reason*". Taurus also has virtue in trees which are planted. And it is said that Taurus rules the neck, since the bull's power thrives here more so than in any other part of him. And of regions it has: Alzemiet, Almechin and Aricorad. And it is said that Taurus has these regions since its significations appear more in these regions than anywhere else.

On Gemini

Of the body of man, Gemini has the shoulders, from their beginning onwards, along with the arms and the hands. Whence it is said "*Striving from the shoulders, possessing two twins*" - from there because men are doubled from the shoulders. And it signifies the generosity and goodness of the soul of the native born with Gemini as their Ascendant. And of regions it is said to have,

Iurgen, Greater Armenia, Azerbaijan, and Egypt. And it is said to have the shoulders, arms, and hands since men are doubled from the shoulders onwards towards the hands. And it is said to have these regions since its significations appear more in these regions than anywhere else.

On Cancer

Of the parts of the body of man, Cancer has the chest up to near the diaphragm, and the parts adjacent to this, and the lungs. And Alchabicius says that it also rules the spleen, whence is said of Cancer "*The celestial sign so called the Crab, for it holds the heavens chest, in the hollows of its bosom*". And of regions it has Lesser Armenia, and the eastern parts of Khoracen, China, and has parts of Balkh and Azerbaijan. And it has virtue in tall trees which lose their leaves in autumn, such as the poplar tree and others like it. And it is said to have these regions as its significations appear more in these regions than anywhere else.

On Leo

Of the parts of the body of man, Leo rules the stomach, the heart, and the lower part of the chest (where courage thrives), and the diaphragm and the sides of spine. And it signifies cunning, wily men, and those who sorrow and worry a lot; and similarly the dorsal region, and around the iliac crest. Whence it is said "*Leo, equally ruling of the lower breast, where bravery blossoms below*". And it has virtue in noble trees, such as firs and other trees which make many leaves and are without fruit, and keep their leaves in the winter. And of regions it is said to have the land of the Turks up to the ends of the habitable regions, along with Mauritania and all its bounds. And it is said to have these regions since its significations appear more in these regions than anywhere else.

On Virgo

Of the parts of the body of man, Virgo has the stomach and the navel, and the parts adjacent to the navel, and the intestines. From which it is said: "*The navel has the borders of virginity*" - for it is cherished by the sign of Virgo. And it signifies the generosity and good will of those born with this sign on the Ascendant. And it signifies all seeds which are sown. Of regions it has Garamaqa, Syria, and the regions next to the Euphrates, and Great Spain, and Persia. And it is said to have these regions since its significations appear more in these regions than anywhere else (besides those relating to seeds, which it signifies for the whole earth).

On Libra

Of the parts of the body of man, Libra signifies the lumbar region, the haunches, and the lower part of the belly up to the upper part of the thighs, and it has the inferior parts of these, along with the buttocks. And it is said to have the haunch, since man almost begins to be balanced from this part of the body, since they are in a certain way made similar to a balance-scales. From which is said "*Level to this the man begins to fork, and from this omen the Scales take their name*". And Libra has all of the trees which Leo has, and in addition to these it also has those which grow quickly and bear fruit quickly, such as peach trees, and almond trees and the like. And it also signifies generosity and a good mind, like Virgo. Of regions it rules Apulia, Rome, and Roman lands and their borders, up to the province of Africa, and Egypt, and up to Aethiopia and Barchan; as said by Alchabicius. And it has Kirman and Sigistan, Kabul, Tabaristan, Balkh and Herat. And it is said to have these regions since its significations appear more in these regions than anywhere else.

On Scorpio

On the parts of the body of man Scorpio signifies the private parts, *the whole thigh, and the bladder. Whence is said "The Scorpion, stinging itself with tail raised above, ruling the penis and Venus by one member*" And it signifies generosity and goodness of the soul, as do Virgo and Libra. And it signifies the trees ruled by Cancer, those being the poplar tree and those which are very wide and lose their leaves in the autumn. Of regions it has Hejaz, and the Arab lands, and their limits up until Yemen. And it has participation in Sind. And it is said to have these regions since its significations appear more in these regions than anywhere else.

On Sagittarius

Of the parts of the human body Sagittarius signifies the upper thighs. Whence it is said "*Venus and the arrow equally shot from the bow; by mighty thighs the horse governs their flow*" And it signifies an ingenious, cunning man who knows how to do many things, and how to handle affairs he is involved in so that they reach his desired end; and who know how to seduce and lead men to whatever he wishes (whether he wants to do good, or bad); and will be trusted by men on account of this, and will often deceives them (albeit not always under the pretext of pretending to do good, when he is actually a seducer), and he is not believed to be a seducer, but rather he is believed to be lawful; but he is neither believed to be entirely faithful nor entirely unfaithful. Of regions it has Aethiopia, Mahruban, and India. And it is said to have these regions since its significations appear more in these regions than anywhere else.

On Capricorn

Of the parts of the body of man, Capricorn has the knees. Whence it is said *"The goat grazing on the bank kneels on his knees*".

And it signifies a man who knows how to lead a good life, and is irritable, and who knows how to look after his own business well, and also the business of others. And he will know well how to counsel those seeking advice from him. And he will be clever, both in good things, and in bad things (if he wishes), and similarly a man who is easily and often saddened. Of regions and countries it rules the western part of Aethiopia up to Yemen (where two seas are joined), and up to Iacinthum and Lower India. And it is said to rule these regions since its significations appear more in these regions than anywhere else.

On Aquarius

Of the parts of the body of man, Aquarius has the leg from the knee down to the ankles of the feet, so that it has the entirety of the ankles. Whence it is said *"Denoting the legs making long forms of vessels, a man like a pourer water in the cold*". Of regions it signifies Azenguch, and a part of the black land of Ceclem, and Kuda, and the areas bordering on it, and all of Elfigem, and the western western part of Egypt, and the western part of Sind. And it is said to have these regions since its significations appear more in these regions than anywhere else.

On Pisces

Of the parts of the body of man, Pisces rules the feet, whence it is said "*Fortune makes feet like the Fishes, put together as though with spiny bones*". And it signifies a clever man, of mixed nature and not lasting long in his proposals. And sometimes signifies a very coloured man, and sometimes a man of mixed colours. Of regions it has Tabaristan, and the northern part of Gurgan. It also has signification over the lands of the Romans up to Syria. And over Italy. It similarly signifies, and especially Romaniola and up to Marche and up to Venice. And it partly rules Egypt, Alexandria and the sea of Aluven.

XXII

What Part Of The Body Is Signified By Each Planet In Each Sign

It has been discussed above regarding what parts of the body are ruled by each of the twelve signs; now we shall discuss what part of the body each planet signifies in every sign. And we will begin from Saturn, who is the first planet, and from Aries, which is the first sign. Whence if you were asked a question about some illness or pain which someone was suffering: look then in what sign the significator of the querent (namely the sick person) is in, and who the significator is.

If it is Saturn, and he is in Aries, it signifies the illness or pain, is in the chest: since Saturn in Aries signifies the chest; Jupiter in Aries the stomach; Mars the head; the Sun the thighs; Venus the feet; Mercury the legs; the Moon the knees. And understand thusly for all the signs.

In Taurus Saturn signifies the stomach; Jupiter the back; Mars the neck; the Sun the knees; Venus the head; Mercury the feet; the Moon the legs.

In Gemini, Saturn signifies the stomach; Jupiter the private parts and what follows them; Mars the chest; the Sun the legs and ankles of the feet; Venus the neck; Mercury the head; the Moon the thighs.

In Cancer Saturn signifies the male genitals and what follows them; Jupiter the thighs; Mars the chest; the Sun the feet; Venus the shoulders, arms, and hands; Mercury the eyes; the Moon the head.

In Leo Saturn signifies the private parts and what follows them; Jupiter the thighs and knees; Mars the stomach; the Sun the head; Venus the heart; Mercury the shoulders and throat; the Moon the neck.

In Virgo Saturn signifies the feet; Jupiter the knees; Mars the stomach; the Sun the neck; Venus the navel and the parts adjacent to it; Mercury the heart; the Moon the shoulders.

In Libra Saturn signifies the knees are what follows them; Jupiter the eyes and what is around them; Mars the private parts and what follows them; Sun the shoulders; Venus the head; Mercury the private parts; the Moon the heart.

In Scorpio Saturn signifies the ankles of the feet and what follows them; Jupiter the feet; Mars the head, arms and thighs; the Sun the heart; Venus the private parts and what follows them; Mercury the back; the Moon the stomach.

In Sagittarius Saturn signifies the feet; Jupiter the legs and head; Mars the feet and hands; the Sun the stomach; Venus the thighs and arms; Mercury the private parts and heart; the Moon the back.

In Capricorn Saturn signifies the head and the feet; Jupiter the knees and eyes; Mars the legs and shoulders; the Sun the back; Venus the thighs and heart; Mercury the private parts and what follows them; the Moon the thighs and what follows the private parts.

In Aquarius Saturn signifies the head and neck; Jupiter the shoulders, chest and feet; Mars the ankles and the heart; the Sun the private parts and what follows; Venus the knees and what follows; Mercury the thighs and the heart; the Moon the private parts.

In Pisces Saturn signifies the neck, shoulders, and arms; Jupiter the head and heart; Mars the stomach and ankles of the feet; the Sun the thighs and what follows; Venus the neck and back; Mercury the legs and private parts; the Moon the thighs.

XXIII

On The Masculine And Feminine Degrees In Each Sign

Albumashar and Alchabicius said that in each sign there are certain degrees which are called masculine, and certain degrees which are called feminine. For the first eight degrees of Aries are said to be masculine, and the next five are called feminine, followed by six masculine, followed by seven feminine, followed by four masculine up to the end of the sign. And the first five degrees of Taurus are feminine, followed by six masculine, followed by six feminine, followed by four masculine, followed by three feminine, followed by six masculine.

And not to have our work overly prolonged, and to avoid prolixity, I have written everything in the table below, according to what the philosophers have said on this matter.

Aries	8-M	5-F	6-M	7-F	4-M	0	0
Taurus	5-F	6-M	6-F	4-M	3-F	6-M	0
Gemini	5-F	11-M	6-F	4-M	4-F	0	0
Cancer	2-M	6-F	2-M	2-F	11-M	4-F	3-M
Leo	5-M	3-F	7-M	8-F	7-M	0	0
Virgo	8-F	4-M	8-F	10-M	0	0	0
Libra	5-M	10-F	5-M	7-F	3-M	0	0
Scorpio	4-M	10-F	3-M	8-F	5-M	0	0
Sagittarius	2-M	3-F	7-M	12-F	6-M	0	0
Capricorn	11-M	8-F	11-M	0	0	0	0
Aquarius	5-M	10-F	6-M	4-F	2-M	3-F	0
Pisces	10-M	10-F	3-M	5-F	2-M	0	0

You might ask why these degrees are called masculine, and why those degrees are called feminine; the reason for the philosophers calling them so is as follows: that when you are asked a question on any matter where it is necessary for you to discern the sex of something, such as if you are asked whether a pregnant woman's' baby is male or female; or a question about a thief, as to whether they are male or female, and other such questions - you will be able to answer them. And if the significator of the individual in question, or the Moon, is found in one of those degrees which are said to be masculine, it is attested that the individual in question is male. And if they were found in any of the degrees which are said to feminine, it attests that the individual in question is female - especially so if the other signs of masculinity or femininity concord with the degree, just as will be said in the Tractate on judgements in the chapter on children and in the chapter on robbery.

XXIV

On The Bright, Dark, Smoky, And Empty Degrees

Albumashar and Alchabicius said that there are certain degrees in the signs which are said to be bright, others which are said to be dark, others which are said to be smoky, and others which are said to be empty. Whence the first three degrees of Aries are said to be dark; the next five bright; the next eight dark; then four bright; then four dark; then five bright; then one dark. The first three degrees of Taurus are dark; the next four bright; then four empty; three bright; five empty; eight bright; three dark. And to explain things quicker, I give you this table, following from what these two philosophers have said on these degrees.

Aries	3-D	5-B	8-D	4-B	4-D	5-B	1-D
Taurus	3-D	4-B	4-E	3-B	5-E	8-B	3-D
Gemini	4-B	3-D	5-B	4-E	6-B	5-D	3-E
Cancer	12-B	2-D	4-E	2-S	8-B	2-E	0
Leo	10-D	10-S	5-E	5-B	0	0	0
Virgo	5-D	3-B	2-E	6-B	6-S	5-E	3-D
Libra	5-B	5-D	8-B	3-D	6-B	3-E	0
Scorpio	3-D	5-B	6-E	6-B	2-S	5-E	3-D
Sagittarius	9-B	3-D	7-B	4-S	7-B	0	0
Capricorn	7-D	3-B	5-S	4-B	3-D	3-E	5-D
Aquarius	4-S	5-B	4-D	8-B	4-E	5-B	0
Pisces	6-D	6-B	6-D	4-B	3-E	3-B	2-B

The degrees above have been so called for this reason: for if it appears from the Ascendant Lord of someone's nativity (or the Lord of someone's nativity, or through the Moon) that the native (or the person who is quesited) ought to be of a bright colour and a beautiful face; and if these significators are in any of the bright degrees: then the person will be clear and very beautiful. If any of them are in a dark degree the person will be less beautiful. And if any of them are in a smoky degree, the person will be between the two (that is neither beautiful nor overly ugly). And so if the aforementioned significator and the Moon were in a dark degree, if the native ought to be ugly, he will be uglier and more unsightly. And if one is in a bright degree he will be less ugly and less unsightly than he ought to be according to the Lord of the Ascendant. And if they are in an empty degree, whether the native is beautiful or ugly, they will be of little sense and little intelligence - even to a worse degree than they appear. And the more you inquire into the sense and intelligence of these individuals the more you will be displeased, and they will seem even less strong to you with respect to other people, and will be called empty by everybody.

XXV

On The Welled Degrees

And the same philosophers said that there are certain degrees in the signs which are said to be "welled". Of which I have put together the following table for you

Aries	6	11	16	23	29	
Taurus	5	12	24	25		
Gemini	2	12	17	26	30	
Cancer	2	12	17	26	30	
Leo	6	13	15	22	23	28
Virgo	8	13	16	21	22	
Libra	1	7	20	30		
Scorpio	9	10	22	23	27	
Sagittarius	7	12	15	24	27	
Capricorn	7	17	22	24	29	
Aquarius	11	12	17	22	24	29
Pisces	4	9	24	27	28	

They are called welled degrees, since when a significator of someone's nativity, or the significatrix (which is the Moon; who has participation in all matters) is found in any of these degrees, it is said to be "in a well" - that it is in a certain form of debility, like someone who wishes to travel to some place, and is in a great pit, or in a valley, or cavern made in the manner of a well: so that he cannot travel as freely, nor as quickly as he wants to; nor as quickly as one who is in a flat place outside of "the well"; for he who is outside of the well is not impeded, so he can travel faster than someone who is in the well. And so the native or querent is impeded in their business when their significator (or the Moon) is in any of the welled degrees, so that they will not be able it to effect as quickly; and he will only perfect it with greater burdens and greater difficulty than another who is not impeded in such a manner.

XXVI

On The Azemena Degrees

Ptolemy, Alchabicius, and others have said that there are certain degrees in certain signs which are called azemena degrees, and they are debilitating. Azemena is a certain illness inseparable from the body of the native, which is often acquired while they are in the womb; and as long as the native lives he will have this illness with him. And it is an illness inseparable from the body, such as natural blindness, natural deafness, lameness, or natural gibbosity and similar things. Of which degrees I have made the table written below.

Aries							
Taurus	6	7	8	9	10		
Gemini							
Cancer	9	10	11	12	13	14	15
Leo	18	27	28				
Virgo							
Libra							
Scorpio	19	28					
Sagittarius	1	7	8	18	19		
Capricorn	26	27	28	29			
Aquarius	18	19					
Pisces							

XXVII

On The Degrees Of Increasing Fortune

And the same philosophers said that there are certain degrees in the signs which are called degrees of increasing fortune; regarding which the table below was made.

Aries	19				
Taurus	5	15	27		
Gemini	11				
Cancer	1	2	3	4	15
Leo	2	5	7	19	
Virgo	3	14	20		
Libra	3	15	21		
Scorpio	7	18	20		
Sagittarius	13	20			
Capricorn	12	13	14	20	
Aquarius	7	16	17	20	
Pisces	13	20			

XXVIII

On The Degrees Having Power Together And Conforming In Virtue

Alchabicius says that two degrees which are equidistant from the beginnings of the mobile signs are said to be "having power together"- that is they are said to be of equal strength, and to participate and conform in virtue: such as the twentieth degree of Capricorn (so that the twentieth is included), and the tenth degree of Sagittarius (so that the tenth is included): and the twentieth degree of Cancer and the tenth degree of Gemini. The tenth degree of Sagittarius is the same distance from the beginning of Capricorn as the twentieth degree of Capricorn; and in like manner the twentieth degree of Gemini and the tenth degree of Cancer are the same distance from the beginning of Cancer. Between the tenth degree of Sagittarius and the beginning of Capricorn are twenty degrees, and between the twentieth degree of Capricorn and the beginning of Capricorn are twenty degrees. Similarly the tenth degree of Gemini and the twentieth degree of Cancer are an equal distance from the beginning of Cancer. And likewise the twentieth degree of Aries and the tenth degree of Pisces are the same distance from the beginning of Aries. And likewise the twentieth degree of Libra and the tenth degree of Virgo are the same distance from the beginning of Libra. And similarly equidistant from the beginning of Libra are: 21 Libra and 9 Virgo; 22 Libra and 8 Virgo; 23 Libra and 7 Virgo; 24 Libra and 6 Virgo; 25 Libra and 5 Virgo; 26 Libra and 4 Virgo; 27 Libra and 3 Virgo; 28 Libra and 2 Virgo; and 29 Libra and 1 Virgo. And understand the same for all the degrees of Capricorn and Sagittarius, Gemini and Cancer, along with Aries and Pisces.

I will not point them out to you as it would be excessively long winded and laborious, and all of the degrees are distinguished in the same manner as those of Libra and Virgo (which ought to suffice as an example). And they are called "having power together", since each of them has as much strength in the matters which it signifies as its correlate: such as the first degree of Aries and the last degree of Pisces, the second degree of Aries and the twenty eighth degree of Pisces, the third degree of Aries and the twenty seventh degree of Pisces, and so on for all the other degrees.

THE THIRD PART OF THE SECOND TRACTATE

On The Nature Of The Accidental Circle

I

On The Division Of The Circle By Houses

A division is made of the circle of signs, which divides it into four equal parts, according to its division into two great circles: one of which is called the horizon or circle of the hemisphere. And the other is called the circle of the meridian, or the Midheaven. And each of these quarters is divided into three unequal parts, and thus the whole circle is divided into twelve unequal parts. And the inequality is due to the refraction of the horizon in different climates and the diversity of regions, as is demonstrated well by Thebit in his introduction to the celestial sphere, in the tractate on how the circle in the sphere is imagined. And you will also find in this book "*Rules on the Equations of the Stars*". And this division always begins from the line of the Ascendant.

And each of these divisions is called a house, or a cusp, or a tower, and not simply "a sign". And the first of these houses is the sign on the Ascendant, namely that which is in Aries. And Ptolemy says that there are five degrees which have crossed over the line of any division of one house from another, are counted as, and said to belong to, the same house given to the line in question. So that if the Ascendant was twenty-five degrees of some sign, the five degrees which have crossed the line of the Ascendant would be counted as, and said to belong to, the 1st house (and likewise for the twenty five degrees under the line). And you ought to understand this for the other houses. For the five degrees which have crossed over the line of any given house are always counted as being in that house, and the twenty five which have not yet reached the line (namely on the condition that each house is thirty degrees). Then follows the 2nd house, then the 3rd house, then the 4th house, then the 5th house, then the 6th house, then the 7th house, then the 8th house, then the 9th house, then the 10th house, then the 11th house, and finally the 12th house (which is the last of all the houses).

II

On The Division Of The Quarters Of The Circle

Alchabicius and Haly said that the quarter part of the circle between the Ascendant and the Midheaven (which contains the twelfth, eleventh and 10th houses) is said to be the oriental, masculine, advancing, sanguine, vernal, puerile quarter, and signifies the beginning of life natives life up until the end of adolescence (which is from the beginning, or the day of birth, up until the twenty-first year inclusive).

The quarter which is from the Midheaven up to the occidental line (which contains the ninth, eighth and 7th houses), is said to be the southern, receding, summery, choleric, youthful, quarter, and signifies the middle age (that is the complete age of youth), and is called the advancement of youth. And this quarter is said to relate to the other quarters in the same way that youth does to the other ages of life (youth being from twenty-two years old to forty-one years old inclusive).

The third quarter, that is from the 7th house to the 4th house (namely the sixth, fifth and 4th houses) which is below the earth, is said to be the western, masculine, advancing, the autumnal, melancholic and senile quarter. And this quarter is said to relate to the others in the same way that old age relates to the other ages of life (old age being from forty one years old to sixty years old). And certain men say it signifies old age up until the end of life, which to me does not seem correct. But for their part, they considered that men often pass away around the age of sixty, or a little past it.

The final quarter, namely that from the 4th house to the Ascendant (which is the third, second and 1st houses), is said to be the northern, feminine, receding, phlegmatic, vernal, defective quarter, and it is called decrepit. And this quarter is said to stand in respect of other quarters as the decrepit final years of life stand in relation to the other ages: the decrepit years being from the end of old age, that being from sixty years old, up until ninety years old; and also up to the end of life, should anyone live past ninety, which few do; although some say they are one hundred years old or more, and there are those who are ninety or a small bit older); since the general life of man contains three reigns of

Saturn, which are ninety years. And this quarter also signifies what happen men after their death; that is what happens to their goods and their estate, what will be said about them (whether they will be praised or blamed), and whether their body will be cremated or buried, or buried honourably or shamefully, or whether their relatives and friends will cry and suffer from their death, or laugh and rejoice from it.

III

Which Half Is Called Ascending, And Which Descending, And Which Part Is Called Right, And Which Left

Two of the above mentioned quarters, those being the quarter from the Midheaven to the Ascendant, and the quarter from the Ascendant to the line of the 4th house, are called the ascending half. The remaining quarters, those being the quarter from the line of the 4th house to the seventh, and from there to the Midheaven, are called the descending half.

And that part of the heavens which is above the earth is said to be "right of the heavens", and is stronger and more noble. And that part which is below the earth is said to be "left of the heavens, and is weaker and less noble; and this according to how the circle of the horizon of any region divides the heavens in two halves.

And that part of the heavens which is from the Ascendant up to the 7th house below the earth is said to be "right of the Ascendant", while the corresponding part above the earth is said to be "left of the Ascendant".

And that which is from the Ascendant passing through the north to the 7th house, (according to how the horizon has divided the heavens into the part above the earth and the part below the earth), is said to be "right of rising". And that which is from the Ascendant passing south up to the 7th house is said to be "left of rising".

And the right of the heavens, the right of the Ascendant, and the right of rising, differ from each other in this.

IV

On The Angles, Cadents, And Succeedents

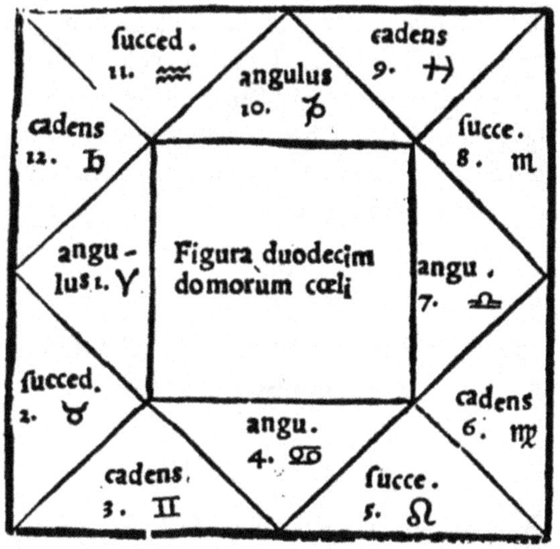

Out of all the halves and quarters mentioned above, twelve houses come to be, four of which are called "angles": namely the first, fourth, seventh, and 10th houses. And these houses are the stronger and firmer parts of the heavens; and they also differ in strength amongst themselves. For the first is stronger than the tenth (except in dignities which pertain to secular glory, such as kingship, dukedoms, positions of power, and so on; in which the 10th house is preferred to all others). And the tenth is stronger than the seventh; and the seventh is stronger than the fourth.

The second, fifth, eight and 11th houses are called "succeedents" of the angles, since they immediately follow the angles and are less strong than the angles by half; except for the 11th house, which is very strong in matters related to fortune, and of things in which we have hope (for this is the house of fortune, faith, and hope, as is said in the tractate on houses).

The third, sixth, ninth and 12th houses are called "cadent from the angles. And they are very weak houses, and do not promise good, nor firmness, nor durability, nor prolongation of any matter; except that the 9th house is preferred in religious matters, and is more suited to these matters than any other house, along with matters which look to clerical dignities (such as bishoprics, abbacies, priories, and similar things).

Whence if a planet signifying some matter is in an angle, it promises good, and will be said to be successful. But if this planet were in a succeedent house, it would be less successful than in the angle. And if this planet were in a cadent house it is said to fail, and to be weak and useless (with the exception of that which I said to you about the ninth and 11th houses). And each one of the houses mentioned above has their own unique significations in things, and in the lives of men, just as I am about to narrate to you in what follows.

V

On The Significations Of The Twelve Houses

On The First House

The 1st house, which begins from the direction of the east, is called the Ascendant. And (according to Adila, Zael, Alchabicius, and all other wise men) signifies the life and body of the native, or of the querent. And it signifies the beginning of any given work, and has signification over all elections, and over all beginnings, and over the beginning of the life of the native or querent. And from this the 1st house is said to be the beginning of all houses.

And there is a certain similarity between the 1st house and the birth of a native, and asking a question: for just as this house ascends from that part of the heavens which is hidden from our view below the horizon, toward the superior part of the heavens visible to us above the earth, and comes from being hidden into the light, and from the hidden parts to the manifest: in like manner when a native is born they come out from the darkness, and the distresses of their mother's womb, and arrive into the light of this world, and into the open air. And he who asks a question brings his intention and the secrets of his heart to light, and that which was at first hidden in darkness is now revealed in the light.

And Adila and Alezdegoz say that in nativities, the first triplicity Lord of the 1st house signifies the life and nature of the native or querent, and his pleasures and in what he delights, and what he loves, and what he hates. And also what happens to him, both good and bad, in the first third part of his life. The second triplicity Lord signifies the robustness of the native, or his strength and virility, and what happens to him in the second third of his life. And the third triplicity Lord signifies what the first two signify, along with the end of life, and what happens to the native in the final third of his life. Whence if you are presented with someone's nativity, or if you are asked a general question about fortune (or about the general condition of someone): examine the triplicity Lords of the 1st house, namely the first, second, and third; and judge according to the quality of each of them. If the first Lord signifies good, judge that good things will happen to the native, or the querent, in the first third part of his life. And if the second Lord of the same triplicity signifies good, it will befall the native in the second third of his life. And if the third triplicity Lord signifies good, it will happen in the final third of the natives' life. The same can be said about evil, so that if any of the above significators signify evil, it will befall the native in the third of his life signified by the significator in question, just as said about nourishment.

On The Other Significations Of The First House

And the 1st house signifies the substance, or assets of hidden enemies, since it is the second from the twelfth. Hidden enemies are those who pretend to be a friend, who laugh and appear to rejoice with men, and say they love them, and publicly announce good things to them, while at the same time being jealous, and being pained at others prosperity, and rejoicing in their adversity, and striving to secretly harm them in every way possible.

And it also signifies brothers of friends, since it is the third from the eleventh. And parents of kings, since it is the fourth from the tenth. And children of the religious, since it is the fifth from the ninth. And infirmities of the household members of the natives associates, public enemies, and wives not staying with their husbands, since it is the sixth from the eighth. And the wives of these people, since it is the seventh from the seventh. And the death of slaves, since it is the eighth from the sixth. And the religion of children, and their long journeys, since it is the ninth from the fifth. And the profession or dignities of the father, since it is tenth from the fourth. And friends of brothers, since it is the eleventh from the third. And hidden enemies of associates, and their large animals, since it is the twelfth from the second.

On The Second House

The 2nd house, as Alchabicius said, signifies substance, acquisition, attendants, and the end of youth. And Adila said that it signifies the aggregation of substance, or possessions, and money, and things given and things received. And Zael said that the 2nd house signifies property, letters and assistants, and doesn't aspect the Ascendant.

And Alezdegoz said to examine the triplicity Lords of the 2nd house (namely the first, second and third triplicity Lords), and see which of them is stronger by condition and place, and give this planet authority over the substance and acquisition of the native or querent. Which, if placed in the Midheaven will signify acquisition from kings; or if it is in the domicile of a luminary, the acquisition will be from religion: and understand similarly for the rest of the houses. Likewise the first triplicity Lord of the 2nd house gives substance in the beginning of life, that is in the first one-third of life; the second in the middle part of life (namely in the second third of life); while the third gives substance in the final third of the natives life. However this thing which Alezdegoz has said about the above mentioned significators, should be understood as meaning that the significator of substance will signify it at whatever age.

If the significator is in the 1st house, the native will obtain substance by means of his own body, namely by the work of his own hands, his own industry, and his own solicitude.

However, if it is in the 2nd house, he will obtain substance by means of his own substance, such as from the profits of his possessions and goods, and also from commerce, and other mechanical arts and trades such as carpentry and the like, where the native works with moveable substance, such as in the case of cobblers, or leather workers and so on; or through other things signified by the 2nd house.

If it is in the 3rd house, the native will obtain substance through his brothers, or sisters, or neighbours who are not related to him, or through short journeys, or through those lesser than him in wealth, power, or age (namely those who hold him as their senior, as will be discussed in the chapter on the 3rd house).

And if it is in the 4th house, he will obtain substance by means of his father and grandfathers, or other relatives who are senior to, or older than the native, or through his father in law, or possibly through a hidden or buried treasure, or from underground, or through some other signification of the 4th house.

And if it is in the 5th house the native will obtain substance through children, and through medium length journeys (which are those between two and five days long), or through foods and drinks which are sold in taverns and similar places, or through games, or some other thing which is signified by the 5th house.

If it is in the 6th house, the native will obtain substance through slaves, or slave-girls, or dogs or birds (as do hunters), or through other small animals which cannot be ridden, such as sheep and similar creatures; or through some other thing which is signified by the 6th house.

If it is in the 7th house the native will obtain substance though wives, or associates or enemies, or through something else signified by the 7th house.

If it is in the 8th house the native will obtain substance because of death, or through goods inherited from the dead, or through his wife's goods, or the goods of his associates or enemies, or through something else signified by the 8th house.

If it is in the 9th house the native will obtain substance through long journeys (as you will often find to be the case with merchants or sailors who travel for long durations to gain profit), and also by means of bishoprics, abbacies, or other religious matters, and so on; or something else which is signified by the 9th house.

And if it was in the 10th house, the native will acquire substance through a magistracy, or kingship, as was said, or through other lay dignities, as are positions of power, and the like.

And if it is in the eleventh the native will obtain substance through friends, or the king's soldiers, or the king's substance, or through unexpected good fortune, or through something in which the native has hope; or something else signified by the 11th house.

And if it is in the 12th house, the native will acquire substance through hidden enemies, or through prisons, or prisoners, as you sometimes find in the case of guards of prisoners, and the like. Or by means of cattle, or camels, or horses; or something else signified by the 12th house.

And the 2nd house also has other significations besides the substance of the native: since it signifies hidden enemies of the natives brothers, since it is the third from the twelfth. And fathers and grandfathers, etc. of friends, since it is the fourth from the eleventh. And it signifies the king's children, and his medium length journeys, since it is the fifth from the tenth. And it signifies infirmities of the religious, since it is the sixth from the ninth. And it signifies the wives, associates, and enemies of the household members of enemies and associates, since it is the seventh from the eighth. And it signifies the death (and absences) of wives, associates, and enemies, since it is the eighth from the seventh. And it signifies the religion and long journeys of slaves, since it is the ninth from the sixth. And it signifies the professions of children, since it is the tenth from the fifth. And it signifies the friends and fortune of the father etc., since it is the eleventh from the fourth. And it signifies the hidden enemies and large animals of the native's brother, since it is the twelfth from the third.

On The Third House

Alchabicius says that the 3rd house signifies brothers and sisters, and close friendships and loves, faith and religion, orders (or contracts), and legates, changes, short journeys, and it signifies the condition of life before death. And Adila said that it signifies blood relatives, and changes from dwelling to dwelling, and patience, and similar things. And Zahel says that it signifies contentions in sects, letters, and dreams. And it signifies all sects and heretics. And Alezdegoz said that the first triplicity Lord of the house of brothers signifies younger brothers; the second signifies middle brothers; and the third signifies older brothers. And he said that the condition of these brothers will follow from the placement of their significator.

And it seems the same to me, that it signifies all of the above things, and that it signifies all blood-relatives and other relations who are younger than the native or querent, and neighbours, and also fellow citizens (both masters and slaves, matrons and women and rich and poor). It signifies blood-relatives and other relations who consider the native as their senior, and who revere and obey him, and who are lesser than him in wealth, power, and wisdom; and who consult him in their affairs and necessities, and who often want to manage their own affairs based off of the counsel and assistance of the native.

Whence if you are given a question on any of the things said above, you always ought to give the 3rd house to it, and give the 1st house to the querent: so that if anyone asks about his relatives, or about one of the above mentioned people, and the Ascendant is Aries (or any other sign), give the Ascendant to the querent, and give the 3rd house to the quesited. And according to what you see as regards the Lord of the 3rd house (as to whether it signifies good or evil): judge according to that.

And if someone is born, and you wish to know what kind of fortune he is to have from his brothers, or any of the matters mentioned above: see how the Lord of the first and the 3rd house interact with each other, and how they aspect each other. Since if they aspect each other by a loving aspect, and receive each other, there will be love and goodness between the native and the person in question; however if they aspect each other by an inimical aspect, the native will not rejoice because of them, nor with them, nor will there be good from them, nor to them from the native.

Moreover, you ought to examine the triplicity Lords of the 3rd house: since if one of these aspects the Lord of the Ascendant by a good aspect (namely a trine or a sextile), or receives him, there will be good things for the native from the brother signified by the planet in question, and understand the same for the other two triplicity Lords.

And should one of them aspect the Lord of the 1st house by an evil aspect, things will be bad for the native regarding the brother signified by the planet in question.

And if the Lord of the first does not aspect any of these planets, the native will be like a stranger with all of his brothers, and will benefit from them as if he were a stranger.

Understand the same for the Moon as has been said for the Lord of the first.

And if one of these significators is in better condition, the brothers which are signified by this planet will be similarly in better condition, and have better fortune than the rest. And should one of the significators be in worse condition, the brothers which are signified by it will be in a similarly worse condition themselves.

Besides this you ought to know that the 3rd house is always the Ascendant of brothers and younger relatives, neighbours, and other persons signified by this house; and the 1st house is always the querent's, apart from excepted cases, which you will find in their own place.

Posit that someone enquired about the affairs of their brother or sister; and the Ascendant was Leo, and the 3rd house was Libra . By this method the first is the Ascendant of the querent, and the third is that of the quesited; whence you ought not to judge according to the Lord of the Ascendant, but according to the Lord of the third. And according to what you see regarding the condition of the Lord of the third, so you will judge regarding the affairs of the querent's siblings.

Moreover, if the first triplicity Lord of the 3rd house interacts well with the Lord of the Ascendant, things will be good for the native or querent with his brothers, neighbours, younger relatives, and other things which are signified by the 3rd house, in the first third of the natives life (and these people will do well from the native in this time also). And if this is true for the second triplicity Lord, the native will do well from these people, and them from him, in the second third of his life. And if this is true with the third triplicity Lord, the native will do well from these people, and them from him, in the final third of his life. And it will be to the contrary if the two planets in question interact badly with each other.

And the 3rd house has other significations: since it signifies the substance of household members, since it is the second from the second. And fathers, homes, etc. of hidden enemies, since it is the fourth from the twelfth. And it signifies children of friends, since it is the fifth from the eleventh. And infirmities of the king, since it is the sixth from the tenth. And enemies of the religious. And associates of the religious, and also lovers of the religious, since it is the seventh from the ninth. And it signifies the death of absent people, and the household members (and assistants) of their enemies, since it is the eighth from the eighth. And it signifies the religion of wives, since it is the ninth from the seventh. And the professions of slaves, since it is the tenth from the sixth. And the friends and fortune of children, since it is the eleventh from the fifth. And the fathers large animals and hidden enemies, since it is twelfth from the fourth.

On The Fourth House

Alchabicius said, that the 4th house signifies fathers, houses, countries, ancestors, and all ancients on the direct line of ancestors (older men, and father in laws), and all inheritances apart from what is inherited from the dead, and those things which will be discussed in the 8th house. And it signifies all immoveable things which are in the ground, or above the ground, such as buildings, towers, shelters, cities, castles, and similar things. And it signifies hidden treasure, and anything that is buried or underground. And Adila said that it signifies hidden things and concealed things, and prisons, and prisoners, and things hidden or placed in the earth, and what happens to the dead regarding their burial, and after burial, and whether he will be buried or cremated, or if their corpse is disregarded, so that it nobody cares what happens to their body, as often is the case with those who die from hanging, or decapitation, or who are otherwise killed.

And Mansor said that it signifies the end of things.

And Alezdegoz said that the first triplicity Lord of the house of the father signifies fathers; the second cities and countries; the third the end of things and prisons. Whence it should be kept in mind regarding someone's nativity, or any question which is asked of you about any of the above mentioned things: that you ought to look to the 4th house if you want to know what ought to happen to the native or the querent in regard to these things which are signified by the Lord of the 4th house, or by its triplicity Lords. And see which one is in better condition, and judge on the matter accordingly. And so if the first triplicity Lord of the 4th house is in good condition, and aspects the Lord of the Ascendant by a good aspect, namely a trine or sextile (or if the Ascendant Lord aspects him in like manner): the native will do well from his father, and his father from him, and the same for his grandfather, great grandfather and father in law, and all his ancestors, (even if the father in law is signified by the 4th house by accident). And likewise if the second triplicity Lord is in good condition, the native will do well from houses, land, and from things inherited from the people mentioned above. And if the third is in good condition, the native will do well from prisons and prisoners (as often happens with guards of prisoners, and the like); and the native will also do well from the ends of things - as often happens when someone resolves a legal case, or a conflict, or who mediates between those in the marketplace, as is often the case with horse traders, or with other matters whose sellers are in need of a mediator, and so on. And if the significators are unfortunate or in bad condition, things will go badly for the querent with the things they signify. And consider in what part of life this will happen to him, since the first Lord of this triplicity signifies what happens to the native regarding these things in the first one third of his life, the second in the second, and the third in the third, as is said for the other houses.

And the 4th house also signifies the substance of brothers, since it is the second from the third. And brothers of household members and assistants, since it is the third from the second. And the children of hidden enemies, since it is the fifth from the twelfth. And infirmities of friends, and of the king's household members, since it is sixth from the eleventh. And it signifies enemies of the king, since it is the seventh from the tenth. And it signifies the death of the religious, since it is eighth from the ninth. And the religion of absent people, since it is the ninth from the eighth. And the professions and mothers of enemies and associates, since it is the tenth from the seventh. And the friends and fortune of slaves, since it is the eleventh from the sixth. And it signifies the hidden enemies and large animals of children, since it is the twelfth from the fifth.

On The Fifth House

Alchabicius said that the 5th house signifies children, pleasures, legates, gifts, and what is said about a man after his death. And Adila said that it signifies joy and clothes. And Valens said that it signifies papers, books, messengers and novel things. And Alchaiat said that it signifies all things in which one has trust, along with honour, requests, women, friends, the condition of citizens, and the profits of inheritances.

And Alezdegoz said that the first triplicity Lord of the 5th house signifies children and their life; the second signifies pleasures; the third legates. Whence you should examine the Lord of any nativity or question and see how it interacts with the first triplicity Lord of the 5th house (which is called the house of children), since if they interact well together, this will be good for the native regarding children, and good for children regarding the native, in the first third of his life. If the second triplicity Lord is placed as described above, these things will be good in the second third of the native's life, and similarly for the third Lord in the final third of the native's life. However, the life of children will be seen more so from the first triplicity Lord than from the second or the third.

Now examine the Lord of the 5th house, and see how it interacts with the Lord of the first. Since if the Lord of the fifth is joined to the Lord of the first by a praiseworthy aspect, (namely a trine or a sextile), or if the fifth Lord is in the first, or the first Lord is in the fifth: the native will have children, especially if Jupiter is in the fifth, or is joined with the Lord of the fifth (or to the Lord of the first) by a good aspect. And if Jupiter is in the third, or the eighth, or the eleventh, with the Lord of the first, or with the Lord of the fifth, or with the Moon: the children will live, and things will be good regarding them. However, if Mars is in the place of Jupiter, the native will have children (as we will see in the chapter on children), but they will die; just as will be more broadly discussed in the chapter on children in the Tractate on Judgements and in Nativities.

Moreover, you should examine all of the triplicity Lords of the house of children, and see which of them best aspects the Lord of the 1st house, or the Lord of the 5th house, or the 5th house itself. For if the first triplicity Lord aspects it best, the native will have children in the first third of his life; if the second triplicity Lord, in the second part of the natives life. And if one of the triplicity Lords is the Lord of the 1st house, or the Lord of the fifth (as sometimes happens), it signifies children in that third of the natives' life.

And the 5th house also has these other significations. One of which is the goods of the father and other older relatives, since it is the second from the fourth. Whence if the Lord of the fifth is joined to the Lord of the first, or Lord of the second, and is received by either of them, the native or the querent will obtain all of their fathers positions, or a good part of them. And if the Lord of the second is joined to the Lord of the fifth, and the Lord of the fifth receives him, the native's parents will obtain his goods. And it signifies brothers of brothers (if the native has brothers from another mother, or another father), since it is the third from the third. And it signifies infirmities of hidden enemies, since it is the sixth from the twelfth. And enemies of friends, since it is the seventh from the eleventh. And the death of the king, and all those who are signified by the 10th house, since it is the eighth from the tenth. And it signifies long journeys of the religious, since it is the ninth from the ninth. And the professions or dignities of absent people, since it is the tenth from the eighth. And it signifies friends of the natives or querent's enemies and associates, since it is the eleventh from the seventh. And hidden enemies of slaves, since it is the twelfth from the sixth.

On The Sixth House

They said that the 6th house is the house of infirmities, slaves, and slave-girls. And this house is said to be the house of sickness, since it is outside of the house of games and delights (which is the fifth), and goes towards the seventh, which is the house of public enemies. And Alchabicius said that it signifies whatever will happen before old age, and that it signifies the end of life. And Adila says that it signifies servants and beasts which are not ridden. And the 6th house signifies vassals and justices, and it signifies changes from place to place. And Zahel said that the 6th house is cadent from the Ascendant, and that it doesn't aspect the Ascendant, and that it is a malignant place.

And Alezdegoz said that the first triplicity Lord of the 6th house signifies infirmities, and recovery from them, (and from evils). The second signifies slaves and domestic servants. The third signifies what comes from slaves, and their utility and work, and it is also the significator of beasts, cattle, sheep, and other small animals, and all four-footed beasts, and their strength, their number, and whether they remain in his possession or leave his possession, prisons also and restraints.

Whence it should be examined how the Lord of someone's nativity or question interacts with the Lord of the 6th house, namely whether it is joined to it by a trine or sextile aspect, or by body with mutual or perfect reception: for if so, the native or querent will have good fortune with all, and from all things that are signified by the 6th house. However, if they aspect each other by the above aspects without reception, the fortune from these things will not be as great, although there will still be some kind of good fortune from them. However, if they aspect each other by square or by opposition, without reception, there will be evil in all, and from all of the things mentioned above. If with reception, less evil will come from these things. If the Lord of the 1st house receives the Lord of the 6th house, and the Lord of the sixth does not receive him, slaves and domestic servants will do better from the native than he will from them: for they will be unfaithful and fraudulent towards the native. If the Lord of the sixth receives the Lord of the first, and the Lord of the first does not receive him, the native will do better from his slaves than they will from the native: for he will not love them, nor do good for them; not even if they do good for him, and show loyalty to him, and handle all of his business well.

And examine at the triplicity Lords of the 6th house: for if the first is in better condition than the rest, the good things mentioned above will happen to the native in the first third of his life; if the second, in the second; if the third, in the third or final part of his life. And vice versa if they are in bad condition.

And slaves differ in condition from the domestic servants: for slaves are under the native due to slavery; the domestic servants without slavery, and they belong to him in his family.

And even if Alezdegoz said that this house signifies quadrupeds, his intention was for only for the beasts which cannot be ridden to be signified, such as sheep, goats, pigs, dogs, and so on. And also included under the 6th house are chickens, geese, ducks, hawks, bees etc.

Besides these things, this house has certain other significations: since it signifies children's substance, since it is the second from the fifth. And brothers of fathers, since it is third from the fourth. And the fathers of brothers who are from another father, since it is the third from the fourth. And children of household members, since it is the fifth from the second. And enemies of hidden enemies, since it is the seventh from the twelfth. And the death of friends, since it is the eighth from the eleventh. And the religion of the mother, and long journeys of the king, since it is ninth from the tenth. And the professions and lay dignities of the religious, since it is the tenth from the ninth (for it sometimes happens that bishops and other religious figures receive positions of power, and lay dignities of this kind. And it signifies friends of absent people, and of the household members of enemies and associates, since it is the eleventh from the eighth. And hidden enemies of wives, enemies, and associates since it is the twelfth from the seventh.

On The Seventh House

Argaphalon said that the 7th house is the house of women, and signifies marriages and contentions. And Albategni said it signifies participation, opposition, and all opposite matters. And Adila said that it signifies wives, war, and inimical things. And Alchabitius said that it signifies the middle of the end of life, towards old age. And Ven said that it signifies thieves, legal sentences, and associates, and is the house of buying and selling, and signifies marriage, and matters related to marriage, and fugitives, and brigands, and highway bandits, and missing things. And Zahel said that it signifies battles, since it is the setting angle, and the seventh is opposed to the Ascendant; and it signifies contrarieties which happen between people, and between the querent and the quesited.

And according to some it signifies journeys of moderate length, just as the 1st house signifies very brief journeys, which are from one district to another in the same land, or from the city to the gardens, or to cloisters or a pleasure garden bordering on (or almost bordering on) a city. And pure and simple veneration of God, and all houses of philosophers, and foreknowledge of things, and the science of the stars, and divination, and letters, and legates, and dreams, and divine wisdom, and health, and religion, and rumours, and all things past and preceding. And it signifies man relieved of his burden or his work, and foreknowledge of the future, and matters of future ages, and bandits, and those similar to bandits, and pilgrims and exiles, and the loss of things, and their purpose. And this sign is the enemy of the Ascendant.

And Alezdegoz said that the first triplicity Lord of the 7th house signifies women, the second contentions, and the third comminglings.

And this house also has these other significations: since it signifies the substance of slaves, since it is the second from the sixth. And brothers of children from another father, since it is third from the fifth. And fathers of fathers (for living fathers), since it is the fourth from the fourth. And children of brothers, since it is the fifth from the third. And infirmities of household members, since it is the sixth from the second. And the death of hidden enemies, since it is the eighth from the twelfth (and it is could be said that it signifies the death of large animals). And it signifies the religion of friends, and their long journeys, since it is the ninth from the eleventh. And it could be said that it signifies the profession of the king (although this is not wholly fitting), since it is tenth from the tenth. And it signifies friends and fortune of the religious since it is the eleventh from the ninth. And hidden enemies of absent people, and of household members of enemies, since it is the twelfth from the eighth.

On The Eighth House

Adila said that the 8th house is the house of fear, and it is said to be the house of death, on account of it belonging to the assistants of public enemies, and that it follows from the seventh (which is opposed to the Ascendant). And Alboali said that it signifies labour, sorrow, war, despisers, bellicose people, and clients of adversaries. And Alchaiat said that it signifies anything deposited for safekeeping, and estate management, and shrewdness and skill. And Zahel says that the eighth house succeeds the occidental angle, and signifies killing and lethal poisons, and whatever is inherited from the dead, and everything that perishes, and labour and sorrow, and assistants of enemies or adversaries. And Alchabicius said that it signifies Almuerith, that is, everything inherited from the dead, both from strangers and those connected to us, which heirs ought to possess after their deaths. And it signifies the final years of life after old age.

And Alezdegoz said that the first triplicity Lord of the house of death signifies death, the second ancient things, the third Almuerith, and whatever is associated with it. And I assent to that which has been said by the above mentioned wise men, and I say that the 8th house signifies dowries, and thè goods or assets of enemies and associates. Certain men say it signifies usury.

And it also has other significations: since it signifies brothers of servants, since it is the third from the sixth. And illnesses of brothers, since it is the sixth from the third. And the enemies, wives, and associates of household members, since it is the seventh from the second. And the religion and long journeys of hidden enemies, since it is the ninth from the twelfth. And the professions and dignities of friends, since it is the tenth from the eleventh. And friends of the king, since it is the eleventh from the tenth. And hidden enemies of the religious, since it is the twelfth from the ninth.

On The Ninth House

And Tiberiadis said that the 9th house is the house of faith, religion, and long journeys. And Adila said that it signifies visions, wisdom, veneration of God, all religious houses, and foreknowledge of things. And Alchabicius said that it signifies wisdom, philosophy, writings, books, letters, legates, narration of the future, dreams, and the middle of life. And Zahel says that the 9th house is cadent from the angle of the 10th house. And I say that it signifies fame, in accordance with how the house itself and its Lord are disposeed. For if the Lord of the 9th house is in good condition, and well placed, and if there is a benefic placed in it (namely Jupiter, or Venus, or the Caput Draconis), and they are free and unimpeded, it signifies the fame of the native and great honour. However, if malefics are placed there (namely Saturn, Mars, or the Cauda Draconis), it signifies the infamy of the native; and the more the malefic is impeded, the more the natives' infamy will be increased.

Alezdegoz said that the first triplicity Lord of the 9th house signifies pilgrimages, and what will happen to the native or querent on their long journeys. The second signifies faith and religion, and their condition and manner. The third signifies wisdom, dreams, knowledge of the stars, and the truth of these things, and also augury and practice of these things.

And the 9th house also has these other significations, namely the substance and assistants of missing people, and of the household members of enemies, associates and wives, since it is the second from the eighth. And brothers of enemies since it is the third from the seventh. And parents of slaves, since it is the fourth from the sixth. And children of children, since it is fifth from the fifth. And infirmities of the father, since it is the sixth from the fourth. And wives, associates, and enemies of brothers, since it is the seventh from the third. And the death of household members, since it is the eighth from the second. And dignities of hidden enemies, since it is the tenth from the twelfth. And friends of friends, since it is the eleventh from the eleventh. And hidden enemies of the king, since it is the twelfth from the tenth (and this is the reason why prelates and other religious figures are always secretly inimical to kings).

On The Tenth House

Albuas and other ancients said that the 10th house is the house of kings, and signifies imperium and kingship, and professions, dignities and offices, and all arts in which their practitioners are known as "masters". And he whom God willed to be a master said that it signifies mothers, grandmothers and all such older female ancestors, and mothers in law. And Adila said that it signifies divine things, honours, positions of power, and similar things. And Alkindus said that it signifies the king, glory, and the reputation of one's worth. And Albategni said that it signifies judges judging cases, and overseers of work. And certain ancients say that it signifies substance stolen by thievery. And Alchabicius said it signifies the middle of life.

And Alezdegoz said that the first triplicity Lord of the house of kings signifies power and exaltation, and the loftiness of the seat of power, and the highest dwelling. The second signifies the voice of command, and valour in this. The third signifies the stability and durability of the native.

Moreover, the 10th house signifies these other things: namely the substance of the religious, since it is the second from the ninth. And brothers of enemies' household members, since it is the third from the eighth. And the fathers of enemies, associates and wives, since it is the fourth from the seventh. And children of slaves, since it is the fifth from the sixth. And infirmities of children, since it is the sixth from the fifth. And the enemies, wives, and associates of the father, since it is the seventh from the fourth. And the death of brothers, since it is the eighth from the third. And the religion and long journeys of household members and absent people, since it is the ninth from the second. And the friends of hidden enemies, since it is the eleventh from the twelfth. And the hidden enemies of friends, since it is the twelfth from the eleventh.

On The Eleventh House

The 11th house is the house of fortune, trust, and hope. And Zahel said that it succeeds the angle of the Midheaven, and that it signifies the substance of the king, and his returns, or tributes, and his soldiers and foot-soldiers, or assistants, and the man who succeeds the king, or is the first prince after him; and it signifies commendations and children. And Alchabicius said that it signifies ministers, and the final years of middle age, and from middle age onwards.

And Alezdegoz said that the first triplicity Lord of the house of trust signifies trust; the second signifies true friends, and the third what benefits they bring, or their utility.

And the 11th house has these other significations: namely that it signifies the substance of the king, since it is the second from the tenth. And brothers of the religious, since it is the third from the ninth. And fathers of the household members of enemies, since it is the fourth from the eighth. And children of enemies and associates, since it is the fifth from the seventh. And impediments and infirmities of slaves, since it is the sixth from the sixth. And the wives and enemies of children, since it is the seventh from the fifth. And the death of fathers, since it is the eighth from the fourth. And the religion and long journeys of brothers, since it is the ninth from the third. And the professions of household members, since it is the tenth from the second. And hidden enemies of hidden enemies, since it is the twelfth from the twelfth.

On The Twelfth House

Adila said that the 12th house signifies hidden enemies, deceivers, and the envious; it also signifies cows, horses, asses, camels, and the like, and all animals which can be ridden. And it signifies grief, sorrow, bewailing, weeping, lamentations, and whisperings. And similarly blasphemies, prisons, and malevolence. And Zahel said it signifies slyness and evil thoughts. And Alchabicius said that it signifies labours, evil nature, and the end of life, and what happens to women from conception, and from giving birth (whether good or bad).

And Alezdegoz said that the first triplicity Lord of the 12th house signifies enemies, the second signifies labours, and the third beasts and livestock such as cattle.

And certain others said that all triplicity Lords of the 12th house, and the Lord of the 12th house itself, signify prisons and the incarcerated. And others said that the 8th house signifies the incarcerated. And others said that the 4th house signifies prisons. However they do not contradict each other, since the 4th house signifies prisons, because it signifies capture and the act of capturing. The eighth signifies prisons because it signifies the act of incarcerating itself. The twelfth signifies prisons because it signifies the place of the prison, and the captive person now incarcerated. And in this they differ. However all the sages agree on this matter: that the 4th house signifies prisons, because this is the beginning of imprisonment and incarceration: since if there is no capture and the act of capturing, there is no incarceration nor act of incarcerating. And if there is no capture, act of capturing, or incarceration and the act of incarcerating - there is no place of imprisonment, nor anywhere that prisoners stay.

And the 12th house is said to be the house of the actions of prisoners, on account of it falling from the oriental line, and since it is the joy of Saturn; who rejoices in bewailing and lamentation and similar things.

And the 12th house has these other significations: namely, the substance of friends, since it is the second from the eleventh. And brothers of the king, since it is the third from the tenth. And fathers of the religious, since it is the fourth from the ninth. And children of household members of enemies, since it is the fifth from the eighth. And infirmities of wives, since it is the sixth from the seventh. And enemies of slaves, since it is the seventh from the sixth. And the death of children, since it is the eighth from the fifth. And the religion and long journeys of the father, since it is the ninth from the fourth. And the professions of brothers, since it is the tenth from the third. And friends of household members, since it is the eleventh from the second. And hidden enemies of the native or querent, since it is the twelfth from the first. And I came across a certain Florentine who gave the 12th house to pilgrims.

Summary

All of the significations of any of the houses mentioned above ought to be considered and known, so that if a question is asked to you about any of the things mentioned above, or if you are presented with someone's nativity, or a general question, you will be able to judge over this questions regarding all of the accidents that will befall a native, querent, or any of the above mentioned people, under one Ascendant - even if it is difficult. However it will be easy to discover whatever matter you ought to consider in your judgement; since if you have a nativity for someone, or a general question (or even another question), you will be able to judge as to what ought to happen to the person regarding all the above significations, and regarding all the above people, and what happens to the querent from them, and what happens to them from the querent.

For you will be able to judge for them as to what ought to be the condition of their own person. And on their substance and those things signified by the 2nd house. And on their brothers, and what is signified by the 3rd house. And on their fathers, ancestors, and all of those things which are signified by the 4th house. And on their children, and all of those things which are signified by the 5th house. And on their slaves, and all of those things which are signified by the 6th house. And on their wives, and all of those things which are signified by the 7th house. And on death, and all of those things which are signified by the 8th house. And on their religion, and all that is signified by the 9th house. And on their professions and their mother (and similar older female relatives) and all that is signified by the 10th house. And on their friends, and all that is signified by the 11th house. And on their horses, and beasts, and all that is signified by the 12th house.

And understand this for every house, namely the second, third, fourth, and so on up to the twelfth. And know that each one of the houses is its own 1st house, and has its own second, third, fourth, fifth, sixth, seventh, eighth, ninth, tenth, eleventh, and twelfth. And according to each of them it has its own other eleven houses apart from itself, from which it receives its significations, just as the first rising house receives its significations from each of its houses, which you will be able to discern well using your own industry.

VI

On The Significations Of The Twelve Houses Taken In The Opposite Direction

First on the Twelfth House

Another chapter, namely the sixth, on the significations of the planets in the house, who take the contrary direction through the houses to the one we took above: by which it is known what the planets do in each one of the houses in nativities, or in questions, starting from the twelfth and going backwards to the first.

Thus, if you are presented with someone's nativity, or a question is asked to you about wealth, and the twelfth Lord was in the 1st house: it signifies that the native or querent will profit through his household members, or through one of the things signified by the 12th house (which were stated to you above).

And if the twelfth Lord is in the 2nd house, it signifies that the native or querent will make a short journey or small move, in the hope of utility; or that he will journey to one of his absent neighbours, or to one of his younger relatives. If it is a nativity, the native will spend time performing the same actions. And if the twelfth Lord is in the third, it signifies that whatever the question is about, it will be concealed, hidden in a house, or in an estate. And if the matter was something to be buried, it would be underground in one of the above mentioned places.

If the twelfth Lord is in the fourth, the whole of its significations is in children or similar things. And if it was a question about a journey that isn't too long, it would signify that the journey would not be pleasant; since contrary things would befall him, and it would not be perfected for the good of the querent. The same could be said about what would happen to a native in similar situations.

If it is in the 5th house, and it is a question about an absent person, it signifies that he is in the hands of certain people who are, or who were, his slaves; and thus they are hidden enemies.

If it is in the 6th house, and it is a question about an absent person, it signifies that the quesited is in the hands of enemies, or robbers, or highwaymen, or exiles, or paid men.

If it is in the seventh, and if it were a question, as said, about an absent person; it signifies that he is dead, or struggling with a deadly illness.

And if the twelfth Lord is in the eighth, it would appear that he is far from that place, or on a long journey, or that some cleric or religious figure is holding him against his will.

If it is found in the ninth, it signifies he is in the hands of some powerful person, or that his mother is making him stay where he is against his will.

If it is in the tenth, it signifies he is in a place agreeable to him, and with friends and those who love him.

If it is in the eleventh, it signifies that he is not in a good state, in fact it could be said that he is in the hands of certain people inimical to him due to envy, or those wanting to harm him for some unknown reason, or that he is labouring and distressed, or in prison.

On The Eleventh House And Its Lord

If the eleventh Lord is in the twelfth, and it is a question about wealth, it signifies this: that the querent will earn wealth in his absence through his household members or people of an equivalent sort.

If it is in the 1st house, and the question is about a short journey, it signifies that the journey will be useful and profitable.

If it is in the 2nd house, and the question is about a hidden thing, it signifies that it will arrive into the hands of the querent. Say the same for immovable things. And if it is a question about older parents; their status will be signified according to the condition of the planet in question.

If it is in the 3rd house, and the question is about children, it signifies they are in good condition, and that goodness and joy will come from them, and also useful garments, and all good things.

If it is in the fourth, and if it is a nativity or a general question, it signifies that the native or querent will be irritable and laborious and beset by infirmities. If it is a particular question, it signifies that the querent will lose his small animals, servants, slaves, and the like.

If it is in the fifth it signifies that the native will be litigious, and that things will go badly for him in his lawsuits, and it will be likewise for a querent. If the significator is Venus, he will marry a beautiful woman. If it is Jupiter, it signifies he will have good associates and good fortune in commerce. If it is one of the other planets, the prediction will be according to their disposition. If they are well disposeed, they will signify good things. If they are badly disposeed, they will portend evil; and even the loss of his goods, or expulsion from them.

If it is in the sixth, and is one of the aforementioned malefics, it signifies the querent's death. And if it is a nativity it signifies that the native will die an evil death. But if it is Jupiter, or the Sun, or even Venus, it signifies wealth on account of dowries, or perhaps the obtaining of other goods. If it is Mercury or the Moon, and if it is a question about something that is feared, it signifies its evacuation and annulment.

If it is in the seventh, and it is a nativity or a general question on a journey, and it is one of the benefics, it signifies profitable and advantageous journeys. However if it is a malefic, predict the contrary.

If it is in the eighth, it signifies he will attain rulership and honour, or that he will adhere to a profession (or to a great man) according to the nature of the significator - insofar as it pertains to the native. Or that his mother loves him more than her other children.

If it is in the ninth, it signifies that the native or querent will fulfil much of his wishes, and things in which he has hope, as much because of his friends as of other things.

If it is in the tenth it signifies sorrow, alterations, tribulations and prison, and also the taking away of large animals, as much for nativities as for questions.

The Tenth House And Its Lord

If the Lord of the 10th house is found in the eleventh in any question or nativity, it signifies that he will enter into the household of the king, or that of some other magnate fit to rule, or that he will have wealth appropriate for himself.

If it is in the twelfth, and it is a question about short journeys, it signifies that they will not be useful to the native, especially if it is a journey to neighbours or younger relatives. And it will cause fear for the native, unless it is a journey related to large animals.

If it is in the first, it signifies the acquisition of houses and other estates; and they will be useful for the native or querent. And it also signifies a long and good life, and fortune from his ancestors and relatives.

If it is in the second it signifies that the native or querent will be fortunate with children, and rejoice from them, and he will also be fortunate regarding food and drink, clothing, and profit from substance; especially if the Part of Fortune is there.

If it is in the third it signifies anger, labour, sorrow, and infirmities, and that he won't be fortunate in small animals, nor in persons subject to him (nor will these people be fortunate from him).

If it is in the fourth, and it is Venus or one of the convertible planets, and it is a question about marriage, it signifies it will take place. If it is Jupiter it signifies that the native will have good wives, good associates, and fortune in commerce. If it is one of the malefics, it signifies he will have lawsuits and discord, or separation in life from the place in which you found him, or from his own goods (and even more so if it is one of the lighter planets, and even more so again if the 4th house is a mobile sign).

If it is in the fifth, and it is a malefic, it signifies that the native is in bad condition; and this is true also in the case of the querent, for whom it additionally signifies his death and destruction. However, if it is a benefic, it signifies the native or querent will have good fortune in dowries of women, and in obtaining the goods of others. And if it is a question on wealth, it signifies fortune in foreign lands.

If it is in the 6th house it signifies that long journeys will not be good for the native or querent, in fact they will be laborious and unfortunate; unless they are in relation to slaves, servants, or animals. Nor will he be fortunate with clerics.

If it is in the seventh, it signifies that the native or querent will acquire honour, an art, and wealth with women, and by reason of women.

If it is in the eighth it signifies the fulfilment of much of his wishes, and of those things which he hopes for, and especially for matters relating to death; particularly so on the occasion of friends, or some other fortunate matter.

If it is in the ninth it signifies anger and tribulations for the native or querent, which will come from matters which are usually good and useful for him, and in which he has trust.

On The Ninth House And Its Lord

If the Lord of the ninth is in the tenth in someone's nativity, or in a question, it signifies the native or querent will have good, decent and honourable familiarity with men, and especially so with noblemen, magnates, and the household members of magnates, and will contract a stay with them, or will have it from them, or by other magistrates

If the Lord of the ninth is in the eleventh, and it is a question about a journey, it signifies that it will be fortunate and fruitful, and to an even greater extent if the journey is to friends, or with friends. It also signifies that much of the native or querent's thoughts and wishes will come true to his liking, and that he will adhere to some great relative who is known.

If it is in the twelfth it signifies that the native or querent will come upon some immovable and unfortunate things which will be harmful to him, although the misfortune won't last for long; or that he will be struck or injured by large animals

If it is in the 1st house, and it is a question about children, it signifies that the native or querent will have good and useful children, and good fortune with them and from them. And also he will be fortunate in clothing; and the joy which he experiences will be long lasting, and he will delight in all pleasures and live well and honourably.

If it is in the second and it is a question on children, slaves, or small animals, it signifies profit, advantage and utility from them; and you can judge the same for a nativity.

If it is in the third, and it is a question about marriage or about contracting a partnership, or about some business deal: it signifies good fortune for all of these things; and this will be greater and more certain if the significator is fortunate. And it also signifies that the native or querent will be fortunate in relatives, especially older ones, and in neighbours; and that he will be fortunate in lawsuits, and he will meet with great lawsuits, and he will be fortunate in associates and commerce. If it is Venus, it signifies that he will be fortunate in women. However if the significator is one of the malefics, it signifies the contrary.

If it is in the fourth, and if it is a question about death, it signifies that it is going to arrive, and it will be according to the nature of the planet who is the significator of the matter. It also signifies that the native or querent will inherit the goods of the dead, especially the immovable ones, and he will acquire goods from dowries or because of women. And if he does not gain wealth from any of the things above, it appears that he will gain wealth in a foreign land. If one of the malefics (namely Saturn or Mars) are the significator of death, it signifies a blameworthy death which will befall him in some dwelling.

If it is in the fifth, it signifies that he will make a praiseworthy journey because of children, or clothing, or food and drink, or because of messengers, or announcements; and that he will be fortunate in medium length journeys.

If it is in the sixth, it signifies that the native or querent will be in command of lower class and lesser people, or advocate for them; or that he will profit from small animals or on occasion of them.

If it is in the seventh, it signifies his good fortune in marriage or women, and additionally in commerce and associates, and similarly in lands that are not his own.

If it is in the eighth it signifies that the native or querent will fall into imprisonment, or a serious or fatal infirmity, or tribulation. And similarly if he finds himself involved with large animals, injury and harm will follow from it, and things will not come to be in his favour, and it will be feared lest they injure him or dash him against something.

On The Eighth house And Its Lord

If the Lord of the eighth house is in the ninth, and it is a question about an absent person, it signifies that the absent person is well, and especially if his significator is a benefic. For if it is Jupiter it signifies that he is enjoying himself with certain judges, or with those belonging to the church, or is studying in the sciences to advance his knowledge. If it is Venus it signifies that he is enjoying himself with women, or with those who are liberally eating and drinking. If it is the Moon or Mercury, it signifies that he is enjoying himself with various and diverse persons, and that he does not remain stable, nor firm, in one location or land. If it is Mars, and he is fortunate and strong, it signifies that he is practicing some art which is performed with fire and iron and the spilling of blood; and it seems that his activity with these people is useful and fruitful for him.

If it is in the 10th house, and it is a question on short journeys, especially those to some magnate or on occasion of some profession, or any occasion bringing the querent honour: it signifies that things will happen as the querent intended.

If it is in the 11th house it signifies that his friends are striving so that he acquires some immovable thing that will be useful and honourable for him - if the question were about this.

If it is in the twelfth, and it is a question about children, it signifies their bad filiation, or that they will not live; and if they do live, the native will not rejoice with them or from them. It also signifies that the native or querent will be fed poisoned food, and that he will not be fortunate in clothing, and that many displeasing things will be brought to him from embassies, and in terms of news.

If it is in the first, it signifies that he will have moderate good fortune in slaves and small animals; and that he will not be burdened with very many, or very serious infirmities.

If it is in the second it signifies that the native or querent will get a wife on whose occasion profit and utility will follow; and that he will have good fortune in trading moveable goods. However, should he form a partnership with someone, it will not last long, and he will also have lawsuits with his own family.

If it is in the third, and it is a question about a short journey, it signifies death on the journey in question. And if it is a question about a dowry, it signifies that he will get it, and with neighbours or in the area where the querent lives (but not with regard to an inheritance).

If it is in the fourth and it is a question about a long journey, it signifies that the journey will be bad, troublesome and oppressive; and it also signifies that the querent will acquire a bad reputation on this journey. And if it is a question about some cleric, it signifies that he is evil, dishonest, and with little faith in divine matters. You could say the same about an absent person, should the question be about them.

If it is in the fifth, it signifies that the native or querent will have good fortune with children, food and drink, and clothing. If it is a question about marriage or letters, it signifies good tidings, and letters containing good news.

If it is in the sixth, and it is a question about fortune, it is signified to be weak and not having good stability. Nor will the native or querent have good fortune in friends, nor will they be truthful; however the native or querent will be fortunate in servants, slaves and small animals.

If it is in the seventh, and it is a question about prison, or about an infirmity which is long lasting, it signifies that the querent will see or encounter that which he fears or is uncertain about, and this will befall him because of women, associates, or merchants; and he should fear trouble from bandits, or from exiles or those expelled, or from games, and betrayal by women.

On The Seventh House And Its Lord

If the Lord of the 7th house is in the eighth in a nativity or a question, it signifies that the native or querent will profit on the occasion of someone's death, or that he will inherit the goods of the dead. And if it is a question about the death of a business partner, wife, or enemy, it signifies this. And if it is a question about an absent person: it signifies that he has taken a wife in his absence, and it is possible that he is imprisoned on the occasion of women.

If it is in the ninth, and it is a question about a journey, it signifies that the journey will be useless and unprofitable; and in fact it might be damaging, and all the more so if the ninth is the house of a malefic, or if there is an impeded malefic placed there. If it is a question about whether a man will be joined to a woman, or if someone is seeking to enter the church, it signifies that they will. If it is asked whether someone will meet an enemy on the road, or if a wife is suspected of committing adultery with some cleric; or if she herself intends to travel to another land, or to another place; or if a specified cleric is inimical to the querent: it signifies these things. If it is a question about an exile or expelled person, it signifies his return.

If it is in the tenth and the querent is uncertain about whether a king or any other layman in command of them is inimical towards them, or if his enemies have power over him, or if his adversaries will triumph over him in a lawsuit or contention, or if a Lord or judge favours his enemy or adversary over the querent: it signifies these things to be true. If it is a question about whether a Lord, or someone placed in command of the querent, or a doctor, has corrupted or is pursuing his wife: it signifies these things. But if it is a question about forming a partnership with these people, it signifies that the partnership will be good, useful, and honourable; and it will be all the more useful and honourable, if the partnership is related to some immovable things, and that the querent will come upon some art or profession on the occasion of this.

If it is in the eleventh, and the question is about children, it signifies that his children will be fortunate, and he will be fortunate with them and from them, and also with garments. In addition to this; if the significating planet is a benefic, and is fortunate and strong, fortune will follow the native or querent everywhere he goes. The same can also be said in relation to friends, and of the household members of the king, and of magnates who are fit for kingship.

If it is in the twelfth it signifies anger, sorrow, and infirmity will befall the native or querent - I say this, if the significator is a malefic or unfortunate. If the significator is a benefic, it signifies that the native will obtain animals both great and small; and even that he will seize and incarcerate his enemies.

If it is in the first, and it is a benefic, and fortunate: it signifies such good fortune for the native or querent, so that it is hardly possible to improve his status. However, if it is a malefic and unfortunate, it will not be possible to make his status any worse, nor to make his condition in all actions any worse, except if he is an exile or expelled; for then it signifies his return to the land from which he was expelled. So that if a woman was thrown out of the house by her husband, or she removed herself by her own free will, and a question was made about this, it signifies that she will go back inside the house.

If it is in the second, and it is a question about the death of enemies, wives, or associates, it signifies these things. It also signifies the loss of moveable objects due to bandits, or injury due to friends or games, and the native or querent will even find that his own family are inimical to him.

If it is in the third, and it is a question about a journey or relatives, it signifies that it will be good and useful, provided the significator is not one of the malefics, especially the Cauda Draconis. However if it is one of the benefics, and the journey was by land, it's goodness will be increased; and this will be all the greater if the third is an earth sign. If the journey was by water, a water sign would be better than an earth sign.

If it is in the fourth, it signifies that the querent's enemies will occupy his immovable objects, should the question be about this. If the question is about whether the father, or grandfather, or father in-law will take a wife, it signifies that this will happen. It is also possible that one of these men will be going into litigation about some matter.

If it is in the fifth and it is a question about something which the querent is striving to get or acquire, it signifies he will be fortunate, and it also signifies that his friends will be strong and consistent for him. And it will also be possible that his children, or someone who is like a child to him, will be inimical to him. And if it is a question about taking a wife, it signifies this. And if his wife is suspect, it appears that she is not without blemish. And it appears that his enemies will take away his clothing, or it may be taken by bandits, or his enemies might capture his child.

If it is in the sixth, and the question is about imprisonment, it signifies this. The same can be said about infirmities. And if he has a suspicion about his wife, it appears that she is carrying on with a certain young man. or that she is otherwise inimical to the querent. And if it is a question about small animals, it appears that his enemies will take them away from him. And if a woman asks whether her husband is carrying on with a certain young girl who she is suspicious of, it appears that this is true, and it also seems that children will result from this affair.

On The Sixth House And Its Lord

If the Lord of the 6th house is in the seventh, and it is a question about an infirmity, it signifies that its cause is love (namely lovesickness). And if it is a question about a servant, it signifies that he will be obtained; but it doesn't appear that he will be very faithful to the querent. And if it is a question on trade or commerce, it signifies that there will be good profit from it, however it should be guarded against lest the querent stays at it too long, lest it ends in a loss.

If it is in the eighth, and it is a question about the death of slaves or small animals, it signifies this. And if it is a question about dowries, or inheritances of the dead, or about wealth from relatives or neighbours (especially if they are younger), it signifies that the quesited matter will come to the querent.

If it is in the ninth, it signifies that the querent will travel, or make a journey because of immovable things, and that he is going to obtain these things; or that he will travel to enter some church or religion, or to converse with some clerics.

If it is in the tenth in a nativity or a question, he will have good and honourable children. And if anyone asks whether their master is going to fall ill, or be deposed from his position, it is to be feared that it will happen. And if it is a question about whether the querent's mother or master is sick, it signifies that they are.

If it is in the eleventh, and it is a question about animals, it signifies they are useful. And if it is a question on whether a friend is infirm, it signifies this. And in other matters the fortune of the querent will not be well disposed.

If it is in the twelfth and it is a question about the infirmity of slaves, prisoners or animals, it signifies these things.

If it is in the first, and it is a question about servants or small animals and what will happen to them in the future, it signifies that they will not remain in the hands of the querent for much longer; and if they do remain, they will become infirm; however it will be useful in the person of the querent.

If it is in the second, and it is a question about entering into some church, or about a long journey, it signifies that these things will be good, useful, and profitable.

If it is in the third, and it is a question about dignities or an art with neighbours, or on a profession with relatives, it signifies that things will go according to what was asked, and it will not be long before this happens.

If it is in the fourth, and it is a question about stable things, or about the querent's older relatives, it signifies fortune in these things. But if it is a question about a city or a castle, it signifies that infirmities will come to these places, and evil men will live in them, and those striving and labouring at evil deeds.

If it is in the 5th house, and it is a question on matters which the querent ought to rejoice or be elated from, or on clothing, or on pregnancy, it signifies these things. And if it is a question about any infirmity, it signifies that it is from sorcerers or something created.

On The Fifth House And Its Lord

If the Lord of the 5th house is in the sixth and it is a question on whether a child will fall ill, it signifies it will happen. And if it is a question on the commanding of servants or small animals, it is signified to turn out according to how it was asked. If it is a question about food and drink, or garments, it signifies something unfortunate will happen to the querent from them. If it is a question about a messenger, it signifies that he is infirm, or angry on the road, and that he carries a bad letter or errand.

If it is in the seventh, and it is a question about the condition of a child, it signifies that he is going to copulate, and it appears that this is being done against the parents' wishes. It is also to be feared that the son has fallen into the hands of enemies (if he has them), or that he himself becomes a troublemaker, or goes astray with prostitutes; or perhaps he will adhere to merchants. And if Mars, Saturn, the Cauda Draconis, or Venus, is there, it signifies evil for all of the above things. And if there is a question about a thief, it would appear that the thief is his son. If it is a question about an expelled person or an exile, it signifies good for him; for it portends his joy and return to his own land.

If it is in the eighth, and it is a question about hereditary goods, and especially immovable things, it signifies that the querent will obtain them; and the same can be said regarding dowries. If it is a question about an absent person, it signifies that he is well. And if it is a question about whether an inheritance will arrive into the hands of a child, it signifies this. And if it is a question on a pregnancy, it will signify that the baby will not live.

But if it is in the ninth and it is a question about whether a child is going to enter into the church, or if he is going to make some great journey, it signifies these things. And this all the more so if he is the son of some cleric. And it appears that all of these things will be good and useful for the person in question. And if the question is about the Roman Church, it signifies they will rejoice and be elated regarding the quesited matter.

If it is in the tenth, and it is a question about whether a son is going to attain an art, or an office, it signifies this, albeit with labour and fatigue; and it would appear to be a position more related to beasts or low class persons.

If it is in the eleventh, and if it is a question about trade, or forming a partnership, or coupling, and Mars is the significator: it signifies anger and sorrow regarding all of the above. And the querent might even be incarcerated on this occasion.

If it is in the twelfth and it is a question about whether a child will be incarcerated or not, and there is uncertainty about this matter, it signifies that it will happen. If it is a question about this child's infirmity, it signifies its prolongation. If it is a question about large animals, it signifies good and utility from them; however it is to be considered if an auditor may carry them off under a certain pretext of being in the right.

If it is in the first, and it is a nativity or a question about life, it signifies that it will be long, honourable, and appears to be so because of the Church.

If it is in the second, and it is a question about profit, it signifies this, and especially from moveable things, or from some profession or office, or perhaps from some Lord or magnate. And if it is a question about children, it signifies them. And is it a question about whether a messenger, or a letter will arrive, it signifies this, and for it to be with utility and honour. However care should be taken if the native or querent has children, so that they are not harmed on occasion of moveable things. And if it is a question about affairs of the family, it signifies that all of his household members will rejoice, and strive to profit in good faith.

And if it is in the third, and it is a question about a journey to neighbours or relatives, it signifies this, insofar as it is fortunate and for the good. And it signifies joy because of clothing and food drinks, and it will be good in all things.

But if it is in the fourth, and it is a question on hidden or concealed things, it signifies these. And if it is about stable things, it signifies anger, trials and tribulations from them. And if it is a question about the father, grandfather, father in law or stepfather, as to whether they will have children, it signifies that they will have them. And if the Cauda Draconis is there, then it signifies detriment and evil, especially because of fire and spilling of its inhabitants' blood . And if it is a question about the end of any affairs, joy will follow for the querent from them on the occasion of food and drink, garments, or marriage, and similar things (unless the aforementioned Cauda works against matters). And if Venus is the significatrix and she is impeded, and it is a question about fear in the city in which the querent lives, or about something which the querent, it will be feared that it suffers detriment from foreigners overcoming it; unless a benefic is in the second from the Ascendant, for then the evil will be lessened, however if there is a malefic there, it will increase the evil, and worsen the condition of the matter.

The Fourth House And Its Lord

If the Lord of the 4th house is in the fifth, and it is a question about younger relatives, it signifies they are rejoicing and in good condition. And if it is a question about their condition in the land in which they are staying, or their separation from this land, it signifies their separation.

If it is in the 6th house, and it is a question about a general illness of the citizens or inhabitants of the land in which the question was asked, or that of another assemblage or association, or even a particular house or family; or regarding servants or slaves or small animals, it will signify these things.

If it is in the 7th house and it is a question about an exile or an expelled person, as to whether they will return to their home or not, and by what means, and if Mars is the significator: it signifies that the quesited will return to his own home by fire and iron, or bloodshed. If it is Saturn it signifies that he will return with anger, pain, and sorrow, and not without his own labour and that of the inhabitants of that land, and only after he has practically lost all hope. If it is a question about the state of a stable thing, it signifies the victory of the adversary or the one litigating with the querent. And if it is a question about a planned trade or deal, it signifies that it will about to come to the querent

But if it is in the eighth, and it is a question about an absent person, as to whether he will return or not, it signifies that he will return. And if it is a question about the accidents of a city or another land, it signifies that infirmities and mortality will enter into them. Understand the same for any house which is inhabited, and for older relatives. And if it is a question about dowries, or the inheritance of some dead person, or someone about to die, or matters of enemies or wives, or on commerce, it signifies that it will come to the querent in accordance with what was asked. If it is a question about a magical item, or evil deeds of this manner, it signifies they are in the house. And so if the 4th house is an earth sign, it signifies that they are under the ground. If it's a water sign it signifies that they are in a moist place. However, if it is an air sign, they are elevated from the ground. If it is a fire sign, they are in the most highly elevated part of the house.

If it is in the 9th house, and it is a question about some cleric, or bishop, or similar individuals, as to whether they will die or not, it signifies that they will die. And if it is a question about one of his older relatives, as to whether they will enter into some church or into some religion, it signifies this. However, if it is a question about a journey, it signifies that it will be oppressive, troublesome and unfortunate, unless it is a journey made to obtain some item. And if it is a question on the fame of the querent, it signifies that it will be worthless and practically non-existent.

If it is in the tenth, and it is a question about a profession or an art, or a rulership or dignity, or the honour of some older relative, it signifies that it will come to the person for whom the question was made. And if it is a question about the lives of these people, it signifies they will be long. And if it is a question about a matter which the querent wishes to attain for himself, especially if it is something stable, it signifies that he will attain it. And if it is a question about the condition of some city or land, it signifies its increase and exaltation.

If it is in the eleventh, and it is a question about the fortune of the querent, or another person who is of interest for the querent, it signifies good fortune for them. And if it is a question whether public goods will come into the hands of his older relatives, it signifies this. And if it is a question whether a count, or an envoy of the count, or some person of authority or other magnate will enter the city, or someone's house, it signifies this.

If it is in the twelfth, and it is a question regarding any city or land, as to what will happen in it in the future, it signifies that it will be in bad condition and that there will be treason. And if it is a question made for relatives, it signifies their detriment and bad condition, and it is also possible that they will be led to jail, or fall ill with an illness which will be chronic. If it is a question about large animals, or about a prisoner, or about an absent person, it signifies their return.

However, if it is in the first, and it is a question about the person of the querent, it signifies his bad disposition.

However, if it is in the second, and it is a question about wealth, it signifies there will be wealth attained in the future, especially from friends or stable things. If it is a question about moveable things, it is to be feared that they will be taken away, especially by older relatives.

If it is in the third, and it is a question about wealth, it signifies that the querent will not attain it, unless perhaps from large animals. And if it is a question about the wealth of younger relatives, and also ones of the same age, it signifies that it will come from their own things, or from fixed objects.

On The Third House And Its Lord

If the Lord of the third is in the fourth, and it is a question about wealth. It signifies that the querent will get stable things from stable things. And if it is a question about a city or a castle, it signifies its duration. The same can be said about a house or a province.

If it is in the fifth, and it is a question about children, it signifies that he will have them and rejoice from them. And if it is a question about a child's journey, or those things which pertain to the third, or the 5th house, the question will be good.

If it is in the sixth, and it is a question about an infirmity, or a matter which could anger the querent, it signifies these things. And if it is a question about a servant, or a slave, or a slave-girl, or a dog, or a hawk, or a falcon, or anything similar, it signifies their escape.

If it is in the seventh, and it is a question about whether a relative or neighbour is opposed to the querent, or if one of his relatives will take a wife, or if his wife is having an affair with a relative of hers, or a relative of the querent, or with one of the neighbours, it signifies this.

However, if it is in the eighth, and it is a question about something which the querent fears regarding a death, or a dowry, it signifies that what he fears will come to pass. If it is a question about an inheritance of a dead person, or a woman's dowry, or profit in a land which the querent intends to travel to, it signifies these things, albeit with labour and fatigue. And if it is a question about an absent person, it signifies that he will return, albeit not quickly.

If it is in the ninth, and it is a question about entering into a church or a religion, it signifies this. And if it is a question about the death of someone, and the significator is a malefic, or if there is a malefic in the 9th house with the significator, it signifies this - if things are otherwise, it won't. And if it is a question about a journey, it signifies that it will be good, unless a malefic works against it. And if it is a question about whether a bishop or another prelate is friendly to the querent, it signifies this. The same can be said if the question is about stable things; that is, they will be good for the querent.

If it is in the tenth, and it is a question on an art, or some other dignity, of office, it signifies these things. And if it is a question about the journey of his mother or a magnate, or someone in command of the querent, it signifies this. And if it is a question about whether the querent will complete or contract a relationship with someone older than him, it appears that it will come to be.

If it is in the eleventh, and it is a question about whether the querent will become a household member of the king or governor, or if he will obtain some royal or public goods, it signifies this. It also signifies fortune coming to the querent, and that he will cherish it. And if it is a question about a journey, it is signified to be fortunate and good.

But if it is in the 12th house, and it is a question about relatives, it signifies that they will become infirm or imprisoned, or even overcome by treachery. And if it is a question about large animals or a prisoner, it signifies good things for them.

If it is in the 1st house, and it is a question about the querent's life, or the life of another quesited person, it is signified to be long, useful, and good.

If it is in the 2nd house, and it is a question about moveable things, it is to be feared that the querent may be defrauded by relatives or neighbours, or even his own household members.

On The Second House And Its Lord

If the Lord of the second is in the third, and it is a question about the condition of the querent's missing things, it signifies that he will lose them, and this will happen due to neighbours, relatives, or short journeys.

If it is in the fourth, and it is a question about the querent's assets, it signifies that the querent will lose them on account of his father or one of his relatives. And if it is a question on stable, hidden, or underground things, it signifies a good status for the querent.

If it is in the fifth, and it is a question about children, it signifies that the querent will have them. And if it is a question that he does not wish to reveal to you, it signifies his intention is about children, or for his children. And if it is a question about a messenger, it signifies that he is going to come. And if the querent is uncertain as to whether his son or daughter took away his goods, it signifies this. However, if it is a question on the state of the family, the quesited matter will be good.

If it is in the sixth, and it is a question about whether servants or slaves took away the querent's' goods, or whether his household members will fall ill, it signifies these things.

If it is in the seventh, and the querent is uncertain as to whether enemies, or bandits, or expelled people have taken away his goods, it signifies this. And if it is a question about an expelled person, it signifies that he will return to his own land. And if it is a question about matrimony, or a dowry, or commerce, it signifies that things will happen for the querent as intended, but no great utility will follow from it. And if the question is about a game, it signifies that it will be harmful to the querent. The same can be said if there is suspicion of the querent's' wife or lover stealing something from him.

If it is in the eighth, and it is a question about a dowry, or recovering a deposit or debt, or an inheritance of the dead, and if the Lord of the 1st house is stronger than the Lord of the seventh, it signifies the acquisition of these things. And if it is a question about an absent person, it signifies that he will return.

If it is in the ninth, and it is a question about assets, it is to be feared that they will be taken away, especially by the Roman Church.

If it is in the tenth, and it is a question about wealth, it signifies that the querent will get it from an art, or from a Lord. Nevertheless it is to be feared that the querent's' profits might be taken away by a person in a position of power or rulership; and more seriously so if the question is about such things.

If it is in the 11th house, and it is a question about fortune, it signifies good fortune for the querent in the future. And if it is a question about whether the querent will get the goods of an earl, or those of some Lord or magnate, it signifies this, nevertheless it is to be guarded against that this wealth is not taken away from him by his friends.

If it is in the 12th house, and it is a question on behalf of household members, asking if they will become infirm, it signifies this, and that the infirmity will be a long one. Say the same if the question is regarding their imprisonment. But if the question is about a prisoner, it signifies that he will escape. And if the question is about large animals, the quesited will be good and useful for the querent.

On The First House And Its Lord

If the Lord of the 1st house is in the second, and it is a question about wealth, and a benefic is in the second, it signifies this will come from the querent himself, and through the querent himself. And if a malefic is in the second, it will signify the contrary.

If it is in the third, and it is a question about a journey to relatives or neighbours, it signifies it will be good and useful.

If it is in the fourth, and it is a question about the obtainment of substance, the quesited matter will be good; however in all other matters, it will be to the contrary.

If it is in the fifth, and it is a question about the status of the querent, it is signified to be good, and that he will rejoice from children and food and drink, and he will be elated from these matters, and from other things which are signified by the 5th house.

If it is in the sixth, and it is a question about a matter which causes anger or difficulties for the querent, or if he is fearful of an infirmity befalling him, or an unsuitable or little known labour, it signifies that the thing which he fears will befall him. And if it is a question about the acquisition of servants or slaves, or small animals, it signifies these things.

However, if it is in the 7th house, and it is a question about getting a woman, or about commerce or business deal; as to whether it will happen or not, it signifies that it will. If the question is about an expelled person or an exile, as to whether he will return to his own land or not, it signifies that he will return; in all other business the contrary will be signified.

If it is in the eighth, and it is a question about an infirm person, it signifies that he will die, and even more so if Mars or the Moon is there, or an impeded Mercury. If it is a question about the acquisition of the assets of another person, or a dowry, or the inheritance of a dead person, it signifies these things.

If it is in the ninth, and it is a question about travelling, or the entry of someone into some church or religion, it signifies this. If it is a question about a long journey, it signifies that it will not be made at the appointed time; and if it has begun it will not be completed.

If it is in the tenth and it is a question about some position of power, profession, or dignity; it signifies that the querent will get what he intended.

If it is in the eleventh, and the question is about something that the querent was expecting, and it is with friends or from friends; or something in which he has trust, it signifies that things will happen as the querent intended.

However, if it is in the twelfth, and it is a question about imprisonment or on a chronic infirmity, or melancholia, or betrayal, or an injury (whether violent, or one to be done or to come to the querent), it signifies these things. If Venus, Saturn or the Part of Fortune is with the Lord of the first: these will mitigate the aforementioned contrary predictions; especially in matters of imprisonment, in which case they will even signify his exit from prison. But if it is a question about a pilgrim or about large animals, it signifies good things.

Nevertheless, if the significators fall in the above mentioned places, see whether they are aspected by other planets or not, or whether they are joined to them in these places: since benefics will increase the good, and reduce evil, while malefics will increase evil and reduce the good.

On Easily Discovering The Significations Of Each House

I introduced all of these things to you on the significations of the twelve houses, so that you can easily discover the significations of each house. Since there are some (of whom I have seen many) who believe that astrologers ought only to operate through the first and 7th house, giving the first to the querent and the seventh to the quesited person, or quesited thing: which by my judgement is not appropriate. And I listed these things to lessen your labours, as it was difficult to always search through all of the houses to discover the significator of any given quesited matter. And because I did not remember ever finding any of our predecessors who involved themselves in this work: I believe they did not do this out of ignorance, but rather since such work was overly tedious to them, and they left these things to the industry of the wise.

Whence if a question is made to you about some matter, you will be able to know through which house you could find the significator of the quesited matter. And I could tell you about many other significations of the twelve houses, but it would lead you into such prolixity and confusion that it would generate tedium for you. Whence it seems to me that what I said to you shall be sufficient for you, so that you will hardly or never meet with such questions or such nativities that you won't be able to predict well for. For you will be able to predict for a native or querent what ought to happen to him regarding all of the above mentioned things throughout the whole of his life - if you know the hour of his nativity well, and intend to rightly consider all of the aforementioned things with discernment.

And I will tell you in its own time and place how every person ought to be considered, whether the querent asks for himself or for another, and who ought to enquire for another, and in what manner. Since it is one thing to examine for someone who enquires for himself; and another to examine for someone who enquires for another. And another if a citizen or inhabitant of a place asks. Another if an exiled, banished, expelled, or absent person asks. Another if a cleric asks, another if a lay person. Another for a cleric asking about a lay person, and vice versa. Another for a king asking about his subjects, and vice versa. Another if a king asks about the commoners, another if vice versa. Another if the Pope asks about a bishop, another if a bishop asks about the pope. Another if a bishop asks about his priests. Another if a priest asks about his bishop. Another if a master asks about his slave, another if vice versa. And understand this for all the diversity of persons, as to whose diversity, and as to which houses are given to them, I will discuss with you after this, in the business of judgements, for thus everyone will uncover the matter of the question and judgement.

VII

On The Numbering Of The Houses And Why They Begin From The First And Go Towards The Fourth, And From The Fourth To The Seventh, And From The Seventh To The Tenth And From The Tenth To The First

In order to satisfy any questions and queries about the numbering of the twelve houses, we shall explain the reason for numbering them in this manner. For some may wish to say that although they should be enumerated, it is not done according to the correct order. For we enumerate them beginning from the first, going under the earth towards the fourth, from the fourth towards the seventh, and from the seventh towards the tenth, which appears to be to be done from right to left: while it appears that we ought to enumerate them from the first going towards the tenth, and from the tenth to the seventh, and from the seventh to the fourth, and from the fourth to the first. Since then we advance according to the order which we write, beginning from the left and going towards the right.

The reason for this is because even if the heavens turn from the east to the west by the first motion, nevertheless the planets (which imprint on the inferior bodies) are moved from west to east, by a second motion (which is from right to left) in contrary direction to the first motion, and so it is against the succession of the signs. For the signs ascend from under the earth (which is left of the heavens), to that which is above the earth (which is its right).

But perhaps you might say that the planets sometimes run in the direction of the first motion (namely when they are retrograde). The response to this is that the retrograde motion is not natural, but rather accidental, neither is it wholly with the first motion, but rather it is always according to something contrary to the first motion, namely out of the motion of the circles carrying them towards the east, in contrary direction to the first motion.

VIII

Which Houses Are Strong, Which Are Stronger, Which Are Weak, Which Are Weaker, And Which Are Mediocre

I made mention to you above of the twelve houses, which are called "towers" or "cusps", and of their significations, from the first going forwards up to the twelfth, and from the twelfth to the first going backwards in succession. Now it remains to be stated which of them are strong, which are stronger, which are weak, and which are weaker, and which are mediocre.

The strong houses are the four angles, namely the 1st house (which is the oriental angle), the 10th house (which is the southern angle), the seventh (which is the occidental angle), and the fourth (which is the northern angle). And of these four two are stronger than the others - namely the first and the tenth.

The weak houses are four in number, which are cadent from the angles, namely the third, (which falls from the angle of the earth, namely, the 4th house), the ninth (which falls from the northern angle, which is the tenth), the twelfth (which falls from the oriental angle, which is the first), and the sixth (which falls from the occidental angle, which is the 7th house). And out of these four, two are weaker than the others, namely the sixth and the twelfth.

The remaining four (which are the second, fifth, eighth and eleventh) are mediocre, but still have more participation with the strong houses (since they move towards them) than they have with the weak houses. Since even if they are contiguous with them as they are with the strong houses, they still recede from them, and go toward the strong houses. For the 2nd house, which succeeds the fir, goes toward it. The fifth, which succeeds the fourth, goes toward it. The eighth, which succeeds the seventh, goes toward it. And the eleventh, which succeeds the tenth, goes toward it.

And Zahel said that the worthier and stronger places in the circle are the angles; the less worthy and less strong are the succeedents; and those which are weaker than the other places are the cadents.

And he said that the angles (namely the 1st, 10th, 7th, and 4th) signify that which is present; the succeedents (namely the 2nd, 5th, 8th, and 11th) signify what is to come, and what succeeds that which is present. The cadents (namely the 3rd, 6th, 9th, and 12th) signify what was, and what is going away, and what no longer is.

Out of the aforementioned angles, the stronger and more noble is the oriental angle (namely the Ascendant). And a planet which is in this angle, is stronger, and especially so if he has any dignity there (namely domicile, exaltation, term, triplicity or face): apart from in certain excepted cases, or if the Lord of the seventh is in the Ascendant is in the Ascendant, and likewise. Following next in strength is the angle of the Midheaven (namely the 10th house): whence a planet which is in the 10th house is said to be less strong than a planet which is in the 1st house, except in lay dignities, magistracies professions, or other offices which pertain to lay people (as has been said elsewhere). And less strong, than a planet in the tenth, will be a planet in the occidental angle (namely in the 7th house). And even less strong than a planet in the seventh, will be a planet in the angle of the earth (which is the 4th house).

And the strongest after the angles are the succeedents (as I said to you). But the 11th house is stronger than the other succeedents, and follows the fourth in strength, but a planet here will still be less strong than one in the fourth. And the fifth follows the eleventh in strength, whence a planet which is in the fifth will be less strong than one who is in the eleventh, except in the particular significations of each house, in which the Lord of that particular house will be stronger than the others (insofar as the significations are to be distinguished).

But still, even if the succeedents are said to be stronger than the cadents, the ninth (which is one of the cadent houses) is stronger than the second and the eighth (which are succeedent houses). And the 3rd house follows the ninth in strength, and precedes the second and the eighth in some cases. Whence a planet which is in the third will not be as weak as one who is in the second.

Whence the aforementioned seven places are better, stronger, and more praiseworthy than the others: namely the Ascendant, which is stronger than the tenth; and the tenth, which is stronger than the seventh; and the seventh, which is stronger than the fourth; and the fourth, which is stronger than the eleventh; and the eleventh, which is stronger than the fifth; and the fifth which is stronger than the ninth; and the ninth which is stronger than the third.

After these seven places, the stronger, or least weak, is the third, since it is the house in which the Moon rejoices; for then the third prevails over the second and the eighth in such matters as journeys and similar things; just as was said when dealing with the topic of which houses the planets rejoice in. Next is the second, which ascends after the first. But there is said to be great misfortune in the 8th house, since it is the house of death, and it also does not aspect the Ascendant. The remaining two houses, namely the sixth and the twelfth, are bad, very weak, and unfortunate, and are said to be worse than the rest of the houses. And any planet which is in these houses will be of no advantage: for the sixth from the Ascendant doesn't aspect the Ascendant, and is cadent from it, and is the house of infirmity and all defects; and of all illnesses both separable and inseparable. And is the place of Mars' joy, who rejoices in burnings, bloodshed, and in all evil deeds which are exercised through fire and iron.

Similarly the 12th house is cadent from the Ascendant, and it doesn't aspect it, and is the place of hidden enemies (not publicly opposed to the native) and is the place of distress, grief, difficulties, labours, sorrow, bewailing, and lamentation; and is the place of Saturn's' joy, who rejoices in bewailing, sorrow, labour and lamentation.

IX

Which Planets Move Against The Firmament, That Is, Against The First Motion

Albumashar said (and the philosophers agree on this) that all planets run by their own motion against the motion of the firmament; except if they are retrograde, which happens to three of the superior planets (namely Saturn, Jupiter and Mars); and two of the inferiors (namely Venus and Mercury). The luminaries do not go retrograde, however they do go fast-of-course and slow-of-course.

The Cauda and Caput Draconis run in contrary motion to the motion of the planets, namely against the succession of signs. For the planets move from Aries into Taurus, from Taurus into Gemini, from Gemini into Cancer, from Cancer into Leo, from Leo into Virgo, from Virgo into Libra, from Libra into Scorpio, from Scorpio into Sagittarius, from Sagittarius into Capricorn, from Capricorn into Aquarius, from Aquarius into Pisces, from Pisces into Aries.

However the Caput and the Cauda travel contrary to this motion, going from Aries into Pisces, from Pisces into Aquarius, from Aquarius into Capricorn, and so on up to the finish of the signs by retrogradation. And it is said by Cancaph that the Caput Draconis and the Cauda, are nothing else other than the intersection of circles of the luminaries with each other in two opposite places; whence in these places, or in the twelve or so degrees around these places, the eclipse of the luminaries takes place.

X

On The Colours Which The Houses Signify

With the aforementioned twelve houses having the above significations, it is possible for someone to judge that they don't have any other significations. But it is not so, but rather that in addition to the aforementioned things, they also signify diverse colours in turn. For the 1st house and the seventh signify white; the second and he twelfth signify green, the third and the eleventh signify saffron; the fourth and the tenth signify red; the fifth and the ninth signify a honey colour; the sixth and eighth signify black. Whence if it is ever necessary for you to examine any matter in terms of colour: examine in which of the houses you find the significator, and according to that house you can judge on the colour of the quesited thing.

XI

In Which Houses The Planets Rejoice

Albumashar and Alchabicius said that each one of the seven planets has a certain accidental power in one of the above mentioned twelve houses, which is called a "joy".

For Mercury rejoices in the first, since the first signifies the body of the native or querent, and from this Mercury rejoices here: since he signifies knowledge, and that is the thing which is more suited to the person of the native or querent than anything else: for knowledge alone can ennoble man, which no other accident can do.

The Moon rejoices in the third, since the third has the significations of short and fast journeys, and those things which are changed quickly and repealed; whence, since the Moon signifies fast and swift changes from one proposition to another, and from one thing to another, she rejoices in the third, since no other house has this signification.

Venus rejoices in the fifth: since this is the house of joys, delights, and dancing, and Venus herself signifies this; and for this reason she rejoices here, since the other houses do not signify this.

Mars rejoices in the sixth, since it is the house of deception, infirmity and slaves, and he himself signifies slaves, deceivers, the mendacious, and liars; and therefore rejoices here, since the other houses do not signify this.

The Sun rejoices in the ninth, which is the house of religion, and the Sun himself naturally signifies religion; and thus rejoices here, since the other houses do not signify this (even if he also signifies other things).

Jupiter rejoices in the eleventh, since he is a benefic, and has the signification of fortune and wealth, and is naturally a significator of money and profit, and the 11th house signifies these things.

Saturn rejoices in the twelfth, since this is the house of mourning, sorrow, labours, lamentations, and tears, and Saturn rejoices in these things, and things similar to them.

XII

On The Significations Of The Houses, Or Of The Angles And Succeedents, And Of The Lords Of The Angles, Succeedents And Cadents

It was said in the significations of the twelve houses that the angles signify strength and perfection, and the fast arrival of things, and greater swiftness; and that the angles and their Lords signify great honours, value, and fortune.

The cadents from the angles signify weakness, detriment, misfortune, and the covering of things (apart from the ninth and the third which signify the apparition of things); and the sixth and the twelfth signify concealment, covering up, base things, disgrace, and hastened falls.

The succeedents of the angles signify moderate strength and fortune. For the eleventh (which succeeds the tenth) is stronger and more deserving than the others, and signifies moderate fortune from friends, and from things in which one trusts, or from any other things signified by the 11th house. The 5th house (which succeeds the fourth) signifies moderate fortune through gifts, and by reason of children, gaiety, or happiness, or by any other things signified by the 5th house. The 2nd house (which succeeds the first) signifies moderate fortune because of substance, assistants and household members, and indeed any of those things signified by the 2nd house. The 8th house (which succeeds the seventh) signifies moderate fortune from substance which is inherited from the dead, which the Arabs call "almaverith". And Alchabicius said that it signifies moderate fortune from hidden matters, or at least from another one those things signified by the 8th house.

XIII

On The Significations Of The Lords Of The Angles In The Angles, And First On The Lord Of The First In The Angles

When the Lords of the angles are in the angles, they have these significations: since when the Lord of the first is in the first, it signifies good fortune, and acquisition through the native himself, from his own industry, the exhaustion of his own body, through his own family, through his own striving, through his own concern, and through those things which are signified by the 1st house.

However when it is placed in the 10th house, it signifies his (the natives or querent's) fortune through his profession, and offices, and positions of power or authority, and through sublime and lofty professions, and even through the king, and communicating with kings or magnates and similar people; and through those things which are signified by the 10th house.

However, if it is placed in the seventh, it signifies his fortune through agreements and contracts which he makes with men who will be useful to him; and even through wives and because of women and associates, and through those things which are signified by the 7th house.

However if it is in the fourth, it signifies his fortune because of his father, or grandfather, or father in law, or because of some inheritance which reaches him (from which he will gain wealth); and through the regulation of rivers or other waters, and by planting trees, and building houses; and because of ancient things, and things having roots, or through hidden treasure which he will find underground, and similar things; or through any other things signified by the 4th house.

On The Lord Of The Tenth In The Angles

When the tenth Lord is in the tenth, it signifies fortune through great kingship, and through kings and lofty magistracies, and through those things which are signified by the 10th house.

And when the Lord of the tenth is in the seventh, it signifies fortune through kings or kingship, and through victory in contentions, and through those who have disputes against him, and from reasons of women, or through those things which are signified through the 7th house.

When the Lord of the tenth is in the fourth, it signifies fortune through kingship and through collection of tributes, and through reasons of tributes or on the occasion of tributes, and by cultivating land and the building of cities, castles, and similar things. And through the draining and division of waters and rivers, and by the guarding of cities, castles, and similar things. And through ancient things, and diggings under the ground, or through any other things which are signified through the 4th house.

However if it is in the 1st house, it signifies fortune through a kingship, through praiseworthy and famous matters, through the talents of his own person, and through staying with kings and magnates, and in their vicinity; and by reason of common people, or though those things which are signified through the 1st house.

On The Lord Of The Seventh In The Angles

If the Lord of the seventh is in the seventh, it signifies fortune through business deals, and agreements, and through exchanges. And if the person in question is a woman, through wet-nursing; and if it is a man in question, through women, associates, and through feminine activities, and similar things; or through anything signified by the 7th house.

If it is in the fourth, it signifies fortune through agreements with women, and that women will earn wealth for him, and in his utility; and through business of his father and grandfather, and their things, and because of inheritances, and planting trees, vineyards, cultivating the land, and similar things; or through any other things signified by the 4th house.

However if the Lord of the seventh is in the first, it signifies fortune and acquisition, and business because of medicine, and through astronomy, and through matters and labours in spiritual matters, and even through natural talent, or any other things signified by the 1st house.

However if the Lord of the seventh is in the tenth, it signifies fortune on occasion of the king, or through those things which are signified by the 10th house.

On The Lord Of The Fourth In The Angles

If the Lord of the fourth is in the fourth, it signifies fortune because of chief offices, and mechanical arts. And if the native is of farming stock, it signifies his fortune through cultivation of the land, because of produce or profits, through reason of his father and similar people, and ancient things, or through any other things signified through the 4th house.

However if the fourth Lord is in the Ascendant, it signifies fortune from cultivating the land, and produce, and through natural talent, and profound plans, and through other things signified by the 1st house.

However if the fourth Lord is in the tenth, it signifies fortune from cultivating the land, and from produce, or from profits by employment of kings and great men, or noblemen or rich men, and through profits of professions, and from their causes and similar things: or through any of those things signified by the 10th house.

When the fourth Lord is in the seventh it signifies fortune and wealth, or profit and success, from cultivating the land, and from profit because of wives, associates, enemies, contentions, business, and similar things which are signified by the 7th house.

On The Significations Of The Lords Of The Succeedents In The Succeedents

The Lords of the succeedents in the succeedents signify moderate fortune (in the case of one succeedent Lord placed in any of the succeedents), through the matters signified by that succeedent, as was said on the Lords of the angles in any of the angles according to their significations.

On The Significations Of The Lords Of The Cadents In The Cadents

However if the Lords of the cadents are placed in cadents, they signify misfortune and impediments through the matters signified by that cadents, as was said on the Lords of the angles in each of the angles according to what is signified by them.

These things are those which the aforementioned Lords signify in the aforementioned houses, but what was exemplified by the Lords of the angles can also be used for the Lords of the succeedents and the Lords of the cadents.

XIV

On The Discovery Of The Significator Of The Quesited Matter

And so that you don't fall into error, nor into ambiguity on the significators of matters which are signified by each house, I will teach you how to find the planet who is the significator of the matter which you seek. The Lord of the sign is not always the significator of the matter which is signified by the house of the quesited; but rather it is sometimes a planetary Lord of the house, and sometimes another who is not the Lord of the domicile, is stronger in the house.

The stronger planet is said to be the one which has more dignity or fortitudes there, and who has more fortitudes in the house of the quesited matter, or who signifies the quesited matter. And that planet is called the significator, which Alchabicius called the "*almutem*", that is, "*the victor*". And it is said to be the victor, since it exceeds the other planets in fortitudes in the house in question.

For example: a certain question is made about substance, whose Ascendant was the first degree of Pisces. Aries was the 2nd house (which is the house of substance), namely its sixth degree; and so it appears that Mars, who is the Lord of Aries, is the significator of substance, but it is not so. Mars only has six fortitudes here: since he has five from domicile, and one from face, and so there are six fortitudes of Mars here. And the same sign is the exaltation of the Sun, who has seven fortitudes there: four from exaltation and three from triplicity;

and so the Sun has seven of the above mentioned fortitudes. Whence he will remain the significator of substance, and not Mars; on account of the greater number of fortitudes which the Sun has there. Still, even if the Sun is the ruler over substance in this question, Mars will still be his participator, but he will be able to do less here than the Sun.

And if the Sun is so impeded that he cannot be the significator, it will then come to Mars; and similarly to Jupiter, if Mars is so debilitated that he cannot be the significator. And the Moon is always a participator.

Moreover, Jupiter will have something to do here (whence he has some kind of participation with them), for he has two fortitudes on account of the terms which he has there; and is also a participator for another reason - since he is the natural significator of substance.

And the 3rd house in this question is at twelve degrees of Taurus. Whence, if there is a question about brothers, or any of those things which are signified by the 3rd house: then you ought to then discern which planet is stronger in this house. And understand this for the rest of the houses and for the rest of their significations.

And in questions related to substance you also ought to examine the Part of Substance, which you can find in this manner: see which of the planets is the significator of substance, and see in what degree of any sign he is in; and subtract this many degrees from the house of substance; and that which remains is the place of the Part of Substance; just as you will find when we deal with Parts in their own place. Nevertheless, I shall give an example to you of the 2nd house of this question (which is the house of substance), which is the sixth degree of Aries. And Mars, (who is the Lord of Aries) is found in eighth degrees Scorpio. You ought to subtract Scorpio from Aries, but you will not be able: since you cannot subtract eight from one. So add twelve signs to the 8; and subtract the eighth degree of Scorpio from the twelve signs and six degrees; and four signs and twenty-eight degrees will remain for you. Then project four signs and twenty-eight degrees from six degrees of Aries (which is the beginning of the house of substance): and the Part of Substance will fall in Leo, in twenty-eight degrees of the same. And thus you will do for the Part of Fortune and the rest of the parts. But the Part of Fortune is taken in a different and easier way, just as will be said in the Tractate On The Parts. And thus you will do for the other houses, namely the third, fourth, fifth, and the rest. And thus you will find the significator of the quesited matter, always determining the significator by the planet which has greater strength in the house signifying the quesited matter.

XV

On Accidental Powers

It is said of the planets that they are in their own likeness, (nevertheless having observed the method according to what will be stated in the Tractate On The Parts) or what Alchabicius and other philosophers call *"Aym"*: when a diurnal planet is above the earth in the day, and below the earth at night, and a nocturnal one above the earth at night, and below the earth during the day. And a masculine planet, when it is in a masculine sign, and a feminine planet when it is in a feminine sign. When this is so, a planet is said to be in its own likeness. Since diurnal planets rejoice in the day time; nocturnal planets in the night-time; masculine planets in masculinity; feminine planets in femininity. Whence if a planet is the significator of any matter, and it is in its own likeness: it will perfect the matter which it signified better and more completely than it would if it wasn't in its own likeness. And aym is a certain strength, so that if a planet is in its aym, it will be a certain amount stronger than when it is not in its aym, as is someone who is in a state in which he profits, and can satisfy his intentions, with profit and fortune appearing to favour him.

THE THIRD TRACTATE

ON THE NATURES OF THE SEVEN PLANETS

And What Are Their Characteristics, And What Things They Signify According To Their Own Being, And According To Their Own Natures, And What They Imprint On Inferior Things According To The Diverse Qualities Of Their Own Motions

I

On Saturn And What He Signifies

After having arrived at the completion of what was intended regarding the circle of the signs and its division, and its accidents, what is to be done now is the following: a commemoration of the seven planets and a narration of their natures, their significations, and the impressions which they imprint on the inferiors things - and first on Saturn.

Alchabitius said Saturn is a masculine, diurnal planet, and he works on a distemperate coldness and dryness, and is the significator of the father, grandfather, and all ancestors who are signified by the 4th house - but this is rather by accident, than by nature. He himself naturally has the signification of the person or body of the native: because the first thing that happens to man is the (physical) person, through which he is given being.

And Saturn is the first in the circle of Planets, and is the first planet in their order, and the one whom all other planets follow, and also the first who exercises his operations in a conceived child after the fall of the seed into the womb; binding and uniting the material out of which the conceived child is formed. For the operations of the fixed stars, (which are principal agents) are not manifestly perceived in these things, but only the operations of the planets (who are secondary agents).

Alchabitius and others that said that Saturn is the significator of the father, and old things, and burdensome things - having a view to his slow and burdened motion, and his heaviness; and therefore they posited him as the significator of older parents, and of old and burdensome things, and not without a suitable reason.

Because if he was the significator of someone's nativity, and he was oriental, and the nativity was diurnal, the native would not reach the completion of his natural life: nevertheless he could arrive up to the beginning of old age (which is from the sixtieth year onwards), unless otherwise impeded against nature, just as we see with the majority of men who die before their time, as by iron, fire, a fall, a collapse of a structure, drowning, and of many other causes which are not of the consideration of nature, nor of its intention (just as was said above). However, if Saturn was oriental and the nativity was nocturnal, it signifies that the native will live up until the end of old age, unless impeded by the aforementioned things, as I said, regarding which it will be spoken of below in the Tractate on Nativities.

And he said that Saturn signifies all things of distemperate, severe, coldness and dryness. And of the humours he signifies melancholy. And of the complexions of the body he signifies melancholy, and perhaps this melancholy will be mixed with phlegm, and with the slowness and heaviness of the natives body, such that he will not have a light gait, nor will he jump lightly, nor will he learn to swim or do similar things which are done to show the lightness of the body. And he will be disgusting and bad smelling, and will smell like a goat, and he makes men who eat a lot. And if a Saturnian begins to esteem someone (which rarely happens), he esteems him by true esteem. And if he begins hating someone (which frequently happens), he hates him with the ultimate hatred, and will hardly or never desists from this hatred.

And Albuaz said that if he is in good condition, he signifies profound knowledge, and profound and good counsel; so great that rarely or never will anyone know how to improve on it.

And of professions, he signifies ancient, laborious, serious, and valuable things, and aquatic works, or works which are done near water, such as mills, bridges, boats, and the like, and also the regulation and management of waters, and cultivating the land (namely fields, and tree plantations), and the building of houses, and especially houses of the religious who wear black vestments - if he is fortunate and in good condition. However, if he is unfortunate and in bad condition, he signifies old and worthless things, such as hoeing, digging of worthless pits, foul-smelling places, laboriously carrying rocks and stones with labour to walls, especially to subterranean walls, or the walls of cities, and those which are next to pits, and the making of many things which are made from bricks, and similar things. And many such men live in labour, tribulations and poverty, eating bad and foul smelling food.

And Alchabitius said that he signifies sailors, namely poor, lower class ones, when he is in bad condition. And when he is in good condition he signifies great and rich sailors, namely those who are enriched from navigation, and these men will be of true esteem, ample and patient. And if Saturn is in bad condition the native will be undistinguished, sad, mournful, of evil suspicion, eager to suspect every evil, and to rouse men by whispers and inciting evil. And if he is in good condition he signifies old and durable things, such as inheritances which come from any source (and especially from the dead), and estates which are acquired by right more so than by wrong. If he is in bad condition it signifies that the native will make use of water which is putrid, dirty, swampy, foul smelling, and old, which has remained long in one place (such as in ponds and the like), and bad tasting and changeable water; nor will he recoil from drinking this water: and he will eagerly remain in swamps, or near these places, and he will eat rotten fish and meat, and will not seem to sense any harm from them.

And of infirmities he has the signification of epilepsy, falling illnesses, and phlegmatic, melancholic, freezing, hard, earthly and locking-up illnesses. And many illnesses which are incurable, such as leprosy, white morphew, deep, hollow, and hard fistulas, and illnesses in places of nerves, and other similar illnesses. And he signifies that these illnesses will happen to the native, when Saturn is his significator and is in such a condition. And in questions about illnesses he often signifies ones of these kinds.

And he signifies long and laborious travels, and (when he is in bad condition) journeys which are barely completed, and if he is the significator of a journey it will be laborious, harsh, and almost intolerable.

And he signifies harsh and oppressive prisons.

And he signifies that the native will accept into his custody the debts of those pledging their substance to each other, but he will not care to make arrangements between them.

And he signifies heaviness of the body, its slowness, and labours; and mental torment, evil thoughts, and the substance of the dead which remains after them; and fathers, grandfathers and brothers older than the native, and slaves, eunuchs and low class persons.

And if Saturn alone is the significator of any nativity, so that he is not combined with any other planet, the nature of the natives duties will be those of a leather-worker, and his labours will be from this.

The Complexion Of Saturn With Jupiter And Other Planets

If Jupiter is joined to him it signifies the working of papers in which are written ecclesiastical books, divine words, and treatments divine matters; and those in which are written words on superior and heavenly matters, like the judgements of the stars(both theoretical as practical), and also on all high arts, and judgements of the law, and similar matters.

And if Mars is joined to him it signifies leather-work from which shoes are made.

And if the Sun is joined to him it signifies leather-work which is taken up and sewn together, such as in the case of pelts and cruppers and similar things.

And if Venus is joined to him it signifies leather-work from which is made drums, cymbals, and all instruments which are made to sound pleasant, and those for games and similar things.

And if Mercury is joined to him it signifies leather work, specifically parchments, on which are written text aimed at perpetuating memories (as are wills, instruments of sale and purchase, and similar things); and parchments in which are written accounts of expenses, which happen in the courts of magnates and rich men and others who wish to have memory of their expenses; and those in which the accounts of merchants and money changers, and similar things.

And if the Moon is joined to him it signifies work or preparation of the hides of wild animals, and also domestic animals which have died.

Whence if the native wishes to perform leather-work, judge according to the complexion of Saturn with other planets and according to this method you will see what leather work he should involve himself in.

And of sects he signifies Judaism, that is the Old Testament, and all sects which confess the unity of God. And if he is in bad condition, he signifies belief in unity with much hesitation or much doubt. And Messala (who was one of the most experienced astrologers, and in very perspicuous in this science), said that Saturn signifies Judaism because it is one of the ancient ones, and no positive law older than it can be found, and all other laws and all other sects, confess it, and Judaism itself does not confess to any other law, neither does it confess to any other sect, just as all the other Planets join to Saturn, whereas Saturn himself doesn't join to any of them.

And he has the signification of black vestments, and those who naturally use black vestments (as much in the case of the religious and those in cloisters, as for anyone else).

And of metals he signifies iron and lead.

And Albubetri said that it signifies the interior of the ears, the spleen, and the stomach. Of colours he has black. And of tastes he has astringent and sour. And of days, Saturday, and of nights, that which precedes Wednesday. And the quantity of his orb is nine degrees.

And the years of his *fidaria* are twelve. His maximum years are 464, his greater years are 57, his medium years are 43 ½. And his lesser years are 30. And his greater years are said to be 57, since they were considered according to the quantity of the degrees of the terms which are assigned to him as his terms out of the degrees of the twelve signs. The medium years are said to be 43 ½, since they were considered according to his greater years and lesser years added together, which are 87, half of which is 43 ½. The lesser years were considered according to his slow course, since he completes it in 30 years; and from this was taken the number of his lesser years, namely 30.

His strength in the regions of the circle is in the northern parts.

And Messala said that of the figure of man Saturn signifies a man between black and yellow, who sinks his eyes ponderously to the earth while walking, and who holds his feet crooked, and joins them together when he walks. And he has small eyes, dry skin, sinewy; with a thin beard on his chin, thick lips, and is crafty, ingenious, a seducer, killer (especially in secret). And Dorotheus said that it signifies a man with a very hairy body and a unibrow.

And of the parts he has the Part of Strength and Stability. And it signifies matters of lands and inheritance, and those who preside over works; and bravery, labour and talent, and reasons for death.

And Adila said that Saturn gives men a dark complexion, a thin beard, and makes them hairy, often working in water, serious, lazy, and never or hardly laughing. And those who Saturn has as subjects (namely those for whom he is the significator) frequently suffer fissures in the heel, which the commoners call "rays". He gives men a grey colour, and often makes the chest thin, and the hair on the head rough and unkempt. Ordering his men to wear ugly black clothes; which orders will always be carried out, since Saturnians always appear to be sorrowful and to have ill will.

Whence if you wish to judge anything on any Saturnian man, in a nativity or a question, consider what was said above and judge accordingly.

Whence, if anyone should ask why Saturn has these significations, and causes these impressions; even if it appears more fitting of a natural philosopher than an astrologer, still a reason appears possible to assign: this reason being that the motion of the eighth sphere is found to be from east to west - not on account of it having such a being, but on account of its nature being suitable to be able to be moved. And it is said to have an external mover, and so to certain men it appeared to be moved by the first cause. The planets are moved from the west to the east in the contrary direction of the first motion (or the motion of the eighth sphere). And they are said to have an internal mover, namely an intellect, as it appeared to certain men. And with this, discord, contrarieties, rebellion, and enmity shall arise; and Saturn is closer to these contrarieties, and therefore signifies this more than the others which are further away from the contrarieties

II

On Jupiter And What He Signifies

Alchabicius said that Jupiter is benefic, masculine, and diurnal; and is the natural significator of substance, since substance is the second accident which happens to the native after his birth, and is one of the first of the necessary things which occurs to him; and in like manner Jupiter is the second planet, since he is second in the order of planets (after the first, which is Saturn). And similarly Jupiter is the second planet who exercises his operations on the conceived child, namely bestowing spirit and life on him. And he works by temperate, airy, and sanguine hotness and moisture through his own nature. And of the ages he signifies youth, which is from the 14th or 21st year up to the 40th or 45th year.

And of the professions, he has those which pertain to law and just and honest judgement. And he gives regard when he sees any people having an altercation or litigation between each other, to place peace and concordance between them, and he always strives for good. And he signifies the abundance of substance. And of business he signifies that which is done without seduction. And he signifies the soul, life, joy, religion, truth, patience, and all good, beautiful, and valuable precepts, and whatever pertains to honesty. And he signifies the abundance of Venus.

And of infirmities he signifies whatever comes from the increase of blood, or through means of augmentation, which is not excessive in such a way that it exterminates nature, nor from inflamed or changeable blood. And he is the planet of wisdom, intellect and good custom.

If Jupiter is well disposeed, and is oriental and in an angle, the native will be of good quality, pleasant, just, honouring of his elders, and also a good advisor, a helper of the needy, well known, loving his friends, and of good intellect.

But if he is unfortunate, as Ptolemy attests, the native will: be ignorant of doing good, experienced around diabolical operations, striving under a feigned sanctity, staying in houses of prayer, wilfully living solitarily, and in crypts and cavernous places, and even in caves, and he will predict the future in these places. He will not esteem anyone, and will have no friends, recoil from children, flee from association with men, nor will he want to be honoured by anyone, he will be unfaithful, nothing could be trusted to him; for he will be evil, weak, foolish, laborious, and will make wicked choices.

On His Complexion With Saturn And The Other Planets

Which if he is joined with Saturn, signifies knowledge of necromancy, the art of magic, and incantations and exorcisms and similar things.

However if Mars is joined to him, it signifies knowledge of medicine, especially surgery.

If the Sun is joined to him it signifies the knowledge of sects, and prudence in contentions and disputations, and knowing how to defend the right faith, and fight against heretics of the faith, and also of the arts; nor will he permit himself to make a false conclusion. And in all things he will be a good and ordered disputer, and he will not be a prattler.

And if Venus is joined to him it signifies composition of music and other delightful sciences. The native will also be a cithara player, trumpet player, and wise in musical instruments.

If Mercury is joined to him it signifies knowledge of arithmetic, and all those things which pertain to number; and knowledge of writing beyond all other writers (if he wishes to study in this), and philosophy - namely astronomy and the other sciences of the quadrivium.

If the Moon is joined to him, it signifies knowledge of the management and measurement of water, and also of land, and swimming places, and the regulation of rivers, and similar things. And of the qualities of the mind it signifies generosity, modesty and justice. And of sects it signifies pluralities and insincerity: for the native whose significator is Jupiter (when Jupiter is joined with the Moon) will want to hold this sect and that sect, and will not serve either of them well, nevertheless his intention will not be evil.

And Cancaph and Valens said that he signifies the liver, stomach, the left ear, the arms and the belly (namely from the navel below), and the lower parts of the pubic region.

And of colours he signifies ashen, green and similar colours.

And of tastes he signifies sweetness.

And the quantity of his orb is nine degrees.

And of the days he has Thursday; and of the nights he has that which precedes Monday.

And the years of his fidaria are 12. And his maximum years are 428. His greater years are 79. His medium years are 45 and a half. And his lesser years are 12.

And his strength in the circle is in the west.

And his greater years are said to be 79 since they were considered according to the quantity of degrees in the terms which were assigned to Jupiter as his terms from the degrees of the twelve signs. His medium years are said to be 45 and a half, since these were considered according to the number which is reached from the addition of his greater and lesser years, which is 91; half of which is 45 and a half. His lesser years were considered according to his course in the eccentric, which he travels through in 12 years - and the number of his lesser years (12) was taken from this.

And Messala said that of the human figures he signifies a white man, having eyes not exactly black, unequal and narrow nostrils, bald, having blackness in one of his teeth, a beautiful stature, a good mind, good character, and a beautiful body. And Dorotheus said that he has big eyes, wide pupils, and a curly beard.

And of the parts he has the Part of Beatitude and Profit. And he signifies faith and an appetite for good.

And of works, wholesomeness, security and participation.

And of regions he has Iraq, Babylonia, Isfahan, Persia, Ctesiphon, and al-Ahwaz.

And Sacerdos said that Jupiter makes good and honourable men, to whom he gives a round beard, beautiful eyes, and two front teeth bigger than the others (and sometimes a small bit different to this). To the faces of men he gives a golden colour, mixed with white. He also makes men who eagerly wear beautiful clothing, having somewhat long hair, which is also beautiful, religious in their being, looking far off into the land while they go about.

III

On Mars And What He Signifies

Alchabitius said that Mars is a masculine, nocturnal, malefic planet, working through his own nature by distemperate heat and dryness; and is fiery, choleric, and bitter tasting. And he is the natural significator of brothers and pilgrimages. And Mars is the natural significator of brothers since brothers are the third accident which befalls the native after conception (namely after the nativity), and who the native loves more greatly than all those things which he met with before. And Mars is likewise the third planet in the order of planets, and is the third that follows from Saturn in their order. And Mars is similarly the third planet which exercises his operations on the conceived child, namely operating on him through blood and reddening. And he is the significator of pilgrimages, since on pilgrimages travellers suffer many inconveniences, and many tribulations, plunderings, impious labours, and similar things which are considered as being similar to the significations of Mars.

And of the ages of man he has completed youth, namely from 22 years up to 45 inclusive. And of professions, all professions which are exercised by fire and iron; such as by striking iron with hammers on an anvil, or by other means; and practicing the work of craftsmen, bakers, furnace workers, butchers, barbers, and the like.

On His Complexion With Saturn And Other Planets

If he is joined to Saturn, it signifies the work of craftsmen which is done using iron alone, and especially tools by which the land is worked, as with hoes, motors, ploughshares, and similar things

However if he is joined to Jupiter, it signifies works of craftsmen which are made from copper ore and lead, as are works from pewter and similar things

If the Sun is joined to him it signifies works of craftsmen, which are made from gold not having been worked on, as with Bizantii, gold florins, small medals, and all other works from raw gold.

And if Venus is joined to him it signifies works of craftsmen which are made for women's jewellery, such as rings, necklaces, and similar things.

And if Mercury is joined to him it signifies works of craftsmen which are done to stitch things together, and joining things together, such as awls, needles, and similar things.

If the Moon is joined to him it signifies the works of craftsmen which make scales, plates, balances, bowls, silver goblets, and vessels with which drinks are measured in taverns and which are used for drinking in the courts of the wealthy, and similar things.

On His Significations When He Is The Sole Significator

And when he is the sole significator, it signifies the work of medicine, as much for surgery and for the other parts of medicine. And if no other planets are complected with him, it signifies works of medicine which are done through the opening of veins, as is with phlebotomy, and the opening of abscesses, and similar things.

And Alchabicius said that if he is involved with Saturn, it signifies works of medicine on wounds and similar things.

And when he is complected with Jupiter it signifies works related to childbirth, and care of the eyes.

And if he is complected with Venus it signifies works of decoration which pertain to barbers, such as cutting hair, trimming beards, and cutting nails.

And if he is complected with Mercury, it signifies the cutting of veins.

And if he is complected with the Moon it signifies the extraction of teeth, and cleaning of the ears, and similar things.

And when he himself is the sole significator, it signifies injuries of wretches, and that he shall wilfully injuries those lesser than him; and spilling of blood, wounds, slaughters, burnings, decapitations, abuses, thieves, tavern-keepers, daylight bandits, arrogant people, liars, perjurers, scoffers, forgers (of both money and writings), and oppressions by force, those harming whoever they can, irritability, highwaymen, rushing, leaders of armies, immodesty, inconstancy, those not ashamed of any evil they have committed, travels outside of the land, and out of one's own land, and an abundance of sex.

And if he is in bad condition, and is the significator for women, she will miscarry a child; and in some cases she herself will be culpable for this.

And he signifies middle brothers, and knowledge and discernment in the care of animals; for he will be a chief shepherd.

And of illnesses he signifies hot fevers, namely those which happen from choler not burned, and without a cause. And madness (both true and false), and blisters of blood, impetigo, albaras, and unusual rednesses which come to be in the body apart from nature with harshness and foulness; and itches and lentigoes; and sicknesses from eating flesh of the body (such as Kings Disease (gout), cancers, and similar things). And he signifies migraines, St. Anthony's Disease, and similar things.

And he signifies that the native will eat rotten meat, and meat that is not well cooked. And it signifies terrors, and horrible thoughts disturbing men, which move and impede men, rendering them useless. And it has the signification of anything which happens by inflammation of heat. Of the qualities of the mind he signifies agitation and confusion.

On His Complexion With Saturn

If he is joined with Saturn it signifies the greatest hatred and enmity, and that the native will be very envious, and he will rejoice and be happy when he sees evil, or any tribulation or harm befall someone. And of sects he will love those in which there is discord and war, and he will eagerly attach himself to these and quickly change from sect to sect, and from one faith to another; nor will he persevere well in any of them, unless perhaps through accidental circumstances constraining his will. And he will experience uncertainty, and swiftly change from one obligation to another, as those men do who always are held in debt, and remain implicated in them, not knowing how to free themselves from these debts; and when they avoid and free themselves from one, they run into another. And when they want to satisfy one of their creditors, they take money from another, and always remain wrapped up in these debts, and in tribulations because of them. And sometimes they do one thing, other times they destroy the same; and they change their wills and make others, and never remain long nor persevere in the same proposition: nevertheless these things are all under the one heading.

And Alchaiat and Albubeter said that of the parts of the body he has the gallbladder, kidneys, veins, spermatic ducts, and the back.

And of colours he has red, and of tastes bitterness.

And the quantity of his orb is eight degrees.

And of days he has Tuesday, and of nights he has that which precedes Saturday.

And the years of his fidaria are seven. His maximum years are 214, and his greater years are 66. His medium years are 40 and a half. His lesser years are 15. And it is said that his greater years are 66, since they were considered according to the quantity of the number of degrees which were assigned to him as his terms from the degrees of the twelve signs. His medium years are said to be 40 and a half, since they were considered according to being half of the number of the sum of his greater and less years; the sum being 81, which when halved gives 40 and a half. However the lesser years were considered in a different manner than the aforementioned: since he completes his epicycle 8 times in 15 years, and from this they took the number (namely 15): since he does this in no other number of years.

And his strength is in the southern part.

And Messala said that of the images of man he signifies a red faced man having red hair, a round face, easily doing all dishonourable things, having saffron eyes, a horrible glance, bold, having a sign or mark on his foot. And Dorotheus said that it signifies a man with a sharp gaze.

And of regions he has Jerusalem and the Roman lands up to the west.

And of the parts he has the Part of Boldness.

And he said that it signifies perseverance and agreement, and a mind which is desirous, cunning, arrogant, audacious, defiant, sharp, and hastening in all matters.

Adila said that Mars gives men a crooked and thick body, and makes men schismatic, and sowers of discord amongst men, whose faces colour is red mixed with black (that is, Martial), so that it could be said he has a brown colour, as one does who walks in the Sun and heat, so that he isn't black, nor truly red, but has a horrible colour: and sometimes has freckles on his face and thin hairs, giving him a beard somewhat like that of a eunuch.

IV

On The Sun And What He Signifies

Alchabitius said that the Sun is a masculine, diurnal planet, benefic by aspect, malefic by bodily conjunction. Operating by heat and dryness though his own nature. And he is the natural significator for the father if the nativity is diurnal. And the Sun the natural significator of the father since the 4th house is the significator of the father, and the Sun is the fourth planet following from Saturn in their order (namely the third after him); and also since the Sun is the fourth planet which exercises his operations on the conceived child, namely operating on the child through natural heat or something similar, in giving spirit and the official members to the conceived child: and the vital soul and features of the face. And the father is someone who the native loves before all others (besides brothers) of those things which can happen to him before children, except the two aforementioned things after the nativity.

And the Sun signifies light and splendour, and beauty, intellect and faith. And he also signifies great kingship, and all other lay dignities, as much in the case of magnates as of others. And this is because the Sun is placed in the middle of the other planets (just like a king), and the others stand next to him: certain ones on one side, certain on the other side - namely the superiors to his right, and the inferiors to his left. And he himself has power in all planets, since he burns them all up. Moreover, his motion is practically uniform, and not varying or alternating, but always keeping the same similar annual advancement. And his motion is the most noble above the motions of the other planets, nor does he go retrograde like the others do.

But you might say that the Moon doesn't go retrograde, which is true, but still, even if she doesn't go retrograde, she still receives such a slowing of her movement which is almost possible to put on a level with retrogradation. But you might say that the Moon sometimes eclipses the Sun. The reply to which is that the Moon sometimes signifies kingdoms and magistracies.

And the Moon naturally signifies the king of the Romans, who has power over the king of Babylonia (of whom the Sun is the natural significator) by law. And the Sun has a certain prerogative over the Moon, namely since the Moon is not a splendid body, nor a luminous one, but rather she receives whatever luminosity and splendour she has from the Sun, and from this she renders less and impedes less. Why this is, I do not dare to say, lest a certain, or rather multiple, fools in tunics surge up against us, wanting to use true reason, and a purpose consonant with truth - things which they are ignorant of. However the wise men among them are not ignorant of these things, nor do they condemn astrologers, in fact they commend them and esteem them, but the fools among them will say that it is a heresy, ignorant of what a heresy is.

And of the ages of man he signifies the end of youth, which is from the forty fifth year up to the sixtieth. He participates with the generality of planets in the disposition of the years.

And of the professions he has kingship, rulership, and the chief place. And he has signification over those who know how to joust lances or throw javelins well, and over hunting, and hunting which is done by means of poisoning (as is done sometimes when someone hunts using poisoned arrows by which he kills wild beasts). And it signifies purging of the body, with every kind of purging with which human bodies are purged inside and outside.

And of infirmities he signifies hot and dry infirmities appearing on the bodies of men. And of substances he signifies much gold, especially raw gold. And Alchabicius said that he signifies all kinds of substance. And of the qualities of the mind he signifies loftiness and sublimity, and that which pursues honour, generosity and glory; and great extent of mind.

And of sects he signifies good worship and similar things. And Alchabitius said that he signifies the command of the voice and strength of speed.

On His Significations With Saturn And Other Planets

If the Sun is joined to Saturn it signifies management of estates, and chief positions of this kind.

And if he is joined to Jupiter he signifies a chief position in faith and religion, and he also signifies all judgements between men, judgements of the works of lesser people, or those of the oppressed, and similar things.

However if he is joined to Mars, it signifies the leadership of an army, and the seeking out of wars: for the native will be efficacious in these things.

If Venus is joined to him it signifies kingship through allegiance with the powerful, and through women.

If Mercury is joined to him it signifies counsellors of the king, and those taking care of libraries and great works of inheritances.

And if the Moon is joined to him it signifies works of legates and revealing of plans, and similar things.

And Valens and Atabari said that the Sun signifies the image of a man's countenance: and particularly the right eye of men, and the left eye of women. And Ben and Alboali said that of the body parts it signifies the heart, the marrow, and the thighs.

And of infirmities those which appear in the mouth, as are cancers and others which eat the flesh of the mouth; and all detriments of the mouth, and descent of water in the eyes. And his virtue and authority is maximally in the head. And the Indians said that when he is in the Ascendant, the native will be burnt up. And that whoever has the Sun as their significator will have a sign on his face.

And of colours he has the emulating colour, which appears to participate in all colours, and according to certain men he signifies the colour white.

And of tastes he has a sharp taste.

And of days he has Sunday, and of nights, that which precedes Thursday.

And the quantity of his orb is 15 degrees, in front and behind.

And the years of his fidaria are ten. And his maximum years are 461 and according to some, they exceed this, and are 1000. And his greater years are 120, and this was considered according to the number of degrees which were assigned to him for his terms from the degrees of the twelve signs: since even if the Sun doesn't have terms assigned through the signs like the five wandering stars; he still has virtue in the above mentioned half of the circle, which is from the beginning of Leo up to the end of Capricorn, just as the other planets have in their terms, and this is 180 degrees. But since two domiciles of the two malefics (which are Scorpio and Capricorn) are in this half, 60 years were subtracted (30 for each of these domiciles); and only 120 remained, out of which the trine aspect results. His medium years were extracted using a different method to the others. His greater years and one half of his lesser years were added together, which made 79, and then halved, which made 39 and a half: and these are the medium years of the Sun. His lesser years were considered from the number of degrees of his exaltation in the nineteenth degree of 6Aries (as was said above), and this is the number of the lesser years of the Sun.

And his strength is in the oriental parts.

And Messala said that of the figures of man he signifies someone who has a colour between saffron and black, with a touch of red; of short stature, bald, (and some say curly hair), but having a beautiful body. And Dorotheus said that the figures of the Sun and the Moon are like the figures of the planets which they are with, and of the planet who is more deserving in their places.

Therefore if you wish to know the figure of the Sun, know that he is saffron, has partly red hair, and his eyes are somewhat saffron.

And of regions he has Samarkand, Khorasan, Persia, and the Roman lands.

And of parts he has the Part of the Future and Divination.

And is the significator of things about to be, and the spirit of wisdom, and elation, perfection, faith, sciences, and joy.

And Adila said that the Sun makes a man full of flesh, having a beautiful and white face, eyes sometimes big; the colour of his face being a mix of white and citrine. Indeed the solar man has a full and beautiful beard, and his hair will be worn long.

V

On Venus And What She Signifies

Albumashar and Alchabitius said that Venus is a benefic, feminine and nocturnal planet, and signifies women and wives. And if it is a diurnal nativity, as Alchabitius says, she signifies mothers. And as Sacerdos says, she signifies younger sisters. And she is the natural significator of children: since children are signified by the 5th house, and Venus is the fifth planet from Saturn, namely the fourth following from him in their order. And also since she is the fifth planet, who exercises her operations on the conceived child, namely completing the sex of a male and female (of whichever sex the conceived child is), and perfecting its nose and eyebrows, and the whole disposition of the face. And since Venus is the planet of delights and joy, and the 5th house is similarly attributed to children, she signifies them - since children are an accident in which the native more greatly rejoices, and nature delights in them more than in other things.

In the Tractate on Nativities what has been said above will be discussed more widely, nevertheless I will say something on these things to you now. Since if you want to know the condition of the native, and want to know what will happen to him from women (namely his mother, wives and younger sisters, and the like): see in the hour of the nativity if Venus is almutem in the nativity: if so, then you will know that things will generally be good for the native with regard to women. And if she is not the significatrix of the nativity, so that she is not the almutem over it, see how and from where she aspects the Lord of the first.

For if she aspects him from the seventh by a trine aspect, the native will be loved by wives by a perfect love. And if she aspects him by a sextile aspect, the native will be loved by wives, but not by a perfect love; but rather there will sometimes be altercations and quarrels between them, and sometimes they will mutually love each other, sometimes not; now this, now that. And if she aspects him from the seventh by a square aspect, then the native will rejoice very little with his wife, and there will be many altercations of all kinds between them, and they will not associate well with each other. If she aspects him from opposition, the native will never rejoice with his wife (and this is to be more greatly feared with the first), neither will things be good for the wife from the native, and there will always be disputes and discord between them.

And if Venus aspects the significator of the nativity from the 10th house by any of the aforementioned aspects: say that it will be so for the native and his mother, as I said it was going to be for him and his wife.

Since if Venus aspects the significator from the 7th house by a good aspect, say that things will be good for the native regarding his mother, if it is by a bad aspect, say that things will be bad from the mother.

And if Venus aspects the significator of the native from the fourth by any of the above mentioned aspects, say that things will happen like this for the native regarding his younger sisters, according to the aspect by which she aspects him, in the same manner that you said regarding the mother.

And Venus works through her own nature by a temperate cold and moisture. And of the ages of man she signifies adolescence, and especially in sheer youth, which is from the fourteenth year to the twenty second. And know that of the professions she has the making of instruments of luxury, and of games and fun, and playing draughts, and playing dice. These will be the offices of a man who has Venus as his significatrix, and which are drawn nearer to him, and which he will know better how to do if he wishes to involve himself in them. And if he involves himself with other things, he will not learn them, nor will he know them as well as he would know these. And he for whom Venus is his significatrix will live in leisure, and will know how to lead his life well, and live more delightfully and in a more courtly manner, than others - who are much worse off than him. And he will be a fornicator and wholly a son of fornication, and will eagerly exercise all venereal pursuits, and will abound in sex, so that sometimes his own nature will be destroyed for this reason. And he will know how to make crowns, and garlands and all ornaments, especially those related to women, and will eagerly ornament his body, and go about clothed in beautiful and elegant garments, and will know how to work with gold and silver, and how to make necklaces, and all such things which pertain to adorning the body, and especially those which pertain to the ornamenting of women (should he adhere to these professions).

And this is what sometimes does not allow someone to arrive at the perfection of their professions or offices: since they perform arts and offices which are not of their nature; and they never learn them perfectly, and only with labour do they learn anything regarding them. However they learn those which pertain to them naturally easily and well.

And Venusian men are playful, and fond of laughing and dancing, cheerful and rejoicing; eagerly enjoying food and drink in company, and they get drunk quicker than others. And they are trusting of others, often being deceived by them. And Venus signifies esteem, generosity, love, justice, and similar things. And Venusian men abide in houses of prayer, so they can appear to be that which they are not; and they restrain their faith. And Venusians desire to hear the sounds of musical instruments, and are more effective in these than other people.

On The Complexion Of Venus With Saturn And Other Planets

If Venus is joined with Saturn signifies the songs of incantations, lamentations and of those who weep for the dead, and those used while building, and the like.

If she is joined with Jupiter, it signifies that the native is learned in sounds of ecclesiastical reading and songs, and in all songs which pertain to clerics and the religious, and those used in houses of prayer, and altars, and in praising Our Lord Jesus Christ.

If she is joined with Mars, if signifies sounds or songs of the lay and masters of war, and songs which are made in battles, such as those made using trumpets, flutes, cymbals and similar things, And sounds or songs in which mention is made of capture, imprisonment, labours, murders, and the clashing of arms and whips: just as happens in the commemoration of the deeds of the ancients, such as in the remembrance of the deeds of Troy, France, Rome, Britain, and the like: for the native will know how to sing these songs.

If she is joined to the Sun, it signifies that the native knows the sounds or songs which are made with wooden instruments which men use in the presence of kings and magnates, such as rotes, violins, citharas, sambukes, lutes, and similar things.

And if Mercury is joined to her, it signifies sounds by which melodies arise and verses are composed, such as those of lyres and similar things.

If the Moon is joined to her it signifies songs which sailors use in sailing or raising the main sails, and similar things.

And of infirmities she signifies cold and moist infirmities, which often happen in the genital members or around them, and the like.

And she signifies that the native is suited for knowing how to adapt and prepare those things which pertain beauty, such as cloaks, women's garments, and their jewellery, and those things with which ornaments are decorated with, such as gold, pearls, fringes and the like.

And of the qualities of the mind she signifies charm, and she signifies friendship, food and drink, and the desire for eating, drinking, sex, and similar things.

And of the sects she signifies idolatry, and those in which eating and drinking are practiced.

And Valens and Cancaph said that of the human body she signifies the haunches, the spine of the back, and the sperm and their course. Albuam and Atabari said that she has the signification of fat, kidneys, the navel and belly; and the vulva and the womb.

Off colours she has white, and of tastes she has greasy.

And of days she has Friday, and of nights, that which precedes Tuesday.

And the quantity of her orb is seven degrees in front and the same in the back.

And the years of her fidaria are eight, and her greater years are 82, her medium years are 45, her lesser years are 8, and her maximum years (according to Alchabiium) are 1151. And her greater years are said to be 82 on account of the number of degrees of the twelve signs which are assigned to her as her terms. Her medium years are said to be 45 since they were considered according to half of the sum of her greater and lesser years - which, added together give 90, half of which is 45. Her lesser years are said to be 8, which were taken from Venus completing her epicycle five times in eight years, which she cannot do in any other number of years.

She goes around the eccentric in 348 days. And her strength in the regions of the world is in the right of the west.

And Messala said that of the figures of man, she signifies a white man leaning to blackness; having a beautiful body, beautiful hair; having a round face and a small chin, and beautiful eyes - with their blacks greater than their whites. And Dorotheus said that he will have a beautiful face, beautiful eyes with their blacks bigger than they should be, and having a lot of hair on their head. And he said that she signifies a man who is white with a mix of red, and who is thick, and he shows benevolence.

And of regions she has Hejaz, Yemen, and all Arab lands, since her significations appear more in these parts than in others.

And of the parts she has the Part of Desire. And she signifies friendship, esteem, patience and games, and also the joining of men with one and other by disgraceful, prohibited, wicked, and abhorrent means.

And Adila said that Venus makes beautiful hair and beautiful eyebrows. The Venusian man pours out sweet and tender words, having eloquence through the sweetness of his words; also joining his girlfriend with kisses.

However in his countenance and the whole composition of his body he is anxious; moving himself lightly in going about and doing whatever which he has to do; of medium stature and lascivious.

VI

On Mercury And What He Signifies

Alchabitius said that Mercury is a mixed, masculine, diurnal planet, inclining his own nature to those he is complected with from the planets and signs: so that if he is joined to a good planet, he will be made good, and if he is joined to an evil planet, he will be made evil. And if he is joined to a masculine planet, he is said to be masculine, and if he is joined to a feminine planet, he is said to be feminine; and if to a nocturnal planet he is said to be nocturnal, and diurnal if with a diurnal planet.

And he has the signification of younger brothers: whence examine someone's nativity, and see how Mercury interacts with the Lord of the first, or the significator of the nativity: since if Mercury aspects him by a trine or sextile aspect, things will be good for the native from his younger brothers, especially if there is reception. And if Mercury aspects him by a square aspect, or from opposition, things will be bad regarding the natives brothers, especially if reception doesn't intervene. Say likewise for a bodily conjunction, and understand the same for Mercury's aspects with the Moon.

And the Mercurial man loves his lovers more than his wives, and more eagerly adheres to them. And Mercury signifies valuing and thinking about the love of God, insofar as it is in his own conscience; even if otherwise he is wanton in illicit matters. And he will have good belief, and devoutly spend time in temples and in other ecclesiastical oracles. And he will be of good faith and Catholic beliefs. And if Mercury is the sole significator of a nativity, and is in his own nature, so that he is joined with no other planets, nor having any of them participate with him: the native will be of his own understanding in the beginning of youth, and growing in his own will and his own unique character; and this will happen him in the first ten years of his youth (namely adolescence).

And Alchabitius said that he signifies terrestrial things, and the augmentation of things which grow. And of the ages he has youth, and success in it, and of works he signifies those which generate cognition of truth; and rhetoric, for he is orderly in his speech. And Mercury has the signification of geometry, and knowledge of business, and he knows how to arrange many forms of5*6 business, and involves himself in many of them, and knows how to bring them to effect. And he has cognizance of many things, and knows about sales related matters, and other things in which there is utility. And if he is made a cleric, he will be a good and pleasing preacher. And Afla said that he signifies philosophy, augury, writing and proverbs: he will be a good moral philosopher: and will also learn the science of arithmetic. A Mercurial man will be a good prover of things, and will work especially in this.

On His Complexion With Saturn And Other Planets

Mercury, if he is joined with Saturn, signifies works of dividing and measuring land, and dividing substance and inheritances between kin and heirs of the dead. And knowledge of counting and estimation which is fitting for someone to have in order to construct a building, such as a tower, or a house, or something similar. And knowledge of organising looms, as have those who weave woollen, linen garments, or other kinds of garments.

If he is joined to Jupiter, it signifies the work of counting and making melodies of ecclesiastical books, and he will know other songs equally well, and dancing in games and similar things.

If he is joined to Mars, he signifies that the native for whom he is the significator knows how to lead armies, and knows how to organise them well, pay the income to warriors and fighters that they ought to receive. And he also knows who to battle well and how best to strike those with whom he is fighting, with lances, swords, clubs and other deadly arms, and similar things.

If he is joined to the Sun, it signifies that the native will preside over the accounts of the king, and the substance of Lords, magnates, noblemen, and the wealthy; for he will know how to arrange their affairs and manage their households, and how to bring forth their household affairs.

If he is joined with Venus it signifies that the native will know the rhythm of the chords and sounds of musical instruments, such as citharas, viols, pipes organs, harps, drums, and similar things.

If the Moon is joined to him it signifies the native will know how to serve in the courts of kings, magnates, noblemen and others: such as putting down the plates in front of the diners, cutting the bread and meat in front of them, and similar things.

And of infirmities he signifies infirmities of the mind, such as magnanimity by making small things out to be big, and faint-heartedness by magnifying small things; and horrible thoughts, and disturbances of the mind and uncertainty, so that he will sometimes appear to be insane, and similar things.. And if the planet which he joins is well disposeed, it signifies the good quality of the mind, and if badly placed, it signifies the bad quality of the mind.

On Mercury When He Is Fortunate

However when Mercury is fortunate, his goodness and fortunateness will be in accordance with the goodness and fortunateness of the planet which makes him fortunate, and according to the place in which he himself is well disposeed. And when he is malefic and unfortunate, his maleficence and unfortunateness will be in accordance with the nature, the condition, and unfortunateness, of the planet which makes him unfortunate, and according to the place in which the malefic is, which makes Mercury unfortunate.

And Alchabicius said that of sects he signifies the worship of true unity, and rational law, and similar things. And this worship is signified to be done with hypocrisy and simulation, making himself appear better than he is; nevertheless, he will do this without heresy.

And Albuas and Ebrianus said that of the human body he signifies the navel, thighs, legs, nerves, veins and arteries.

And of colours he signifies all colours which are mixed and varied. And Valens said that he signifies alezeminium, which is a certain colour similar to that of wild lilies.

And of tastes, he has acidic.

And the quantity of his orb is seven degrees. And of days he has Wednesday; and of nights he has that which precedes Sunday.

And the years of his fidaria are 13. And his greater years are 76, his medium years 48, his lesser years are 20, and his maximum years are 460. And his greater years are said to be 76, since 76 degrees are assigned to him as his terms from the degrees of the twelve signs, and his greater years were considered according to this number. His medium years are said to be 48 since they are considered according to half of the sum of his greater and lesser years (the sum being 96; half of which is 48). His lesser years were 20 because Mercury is found to make 63 revolutions in his epicycle in 20 years, which he does not do in any other number of years, and from this was drawn the number of minor years.

And he goes around the eccentric in approximately 10 months.

And his strength in the parts of the world is in the north.

And Japhar said that Mercury signifies childhood from the middle of his retrogradation up to his second station.

And from his second station up to his bodily conjunction with the Sun he signifies youth, esteem, friendship, concordance, and the seeking and imitation of love.

And from his conjunction with the Sun up to his first station he signifies old age.

And from his first station up to the middle of his retrogradation he signifies decrepitude, contrarieties, dissimulation, slowness and bashfulness - except in the acquiring of money and taking possession of things; for the native will accumulate these things through all possible means, both rightly and wrongly.

And when Mercury is in the middle of his retrogradation and he is the significator of a native, the native will be of mediocre quickness, on account of the weakness of his natural intelligence.

And when he is near his second station, it signifies that the native will be quick witted, but not the quickest: and that he will be well gifted in the knowledge of uncovering men's way of thinking through flattery, so that they will reveal their secrets to him.

And when he is joined to the Sun by corporeal conjunction to the Sun, and is direct, and is someone's significator: he signifies the native to be quick witted, with an expansive, wide reaching, great, and profound mind, and having a good memory: and the same happens with the other planets, besides the Moon.

And Messala said that of the figures of man Mercury signifies a man having a colour not very white, nor very black; having a high forehead, a long face, a long nose; beautiful eyes, which are not totally black; a thin and black beard on his chin, and having long fingers.

And of regions he has Daylam, Makran, and all Indian regions.

And of the Parts he has the Part of Business: since he has the signification of business on account of over-agitation, which he signifies; and on account of his over enthusiasm for inquiring into diverse things which thrives in him.

And he signifies fear, disturbances, war, enmity, insurrections and contrarieties. And indeed he signifies advancement, professions, and subtlety in all operations and in all investigations which the native wishes to involve himself in. For he will know how to subtly enquire from all men about whatever he wants, and how to subtly inquire about everything which anyone inquires about, whether these things are deeds or words.

And Sacerdos said that Mercury gives men a slender body. And Mercurial men are wise, eagerly reading when at leisure; often of average stature, acquiring sufficient friends, not easily retaining them. And he said that he will have a beautiful beard, but thin and short; sometimes having thin lips, and likewise a thin nose.

VII

On The Moon And What She Signifies

Albumashar and Alchabisi said that the Moon is a benefic, feminine and nocturnal planet, operating by coldness and moisture through her own nature, and is the significatrix of the mother. Whence if the nativity is nocturnal, she signifies what happens to the native from their mother. Whence you ought to consider how the Moon interacts with the significator of the native: for if she aspects it by a good aspect (namely a trine or sextile), or receives it with perfect reception, things will be good for the native from his mother. However, if she aspects it by a bad aspect without reception, things will be bad for the native from his mother. And understand the same for the mother from her child: since if the significator of any nativity receives the Moon, things will be good for the mother from the native; however if it aspects her by a bad aspect without reception, things will be bad for the mother from the native.

And Alcabitius said that the Moon is of temperate phlegm. And she signifies the age of childhood, and the beginning of growth (namely the first four years from the nativity), on account of her repeated and fast changes - in the manner of changes in childhood.

And the same philosopher said that of works she has legations, commissions, and works of water and land, and cultivation of the land: according to the quantity of her goodness or badness. And she signifies the chief place, for she knows how to manage the affairs of kings, princes, and magnates (if she presides over them), and similar things: if she is fortunate and in good aspect to the Sun or the Lord of the 10th house (namely by trine or sextile).

And of substances she signifies silver.

And if she has dignity in the 4th house at the hour of the nativity she signifies fortune in cultivation of the land.

And of faith she signifies religion, wherefore many Lunarians are religious, especially in their youth. Yet sometimes they do not maintain their promise to God well; and they rarely persevere well in religions; and thereafter make folk tales.

And of infirmities she signifies epilepsy and contortions of the face, and those which pertain to paralysis, and especially of particular parts, and particularly those which arise in the tongue, the lips, and the eyes. And she signifies the agitation of the limbs which arises from certain illnesses, which often happens from cold and moist illnesses, such as phlegmatic ones.

And she signifies the quality of the mind according to her mixture with planets: since if she is joined to benefic planets, the quality of the natives' mind will be good; however if she is joined to malefics, its qualities will be bad.

On The Complexion Of The Moon With Saturn And Other Planets

If the Moon is joined to Saturn in the nativity of any man or woman, it signifies that the native has hatred for people, and feigns that he esteems them; and he will be envious, and will rejoice when others are harmed, and suffer from their advantages: and it will seem to him that every good thing of another, is a harm to him.

And if she is joined to Jupiter it signifies that the native is careful, honourable, and benign in all things, and will lead a good, fine, honourable and pleasing life, and will be praiseworthy in all matters.

And if she is joined to Mars it signifies that the native will be a whisperer; and envious; and that he will apply himself to evils and whisperings, and to sowing discord amongst men in all matters, and to doing those things which are harmful to others; nor will he care if these things are not useful to him, provided that he believes them to be harmful to others - with the proviso that reception will shatter all of the malice mentioned above.

But if she is joined to the Sun by trine or sextile aspect or with perfect reception, what is signified will be fulfilled more completely; and it signifies that the native or querent will involve himself with management of royal affairs, and those of magnates, noblemen, the wealthy, and those who are fit for a kingdom.

If she is joined with Venus it signifies that the native will be courtly, benign, pleasant, and of a good mind and honourable habits. And he will be quick, light, and swift moving; and he will act with divine obedience, and he won't speak ill of anyone, nor will he say anything unseemly by his own fault.

If she is joined with Mercury with reception it signifies that the native will be an eloquent preacher; and that he will adhere to writing and rhetoric; and that he will be ordered in all of his speech, and in all of his statements, as much metered as prosaic. However, if this by a trine or sextile without reception, it will be below this. If it is by a square aspect or opposition, the native will be loquacious, and pour out many needless and useless words; neither will he want to give anyone else a chance to respond, and will interrupt their speech, while not wanting his own to be interrupted. And Valens and Albua said that it signifies thoughts and novelties of the mind, and weakness of the natural intelligence and sense; and heaviness of the tongue, and honourable women. Whence you ought to examine in the nativities of women if the Moon is joined with Mercury as said above, since then it signifies that this woman is honest, good, and of a good mind, and will eagerly nurse children; and she will be fortunate in this, and will be a midwife. And it signifies mothers and mothers in law, and purveyors of food, for the native will know how to supply food to others.

And Toz of Greece and Albua said that she signifies the lungs and the brain.

And of colours, she signifies citrine.

And of tastes, salty.

And she signifies the right eye in women, and the left eye in men. Whence you ought to examine in nativities to see if the Moon is impeded: since it signifies an impediment of the eye; which happens more so when it is impeded in Aries. And in men it will impede the left eye, in women the right. For either the native will be born with an eye impediment, or his eyes may be impeded before his natural death by an inseparable impediment, and sometimes the native will lose an eye completely. And of days she has Monday, and of nights, that which precedes Friday.

And the quantity of her orb is twelve degrees.

And the years of her fidaria are nine, her lesser years are 25, her medium years are 39 and a half. And certain men wish to say that they are 66, in whose opposing view I do not see any reason to assent. Her greater years are 108, and her maximum years are 430. And her greater years are said to be 108 since she has as much virtue in the half of the circle of signs which is from the beginning of Aquarius to the end of Cancer, as the other planets have in their terms, and this half of the circle is 180. But 60 were taken from her on account of the two domiciles of two malefics (which are Aquarius and Aries), and another 12 years were taken on account of this half taking away 12 degrees in its elevations from those which are in the beginning of the first clime up to the end of the seven clime (which is attributed to the Moon): whence only 108 will remain. Her medium years are said to be 39 and a half, for the same reason as was given for the medium years of the Sun: and the aforementioned 12 degrees are not taken away from this. The lesser years are 25, and this because when the Moon is at the end of 25 degrees of Aries, which belongs to each luminary (for it touches the nineteenth degree of Aries, which is the exaltation of the Sun and it touches 3 degrees of Taurus, which is her own exaltation) and on account of the subtraction of the aforementioned 12 years from her greater years, it adds a second half of them (6) to the lesser years of the Sun, and thus there are 25 years.

And her strength in the parts of the world is in the right of the west.

On The Forms Which The Moon Signifies

And Messala said that of the figures of man she signifies a snow white man, mixed with redness, having a benevolent brow, eyes not wholly big, a round face, and a beautiful stature. And of lands Artore, Exthomama and Daylam.

And Sacerdos said that the Moon gives men of no service, since day and night they want to run here and there, not easily remaining stable anywhere - which is true, if she is slow-of-course in a nativity, without perfect reception, and joined to a planet which is fast-of-course (especially if it is one of the inferior planets). And he said that the Lunar man has a round face, and a mediocre stature. However he has a great alteration in one eye, or one is pierced through. And to explain it clearly and briefly, the other eye will not lack imperfection either.

And Sarcinator said in one of his tractates: that from the beginning of its New Moon up to seven days, the Moon signifies the years of childhood. From the seventh day up to the fourteenth she signifies the years of youth. And from the fourteenth up until the twenty-first she signifies the years of old age. And from the twenty-first day up to the end of the month she signifies the years of senility.

And when she is under the rays of the Sun, she signifies secrets and hidden things; and also signifies that which ought to be hidden - and so it is good to handle, and to do those things which is to be hidden (namely those which we want to hide from the public), before she is separated from the Sun. We should do those things which we want to hide for the time being after she is separated from the Sun, but before she exits out from under the rays of the Sun.

And from the beginning of the month up to the opposition, she signifies all that will come to be; and from the opposition up to the end of the month she signifies all that is going to be destroyed. And from the beginning of the month up to the Full Moon, herself and the Sun signify accusers. And from the beginning of the lunar month up to the opposition she signifies profit and holding on to it. And from the opposition up to the end of the month she signifies payments and dispersion: and so if there is a birth in the beginning of the month, the native will be intent on profit and the retention however much wealth there is in this. And if there is a birth at the end of the month, the native will be intent on spending, and the dispersal of substance, so that his method of spending will decline to prodigality.

And in the beginning of the month (with respect to judgements) she signifies the manager and the quesited matter, and the prosperity of the manager, and that of the quesited matter; while at the end of the month she signifies the contrary, as Alcabichius says.

And in the opposition she signifies contrariety. And when there are 15 degrees between the body of the Moon and her opposition with the Sun, it signifies the condition of the beginning of contrarieties and their causes. And when she is separated from her opposition with the Sun, she signifies salvation from contrarieties, and the reason for this. And in her exit from under the rays of the Sun, she signifies exit from concealment, and detection of hidden matters, and things similar to these. And in her entrance under the rays of the Sun, she signifies suitability for concealment, especially regarding those things which we want more greatly to be concealed and hidden. And from the hour of her separation from the Sun she signifies suitability for exiting from concealment. And from the hour of her exit from under the rays of the Sun she signifies revealing, and arriving from absence; for then she seems to signify the arrival of an absent person, if a question was made about an absent person when the Moon was so disposeed.

On The Signification Of The Moon In The Square Aspect Of The Sun

Alchabicius said that as long as the Moon is in square aspect to the Sun she signifies descent from a height to the lowest point, just as often happens to those who have great dignities and high magistracies, and are unwillingly and reprehensibly deposed from them. And the same thing happens with the second square aspect; and indeed the second square aspect is even worse than the first: since even if the first square signifies diminution of status, it still signifies the apparition of things, wealth, and an increase of holding on to things: while the second square aspect signifies the contrary.

On The Signification Of The Moon From The Conjunction Up To Half Of Her Light

Ptolemy, Arthephius, and Archaphala (who were found to have been very effective in this science) said that from the Moon's conjunction with the Sun up to half of her light, her nature will be moist, since at that time she signifies moisture.

And from half of her light up to the full moon her nature will be hot, since at that time she signifies heat.

And from the full moon up to the second half of her light, her nature is dry, since at that time she signifies dryness.

And from the second half of her light, her nature will be cold, since at that time she signifies coldness.

Moreover, they said that the rest of the planets (namely Saturn, Jupiter and Mars), from their rising up to their first station, are more moist in nature, and signify youth - which is from the fourteenth year up to the forty-first.

And from their first station up to their opposition with the Sun, when they are in the middle of their retrogradation, they are more hot in nature, since at that time they signify heat, and they signify the completed age - which is from the forty-second year up to the sixty-second.

And from their opposition with the Sun, namely from the middle of their retrogradation up to their second station, they are more dry in nature, since at that time they signify dryness (although not a true dryness); and they signify old age - which is from the sixty-second year up to the ninetieth.

And from their second station up to their concealment under the rays of the sun, they are more cold in nature, since at that time they signify coldness; and they signify senility or decrepity - namely from the ninetieth year up to the end of human life, which can sometimes reach 120 years; and a few are found that have gone past this (although sometimes people lie about this).

Whence only the inferiors (namely Venus and Mercury), from the middle of their furthest longitude up to their first station, signify that which the Moon does in the first half of her light.

And from their first station up to the middle of their longitude, they signify that which the Moon does from the first half of her light up to the full moon.

And from the middle of their nearer longitude up to their second station, they signify that which the Moon does from her fulfilment up to the second half of her light

And from their second station up to the middle of their further longitude, they signify that which the Moon does from the second half of her light up to her conjunction with the Sun.

The Sun from the beginning of Aries up to the end of Gemini signifies childhood. From the beginning of Cancer up to the end of Virgo he signifies youth. From the beginning of Libra up to the end of Sagittarius he signifies the completed age. From the beginning of Capricorn up to the end of Pisces he signifies old age.

And Arthephius and Argasala said that the Sun signifies the soul, and the Moon signifies thoughts. Whence you ought to consider in someone's nativity if the Sun is well disposeed and in a good place from the Ascendant: for if so, it signifies that his soul is naturally benevolent. And if the Sun is badly disposeed, and in a malignant place from the Ascendant, it signifies that the natives' soul is of naturally malevolent; however, by accident he might be able to constrain and correct his own evil will by means of his own free will: as happens sometimes, and oftentimes in these religions and religious people, and also in other discerning people recognising their own evil thoughts.

And if the Moon is well placed, as said of the Sun, the natives' thoughts will be on the good and for the good. And if she is badly disposeed, his thoughts will be evil, and on evil, and for evil.

And they said that Saturn signifies mourning, sorrow, bewailing, lamentation, labour and evil.

And Jupiter signifies wisdom, rationality, honour, and goodness.

And Mars signifies anger, fury, contrarieties, and changes (more to evil more than to good).

Venus signifies pleasure, games, and joy, and gaiety.

Mercury signifies rationality, discernment, logic and learning.

And the Moon is said to be a pedagogue, and has signification over every matter, and participates with every planet in nativities, questions, journeys, and the beginnings of all things, and their middles and ends: since she is the mediator between the heavens and the other planets, and the elements. And even if the heavens or the supercelestial bodies act on the elements, still they always do this by the mediation of the Moon, since she is located between the other planets and the elements, so that the elements can neither be corrupted, nor changed by them, or by any one of them, without that changing or altering of virtue being transferred through her rays, or through her power.

VIII

On The Caput And Cauda Draconis And What They Signify

The Caput Draconis is naturally benefic, and masculine by nature; but sometimes by accident he is made a malefic. His nature is composed of the nature of Jupiter and the nature of Venus, and this signifies increase and things which are susceptible to increase, namely kingship, dignities, substance, sublimity, and good fortune. And Adila and Argasala said that the particular property of the Caput is augmentation; except in the giving of years (for he subtracts one-twelfth of them when he is with the significator). Whence if he is with benefics, he increases their beneficence, and when he is with malefics, he increases their maleficence - and then is made malefic by accident.

And the years of his fidaria are three.

The Cauda Draconis is naturally malefic, and feminine in nature, but is sometimes made benefic by accident. And her nature is composed of the natures of Saturn and Mars. And she has the significations of decrease, dejection, falling into poverty, and the decrease of all good things and of all fortune.

And the same philosophers said that the particular property of the Cauda is diminution, since when she is with benefics she reduces their beneficence, and when she is with malefics she reduces their maleficence - and then is made benefic by accident.

Whence it is said that when the Caput is benefic with benefics, and malefic with malefics; the Cauda is malefic with benefics, and benefic with malefics. And the years of the Cauda's fidaria are two.

IX

What Each Of The Planets Do In The Conception Of Children

Here I will put forth certain things which the planets do in the conception of children.

As in the first month, Sacerdos said, Saturn coagulates and binds together the material, and dries it out, although not withering it. Whence if Saturn is well disposeed, then the preparation of this conceived child will be well ordered and well disposeed, so that any of the other planets will be able to operate well on that which pertains to them in the conceived child, according to their own condition and according to their own disposition. However, if Saturn is at this time badly disposeed, the compacting or putting together of the conceived child will be badly disposed, and it will never be possible for the form or disposition of the conceived child to be well ordered, even even if the other planets are well disposeed.

In the second month Jupiter bestows the spirit and members. Whence, if Jupiter is well disposeed and in good condition, the limbs of the conceived child will be well disposed and well ordered, and everything will be formed in a natural way, and his spirit and breathing will be good, and he will inhale and exhale pleasantly, and will breathe free from labour and impediments. However, if Jupiter is in bad condition and badly placed, it will be to the contrary.

In the third month Mars operates on it through reddening of the blood, and by leading it to the form of blood. Whence if at this time Mars is well disposeed and in good condition, the blood of the conceived child will be good and abounding in purity, and will nourish the body of the conceived child well, and hardly and rarely overabounding in such a way that it causes lesions (unless perhaps on account of an inordinate life), so that it can carry out the force of nature. However, if Mars is badly disposeed at this time, predict the contrary.

In the fourth month the Sun bestows, or completes, the principal members, and gives heat to the limbs, and strengthens the natural heat and augments it, and regulates it to exercise all of its operations. Whence if the Sun is well disposeed at this time, the natural heat of the conceived child will be good and useful, and well preserving of the native, and will complete all of its operations well, and will most rarely allow itself to be overcome by unnatural heat, and will be long lasting in the native's body. However, if the Sun is badly disposeed at this time, these things will be to the contrary.

In the fifth month Venus completes the ears, nose, and eyebrows of the conceived child; and the whole disposition of the face, and the testicles; and assists the operations of the other planets. Whence if Venus is well disposeed at this time, the conceived child will be comely, having beautiful eyes, beautiful eyebrows, a beautiful nose, beautiful ears, and the whole disposition of his face will be blessed with gladness. If Venus is badly disposeed at this time, it will be to the contrary.

In the sixth month Mercury composes the kidneys, tongue, lungs, and completes all of the apertures and all hollows of the body which are not yet completed, and all of these will be completed according to the disposition of Mercury.

In the seventh month the Moon opens all of the channels of the lungs, and completes them if they lack anything; and completes the trachea, arteries, and the uvula. And she divides all of the parts of the body (which are not yet divided) with limits. Whence if she is well disposeed, all of these will be fit for purpose, each one of them apt for the duties assigned to it. If she is badly disposeed it will be to the contrary.

And this (the impediment of the Moon) is the reason why certain children are born impeded in some part of their body. This happens due to the impediment of the Moon, and the impediment will occur in the body part deputed to the sign in which the Moon is impeded.

And if she is in the first half, she signifies that the impediment will be on the right part of the native. If she is in the latter half, it will happen on the left part of the native.

And since in seven months each planet has operated on the conceived child with their own power, and on what belongs to each of them in the conceived child, if the child is born (after seven months) it can be vital by right. And I see many who were born at the end of the seventh month after conception and lived for a long time. And my father, who lived to 107 (according to him) was one of these, as his mother used to report.

Finally the disposition returns to Saturn, who in the eighth month, and by his own coldness, solidifies, binds together and condenses the members of the infant. From which still-births can happen, and this occurs on account of the distemperate coldness of Saturn, which disposes the child's condition at this time.

However in the ninth month Jupiter rules, who at this time, and through his temperateness, draws out the members of the infant, separating him from the mother's womb with the cutting of the umbilical cord in a safe manner, and so children born at this time are believed to be vital.

It is possible to say, as Hermes did and Ptolemy assented to, that the periods of the conceived child in the womb are three: the greater, which consists of 188 days; the middle, which is from 173 days; and the lesser, which consists of 258 days. And none of these are divided by any number of the aforementioned months. To which you could respond, that Ptolemy and Hermes considered those births, which universally occur, not considering which children will be vital or not : but only the common periods of infants in the womb. And they spoke likewise of those who go beyond the seventh month. Nor indeed was their rule so universal that it could not be repealed by a specific case. For they were not able to cross the street with dry feet; but it is not part of my interpretation to dispute over these things, since it seems that each opinion can be observed and maintained well enough. But enough on this, we must return to what was proposed according to the intention of this work.

X

How The Life Of The Native Is Disposed According To The Years of Nourishment Of Each Of The Planets

And there is something to be said on the disposition of the natives' natural life, as to how each of the planets disposes it from its beginning up to its end. Their order is as follows:

For the Moon, which is said to be closer to the earth and faster than all planets; and who, beginning from the inferiors, is the first of the planets in their order, disposes the life of the native for the first four years, which are her years of nourishment.

Then Mercury disposes ten years, which are his years of nourishment.

Then Venus disposes seven years, which are her years of nourishment.

Then Mars disposes fifteen years, which are his years of nourishment.

Then Jupiter disposes twelve years, which are his years of nourishment.

Then Saturn disposes thirty years, which are his years of nourishment.

If any native should surpass these years, the disposition returns to the Moon, and afterwards to Mercury, and so on for the rest of the planets, as has been said. Whence, in whichever disposition one of the above mentioned disposeors is well disposed at that time, the life of the native will be well disposed; and if one is badly disposed, it will be to the contrary. And it adds or subtracts in those years from the significator of the native at that time, according to its disposition and condition.

XI

Which Of The Days And Which Of The Nights Each Planet Has, And Why They Were Named From Them, And On The Unequal Hours, And On The Masculine And Feminine Hours

Each one of the planets has its own day and its own night assigned to it, whence when there is some day assigned or some night to a certain planet, the first hour of that day or night will belong to that planet from which the day or night is named; and the second hour will belong to the planet which succeeds the first in the order of planets.

To demonstrate:

Sunday belongs wholly to the Sun, and so the first hour of Sunday belongs to the Sun.

Monday belongs wholly to the Moon, and so the first hour of Monday belongs to the Moon.

Tuesday belongs wholly to Mars, and so the first hour of this day belongs to Mars.

Wednesday belongs wholly to Mercury, and so the first hour of this day belongs to Mercury.

Thursday belongs wholly to Jupiter, and so the first hour of this day belongs to Jupiter.

Friday belongs wholly of Venus, and so the first hour of this day belongs to Venus.

Saturday belongs wholly to Saturn, and so the first hour of this day belongs to Saturn.

Moreover, I say that the first hour of Sunday belongs to the Sun, and the second to Venus, since she succeeds him in the order of the planets. The third to Mercury, who succeeds Venus. The fourth to the Moon, who succeeds Mercury. Then it begins from the superiors, and its fifth hour belongs to Saturn, from whom it is begun after the Moon. The sixth belongs to Jupiter, who succeeds Saturn in the order. The seventh belongs to Mars, who succeeds Jupiter in the order. Again, the eighth belongs to the Sun, who succeeds Mars. The ninth belongs to Venus, who succeeds the Sun. The tenth belongs to Mercury, who succeeds Venus. The eleventh belongs to the Moon, who succeeds Mercury. The twelfth belongs to Saturn, who (as it was said) succeeds the Moon. And thus you have the twelve hours of the day, both equal and unequal.

On The Hours Of The Night, Equal And Unequal

Just as each planet has its own day assigned to it, so does each one have its own night assigned to it, and named after it. For the whole night which follows the day of Sunday is said to belong to Jupiter; and so the first hour of this night belongs to Jupiter; the second to Mars; the third to the Sun; the fourth to Venus; the fifth to Mercury; the sixth to the Moon; the seventh to Saturn; the eighth to Jupiter; the ninth to Mars; the tenth to the Sun; the eleventh to Venus; and the twelfth to Mercury. And so you have the twelve hours of the night, both equal and unequal.

On The Masculine And Feminine Hours

Of the hours of both the day and the night, there are certain which are masculine, and certain which are feminine. For the first hour of every day, and the first hour of every night, is said to be masculine; the second feminine; the third masculine; the fourth feminine; the fifth masculine; the sixth feminine; the seventh masculine; the eighth feminine; the ninth masculine; the tenth feminine; the eleventh masculine; and the twelfth feminine.

Whence you ought to consider as to whether the hour of a males' nativity is masculine, for if it is, it makes him have strong masculinity, and if it is feminine it makes his masculinity poor, since it makes him decline somewhat towards femininity.

And if the nativity of a female is in a feminine hour, it makes her femininity good, and makes her nature feminine. And if it is in a masculine hour, it makes her decline somewhat to masculinity, and makes her somewhat of a virago, not entirely however.

XII

On The Forms Or Figures Which The Signs Give The Native

We have already discussed the forms or figures which the planets give to those for whom they are the significators. However something remains to be said on the assistants to their forms or figures, which appear to pertain in some way to the ylem, which is said to be the "root of life". For just as the planets bestow their figures to the native, so do the signs. Indeed, it is not that one of them bestows the complete form of the native by itself, but both of them do so together, namely one with the other; since a planet cannot give the native its likeness by itself without a sign, nor can a sign do so itself without a planet - just as a mother cannot generate a child without a father, nor a father without a mother. Nobody can be born without a sign ascending, nor can anybody be born without a planet being the Lord of the sign ascending at that time: and so it is necessary that one participates with the other in the nativity of every native. Whence the signs modify and restrict the Planets so that the figure of the native will not be wholly like that which the planet bestows. And in a similar manner the planets modify and restrict the signs, so that the figure of the native is not entirely like that which the sign bestows: and in this manner one assists the other.

And these are the figures which the signs give men.

Aries makes a man having a long neck, a long face, much hair, eyes sometimes heavy, small ears, and often a curved body.

Taurus makes a man having a full face, sometimes curved; and if he doesn't have a full face he will have a large nose, and if he don't have a large one by nature, by the passage of time he will get a long nose by accident. He will also have black and heavy eyes, shaggy or raised hair; a thick and fat neck, almost more than is seemly. Modest, looking at the ground while he walks, honourably proceeding; not stable, almost wandering; but you wouldn't trust him alone with your wife.

Gemini makes a man of moderate stature, a full chest, and an agreeable person.

Cancer makes a man having a disordered body, thick flesh all over his body; thin above, thick below, with crooked teeth and small eyes.

Leo makes a man industrious, well known, and intelligent; thick above, thin below, yet not being made unsightly from this; magnanimous; with slender legs.

Virgo makes a man having a beautiful person and good will, with beautiful eyes and a decent face.

Libra makes a man having an agreeable face; moderately fleshy; and someone who will love women.

Scorpio makes a man having a ruddy and small face; with much hair on his head, small eyes, long legs, big feet; quickly changing And one in whose mouth the truth will rarely or never be found; irritable and a litigator, quarrelling and disputing with everybody, and doing this for practically nothing.

Sagittarius makes a man having long thighs and a long face, having a full jaw on his face; a keen mind; much more beautiful from behind than from the front; having thin hair; sometimes having a bigger belly than he ought to; and delighting in horse riding.

Capricorn makes a man having slender feet, a dry body, and a face like a goat, with lots of hair.

Aquarius makes a man tall, vain, conceited, and arrogant; who will be a great expounder, often wasteful, and a devastating of goods; having a beautiful and coloured face; and sometimes with one leg longer than the other.

Pisces makes a man having a full chest, a small head, a beautiful and flourishing beard, and a full jaw on his face in respect of his head, of white colour, having round eyes, magnanimous.

Still it often happens that men are found not to be made like this - and this is by accident, not by nature; for sometimes the significator of a nativity will be found so disposeed that it will contradict the sign, and does not permit its significations to be perfected as they should be perfected according to the nature of the sign. And sometimes it will be found so disposeed, and so debilitated, and so remote from the power to complete its own significations, that the sign will contradict it to such an extent that its significations are not perfected as they ought to be perfected according to the nature of the planet. Still, from your own industry you will be able to consider these things as to why and how they happen. For I cannot write down all of the particulars which could possibly happen in times to come.

XIII

On The Diverse Accidents Which Happen To Men

There are certain accidents which happen to men, regarding which I have found nothing to be said by any of the philosophers from which my soul would be quieted. Nevertheless, I still do not believe, nor does it appear similar to truth, that this was on account of them being ignorant of these things, but rather that it appeared to them to be a difficult and drawn out work, from which they feared that they might generate weariness in their audience; and so they left this to the industry of the wise (such as yourselves). For we see a small child being born out of a large father and a large mother; and a large child being born from a small father and a small mother; and from whites a black, and from blacks a white, from fat skinny and from skinny fat. We see some people are fat, others fleshy, some skinny, others between the two. We see some fat people are strong, virtuous, audacious, easy, and proceeding lightly. Some of the same are weak, serious, proceeding heavily, vile, and timid. Some are wise men, some are fools, indeed from the same parents are sometimes born both wise men and fools. Some from the lower class and the poor arrive to great wealth, dignities and fame. Some from magnates and nobles arrive to the greatest depression and poverty, so that they are reputed to be almost nothing. We see some who are in no way similar to their fathers, whence the mothers are often accused due to this (although they are not culpable). Some who are similar to their fathers, some who are similar to their grandfathers, or great-grandfathers (both maternal and paternal).

And we see diverse people practicing one and the same art at one and the same time, and one is made rich from it, while another is impoverished from the same - sometimes knowing it better and having less expenses, and living more miserably, yet still not becoming wealthy; and some to the contrary. We will see some who, although not having much wisdom, their words still are heard and believed, and are counted as being more wise than those of others who are actually wise, and also vice versa. We see some who always remain healthy, some who always remain ill, some moderately healthy, some who are benefited by medicines and cures of doctors in their illnesses and cured by doctors, some who are harmed by these things. We see some who abound in wealth and lack children, some who abound in children and lack wealth; some who abound in both, some who lack both; some who abound in the aforementioned for a time, others who lack the aforementioned for a time. Some who at one time abound in children, and who see their deaths and sorrow from them; and some who leave their goods and inheritance to their children after death.

Similarly there are certain men who carry out womanly duties, and certain women who carry out many duties, and wage war and do many things which pertain to men: as was a certain Maria of Cremona, who used manly arms (such as the hunting spear) like a man, and hunted boars; and the daughter of Girzavensis who was called Fredona; and many others. And certain people who are excellent signers and have good sounding voices. And some who know nothing of singing. And some who know how to play and use musical instruments very well, and others who neither know nor are able to know, nevertheless they know how to do other things better than other men. And we see some rejoicing on one day and sorrowful on another, even without an obvious reason. And some rejoicing on a day on which another is sorrowful, and some who are sorrowful on a day on which another rejoices, and some who rejoice on a good day and are sorrowful on a bad day, and some who are sorrowful on a good day and rejoicing on a bad day. We see some who stutter, others who are loquacious, some wise men having few words, and those poorly ordered, some having many, and those well-ordered, some who have many words which are not well ordered, both wise and foolish.

And we see many other accidents happen to men, of which it would be troublesome to mention each individually; nevertheless, whence they come, and why, I will mention and explain them in the tractate of nativities, God willing.

And even if the work appears diffused, nevertheless it will be of such great utility that it will not generate boredom for you in its reading or its study, and certain unusual and almost unheard of things will be said there, such as are these; since we will see that no man's face is so similar to that of another that there couldn't be some dissimilitude between them, and similar things.

THE SECOND PART

On That Which Happens To The Planets In Themselves, And What Happens To One From Another

I

On Those Things Which Happen To The Planets In Themselves

In this second part of the third tractate our discussion will be on certain accidents which happen to the planets in themselves, and to one and other. I will now speak to you now, as someone already introduced, and not as someone to be introduced. And, following in the footsteps of the philosophers, I will tell you first about these things which happen to the planes in themselves. And they are about those accidents, namely when one planet is ascending in its circle of the auge, and when he is descending in the same circle, and when he is neither ascending in it nor descending.

And Alchabicius said, that the significations which happen to the planets in themselves, is like when a planet is ascending in the circle of its auge, in less in light, magnitude and course. For when a planet is in the more remote part of its eccentric from the earth (which its auge is in), then it appears less in its light and in its magnitude of its body, and appears to be slower in course: not that it runs less in one day than another, in terms of it running through the line of its epicycle, but it appears so on account of the position of the parts of the epicycle.

And when it is in opposition to its auge, namely in that part of its eccentric which is closer to the earth, then it appears of greater light and magnitude of its body, and faster in course. In the more remote part of its eccentric it appears slower in course, on account of the lesser span of degrees in this part than in the other. In the closer part of its eccentric it appears faster in course, on account of the lesser span of degrees here than in the other part. Since it runs faster through a lesser span of degrees than a greater one, while it actually always runs equally fast, as I said.

Whence it then appears then to be faster in course when in the direction of the eighth heaven, than it is in the direction of its own eccentric. In the more remote part it appears slower in course in the direction of the eighth heaven, on account of it moving through the greater span of degrees which are in this part compared to the other; slower than it does through a lesser span. For the degrees of the eccentric are greater on the side of the auge than those of its opposite point, which happens on account of the declination of the centre of the eccentric from the centre of the earth, which is the centre of the eighth spheres.

And certain men, not making perfect sense concerning the auge, but perhaps by speaking generally they were of one voice on it, thought that the auge is the most remote place on the epicycle. But the true auge is the most remote place on the eccentric, and not the epicycle. In the epicycle only the further longitude and nearer longitude are considered. The further longitude is the part of the epicycle which is above the line of the eccentric. The nearer longitude is that part of the epicycle which is below the line of the eccentric: and so in this the auge and longitude differ from each other. Moreover, that the auge is not considered in the epicycle is shown by this: since the epicycle goes around the entire eccentric. Whence sometimes it is in the auge (namely the most remote part of the eccentric), sometimes in opposition to the auge (namely in the closest part of the eccentric), sometimes between these places (namely the auge and its opposition). And the epicycle goes around all of the signs, but the auge of the eccentric always remains fixed in one sign and in one place, and so the auge is only considered in the eccentric.

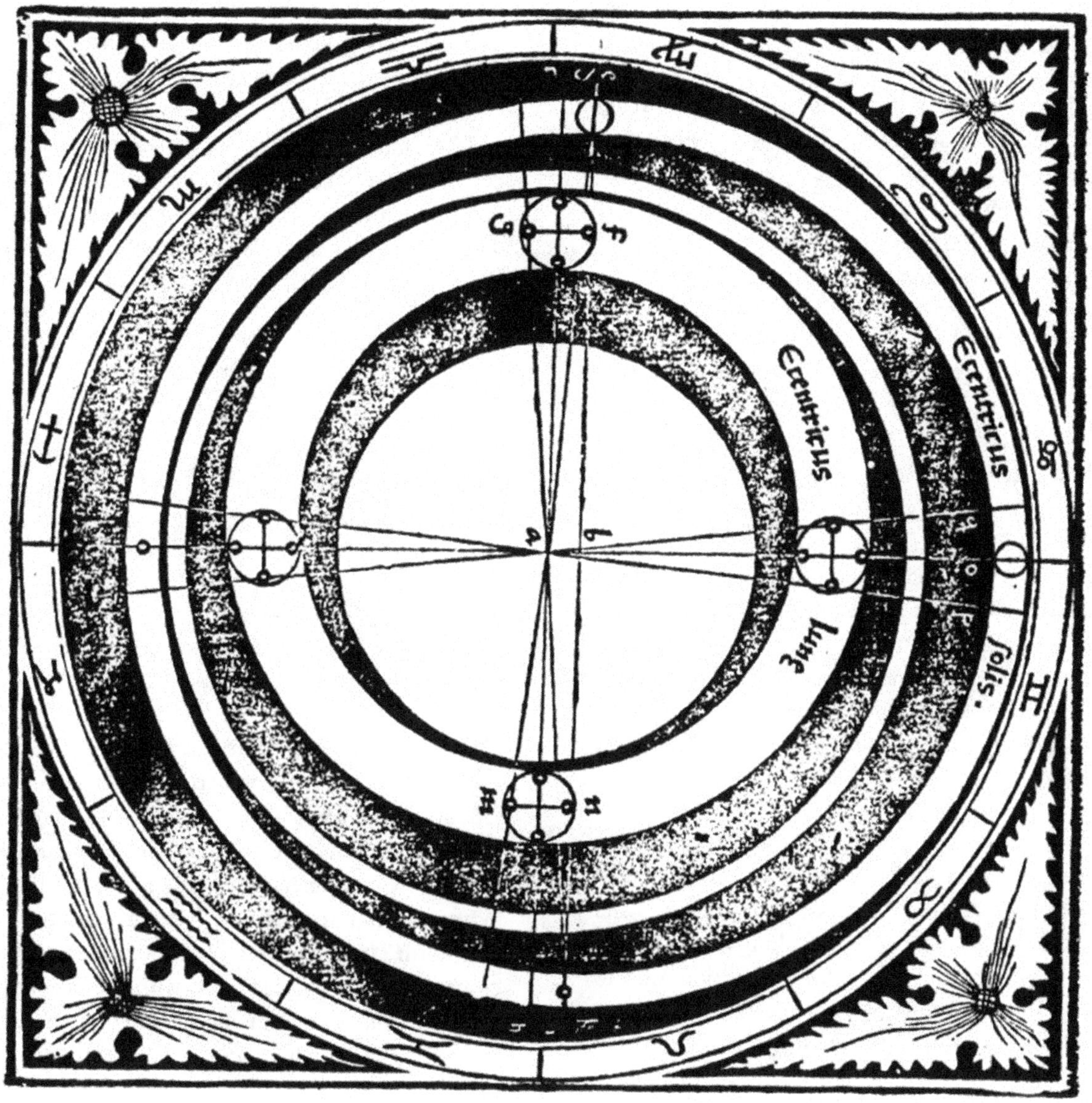

The auges are (as I tell you in the present work) as follows. For the auge of the Sun and the auge of Venus are in one and the same degree, namely in eighteen degrees and fifty minutes of Gemini. The auge of Mars is in the second degree of Leo, namely its fifty first minute. The auge of Jupiter is in the fifteenth degree of Virgo, namely in its thirtieth minute. The auge of Saturn is in the first degree of Sagittarius, namely in its fifth minute. The auge of Mercury is in the eighteenth degree of Libra, namely in its tenth minute. The auge of Moon is not distinguished in the same manner as the auges of the other planets, since she does not withdraw from her average course in her equations, as is done with the other planets; which happens on account of the course of the centre of the eccentric in a small circle, whose centre is the centre of the orb of signs.

When a planet is in the middle of the circle, so that as much of the circle of the fixed stars is above the planet as there is below, or in front, or behind, the auge: then it appears to be equal in body and light; in all other places it appears either greater or lesser in light and body. And when it is moving toward the auge, and there are ninety degrees or less between it and the auge, then it begins appearing lesser in light and body, and thus it gets smaller bit by bit, until it arrives at the auge, which is the most remote part of the eccentric. And when it begins to separate itself from the auge, it begins to appear greater in light and body, and thus it doesn't cease getting bigger, insofar as it is in view, up to when it is elongated from the auge by 90 equal degrees (which are considered in the circle of signs), and appears equal, just as was said. From this point forwards its light and body are made greater in a more perceptible than they were before, until it arrives to the opposition of the auge (which is the part of the eccentric closest to the earth).

And if the equated argument of the planet is from one degree up to six signs, it will be an increasing number, or course. And if it is from six signs up to twelve there will be a decreasing course. And if it is exactly six signs, or only twelve, the planet will neither be increasing nor decreasing in course.

And it is considered like so in the epicycle, the direction, retrogradation, and stationary and the fastness and slowness of the course. As when a planet is in the part of the epicycle which is above the eccentric, it is said to be direct. And when it is in the part of the epicycle which is below the eccentric it is said to be retrograde. And when it is in the places of contact between the line of the eccentric and the line of the epicycle, it is said to be stationary. And when it is between these two places of contact (namely from the top of the line of the diameter of the epicycle which is a small distance from the line of the eccentric) it is said to be slow-of-course.

But since this work is not about the consideration of these things, I will say no more on them, and will return to the original proposition, and especially since all of these things are widely discussed in Alfraganus, whose intention was to deal with the motions of the supercelestial bodies and their diversity. And when the equated equation of some planet is added on to its average course, then the course or number will increase. And when the equated equation is subtracted from the average course of a planet, then its number, or course, is decreased. And this equation is to be considered according to the epicycle, and not according to the eccentric.

And when Saturn, Jupiter or Mars go over their average course, they are said to be increasing their course or their number. The average course of Saturn in one day is two minutes and 35 thirds. The average course of Jupiter is four minutes and 59 seconds. The average course of Mars is 31 minutes and 26 seconds. And when any one of them goes this far from their average course, it is said that their course is equal, which is, neither increasing nor decreasing. And when the Sun, Venus, or Mercury go more than the average course of the Sun (which is 59 minutes and 8 seconds) in one day, they are said to be increasing in course, and when they go less than 59 minutes and 8 seconds they are said to be decreasing in course. And when the Sun is 90 degrees before or after his auge, his course is said to be equal or average. And when it is less than 90 degrees he is said to be slow-of-course. And when he is more than 90 degrees before or after it, he is said to be fast-of-course. And when he goes 59 minutes and 9 seconds exactly, he is said to be equal of course. And when the Moon goes more than 13 degrees ten minutes and 35 seconds, she is said to be increasing in course. And when she goes less than 13 degrees ten minutes and 35 seconds, she is said to be decreasing in course. And when she goes 13 degrees ten minutes and 35 seconds exactly, her course is said to be equal.

II

When The Planets Are Northern And When They Are Southern

It happens the planets are sometimes northern, and sometimes southern. A planet is made northern, when it crosses its own genzahar - which is in the place in which the line of the eccentric of a planet intersects the path of the Sun. Whence, when the planet crosses from the south to the north, his crossing is through the point of contact of his own eccentric with the eccentric of the Sun. And as long as he remains in that part of the eccentric which is on the northern side of the path of the Sun, he is said to be northern, until he comes to another point of contact, which is opposite to his crossing, and returns to that part of the eccentric which is on the southern side of the eccentric of the Sun: and in all of this half, the planet is said to be southern. And from when he has crossed the aforementioned first point of contact up to three full signs, he will be "northern ascending", and from three signs up to six he will be "northern descending". And when he crosses the same point of contact again, returning to the south up to three full signs, he will be "southern descending", and from the three up to the six full signs (which is the place of his genzahar from which he begins to be northern), he will be "southern ascending". These are the things which happen to the Planets in themselves.

III

On Those Things Which Happen With The Planets To Each Other, Namely, To One Of Them From Another

Those things which happen to one planet by another (that is, to one another) will be discussed in this chapter according to the utterances of the philosophers. And the first point of discussion is those things which happen to Saturn, Jupiter, Mars, Venus, and Mercury, from the luminaries, and in relation the luminaries.

And Ptolemy said, that when a planets sees itself face to face, then the planet is said to be in the *"almuguae"* of a Planet. Almuguea, means viewing face to face - these are the words of Ptolemy, and they seem to be somewhat difficult, but they should be understood in this manner: namely, that when a planet is occidental from the Sun, it is said to be in the almuguea of the Sun. And take care not to be deceived by Ptolemy saying "occidental": do not understand by this that the planet sets after the Sun, as you would understand otherwise by "occidental". But by "occidental from the Sun" Ptolemy understood that a planet is on the western side of the Sun, so that it sets before the Sun sets. And understand Ptolemy, when he says "face to face", that is, that there is as much distance between the planet and the Sun as there is between the domicile of the Sun and the domicile of the planet: understand this as when a planet in any place which as far from the Sun, as his own domicile is from Leo (which is the domicile of the Sun).

To give an example, posit that the distance from Saturn to the Sun is as much as the distance between Leo and Capricorn, which is the domicile of Saturn; namely that the Sun is in one sign (whatever that sign may be), and Saturn is in another sign which is as distant from the sign the Sun is in, as Capricorn is from Leo - that is to say that one of them is in the sixth sign from the other, just as Capricorn is the sixth sign from Leo. And there is between them in signs, degrees and minutes, as much as there is between those two signs, including one of them in number, excluding the other, which is five full signs: then Saturn will be in the almuguea of the Sun.

To give an example, posit that the Sun is in the twelfth degree of Leo, and Saturn is in the twelfth degree of Pisces: now Saturn is in the sixth sign from the Sun, calculated from the sign in which each of them is placed; namely Leo, Cancer, Gemini, Taurus, Aries, and Pisces. Now the distance from Saturn to the Sun is the same as that from Leo (which is the domicile of the Sun) to Capricorn (which is the domicile of Saturn), so that five whole signs fall between them: since from the twelfth degree of Pisces up to the twelfth degree of Leo, there are five whole signs (namely Aries, Taurus, Gemini, Cancer, and Leo), just as five whole signs fall between Leo and Capricorn, which are Virgo, Libra, Scorpio, Sagittarius and Capricorn. For from the twelfth degree of Leo up to the twelfth degree of Cancer is one whole sign. From the twelfth degree of Cancer up to the twelfth degree of Gemini is one whole sign, and so there are two signs. From the twelfth degree of Gemini up to the twelfth degree of Taurus is one whole sign, and so there are three signs. From the twelfth degree of Taurus up to the twelfth degree of Aries is one whole sign, and so there are four signs. And from the twelfth degree of Aries up to the twelfth degree of Pisces is one whole sign, and so there are five whole signs. For a sign is not completed in the sign in which it begins, but is completed in the sign following it.

Similarly it is necessary that for Jupiter to be in the almuguea of the Sun there falls as many signs, degrees, and minutes, between him and the Sun, as there are between Leo and Sagittarius (which is the domicile of Jupiter), and this is four whole signs - namely that Jupiter is in the fifth sign from the Sun.

To give an example, say that the Sun is in Gemini, it is now necessary for Jupiter to be in Aquarius, so that he is distant from the Sun by four whole signs, neither more nor less. For Aquarius is the fifth sign from Gemini (in a similar degree and minute). Therefore the Sun is in the third degree of Gemini, so from the third degree of Gemini up to the third degree of Taurus is one whole sign, and from the third degree of Taurus up to the third degree of Aries is one whole sign, and so there are two whole signs. And from the third degree of Aries up to the third degree of Pisces is one whole sign, and so there are three whole signs. And from the third degree of Pisces up to the third degree of Aquarius is one whole sign, and so there are four whole signs, and so Jupiter will be in the fifth sign from the Sun.

Similar to this, for Mars to be in the almuguea of the Sun, he ought to be in the fourth sign from the Sun, so that there falls between them in signs, degrees and minutes the equivalent of three whole signs: just as there falls between Leo and Scorpio (which is the domicile of Mars); and, as was said, with one included and one excluded. Let's say that the Sun is in the fourth degree of Aries: it is now necessary for Mars to be in the fourth degree of Capricorn, since there are three whole signs between the fourth degree of Aries and the fourth degree of Capricorn. For from the fourth degree of Aries up to the fourth degree of Pisces is one whole sign, and from the fourth degree of Pisces up to the fourth degree of Aquarius is one whole sign, and so there are two whole signs. And between the fourth degree of Aquarius and the fourth degree of Capricorn is one whole sign, and so there are three whole signs: and so Mars will be in the fourth sign from the Sun.

With Venus however, the almuguea is not considered in the same way as it is with the other planets: since she is not elongated as much from the Sun as much as her domicile is distant from the domicile of the Sun. But she is said to be in the almuguea of the Sun when she sets before the Sun sets, and is in her furthest elongation from the Sun, so that she cannot be any more elongated from him.

Regarding Mercury however, it is said that for him to be in the almuguea of the Sun, it is necessary for him to be in the second sign from the Sun, so that one entire sign falls between him and the Sun, just as there is one entire sign between Leo and Virgo (which is the domicile of Mercury). Let us say that the Sun is in the ninth degree and twelfth minute of Capricorn: now it is necessary for Mercury to be in the ninth degree and twelfth minute of Sagittarius: since between the ninth degree and twelfth minute of Capricorn and the ninth degree and twelfth minute of Sagittarius is one whole sign.

The Moon is not said to be in the almuguea of the Sun, on account of the luminaries not said to be in the almuguea of a luminary; and indeed it would be necessary for her to be distant from the Sun by one sign exactly, for her to be in the almuguea of the Sun, if he was supposed to receive her, and if she was able to receive almuguea (which would be able to introduce or confer perceptibility).

On Almuguea

With the almuguea of the Moon it ought to be considered (and you ought to know), that just as a planet which is in the almuguea of the Sun is occidental from the Sun (that is, the planet sets before the Sun): so it is necessary that on the other hand, a planet, which is in the almuguea of the Moon is oriental from her in such a way that it sets after the Moon, and not before her, and the Moon sets before it, and not after.

And Ptolemy said, that when a planet is as exactly the same distance from the Sun as its domicile is from the domicile of the Sun, and from the Moon as its domicile is from the domicile of the Moon, and is safe from their rays, then it is in almuguea.

On The Almuguea Of The Other Planets

Regarding the almuguea of the other planets, the sages did not care to make mention of, since they did not believe there was great power in this. Nevertheless, each one of the other five planets has its own almuguea. The almuguea of the three superior planets is considered just as the almuguea of the Sun, and the almuguea of the two inferiors is considered just as that of the Moon. And any one of them can be in the almuguea of another, namely when the distance between them is the same as the distance between the domicile of one from the (closer) domicile of another. And the inferiors always receive almuguea from the superiors, except for Saturn, who receives his almuguea from Mercury.

IV

On The Alitisal Of The Planets

There is another condition of the planets toward one another, namely the corporeal or aspectual conjunction or application, which Alchabicius calls 'alitisal", or "continuation". For a corporeal conjunction is when a planet is joined to a planet in the same sign. An aspectual conjunction is when two planets are in two different signs aspecting each other by a trine, sextile, or square aspect, and the lighter planet has fewer degrees in its sign than the heavier planet has in its sign, in such a way that there are six degrees or less between them (namely, between the rays of one and the body of the other).

To give an example, posit that Venus or Mercury is in the fourth degree of Aries, and Mars, Jupiter, or Saturn is in the tenth degree of Gemini, Cancer, or Leo in front of it, or in Aquarius or Capricorn or Sagittarius behind it. Then Venus or Mercury will be joined to the planet in question by aspect, until she reaches the aspect degree for degree. And understand the same for corporeal conjunctions: that if Venus or Mercury are in the fourth degree of Aries, and one of the superior planets is in the tenth degree of Aries: thus the lighter planet is joined to the heavier one by body, and it is always said to be joined to the other until it completes its conjunction with the other in the same minute: but after it has transited the other by one minute, it is said to be separated from the other.

Understand the same for all the others as I said to you on Venus on Mercury; since the lighter always joins the heavier, and the less heavy to the heavier, until it arrives at Saturn: for Saturn, since he is heavier than the rest, is not joined to any other planet (as has been said elsewhere), but all other planets are joined to him.

However Alchabicius said that a planet is not said to be joined to another planet, unless it is joined to it degree for degree (whether the conjunction is made by body, or by aspect): nevertheless he understood this regarding the act of perfecting the matter.

Messala, who was highly trusted by the wise, said that a planet which projects its rays upon another planet is said to be joined to it; which is true, unless another planet prohibits their conjunction. Other than that, one planet will be joined with another, and the effecting of matters will be signified. Whence, when one planet projects its rays upon the rays of another, and is as distant from it as their orbs are distant from one another, it is said that one "seeks the conjunction" of the other, and it signifies the effecting of the quesited matter, unless another planet destroys it or impedes it, and this conjunction is said to be burdened. And when the distance between them is as much as the orb of one of the planets, it is said to be a "complete conjunction", and unless something impedes it (as was said above), it signifies the effecting of the matter. And when the orb of the lighter planet touches the orb of the heavier planet, it is said that the heavier planet is in the degrees of the lighter one. And all of this is to be considered as much with aspects as with corporeal conjunctions.

V

When The Planets Are Said To Be Oriental And When They Are Said To Be Occidental

Saturn, Jupiter, and Mars, after they exit from under the rays of the Sun (as Alchabicius says) are said to be "oriental", and are said to be increased in strength up until they are elongated from the Sun by thirty degrees; just as an ill person who, after the crisis, is increased in his strength and health, until he recovers his former vigour, and returns to his state in which he was in before he began to fall ill, and stays more secure. Then from those thirty degrees up to another thirty, these planets are said to be "oriental-strong", since they are now in greater security from the Sun than they ever can be otherwise: for now they don't fear the Sun at all; just as he who has escaped an illness and has recovered all of his strength no longer fears the illness; in fact, after his complete liberation and recovery of his strength he is often made somewhat fleshier and stronger than usual, (however only if his complexion is well disposed to receiving this).

And when they have transited the Sun by sixty degrees, namely that the Sun is elongated from them by this much, they are said to be "oriental going toward weakness", until they come to an elongation of ninety degrees from the Sun, at which time they are said to be "oriental-weak"; until they come to retrogradation. And once they has begun their retrogradation, they are said to be "oriental-retrograde", until they come into the opposition of the Sun degree for degree. And after they have transited the degree of the Sun's opposition, until they go direct, they are said to be "occidental-retrograde". Then from the degree they go direct up to sixty degrees after, they are said to be "occidental-strong" - which isn't truly strong, but is less weak. Then from the aforementioned sixty degrees until their longitude is thirty degrees from the Sun, they are said to be "occidental going toward weakness". Then until they come to the beginning of combustion, they are said to be "occidental-weak". And after they have begun to enter under the rays of the Sun, until they reach the degree of the Sun, they are said to be "occidental-combust". And all of these degrees are to be considered according to the zodiac and its degrees, and not according to the eccentric or according to the epicycle.

VI

On The Two Inferior Planets, When They Are Oriental, And When They Are Occidental

Venus and Mercury, when they are separated from the Sun and retrograde, are said to be oriental-weak. And from when they first go direct up until they are close to the Sun, so that there are as many degrees between them and the Sun, as there were between the Sun and them when they began their retrogradation, they are said to be "oriental-strong". Then, up until the middle of those degrees which remain between the aforementioned place and the rays of the Sun, they are said to be "oriental-weak". And after they begin to enter under the rays of the Sun until they are in the same degree as the Sun, they are said to be "oriental-combust". Then, until they move through all the other degrees of combustion, they are said to be "occidental-combust going towards appearance". And after they begin to appear from under the rays of the Sun, and are direct, up until fifteen degrees after their appearance, they are said to be occidental-strong. Then up until the middle of the degrees which are between that place and their first station, they are said to be "occidental going toward weakness". Then up until the beginning of their retrogradation, they are said to be "occidental-weak". Then up until they come to the beams of the Sun, they are said to be "occidental-retrograde", or "occidental-very-weak". And after they begin to enter under the rays, until they come to the degree of the Sun, they are said to be "occidental-combust". And every planet, after it has exited from under the rays of the Sun, until it is joined to another planet (either by body or aspect) is said to be in its own light. These are the conditions of planets with the luminaries.

Whence you ought to consider in nativities and questions, and see whether the significator of the native (or the question), signifies good or bad. For if it signifies good, and is in a good location of its epicycle, or its eccentric, it signifies that whatever good there is will be completed well. And if it is one of the superiors, and is oriental-strong, and is ascending to its further longitude, or to its auge, or if it is fast-of-course, and especially if it is northern: then the matter will come to be better, more perfectly, faster, and with less labour. If it is oriental-weak, or oriental moving towards weakness, or is descending in any of the above mentioned circles, it signifies the effecting of matters, but more slowly, with labour, perseverance, worry, and with some king of diminution: and this is true for both nativities and questions. If it is occidental, the good will be reduced again. And if it is occidental-weak, it will reduce more again from the significations. And if it is retrograde or combust, it will reduce even more again, and what ought to be given will only be given with labour, perseverance, worry, and difficulties, especially if it is southern.

VII

On The Dustoria Or Aym Of The Planets

Alchabicius said that a planet is said to be in its dustoria when it is in its aym, or its likeness: that is when a masculine planet is in a masculine sign, and a feminine planet is in a feminine sign. And a diurnal planet above the earth during the day, and below the earth at night, and a nocturnal planet above the earth at night, and below the earth during the day; and also oriental from the Sun in the day, and occidental from the Moon at night. And if a planet is in one of the angles of the Ascendant, and one of the luminaries is in one of the angles in a square aspect to this planet.

For example: posit that the Ascendant is five degrees of Taurus, which is then the 1st house: now it is necessary that a planet should be in the 4th house, or in the tenth from the Ascendant, so that it is in an angle of the Ascendant, namely in the fifth degree of the sign making that house: so that three whole signs fall between these houses and the Ascendant, and that one luminary is in square to this planet, so that ninety degrees falls between them (namely the planet and the luminary).

There is also said to be another form of dustoria, and it is interpreted as being "on the right" or "security". This is when a planet is oriental from the Sun during the day, and occidental from the Moon at night. Oriental from the Sun being when the planet rises before the Sun, and occidental from the Moon being when the planet sets before her, namely when there are sixty degrees between the planet and the Sun or Moon. And in a similar manner the luminary should be in its aym: namely the Sun in the day being above the earth, and at night below the earth; and the Moon has it by necessity at night above the earth, and in the day below the earth.

And therefore the sages said that is when a planet is safe from the rays of the luminaries: since after a planet enters under the rays of the Sun, so that it is covered by them, it is said to be burnt up, until it exits from under the Sun's rays and appears. And when it begins entering under the rays, it is said to begin burning, or falling into fire, while it is under the rays near the Sun by twelve degrees, moving towards him (if it is an inferior planet), or separated, receding from him by two degrees or less; or if it is a superior planet and the Sun is moving towards it, and is close to it by twelve degrees, or if he was to be ahead of the Sun by two degrees or less, it is said to be *"oppressed"*. And when the planet is with the Sun in one degree, so that there is seventeen minutes or less between them, both by longitude and latitude (which rarely happens), the planet is then said to be "united" and then is made strong, since it is said to be in the "forge" of the Sun, that is, in his heart. And many of those who deal with the stars, and especially in my time, agree on this matter, that when a planet is sixteen minutes or less away from the Sun, it is made strong, and is said to be in the heart of the Sun. I agree with them on this, but not completely. Since for a planet to be in the forge or the Heart of the Sun, it ought to be less than sixteen minutes from the Sun according to longitude and latitude - and this was the intention of the philosophers. Since if a planet was less than sixteen minutes away from the Sun by longitude, and according to latitude it was more than sixteen minutes away from the Sun, nevertheless it is combust, since the difference of combustion of latitude, from combustion of latitude. is almost imperceptible.

And Alchabicius said, that when a planet has transited this union, namely that the three superiors remain after the Sun for five degrees, and the three inferiors are elongated from him by five degrees, they are said to have escaped, whether they are direct or retrograde. And the philosophers spoke on this with greater caution, and more certainty, lest anyone be deceived. However I believe that a planet has escaped, when it is separated from the Sun by two degrees or more, whether ahead or behind him. And a planet who has escaped is said to be similar to a sick person, who is no longer in the grip of a fever, but is still not healed to the extent where he is said to be free, nor is he fully free; however he is out of danger until be heals, after which he is said to be free. And when a planet enters combustion, it is like a man who begins to fall ill. And when it is in the ultimate part of combustion, he is like a sick person in a state of paroxysm, that is, when a fever is overcoming him, and is in the process of happening. And when a planet is separated from the Sun, up to two degrees, it is like a sick person, whom the crisis has come over, and is as yet completed (experiencing things like sweating, sleeping, fluid loss, and similar actions of the crisis). And when a planet is from these two degrees up to another three (that is, the remainder up until five degrees), is like a sick person who has suffered a crisis, and overcome it. And when a planet is from these 5 degrees of elongation from the Sun, up until it exits from under the rays, it is like a sick person whose illness has ceased and is manifestly diminishing; and when a planet is totally free from combustion, it is like a sick person completely freed from illness, but has not yet recovered his former powers; however is still safe from that illness.

VIII

On The Three Superiors, When They Have Appeared From Under The Rays Of The Sun

And after Saturn, Jupiter and Mars have appeared from under the rays of the Sun, and are fully out of combustion, so that they appear in the east in the morning before the Sun, they are said to be "oriental-right", until they come to the opposition of the Sun. And their strength is increased, up until they are elongated from the body of the Sun by 30 degrees. And from here up to another 30 degrees, so that their longitude from the body of the Sun is 60 degrees, they are "oriental-strong". And from these sixty degrees onwards they are "oriental moving towards weakness", until they reach their first station and begin their retrogradation. From their first station up until the Sun is opposed to them by a straight line, degree for degree, they are "oriental-retrograde". But after the Sun has transited past them by opposition, they are "occidental-retrograde", until they come to their second station and begin to go direct. And from here up until the Sun approaches them by 30 degrees, they are said to be "occidental-strong". From this point up until the Sun approaches them by 15 degrees, they are said to be "occidental moving toward weakness". After that they are "occidental-weak" until they enter under the rays of the Sun. From here they are "occidental-combust", until they are united with the Sun in the same degree. And when they are in the opposition of the Sun, they are called "opposite". And when they have transited the opposition, they are called "occidental-right". And is it a certain form of impediment for them, and not a small one, since the planet begins to fear that he might come into combustion again: like a man who is being followed by someone, and begins to tire in his flight, and sees his pursuer catching up to him, and sees that his pursuer is faster than himself, and approaching him: for he fears that he cannot escape his clutches.

On Venus And Mercury When They Are Separated From The Sun

Venus and Mercury, from when they are separated from the Sun, and are retrograde, are oriental up until they come to their first station, and begin going direct. From when they go direct until they are elongated from the Sun by as many degrees as they were when they began their retrogradation, they are "oriental-strong". Then until they approach the Sun by twenty degrees, they are "oriental-weak", until they enter under the rays of the Sun. After they are under the rays, they are "oriental-combust", until they are united with the Sun. And Alchabicius said that then they are "combust moving toward appearance", whenever they are seen. And from when they are separated from the Sun, and direct, they are said to be "occidental-strong", until they come to retrogradation. And from when they begin going retrograde, until they are united with the Sun, they are said to be occidental-weak. And he said that when a planet exits from under the rays of the Sun, and is joined to no other planets, it is said to be in its own light. These are the conditions of the planets with the luminaries.

IX

On The Conjunctions Of The Planets According To Latitude

Mention was made in the preceding chapters of the conjunction of the planets, and this mention was on their conjunction according to longitude, considering their conjunction from east to west, or vice versa.

Now however it remains for us to speak about their conjunction according to latitude, and this is the conjunction which is made between them from south to north, or vice versa, or on either side.

However, it is a conjunction in latitude when one planet is conjoined to another according to its latitude, namely, when one Planet is joined to the other by body, and both are in one degree, their conjunction will be by latitude and equal, whether this conjunction or application is northern or southern, since the latitude of both of them is to one and the same area. And if their conjunction is by opposition (namely that the latitude of one is ascending in the north, and the other is ascending in the south) their latitudes will be equal.

And even if this may seem hard to understand, still, in itself it is easy: since when a planet moves toward a further longitude, then it is ascending in the north. And it is necessary that in order for one to be joined to the other by opposition, that one is in one quarter of its epicycle, and the other is in the quarter of its own epicycle which is opposite to that of the first planet. All other conjunctions which are made by other means than this, are conjunctions in longitude and not latitude. And this way is that one planet is northern ascending in the north, and the other is southern descending in the south. This is a conjunction in latitude. Nevertheless, the sages of this art, and especially those who use an almanac, do not care much for these conjunctions of latitude in their judgements; which does not seem appropriate in my opinion, especially in great matters, such as nativities, general questions, revolutions of the year, and similar things.

X

On Planets Void-Of-Course

After one planet is joined to another, and their conjunction is perfected, and after the perfection of the conjunction is transited, so that one of them is separated from the other, and after the separation is joined to no other planet, it is said to be void-of-course, since it then runs alone. And it will remain in the condition of being void of course, until it is joined by another planet, or seeks the conjunction of another planet, just as was said elsewhere; and this is a form of impediment.

And Alchabicius said that as long as any planet is in any sign on its own, and another planet does not aspect that sign, it is said that the planet is feral or wild: and similarly this is a great impediment for the planet, and is a very horrible thing.

XI

On The Transfer Of The Nature Of The Planets

It was the opinion of certain philosophers, that a planet transferred the nature of one planet to another unconditionally. For they said that when a light planet separated from a heavy planet and joined to another (whether heavier or lighter than it), that it transferred the nature of the first to the second. Which appears to be somewhat obscure to me, to confess plainly. For it does not seem similar to the truth, that even though one planet is joined to another (unless it is joined to it from one of its own dignities) that it would give its own virtue to it, or commit its own nature or disposition to it, according to this saying of the philosophers: “a planet will not give something in a place where it promises nothing”. Whence if a planet doesn't give another his own nature or virtue, it doesn't appear that he can carry the nature of one planet to another. And even if it did, by the same logic it does not appear that this planet would give it to another unless it joins the same from one of his own dignities. And I believe that this was their intention, even if they didn’t express it.

But if a lighter planet is joined to a heavier planet from one of the dignities of the heavier one, the heavier will commit its nature and disposition to it, and it will be able to carry these with itself, until it joins another planet which it finds in one of its own dignities, and it will commit what it accepted to this planet, unless perhaps that virtue were to be intercepted by the conjunction of another planet, even if it did not commit to this planet. For it does not seem similar to the truth that someone would give something to a stranger in a foreign land that he had acquired for himself. Still, since these men were wiser than me, their statements stand, whatever might have been their intention.

And they said that a planet carries the nature of one planet to another, below is such an example.

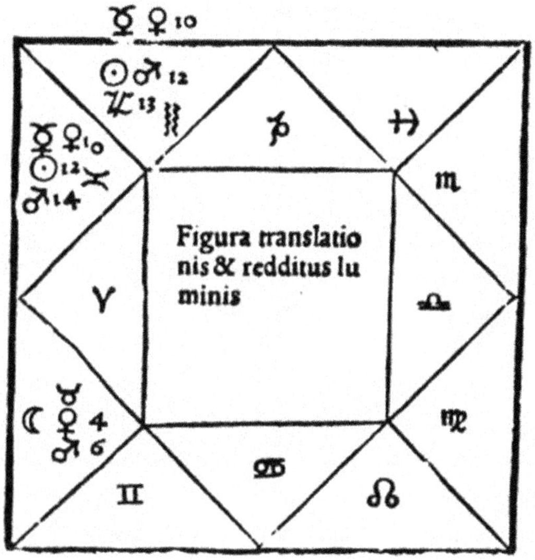

The Moon was joined to Venus in one sign, and in one degree (let's say in the fourth degree of Taurus), and when the Moon separated from Venus (or Mercury, who is lighter than her), she joined Mars (in 6 degrees of the same Taurus, or in whatever other degree he is), who is heavier than Venus. Thus the Moon transfers the nature of Venus to Mars, or to another (whichever she encountered, or joined to first). For Venus commits her disposition and nature to the Moon, and the Moon carries it to the planet which she first encounters, and to whom she is first joined (that which she carries was from Venus).

And they said that there is another method of transferring the nature of one planet to another, namely that a lighter planet is joined to a heavier one, and this heavier planet is joined to another planet heavier than himself: and so the heavier planet who is in the middle of the light planet and the heaviest, transfers the nature of the light planet to the heaviest.

To give an example: Mercury was joined to Venus in 10 degrees of Pisces (or in any other sign), and after separating from Venus, he was joined to the Sun in 12 degrees of Pisces (or in any other sign), and the Sun was again joined to Mars, in 14 degrees of the same Pisces (or in any other sign, provided that the degrees are correlated to one another): and thus Mercury transfers the nature of Venus to the Sun, and the Sun transfers it to Mars. But if neither of the two heavier planets were by themselves joined another planet, but both joined one planet at the same time, then this third planet would be said to render their light, to that place in the circle which he aspects.

And this is called "rendering of light", and below is an example of this.

Mercury was separated from Venus from the tenth degree of Pisces (or from any other sign), and after separating from Venus, he was joined to the Sun and Mars in 12 degrees of the same Pisces (or in any other sign); and they were again joined to Jupiter in the thirteenth degree of Pisces (or in any other sign). But Jupiter is joined to no other planet: thus Jupiter transfers the light of Venus to that place in the circle, which he aspects - namely to 13 degrees Taurus in front of him by sextile aspect; and to 13 degrees of Gemini by square aspect; and to 13 degrees of Cancer by trine aspect; and to 13 degrees of Capricorn behind him by sextile aspect; and to 13 degrees of Sagittarius by square aspect; and to 13 degrees of Scorpio by trine aspect.

XII

On The Return Of The Light Of The Planets And Its Cutting-Off

Having spoken about the transfer of the nature of the planets, what is to be spoken of next is the return of their light, and its cutting off. And this is when one planet seeks the conjunction of another, but they are not yet joined together, and another planet besides them is joined beforehand to that planet whose conjunction was being sought by the first, and the third one returns the light of the first to the first: it is called the "return of light", and it is called the "cutting off" of light.

To give an example: posit that the Sun is in 12 degrees Cancer, and Saturn is in 18 degrees Libra, and Jupiter is in 15 degrees Gemini: thus the Sun is applying to a conjunction with Saturn from a square aspect. But Jupiter, who is closer to a conjunction with Saturn than the Sun, by joining him from a trine aspect, cuts off the Suns' light from Saturn, and this is called the "cutting off of light".

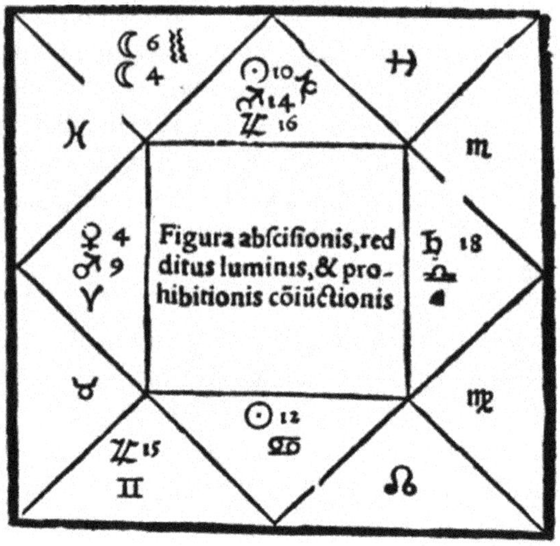

And this is similarly said to be a "return of light": since Saturn returns the light to the Sun, which he had begun to receive from him, and instead received the light of Jupiter, who is closer to him: since Jupiter is in the fifteenth degree of the sign which he is in, and the Sun is only in the twelfth degree of the sign he is in - and thus the quesited or hoped for matter can be destroyed. And this comes to be by a method which certain merchants use, or others who are accustomed to buying and selling things: for one seeks someone else in order to buy something for himself, and he who seeks the thing hopes that he will get it in the manner which he seeks it; and he does not believe that anyone else will interpose themselves in this, and then another person comes along and gives more to the seller than the first buyer promised, and acquires the thing for himself: and thus he frustrates the matter, or it is done by someone else placing themselves among things, so that they frustrate the first buyer, and acquire the thing for themselves.

And this is something that is very much to be considered in questions, since matters are often frustrated, even after they appear to be arranged. And you ought to know that returning of light is considered according to aspects. The transfer of nature or strength is considered according to corporeal conjunctions and aspects, but more so according to corporeal conjunctions.

XIII

On The Prohibition Of Conjunction, And Why Matters Are Sometimes Not Perfected

The prohibition of conjunction, and that matters are sometimes not perfected, happens in two ways. One of which is when three planets are in one sign, in different degrees, and the heavier planet has more degrees than the others, and one of the other two seek the conjunction of the heavier planet; and between him and the planet whose conjunction he seeks, there is another in the middle. He who is in the middle prohibits him who has less degrees from joining the other (which has more degrees than them both). Nor will the first planet join the heavier planet, until the middle planet transits his conjunction with the heavier planet, and leaves him behind him.

To use the previous figure as an example: the Sun was in 10 degrees Capricorn, and Mars was in 14 degrees of the same Capricorn, and Jupiter was in 16 degrees of the same sign. The Sun now seeks to join Jupiter; but Mars (who was between them and closer to Jupiter than the Sun was) prohibited the Sun from joining Jupiter, and Mars himself was joined to Jupiter. And so Mars did not stop prohibiting the conjunction of the Sun with Jupiter, until he had transited Jupiter, and left him behind him - and then Sun joined Jupiter, after Mars had transited him. Whence if the quesited matter was not totally destroyed at that time, it would be possible to bring to completion, when they (the Sun and Jupiter) are conjoined.

The second way is when two planets are in one sign, and the lighter is joined to the heavier by body, and another is also joined to the heavier one by aspect, from a similar degree to that degree from which the planet which is with him (the heavier planet) in the same sign is joined to him: thus he who joins that planet in the same sign annuls the conjunction of the planet aspecting, and prohibits him from it (namely the conjunction with the heavier planet): since a corporeal conjunction is stronger than an aspectual conjunction.

To give an example: Venus was in 4 degrees Aries, and Mars in 9 degrees of the same Aries, and Moon in 4 degrees of Aquarius, wanting to join herself to Mars by aspect. And would be joined to him, unless something else impeded her. But Venus, who was corporeally joined to Mars, prohibited the conjunction of Moon and Mars for the aforementioned reason - namely, that a corporeal conjunction destroys an aspect: however an aspect does not annul a corporeal conjunction. It is different if the aspect has more degrees in its own sign than he who joins by body: since then the aspecting planet will make the conjunction, not the one joined by body.

Here is an example: Venus as said was in 4 degrees of Aries, and Mars in 9 degrees of the same Aries, and the Moon in 6 degrees of Aquarius. Thus the Moon joined Mars, and annulled the conjunction of Venus to Mars, since she aspects him from a closer degree than Venus was joined to him.

Reception and Committing Disposition

And it is said that if any planet is joined with the Lord of the sign in which it is, or with the Lord of the exaltation of the same sign, or with the term, triplicity, or face Lord, either by body or by aspect: it (namely the Lord of the sign, or whatever other dignity) will commit and give its disposition, nature, and virtue to the other planet.

This is true, if a planet is joined with the Lord of the house, or exaltation, or with the Lord of two of the other lesser dignities - namely with the Lord of the terms and triplicity, or with the Lord of the terms and face, or with the Lord of the triplicity and face. But if he is only joined with the term Lord, or the triplicity Lord, or the face Lord; then the Lord of only one of these dignities or terms does not receive the other planet, since these dignities are not strong enough that one of them is able to make reception without the support of another. Whence a planet who receives another from these dignities, as I said, commits his own disposition to that planet, even if they were enemies, from any aspect or by conjunction.

To give an example, the Moon was in 3 degrees of Aries, and Mars (who is the Lord of Aries) was in 8 degrees of Gemini (or Cancer, or Leo)) in front of her, or Aquarius (or Capricorn or Sagittarius) behind her: so the Moon was being received by Mars by aspect, and he received her from his own domicile and committed his virtue and disposition to her.

Or the Moon was in the above mentioned third degree of Aries, and the Sun (who is the Lord of the exaltation of Aries), was in the eighth or ninth degree of Gemini (or Cancer, or Leo) in front of her, or in the eighth or ninth degree of Aquarius (or Capricorn, or Sagittarius) behind her: so the Moon was joined to the Sun by aspect, and he received her from his own exaltation, and committed his own strength to her.

Or the Moon was in the same third degree of Aries, and Jupiter (who is the Lord of the first terms of Aries, and is also the triplicity Lord of Aries) was in the fifth degree of Gemini (or Cancer, or Leo) in front of her; or in the fifth degree of Aquarius (or Capricorn or Sagittarius) behind her: so the Moon was joined to Jupiter by aspect, and he received her from his own terms and triplicity, and committed his own virtue and disposition to her, just as if he received her by domicile or exaltation. This is the committing or bestowing of the strength and disposition of the planets.

But if the Moon was joined to Saturn (who is the triplicity Lord of Aries, but does not have any other dignity here), he would not have received her, since he only has one of the lesser dignities here, from which perfect reception cannot come to be.

Alchabicius still appeared to want to say that a planet which is in domicile, exaltation, or any dignity of another planet, if he is joined with this planet, that he whose dignity it is, bestows and commits his own nature to him: of whose opinion I do not diminish, nor do I say that it is to be cast aside, considering he was an introducer, whence it is more deserving to be upheld, than if it was said by anyone else, and when he himself is of great value in introducing.

And he said that when a planet is in any of its own dignities, and is conjoined to some planet by body, he will give this planet his own strength, and this is also explained by the method above.

And if a planet is in such a dignity of his own, that another planet also has dignity there, and is joined to him in it, he will give him his own strength, so that he to whom the planet joins will have the strength and nature of both.

To give an example: Jupiter was in 9 degrees of Aries and Mars was in 5 degrees of the same Aries: and so Mars is joined to Jupiter, and receives him from his own house, whence he commits his own strength or disposition and nature to him; and Jupiter has triplicity dignity there; whence he therefore had the dignity of both - namely that which he has there from triplicity, and that which is given to him by Mars from domicile. And this mixture which Mars makes here is said to be reception, which the philosophers called "*alcobol*".

XIV

On The Return Of Virtue, When A Planet Returns It To Him Who Gave It To It

When some planet is joined to another, and bestows or commits his own virtue or disposition to it, and he who is given virtue or disposition is retrograde or combust, he will not be able to retain this virtue - whence he will return it to that planet who gave it to him: since he cannot keep it on account of the weakness which he has from his retrogradation, or combustion. And if both are in angles, or in succeedents to the angles, the return will be good and useful, and with benefit. And even if he who is joined to the other is in an angle, and he to whom he is joined received him, or was in an angle, or in a succeedent: the return will be with benefit and utility.

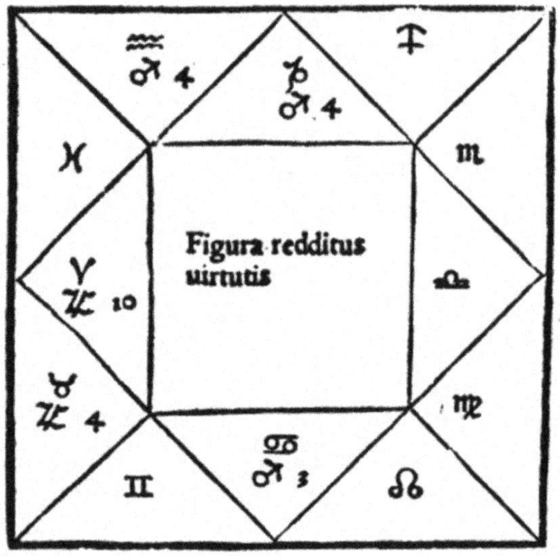

To give an example: Jupiter was in Aries, placed in the tenth degree, but he was retrograde, or combust, and was placed in an angle. Posit that the Ascendant was at 5 degrees of the same Aries, and Mars was in the fourth degree of Capricorn, in the angle of the 10th house (or was in the fourth degree of Aquarius in a succeedent). Mars was joined to Jupiter by aspect and received him from his own domicile and committed his own disposition and virtue to him; but Jupiter (who was retrograde) couldn't retain this virtue, whence he returned it to Mars. And such a return was good, useful, and with benefit, since Mars was in an angle or a succeedent, so that he was well able to retain the virtue returned to him by Jupiter, and all the virtue of Mars remained afterwards, so that the quesited matter proceeded well as a result of his virtue and power. If the planet who was joined (the light one), or he to whom the virtue is returned was cadent from an angle, wherever the heavier planet, or he who returned virtue was (whether in an angle or a succeedent or a cadent), the return will be useless, bad, and with detriment.

To give an example, the Ascendant was the fourteenth degree of Taurus, and Jupiter was in the fourth degree of Aries, cadent from an angle, and Mars was in the third degree of Cancer, likewise cadent. Mars received Jupiter and committed his own disposition to him, but Jupiter since he was cadent, he was not able to retain the virtue given to him by Mars - whence he returned it to him. But Mars, since he was similarly cadent, was not able to retain the virtue that Jupiter returned to him (on account of his weakness from falling from an angle) - and so it did him more harm than good. For example, he who has a package in his arms which he is not able to carry, gives it to another: who, not being able to carry it, returns it to him. This return was not useful to him, but harmful. And so, if a question was made about any matter, the quesited matter was destroyed, and was annulled on account on the weakness of Jupiter, who could not retain the virtue committed to him by Mars. However with Mars being weak, he could not retain what was returned to him, nor could he lead the matter to its effecting, which happened on account of the weakness of both planets.

However I found certain men, who seemed to be different from others, and who were of a certain opinion that they didn't believe that the return of virtue or disposition existed, as was the case with that tyrant Ezzelino da Romano, and his astrologer named Salonus, who I believed agreed with this opinion more so out of fear, than out of believing it to be so. And I believe this on account of Ezzelino having one of Salonus' brothers in shackles, and Salonus fearing that Ezzelino might kill him. And he said that the Moon, and any light planet, accepted the nature of that planet to which it was joined, and any heavy planet would give its virtue to a lighter planet, whether he received him or not; and had many other such erroneous opinions.

XV

On The Refrenation Of The Planets

One planet is refrained from a conjunction with another in this way: namely when one of the planets wants to join another planet or to be applied to him, and it is believed that the conjunction will perfect, and meanwhile, before this conjunction is perfected, he goes retrograde, and so does not complete the conjunction which he sought, and which was believed that the planet would perfect - just as someone holding the reins restrains a horse wishing to run, and does not permit the horse to run where he intended. Whence a planet is therefore said to be refrained from a conjunction with the other planet.

To give an example, Jupiter was in the sixteenth degree of Pisces, and Mars was in the seventh degree of the same sign, wanting to be joined to Jupiter. But when Mars reached the fourteenth degree of Pisces, he went retrograde: whence this retrogradation refrained him from Jupiter, so that he couldn't perfect the conjunction, and so all of his significations were annulled, so that if the querent thought he would perfect a matter, he would be in the hope of perfecting it until Mars went direct; but it would be uncertain, and he would always have a nagging conscience, that the matter would not be perfected. However, the hope that the matter would be completed will be greater than the suspicion that it won't be completed: and so he will not cease to hope in the completion of the matter until Mars goes retrograde, for then he will lose all hope of the matter being perfected. And this is called "refrenation", which Alchabicius called alicichae.

XVI

On The Contrariety Of The Planets

Sometimes contrariety happens to the planets, and this happens in the following way: namely when some light planet is in any sign in many degrees, and another heavier planet is there with fewer degrees than the lighter one; and a third planet which is lighter than the first has less degrees again than the heavy planet, and is moving towards the heavy planet wanting to be joined to him. But before he is joined to him, the other planet (who has more degrees than the rest) goes retrograde, and in this retrogradation joins the heavier planet before the light planet who sought the conjunction of the heavier planet does. And after the retrograde planet leaves the heavier one, it joins to the other light planet - therefore destroying the conjunction of the direct light planet, which sought a conjunction with the heavier; and also destroying the matter which was signified by this conjunction, even if it were completed.

To give an example, Jupiter was in the sixteenth degree of Aquarius, and Saturn was in the twenty-fourth degree of Aquarius, and Mars was in the fifteenth degrees of the same sign, seeking a conjunction with Saturn, wanting to join him; meanwhile Jupiter goes retrograde and joins Saturn by his retrogradation, and transits him in this retrogradation, and leaves Saturn behind him, and then in his retrogradation he joins Mars, and does not allow Mars to join with Saturn. And this is called "contrariety" since what happened was the contrary of what ought to have happened: for Jupiter ought to have gone his own way, and not to have joined Saturn, since he is less heavy than Saturn, and had transited him; but rather Mars, who was pursuing Saturn, ought to have joined him. For he was less heavy than Saturn, and less heavy than Jupiter. Whence if a question was made about any matter, and it was signified as being set to come to be, or to be perfected by the conjunction of Mars and Saturn; the matter would be destroyed on account of the retrogradation of Jupiter, who joined Saturn by retrogradation, before the conjunction of Mars and Saturn was completed; even after the querent thought that the matter was in order, and ought to be completed. And Alchabicius called such contrariety "Halyntirad".

XVII

On The Frustration Of The Conjunction Of Planets

The frustration of a conjunction of one planet by another happens in this manner: namely when one planet wants to join another planet heavier than itself, and seeks its conjunction in any sign, but cannot join him in this sign, but rather the heavier planet moves into another sign, and some other planet aspects this second sign, so that he to whom the first wanted to join meets the rays of the aspecting planet (so that this planet is joined to him), before the first planet (who wanted to be joined to the heavier one) can join the heavier planet. Since the rays of the aspecting planet were in the beginning of the sign, it was necessary that the planet whose conjunction the other sought was first joined with the aspecting planet, rather than being joined with the planet who sought to join him by body - and thus this conjunction was destroyed and "frustrated".

And for you to more easily understand this, I will give you an example of this matter, since the text is very difficult.

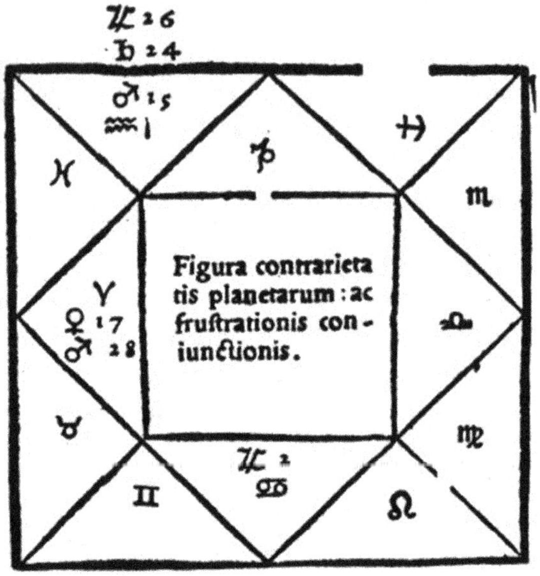
Figura contrarietatis planetarum : ac frustrationis coniunctionis.

Mars was in the twenty-eighth degree of Aries, and Venus was in the seventeenth degree of the same Aries, seeking a conjunction with Mars, and Jupiter was in the second degree of Cancer. And the rays of Jupiter were in the beginning of Taurus, so that whenever Mars left Aries, and touched anything of Taurus, he was immediately joined to Jupiter by aspect, namely, before Venus could pursue Mars, whose conjunction she sought. And this frustrated the conjunction of Venus with Mars, so that Venus sought the conjunction in vain, since she could not perfect it on account of the presence of Jupiter's rays, and his conjunction with Mars: just as sometimes happens in cases of hunters, when one of them is pursuing a wild animal, and following him in order to catch him; and before he catches it, another person catches it: and thus his hunt is frustrated.

Whence if some question had been made about a matter which appeared that it ought to be perfected by the bodily conjunction of Venus and Mars, it will be frustrated and destroyed by the aspectual conjunction of Mars with Jupiter. And so it often happens that when someone has laboured and strived for a long time in order to perfect some matter, and they always believed and had hope that they could perfect it; and meanwhile another person comes out of nowhere, and perfects the matter without labour, and snatches it away. And below is an example of such a thing.

A question was made on a marriage, with Libra ascending, and Venus was in Aries, wanting to join herself to Mars (as was said), and it appeared that Mars ought to receive her from Aries. And he who had Mars as his significator, gave a good intention to her (whose significatrix was Venus) of perfecting what was sought: and proposed in good conscience, and believed that he would do what was sought from him. And after several long discussions, a certain other matter appeared that he had not planned, and which perhaps appeared more useful than the marriage, or that he didn't know what to say, as often happens. And thus it was dismissed after long examination, and undisturbed by this, he perfected the new thing that happened to him unexpectedly.

XVIII

On The Cutting-Off Of The Light Of One Planet By Another

The cutting-off of the light of one planet by another is done in this manner: namely that if one planet wishes to join to another who is heavier than him, and another planet is in the second sign from the sign in which the heavier planet is in; and before the first planet joins that planet who he wishes to join (and who is heavier than him), the third planet (which is the heaviest of them all), goes retrograde, and in its retrogradation joins the planet which the first, lighter planet wished to join. In this manner the heavier planet cuts off the light of the lighter planet from the other who is less heavy than him; and does not allow this conjunction to be perfected: and thus the quesited matter is destroyed.

To give an example: Mars is in the fourteenth degree of Aries, and the Sun is in the fifteenth degree of Sagittarius, seeking the conjunction of Mars, and wanting to be joined to him by aspect; and he projects his own light upon the light of Mars. And Jupiter was in the third degree of Taurus, and meanwhile went retrograde; and Jupiter was joined to Mars in this retrogradation, before the Sun could perfect his conjunction with Mars; and Jupiter cut off the light of the Sun from Mars, and so the conjunction was destroyed and annulled. Whence if there is a question about some matter which appears as if it ought to be perfected by the conjunction of the Sun and Mars it will be destroyed, on account of the conjunction of Jupiter with Mars.

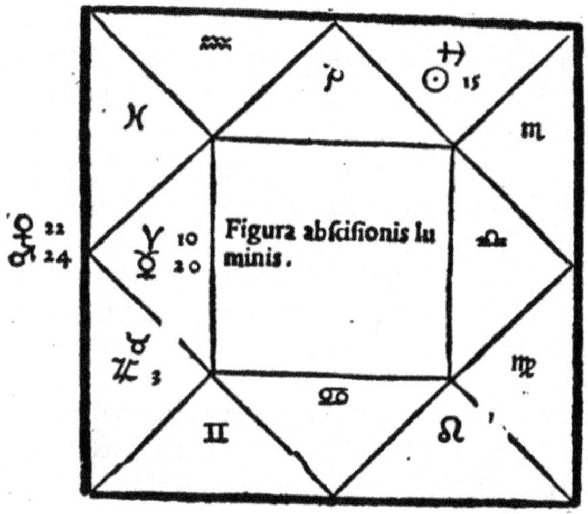

The cutting-off of the light of one planet by another can also happen in another way: namely, that if one planet seeks a conjunction with another heavier than it, and this heavier planet again seeks a conjunction with another planet heavier than itself, and before this first light planet joins the second heavier planet, the second joins the other (namely the third planet heavier than itself). Thus, the third cuts off the light of the second from the first, lighter planet: thus, the thing which was signified by this conjunction is destroyed, as was said above.

To give an example, Mercury was in the tenth degree of Aries (or of any other sign), seeking the conjunction of Venus, who was in the twentieth degree of the same sign, and Mars was in the twenty-second degree of the same sign. Mars is joined by Venus before Mercury is joined to her - and thus Mars cuts off the light of Venus from the conjunction of Mercury with Venus.

XIX

In Which Places The Planets Become Strong, And In Which They Become Weak, And In Which They Become Benefic, And In Which They Become Malefic

There are certain places, in which the planets gain strength and become strong, and certain places in which they become weak, and certain in which they become good and fortunate, and certain in which they become bad and unfortunate.

The places in which they are strong and fortunate are those which are aspected by good and fortunate planets by trine or sextile, or at least square; and especially if the aspect is with reception: since then they are made fortunate, even if they are malefic.

And if they are in places, in which malefic planets are cadent from them, so that they are not joined by them, nor joined to them.

And if they are separated from benefics and joined to benefics; or are between two benefics; or between the rays of two benefic planets.

To give an example, Jupiter was in the tenth degree of Aries, and Venus was in the twentieth degree of Sagittarius, and the Moon was in the fifteenth degree of Leo: thus, the Moon was separating from Jupiter by a trine aspect which was made from Aries and Leo, and was similarly joined to Venus by a trine aspect, which was made from Leo to Sagittarius.

Likewise if they are in houses in which they rejoice (as was said elsewhere), namely: Saturn in the twelfth, Jupiter in the eleventh, Mars in the sixth, the Sun in the ninth, Venus in the fifth, Mercury in the first, and the Moon in the third.

Similarly if they are in signs in which they rejoice when they enter, namely Saturn in Aquarius, Jupiter in Sagittarius, Mars in Scorpio, Venus in Taurus, and Mercury in Virgo.

And if they are in angles or succeedents from angles.

And if they are united with the Sun, as was said elsewhere: since a planet is not united, unless it is joined to the Sun by less than 16 minutes in front or behind, to the right or the left: since a planet is not said to be in the heart of the Sun, unless it is as described here. Even if it is in the same minute with the Sun according to longitude, and is more than 16 minutes away from him by latitude, it is still combust, and the planet cannot be said to be strong from this.

And if the planet is in the trine or sextile aspect of the Sun, or in the trine or sextile aspect of the Moon, and she is fortunate at that time.

And when they are fast-of-course, increasing in light and number.

And if the planets are in their own dignities: namely in their domiciles, exaltations, terms, triplicities, or faces.

Or, if they are in their own likeness as mentioned above: that is, masculine planets in masculine signs, feminine planets in feminine signs, diurnal planets above the earth in the day, and below the earth at night, and vice versa.

Or if they have reception.

Or are in bright degrees.

And if they are ascending northerly, and ascending in the circles of their auges.

And if they are direct, or in their second station when they want to go direct.

And if they are exiting from under the rays of the Sun; or if Saturn, Jupiter and Mars are oriental from the Sun, while not being so remote from him that they are moving toward weakness.

And if masculine planets are in masculine quarters - which are from the Ascendant to the tenth, and from the seventh to the fourth. And if feminine planets are in feminine quarters, which are from the tenth to the seventh, and from the fourth to the Ascendant. And the Sun likewise rejoices in masculine quarters, except if he is in Libra (which is his fall).

And if Venus, Mercury, and the Moon are occidental from the Sun, so that they set in the evening after him. And when they are in feminine quarters. And when the Moon is under the earth in the day and above the earth at night. And if she is in a feminine sign and a feminine place; or if she is in the exaltation of the Sun.

These are the places in which the planets are made strong and fortunate, provided that they are otherwise free from impediments.

XX

When, And In Which Places The Planets Become Weak

Strength and fortune have been spoken of, now weakness and misfortune shall be discussed. And this happens in many ways, namely if they are in corporeal conjunction with malefics, or in any of their aspects without reception, or are close to malefics or their rays - however this will be less debilitating if it happens in the terms of the planet: such as if Jupiter is in Aries, and Saturn, or Saturn's rays, are close to him by less than six degrees, which are the terms of Jupiter in Aries. Or if Venus is there, and Saturn or his rays, are close to her by less than the 8 degrees which are in the second terms of Aries (which belong to Venus). Or if Mercury is there, and there are less than the seven degrees which are the third terms (and his terms) in Aries between him and Saturn, or Saturn's rays. And you ought to understand this for any planet, and for any terms of any planet, and for any sign.

Or if the planets are in the terms of malefics, and when they are in the domiciles of malefics without reception.

Or if the malefics are elevated above them, namely that they are northern from them, or aspected from the 10th or 11th from their places (namely, by a square or trine aspect, the hindmost, which is made from the back); and this will be worse if the malefics do not receive them; however they receive them, their malice will be lessened by reception.

Or if the planets are under the rays of the Sun (which are degrees of combustion), or in his opposition, or in his square aspect without reception.

Of if they are with the Caput or Cauda Draconis, or if they are in their genzahar, so that there is between them and the Caput or Cauda Draconis, or their zenzahar, 12 degrees or less before, or 10 degrees or less after. And of the planets, those more greatly impeded by their genzahar are the Sun and the Moon, when there are between them and the Caput or Cauda Draconis 12 degrees or less before them - since there they suffer an eclipse, which is a great detriment to them.

Or when planets are besieged by malefics, or their rays.

And among the misfortunes of the planets is when a planet is retrograde, or is cadent from the Ascendant so that it doesn't aspect it, or if it is slow-of-course, or in its first station, namely so that it becomes retrograde; or is in the dark degrees; or if a masculine planet is in feminine degrees, or in a feminine sign, or is under the earth in the day, and above the earth at night; or if a feminine planet is in a masculine degree, or in a masculine sign, or is above the earth during the day, or below the earth at night; or if they are in opposition to their own domiciles or exaltations; or if they are southern; or descending in the south; or cadent from the angles, or from their succeedents; or are in houses cadent from the Ascendant; or if they are in the *via combusta* (which is from the middle of Libra up to the middle of Scorpio); or if they are joined to a retrograde or combust planet, or a planet impeded in some other way; or if they are not received; or if the three superior planets are occidental from the Sun, in feminine quarters; or if the three inferior planets are oriental from the Sun, in masculine quarters; or if the Sun is in a feminine sign, or in a feminine quarter, unless he is in the ninth, which is the house of his joy, since he has the signification of religion, just as the 9th house does, as the philosopher testifies.

Or if the Moon is combust, or in the degrees of her descension, or joined to a planet which is in its own descension, or is in opposition to the Sun, or if she is joined to malefics, or in their opposition, or their square aspect without reception, or is besieged by two malefics, or their rays. Or if she is with the Caput or Cauda Draconis, as was said, or is in Gemini, and not received by Mercury; or is in the terms of malefics, or is cadent from an angle, or joined to a planet falling from an angle, or if she is in the via combusta, or if she is slow-of-course, or is in the end of the lunar month without reception, or is in smoky, dark, welled, or azmena degrees.

Whence the wise men said, that when the Moon is thus impeded, it is hardly possible but that she has one of the above impediments, so that it is not good to begin any work from which good is hoped, nor any journey or pilgrimage, nor is it praised in nativities. Whence if someone is born at a time when the Moon is impeded by one of these impediments (which rarely happens but that she is impeded by one of them), if the nativity is good in itself, she will reduce the good signified in the nativity, according to the quantity or quality of the impediment; and if it is bad in itself, she will increase the evil for the native. And so too for journeys or pilgrimages: if it is a good journey she will reduce the good, and if it is a bad journey she will increase the bad, according to how she is impeded.

XXI

On The Besieging Of Planets, And Of Signs

Sometimes a planet is said to be "besieged", and this happens in two ways. One which is called "veneration" (and this besiegement is said to be good and in a good part), and is when a planet is between two benefics, or their rays, so that it has one benefic (or its rays), in front of it, and one benefic (or its rays) behind it, so that it is separated from one (or its rays), and joined to another (or its rays).

The other way a planet is said to be besieged (and this besiegement is evil, and in an evil part), is when a planet is between two malefics or their rays, namely that it has one malefic (or its rays) in front of it, and another malefic (or its rays) behind it.

In the same way that a planet is said to be besieged, so too is a sign said to be besieged, as Alchabicius said. And he said that if the Sun or another benefic aspects a besieged planet or sign by a trine or sextile aspect, so that there are less than 7 degrees between the planet and the Sun (or the Sun's rays), or between the planet and another benefic (or its rays): this will shatter the malice or besiegement. And a sign is said to be besieged if one of the benefics (or its rays) is in front of it, and another benefic (or its rays) is behind it: and this besiegement is good. And a sign is also said to be besieged if one of the malefics (or its rays) is in front of it, and another malefic (or its rays) is behind it: and this besiegement is said to be evil.

XXII

How One Planet Loves Another, And How One Is Loved By Another; And How They Hate One Another

Indeed, the ancient sages said that certain planets love one another, and certain planets hate one another.

For they said that Jupiter loves all planets, and is naturally a friend of them all; and all of them love him; and all of them are his friends except for Mars.

Venus loves all planets, and all of them love her, except for Saturn.

Saturn loves Jupiter, the Sun, and the Moon; and they love him; and he hates Mars and Venus, and they hate him; and Venus has more hate for him than Mars does. Mercury, when applied to by lovers of Saturn, loves him; when applied to by his haters, hates him.

Mars only loves Venus, and she loves him; he hates the rest, and they hate him; but Jupiter and the Sun hate him more than the others.

The Sun loves Jupiter and Venus by a perfect love, and they love him; and he hates Mars, Mercury, and the Moon, and they hate him.

Mercury loves Jupiter and Venus, and they love him; and he hates Mars, the Sun, the Moon, and Saturn (as I said).

The Moon loves Saturn, Jupiter, and Venus, and they love her; and she hates Mars, the Sun, and Mercury.

The Caput Draconis loves Jupiter and Venus, and they love him; he does not care for the others.

The Cauda Draconis loves Saturn and Mars, and they love her; and she hates Jupiter, Sun, Venus, and Moon, and they hate her.

The same sages said that there is a certain other kind of enmity, namely that when two planets have their domiciles or exaltations in opposition, as I do Saturn and the luminaries, Jupiter and Mercury, and Mars and Venus: who have their domiciles in opposition. And so too for Saturn and the Sun, and Jupiter and Mars: who have their exaltations in opposition. But such enmity is more by accident than by nature.

Whence you ought to consider in judgements, whether questions or nativities or whatever sort they are, that whatever is signified by any of planets, regarding those things which appear like they ought to happen to the native or querent, if good is signified, and it is signified by a planet inimical to the Lord of the Ascendant of the nativity or question, that it will not freely give or do that matter which it ought to give or do, and it will always come to be with some diminution. But even if the planets are inimical to one another (as was said), nevertheless if one of them were joined to another, or one of them found the other in its own domicile or exaltation, and it receives him: it will look on him with a good spirit, and with good will, and will forget all enmity, nor will the other remember anything of it. Such as when someone finds one of his enemies (who is not an enemy by ultimate or capital enmity) in his own house, or in a place where he has dignity, or a magistracy (such as a position of power, and similar things): he receives him, and honours him with a cheerful face - fearing lest he be reprehended if he does otherwise - unless he is a man of the forest, and very wild, who is not of a mind to associate with men, or to allow himself any such association: such as that tyrant Ezzelino da Romano, whose tyranny was like no other, who spared no rank, no religion, no nobility, no age, no sex, no blood of his own nor that of strangers, indeed he killed his own brother and his own nephew with his own hands and without a reason. And I saw all of these things.

And such reception as this, and such a show of good will, that it is said to be the "opening of the gates": since it opens the gates and entrances for him, and makes him secure; for you cannot say "come into my home" to someone more clearly than by opening the gates for him.

XXIII

On Their Friendship

Just as sometimes enmity falls between Planets, so does friendship fall between them, namely when one planet, concords with another planet in nature, quality, substance and power: just as Mars and Sun concord in heat and dryness, and Mars is the Lord of the Sun's exaltation, in which his strength appears great.. And stronger than all of these friendships is that of concordance in nature. Whence you always ought to consider in nativities, or questions as to what is signified by one of the planets regarding those things which ought to happen to the native or querent: for if it is good, and is signified by one of the planets who is friendly to the Lord of the Ascendant of the nativity or question, he will eagerly, happily, perfectly, and always without diminution, give, or do that matter, which he had ought to do or give. Just as when anyone divides something, between several people, they will strive to give their friend a better part of that thing which they divide; and when he gives to someone who isn't totally his friend, or who is inimical to them, even if they give something, they will strive to give him a less good part of the thing which was divided. And just as Venus and the Moon concord in coldness and moisture, and Venus is the lady of the exaltation of the Moon: so Jupiter and Venus concord in benevolence and the collecting of good, and fortune, and time.

THE FOURTH TRACTATE

On The Consideration Of Certain Conjunctions, And Certain Other Things, Which The Astrologer Ought To Know And Consider

I

On The Exposition Of Certain Terms Used By Astrologers

This tractate is on the more powerful things which are in a complete consideration of astronomy, which appear to pertain to judgements: whence it is fitting that you apply your whole mind, and the whole of your intention to them, in such a way that you are not given to any other topics, until you understand their purpose. For if you do otherwise, you are only fooling yourself, and wasting your work and your time; and perhaps (even if it is unduly) reproaching me, affirming that I have said nothing.

The true beginning of this tractate is about the conjunctions signifying matters which come to be in this world; and there are six of these conjunctions, of which the first, and greatest, of them all is the conjunction of Saturn and Jupiter, in the first terms of Aries, or in the beginning of Aries itself: and this only happens once in 960 years, and signifies great events to come into the world.

The second of these conjunctions happens in the first terms or degree of each triplicity, as much for the fire triplicity, as the earth, as the air, as the water; and this happens only once every 240 years.

Besides this, they make other conjunctions in each triplicity; and it is sometimes possible that they make 13 conjunctions in one triplicity, in this way: one conjunction ends in the beginning of some triplicity, which began so close to the end of another triplicity, that they could not complete the conjunction in it: whence it is designated as being in that triplicity in which it finished. And it ends in the beginning of this triplicity in such a way that another 12 are all able to begin and end in the same triplicity, and thus there come to be 13 conjunctions in the same triplicity. This happens if one conjunction ends in the beginning of some triplicity, in such a way that it does not go beyond 54minutes of the first degree of this triplicity. And these 13 conjunctions happen in one triplicity, just as sometimes two conjunctions of the Sun and Moon happen in one sign, and in one solar month.

To give an example: a conjunction of the Sun and Moon was made in the first degree of Aries, and this conjunction was in Saphar, (which is the second month, consisting of 29 days), and before the Sun left Aries, another conjunction was made in the thirtieth degree of Aries, or perhaps in the twenty-ninth degree. And in this manner two conjunctions were made in Aries. Similarly one conjunction was made in the first day of August, and before the Sun left August (so that a lunar month was completed), there was another conjunction made of the Sun and the Moon on the 30th of August; and so two conjunctions of the Sun and Moon were made in one month: not that both of them began in it, but because both finished in it. And it is like this with the conjunctions of Saturn and Jupiter when they make 13 conjunctions in one triplicity.

Afterwards the conjunction moves to the triplicity which succeeds the first; so if their first conjunction was made in the fire triplicity, they move to the earth triplicity, and from earth to air; air to water; and again from water returning to fire, namely to the triplicity of Aries; and from the triplicity of Aries to the triplicity of Taurus; and from the triplicity of Taurus to the triplicity of Gemini; from the triplicity of Gemini to the triplicity of Cancer; and again from the triplicity of Cancer to the triplicity of Aries, and so on ad infinitum.

II

How The Supercelestial Bodies Are Moved, According To The Diverse Motions Of The Planets

The conjunctions of the superior, perceptibly changing bodies come to be according to the diversity of their motions (both natural and in place); and thence their effects come to be, imperceptibly in individual inferior things. And these natural motions are considered according to three divisions, which are named and considered according to the successive order of the circles of the 7 planets in this manner: namely, that the first division is considered according to the motion of the three superior planets (which are Saturn, Jupiter, and Mars), according to which you will find sufficiently defined below, in the tractate on nativities. The second is considered according to the planet located in the middle of the others, which is the Sun. The third to be considered, is according to the motion of the three inferiors, which are Venus, Mercury, and the Moon.

The first division of the planets (namely that of the superiors) is three fold, and imprints on the inferior individual things in three ways, according to three diverse motions, namely the first, second and third. The first motion is moved about the middle. The second is moved from the middle. The third is not moved about the first, nor from the first, nor about the middle, nor from the middle, but toward the middle.

Whence the first division of the superior planets is considered and referred to the first motion, which presides over the middle motion, because those planets approach the first motion, and are elongated from the third motion, which is toward the middle motion. And these divisions of motions are considered to be over individual particulars of which durability is expected: such as structures of houses and similar things, which have a beginning, and whose middle does not come quickly, and whose end comes a long time after their beginning. And these things are attributed to Saturn, who has more affinity than the others with the first motion. And their middle is attributed to Jupiter, since just as Jupiter is in the middle of the other superiors, and located in the middle of them, and among these motions, his is the middle one: therefore the middle of those things is attributed to him, and even their completion is attributed to him, and is considered according to him. And because he is closer to Mars (to whom the end of matters is attributed) than Saturn; and closer to Saturn (to whom the beginning of things is attributed) than Mars, therefore the middle is attributed to him, and the completion of matters is considered according to the same consideration. The end is attributed to Mars, since he is placed at the end of the first division, and since the end makes for the destruction of matters: and on account of this wars, battles, and contentions are attributed to him, since they do more towards consumption, diminution, and destruction, than the rest.

The beginning indicates the being of things; the middle their perfection; and the end their destruction. And since the multitude of diverse motions are multiplied, and diversity amongst men, and dissension of their wills: and from which arises wars and contentions, which make for the destruction of things, and to their ends. And whatever may be said by certain men, ignorant of their Creator (who disposed everything in order, and did nothing without reason), this was the reason why these three significations were attributed to the three superior planets, as many as there are principles in the first signification, preceding those which follow from the second signification, which are signified by other planets.

And so, by the testimony of the philosopher, the second motion is moved from the middle: and the third motion is moved toward the middle. And the second, middle motion is naturally attributed to the Sun (who is the greater luminary), and to his effects; and this motion is from the middle, through a relationship, since he has affinity to that motion; and his circle is placed in the middle of the others in the order of the circles; and whatever is referred to him is between the first motion and the third motion. And since his motion is less slow than the superiors, and less fast than the inferiors, for this reason he is said to be the significator of kings, the wealthy, magnates, and others who want to be in charge and to rule over others; and since he participates with the first division, and his signification is considered to be stronger in the second than any of the others; and he succeeds Mars in the order of the circles.

However the third motion (toward the middle) is attributed to the three inferior planets, on account of their remoteness from the first motion (which is above the middle motion); and their effects are over lively matters, and those of which a long duration is not expected; and on account of their swift motion having an affinity with lively matters, even if they have some resemblance with the first motion, nevertheless they have an affinity with the third motion. And their natural motions are considered according to the three divisions of the motions of the three superior planets. For to Venus is given the significations of marriage, the arrangement of clothing of bodies, and similar things, on account of her correlation to Saturn. For just as Saturn, is the first and highest of the three superior planets, and from him are considered the beginnings of things of great durability, and great age: so Venus is the first of the three inferior planets, and according to her are considered the beginning of things, of which great durability or great extent are not expected; and she succeeds the Sun in the order of the circles.

Mercury is given signification over things signifying the perfection of things which are not of great durability, as are numbers, writings, measurements, sculptures, and similar things; even if some of these things last long, but only when they are used for the memory of things, and to assist men's' forgetfulness, and so his significations are associated with the significations of Jupiter, and Mercury is correlated to him, since he signifies the perfection of long lasting things. For just as Jupiter is the middle planet of the three superiors, so too is Mercury the middle planet of the three inferiors, and succeeds Venus in the order of the circles.

The Moon is given signification over moveable things, things which change themselves swiftly, travels, and over all matters receiving change quickly, and whose end comes quickly; and the Moons significations are correlated to the significations of Mars: for just as Mars is the third and final planet of the three superiors, and signifies the end of long lasting matters: so too is the Moon the third and final planet of the three inferiors, and is akin to the third division, signified by Mars, and signifies the end of things which swiftly arrive at their end, and thus the Moon falls the order of circles, just as will be more widely discussed below in the tractate on nativities.

Nor should you believe, these significations to be attributed to these planets otherwise than by reason of the need for those things which natural necessity impelled toward them, just as are the customs of men, and oppositions, and conditions, and laws, and according to particular stories of the living, which were all completed by number and writing; and into whose debt they plainly fall, as much in those, as to wars, contentions, journeys, and other changes, which they do not take up except by perfected motion. And the aforementioned significations were attributed to the three inferiors, since they are secondary, through a relation to the first motion or being: and on account of this they follow from thence. And wherefore, from their significations, and those of others, foreknowledge is had of their effects, which generally come to pass according to their course; and though which we arrive at their particular cognitions; the which aforementioned conjunctions we would be able to judge, if we wished to understand them correctly - namely that of Saturn with Jupiter and Mars, in the aforementioned places. Nevertheless, these motions and their significations, will be discussed more widely, and to a finer point, in the Tractate on nativities.

III

On The Conjunction Of Saturn And Mars

The third conjunction is the conjunction of Saturn and Mars which they make in the beginning of Cancer, or in its first degree, or at least in its first terms; and this happens once every 30 years.

But you might say, "why is the conjunction of Saturn and Mars in the beginning of Cancer the only one considered, when they make conjunctions in the beginnings of other signs, and likewise in other triplicities, just as they do in the beginning of Cancer?" To which question we have the following reply: that their conjunction is considered in the beginning of Cancer more so than elsewhere, since it is worse than all the other conjunctions which they make, even if all of the others are bad; and the one which they make in the beginning of Capricorn is less malicious, since they have mutual reception, and their malice is reduced. Capricorn is a dignity of both, namely being the domicile of Saturn, and the exaltation of Mars: while Cancer is the detriment of both of them (namely Saturn and Mars), since it is their greatest impediment. And the greater the impediment of the malefics is, the more they do worse things, and the more their malice and detriment is increased. For in other signs, they don't have such manifest detriment. And even if they harm, and injure in others, still they don't harm as much as they do in Cancer: since at this time the greatest changes in the world take place, as well as the greatest accidents, which do not happen in the other conjunctions which they make elsewhere. For kingdoms are changed, and terrible wars happen, from which follow suffocations, killings, wicked captures, destruction of kingdoms, burnings by fire, and much spilling of blood, famine, mortality, sterility, and many pestilences.

And if they are oriental, their significations will happen faster, according to how close they are to the Sun, or how remote they are from him. And if they are occidental, their significations will be prolonged and delayed. Whence you will consider the Ascendant of their conjunction, namely when they come together in the same minute; and see the number of degrees of longitude which are between them and the Sun, out of which you will make the signs, namely giving each sign 30 degrees. If the Ascendant is a fixed sign, and the planets are occidental, it will signify the amount of years before the arrival of their significations, according to the number of signs and degrees of distance which you find between them and the Sun. And if the planets are oriental, in place of years put months. And if it is a common sign, and they are occidental, in place of years put months. And if they are oriental, in place of months put weeks. And if it is a mobile sign, and they are occidental, in place of years put weeks. However if they are oriental, in place of weeks put days. And when you give one sign per year, give a month for every 2 degrees and thirty minutes, and a week for every 37 minutes 30 seconds, and a day for every 5 minutes and 11 seconds, since their significations will happen within these times (if you have calculated the Ascendant of their perfect conjunction well).

However you should consider whether the angle of the 1st house is correct or remote. Since if it is correct (namely that it is one sign, and only makes one house), these things will occur according to what I said to you in the stated equal times. If it is remote, they will occur in another way: since if the angle contains less than 30 degrees, it will delay the significations - that is, if one sign makes two houses (as often happens). If it contains more than 30 degrees, that is, that it includes more than one sign which is not specifically named; or if it contains more than 30degrees in another manner: the significations will be accelerated and arrive more quickly.

Let us say that the fifth degree of Leo is the 1st house, and the twenty-seventh degree of the same sign is the 2nd house. In this way this sign makes two houses, and the significations are delayed by one-tenth, just as one-tenth of the sign falls in another house; and if more of it falls in another house, the significations will be delayed even more; and if one-ninth of the sign falls in another house, its significations will be delayed by one-ninth of their time; if one-eighth, they will be delayed by one-eighth, and so for the other fractions of the signs. But if it encloses one sign, such as if the twenty-eighth degrees of Pisces is the 1st house, and the third degree of Taurus is the 2nd house: in this manner all of Aries will be enclosed in the 1st house, and the significations will be accelerated according to the quantity of degrees which the 1st house contains above 30, and which ought to have been in the 2nd house, which are 2degrees of Pisces and 3degrees of Taurus: and so the significations will be accelerated by one sixth of their time, just as one sixth of one sign falls in that house beyond what ought to according to the correct size of the angles. And understand the same for any proportion of a sign. Similarly, if there are such a number of degrees between them and the Sun that they cannot make up one entire sign (that is, that there are less than 30).

And if such a sign is rising, that it rises in less than two equal hours, it signifies days. And if there are such a number of degrees between them and the Sun that one entire sign can be made from them (namely that there are 30), and the ascending sign is one which rises in two hours, it signifies months. And if the ascending sign is one which rises in more than two hours, it signifies years, according to the proportion subsisting in degrees and minutes, as was said.

You should also know that the significations of their conjunctions often happen to those things which are signified by the sign of the Ascendant at the hour of the middle of their conjunction, or those things signified by its Lord, and also those things signified by the sign in which their conjunction was.

And if they were in the eastern part when they completed their conjunction, namely when they came together in the same minute, or were joined to eastern planets, these significations will happen in eastern parts. And if they are in the south, or joined to planets in the south, their significations will happen in southern parts. And if they are joined to western planets, or are western, they will happen in western parts. And if they are not in any of these parts, but are in the north, or are joined to northern planets, the significations will happen in the north.

As I said, Cancer is the detriment of Saturn and Mars, since it is opposite Capricorn (which is the domicile of Saturn, and the exaltation of Mars); and every seventh sign from the domicile or exaltation of any planet, is said to be the detriment of that planet.

Aries is opposite Libra (which is the exaltation of Saturn;: but is not opposite to any dignity of Mars, but rather it is his dignity.

Taurus is opposite Scorpio (which is the domicile of Mars), but is not opposite the domicile or exaltation of Saturn. Whence their conjunctions in the beginnings of other signs, or other triplicities, are less than their conjunctions in the beginning of Cancer, and less malicious. And Gemini is not opposite to the domicile or exaltation of any of them.

IV

On The Fourth Conjunction: That Of Saturn And Jupiter

The fourth conjunction, of Saturn and Jupiter, which happens once every 20 years, so that there are 12 conjunctions in each triplicity. And that it is true that they make 12 conjunctions in each triplicity, is demonstrated through this, if you attend to its truth well: multiplying 12 by 20 (or 20 by 12 which is the same thing), makes 240; and so, making one conjunction every 20 years, they are conjoined 12 times in 240 years. And thus they make 48 conjunctions between all of the triplicities, before they return to the same point in which they made the first conjunction; whence they make 12 conjunctions in 240 years, and multiplying 240 by 4 makes 960 years; and then their conjunction returns to the beginning of Aries, or to the beginning of some other triplicity. And understand about any place in which they make some conjunction: that they will always return there once every 960 years.

V

On The Fifth Conjunction: That Of The Sun With Other Planets

The fifth conjunction is that, which the Sun makes with planets, in his entry into the first minute of Aries, or of the other planets to him. For this has its own significations: sometimes small, sometimes great, sometimes good, sometimes bad, sometimes middling, such as will be discussed in full in the tractate on revolutions (for it would be long and laborious, and not philosophical or ordered if we touched on it now). And similarly, the entry of the Sun into Aries should be considered, and its Ascendant in that hour, and its minute in every year in which there ought to happen one of the above mentioned conjunctions (namely Saturn with one of the mentioned planets): since in that year the conjunction of the Sun with the planets will show greater significations than in others.

VI

On The Sixth Conjunction

The sixth conjunction is that of the Sun and Moon in the same minute, which happens once at the beginning of every lunar month; and their opposition, which happens in the middle of every lunar month. And similarly, they have their own diverse significations, just as will be discussed in the Tractate on rains, and I will also tell you certain things about them which will seem expedient in the tractate on revolutions.

VII

On The Combust And Incombust Hours After The Conjunctions Of The Sun And Moon, Which Certain Men Call "Albuim" Or "Abiuth"

Certain ancient sages, from whom I do not wish to deviate, said that after the conjunction of the Sun and Moon, from the minute itself of the same conjunction, there are twelve hours which are said to be "combust"; and after these twelve combust hours there are 72 hours which are called "incombust"; and after these 72 hours there are 12 combust; and so on in this manner up to the degree and minute of the following conjunction. And they said that the 12 combust hours are divided into three equal parts, giving each of these parts four of these hours. And they said that he who begins to wage war, or sets out to war, in the first of these four hours, should fear for the life of his body. And who begins to wage war, or sets out to war in the second of these four hours, should fear for his capture, or being wounded, or being struck in some other manner without the loss of his life. And who begins to wage war, or sets out to war in the last of the four hours, should fear the loss of his substance, and those who are with him, and he might also lose the persons who assist him.

And he who begins ploughing, or sets out for ploughing, in the first of the four hours, should fear losing the fruits he hopes for from that ploughing. And he who begins ploughing, or sets out for ploughing in the second of the four hours should fear a great detriment to all things that he has, and even to his own body, without the loss of life. And he who begins to plough, or sets out to plough in the last of these four hours, should fear a diminution of his seeds.

On The Duodena Of The Moon

Another division of these hours is made which is called the 12 hours of the Sun and Moon - namely 12 of the Moon. And this is a matter which is very important to observe, namely that you ought to know the hour of the conjunction of the Sun and Moon and its minute, and take the 12 hours after the conjunction and divide them into three equal parts, namely giving 4 hours to each part; and give the first division to the Sun, who is the first Lord of the first triplicity, namely the fire triplicity; and you ought to give the second hour to the second Lord of the same triplicity, namely Jupiter; and the third hour you ought to give to the third Lord of this triplicity, which is Saturn. And you ought to judge according to the condition of these Lords, just as I will explain to you in what follows.

Then you ought to give the next 12 (after those which you gave to the Lords of the first triplicity) to the second triplicity, namely the earth triplicity, giving the first four hours to Venus, who is the first Lord of the second, triplicity (namely the earth one); the second four to the Moon, who is the second Lord of the same triplicity; and the last four to Mars, who is the third Lord of this triplicity.

Next you ought to give the 12 hours (after those 12 which you have to the second triplicity) to the Lords of the air triplicity, namely the third; giving the first 4 hours to Saturn, who is the first Lord of the third triplicity; the second 4 to Mercury, who is the second Lord of the air triplicity; and the final 4 to Jupiter, who is the last Lord of the same triplicity.

Then you ought to give another 12 hours to the Lords of the fourth triplicity (namely the water triplicity); giving the first 4 hours to Venus, who is the first Lord of the fourth triplicity; the second 4 to Mars, who is the second Lord of the same triplicity; and you ought to give the last 4 to the Moon, who is the last Lord of the fourth triplicity, namely the water triplicity.

And so you ought to do with all of the Lords of every triplicity, until the disposition reverts back to the Sun, and it arrives to the degree and minute of the following conjunction. And you will consider all of these hours according to unequal hours and not according to equal hours.

And so, Ptolemy said "observe the duodena of the Moon", since this is the duodena he understood. For when the Moon is in one of these duodena, her condition and disposition will always be according to the condition of that planet to whom was assigned that third part of the duodena which the Moon was then placed. Whence a duodena of the Moon should be avoided; according to the disposition if that planet which was attributed those 4 hours, who is not to be placed for him for whom you elect, if you can ever avoid it; or else things will turn out badly for he who begins his war, or his journey to war: for if it does fall in any of those combust hours, he should fear the aforementioned dangers. And this is more likely to happen with those four hours of the duodena of the Moon, if she is badly disposeed at that time: since then there is no remedy, even if he had a good election for war; only God could avert the disaster.

However the aforementioned 12 combust hours are to be avoided even more, since the duodenae are subordinated to these. And so each planet is assigned twelve degrees, by dividing the duodenae equally amongst the planets; whence are produced 84 between them all (since 12 multiplied by 7 is 84). Then the eighth duodena is returned to the Sun, and the divisions of the duodenae are made again as said above, until they arrive at the second conjunction.

Then the wise men said that after the aforementioned 12 combust hours (in which it is not good or useful to begin or to do any of the things mentioned above) there are 72 incombust hours, which are useful for beginning or doing anything, unless impeded by something else. And so on until the second conjunction is reached. Whence you ought to consider in judgements, and especially in those things which I mentioned to you, lest the beginning of any matter, which you or someone else intends to do or begin falls in one of these prohibited hours, whether it is a journey or something else; and avoid this as much as it is in your power to do so.

VIII

On Finding The Degree Of The Ascendant Of A Nativity, Or Of Any Question, Or Of Any Beginning Which Has A Semi-Certain Indication

I have spoken about the conjunctions, and about the combust and incombust hours, and even if it doesn't appear to be of a philosophical order, I will still make mention to you of how to find the degree of the Ascendant of any beginning for which certainty is not had; provided that there is some indication of it which appears to show the approximate time, even if it doesn't seem very certain, but almost semi-certain. Since it happens sometimes that the mother, or midwife, or another person present at childbirth, does not know the hour of a child's nativity very well; nor even those who are present for some matter: but they have something close to the truth, not too far off, possibly by an hour, or a half an hour or thereabouts. Whence they say "this child was born around the third hour, or the sixth, or the ninth": or they might say "around midnight", or "around dawn", or "around the first hour of the night", as the lay are accustomed to say; or as others say "it was around such an hour, as when the banner was given", or when some building was begun, when something was managed, and similar things. And they cannot give you certainty of the hour for these judgements; but they can give you a time close to the hour.

Whence in order for you to find the exact hour of this nativity or matter, you ought to calculate the planets to this hour as closely as you can, so that you aren't more than an hour off from that hour which the midwives, or the mother, or someone else said. And see what sign is then ascending, and consider whether that nativity (or the beginning of whichever matter it is) is conjunctional or preventional. And see what degree that conjunction or prevention was made in; and consider which planets were stronger and powerful in the number of dignities or fortitudes in that degree, and see how many degrees it has transversed in the sign it is in, and make the degree of the sign which seems to be ascending at that time similar to the degree of the planet which is the almutem in the degree of the conjunction or prevention.

To give an example: it seemed to you according to the calculation which you made for some uncertain hour, that you had initial indications that the Ascendant was in the fourth degree of Aries, by your estimation, as I said, since you were able to understand concerning the nativity or the uncertain matter; and the conjunction or prevention was in the tenth degree of Aries: in which case the Sun is stronger in the degree of the conjunction than the other planets, by his number of dignities, just as was said elsewhere. Therefore calculate the Sun for that hour, and see in which degree of whatever sign he is in. Say that he is in the seventeenth degree of Aquarius; now you ought to change the Ascendant that you found first (which was the fourth degree of Aries by your judgement), from the fourth degree to the seventeenth degree of the same sign; and in this way you will verify the Ascendant which you sought. And if you find through your judgement that the Ascendant is greater than the planet which is the almutem of the sign: reduce the quantity of its degrees, so that if it was the twenty-fourth degree, or more or less, reduce it to the seventeenth - just as the Sun is in the seventeenth degree of the sign he is in. And thus understand for any other cases, and make the other houses according to this Ascendant. But since I, with the help of God, will make a special Tractate for you on nativities, in which I will explain all these things to you, and explain them more to the point, I will not spend any more time on it here, so that the order of topics may be observed more correctly.

THE FIFTH TRACTATE

On The Considerations Which Concern Judgements, According To The Motions And Significations Of The Stars, And On Certain Chapters Pertaining To The Introduction Of Judgements

And In This There Are 146 Chapters, Or Considerations

However from those things which pertain to judgements, there are six that are to be initially considered, as will be discussed below in its own place. The first is nations, and generations of nations. The second is the constitution of families, and households, and the arranging of individual households. The third is the disposing of wealthy and powerful people. The fourth is the consideration of individuals of the human race. The fifth is elections, or the beginnings of actions. The sixth is questions, as much general as particular; and from this it is possible for astronomical judgements to be reached. But before they are reached there are certain things to be set out in advance, which appear to have to do with the subject of them, such as considering the manner of inquiry for someone who intends to ask about something, and also to observe other considerations, and other ways which it is necessary for you to consider in the business of judgements.

And there are 146 considerations, which are impossible to apply all together and at once. But after I have named them all out to you, I will tell you at the end the ones without which an astrologer cannot judge perfectly. Nevertheless, first I will tell you the way by which whoever wants to ask anything from an astrologer ought to observe: since judging on future matters, as it is sometimes called, is a most difficult task, nor can it be judged to a fine point about these future matters; however it can be judged close to the truth; to which it is likened to and closely approaches to. Nor will it differ from the truth by much, in fact it will be almost imperceptible. And even if it is most difficult to judge on the future, nevertheless it is not a labour to be avoided, for indeed we strive to know everything on a judgement which can possibly be attained by the human mind. And since inferior things are ruled by superior things, as everyone unanimously agrees (and is true, as is said elsewhere), and the disposition of the superior bodies can be known by the dimensions of their motions, which have been discovered exactly by experienced people, and publicly proven, we can judge on future things, and which of these motions falls together with these things, and predict what is to come.

For this art has precepts: for the precepts of astronomy are its end, and its end is judgements (as is touched on elsewhere), which she makes regardless of those who strive to condemn astrology say (who appear to want to say that she is nothing). For something is not an art if it doesn't have its own precepts. But indeed she is an art (as was said elsewhere), which nobody will deny; therefore she has an end: and her end is judgements. And the astrologer has to consider judgements, and judgements are about accidents which are imprinted on the inferior things from the motions of the superior bodies, and from their qualities on account of their effects in them.

Consideration One is of those things which move men to make questions: and there are three motions.

The first is a motion of the soul, when someone is moved from their own intention to make a question.

The second is a motion of the superior bodies, namely when someone enquires about what they are imprinting on the quesited matter, and what will become of the quesited matter.

The third is a motion of free judgement, which can possibly be the act of enquiring itself: since even if the mind is moved to enquire, it is not sufficient, unless it is led to make a question by the superior bodies: nor are the motions of the stars sufficient, unless the act of enquiring is reached by the motion of free judgement.

Consideration Two is on the manner in which anyone who wishes to ask anything of an astrologer ought to observe. And when he wishes to ask an astrologer about the present, or the past, or the future, he ought to follow this manner of enquiry, namely that he ought to pray to the Lord, from Whom every good beginning is drawn, and with all devotion, and a contrite spirit, entreat Him, to allow him to arrive at an understanding of the truth of the matters which he intends to enquire about. Then by this truth he ought to go to the astrologer with intention concerning that about which he is going to ask, and about that which he proposed to ask, and the intention for which he holds in his heart for a day and a night (or more), not touched by just any motion of the mind, as sometimes many inexperienced men are in the habit of doing, as is said elsewhere. And thus He who spoke, who gave so that you may seek, will add so that you may find.

I recommend that all questions on all matters should be made in this manner, unless perhaps in the case of some sudden matter, suddenly emerging, which requires a sudden question and a sudden response not admitting of delay; however the beginning of which, is always the name of the Most High, for indeed certain people sometimes do otherwise, and for this reason they themselves come to be deceived, and they sometimes pressure the astrologer, in fact they often lie to him; for a stupid querent makes the responding sage err sometimes; and these men, not knowing the foolishness of the querent asking poorly, sometimes defame and scorn the astrologer, when the astrologer is not deserving of being defamed or scorned.

Consideration Three is to see how many ways the planets operate on the inferior bodies, following the diverse qualities of their aforementioned motions. And there are 16 modes by which diverse operations and effects of all things which are made and perfected happen, and of those which are not made, and which do not perfect, and of those which are party made and perfected, and partly not made or perfected, which will be discussed below.

Consideration Four is of the causes of helping matters to be done and to perfect, and which are prohibiting of matters, so that they are neither done nor perfected: and which are the causes of the destruction of matters after they are perfected, which befalls many things. And these things are done in 16 ways, as said, according to the 16 diverse motions, and so on.

Of which the first is the arrival or perfection of matters, or in things which philosophers call "*Alcocohol*".

The second is deterioration, which they call "*Aliber*".

The third is conjunction or turning back, which they call "*Alitisal*".

The fourth is separation, or disjoining, which they call "*Alinchirat*".

The fifth is transfer of light, which they call "*Annecad*".

The sixth is collection or aggregation, which they call "*Algemei*".

The seventh is vetoing, or prohibition, which they call "*Almana*".

The eighth is reception, which they call "*Alcobol.*"

The ninth is void-of-course, which they call "*Galaalocir*".

The tenth is concession or permission, which they call "*Gafralcobol*".

The eleventh is returning of virtue or disposition, which they call "*Alteat*".

The twelfth is the pushing of virtue, which they call "*Dalpha Alchoa*".

The thirteenth is the pushing of disposition which they call "*Dafaaredbit*".

The fourteenth is virtue or strength, which they call "*Alcovah*".

The fifteenth is debility, which they call "*Adirof*".

The sixteenth is the condition of the Moon, which they call "*Gnaymel Alchamaur*", which is a bad condition and a corruption of the Moon, as the wise men of antiquity said.

Consideration Five is how many ways such a condition of the Moon occurs. Philosophers said that this happens in ten ways. However to me it appears possible to add another seven, and so there will be 17 ways, by which impediments and detriments happen in all matters which are impeded, and in all beginnings, and in all questions, and in all journeys, and in all nativities, and in all things which we wish to do, or which we intend to do.

The first of which is if the Moon is combust, namely under the rays of the Sun, before him by less than 15 degrees, namely from behind the Sun when she moves towards him: and after him by less than 12 degrees, that is, when she recedes from him, so that she exits from under his rays. Since it is possible that she appears from under his rays. And she is more impeded when she moves towards the Sun, than when she recedes from him: since when she recedes, and is separated from him by 15 degrees, she is said to have escaped, even if she is not completely liberated - just as when a fever leaves an ill person, who, even if he is weak and broken, nevertheless is said to be free, since he is now untroubled about the strength that is about to arrive.

The second is, if the Moon is in the degrees of her descension, namely in the third degree of Scorpio, or all of Scorpio, and in all of Capricorn: or is joined to a planet in its descension, or in the descension of the Moon: so that if she was joined to Sun, and he was in Scorpio, or in Capricorn, or in his own descension, namely Aquarius, or Libra, specifically in its 19th degree, or in all of Libra: or if she is joined to Mars and he is in Libra or Taurus, or in the twenty-eighth degree of Cancer, or in all of Cancer. And understand this for all of the other planets.

The third is when she is in the combust degrees, the worst of which are the 12 degrees which are before the degree which is directly opposite the degree where the Sun is (wherever he may be).

The fourth is when she is joined to any malefics, or in their opposition, or square aspect without perfect reception. For it is different if she joins Saturn and Mars with the intervention of perfect reception, as if this is the case, she will be less impeded. In all other places she will be impeded by the aforementioned aspects, and by a bodily conjunction, unless she is in a place where the malefics have two of the lesser dignities, as Saturn has in the last four degrees of Aries, in which he has term and triplicity. And in the last four degrees of Gemini, in which he similarly has two dignities. And as Mars has in the last 10 degrees of Pisces, in which he has face and triplicity. And understand this for all the other signs, and places, in which the malefics have two of the lesser dignities.

The fifth is when she is with the Caput Draconis, or the Cauda, so that there is less than 12 degrees between them, since this is the boundary within which the Moon is eclipsed.

The sixth is when she is in Gemini, which is the 12th sign from her own house.

The seventh is when she is in the final degrees of signs, which are the terms of malefics, the last six degrees of Leo excepted, which are the terms of Jupiter, but she is impeded in the first six degrees of Leo, which are the terms of Saturn. But you might say that she is impeded in the first six degrees of Cancer, which are the terms of Mars - nevertheless she is not impeded here, as she is in the other terms of malefics, for something is removed from it: since Cancer is her house, and her greatest strength.

The eighth is when she is in the sixth, eighth, ninth, or twelfth from the Ascendant, without reception: or if she is joined to a planet in any of these places: or if she is in the third, since the third is cadent from the angles: but since she is said to rejoice here, she is not as impeded here as she is in the other cadents.

The ninth is when she is placed from the fifteenth degree of Libra up to the end of the 15th degree of Scorpio - these 30 degrees being the *via combusta.*

The tenth is when she is void-of-course, namely joined to none of the planets by body or by aspect, or if she is wild, or feral, which happens when she is void-of-course, and in a place in which she has no dignity.

The eleventh is when she is slow-of-course, for then she is considered as being similar to a retrograde planet.

The twelfth is when she is deficient in light, so that little or nothing is seen of her, while she is going towards combustion, which happens at the end of the lunar month.

The thirteenth is when she is besieged between two malefics impeding her.

The fourteenth is when she is in the azemene degrees.

The fifteenth is when she is in the welled degrees.

The sixteenth is when she is in the smoky degrees.

The seventeenth is when she is in the dark degrees, all of which you have noted in the tables above, in the First Tractate of this work.

Consideration Six is another method of weakening the planets, not differing much from the abovementioned, which happens in ten ways.

The first of which is when a planet is cadent from the angles, and from the Ascendant, so that it doesn't aspect the Ascendant.

The second is when a planet is retrograde.

The third is when a planet is combust, that is 15 degrees before the Sun, and less after him: indeed the inferior planets, when they are direct, are impeded more when they are after the Sun, and less when they are before him. When they are retrograde it is to the contrary.

The fourth is when any of them are in opposition, making a bodily conjunction, or a square aspect, to one or more malefics, without reception.

The fifth is when they are besieged by two malefics, namely if it is separating from one and joining to another without perfect reception from house, or exaltation, or two of the lesser dignities - which are term, triplicity and face.

The sixth is when a planet is joined to another planet in its own descension, or its own fall, namely in opposition to its own house or its exaltation.

The seventh is when it is joined to a planet cadent from the Ascendant, or separating from a planet who receives it, and joining to another who doesn't receive it.

The eighth is when it is peregrine, that is, if it is in a place where it doesn't have any dignity: or if it is a superior planet being followed by the Sun, or if it is an inferior following him.

The ninth is when a planet is with the Caput Draconis, or the Cauda, without latitude.

The tenth is when a planet impedes itself, that is, if it is in the seventh from its own house (namely feral) or without reception.

These are the ten impediments of the planets, by which impediments happen in nativities, in questions, journeys, and in all works which we intend to do or begin. You ought to know all of these kinds impediments of the planets.

And there are other ways which are necessary for you to know, certain of which I will make mention to you, which appear more necessary for you to know. Since it would be difficult, in fact most difficult, to consider all of those ways; for, as I said, it would be impossible for you to apply them all at the same time. But I will tell you the ones which are more necessary for you, and without which you cannot judge perfectly. I may name others for you, but I will not expound them all, lest it generate weariness in you. Of which certain ones are most strongly good, certain ones weakly good, certain ones more weakly good, certain ones most weakly good, certain ones hidden, certain ones manifest, certain ones are most strongly evil, certain ones more strongly evil, certain ones strongly evil, certain ones weakly evil, certain ones more weakly evil, certain ones most weakly evil.

Consideration Seven is to guard yourself against these ways by which the astrologer can err, of which the wise men named four.

The first is if the querent doesn't know how to ask his question.

The second is if the astrologer takes the shadow in an uneven place, or with a false instrument.

The third is if he is ignorant of whether the Sun had already receded from the line of the Midheaven, or whether he is on the line, or before it (earlier degree), or after it (later degree).

The fourth is if benefics and malefics are equal, whence at that time you ought not to receive the question, if you can avoid it.

To me it appears that they can add another three ways by which an astrologer can err. One, namely if the querent comes to him in order to test him, as some people do sometimes, who say "we will go to such an astrologer, and we will ask about such a matter, and we will see if he tells us the truth" - as the Jews used to do to Our Lord Jesus Christ.

Similarly, there is another way which appears possible for an astrologer to err, namely when the querent does not ask out of intention, as certain people sometimes do when they meet an astrologer, or when they go to enquire about the affairs of another, and they think of a matter of which they want to ask an astrologer about, and in this manner they unexpectedly enquire - and here it is possible to fall into error.

And you might say, how will I be able to know, whether a querent asks out of intention or not: or asks for reason of testing. To which I say to you, that it appears to me to be a truly arduous matter, and truly difficult: but still this is of much experience, and I have found it to be true, since I looked at the hour of the question, and I looked at its Ascendant, and if I found any sign on the oriental line, (which is the Ascendant) between the end of any sign and the beginning of another, I said that the querent didn't ask out of intention: or that he was asking for reason of testing : and I found many who confessed to me that this was so, and they reflected afterwards that I knew something, which they believed before: and they were brought to have faith in the art, whereas before they had none. And when I found any such Ascendant, I said to him "brother, don't exhaust me unless you enquire from intention: as I suspect that you wish to deceive me, by not proposing this question as you ought to: but if you wish that I work on your affairs, provide me for my labour" - and if it was a deception, he immediately went away.

Another way, namely the third, by which the astrologer can err, is that if the Lord of the Ascendant and the Lord of the hour are not of the same triplicity: or are not of the same complexion as the Ascendant. If you find them like this, it is not a question with roots, just as I have experienced many times.

I recite these to you so you may know which men you ought to examine for: since, as the philosopher says, matters turn out according to the quality of the querent's concern: and according to how he came to you by necessity, almost sorrowful, or meditating, and as if he hoped that you could respond, and that you knew the true response to his question: these are the men that you can examine securely.

Consideration Eight is that you examine and consider, as to how many out of the above ways, or of the above considerations that you ought to use in judgements. You ought to consider that there are 30, namely the aforementioned 16 on the impediments of the Moon: and 10 by which planets are impeded and debilitated, and four by which the planets rejoice, as I said to you above in the chapter on the joys of the planets.

The first of the four lesser ones is to see the place in which a given planet rejoices, just as Mercury rejoices in the Ascendant, the Moon in the third, Venus in the fifth, Mars in the sixth, the Sun in the ninth, Jupiter in the eleventh, and Saturn in the twelfth.

The second is if a planet is in its own house, in which it rejoices (as was said elsewhere), as with Saturn, who rejoices in Aquarius, Jupiter in Sagittarius, Mars in Scorpio, the Sun in Leo, Venus in Taurus, Mercury in Virgo, and the Moon in Cancer. And do not be annoyed if sometimes I repeat certain things to you which were said elsewhere, because it is easier for you to see what you want, where and when it is necessary, rather than to be looking elsewhere.

The third is that those diurnal planets (which are Saturn, Jupiter, the Sun, and Mercury) are with diurnal planets in the east, and they are oriental from the Sun, and they are next to the oriental line; and the nocturnal ones (who are Mars, Venus, the Moon, and Mercury) are with nocturnal ones in the west, and are occidental from the Sun, and especially next to the occidental line.

The fourth is if the three superior planets, namely Saturn, Jupiter and Mars, are in masculine quarters, which are from the cusp of the 10th house up to the cusp of the 1st house, and from the cusp of the 4th house up to the cusp of the 7th house. And if Venus and the Moon are in feminine quarters, which are from the cusp of the Ascendant up to the cusp of the fourth, and from the cusp of the 7th house up to the cusp of the 10th house. Mercury rejoices with masculine planets in masculine quarters, and feminine planets in feminine quarters.

Consideration Nine is to observe the ways of helping and harming in matters, if they come to be, or do not come to be, as much the manifest as the hidden, as much the good as the bad. Indeed there are 21 of these ways.

The first of which is the strongest, hidden, helper.

The second is stronger, hidden, helper.

The third is strong, hidden, helper.

The fourth is weak, hidden, helper.

The fifth is weaker, hidden, helper.

The sixth is the weakest, hidden, helper.

The seventh is the strongest, manifest, helper.

The eight is stronger, manifest, helper.

The ninth is strong, manifest, helper.

The tenth is weak, manifest, helper.

The eleventh is weaker, manifest, helper.

The twelfth is the weakest, manifest, helper.

The thirteenth is the strongest, hidden, harmer.

The fourteenth is stronger, hidden, harmer.

The fifteenth is strong, hidden, harmer.

The sixteenth is weak, hidden, harmer.

The seventeenth is weaker, hidden, harmer.

The eighteenth is the weakest, hidden, harmer.

The nineteenth is the strongest, manifest, harmer.

The twentieth is stronger, manifest, harmer.

The twenty first is strong, manifest, harmer.

All of which I will make mention to you. And these are hidden matters, and secret ones, from the secret judgements of the stars, of which the ancients were not concerned: and said nothing about openly which I found, besides what Haly appears to touch on of them in his exposition of the 29th saying of *Ptolemy's Centiloquium.* Nor do I believe they dismissed them on account of ignorance: but more so on account of being unaccustomed to them, and since they did not want to generate weariness in their audience or readers, nor weigh down their minds. They judged them according to how they found planets disposed in houses and signs, and according to their strength, and their debility: and similarly according to the Part of Fortune: and similarly according to certain other things which appear to them as being among these things. However you ought to consider in your judgments those things which the wise men considered in theirs, and furthermore whatever else which you may be able to consider.

Indeed when you erect any figure you ought to consider and to examine the ruler of the quesited matter, or the thing undertaken, or the thing to be begun, or to be done, to see if one of the fixed stars, which are of the nature of the matter are in a place where the ruler has house, or exaltation, and is with the ruler in the same minute, since this star will then help the significator so greatly and to such an extent, that the matter will be perfected, indeed beyond what was the intention of the querent, or the person beginning or doing it. And this is the strongest hidden helper. For he won't know from where it will happen to him. If this star is with the significator in the same degree, from one minute up to 16 in front, or up to 5 behind, it will help him, but not as much. And these are stronger hidden helpers. If it is with him in the same degree from 16 minutes up to 50, it will help even less, and these are strong hidden helpers. If it is with him in the same degree in a place where the significator has two of the lesser dignities, in the same minute or from one minute up to 16, it will help him even less. And this will be a weak, hidden, helper. If it is in the same degree, more than 16 minutes, up to 50 minutes away from the significator it will help him even less again, and this will be a weaker hidden helper.

If it is in a place, in which the significator does not have any dignity, it will help him somewhat, but almost imperceptibly. And this will be the weakest hidden helper.

And the harmers are in contrary to the helpers: for if a planet which is the significator of any matter is in such a place where it does not have any dignity, with one of the fixed stars which are contrary to its nature in the same minute, it will harm him, and will not permit the matter to be perfected, and it will appear through the figure erected above this matter that it ought to be perfected, and then the astrologer will be unjustly blamed and condemned, and for an unmerited reason: and astronomy will be said to be deceitful and to be nothing at all by idiots and those who condemn it. And this will be the strongest hidden harmer.

If it is with him in a place where he has one of the aforementioned lesser dignities, outside of the first minute, up to 16, then it will harm him less, and impede him less. And this will be a stronger hidden harmer.

But if he is in a place in which he has two of these lesser dignities, in the same degree with any of these stars from beyond 16 minutes, it will harm him even less. And this will be a strong hidden harmer.

If this star is in the domicile, or exaltation of the significator, not in the same minute, but in any of those outside of it up to 16 minutes, it will harm him even less again. And this will be a weak hidden harmer.

However, if the star is with the significator in his house or exaltation from 16 minutes up to 50, it will harm him even less. And this will be a weak hidden harmer.

If the star is with the significator in the same degree, in any of the greater dignities, from 50 minutes up to the end of the degree, it will harm him even less. And this is the weakest hidden harmer.

However the fixed stars which are of the natures of the planets, and of their contraries, will not be named here (indeed it would be long drawn out); but in the *Tractate On Revolutions*, I will tell you some of them which you ought to consider in any revolution: some I will tell you in the *Tractate On Nativities*: and some others in the *Tractate on Rains*, if the goodness of the Lord bestows me the life and bodily integrity to complete this work.

On The Above-mentioned Ways, Which Are The Strongest Good Ones, And Which Are The Strongest Bad Ones

But I do not want to forget before I tell you the ways (about which I made mention of above), namely which are the strongest good ones, and which are the strongest bad ones, and all of which are manifest and not hidden, whether they are good or bad

The strongest manifest good one is when a planet who is the significator of any matter is in its own house, in an angle, in the minute itself of the cusp, direct, fast-of-course, with reception, free from all impediments - which is very rarely attained.

The stronger manifest good one is when a significator is in its own house or exaltation, in an angle, one degree before the line or two after: free from malefics, and with reception, which is rarely attained.

The strong manifest good one is when a significator is in an angle, in its own house or exaltation, three degrees before the line, or five degrees after it.

The weak manifest good one is when a planet is in two of its lesser dignities, in the 5 degrees before an angle, or the 15 degrees after, or is in its own house or exaltation in a succeedent, free from malefics.

The weaker manifest good one is when a significator is in its own house or exaltation, or in two of its other lesser dignities, in a cadent, aspecting the Ascendant.

The weakest manifest good one is when a significator is in one of its greater dignities, or in two of its lesser dignities, not aspecting the Ascendant, or in only one of its lesser dignities aspecting the Ascendant, or joined to a planet aspecting the Ascendant, and having testimony in it.

The strongest manifest evil one is when a significator is in a place where it has no dignity, no joy, no reception, besieged by two malefics, cadent from an angle and cadent from the Ascendant, and this even more strongly if it is joined to any of the malefic fixed stars.

These and other ways besides, which have been mentioned above, both helpful and harmful, as much hidden as manifest, and made by conjunctions, and by aspects of the planets, of which would take a long time to list individually here, about which I will not make mention, but it will happen with certain ones of them in this treatise, for indeed the account would be overly long, and generate weariness in the listener and the reader. Nor will I give examples of all the aforementioned ones to you, because of the over prolixity of words. But I will tell you in the end about the considerations or chapters which principally pertain to a first glance at a judgement.

The first of which is Consideration Nine, which is that you know that the Moon, above all other planets, has a similarity with inferior generated things, namely to the kings of genera and the individuals of kinds; this befalls her on account of her own effects, which she has on all terrestrial things: and from the frequent revolutions - which revolutions she makes around the elements and elemental things, which is on account of her closeness to the earth.

She herself has a smaller circle than the other planets. Indeed within her circle there is not contained any other circle, but only the elements and other corruptible things. The Moon is the mediator between the stars and the inferior bodies: indeed her circle is contained by the circle of Mercury.

Moreover, the circle of Mercury is contained by the circle of Venus.

The circle of Venus is contained by the circle of the Sun.

The circle of the Sun is contained by the circle of Mars.

The circle of Mars is contained by the circle of Jupiter.

The circle of Jupiter is contained by the circle of Saturn.

The circle of Saturn is contained by the circle of the fixed stars, beyond which it is not of interest of the astrologer to admit himself, even if it appears to be so for certain people, which is an issue I do not intend to dispute here.

For you see that the Moon at a new Moon appears small, fine, and little: then her light is increased, and she appears that to grow little by little, until her entire body is illuminated, from the part which we observe, and is made full in her light: next her light is reduced little by little, and step by step, until she arrives at nothing. And bodies act the same way, as much rational as non-rational and all vegetable life. For observe how men are born, grow and are increased, until they are perfected in their own designated size, next they are decreased, and similarly begin to decline, and they decline until their life ends, and the same happens to the rest of things. Whence the Moon is always to be placed as the significatrix in all matters, all beginnings, and all nativities: and her good condition is good for all matters: and her bad condition is bad for all matters. And her virtue, and her power is so great, that indeed even if the Lord of the Ascendant, or any significator of any matter is so impeded that it cannot do or perfect what it ought to, and the Moon is found to be strong, the matter will be perfected nonetheless. Indeed she is the governess of all matters, and is the bearer of the strength of all planets towards planets, that is, from one to another, so that she receives the disposition of one planet, and carries it to another. And it appears to certain people that she always does this. In which opinion was that tyrant Ezzelino da Romano, namely that when she separated from one planet, she received its virtue, and carried it to another, and commits it to the planet which she first encounters. And it appeared to certain men that Zael said the same, but the intention of Zael was not absolute. He himself believed that the Moon carried that which was committed to her: and if something was not committed to her, she didn't carry anything to anyone, to which I assent.

For when the Moon joins any planet who receives her, at that time the planet commits its disposition to her, and she carries it with her, and commits it to the planet which she first encounters in one of its own fortitudes, and not to another. According to this, a planet does not give something in a place where it promised nothing.

Consideration Ten is to look out for the helping or harming fixed stars, on which will be discussed in the Tractate of Revolutions in their own place and time, which have much work to do concerning judgements, and often lead the astrologer into error.

Consideration Eleven is to observe and consider the malefic planets, and see what they signify. As Saturn and Mars, as I said to you above, are naturally malefic. Saturn on account of excessive cold, Mars on account of excessive heat - predominating, or ruling in them, not that either of them is in truth hot or cold, but they have this in virtue, and these are their effects: and from this they signify evil, detriment and impediment in matters, except if they receive the significator, or the Moon, from house, or exaltation, or from two of their lesser dignities, or if the malefics themselves are significators - since then they refrain all their malice from the planet which they receive, nor do they impede him by whatever aspect they aspect him from (still it is better if they do so by a trine or sextile). If they don't receive the planet their malice is increased, and this more strongly if they aspect by opposition or square aspect. If they aspect by trine or sextile, even if it is without reception, the impediment will be less.

Still, Zael appeared to want to say, that the malefics refrain their malice, if they aspect by a trine or sextile aspect: but his intention was that they impede less, yet he did not say that their malice was entirely refrained.

Consideration Twelve is to observe the benefics, and see what they signify. As Jupiter and Venus are naturally benefic, and are temperate: and from this they are said to be removed from all evil, since they harm nobody, unless perhaps sometimes by accident (which does not happen from their intention, and rarely happens). For they have advantageous and temperate impressions, always striving to help both what is their own and what is not their own, whether with reception, or without: still it is better if they have reception, and if they aspect by trine or sextile it is better, and more useful than a square: and a square is better than an opposition.

Consideration Thirteen is to observe the Sun and his significations, since he is said to be benefic, and he is, namely by aspect, whatever that aspect may be. Except if it is by opposition: but by bodily conjunction evil is effected, since then he is said to burn up and make unfortunate every star, except if that star is in the Cazimi of the Sun, as was said above: since then the star is in the heart of the Sun: and every star in the heart of the Sun is made strong.

Consideration Fourteen is to observe Mercury and the Moon, and see which planets they are conjoined to: since they have the signification of that which is signified by the planet whom they are joined to. For they are of convertible nature.

Consideration Fifteen is to consider the ways by which the planets imprint on the inferiors, and there are two: one good, another bad : since the benefics naturally imprint good things, and the malefics naturally imprint bad things, or introduce evil naturally. Whence when you see benefics you always ought to hope for good: and when you see malefics you always ought to fear evil, unless the aforementioned things decrease it.

Consideration Sixteen is to examine whether a planet signifying any matter is impeded by any malefics; since a planet is not said to be impeded by a malefic unless the malefic projects its rays over his rays according to the quantity of the orbs of their light. From which, when a malefic projects its own light, or rays, over the light or rays of another planet, the other planet is said to be impeded until the malefic transits him. And Zael said that from when the malefic planet transits the planet which he impeded by one full degree, the planet is said to be freed from the malefic. Yet it appears to me, that from when the malefic transits the other planet by one minute, the planet may be said to be free, and to have escaped, since afterwards the malefic can introduce nothing to him except for fear.

Moreover, he will introduce greater fear when he is only transited by one minute, than when he has transited him by one degree: but still this fear which is sent forward by the malefic is so great than when it has transited the planet by only one minute, it does not appear to him to whom it pertains to, that he can escape, yet he is not without some sliver of hope.

Below is such an example, a question was made by a certain man wishing to set out to battle, asking whether he would return safely from the battle or not: and the Ascendant was Gemini 13 degrees, and Mercury was in 7 degrees and 54 minutes of Aquarius, in the ninth joined to Saturn, who was similarly in Aquarius, at 7 degrees and 53 minutes. And Mercury was separating from Saturn, who was the Lord of the house of death, by one minute. Therefore it appeared that he ought to die in this battle, on account of the conjunction which Mercury made with Saturn in 8 degrees of Aquarius: from which he was in danger of death, and feared it with a near ultimate fear, and believed he would be killed by his enemies. And he was pursued by them, so that it did not appear that he could escape, and they often laid their hands on him. Nevertheless ultimately he escaped from them, after having lost almost all hope: since he did not believe he could escape. And this happened to him on account of Mercury, who had already separated from Saturn.

And Zael said that if a malefic planet who was impeding some business was cadent from the Ascendant, so that he did not aspect it, he would not impede the matter, but would only introduce fear.

COnsideration Seventeen is to examine whether the significating planet is safe, in such a manner that he is not impeded by any malefics: and that one of the benefics projects its rays or light, over the rays or light of the significator: since then the planet is said to be safe, until that benefic transits by one minute: and it signifies the perfection of the matter.

After the beneifc has transited the significator by one minute, it won't be perfected, nor will the matter send forth anything except for hope, just as a malefic will not send forth anything except fear, as I said. And the hope that the benefic gives is so great, that the querent will believe that the matter will be perfected, and it will appear certain to him that his matter will be perfected: yet not without the rendering of some kind of doubt.

To give an example, a certain question on some arduous business was posed - whether the matter would be perfected or not. And the Ascendant was 17 degrees of Scorpio, and Mars was in 12 degrees and 13 minutes of Taurus, and Venus was in 12 degrees and 14 minutes. For indeed Venus was joined to Mars by a trine aspect, and received him from her own house, and Mars received her from exaltation: and it appeared to the querent, and everyone handling the business, that it ought to perfect according to this aspect of perfect friendship: and they remained in this hope until Venus transited the aspect of Mars by one full degree : nevertheless the matter was ultimately destroyed, on account that Venus had transited the aspect of Mars by one minute at the time of the question.

It is possible that sometimes a matter might perfect in such a case, but not without great perseverance, great labour, great complications, and great effort and inconvenience. And Zael said that if a benefic it cadent from the Ascendant, so that it doesn't aspect the Ascendant, it only gives hope and does not perfect the business.

Consideration Eighteen is to consider when a planet is in the angles of the malefics: since unless the malefic receives him, he is said to be in evils, and in trials and tribulations, just as is a man whom some people attacked and perpetrated an insult on, whom nobody helped, who fights and defends himself from many attackers; and just as one who strives and labours against fortune, and everything turns out adversely for him, and just as he who falls in a whirlpool, and doesn't know how to swim, yet thrashes his hands and feet in such a manner that at some time he arrives at the bank, and escapes, even if this doesn't always happen.

And a planet is said to be in the angle of a malefic, when a malefic is in one sign, and the planet is in the 4th from him, or in the 7th, or in the 10th, so that if a malefic is in Aries, and another planet is in Cancer, or in Libra, or in Capricorn, this planet is said to be in an angle of the malefic. Understand the same of a bodily conjunction. But if it is received, it is not impeded, since reception shatters all evil, as is said elsewhere. After (as was said) he has transited him by one whole minute, it is said the planet has escaped from the danger of this malefic, and from its impediment. And after transiting him by one degree, it is said to be secure, since the malefic has no power over him, even if he sends forth some fear. And don't forget this which I tell you, since it could prove useful to you, as much in nativities, as in questions, and for inceptions of all matters.

Consideration Nineteen is to examine the Moon, when she is void-of-course, since then she signifies impediments: and that the quesited matter, or which was begun, or what is being handled, will not come to a good end, and the matter will be annulled, and will not come to be, nor be completed for the one wishing to do it and he will return from that matter similarly void (of results), disgraced, and impeded.

Consideration Twenty is to examine if the Moon, or a significator, is joined to one of the planets, since this will signify that it is going to happen. Whence you should consider whether that planet to whom the Moon, or the significator of the matter or question is joined, receives the significator or the Moon: for then it signifies the completion and perfection of the matter, and that its end will be good, and praiseworthy - I say this, if the receiver is benefic. However, if it does not receive, and the Moon, or the Lord or significator of this matter commits their disposition to it, nevertheless the matter will be perfected. But if it is a malefic, even if the Moon or significator commits their disposition to it, and reception does not intervene, the matter will not be perfected- and evil and detriment will be introduced amongst its parts. However if there is reception, and the planet is not otherwise impeded, it signifies the perfection of the matter, even if it will happen with labour, perseverance, and fatigue.

Consideration Twenty-One is to examine from which planet the Moon is separating, since this signifies what already was, and what is past: for if she separates from a benefic she signifies good, which already was. If she separates from a malefic, it signifies evil which already was. Whence if you want to judge on what already was, and what is past, you will be able to speak about it according to how you observe the Moon separating from one of the planets.

Consideration Twenty-Two is for you to consider which of the planets the Moon is conjunct with, for this signifies what is present. Whence if you wish to judge something on a present matter, it is necessary for you to consider to whom the Moon is joined to at that time, degree for degree, or by less than one degree, and you ought to judge good or evil according to whom she is joined to.

Consideration Twenty-Three is to examine who the Moon is now joined to, yet joined in such a way, that her conjunction is not yet completed: since this signifies what is going to be. Whence if it is necessary for you to judge on a matter which does not yet exist, and is hoped to come into act, you ought to observe to whom the Moon wants to join at this time - and you ought to judge good or evil according to its significations (it being who she appears to wish to join).

Consideration Twenty-Four is to examine if a significator is in its descension, since then it signifies impediment of that matter for which it is the significator, along with difficulties and sorrows because of it. And if it is a question about a prison, which someone one fears, it signifies his fall into prison, and similarly his disgrace and detriment. And if it is on a prisoner, it signifies his long stay in prison, and remaining in there longer than the prisoner believes.

Consideration Twenty-Five is for you to consider whether a significator of any matter is retrograde, or stationary in his first station: since then it signifies evil, and impediment, and discord, diversity, contradiction, and repetition in evil, and disobedience, and turning back to evil from whatever the reversion was, and in a bad direction. But in its station it doesn't signify as much evil as it does in retrograde: since retrogradation signifies a present evil, and a past evil which is virtually present, and a future one which is as if it is already in progress. The first station signifies evil which is now completed, according to imperfect time.

Consideration Twenty-Six is to examine whether a significator is in its second station, which then signifies impediment and evil, which already was, and is past. Yet certain men say, that the second station signifies the same things as direct motion, but this is to be understood according to a certain manner of speaking, just as is said of someone who was sick and is now healing, that he is already freed and healthy - but this is not plainly true, even if it is close to the truth: indeed just as the first station doesn't signify as much evil as retrogradation, so does the second station, not signify as much good as direct motion.

Consideration Twenty-Seven is to examine whether a malefic planet is the significator of any matter, or of any work, or any beginning, or of any nativity, or of any of the things which happen every day, or pass through men's hands, for if they signify evil, it will be greater, and if they signify good, it will be diminished, and imperfect, and with sorrow, trials, difficulties and oppression, so that he whose business it is will hardly believe that it will be perfected for him, unless perhaps the malefic is in very good condition and well disposeed.

Consideration Twenty-Eight is to examine if a planet signifying any matter is slow-of-course: for then the effect of the quesited matter will be prolonged, and if it is the beginning of any building, it will prolong and delay its completion in such a manner that it will hardly or never be perfected. And if it is a promise made to someone, the thing promised will be delayed, and will hardly or very slowly be perfected for who it was promised to. And if a threat was made, it will not hasten its effects, or they will be bad promises.

Matters will also be delayed if the significators are in Sagittarius, Capricorn, Aquarius or Pisces, whether or not their Lords, namely Jupiter and Saturn, are slow-of-course or not: but if they are slow of course, matters will be further postponed. If they are in Aries or Scorpio, they will be postponed less than in the aforementioned signs. If they are in Leo they will be accelerated. If they are in Taurus or Libra they will be accelerated further. If they are in Gemini or Virgo they will be accelerated more than they are in other signs.

Consideration Twenty-Nine is to observe whether the Moon is making a corporeal conjunction, or a conjunction by aspect with any of the planets, and her conjunction is complete, minute for minute. Since then it signifies what concerns the matter is present. And when she transits this minute, you should observe which of the planets she joins to first: since this signifies that which ought to come of that matter. Indeed also examine the planet from which the Moon is separating from at that time, before she joined the aforementioned planet minute for minute. Since this signifies what had already been for the matter.

Consideration Thirty is to observe when a significator or the Moon has transited the 29th degree of the sign in which it is in, and is touching the thirtieth degree of that sign: and especially if it transits past the first minute of the same degree: since then the planet has no strength in that sign, but will have strength in the following. Whence if it had first signified something bad, it would not have harmed the one which it seemed it ought to have harmed, similar to if some house had threatened to fall, it would not injure the person who had left it, and had already put one foot on the threshold of the door, and had the other advancing beyond the threshold itself, and had the other advancing beyond the threshold itself, leaving quickly, and the house fell down at that time. And if anything good was signified for someone, it won't benefit him, similar to someone who throws a net at any bird, and only touches his tail-feathers, not catching him.

Whence Zael said, if a planet or the Moon is in the 29th degree of some sign, that its strength exists thus far in the sign in which it is placed; since it did not yet transit the 29th degree entirely, and also in the degree which is before it, and the degree which is after it.

Consideration Thirty-One is to note when one planet, seeking a conjunction of another, is itself next to the end of the sign in which he himself, or the planet to whose conjunction he seeks, is placed; in such a way that the second planet leaves from that sign before the conjunction is perfected. And then see if he is joined to this planet in the following sign (into which he moves); for then the matter will be perfected if the planet gives him something in the sign where the joining takes place (this is, if reception intervenes) - unless he or the planet to whom he wishes to join, is first joined to yet another planet, since in this case the matter will be annulled and will not be perfected. Even if it joins to the original planet from which the conjunction was sought, after he separates from the planet to whom he joined when he moved sign, since the other planet interposed itself before the conjunction could be perfected. Nor should you forget this, since a corporeal conjunction will prohibit an aspect, and cuts it off, but an aspect will not prohibit or cut off a corporeal conjunction.

Consideration Thirty-Two is to observe what condition a malefic planet who is the significator of any matter is, since if he is in good condition, the matter will be good. However, if he is in bad condition, the matter will be bad. Sarcinator said something similar in Pentadeca:

"A malefic planet, when it is oriental in its own house or exaltation, and if it is not joined to a malefic who impedes it, is better and more worthy than a retrograde and impeded benefic".

Consideration Thirty-Three is to observe whether any malefic is the significator of any matter, and is joined to another malefic which impedes him: or is joined to the Lord of the Ascendant, or the Moon by a bad aspect, namely by a square, or from opposition: for the malefic will perfect the thing, but will not make it arrive at a good end, in fact it will be destroyed after it appears to be arranged and is believed to be perfected. But if the impeding malefic is lighter, so that it sought the conjunction of the significator, it will impede less than if the significator was seeking the conjunction of the impeding malefic; so that it will be worse if the significator pushes, than if it itself is pushed.

Consideration Thirty-Four is to observe in questions or in nativities, or in any other matters over which you have to judge, whether the significator of the business at hand, is a malefic, and is also the Lord of the Ascendant, and is himself in the Ascendant, direct, and in good condition. Since if this is so, it will perfect the matter, and will cause it to arrive at a good end: and indeed if he is not the significator, nor the Lord of the Ascendant, and is in the Ascendant: and the Ascendant is his exaltation, all his malice will be dismissed, and he will be refrained from causing an evil impediment. However being impeded will increase his evil, and multiply his harm, and his contrariety, and he will try in every way to destroy the business.

Consideration Thirty-Five is to examine whether a malefic planet is in a sign similar to him, since then his own malice will be reduced: and he is like a person who has what he wants : who will then be found to be of good will, more pious, more merciful, and less malicious. Just as when Saturn is in Capricorn, or Aquarius, or Libra, or in a cold sign: and especially if he has any dignity there: and like when Mars is in Ares, or Scorpio, or Capricorn, or a hot sign: and especially if he has any dignity there, since then he will perfect the matter.

If Saturn is in a hot sign, outside of his dignities, or Mars in a cold sign, outside of his dignities, it will be evil, and the matter will not be perfected, like how the mixture of water with oil is not easily perfected, and how they do not embrace each other. If he is in good condition, and well disposeed (as I said), they will then be able to mix together well, and they will perfect the matter, just like a combination of water with wine, or honey with milk.

Consideration Thirty-Six is to consider when a malefic signifies impediment, whether a benefic aspects him from a trine, or a sextile aspect, since then his impediment will be reduced, and much more strongly so if he is received.

Consideration Thirty-Seven is to examine if benefics are significators, whether malefics aspect them from opposition, or by square aspect, since then the malefics will reduce their fortune and goodness.

Consideration Thirty-Eight is to examine if benefics are significators, if they are cadent from the angles, or from the Ascendant, so that they do not aspect it, and if they are also retrograde: since then they are impeded, and will be almost similar to malefics, unless they are received.

Consideration Thirty-Nine is to examine if the planet who is the significator has reception: for if it is a benefic, his significations will be better than they would be otherwise. However, if he is a malefic, his impediment will be less; however if he ought to impede, he will even impede after he is received.

Consideration Forty is to examine if a malefic planet (whether he is the significator or not) is peregrine: "*peregrine*" being if he is not in any of his own dignities: since then his malice will be made greater: and likewise for the evil and impediment he signifies. And when he is in its own dignities, his impediment will be reduced, and his malice is restrained, namely in his own house or exaltation, or terms. In triplicity and face, it is restrained less. In haym even less again.

Consideration Forty-One is to examine if a malefic planet is the significator of any matter, or any beginning, and is in its own house or exaltation, or in its terms, or triplicity, and in an angle, or a succeedent, since then it is said to be strong and like a benefic.

Consideration Forty-Two is to observe if a benefic is the significator, or offers its support to one of the planets, and is in a house in which it has none of the above mentioned dignities: since then its good and its fortune will be reduced. And if it is in any of these dignities, it will perfect the matter and increase its strength, and its good, and its fortune is made greater.

Consideration Forty-Three is to examine if benefics and malefics are in malignant places at the same time, namely in any of the impediments which I have said to you above and on many other occasions - that is in houses in which they don't have testimony, and if they are combust: since then they signify their significations more weakly: and they signify debilitated and despicable things. Nor can benefics signify well: nor malefics evil, on account of their excessive debility. In accordance with this, the Philosopher says that a retrograde and combust planet has no strength in signification.

Whence Zael said, wherefore a planet is combust when it is under the rays of the Sun, or if it is in the

Sun's opposition, it will be debilitated : since in this place it will have no utility: benefic planets do no good: nor do malefic planets do evil: since benefics signify nothing good, or by way of good, when they are combust: and similarly when the malefics are combust, they have little or no virtue in signifying evil, and they can cause less impediment at this time.

C**onsideration Forty-Four** is to examine if the significator, whether it is benefic or malefic, is in its own house, exaltation, or terms, or face: although face doesn't have as much virtue as the aforementioned dignities do. Whence it is necessary that it will be helped by another dignity, namely light or haym. For then malefic is restrained from their malice, just as a wicked horse is restrained from his wickedness by a strong bridle; and whatever evil is in him, is converted to good. And benefics are strengthened and increased in good. And even if this appears almost miraculous: still the vast majority of philosophers attest to this, and I have seen it occur in my time. Whence you ought to consider all of these things which I have said to you in this chapter, and so you will be able to judge truly on this matter; for I myself have not found it to disappoint.

C**onsideration Forty-Five** is to examine if malefics are in the angles of the Ascendant, and are impeding one of the planets by a square aspect, or from opposition: since then they will more greatly impede and afflict: and their harm will be greater: and especially if the malefics are in a stronger place than the planet which they impede. If they aspect from a trine or a sextile aspect, their evil is restrained and their malice reduced, and similarly of their impediments

C**onsideration Forty-Six** is to examine whether a significator is a benefic or malefic: since if it is a benefic, it always naturally signifies fortune. Malefics however, always naturally signify evil, which happens to them on account of the overflowing malignancy of their own nature. Whence you ought to examine the places where the planets are from the Ascendant: for if a planet is in its own light, or in its haym, or in any of its own dignities, or in a good place from the Ascendant, it signifies good. If it is a benefic, it signifies greater good.

C**onsideration Forty-Seven** is to consider whether the significator is in its own light, namely a diurnal planet above the earth in the day, and below the earth at night: and a nocturnal planet above the earth at night and below the earth in the day. And if a nocturnal planet is the significator of any matter and is above the earth in the day: or a diurnal planet is above the earth at night: or if this significator is peregrine, namely that it does not have dignity in the place in which its in: or is cadent from the Ascendant, so that it doesn't aspect it: or if it is cadent from the angles: for then it is impeded, and impedes that matter which it signifies, nor can it perfect that matter.

C**onsideration Forty-Eight** is to examine when a malefic planet is the significator, and is threatening evil, whether Jupiter aspects it, or joins it by his own body: since he shatters the malice, and changes its nature to good, whatever kind of malefic this was. For so great is his beneficence and strength in good, that he shatters all Saturn's evil and changes it to good. Whence if Saturn does not give good in that place, and is not perfecting the matter that he promised, Jupiter will make him give and perfect the matter, whether Saturn wants to or not- unless Jupiter himself is impeded from fall, or combustion, or retrogradation: for then he will help, but will not wholly perfect the matter. Indeed Venus shatters the malice of Mars, on account of the excessive friendship which is found between them, unless it is a truly arduous matter, such as the clashing of arms, and wars, and spilling of blood. However she cannot shatter the evil of Saturn without the support of Jupiter: for when she has this then she will shatter the evil of Saturn, just as she otherwise shatters the evil of Mars: since Saturn does not applaud Venus in any way: since Saturn is slow: Venus is fast. He is heavy: She is light. He rejoices in lamentations: She rejoices in delights.

C**onsideration Forty-Nine** is for you to consider whether one of the malefics is the significator of any matter, and if he joins another malefic, since if it signifies any good, this good will be destroyed. If it signifies any evil, it will be increased and made worse, or change into another greater evil, just as when an ache around the navel changes into dry-dropsy. However if the significator joins to a benefic who receives it, or is received by it, then this evil will be led away to good. But if reception does not intervene, the evil will not be wholly cancelled, but it will be mitigated so that it is made less, according to how that benefic is disposeed, for it is possible that the evil would be so greatly reduced that it will only appear to do the slightest damage.

Consideration Fifty is to examine the Lord of the Ascendant of any matter and the Moon, and see if one or both of them are impeded by the malefics, namely from a conjunction, or from opposition, or by a square aspect: for without the aspect of a benefic this matter will be impeded. But if the significator or the Moon is then aspected by a benefic, namely Jupiter, Venus, the Sun, or the Moon, it will dissolve the malice of the impeding malefic, and he whose significator was the Lord of the Ascendant or the Moon will be freed (if he was threatened by any danger), from the fear of the malefic being let in, even if the aspect is a square (as long as it is with reception). But if a benefic aspects by square without reception, or from opposition, or a malefic by trine or sextile without reception, or by square or opposition with reception, it will then be possible that he whose significator was the Lord of the Ascendant or the Moon will be freed from the impediment which appears to be threatening him, however it will be converted into an evil that is equally bad, or a small bit better, in such a way that his liberation will not seem advantageous to him.

Consideration Fifty-One is to examine whether a planet signifying any matter is cadent from an angle, and from the Ascendant: and not in any of its joys, since then it signifies every evil, every doubt, and no utility and nothing good, and there will be no hope for the matter, and nothing praiseworthy will be signified from a planet so disposeed.

Consideration Fifty-Two is when the three inferiors, namely Venus, Mercury and the Moon, exit from under the rays and arrive at the origin of the evening: namely that they appear in the evening after the Sun sets: since before they exit from under the rays of the Sun, and are elongated from him by 12 degrees, the strength of any of them will be weak - and indeed so too of the others, so that benefics will be only be slightly beneficial, and malefics will only be able to cause a little harm. Whence the benefics will provide advantage slowly and with difficulty, in such a way that only with great labour, perseverance, and great complications will this advantage arrive. And if it is a malefic, its signification will appear slowly. In the superiors (which are Saturn, Jupiter and Mars) the significations will happen when they exit from under the rays of the Sun, so that they rise in the morning before the Sun, and appear before his rising.

Consideration Fifty-Three is to examine whether a significator is under the rays of the Sun, since then it will be debilitated, and of almost no strength in any given matter: nevertheless malefics will be somewhat more powerful in evil than the benefics are in good, even if it is not by much. A planet is said to be under the rays of the Sun when there are exactly 12 degrees, or less, between him and the Sun, and more than 16 minutes. Since when there are exactly 16 minutes, or less, between a planet and the Sun, he is said to be strong, for he is then in Cazimi, or in "the heart of the Sun", as I said to you above. When there are more than 12 and less than 15 degrees between a planet and the Sun, the planet is said to be exiting from under the Sun's rays.

Consideration Fifty-Four is to examine whether a superior planet is elongated from the Sun by 12 degrees, moving to the morning rising place, just as much as an inferior (and direct) planet is while moving to the evening setting place- since the planet is then said to be strong. After it is elongated from him by 15 degrees, so that it appears from under the Sun's rays, it is said to be stronger than it could possibly be otherwise in all matters, just like someone, who exits from a battle having conquered all of his enemies, and now rests and rejoices in his victory: not fearing that anyone else may rise up against him, or that anyone will resist him in anything: for then he is cheerful, of good mind, good disposition, and blessed in every way.

However when the Sun pursues the three superiors, and there is less than 15 degrees between them, their weakness is said to be increased up until there is only 7 degrees between them and the Sun: and after there are less than 7 degrees between them and the Sun, up until they are in the heart of the Sun, they are said to be in ultimate weakness. Indeed the weakness of the three inferiors is to the contrary of this, for their weakness is said to be increased when they pursue the Sun, and when there are 15 to 7 degrees between them and the

Sun: and from 7 degrees up until they are in the heart of the Sun, they are said to be in the ultimate weakness.

Consideration Fifty-Five is to examine whether a significator is peregrine, which will then signify that the individual signified, (whether it is in a nativity, or a question, or in the beginning of any matter), will be sly, astute, malicious - for he will know how to do good and evil, and how to advance cleverly in all matters; however his intention will be inclined more towards evil than towards good. And if the significator is in any of its greater dignities (namely in house or exaltation), and it is direct, and in a good place from the Ascendant (in the tenth, or the eleventh), or in any friendly aspect to the Ascendant, then it signifies a good effecting of the quesited matter, or undertaking, and the good mind and good will of the native, or querent, or the quesited person. If it is in any of its lesser dignities its significations will be below this.

Consideration Fifty-Six is to examine if a planet who is the significator of some matter commits its disposition to another planet, whether the receiver of disposition is oriental or occidental. Since if it is oriental, and the planet is one of the inferiors, and is direct (or if it is occidental, and one of the superiors), and there are less than 20 degrees between it and the Sun, it will be debilitated, as Sarcinator says, and what was judged or shown by it will not be perfected. For it will then be impeded more by such an impediment, so that it will be similar to impediments which impede a man who has begun to fall ill, and the illness has prevailed to the extent that the ill man is thought to have fallen: nor can he help himself without external support; and like a building which has begun to collapse with nobody there to defend it from ruin.

And the greater distance there is between a planet and Sun, the less it will be impeded. And if it is oriental and one of the superiors, or if it is occidental and one of the inferiors, and if it is not retrograde, it will be strong and well suited to perfect the matter which it indicates - like a man who was infirm, and now is totally liberated, and has recovered all of his powers: and like a building which was ruined, and now is reconstructed, and newly raised, and improved in all its parts; and it is like this for all the aforementioned planets disposeed in this manner.

Consideration Fifty-Seven is to inspect whether the significator is in the eighth from the Ascendant: since if it is found here, and it is a benefic, even if it won't operate evil, it won't operate good either. And if it is a malefic it will operate greater evil than in any other place in the whole figure, and it will magnify its malice. And if it is a question about going to war, do not counsel him to set out at that time, even if it is a benefic, for evil, namely death, or to a lesser extent capture, is always to be suspected - for it is the place of darkness and death. However, if it is a malefic, you will be able to judge death for him, unless it is at that time separating from the Lord of the eighth, since then it could signify injury, or beatings, or an occasion where it will appear possible that he could die - even if he might escape. And if it is any journey, and especially a long one, you can judge him to be captured, or at least to suffer the greatest fear on this journey. And this is always to be understood if the significator separates from the Lord of the eighth, and understand similarly, that if a malefic is disposeed as I said, it will always accomplish more evil than fortune.

Consideration Fifty-Eight is to inspect whether the significator is fixed in the sign where it is found.

And Zael said that a planet is not said to be fixed in a sign, unless it had travelled through it by five degrees. However it appears to me that from when a planet has travelled through one full degree of a sign, he is firmly in it, however Zael spoke to greater clarity, and said that a planet is not said to be cadent from the Ascendant unless it is elongated from it by five degrees. To give an example, the Ascendant was 9 degrees Aries, and a planet was in 5 degrees of the same Aries. In this case, Ptolemy, and many other wise men said that such a planet is in an angle- with all of whom I agree.

Certain others wanted it to be so that a planet is said to be in an angle, when it is in the same degree as the Ascendant, or one degree before, or two after. But their intention was in revolutions of the years: and because they wanted to be certain that they could not be deceived on any matter.

However I have demonstrated that a planet is in an angle up to near a full 5 degrees beyond the cusp of any angle; for in a certain year which I investigated the revolution of the year for, I found Mars in the fifth degree past the cusp of the angle of the earth, and he was in Capricorn, and his latitude was southern, and this signified the killing of the Roman Emperor; and it signified this for him at that time, for he was then in Grosseto (while I was in in Forli), and Pandolfo de Fasanella and Tibaldi Franciscus, and many others of their secretaries were then discovered to have formed a conspiracy to kill him - and none of their astrologers found this, since they didn't believe that Mars was in an angle: for he had transited the cusp of the angle by four degrees and 58 minutes according to their opinion. Indeed after a planet was elongated from the cusp or the line of any angle by 5 degrees it is said to be cadent from the angle.

Consideration Fifty-Nine is to examine whether a significator is after the line of an angle by 15 degrees, and not more: for indeed the planet is then said to be in an angle just as much as one who is directly on the angle, according to how it appeared to Zael. From this point onwards he said that it was not in an angle: and he said that it didn't have strength in an angle beyond the 15th degree after an angle. To give an example, the Ascendant was the fourth degree of Taurus; up to the end of the sign was after the angle: but whichever planets were from this fourth degree of Taurus up to 19 degrees of the same, were in an angle: whatever planets were beyond 19 degrees were not in an angle.

Ptolemy appeared to want to hint, even if he did not say it expressly, that all planets which were before an angle by five degrees, and after it up the 25th degree, were in the angle.

Zael wanted to remove the doubt that a great elongation of the planet from an angle impeded its business.

Ptolemy (from whom I do not dissent) appeared to want that no part of any house remained without virtue. To me it seems (and I do not believe this without reason), that every planet which is in some house, and is said to be, and is, in that house in which it is found, from the beginning of that house up to its end. And therefore I say "in a house" and not "in a sign", since one house can enclose more than one sign: sometimes less than one sign. Indeed it seems ridiculous that any part of any house remains shut off, or lacking virtue.

Consideration Sixty is to examine whether a significator is in a fixed sign, or a common sign, or in a mobile sign: since in a fixed sign it signifies the fixity, stability, and durability of the matter undertaken, or of any quesited matter. When it is in a common sign, it signifies he change and reiteration of a matter already undertaken, or to be begun, or of what is quesited: and that the matter will be dissolved and begun again: or that another matter will be combined with it, and will be connected to it: or some alteration or reiteration will happen with the matter. Whence in matters of which we desire an alteration, such as buying, selling and similar things, we ought to place the significator and the Moon, or at least one of them in a common sign. And when it is in a mobile sign, it signifies the quick change or alteration of the matter, or of the thing undertaken, or about to be begun, or the quesited matter, or whatever else there is: and its fast completion, and swift end, whether it signifies good or evil. Whence in matters of which we desire a swift end to, we ought to place the significators in mobile signs. In matters which we desire durability and long fixity in, we ought to place the significators in fixed signs. In those of which we desire moderate duration, we ought to place the significators in common signs. You should understand the same for the nature of the Moon, if you can ever make things like so. And I will repeat to you again that fixed signs signify fixity, durability and unity; common signs signify plurality; mobile signs signify swift change.

Consideration Sixty-On is to examine whether the Lord of the Ascendant, or the Moon, is with the Caput or the Cauda Draconis: since then it signifies impediments in all matters: and the impediment will come from a thing, or out of a thing, which is signified by that house in which the conjunction of the significator or the Moon with the Caput or Cauda took place. And only bodily conjunctions count, since the Caput and Cauda do not have aspects, or oppositions. And it is worse when the significator or the Moon moves towards them, than if they recede from them, as is said elsewhere. For when they move towards them, then it signifies the ultimate evil; as happens to a man who is in a boat, when it is in danger and shatters in the sea, since then there is no hope for him. But when they recede from the Caput and Cauda, it is like when a boat is in danger: in such a way that a sailor can grab onto something, namely a plank, or dross, or similar things which give him a hope of escaping, and sometimes allow him to escape.

And it should be known that when the significator of a matter, or the Moon, moves towards the Caput, the malice is increased; and is greater than when it recedes from him, since his nature is to increase. And when it goes towards the Cauda, it is not entirely the ultimate malice as it is when the planet separates from it, namely less than one degree. From one degree earlier its malice is not as great as it is within one degree (even if it is great). And from one to three, it is said to be less evil, and from three to five, it is said to be even less so, and from five to seven it is said to be small, and from seven up to nine it is said to be smaller, and from nine to twelve it is said to be almost nothing.

Consideration Sixty-Two is to examine whether the Moon is void-of-course: for being void of course signifies that the matter which is quesited will hardly or never be possible to perfect or arrive to a good end. And if it is perfected, it will perfect with labour, and similarly with difficulties and sorrow, unless the Lord of the Ascendant or the significator of the matter is in very good condition: since if this is so, even if it is impeded, it will not destroy the matter entirely. Nevertheless someone can take part in certain things when the Moon is impeded, namely drinking, bouts, baths, feasts, and sand similar things. And similarly it is good to use annora, especially when she is in Scorpio, which is an oil for removing hair, which in Latin is called "*Psilotrum*" while commonly it is called "*Sconapotum*".

Consideration Sixty-Three is to examine whether the Moon is far enough away from a conjunction with malefics, that she doesn't project her rays upon the rays of a malefic, because if this is so, then it signifies good things happening for the matter which was quesited, or which is coming to be, and this will be even better if she projects her rays upon the rays of some benefic: and much more strongly if the Lord of the Ascendant or the significator of the matter is in good condition. If they are not well disposeed, the signified good will be reduced: yet not totally destroyed, for some good part of it will remain.

Consideration Sixty-Four is to examine whether the Moon is in Cancer, or in Taurus, or in Sagittarius, or in Pisces: since if she is, it signifies good in the matter at hand, if she is joined to malefics (even if she is not joined to benefics), nor does being void-of-course harm her as much in this case and being in these places as it would if she was in others - as long as she is not combust: for then these places will not profit her.

Consideration Sixty-Five is to examine whether the Lord of the seventh is impeded or not: since when he is impeded, it signifies the impediment of the quesited matter: whence you then ought to defer judgement, if you can at all, and consider and investigate in every way that you can, so that you see from where this impediment can possibly arrive: first from the conjunction of the Lord of the seventh with the planets : then from his separation from them. Similarly from the Moon, since it hardly ever happens otherwise than you finding the cause of the impediment, from which the cause arrives: and so you will be able to safely judge after this.

Consideration Sixty-Six is to examine in questions, and in all things which you intend to do, when the malefic planets threaten some evil, if the place where this threat falls is the dignity of any of the benefics; and to see then if that benefic aspects this place by a trine or a sextile aspect: since this will take away all of the evil, and annihilate it completely. If the benefic aspects from a square aspect, it will carry away some of the evil, and reduce it, even if it won't be destroyed in whole; it will perhaps be reduced by half, or a small bit less. If it aspects from opposition, it will take away even less, possibly less than one-quarter, or one-fifth, or one-sixth, or even less than one-eighth. However, if it does not aspect, the evil will occur in accordance with was threatened by the malefic impeding the place, and it will happen by means of good and just men, who will not use evil means. And perhaps it will happen because the just men will give testimony against the querent by speaking the truth against him, for which reason he will suffer harm or detriment, or a judge or ruler may judge against him for reasons of justice.

However if the place is a dignity of a malefic, the evil will come from unjust men, and men who do not employ justice or truth, but are in fact wicked men who may bring testimony against the truth; and whether the testimony is true or false, it will be of the kind I mentioned. Or it will come to him from a bad authority or judge, who is a wicked man, even though he may judge justly in the matter, there will be wickedness in him nonetheless; and the man will not be one who loves, fears, or cares about God.

Consideration Sixty-Seven is to examine in questions or in any beginnings, whether there will be an eclipse close to the question or the beginning, which is distant from the significator of the matter, or the Moon, by less than 12 degrees: since this eclipse will bring harm and evil to the querent, and to the matter which ought to have been begun, unless there is a benefic there who has dignity in that place (since then the malice is decreased). Nevertheless, if a benefic is not there, you ought to examine who aspects the place of the eclipse, and in what manner: because if benefics aspect it, they will increase the evil; if malefics aspect it, they will decrease the evil - which appears in a certain way almost miraculous.

Consideration Sixty-Eight is to examine in questions about sick people, or in the beginning of an illness, whether or not the Lord of the seventh, and the 7th house itself, are free from impediments; since if they are free from malefics, so that they are not impeded by any malefics, then the infirm person will be able to safely commit himself to the care of doctors: for the medical art will be beneficial to him. If indeed the seventh and its Lord are impeded, Ptolemy said that then the doctor is to be removed from the patient: for the medical art will not be of benefit to him, nor the care of doctors: for the seventh signifies the medical art, as Zael says: or it may signify that the illness will become chronic. You can say the same if the aforementioned impediments are present at the beginning of the care of any illness.

Consideration Sixty-Nine is to examine in questions about journeys, or in the beginning of journeys, or indeed in any other matters, whether the significators of the Ascendant and the house signifying the quesited matter, or the undertaking, or the thing to be begun, are equal in strength or debility: since you will not be able to judge confidently then. For then it will be necessary to examine the Lord of the conjunction or prevention (insofar as the matter is conjunctional or preventional), which was before the matter, which you intend to do, and you will judge according to this.

That if again the Lord of the conjunction or prevention and the Lord of the quesited matter are equal, you will not be able to judge with confidence: so return then to the Moon, and see to whom she is originally joined, and you will be able to judge according to this. And if she is not joined to any planets in the sign, or from the sign in which she was placed, you will move her from the sign in which she is placed, and see to which planet she first joins in the sign, or from the sign, in which she is set to enter after she leaves the sign in which she was placed at the time of the question or beginning - and you will judge according to this. And this is such an important topic, it is necessary for you to consider it well.

Consideration Seventy is to look at a certain hidden matter, namely one which is not well investigated by astrologers: and sometimes - in fact many times - harms them greatly; and this is, that you examine in questions, or the beginnings of things, whether the Lord of the conjunction, or prevention, which was before the question, or before the beginning, is in one of the angles of the quesited matter or beginning. Since it will then signify that the matter will be perfected, and that it will come to be, lest it is stopped by the querent, or the inceptor, or unless God resists - even if it doesn't appear through any of the other significators that it ought to be perfected.

Which, if it is not in an angle, but in a succeedent, and the other significators, namely the Lord of the Ascendant, and the Lord of the quesited matter, and similarly the Moon, or one of them assists, the matter will come to be with ease; and if it is in a cadent, the matter will hardly ever come to be, even if the other significators appear favourable. If all of them, or at least two of them are not favourable, the matter will never be perfected.

Consideration Seventy-One is to examine in a question which was made to you on any matter (or if you want to make some beginning) whether it is a journey, or something else, whether the significator falls between the Ascendant and the twelfth, since then it signifies the duration of time during which the matter ought to come to be: and if there was made, how long it ought to last, and this duration of time will be days or hours. However, if it is between the twelfth and the tenth it will signify half-weeks. If it is between the tenth and the seventh it will signify months or weeks. However, if it is between the seventh and the fourth it will signify years. And if it is between the fourth and the Ascendant, it will signify halves of years.

Consideration Seventy-Two is to examine when a question is made on a journey, and in the beginning of any journey, if the Moon is then impeded, for if she is, the journey should not be made at that time. If he must make the journey, make the planet who impedes the Moon the Lord of the Ascendant.

Consideration Seventy-Three is to examine in questions, whether the question signifies good or evil, and if good is signified, and benefics aspect the significator of the question, or the Moon: that good will be augmented. However, if, malefics aspect it, the good will be reduced. If evil is signified, and benefics aspect it, that evil will be reduced. However, if malefics aspect the significator, or the Moon, the evil will be increased, and made worse.

Consideration Seventy-Four is to examine whether a significator is in its first station, wanting to go retrograde: since then it signifies disobedience, and that the matter which is quesited will not come to be, nor will it be perfected, even if it appears that it ought to be perfected. And if there is any work or building undertaken at this time, it will not be completed.

And if such a significator is so disposeed that it is under the earth at that time, the building will not be erected, so that if it is said that the building will be erected in 30 years, it will still not be completed then. And if it is erected a small bit, it will not be fully erected for another 30 years. And if it is not completed then, it will not be completed up until 90 years from the day of its first beginning; and if it is not completed then, it will never be completed, unless its ownership was transferred to strangers, and not the usual owners.

And when it is in its second station, wanting to go direct, it signifies that the matter will be perfected, yet with delay, complications, duress, difficulties, effort, and great worry.

And if any building is begun at this time, it will be completed, even if it won't be completed as quickly as was believed at the beginning: as long as the significator is not under the earth: since then the person who begins the building will not perfect it, nor will it even be elevated much above the ground. And understand this - that a planet in its second station when it wants to go direct signifies the fitness, renewal, positive direction, and strength of any given matter: but in the first station when the planet wants to go retrograde it signifies dissolution, difficulty, and the destruction of any given matter. Understand all of this well, for these things will very often pass through your hands.

Consideration Seventy-Five is to examine whether the Moon in any matter, which anyone intends to do, is impeded by any of the planets (for whatever kind of question it is, and whatever kind of beginning); since whatever is done or undertaken at this time will be impeded. However, if the Moon is in a good place from the Ascendant, so that it aspects the Ascendant by a praiseworthy aspect, namely a trine or sextile: and that planet which impedes the Moon aspects the Ascendant by one of the aforementioned aspects, the impediment will be reduced, and it will not harm as much: and may be destroyed entirely, insofar as the impeding planet is well disposeed - so that he is not cadent from the angles, or from the Ascendant, as I said: nor in his own fall, namely in the seventh from his own house; for at this time he will introduce more fear, than he will cause harm.

Zael appeared to want to say, that if an impeding malefic was cadent from the Ascendant, or was retrograde, then it would send forth fear from the part of the querent, or the person making the beginning. However I remember that I always feared the impediment of the Moon more than all other impediments, nor do I remember seeing a good end of any matter, in which the Moon was impeded: for in journeys, if the journey was to war, I feared for the person of the one travelling to it. However, if it was to do business, or to anything similar, I feared difficulties, anger and sorrow on the journey, with the loss of substance.

Consideration Seventy-Six Consideration is to examine from which planet the Moon is separating, and to whom she is joining: since he from whom she separates signifies that which already was. He to whom she is joining signifies that which is going to be, as is said elsewhere. So that if she separates from a malefic and joins a benefic, it signifies that which already was, was not good, in fact it was an evil matter, and impeded the querent; and that which is going to be, will be good, and is a matter from which the querent will rejoice and will be useful to him. But if she separates from a benefic and joins a malefic, the matter will be good from the beginning, but the end will be evil. If she separates from a benefic, and joins a benefic, the matter was good, is good, and its end will be praised. If indeed she separates from a malefic, and joins another malefic, the matter was bad, and is bad, and its end will be bad.

Consideration Seventy-Seven is to examine whether the Lord of the Ascendant of any question, or any other matter, or the Moon, is in opposition to its own house - that is the Moon being in Capricorn, Mercury in Sagittarius or Pisces, Venus in Scorpio or Aries, Sun in Aquarius, Mars in Taurus or Libra, Jupiter in Gemini or Virgo, and Saturn in Cancer or Leo. Since then the Lord of the question or any other matter, will be averse to the purpose which was quesited, or what was being done, nor will the matter be something in which he delights, or which he strives to perfect: and it will appear more likely that he will not want to perfect the matter, than that he wants to perfect it, or to have it come to be.

Consideration Seventy-Eight is to examine the sign which signifies the quesited matter. The first signifies the person. The second signifies substance. The third signifies brothers. The fourth signifies fathers etc. as was said above in the Tractate on the Twelve Houses. And observe its house, and according to what it shows you about the signified matter, and according to the thing to be judged you will be able to estimate each and every thing which I told you, with them all having been diligently inspected.

Consideration Seventy-Nine is to examine whether a significator, or the Moon is joined to a benefic or malefic planet, whether by conjunction or by aspect. And you must diligently investigate this, since the bodily conjunction of the Sun is the greatest misfortune which can befall a planet.

Consideration Eighty is to examine in what sign the significator of the quesited matter is in from its own house, whether it is in the same sign, or the second, or the third, or the fourth, or the fifth, or the sixth, or the seventh, or the eighth, or the ninth, or the tenth, or the eleventh, or the twelfth. Since according to what is signified by that sign in which it is from its own house, according to that you will judge, just as you judge on other planets placed in any of the houses from the Ascendant.

Consideration Eighty-One is to examine whether a significator is in an angle, or a succeedent, or a cadent, since the closer a significator is to the line of an angle, the stronger it will be. And the more remote he is from the line of an angle, the less strong he will be: and so too in succeedents. And the closer a planet is to the line of a cadent house, the more he will be debilitated. And the more remote he is from this line, the less he will be debilitated.

Consideration Eighty-Two Consideration is to inspect whether the significator of any matter accepts disposition from one of the planets, whether it is a benefic or a malefic: since if he receives disposition from a benefic, it signifies good: and this will be all the better, if that benefic is in good condition and well disposeed. However, if it is not well disposeed, it will be less than this. If it is impeded, it will be even less than this again. If it receives disposition from a malefic, it signifies the contrary: and this more strongly, if that malefic is impeded. However, if it isn't impeded, it will be something less than this. If it is well disposeed, it will reduce even more of that malice.

Consideration Eighty-Three is to examine whether benefics and malefics are equal in a question or in any other matter: since then they will not signify any conclusive judgement for good or evil, nor will the matter in question bring in profit or harm.

Consideration Eighty-Four is to examine if benefics are stronger than malefics in questions than, since if both are strong, and the benefics prevail in strength, they will signify some kind of good thing, almost a mediocre kind; if malefics prevail, they will signify some form of evil, almost a mediocre kind.

Consideration Eighty-Five is to examine whether the Part of Fortune falls in a good place in the figure, or in a bad place – namely, whether it falls in an angle or a succeedent, or in a cadent. And see how it is aspected, and by whom, whether by a benefic or by a malefic; and whether or not it is received by that planet which aspects him. Since questions sometimes appear good, and the Part of Fortune falls in a bad place, which greatly debilitates a question, and makes it less useful, for the querent will hope for good from the matter, and it will not turn out in the manner that the question appeared to show. For the good which the question signified will be reduced on account of the Part of Fortune being placed in a bad place of the figure, or joined to a malefic planet. And sometimes the question will appear to threaten evil, and predict evil, nevertheless if the Part of Fortune is in a good place in the figure, and is joined to a benefic planet who receives it, by body or by aspect, this evil will be reduced, and not so much of what the question appeared to threaten will happen to the querent.

Consideration Eighty-Six is to examine in every questions, or journey, or nativity, or any other beginning, whether one of the malefics aspects the significator; and examine if both are retrograde, and cadent, and peregrine, and in signs contrary to their nature; for then they will cause such contrariety, and such harm, that it could never be avoided, nor will anyone be able to avert it, unless God intervenes. And it will be almost a great miracle, if he whom the danger threatens manages to escape. And if anyone is born with the matter appearing this way, he will be poor forever, and a beggar, and lacking food for his stomach, and will never be able to exert himself to escape this indigence. And if a house is built at this time, one shall never rejoice in it, nor collect money which would be of benefit to him; and contrary things will frequently befall him, by which his goods will be destroyed, disappear and come to nothing. And always when such a man believes that his business is going better, and approaching a good and desired end, at that time it will be more likely to be destroyed and frustrated, unless divine goodness interposes itself.

Consideration Eighty-Seven is to examine the ninth-part of the Moon, which is something very much to be observed: since it often impedes the astrologer, so that he cannot understand the truth well, and sometimes errs in his judgements, not knowing what caused his mistake.

Consideration Eighty-Eight is to consider the planet from which the Moon separates, and how it is disposeed, since it has the signification of what already was, as said above. And see which planet she is now joined to in such a way that there is not more than 5 minutes between them: since this signifies what presently is, according to how this planet is disposeed. Also examine whose conjunction she seeks, or to whom she will join first after separating from the planet that she is now joined to, since this signifies what is to come in the future for the matter, according to how the planet is disposeed.

Consideration Eighty-Nine is to examine the twelfth-part of the Moon, which is something very much to be observed in many judgements, indeed more so than the aforementioned ninth-parts, since greater danger can arise from both it, and the most precise and uncommon considerations of astrologers, which is often poorly observed by many, more so on account of laziness than ignorance; from which they sometimes fall into disgrace among laymen on account of their fear of labour which they do not want to sustain.

Consideration Ninety is to examine in questions, or nativities, or journeys, or any other matters or beginnings, whether the Lord of the house where the Sun is, and the Lord of the house where the Moon is: and also the Lord of the Ascendant, are oriental and in angles (even if this rarely happens), and mutually aspect each other from good places, and from good and praiseworthy aspects - namely trines or sextiles: since then they signify the greatest fortune and the greatest good, and the ultimate progress in every matter, whatever kind of matter it may be. If they are not all disposeed in this manner, but only some of them, it will signify good according to the portion which are so disposeed.

Consideration Ninety-One is to examine in questions, or nativities, or in any other matters whatever they may be, whether Mars is in any angle of their figure, especially if the angles are fixed signs: and especially if Scorpio is the 1st house: for then Mars will destroy all the good which is signified by that question, or by that figure. And if it is not totally destroyed, it will be much impeded and diminished: unless perhaps Jupiter aspects Mars from a trine or sextile aspect, since then the evil of Mars will be reduced and mitigated, on account of the aspect of Jupiter- however this will be according to how Jupiter is disposeed in his own strength or debility.

Consideration Ninety-Two is to examine in nativities or general questions, or in questions about death; and see if the Lord of the house of death, or the significator of death, or the Lord of the house where the Lord of the house of death is placed, moves towards the significator of the native or querent, or the significator to him: since the planet so disposeed is made the killer, and kills whether he is a benefic or a malefic, whether reception intervenes or not.

Consideration Ninety-Three is to examine if there is a question on a matter which someone wishes to seek from another, or on a thing which he wishes to dig up, or extract from a concealed or hidden location, whether the significator of the querent or of the quesited matter, aspects Saturn, or is joined to him by body, or if Saturn is in the house of the quesited matter, since then what the querent asked about will hardly be done, and only with difficulty will the hidden matter be extracted from the place in which it is in, and with the greatest labour and complication, and with delay, even if it appears that the quesited matter ought to be done quickly, and with ease. And in many cases, after the querent has thought the matter to be arranged, it will be impeded and delayed, more than the querent himself believed.

Consideration Ninety-Four is to examine in questions or in other beginnings, whether the significator of the quesited matter is cadent from the Ascendant, or from the other angles, or from the house of the quesited matter, or from its Lord, or is retrograde, or in bad condition with the Sun, or if there is a planet in fall in the house of the quesited matter, or a retrograde planet, or in bad condition with the Sun, or in a bad place from him, or in bad disposition with him, since these things signify the impediment of the matter, even if the question otherwise appears good.

Consideration Ninety-Five is to consider whether the planets signifying the quesited matter are joined to each other: since this signifies the perfection of the matter. Nevertheless, don't finish judging the perfection of the matter unless you examine and consider well the nature of the sign in which they are joined, and whether it is of the nature of the planets, since if it is of their nature, the matter will be perfected with ease, and with joy for the querent. If the planets do not concord in nature with the sign, the matter will not be perfected with ease; in fact it will hardly or never be perfected. And it is perfected, it will only happen with the greatest labour and solicitude of the querent: even if it otherwise appears that it ought to be perfected easily. And if they concord in nature, the matter will come to be with little labour, yet not very easily.

Consideration Ninety-Six is to examine in questions which appear to show that the quesited matter ought to perfect, whether the significator of the matter and the Moon are in angles, and are both removed from the cusps of the angles by more than 25 degrees: since this signifies that the matter will not perfect, even if it appears to be arranged. If only one of them (namely the significator of the matter, or the Moon) is removed from an angle as was said, and the other is not removed, the matter will be perfected, even if it will be with difficulty, unless it happens to be a journey, since this will nonetheless be perfected, even if the significators are removed from the angles.

Consideration Ninety-Seven is to consider in what clime you take up a question: since there will be diverse judgements according to the diverse ascensions of climes and regions. For there is not the same order in ascensions or elevations of the signs in one clime as there is in another: nor is there the same Ascendant in one region as there is in another. Whence unless you guard yourself well against this, you might err in your judgements, which would be bad, improper, and very reprehensible. For the signs are raised up one way in the first clime, another in the second, another in the third, another in the fourth, another in the fifth, another in the sixth and another in the seventh.

And from this you ought to guard yourself well against these differences, lest you fall into error in your judgements. Since in whatever direction you travel from one region to another, whether from east to west, or from west to east, or from south to north, or from north to south, by 53 miliaria, and although it is barely detectable, one Ascendant will differ from another by 1 degree, from the east to the west (and in the opposite direction) according to longitude, and from the south to the north (and in the opposite direction), and by a certain amount which is barely more, but still perceptible.

But perhaps some fools in tunics may rise up and say "If judgements diversify according to the location of the region, therefore they are false" – such men are ignorant of what is hidden. Nor are these men to be responded to, nor is there any debating with them, for they have no discernment, they do not understand, they do not believe, and nothing is acceptable to them. Yet there are certain men amongst them who have discernment and good understanding, and with these men you will be able to deliberate well with (even if there are few men like this) - one of which was the venerable brother Conradus Brixiensis of the Order of Preachers, whom I found to be very discerning, and to have a good understanding of all truths, and operating by way of it, who, on account of his profound knowledge was made bishop of Cesenas.

Indeed these things which I have said to you can cause the astrologer to err, and I fear that they have made some men err sometimes; since a judgement cannot be given except according to the Ascendant and the other houses: whence if the Ascendants differ, it must to be necessary that the judgements also differ. And so it is necessary that you do not fear work, nor laziness conquers your concern, but that you make it so that you have tables of the elevations of the signs for every clime in which you find yourself, and for every region, whether they are made by you or someone else, by exact reckoning, or by such a method of inference from one region to another that you are not deceived.

However it is more difficult to find the difference from clime to clime than from region to region (and this is according to longitude). Since if you have tables of the elevations of the signs in some region from the east to the west, you can make an inference and have elevations of the signs from that region to another in the direction which you wanted to travel, whether towards the east, or towards the west from that region, according to that clime, by way of taking the differences as I just mentioned to you; but according to the diverse climes you could make such an inference so easily.

Consideration Ninety-Eight is to examine in questions if that which is signified by any question that it ought to come to be, is signified by planets through a bodily conjunction, or by aspect, or by transfer of light. Since if the significators are conjunct by body, or by aspect, the matter will be perfected and come to be, by the querent and by the quesited, without the interposing of anybody else. If indeed they are not conjunct by body, or by aspect, but one of the planets transfers light between them, the matter will come to be through the hands of legates, or someone else, or by some people who interpose themselves in it, and lead the matter to effect through a person or thing signified by the house whose Lord was the mediator.

For if it was the Lord of the 2nd house who transfers light, the matter will come to be by expenses, or by another manner of interposing the querent's money. If it is the Lord of the third, it will come to be by the querent's brothers (if he has them), or by one of those things which are signified by the 3rd house. If it is the Lord of the fourth, it will come to be through the father, or one of those things signified by the 4th house. If it is in the 5th house it will come to be through a son, or one of those things signified by the 5th house. If it is the Lord of the sixth, it will come to be through slaves, or by one of those things signified by the 6th house. If it is the Lord of the seventh, it will come to be through the wife, or through one of those things signified by the 7th house. If it is the Lord of the eighth it will come to be through death, or through the wife's money, or through one of those things signified by the 8th house. If it is the Lord of the ninth it will come to be through a bishop, or a religious person, or one of those things signified by the 9th house. If it is the Lord of the tenth it will come to be through the king or an authority, or one of those things which are signified by the 10th house. If it is the Lord of the eleventh it will come to be through a friend, or by one of those things signified by the 11th house. If it is the Lord of the twelfth it will come to be through a hidden enemy, or by one of those things signified by the 12th house.

Consideration Ninety-Nine is to examine in questions or nativities, or any other beginnings, what is going to be from them; since sometimes it will appear that some matter ought to come to be, and to be wholly perfected, but is will not be wholly completed, but partially, and sometimes the matter will be perfected in whole: and sometimes it will neither be perfected in whole, nor in part - and why does this happen? Whence astrologers are blamed and blasphemed, and they don't know how to explain themselves, being ignorant as to the reason why this happens; and this is an arduous, difficult and most precise investigation: and this is the reason why our ancients did not involve themselves with this; since it would be a very great labour - all of them except for the most honourable predecessor himself, Albumasar (who is to be imitated in all things), who said more on this than the rest of the astrologers said. And I found his judgements, as much the particular judgements as the ones on revolutions, to be more effective than the others, and more deserving of been striven for, even if Ptolemy (who was the elucidator of this science) is found more to be emulated in general judgements than the rest of the astrologers. And it is this (the consideration of certain fixed stars which are found in certain signs) which I spoke about, of which I will make mention of to you in the Tractate on Revolutions, and in the Tractate on Nativities, and I will touch somewhat on these things there.

Nevertheless I will still name those here, which will fall into your hands more often, and lest you might put off having knowledge of them for too long: of which some are fortunate by nature, or of the nature of the benefic planets (and those which are of the nature of benefics will perfect matter which do not seem like they ought to be perfected based off of the significations of the planets). Certain others are of the nature of the malefics, and these are those which do not permit matters to be perfected by what is signified through the planets - of which stars (those that are of the nature of malefics), certain ones are found in ever sign.

Of which two are in the head of Aries, namely at 13 degrees 45 minutes. Another is at 14 degrees 45 minutes, and these are northerly, and are of the nature of Saturn and Mars.

In Taurus there are six stars at 9 degrees 55 minutes which are called the Pleiades (they all however are said to be one star), and they are all of the nature of Mars and the Moon. And another is at 13 degrees of the same sign. And another is at 13 degrees 2 minutes. And another is at 14 degrees 45 minutes and this is called "*Diabolus*". And there is another at 15 degrees of the same which is called "*Caput Diaboli*". And another is in the belly of Taurus, at 19 degrees 15 minutes, which is called "*Aldebaran*", all of which are of the nature of Mars and Mercury.

In Gemini there is one at 8 degrees which is called "*Humerus Canis*", which is of the nature of Mars and Saturn. And another at 10 degrees 15 minutes which is of the nature of Mars and is called Bellatrix. Another is at 17 degrees 55 minutes. Another is at 18 degrees 52 minutes, which is called "*Malefica*" and is of the nature of the Sun and Mars.

Another is in the 1st degree and 3rd minute of Cancer, which is called "*Camelus*", and is of the nature of Saturn and the Moon. And another is at 7 degrees 55 minutes. And another is at 13 degrees and is of the nature of Sun and Moon, which is called "*Occidens Camelum*". And there is another in the same degree which is of the nature of Saturn and is called "*Pes Canis*". And there is another at 17 degrees 55 minutes, which is also of the nature of Saturn.

In Leo there is one of them at 15 degrees 55 minutes which is of the nature of Saturn.

In Virgo there are two stars, one of which is at 7 degrees 11 minutes, and is of the nature of Mars. And the other is at 15 degrees and is of the nature of Saturn.

In Libra there is one star at 26 degrees of the nature of Saturn.

In Scorpio there are three stars, one of which is in the first degree and third minute. And another at eight degrees 7 minutes. And another at 9 degrees, all of which are of the nature of Mars.

In Sagittarius there are two small stars, one of which is at 19 degrees 2 minutes. Another is at 21 degrees 1 minute, and both are of the nature of Saturn.

In Capricorn there are two stars which are said to be evil, one of which is at 27 degrees 2 minutes. And another is at 29 degrees 5 minutes, and both are of the nature of Saturn.

In Aquarius there is one star at 9 degrees 4 minutes, which is of the nature of Mars and Saturn.

In Pisces there is one star at 4 degrees 7 minutes, which is of the nature of Mars and Mercury.

All the aforementioned stars are harmers and malevolent, and impeding and destroying of matters after they ought to be perfected, and prohibit them so that they are not perfected; whence it is always necessary for you to avoid them in all of your actions if at all possible (which is very difficult). And even if I have made mention of them to you here, you will find a better discussion of this below in the Tractate on the Revolutions Of The Years, if health and life be granted to me.

Consideration One Hundred is to examine in your actions the fixed stars helping matters so that they come to be perfected. These stars are as follows:

In Aries there are two stars, one of which is at 15 degrees 6 minutes, which is of the nature of Jupiter and Venus, whose nature is to assist and benefit. Another is at 16 degrees 1 minute, and is of the nature of Jupiter.

In Taurus there are three stars, one of which is at 1 degree 3 minutes. And another is at 8 degrees 7 minutes. Another is at 9 degrees 1 minute, all of which are of the nature of Venus.

In Gemini there are two stars, one of which is at 19 degrees 2 minutes. And another is at 21 degrees 3 minutes, which are both of the nature of Jupiter, and are of the second magnitude.

In Cancer there are again another two stars which are said to be good, one of which is at 27 degrees 2 minutes. And the other is at 29 degrees 4 minutes, and both are of the nature of Jupiter.

In Leo there is one star at 9 degrees 4 minutes, which is of the nature of Jupiter and Venus.

In Virgo there is one star at 4 degrees 7 minutes which is of the nature of Venus and the Moon.

In Libra there are two stars of the nature of Jupiter and Venus, one of which is at 13 degrees 45 minutes, and the other is at 14 degrees and 45 minutes.

In Scorpio there are four stars, one of which is at 9 degrees 55 minutes. And another is at 13 degrees 1 minute. And another is at 14 degrees 45 minutes. And the fourth is at 19 degrees 15 minutes, all of which are of the nature of Jupiter.

In Sagittarius there are two stars, one of which is at 10 degrees 15 minutes. And the other is at 7 degrees 55 minutes, and both are of the nature of Jupiter.

In Capricorn there are three stars, one of which is at 2 degrees 3 minutes. And another is at 7 degrees 55 minutes. And another is at 17 degrees 55 minutes. All of which are of the nature of Jupiter.

And in Aquarius there is one star, which is at 15 degrees 55 minutes and is of the nature of Jupiter.

In Pisces there are two stars, one of which is at 7 degrees 11 minutes and is of the nature of Venus. And another is at 14 degrees 59 minutes, and is of the nature of Jupiter.

Whence always if you see the significator of a matter corporeally joined with one of the aforementioned helping fixed stars, you will predict good things, and for the increase of the matter, and a good end.

Consideration One Hundred And One is to examine in nativities or questions, which planet is the killer or cutter of life or years, or the prohibitor of the matter so that it does not come to be or be perfected; since he is the planet who destroys the natives life and kills him, and prohibits matters from coming to be, and destroys them, who is stronger by multitude of dignities or powers, in nativities or questions, or the beginning of some matter. Messala concealed this, and it seems that he did it well, since he only revealed this to a certain student of his (along with a certain other very useful secret) and this arrogant student appropriated it for himself.

After you have perceived the planet who is the prohibitor, or destroyer, or killer, see to whom the Lord of the Ascendant or the Moon (who is the participator in every matter) is joined, just as is said to you elsewhere, or the Lord of any quesited matter, undertaking, or beginning, and the Lord of the house containing the Moon, namely one of them, or a few of them: since if it is joined to a retrograde or combust planet, or one cadent from the Ascendant or the angles, or to any malefic which doesn't receive it, or another malefics star, which is made malefic by malefics who cut off the light of the significator, the matter is destroyed and is not perfected, and thus the years of the native will be cut off and diminished and he will not live long. Moreover if the Lord of the Ascendant, or the Moon, or the Lord of the quesited matter is joined to a planet which is free from the conjunction of malefics, and is safe as much as it is in itself, but is joined to another planet who is impeded by any of the aforementioned impediments - the matter will be destroyed, even after it appears to be and is believed to be arranged so that it ought to be perfected; and the life of the native will be cut off, when it appears and is well believed that he ought to live. And this will still happen if it is not conjunct with the cutter, as long as the significator or the Moon is impeded, just as was said, by one of the aforementioned impediments.

Consideration One Hundred and Two is to examine and consider in matters which are signified, how the significations which they signify ought to be discovered, and from which significators they ought to be extracted. For it is extracted from the significator of the querent, and from the significator of the quesited matter itself. Whence if the significator of the querent and the significator of the quesited matter are joined, and likewise the Moon, it signifies that the complete effecting of the matter; if indeed they are not joined it signifies the contrary. And from the conjunction of the significators you ought to know why the question arose, and through the Lord of the house in which the conjunction was made, you ought to know what will be quesited: for if it is benefic, it will be about something good - according to the condition and significations of this benefic, and the house in which it is placed, and the significations of the Lord of this house, and the place in which this Lord is found. However, if the planet is a malefic, it signifies that it will be about something bad - according to the condition and significations of this malefic, and the house which he is in, and the significations of the Lord of this house, and again of the place in which the Lord of this house is in.

For if the Lord aspects the house, or the exaltation Lord aspects the house, or the Lord of any of the two lesser dignities, or if any of them were to make a transfer of light, the reason why the question was made will be known. If it is not known by any of these planets, it will not be determinately known why this question was made, but it will be for a reason which is not yet known; and from the aspects of the benefics or malefics it will be known of what kind of effecting the matter will be.

Consideration One Hundred and Three is to examine in nativists or universal questions, in which house the Part of Fortune is found. Since the fortune or wealth of the native or querent will be from the significations of this house, if the Part is well disposeed that is. If it is badly disposeed, it signifies that these things will be the cause of misfortune and harm.

Consideration One Hundred and Four is to examine in nativities or in general questions, or any other matter, whether the significator of the querent is found in the seventh from its own house, or in opposition to the Lord of the Ascendant, since this will not signify profit for him from the significations of that house, but rather harm and expenses

Consideration One Hundred and Five is to examine in nativities or in general questions, whether an unfortunate malefic is found in the seventh, since this signifies that the native or querent will not rejoice with wives, nor with lovers, nor with associates, but will always have quarrels and malevolence with them; and rarely will things turn otherwise for him from these matters.

Consideration One Hundred and Six is to examine in nativities or in general questions, or in any other matters, if a fortunate, unimpeded, benefic is in the seventh; since this signifies that the native or querent will be fortunate in having good wives, good associates; but nevertheless he will have many rivals, and many who hate him, both with reason and without reason, and more likely from jealousy than from his own fault, so that he will hardly be able to perfect what he wants, and will only perfect the thing with labour and perseverance.

Consideration One Hundred and Seven is to examine in nativities or general questions, or other ones, whether Mars is in the second from the Ascendant, or in the tenth, and well disposeed; for it signifies that the native or querent will have fortune in those things which are operated by iron, or fire, or consuming, as are workshops, furnaces, and similar things: taverns, inns, and so on. However, if it is a malefic or badly disposeed, you can judge the contrary.

Consideration One Hundred and Eight is to examine if one of the planets aspect two houses, since its strength will be in that house in which the planet has more dignity, and more fortitudes, and it will more greatly help this house and what it signifies.

Consideration One Hundred and Nine is to examine in nativities or in general questions, if the Lord of the 5th house is impeded in the seventh; since this has the signification that the native will not be fortunate in banquets, and many disagreeable things will befall him at them, and worse and more detestable dishes will be served to him compared to the other guests - and fouler deserts, and worse wreaths than any of the others, and the wreaths may not even be given to him unless he first seeks them out, even if they are given to almost all the others. And the same will befall him with respect to clothing and other ornaments of the body.

Consideration One Hundred and Ten is to examine in nativities and in general questions, whether the Ascendant is Scorpio: since he who has this Ascendant will not have good fortune in the Roman Church, on account of Cancer, the exaltation of Jupiter, which naturally signifies clerics, which will then be the 9th house which signifies churches, and Jupiter being the enemy of Mars, who is the Lord of the Ascendant.

Consideration One Hundred and Eleven is to examine in nativities and in general questions, and indeed in other questions, and especially on lawsuits and disputes, whether the Cauda Draconis is in the seventh: since this has the signification of the detriment and voiding of enemies, and increasing of the native or querent - since the Caput will then be in the first. If the Cauda is in the eighth, it signifies the voiding and diminution of the wealth and goods of the enemies, and this too in the seventh: and the increase of the goods and wealth of the native or querent, since the Caput will then be in the second. When it is in the third it signifies the voiding of brothers. In the fourth, the voiding of the father. In the fifth the voiding of children. In the sixth, the voiding of servants. In the seventh and eighth, what I said to you above. In the ninth, the voiding of journeys. In the tenth, the voiding of men. In the eleventh, the voiding of friends. In the twelfth the voiding of large animals. And in each one of the houses it also signifies the voiding of the other significations of this house; and Saturn and Mars do the same, but somewhat less than what the Cauda does. And other malefics will void the aforementioned significations, however something less than that which Saturn and Mars do, unless they themselves are the significators - since then much of their malice will be reduced.

Consideration One Hundred and Twelve is to examine the Ascendant in nativities or questions; for if their Ascendant is Virgo; and Mercury is in good condition, or at least that he is not malefic, it signifies that if the native or querent will pursue the medical art he will be fortunate in being a doctor, and things will go well for him in his medical practice or cures, but he will be unfortunate in his salary and profiting by the art of medicine, since those to whom he will offer his services will be unwilling to compensate him for his work, and he will hardly be able to go after them as he ought to, aside from a small number of them, and he will also be unfortunate in his lawsuits. And if he pursues law he will be unfortunate in his advocacy, and he will be despised by worthless men, not to mention others; nor will his words be heard, and even if he speaks useful words or words of wisdom, they will be counted as nothing by those who hear them; for those for whose benefit he speaks will instead hear a fool and an idiot, even though there will be few men who know how to improve on his speech. And for the most part in things he involves himself in, it will be unlucky for him, and men will be inimical to him for no reason, and will speak ill of him, ignorant of their reasons.

But it will be different if the Ascendant is Taurus or Pisces, and Jupiter, Venus, and Mercury are all together in the Ascendant, or if Jupiter and Venus are in the Suns Zamini (regardless of what the Ascendant is); as in this case he will be treated like a prophet, and his words will flow like honey, even though he may say foolish things publicly.

Consideration One Hundred and Thirteen is to examine in nativities or questions, whether any malefic is impeded in the ninth, who does not have dignity there; since this signifies that the native or querent will be accused and found guilty, with cause and without cause. If indeed there is an unimpeded benefic there, and this more strongly if it has dignity there, it signifies that he will be praised and honoured, both with cause and without cause.

Consideration One Hundred and Fourteen is to examine in nativities or questions, whether the Lord of the eighth house is a benefic and is in the second; since this signifies that the native or querent will acquire wealth and gain profit from the goods of the dead, and enemies, and wives, and this more strongly if the planet is not impeded, or if it has dignity there. However, if it is a malefic, it signifies the diminution of the natives or querent's substance unless perhaps it has dignity there. But if it has dignity there and it otherwise well disposeed, and in good condition, it will cause little or no harm. If indeed it does not have dignity there, and is otherwise in bad condition, it signifies the total destruction of the wealth, and the loss of it in every way.

Consideration One Hundred and Fifteen is to examine in nativities or questions if the 8th house or its Lord are impeded; since this signifies that the native or querent will be harmed by the reason of the death of some woman, whose dowry he will have to return, with harm to himself.

Consideration One Hundred and Sixteen is to examine in nativities or questions, which of the houses are impeded or made unfortunate, or which house Lords are impeded or made unfortunate: for this signifies that on account of those things which are signified by the house in question, the native or querent will be harmed. If any of them, or their Lords are fortunate, good and useful things will happen to the native on account of the significations of that house.

Consideration One Hundred and Seventeen is to examine in nativities or questions, and see in which of them the Cauda Draconis is in the fourth: since this signifies that whatever the native or querent acquires or earns will be destroyed, and come to nothing, And in whatever other house the Cauda is placed, it signifies harm and detriment to come to the native in those matters and from those matters which are signified by that house.

Consideration One Hundred and Eighteen is to examine in nativities or questions, in which house there is a fortunate, strong, well disposeed, and not impeded benefic: since it will signify that the native or querent will profit and have good fortune from these matters, and out of these matters, which are signified by the house in question. And in whichever house a malefic is placed, the native will lose, and his misfortune will come from matters signified by that house.

Consideration One Hundred and Nineteen is to examine in nativities or questions if the Lord of the 2nd house is in the seventh, and the seventh is Aries, Scorpio, Capricorn, or Aquarius: since this will have the signification that the enemies of the native or querent will freely take away his goods. And if he has a partnership with someone, this person will rob the native of whatever he contributed to the partnership. Similarly his wife or lover will steal anything that is convenient for them to steal; unless the Lord of the Ascendant is in trine or sextile aspect with the Lord of the seventh, or in any of the other aspects with reception.

Consideration One Hundred and Twenty is to examine in nativities or questions, whether any Lord of any of these eight houses, namely: the third, fourth, fifth, sixth, ninth, tenth, eleventh, or twelfth - is in the 7th house: since whichever one of them is in it, will be inimical to the native or querent, unless perfect reception intervenes from a good aspect, trine namely, or sextile. However, if it is by square or opposition, with reception, it will reduce the evil; however it will not totally destroy it. If it is the Lord of the third, his brothers will be inimical to him. If it is the Lord of the fourth, his father will be inimical to him. If it is the Lord of the fifth his children will be inimical to him. If it is the Lord of the sixth his slaves will be inimical to him. If it is the Lord of the ninth religious people will be inimical to him, and they will oppose him and speak ill of him, and he will not entrust things to them to be perfected. If it is the Lord of the tenth kings, nobles, the wealthy, and the powerful will be inimical to him, nor will he profit with them or from their occasion; indeed he will lose just as much as from another party, or even more. However this will be worse for him with the powerful. And even if sometimes one or more appear favourable to him, nevertheless evil will be shown to him by one of the others, or perhaps by many, so that if the others bequeath him something in a letter, they will recover it in time. And it may happen that a powerful person will expel him from the city on account of the offences he will commit through his taking of a part in the household or a place at the table which a powerful person will appear to offer him; and he will lose the services which he will provide to the powerful or to the general public of the city, or to magnates, and for the most part they will be counted for nothing. If it is the Lord of the 11th he will not have friends who love him, unless on account of his usefulness to them, even if they feign being his friends; for indeed they will promise him much, but will serve him very little, or not at all. However, if it is Lord of the twelfth he will not be able to trust anyone, and if he gives someone anything in deposit they will deny it, and will take part of it for themselves, nor will they reinstate it, even if they are religious, unless perhaps if they are forced.

Consideration One Hundred and Twenty-One is to examine in nativities or questions, whether the Moon is in the eighth, and the Lord of the Ascendant is retrograde in the Ascendant, the second, or the twelfth, since this signifies that the native or querent will not have good fortune in dice games, nor will the dice speak well to him.

Consideration One Hundred and Twenty-Two is to examine in nativities or questions, whether the Part of Fortune is in the first ten degrees of the 4th house, with the Caput Draconis, the Moon, Venus, and Jupiter, and these are direct; since this will signify that the native or querent will acquire an immense sum of money underground. If it is in the second ten degrees, with two of them, he will acquire it, but not in as great a quantity; he will perhaps acquire half as much, or around a half. But if it is in the last ten degrees of the mentioned house, and is only with one of the planets, he will acquire less again; yet he will still acquire a good quantity, perhaps a quarter of it, or perhaps close to a quarter of it. If the Part of Fortune is here alone, and is free from the aspects of malefics, he will acquire less again; for perhaps he will acquire one-sixteenth or less. If indeed none of these significators are there, he will not acquire it, nor anything out of it at all.

If the Sun then aspects this place by a trine or sextile aspect, and this aspect is closer to the first ten degrees than the other aforementioned significators, the treasure will be raw gold. If the Moon is closer, it will be silver. If Jupiter is closer, the treasure will be made up of diverse things, namely gold, silver, and similar things. If Venus is closer, it will be pearls or women's jewellery for the most part. If Mercury is closer it will be coins with sculpted images. But if they are retrograde, it signifies that he will be shown the money, but will not acquire it for himself. But if one is retrograde, and the other is direct, he will acquire it in part, according to how many of them are direct. If the Lord of the 8th house then aspects the Lord of the Ascendant by a square aspect, or from opposition, the discoverer will die because of the treasure. If it aspects from a trine or a sextile it signifies that he will fall seriously ill, but will not die from it. If the Cauda in the place of the Caput, he will find it, but it will be taken away from him; or being led by ignorance and not knowing what he has found, he will give it away for nothing. If the Moon is then separating from the Lord of the Ascendant, and joining a malefic who impedes her, he who is first given that money by the person who found it, will not get any perceptible utility from it, nor will it benefit him much. And if in addition Mars or the Lord of the eighth house then aspects the Lord of the Ascendant, the discoverer of the treasure will be killed by those who take it from him. If Mars and Saturn are in the place of Jupiter and Venus, the treasure will be ore, or copper, or lead, or other things of little value. If the Lord of the Ascendant is with them, or aspecting them by any aspect, he who finds the treasure will be wearied from whatever the treasure is, whether dear or precious, or of low quality.

Consideration One Hundred and Twenty-Three is to examine whether the Sun and Moon are conjunct in one and the same minute according to longitude and according to latitude, and one of the benefics is in the Ascendant, namely by fifteen minutes above or below the line of the cusp; since this signifies that the native or querent will be fortunate in acquiring of much wealth, and in its accumulation, since a benefic will then be on the Ascendant. If the luminaries are then joined together in the same minute according to longitude, but not according to latitude, and their distance, namely from one to the other, is 15 minutes or less, his fortune will be acquiring wealth; but it will be less than this, according to their distance being greater than one minute and less than 15 minutes. But if the benefic which is in the Ascendant is below the line of the cusp by more than fifteen minutes, up to 55 minutes, the fortune of the native or querent will be less this, according with what has been said when it is under fifteen minutes up to one minute, proportioning from 15 up to 45, as the luminaries were proportioned from 1 up to 15. You can say the same as has been said for the Ascendant, if the Moon is in the minute of the Sun's opposition and a benefic is in the seventh: since a benefic will then be in the seventh, namely on the line of the cusp of the 7th house, which has the signification of the fortune of the native or querent because of wives or other women, and because of associates and also enemies. But if at the hour of the nativity the Moon was in Taurus, in the minute of the Ascendant, and Taurus was the Ascendant, or the Ascendant was Leo and the Sun was in the minute of the Ascendant, and one of the malefics do not impede him or her, it signifies that the native will acquire much money, and that he will reach great dignity and at great exaltation. But if one of the malefics were in the place of the benefics, namely in the Ascendant or in the seventh, it signifies the loss and destruction of the wealth of the native or the querent by reason of the aforementioned things.

Consideration One Hundred and Twenty-Four is to examine in nativities or questions, the significator of the wealth of the native or querent, and the significator of his dignity or mastery, which you will be able to perceive from the Lord of the 10th house, or indeed the Lord of the Ascendant - if the Lord of the tenth is not suitable to signify the dignity or mastery of the native, or querent, insofar as the quality of his nature and lineage are fit to assume dignity or profession.

Which if the Lord of the 10th house (or its almutem) are oriental from the luminary whose authority it is, and are elongated from it by sixty degrees or more up to ninety degrees (if it is one of the superiors), or is elongated by thirty degrees if it is one of the inferiors, and is also in the angle of the 10th house or the Ascendant, so that it is not removed from the line of the angle (if it is beyond it) by more than 30 minutes. If indeed it is within it by more than one and a half degrees, or is with the luminary whose authority it was, namely with the Moon and with the others, with the Sun in his heart, and with the Part of Fortune, and it is not impeded, it will signify that the native will reach the dignity, or mastery of his predecessors, and will not exceed it; but he will be greater, more excellent, and more perfect in that dignity, or mastery than any one of his predecessors was. However, if there are any of the aforementioned helping and fortunate fixed stars in any of the above mentioned angles, with the Part of Fortune or one of the planets, he will rise to a much greater dignity than any of his relations had reached. If the star is one of those of the first magnitude, and it is also the sole significator, the native or querent will arrive at immense dignity, and immense honour, and to almost immeasurable wealth. If the Lord of the Ascendant aspects it, his fame and honour will emerge in his own person. However, if it is the Lord of the 2nd house aspecting it, it will emerge in wealth, if the Lord of the tenth, it will emerge in such a title and reign, that it will be the kind that is fit for great kings; even if he is of worthless persons and a humble nation. And the lower his birth, all the more will he rise to a greater height. However this will not last for long; nor will it easily transcend the space of 27 years, and few will arrive at this, or more than thirty years. And the higher his rank, the heavier will be his fall, and his dignity or title will end in evil, for it will come down to the ultimate misery: he will die a most contemptible and deplorable death - which if it does not befall him, it will befall his proximate successor in that dignity.

Consideration One Hundred and Twenty-Five is to examine in nativities or questions, what sign is ascending: if it is the sign of any planet having two houses, the exercises of the native or querent will be in those things, which are signified by the other house of that planet, and its accidents will easily befall him, and he himself will be the reason why these things will happen to him.

Since if the Ascendant is Aries, he will be engaged in such things that he himself will be the cause of his own death or ruin; since Scorpio (which is the other house of Mars), will then be the 8th house. If Mars is then well disposeed, and the Part of Fortune is in the eighth, he will be fortunate in those things signified by the 8th house.

If the Ascendant is Taurus, he will be engaged in such matters that he himself will be the cause of his own illness; since Libra (which is the other house of Venus), will then be the 6th house, whence he will become ill by his own fault. If Venus is then well disposeed, and the Part of Fortune is in the sixth, he will be fortunate in those things which are signified by the 6th house.

If the Ascendant is Gemini, he will be engaged in such matters that he himself will be the cause of his own capture; since Virgo (which is the other house of Mercury), will then be the 4th house. If Mercury is then well disposeed, and the Part of Fortune is in the fourth, he will be fortunate in those things that are signified by the 4th house.

If the Ascendant is Virgo he will be engaged in those matters which have a view to dignity and exaltation: for he will acquire a realm from his own person and industry, and he will do this easily, without great labour or fatigue: since Gemini (which is the other house of Mercury), will then be the 10th house. However, if Mercury is then joined to the Part of Fortune, and is in the Ascendant, he will acquire riches and dignity similar to a kingdom. If Mercury is in the tenth with the Part of the Kingdom, and otherwise well disposeed, namely fortunate and strong, without a doubt he will acquire a rulership or dignity which will be equivalent to a great king. If indeed he is with the Part of Fortune in the tenth, and similarly the Moon, he will infallibly become a great king.

If the Ascendant is Libra, he will be engaged in those things which have a view to his own ruin, and he himself will be the cause, or occasion of his own ruin, since Taurus (which is the other house of Venus), will then be the 8th house. Which if Venus is well disposeed, or the Part of Fortune is in the eighth, it signifies that he will be fortunate in those things which are signified by the 8th house.

If the Ascendant is Scorpio, he will be engaged in such matters, that he himself will be the cause of his own illness, since Aries (which is the other house of Mars), will then be the 6th house. If indeed Mars is well disposeed, or the Part of Fortune is in the sixth, it signifies he will be fortunate in those things which are signified by the 6th house.

If the Ascendant is Sagittarius, he will be engaged in such matters that he himself will be the cause of his own capture, since Pisces (which is the other house of Jupiter), will then be the 4th house. If indeed Jupiter is well disposeed, or the Part of Fortune is in the fourth, he will be fortunate in these things, which are signified by the 4th house.

If the Ascendant is Capricorn, it signifies that he will be engaged in those things which have a view to his own profit, since Aquarius (which is the other house of Saturn), will then be the 2nd house. If Saturn is then well disposeed, or the Part of Fortune is in the second, he will be fortunate in those things which are signified by the 2nd house. However, if he is badly disposeed, he himself will be the cause of the destruction of his own wealth.

If the Ascendant is Aquarius, it signifies that he will be engaged in such matters that the native himself will be the reason why he acquires many hidden enemies for himself, since Capricorn (which is the other house of Saturn), will then be the 12th house. Should Saturn be well disposeed, or the Part of Fortune is in the twelfth, if signifies that he will be fortunate in those things which are signified by the 12th house.

If the Ascendant is Pisces, it signifies that he himself will be the cause of his own reign, his own high title, etc. as has been said above for when Virgo is the Ascendant.

Consideration One Hundred and Twenty-Six is to examine in nativities or questions, whether Mercury is the significator of the nativity, or its participator, and if he is well disposeed (namely fortunate and strong), and is in Capricorn or Aquarius: since this signifies that the native will be of profound and subtle disposition, having a high and great intellect, for he will deeply understand the roots of things, whatever kind they may be; he will see from their principle what end they can come to, and this more strongly if Saturn aspects Mercury (according to the quality of the aspect and if Saturn is not impeded). and more still if Mercury is in Aquarius, which is the joy of Saturn: and greater again if a benefic is complected with Mercury; or if he is with any of the fortunate fixed stars. If he is in Aries, or Scorpio, it signifies that he will be strong through stupidity, and treachery, and the agility of his motion, and magnanimity; and he will be arrogant around many people in his acts of arms; and he will also be prudent, and quick to understand those things which are said to him, or he will understand what is written down more so than through himself, or what he himself thought up of.

Consideration One Hundred and Twenty-Seven is to examine in nativities if the Lord of the Ascendant of the nativity is naturally malefic (as are Saturn and Mars), and rules over the nativity alone, without the participation of any benefic: since this signifies that the taste of the native, or his sense of smell: or his complexion, will not be similar to the taste, sense of smell, or complexion of others. Since if Saturn is the sole significator, his taste will delight in tasteless, bitter, and sour things, as Haly attests in his exposition of the fortieth aphorism of Ptolemy's Centiloquium. However, if

Mars is the sole significator, he will delight in sharp and bitter things: nor will he be averse to agitated wine, nor freshly bottled wine, nor doubtful wine, nor will he delight in sweet things, nor delicate or clear things: nor will he recoil from vile meat, nor even from half rotten meat, nor even from putrid or stinking fish: he will be inclined more to horrible odours than sweet ones, as are those of aloes, galbanum, serapine, oppoponax, quenching candles, burning leather, dung in stables and other locations, and similar things. And his nature will delight in unsightly and ugly women more so than in beautiful ones, and he will be more comfortable with these than with others. You may Say the same for women - that they will delight more in ugly men than in handsome ones.

Consideration One Hundred and Twenty-Eight is to examine in nativities whether the sign of the Ascendant is formed in the image of the sign of a human, or if its Lord is in a human sign, as if this is so, it signifies that the native will be familiar with men and eagerly associate with them. If the Ascendant is a human sign, and the Lord of the Ascendant is in a human sign, he will be even more social, and associate himself even more with men, and will more eagerly converse with them. But if the Ascendant is a sign formed in the likeness of any animals which men use in their labours or their actions (as are Aries, Taurus, the final part of Sagittarius, and Capricorn), it signifies that the native will be humble to men, but will not be very sociable with them. But if it is in semi-feral signs (as are Cancer and Pisces), he will be even less sociable with them. If indeed it is in feral, frenzied and maddened signs, as are Leo and Scorpio, he himself will be feral, frenzied and wild towards men, nor will he want to associate with any of them; he will prefer to remain alone rather than associate with people: indeed, he will not even want to be with his parents or any of his relatives.

Consideration One Hundred and Twenty-Nine is to examine in nativities whether the Moon is exactly in the opposition of the Sun, with any of the stars which are said to be nebulous, which are Athozaic, the Head of the Twins, and the place which falls in the water poured by Aquarius, and the Throat of Leo (which is said to be a small distance from its heart) and others which, on account of their mixture with others, do not sine, when she is not distant from them by more than ten minutes according to longitude and according to latitude, it seems inevitable that the native will have illnesses in his eyes, which cannot be cured by human medical means. Since if the Moon is then waning in an angle, and Mars and Saturn are occidental from her, not far removed from her, and oriental from the Sun, or opposite to each other with the Sun is in one of the angles, it signifies that the native will be deprived of the light of both of his eyes before the day of his natural death, and it does not appear that he will be able to prevent this from happening. If both of the luminaries are not as described, but one of them is, he will be deprived of the light of one eye only. If it is the Sun, and he is a man, he will be deprived of the light of the right eye. If she is a woman, she will be deprived of the light of the left eye. But if it is the Moon, and a man, he will be deprived of the light of his left eye. If she is a woman, she will be deprived of the light of the right eye.

Consideration One Hundred and Thirty is to examine in nativities whether the Moon is joined with Mercury by conjunction or by aspect, or if one of the planets transfers light between them; since if this is not so, and if the Ascendant is not a sign which is of the nature of Mercury or the Moon, and if in addition Saturn is in an angle in a diurnal nativity, or Mars in a nocturnal nativity, the native will be insane or furious, or epileptic, or raving, or stupid, or at least very forgetful, unless a strong benefic were to then aspect the Ascendant or Mercury or the Moon: and this more strongly if the angle in which one of the aforementioned malefics is placed is Cancer (which is the exaltation of Jupiter), or Virgo (which is the exaltation of Mercury), or Pisces (which is the exaltation of Venus). And this is because the Moon in a nativity has the signification of the body of the native, and the planet to whom she is joined signifies the virtues appearing in it, according to its own virtue. However, if she is joined to Mercury, or moving towards him, the native will be wise, and preserve his sense, and he will not lose it. If Mercury is in Capricorn, or Aquarius, not impeded, and he is in good condition, the native will be of great intellect, of deep understanding, wise, and a philosopher. If Jupiter and Venus are in the Zamini of the Sun, he will be a hermit, and almost a prophetic man: and his words will be heard and received before the words of other men.

Consideration One Hundred and Thirty-One is to examine in nativities, if it is the nativity of a man, whether the Sun and Moon are both in masculine signs, or are both in one masculine quarter, or in one masculine sign, since if they are so placed, it signifies that the actions of the native and his workings will be natural insofar as what pertains to men, and he will naturally engage in these things. But if it is the nativity of a woman and the luminaries are so disposeed (as was said), she will be man-like, and will naturally engage in those matters which pertain to men, and she will despise men. And if she marries she will not want to revere her husband, nor be subject to him.

If Venus and Mars are in masculine signs in a man's' nativity, his sexual intercourse will be in accordance with nature and in accordance with the law. If they are oriental, he will abound in sex, and be excessive in it, and will not be content in natural sex; indeed, he will desire impure sex, so that he scorns women and is misused by men. However, if they are occidental and in feminine signs, his sexual intercourse will be unnatural and impure; and this more strongly if they are aspected by Saturn, who has the signification of impure sex. If indeed it is a woman's nativity, and Mars and Venus are in masculine signs, and are oriental, she will recoil from sex with men, nor will she delight in that: she will delight more in the rubbing of women, and especially girls. But if Mars and Venus are in feminine signs, and are occidental, she will love sex with men, and delight in it, and engage in it according to nature. And if Jupiter is in a feminine sign, and is occidental, as much in nativities of men as of women, nor is Mars as was said of him above, the sexual intercourse of the native will be natural and in accordance with the law. If Mars is the sole significator, and Jupiter does not aspect him, their sexual intercourse will often be against both natural and apostolic laws.

And Ptolemy said in Centiloquium, that if Venus is incorporated with Saturn in a nativity, and also if Saturn has dignities in the 7th, the native will be born of impure sexual intercourse.

Consideration One Hundred and Thirty-Two is to examine in nativities whether Mars is corporeally conjunct with a certain red star of its nature, which is in Taurus, and is named "*Algol*"; so that there is a distance of 16 minutes or less between them, with Mars moving towards it, and the Lord of the house (or the exaltation, or two of the other dignities) where the luminary who is the authority is placed, which is called the Anauba Lord, is in opposition to Mars or in his square aspect, and if the degree of the Ascendant is not aspected by any of the benefics, and if there is no benefic in the 8th house, i is far from doubtful that it signifies that the native will be decapitated. If Mars does not differ in latitude to Algol by more than 16 minutes, this will happen infallibly, nor will it be possible to avoid, unless God averts it. If a retrograde or combust benefic aspects the degree of the Ascendant, it will hardly be able to prohibit the native from being decapitated, but he won't be decapitated due to his own fault.

However, if the benefic is not impeded, it will release the native from an evil death; and he will pass away in his own bed, yet he will still die from an illness of the head, which will originate from a hot cause, and this will happen before his fiftieth year. If Mars is not as has been said above, and there is a malefic in the eighth, the native will die an evil death. If there is an unimpeded benefic there, he will die in his own home by a common death. If this benefic is impeded, he will then die from something unpleasant overtaking him.

And Ptolemy said in Centiloquium that if a luminary is in the Midheaven whose authority it was; I say with the aforementioned conditions, the native will be hanged. If one of the malefics is then in Gemini, and the other in Pisces, his hands or feet will be cut off, according to (I say) what is signified by the sign in which you find the more malicious planet. If indeed Mars is corporeally joined to the Lord of the Ascendant, and they are in Leo, and if Mars has no dignity in the Ascendant, and none of the benefics are the eighth, it signifies the native will be burned. If Mars is then retrograde, combust, or cadent, this will happen to the native by his own fault. However, if he is not impeded, this will happen to the native undeservedly.

And Ptolemy said that if Saturn is in the Midheaven in a nativity, and his anauba is in opposition to him, and the fourth sign is dry, the native will die from a collapse of ruins. If it is a moist sign, he will drown. If the sign is in the form of a human, he will be strangled. Again, if one of the malefics (namely Mars or Saturn) is in the Ascendant hour of the nativity, and is peregrine, this native will have a mark or a sign on his face or his head. If the malefic is impeded, retrograde, or combust, this mark or sign will be ugly. However, if the planet is free, it will not be ugly.

Consideration One Hundred and Thirty-Three is to examine in nativities, whether the Ascendant is Gemini or Sagittarius, and the Lord of the Ascendant is well placed (namely fortunate and strong), and similarly the Moon: since this has the signification that if the native survives, he will acquire much wealth. If the Ascendant is Virgo or Pisces, and the Lord of the Ascendant and the Moon are well disposeed, the native will acquire money and spend it in a good way; and he will be generous and live splendidly. However, he who has Gemini or Sagittarius on the Ascendant, will not be a good spender, but stingy. However, he who has Gemini or Virgo on the Ascendant may lose his wealth and become impoverished by it. He whose Ascendant is Sagittarius or Pisces will never destroy his wealth nor become impoverished. Likewise examine if the Ascendant is Aries, Scorpio, Capricorn or Aquarius: for if so, the native will be avaricious and miserable, and shunned. If Jupiter then aspects the Ascendant, he will reduce the misery, yet not remove it.

Consideration One Hundred and Thirty-Four is to examine in nativities whether Mars and Venus are in the sixth, and otherwise well disposeed, for this signifies that the native will naturally become a perfect doctor in any area of medicine. And if Mercury is corporeally joined with Venus, and she is retrograde; it signifies that the native will naturally be a perfect singer. But if Mercury is in the twelfth and not otherwise impeded: it signifies that the native will be naturally wise in all sciences and philosophies.

Consideration One Hundred and Thirty-Five is to examine in nativities whether the Lord of the Ascendant, the Moon, Jupiter, and Venus, are all in the Ascendant, or if Jupiter and Venus aspect the Lord of the Ascendant, and the Moon in the Ascendant from a trine or sextile aspect, and they are not impeded: since if this is so, it signifies that the native will be very strong in his body, and that no man will dare to neglect his commands.

Consideration One Hundred and Thirty-Six is to examine in the nativities of kings, the wealthy, magnates (namely of those who are fit to rule), if both the luminaries are in the degrees of their exaltation, or in their own houses in such degrees that one is in the same kind of dignity as the other, and are free from all impediments : since this has the signification that the native will reach lofty and sublime dignities; for he will become king of the Romans, or someone close to that in a royal dignity below the king of the Romans, so that it will be said of him that he is practically the universal king of the world, and this honour will extend up to the fourth generation of his descendants. But if all the planets who are below Jupiter commit their disposition to him, and he receives every one of them (not ignoring the aforementioned condition); and after the planets commit their disposition to Saturn, and Jupiter also commits his disposition, and Saturn receives them and Jupiter, and both are oriental from the Sun and in angles, it signifies that the native will become a man of a great and powerful name, allowing not a royal one, and his name will be fixed in the earth: and his fame will endure for the entirety of his own time, and after his death for three reigns of Saturn, or it possibly might last even longer.

The One Hundredth and Thirty-Seventh Consideration is to examine whether Mercury is joined with Saturn in the Ascendant; since this has the signification that the native will be foolish, loquacious, and wanting to be counted as wise; he will speak ill of everyone, as much of men as of women. The greater wisdom that is found in him will be used to invent great lies and to use them; he will hardly be able to say a word without some mixture of falsity in his speech; indeed it will be natural for him to lie, and he will have a very filthy tongue, and a malicious one from Saturn, with Mercury providing the sharpness of his malice.

Consideration One Hundred and Thirty-Eight is to examine in someone's nativity if two malefics are in the bounds of the 4th house of this nativity, or if the angles are mobile signs and Mars and Saturn are in them: since this signifies that the native will be poor, miserable, unfortunate, beyond all other unfortunate people for the whole of his life, unless Jupiter or the triplicity Lords of the Ascendant operate against this.

Consideration One Hundred and Thirty-Nine is to examine in nativities, and likewise in questions, in which house the Cauda Draconis is found: since this will have the signification of the voiding and destruction of the matters signified by that house, and especially wealth.

As if it is in the first, it signifies the voiding of wealth which the native will make with his own person. If it is in the second it signifies the voiding of profit which he will make with his own wealth or substance. If it is in the third, the voiding of wealth he will make with his brothers, or on account of his brothers, or with his neighbours or younger relatives. If it is in the fourth, the voiding of wealth which he will make with his father, grandfather, or father in law, or that he inherited, and it signifies that the native will change many houses due to improvements, nor will he remain firmly in them, nor will things turn out well for him in these moves. If it is in the fifth, the voiding of wealth that he will make with his children or on account of children. If it is in the sixth, the voiding of wealth that he will make with slaves or small animals. If it is in the seventh, the voiding of wealth that he will make with women, or associates, or enemies. If it is in the ninth, the voiding of wealth that he will make with religious people, or from religious people. If it is in the tenth, the voiding of wealth which he will make because of dignities or masteries. If it is in the eleventh, the voiding of wealth that he will make with friends, or because of friends. If it is in the twelfth, the voiding of profit that he will make with large animals or because of hidden enemies.

Consideration One Hundred and Forty is to examine whether the significator of the end of the matter, or its completion, is so weak that it cannot perfect the matter, and the Moon similarly. If this is so, then take the significator of the querent and the significator of the quesited matter, and subtract the lesser from the greater; and add the degrees of the sign of the Ascendant to the remainder; and project the result from the Ascendant; and wherever this falls, the Lord of this sign will be the significator of him who enquired according to the content of the quesited or considered topic, and you will judge according to this planets condition, following from whether you find him fortunate and strong, or unfortunate and weak. For if it concerns substance, and the planet is in the second, the substance of the querent will be disposeed according to its condition. If it is in the third, his brothers will be disposeed according to its condition. If it is in the fourth, his older relatives will be disposeed according to its condition. If it is in the fifth, the children will be disposeed according to it. If he is in the sixth, slaves will be disposeed according to it. If it is in the seventh, wives will be disposeed according to it. If it is in the eighth, dowries will be disposeed according to it. If it is in the ninth, long journeys will be disposeed according to him. If he is in the tenth, masteries will be disposeed according to it. If he is in the eleventh, friends will be disposeed according to it. If it is in the twelfth, enemies will be disposeed according to it.

Consideration One Hundred and Forty-One is to look in nativities, and consider gifts or fortunes which are given to men by the fixed stars, and their manner of durability in their subjects, and why they do not endure as long as those which are given by the planets, when it appears that they ought to endure longer than those - regarding which I cannot remember anything being said, except what Ptolemy said in Centiloquium, that the fixed stars give gifts beyond measure, but oftentimes ending in evil. And Almansor said in his chapters (offered to the great king of the Saracens), the fixed stars give great gifts, and lift men from poverty to loftiness, which the seven planets do not do.

The gifts which the fixed stars give to men do not endure in them for as long as those which the planets give. Which happens because the fixed stars are agents and men are patients. Whence the subjects on which the fixed stars act, are not suited to them, nor are they apt to receive their impressions. Indeed it is fitting that between an agent and a patient there is conformity or some accord. The fixed stars are extremely slow moving, and change extremely slowly: and therefore their impressions require subjects or patients suited to them, and which are of the longest durability, and which have conformity with them so that the stars effects can be perfected or completed in them. For the circular motion of the fixed stars is not completed in less than 36,000 years. Indeed the circular motion of men lasts for three reigns of Saturn (who is the slowest of the planets), which is a space of 90 years. Few pass beyond this, which can happen to some people from the addition of the years of some planet to the years of the Alcochoden in the root of the nativity. Whence often, in fact mostly, the length of a man's life is ninety years, even if some octogenarians or possibly nonagenarians lie and say that they are centenarians, when in truth they are not; which does not have true conformity, nor similarity, with the 36000 years to the perfection of the effects of the stars impressions.

Just as an eagle cannot extend, nor exercise the full amount of his flight or his power on a fly, and just a a stone fired from a catapult cannot exercise its action on a bed of moss; so too the fixed stars cannot exercise the full amount or effect of their impressions on men; and therefore their gifts or fortune does not last long in men, since men have much more rapid changes, and are of little durability compared to the circularity of the fixed stars. And from this it was said

"Employ the fixed stars in the building of cities - the planets in the building of homes"

- since amongst corruptible things cities are things of great durability when compared with houses; indeed a house is of long duration in comparison to men. For indeed houses do not always endure by their undivided things. Indeed cities last through the successive building and rebuilding of houses. However castles, even if they are of long duration, are not as long in duration as are cities. Whence we can use the superior planets in the building of castles; still, it is more prudent to use the fixed stars in their construction; since castles are of greater durability than houses, even if sometimes castles are destroyed. And since cities are of greater durability than castles, they are yet closer to the fixed stars, whose subjects they are; for the impressions which something solid makes on something more solid, will last longer than in a less solid thing. They will last much less again in a thing which is not solid than in a thing which is somewhat solid; and will last much less again in a slippery thing than in a thing which is not solid, or which is less slippery.

Whence these impressions which the fixed stars make in cities, are more durable than those they make on castles; since cities are more correlated to them, in terms of their long length of time. And those which they make on castles are of greater durability than those which they make on houses; since castles are more closely correlated to them than houses. Indeed the bodies of men are more removed from the stars bodies than houses are, and therefore more corruptible; and from this the significations of the fixed stars apply less to men; and if they are applied they will last for less time, since the significations of the fixed stars are so great and so noble, and so lofty, and so remote from corruption and mutability, that they cannot quickly sustain a changeable commixture with quickly corruptible or fast changing things; unless in the manner that oil can be mixed with water; for even if they imprint on these things, these impressions will not last long.

For the fixed stars operate with such nobility that on account of their extremely remote elongation from corruptible, base, and quickly changing things, and their approach to the supernal splendour, that is not possible for their significations to remain long in these corruptible things, or with these things, and especially in men, since they are changed and corrupted very easily and quickly - in fact most quickly; and especially in those of low birth, and the feeble and faint of heart; for they do not go beyond the person of who they affect, and it rarely happens otherwise while he is alive (and most of the time for his evil) and in such a manner that only God can avert it, and not others (as I have said many times). Since sometimes they can finish in good, even if this most rarely occurs; just as happens when someone lives according to the maximum years of the Alcochoden, something which I have not seen in my time except for one fellow named Richard, who said he had been in the court of Charlemagne, King of the Franks, and had lived for 400 years. And it was said at the time there was a certain other man who was from the time of Jesus Christ, and was called John Buttadeus, as he had struck Our Lord as He was being led to be crucified, and He said to him,*"You will wait for Me until I have come"*. And I saw Richard in Rennea in the era of Christ 1223, and Johannes himself passing through Forli going to Saint Jacobs in the era of Christ 1267.

Neither do the significations of the fixed stars apply to men nor can they adhere to them, nor last in them perceptibly, unless there was a medium through which the stars act on them (the planets, who are secondary agents, and the fixed stars principal agents); for wherever there are many actions set in order, attributed to diverse agents, it is necessary that the principal act is attributed to a principal agent, since they comport themselves towards the effecting of corruptible things as much as the first cause. The planets indeed are just as much a second cause. The corruption which these inferior bodies undergo is on account of their excessive remoteness, or distance, from the incorruptible superiors, which are not said to have motion, since they do not appear to be perceptibly moved. Yet they sometimes endure in magnates and wealthy men who are fit to rule, and who are magnanimous and great of heart, one such man in my time was Frederick II Emperor of Rome - who, when he was in need and in a position great necessity, was made Emperor with no man able to resist him, and to him went Apulia, the Kingdom of Sicily, Jerusalem, Krakow, Italy, and the Roman Empire except for a part of Lombardy. And he even manages to subjugate all of his treacherous enemies, and rebels, and remained in such a position for almost thirty years. Ultimately however, he died miserably, poisoned by his own men, with all of his family destroyed, so that almost none of them remained unharmed.

There was a certain other Ezzelino da Romano, who, though he was not very lofty, was exalted high above all Italians, in such a way that his fame crossed the seas and sounded out in many regions. For he was the Lord over almost all of the Mark of Treviso, even up to Germany and up to Trent, and up to four or five miliaria from Venice. He remained a tyrant in these parts, and his tyranny lasted for twenty six years. Yet ultimately all these things ended in evil for him. For when it appeared impossible for him to be oppressed, he fell into the hands of the greater of his enemies, whom he had beaten in a certain battle which was waged in defence of the Milanese at Cassianum, and he died miserably, and all of his family were destroyed and none of them remained.

Similarly there was another man from the Kingdom of Apulia, of low stock, by the name of Pierro della Vigna, who when he was a scholar in Bologna was mendicant, and did not have a thing to eat. And afterwards was made a clerk, and then was made chief clerk of the court of Emperor Frederick II. After that he heard laws and was made the greater judge of the court of the Emperor, and ascended to such dignity, that he who could get a little piece of the fringe of his cloak was reputed to be blessed by his grace; and whatever he did, the Emperor would approve. He himself however retracted and infringed upon much of what the Emperor did. And the Emperor made him the Lord or ruler of the whole of Apulia, and in goods was found to have in gold alone 10,000 Augustan livres, apart from his other riches, which were said to be almost immeasurable. In the end however he came to such depression and such misery, that the Emperor had him blinded, and moved by the Emperors disdain, he smashed his head against a certain wall, and in such a manner miserably killed himself, as was said in the common rumours at the time.

There was even a certain Pisan who was called Smerguls, of low stock, practically of the lowliest of people, who was practically made Lord of the Pisans; nor were any of the magnates brave enough to resist him - shortly afterwards he came to nothing.

After him there was another in the same city who was called Oddo Gualduzius, from a small tribe, who ascended to such heights that it was as if he dominated the whole city. Nor did anyone dare to contradict him; ultimately a certain judge named Galiver caused him to be cut up in the city of Pisa; nor did the authorities make any ruling after this, asides from saying that he who had behaved evilly suffered harm.

The same happened in Forli to a certain man named Simon Mestaguerre, who, born of a low father, came to such a high status that the whole populace followed him; nor did anyone dare resist him, except myself alone (who knew him as he truly was) and whatever evil he could do, he did against everyone, and this lasted for almost three years. Yet ultimately he was put down and practically came to nothing, for he was banished and expelled from the city, which happened on account of the vileness of his body and his faint heartedness.

Similarly there was a certain brother of the Order of Preachers, names John of Vicenza, whom I have named elsewhere, who was considered as almost being the holiest man of all the Italians, who confessed the Roman Church: to me however he appeared to be a hypocrite: and who arrived at such status that he was said to have revived eighteen dead men, none of whom could be seen by anyone, and he was said to cure all illnesses, and drive out demons - yet I couldn't see anyone who was freed, even though I put in a lot of effort to see them, nor was there anyone who said firmly that they had seen one of his miracles, and it appeared that the whole world was rushing after him, and he who could get a thread of his cape was considered blessed, and such a thread was revered as a relic of a saint, and the Bolognese followed him carrying arms, and stayed around him in a group, and surrounded him with arched staffs, lest anyone approach him, and if anyone did approach him, they were dealt with in a bad manner; for some were killed, others were injured, while others were driven back with sticks. And he rejoiced and delighted at the dead and injured people, nor did he heal any of them, as Jesus did Malchus. And he used to say openly in his preaching that he spoke with Jesus Christ, and with the Blessed Virgin, and similarly with the angels whenever he wished. And the brothers of The Preachers in Bologna, under such tricks then earned (according to what was said publicly) more than 20,000 silver Marks; and so great was his power in Bologna, that the Bolognese feared him so greatly that whatever he ordered of them they done in whole - indeed one time he pardoned a certain soldier who was named Laurencerius, who murdered the son of one of his neighbours and had been condemned by the authorities to be decapitated; nor did the authorities dare to do anything against his rule, nor was anyone bold enough to contradict his orders, except myself alone - but not the Bolognese; for I knew his tricks and his lies; but the commoners said that I was a heretic, solely out of fear of him, and he remained in this state for almost one year: yet ultimately came to almost nothing, so that hardly one brother would join him when he wanted to go anywhere, and men began to recognise him for who he truly was.

Consideration One Hundred and Forty-Two is to examine in nativities or general questions, the gifts or the fortunes which are given to men by the planets, since they are applied to them, and last a long time with them, and are extended to their successors according to how they are disposeed in the roots of the nativities: but not excessively, unless perhaps they are applied to by any fortunate fixed stars: and this since they are of rapid changeability, whence they will have more affinity with them than those things which are given by the fixed stars, and especially the good fortune which is given by the inferiors, on account of their greater velocity and their conformity with the subjects correlated to them. The good fortune which the superiors give does not last as long in men as the aforementioned: still they are efficacious in the construction of houses more so than the other planets.

On The Fortunes Which Saturn And The Other Planets Give

Saturn, when he is oriental and well disposeed (namely fortunate and strong, and received in the place in which he is), gives great fortune in buildings, plantations of trees, and those things of long durability in the cultivation of the earth, in the management water, and similar things

Jupiter gives great fortune in sciences, such as laws, making decisions and decrees, and in dignities: such as judgeships, bishoprics, and the like.

However Mars gives great fortune in the raisings of armies, and in their command, and similar things.

The Sun gives great fortune in lay dignities such as kingdoms, ruling of cities, positions of civil authority, and similar things.

The inferiors give their good fortune more greatly adhering to men, and longer lasting than the superiors do in corruptible things (which are inferior to cities and castles), on account of their nearness to the corruptible things, and the speed and swift change to those receiving them, and their correlation with these things.

Venus, who is the superior planet of the inferiors, gives her fortune in those things which pertain to the doings of women and their jewellery, and in seducing them so that they do not protect themselves from men, and wealth because of them, and similar things.

Mercury however gives his fortune from mercantile activities, writings, pictures, future things, and the like.

The Moon gives her fortune from sailing and mercantile dealings which are often repeated, writings, paintings; vine plantations, the use of drinks, or the selling of wine and its trade, and similar things.

All of these things are given excellently if the native or querent adheres to those things which are naturally given by the planets, as I said. And even if the significations of the supercelestial bodies adhere to men, still, they do not last forever in men; however the significations of the inferior planets last longer than the significations of the superiors, and the significations of the superiors last longer than the significations of the fixed stars. The significations, or fortune, or wealth, which are given by the Moon, can last up to the seventh age or generation, since she is the seventh planet after Saturn, when beginning from the superiors, and if they go beyond the seventh, they will not be able to go beyond the eighth (by putting an age or a generation from the forty second year up to the forty fifth year, so that both are included). Those which are given by Mercury can last up to the sixth age, since he is the sixth planet after Saturn. Indeed they cannot go beyond the seventh, and hardly reach this point. However those which are given by Venus can last up to the fifth age, since she is the fifth planet after Saturn. They cannot go beyond the sixth, and they hardly reach this point. Those which are given by the Sun can last up to the fourth age, since he is the fourth planet after Saturn. They cannot go beyond the fifth, and hardly reach this point. Those which are given by Mars can last up to the third age, since he is the third planet after Saturn; they cannot go beyond the fourth, and hardly reach this point. Those which are given by Jupiter can last up to the second age; since he is the second planet after Saturn; they cannot go beyond the third, and hardly reach this point. Those which are given by Saturn can last up to one age; they cannot go beyond the second, and hardly or never reach this point. And even if I said that they can last so long, I still do not say that they cannot end before this; for Aristotle said that limits are posited which cannot be passed over; yet he did not say that they could not be prevented from reaching the limits, and so it is with these things. For indeed I say that they cannot go beyond the aforementioned limits, since they will either be completely destroyed, or so greatly suppressed that they will remain in such condition that they will not be likened to the thing before them, unless in the manner that something green or blackish is likened to a brilliant white, unless perhaps something new occurs from another source (which rarely happens). Nor could it truly be said that it would truly be the same, but rather that it was something different than what was at the start.

And of the aforementioned things there were certain men who wanted to say that such wealth or similar things could be said to be bad to seek, and from this it was treated in such a way that the lay would come close to destruction from this profit from bad sources. For they said that profit from such sources does not go beyond the fifth age; and certain men said that it does not go beyond the third, ignorant as to whether they had it, unless they heard it being said by others for a long time, and because they often saw things turn out this way. And by the aforementioned conditions, it is not without reason that profit from bad sources does not go beyond the fifth age. By "profit from bad sources" I understand wealth which comes to someone by way of usury and of things in which many lies and deceptions are committed, and by way of pillage, theft, and similar things.

Consideration One Hundred and Forty Three is to consider the manner of judgement, and by which ways you must arrive at a judgement, so that you can examine it and rightly analyse it, and do so according to how the stars show you their truth to be disclosed. The method of whose consideration is this: to examine it in these fourteen ways.

The first way is whether the querent asks from intention or not. If the Lord of the Ascendant and the Lord of the hour are the same, or the signs in which contain the aforementioned significators are of the same triplicity or the same complexion - the question was made from intention. If indeed they were not as such, or if the Ascendant was in the end of some sign, the question will not be from intention nor will it have roots.

The second is to examine the Ascendant and its Lord, and the Moon, and the planet from whom she is separating, and give these to the querent. You will give the seventh, and the planet whom the Moon is joined, to the quesited, as said elsewhere. And if necessary, descend to the persons according to how things are signified by the houses from the first to the twelfth.

The third is for you to consider the house or sign signifying the quesited matter.

The fourth is the aspects of benefic or malefic planets to the significators of the quesited matter.

The fifth, in what place from its own houses each significator is placed, whether in its own, or the second, or the third, or the fourth, and so on, up to the twelfth, or found in the via combusta, or similar places.

The sixth is whether the significator is found in the angles, succeedents, or cadents.

The seventh is to diligently pay attention to from where the querent's aid will come from, namely whether from a father, a child, a king, relatives, or friends, etc. Since good significators will judge good, bad significators the contrary.

The eighth is to judge for the happiness of the querent if the Lord of the first is found in the fifth, or joined anywhere with the Lord of the fifth away from the impediments of malefics. Or to judge for his sorrow if you find it in the sixth, the seventh, the eighth, or the twelfth, unless the question is about matters signified by these houses: for according to how you find the planet, so you will judge.

The ninth is by benefics or malefics, according to how you find them in places signifying things which are quesited, that if there were more benefics, it will be good; however if there were more malefics it will be bad - and if they are equal, you will predict a middling result.

The tenth is if the Lord of the first is in the house of the quesited matter, or found anywhere with the Lord of that house.

The eleventh is to consider in which house is the Lord of the first is conjoined with the significator of the quesited matter: since you will be able to judge on where the quesited matter will come from by the significations or occasion of this house.

The twelfth is if the significators are not conjoined, and one of the planets transfers light between them, or if a planet accepts their disposition you will judge the same.

The thirteenth is the nature of the significators towards each other in the significations of what they agree in.

The fourteenth is to predict according to whether the receiver of disposition is a benefic or malefic, strong or weak, and if it aspects the significators and the Moon (or one of them) from an aspect of friendship or enmity.

Consideration One Hundred and Forty-Four is to consider in questions, or nativities, or in any other beginnings, when the significators do not clearly show you what you intend to know, and their signification is ambiguous, and you are not able to weigh it up well. When this is so, take the place of the Lord of the Ascendant, and the place of the Lord of the house the Moon is in, and see the distance in degrees between them (beginning from Aries), from which you will make signs. And add from above the degree of the ascending sign, and project the result from the Ascendant (both in the day and at night), and where the number ends, the Lord of that house will be the significator, and you will take the signification of the quesited matter from him, and you can judge according to his disposition.

Consideration One-Hundred and Forty-Five is to examine in diurnal nativities if the "*Cor Leonis*" is on the Ascendant, namely on the oriental line, or above it by one degree or less, or below it by three degrees or less; or if it is the tenth is in similar degrees without the conjunction or aspect of any benefic: since this signifies that the native will be of great name, great power, similarly will be exceedingly exalted, and that he will arrive at sublime dignities, even if he is found to be born from the lowliest of parents. And if this place is aspected by one of the benefics, his sublimity will be increased further. However, if the nativity is nocturnal, it will be something beneath this, yet not by much. If it is aspected by malefics, it will be somewhat beneath this again. If it is aspected by benefics they will increase its good by one-fourth, and they will reduce the evil by one-fourth. Nevertheless, whatever predictions come to pass, it signifies that the native will die an evil death, or at least that all his sublimity, all his greatness, and all his powers will be ended in evil.

Consideration One Hundred and Forty-Six is to examine the place of the Lord of the Ascendant, and the place of the Lord of the twelfth, and subtract the lesser from the greater, and add the remainder to the degrees of the sign ascending, and then project from the Ascendant, and where this number finishes, the Lord of this sign will be a participator with the Lord of the question: and is called the 'First Participator". Again, examine the place of the Lord of the mentioned sign, and the place of the Lord of the Part of Fortune, and subtract the lesser from the greater, and add the degrees of the ascending sign, and where this number finishes, the Lord of this sign will be the participator, and will be called the "Second Participator". If it is one and the same planet, you will only examine him. Indeed you will examine the mentioned First and Second Participators, and subtract the lesser from the greater, and add the degrees of the ascending sign and the planet in whose house this number falls will be the "Third Participator", and whichever of the three participators is stronger will be said to be more authoritative in the participation of the quesited matter.

If the remainders (or two of them) fall in the house of one planet, that planet will be preferred. If the question appears to be good, and the participators are badly disposeed, they will reduce the good which is signified by the question. But if they are well disposeed, they will increase the good. However, if the question is found to be bad, and the participators are found to be well disposeed, they will reduce the evil signified by the question. However, if they are badly disposeed, they will increase the evil.

There are many other considerations which are possible to assign to, and consider with, the aforementioned, but it would be very demanding and severely complicated for you. However from your own industry you can give attention to them in their own place and time, should they occur to you. I will make mention of certain ones in the Tractate on Judgements, others in the Tractate on Elections, others in the Tractate on Revolutions, others in the Tractate on Nativities, and others in the Tractate on Rains and Changes in the Air, just as you, if you diligently attend to them, will be able to investigate them if it pleases you.

THE SIXTH TRACTATE

On The Parts Of Judgements, Or A Concise Introduction To The Judgements Of The Stars

I

If you intend to arrive at judgements of astronomy, let it be your first concern to consider whether he who comes to you with a question asks from intention or not, as has been said elsewhere. Similarly, it is said there *how* you can know whether he asks from intention or not, which has been discussed more widely than here; but certain things are not discussed there; such as if the Lord of the Ascendant and the Lord of the hour are of the same triplicity, or the same complexion, or if the Lord of the Ascendant and the hour are the same planet, the question is from intention and has roots. But if it is otherwise, it does not appear that it is from intention, or that it has roots, unless perhaps in an unexpected case, you will attribute the Ascendant to the querent. And if it is necessary, yield to the person and perceive the sign which signifies the quesited matter, and planet ruling this sign, and aspects of the significators, and also attend to the conjunction of the benefics and malefics to the significators, both by body and by aspect.

And you should know that the corporeal conjunction of the Sun (which is called "combustion") is more harmful than the other impediments. Similarly consider whether the significator of the querent or of the quesited matter is in its own house or in whichever house from that, and whether it is free from impediments or not, or if it is in the *via combusta*. Similarly whether the significators, (among which the Moon is always to be counted), are in strong, weak, or mediocre places, and whether they are in the beginnings of the houses, or the middles, or the ends of them. Similarly examine the helpers and hinderers of the significators of anyone one of them according to their condition.

If you diligently consider all of these things, you will be able to weigh your judgement of the questions proposed to you; since benefics signify good: but the malefics on the contrary will signify evil. However, if you find the benefics and malefics equal, it will portend a mediocre judgement. But if benefics prevail, it will signify good, if the malefics prevail, judge the contrary. Indeed you will even consider the people enquiring, how and in what way it matters to them that they are asking their question, whether the querent asks through himself and for himself, or through another and for another, and by which houses the people enquiring, and the quesited things are signified, and what is signified by whatever house, the significations of which you have in the chapter above on the things signified the twelve houses.

II

How Judgements Are To Be Reached

That judging on the future is difficult, and that this is true, is made clear by the considerations assigned to you above, neither did Hippocrates say by chance that judgements are difficult, since there is nothing more difficult in the world than to truthfully predict future things. Before we arrive at judgements, it is necessary that I say something to you of those things which have a view to the business of judgements, without which I believe it is impossible for you to judge according to the march of truth, (even if I have made mention of some of them to you above).

Wherefore it is fitting to know first, before you presume to judge, what are the causes of perfecting matters, and which of them demonstrate truth, and which are those that prohibit matters from perfecting, and from what causes the effecting of matters will come, and from which occur the detriment of matters; and what is signified by whatever perfecting cause and indeed by the causes of destruction or prohibition; and what signifies the time when they ought to be perfected, or when they ought to be destroyed or prohibited.

And Messala, along with many more, said that the effects and detriment of matters in this world come to be by three principal ways.

Namely the first way is when the Lord of the Ascendant and the Lord of the quesited, and indeed the Moon, are joined at the same time.

The second - when the aforementioned significators are not joined together, that another planet transfers light between them, namely that it separates from one and joins to the other.

The third is when there is a collection of light from another planet which is heavier than the aforementioned significators, and they both join this heavier planet, and any one of them commits their disposition to it:; since this heavier planet will be the one who perfects the matter.

And sometimes a matter is perfected wholly in accordance with the querent's wishes, sometimes it is perfected to a part, other times neither in whole nor in part; and I will explain all of these things to you, so that you can better understand it and that you may comprehend how you can judge about matters that are presented to you.

On The Exposition Of The First Way

The exposition of the first way by which matters are perfected is when the Lord of the Ascendant and the Moon are joined with the Lord of the quesited matter; for then the matter is perfected.

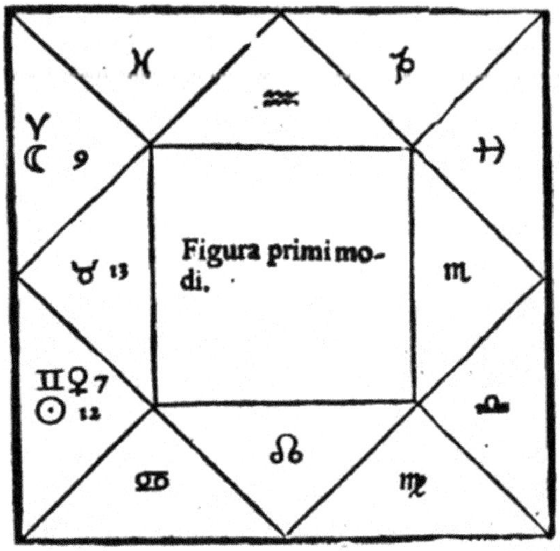

To give an example, a certain question was posed as to whether a certain man was going to attain a certain estate which he wanted to buy. And the Ascendant was 13 Taurus, and Venus was in Gemini at 7 degrees, and the Sun was in Gemini at 12 degrees, and the Moon was in Aries at 9 degrees. And the Lord of the Ascendant (namely Venus, who was moving towards a corporeal conjunction with the Sun), and the Moon (who was moving towards his aspectual conjunction), signified that the matter ought to be perfected. And it would be perfected, if the querent wanted to pursue it so that it would be perfected; and especially, since the Sun who was the significator of the quesited matter received the Moon from Aries by a sextile aspect. And the matter would be perfected not only by sextile, but also by square or opposition, as long as reception intervened, even if it would be with difficulty, anxiety, the greatest labour, and similarly perseverance and unfitness.

On The Exposition Of The Second Way

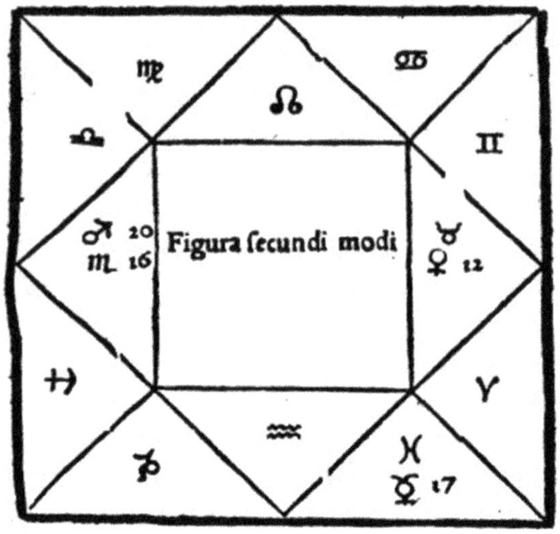

The exposition of the second way is when one planet is separated from another, and is joined to yet another, and commits the disposition which it receives from the first planet, to the one to whom it joins. To give an example, a question was put to me: a certain man asked whether he was going to get the goods of a certain uncle of his (who did not have sons), and this questions Ascendant was 16 degrees Scorpio, and was Mars here at 20 degrees, and Venus at 12 degrees Taurus moving toward Mars' opposition, and Mercury at 17 degrees Pisces, with Mercury separating from Venus by a sextile aspect by which he was joined to her; and she received him from Pisces, which is her exaltation, and committed her disposition to him. And Mercury carried it to Mars, and committed it to him by a trine aspect, and this signified that the querent was about to get the goods of the uncle, on account of Venus, who was the significatrix of the goods of the querent's uncle, who committed her disposition to Mercury, and Mercury carried it to Mars, who is the significator of the querent. For the 6th house is the significator of the uncle, namely the fathers brother, as has been said above in the chapter On the Houses, since the sixth is the third from the fourth (which is the house of the father);

and the seventh (which signifies the uncles possessions) is the second from the sixth. And the transfer of light signified that the matter would be done through the hands of legates, who involved themselves in the matter; and it appeared that it ought to be done by the hands of some familiar* of one of the querent's associates (if he has associates), which if he didn't have associates, it would be done by the hands of some familiar of his enemy or of his wife. If his wife didn't live in the house with him, and if such a familiar was not found, it would be done by the hands of some servant of the querent's brother. And if his brother did not have a servant, it would be done by the hands of some stepson of the querent, and if he did not have a stepson, it would be done by the hands of some friend of his. If he didn't have a friend it would be done by the hands of some soldier or familiar of the king. And if such persons were not found, it would be done by the hands of someone trusted by the querent's hidden enemies. And if such a person is not found it will be done by the hands of someone signified by the house in which the Moon is placed.

On The Exposition Of The Third Way

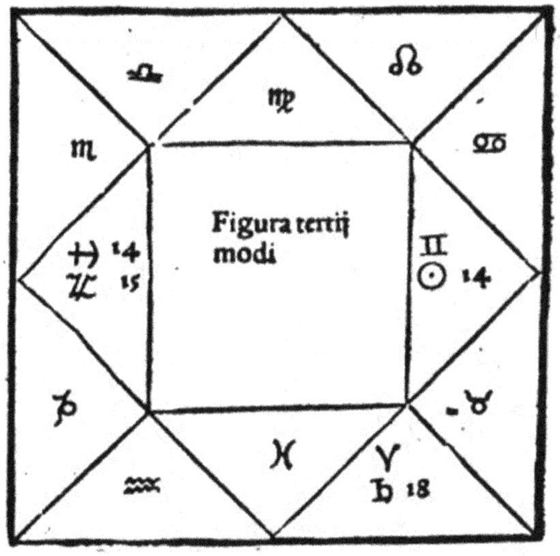

The exposition of the third way is when one planet who is the significator of the quesited matter is not joined to the Lord of the Ascendant of the question, but both are joined to another planet who is heavier than them both, and to whom both planets commit their virtue, and this heavier planet will perfect the quesited matter. Just as in this example. A certain man quesited whether he would attain a certain church position which he was striving for, and the Ascendant was 14 degrees of Sagittarius, and Jupiter was in it at 15 degrees, and the Sun, who was the significator of the church position was in 14 degrees Gemini, and Saturn was in 18 degrees Aries, and both were joining to Saturn, and he collected the light of both of them; this collection of the light of Jupiter and the Sun that Saturn was making signified that the matter would be perfected, and that he will attain the quesited church position. And this because the Sun, who was the Lord of the 9th house (which signified the church position), commits his disposition to Saturn, since the Sun receives him from his own exaltation (Aries), and Saturn entrusted and committed the quesited matter to Jupiter, which was committed to him by the Sun, and the matter would have been perfected more preferably if the querent had sought the quesited matter for another rather than having sought it for himself. For even though Jupiter is joined to Saturn by a trine aspect, Saturn still did not receive him by perfect reception, only receiving him by triplicity. And it appeared that the matter would be perfected by the hands of the querent's brother, and if he didn't have a brother, it would be a brother of someone who makes themselves appear as if they love the querent when they don't love him, and if it is not such a person, it will be the son of one of his friends, and if such a person is not found, it will be a slave of some magnate, and if such a person it not found, it will be some enemy of the church. And if this enemy of the church is not found, it will be an enemy of the querent's' son, and if he doesn't have a son, or if his son doesn't have a friend, it will be some hidden enemy of the querent's' father. If the querent doesn't have a father, or his father does not have such enemies, it will then happen through simony. And this way of perfecting matters is lasting.

On Another Way Of Perfecting Matters

There is another way of perfecting matters, which can be said to be subordinate to the preceding one, which is neither as long lasting nor as perfect, namely that if two planets join another planet heavier than them, and commit disposition and virtue to him (just as has been said of Jupiter and the Sun, and how they commit their virtue to Saturn). And this heavier planet, who receives their disposition was impeded, (namely cadent, retrograde, or combust, or joined to malefics who impede him) or was besieged by malefics, I say that he can perfect the matter, and sometimes perfects it, but after it is arranged and perfected, it will be destroyed and will not remain in its perfection. Whence you will be able to judge for him who asks you, that it appears that the matter will be perfected, but it will be destroyed after it is perfected.

On Certain Other Accidents Of Matters Which Are Perfected

Sometimes it happens otherwise in matters which are perfected, namely that certain ones come to be with difficulty, duress, labour and the greatest complications, while certain come to be with ease, certain are done with striving and inconvenience, certain are done with striving and without great inconvenience, certain are done without striving or any difficulty - in fact they come without any thought whatsoever.

On Those Matters Which Come Easily

Those which arrive easily and without striving, and without any difficulty, as unhindered things, are when the Lord of the Ascendant or the significator of the querent and the significator of the quesited matter are joined by a trine or sextile aspect, and with reception.

On Those Matters Which Come To Be Shortly

Those matters which come to be shortly and without any striving (even the querent doesn't have hope of them coming to be), are when the Lord of the Ascendant joins with the Lord of the quesited matter by a trine aspect without reception, or from a sextile with reception.

On Those Matters Which Come To Be With Striving

Those matters which come to be with the striving and effort of the querent, are when the Lord of the Ascendant is joined with the significator of the quesited matter by a square aspect with reception, or a sextile without reception.

On Those Matters Which Come To Be With Striving, Effort, And Labour

Those which are done with striving, effort, perseverance, labour, and great difficulty, are when the significator of the querent is joined with the significator of the quesited matter by opposition, or from a square aspect without reception.

On Those Matters Which Come To Be With Labour, Yet Are Hardly Perfected

Those which are done with the greatest labour, perseverance, striving, effort, difficulties, anxiety, sorrow, and almost after the desperation of friends and relatives, and yet still are hardly or never perfected, and if they are perfected, their effects will be long delayed (and indeed with expense); are those in which the Lord of the Ascendant or the Moon, and the Lord of the quesited matter are joined from opposition without reception.

When A Matter Someone Wants Comes To Be Without Reception

There is another way which a matter which someone intends to have is perfected, and it is easier than all others mentioned above; namely when the significator of the quesited matter is joined to the significator of the one who wants it from a sextile aspect with reception, or a trine without reception; or if the significator of the quesited matter is in the Ascendant, or in the house signifying the person for whom the matter is sought for. Understand the same for a bodily conjunction as of the aspects, for then the matter will come to be extremely easily.

When The Matter Sought Is A Magistracy Or Dignity

Indeed, if the matter sought is a magistracy or lay dignity which is hoped for by someone, and if the querent hopes to get this from a king or anyone who is his master, and the significator of the aforementioned matter is in the Ascendant, or is joined to the Lord of the Ascendant, or with the Moon from a trine or sextile aspect, or corporeally and with reception, it signifies that the quesited matter will be perfected without his own striving, and without the striving of anyone else on his behalf.

How The Matter Will Come To Be When Someone Hopes For A Matter From Some Magnate

And if someone hopes for any matter from someone who is below king in rank, or from a friend of his, or from the commoners of any land, or the like, the matter will come to be, and it will come to be by some chance occurrence.

When A Conjunction Or Aspect Does Not Intervene

However, if there is not a conjunctional aspect between them, but there is a transfer of light, the matter will be done through the hands of legates, who will involve themselves in the matter to perfect it. To know who these legates are, look to the house whose Lord is the significator of whichever planet it is, or of the houses in which they are found, as I have sufficiently explained to you already. For it would be tedious to explain this everywhere. And then similarly examine the Moon: for if she is then separating from the significator of the person who desires the matter, or even from the significator of the querent, and is joined to the significator of the quesited matter, she signifies that those who will run to and fro between them will come from the side of the querent, and with his knowledge and will. However, if she was separated from the planet signifying the quesited matter, and was joined to the significator of him seeking the matter, it signifies that it will begin from the part of the quested matter, or from those who can perfect it. And if the matter is perfected by legates, these legates will be of those persons which are signified by the houses of which those planets are the Lords. Examine then, to see which persons are signified by those houses, and judge according to them. Whether they are familiars or a brother, or a neighbour, or the father, or a son, or a servant, or an associate, or his familiars, or a religious person, or a king or master, or a friend, or a hidden enemy.

And you should know, even if I said that the matter will be perfected through a trine or sextile aspect, still you ought to understand well: that if the place from which the Lord of the Ascendant or the Moon is aspected by the Lord of the quesited matter (namely by that which the matter itself is signified), or the place from which the Lord or significator of the matter aspects the Lord of the Ascendant or the Moon is the detriment of the aspecting planet; the matter will not be perfected, even if it is a sextile or trine aspect, as is the case with this example.

The Ascendant was Leo and the question was whether a marriage would be perfected or not, and the Sun was joined to Saturn, or the Moon (who has the signification of women), from Aries, which is the detriment of Saturn. Even if the aspect in itself is with reception, nevertheless Saturn will not perfect the matter, but rather he will impede it, so that it is not perfected - not only will he impede it, but in fact he will strive to destroy it if he can. And if the Sun joins him from Cancer or Leo he will do the same, since both of those signs are his fall. Similarly if the significator of any matter, or the Moon, joins the Sun from Libra (which is his descension), or from Aquarius (which is his fall), since then the Sun will not receive any of them and thus he would destroy the matter, and not permit it to perfect. Or if he joins Venus from Scorpio, Aries, or Virgo, or Jupiter from Capricorn, Gemini, or Virgo. And so understand for the detriment of any of the planets: nor will any aspects then have any worth, except if reception intervenes, which shatters this evil. And understand the same if the significator or the Moon joins a planet which is in the detriment of the significator or the Moon; so that if Mercury is the significator and joins a planet which is in Sagittarius or Pisces, or if the Moon joins a planet which is in Scorpio or Capricorn, or if a planet joins any planet placed in its own descension, or he who is in the descension of the other, joins the planet whose fall it is - this planet will always strive to destroy and annul the matter.

And indeed there is another thing which introduces fear into matters, this being if a planet which is the significator of the quesited matter is a malefic, and shows that the matter ought to be perfected from an aspect or from opposition - this will frighten the querent lest any grave incident befall him from the matter, from which he will more strongly hope for that matter not to be perfected, than for it to be perfected.

But if there is a trine or sextile aspect with reception, it will be secure: however if it is without reception, it will not be as evil as he feared, even if it will not be as secure as he wanted it to be. Apart from this if the significator of the querent and he significator of the quesited are the same planet (as often occurs), and it is not received in the place in which it is, it signifies that the matter ought not to be perfected; for if it is with reception, it signifies that the matter ought to be perfected with a good perfection, unless the planet who receives him is impeded by fall, combustion, or retrogradation; since even if it will come to be, it will not be perfected by as good perfection as it would be when it the planet is not impeded.

And there is another thing, this being if the significators are aided to perfect matters, namely if the signs agree in nature with the planets, and will assist them, and other planets exhibit their testimony by them.

And Zael said that it is convenient for us if the Ascendant is a fixed sign, or a common sign. Also understand that the Ascendant is made diverse according to the diversity of persons, by beginning from the 1st house all the way up to the twelfth, and the angles should not be remote, but stable, that is, so that the 10th house is the tenth sign from the Ascendant, and the angle of the earth is the fourth sign from the Ascendant, and indeed so that the 10th house is not the ninth sign from the Ascendant and the 4th house is not the third sign from the Ascendant.

III

By Which Significators It Is Known Whether Matters Ought To Be Perfected

And it is fitting that you know the significations by which it is known whether matters ought to be perfected or not: of which the first is the Lord of the Ascendant. The second is the Moon, since as said elsewhere, she participates in every matter. The third is the planet signifying the quesited matter. Which when they are all joined together, they signify the effecting of the whole matter in the houses signifying the matters.

And always make sure to diversify the Ascendants just as I told you now; for if two of them (namely the Lord of the Ascendant and the Lord of the quesited matter, or the Moon and the Lord of the quesited matter), are joined together, it signifies that the matter will come to be by two thirds. But if only one of them is attested to, it signifies that the querent will perfect the quesited matter by one third. Understand this in matters which are susceptible to partition, since if they are matters which cannot be partitioned, either they will be done in whole, or not done at all. However if in matters which are not partitioned you have two of the aforementioned testimonies, declare the effect of the quesited matter in full. If indeed you only have one of them, the matter will hardly or never be perfected, but if it is perfected it will come to be with hardship, delays, the greatest labour, and complications. as are marriages which either are done in whole, or are not done in whole, and similar things: in the case of a marriage, I am speaking of a single one. For if it is multiple marriages at once, as sometimes happens when it is sought by many women and many men - as when someone enquires for himself, and for his father, or his brother, or son, or anyone else; for then it is possible for some of these to be perfected, and some of them not to be perfected, according to what you see regarding the significators and testimonies occurring in the question.

And these three testimonies or significations are to be considered in any matter; which if they were all safe, without a doubt the matter would be wholly perfected for the querent. Indeed the significators (namely the Lord of the Ascendant, the Moon, and the Lord of the quesited matter) will be safe when they are free from combustion, fall, retrogradation, the square and opposition aspects of the malefics, and their besiegement, and their bodily conjunctions - which is rarely attained. And if, when all of these are safe, they are received by malefics from any aspect, the matter will be perfected, and for the good.

If they are received by benefics, the good will be increased again, so that the querent almost won't know what better result he could strive for, nor will he have believed that what he asked for could have turned out so perfectly. And you should not dismiss these words, since they have proven accurate in all matters, and work for all questions, and for all matters that anyone intends to do. Nevertheless much is discovered by considering the helpful and harmful fixed stars, which help or harm in the manner discussed in their own chapter.

GUIDO BONATTI'S

BOOK OF ASTRONOMY

PART TWO

On the Particular Judgements Of The Stars

I

That Which Has The Signification Of The Person Of The Querent, And What Will Happen To Him In Any Question, And In Any Matter Which He Intends To Undertake Or Begin, Inasmuch As Much As Whatever He Seeks Or Begins Pertains To Him, And Similarly On Those Things Which Appear To Naturally Pertain To This

In this first chapter we must deal with those things which pertain to the 1st house (which is the rising sign, and has the signification of the querent) or which appear to have a view to it, in accordance with how the question pertains to the 1st house. And I will tell you certain things which you ought to know about these things. Indeed diverse questions can be made, and in diverse ways, in accordance with how their qualities diversify them. For questions can be diversified according to their own nature, as when one is on one matter and there is another different from it. Indeed they can also be diverse according to other diverse significations, such as when at one time someone enquires for themselves, and another time they enquire for someone else. And I will tell you how you ought to examine each case, and similarly from what house you ought to examine, when someone asks a question. For it is not necessary that you always examine the 1st house for the Ascendant of the signified matter in every question.

But perhaps you might say "why didn't the sages write down any of these things which you said?" The reason for this was that they left it to the industry of the wise; since they were not speaking at this time as to introduce something, but spoke as if to those already introduced, and for the flourishing, and for the wise and instructed.

If someone asks about himself, you ought to examine the first.

But if he enquires about his own substance or about the other significations of the 2nd house, you ought to examine the second.

If he enquires about siblings or about the other significations of the 3rd house, you ought to examine the third.

If he enquires about his father or any of the other significations of the 4th house, you ought to examine the fourth.

If he enquires about children or any of the other significations of the 5th house, you ought to examine the fifth.

If he enquires about servants or any of the other significations of the 6th house, you ought to examine the sixth.

If he enquires about his wife or any of the other significations of the 7th house, you ought to examine the seventh.

If he enquires about religion of any of the other significations of the 9th house, you ought to examine the ninth.

If he enquires about a kingdom or any of the significations of the 10th house, you ought to examine the tenth.

If he enquires about friends or any other significations of the 11th house, you ought to examine the eleventh.

If he enquires about hidden enemies or any of the other significations of the 12th house, you ought to examine the twelfth.

And you should always remember these things.

II

How You Ought To Look At The Shadow When Questions Are Posed To You

When you are asked about any matter of which the querent wishes to pose a question to you about, take the altitude of the Sun - if it is a diurnal question. However if it is at night, take the altitude of one of the fixed stars inscribed in the astrolabe, or with another instrument suitable for this, as soon as you can, accurately, immediately, without any delay or interval as soon as the words leave the mouth of the querent.

And take care that you do not deviate in anything, lest any error falls in the matter about which the question was posed to you. And observe the method which I told you in the examination of the house which signifies the quesited matter. And similarly beware lest you mix diverse topics together with questions at diverse times.

For if some question is made to you, let us say that it is on marriage, and you examine it' and shortly after that the same querent, or perhaps another, poses another question to you, on whatever topic, don't mix it with the one you already examined. Since the Ascendant has already changed; and so it is necessary for the judgement to be changed; whence you could thereby be guilty of being deceived in your judgement. But nevertheless you will be able to take it up with the required altitude, and it will be a different judgement from the first one. Nevertheless still you will be able to accept more than one question under multiple headings under one Ascendant, if they have been considered by the querent and held in his mind for one day, or for a day and a night, so that the entire heaven has revolved at least once, provided that the questions are diverse, so that one is not on the same topic as another. And similarly beware lest the querent came to you for reason of testing you or catching you out, as certain men tend to do sometimes, or that they did not hold the question in their heart for a day and a night, just as I said to you elsewhere, if you remember correctly. For matters will spring up according to the amount of worry, hope, and money of the querent. For when someone asks you about any matter, the house and places of the planets, and their disposition signifies what will come to be of the matter which he enquired about for the whole of the time of his life. Similarly in nativities, even if nativities are sometimes altered though the revolutions of the years, sometimes being augmented according to them; other times being decreased according to them.

And in general questions about fortune, namely whether someone's question is regarding the whole course of life, or a determinate period of time, such as for one or more years or months, or a week or a day, and so on: since whatever an agent intends to be any end of his acts to be, he acts according to his estimation of his intended ends, and according to the result which he foresees. And you should know this, since every person who asks a question, does not ask except about this, and according to that which the planets and signs (and their disposition regarding any good or evil) prevail over at the root of his nativity.

III

What Is The Trunk And What Are The Branches Of This Tree

Questions are the truck of this tree, and the considerations which you must have about the questions are its branches. And by these considerations you will see how the Lord of the Ascendant of any question, any nativity, any beginning, or of any matter is made fortunate, and how the Moon is made fortunate, and how the Lord of the house signifying the quesited matter is made fortunate. For nobody asks about this otherwise than what I have now told you, and according to that (except perhaps if they ask knowingly, and you ought not to examine those ones, as is said elsewhere). For nobody is born or enquires in a good hour, under a good and fortunate Ascendant, except fortunate people and those who ought to be surrounded by goods and fortune. And nobody is born, and nobody enquires under an evil and unfortunate Ascendant, except unfortunate men and those who ought to be surrounded by evil and misfortune. From which it happens that we see some fortunate men and some unfortunate men.

IV

Why The Astrologer Should Not Examine For Himself

It seemed to the ancient sages, and especially Messala, that the Astrologer ought not to examine for himself, lest he perhaps be deceived in his own matter: since it rarely happens that he would not have some regret over the Ascendant; whence it would be fitting that he should ask someone else according to the aforementioned method. Indeed after the other person has accepted his question, he will be able to examine and judge his own question, or he may give his own question to another person (whether in writing or otherwise), naturally to someone who is concerned about his matter. And he may offer it whenever he wishes after he has posed the question. Or he will place in his own mind saying "when I will meet with such a sign I will make it the Ascendant of the question which I intend to ask for myself, and it will be just as effective".

Whence if there was a question on a matter which ought to last, or be in stable condition, or which ought to be improved or deteriorated, or swiftly concluded, or changed, the Lord of the Ascendant is then to be examined, and it is to be seen whether he joins the Lord of the quesited matter, or if the Lord of the quesited matter joins him, and if so, from what aspect. Since if they are joined by a trine or a sextile, and this is in angles or from angles, or from succeedents, it signifies the effecting of the quesited matter. Indeed it also signifies its durability and stability and improvement, and this will be even better if the aspect is with reception, since then it signifies the complete goodness of the matter without any diminution.

For if it is a square aspect, it will reduce much of the querent's intention, and much of the goodness and durability of the thing itself, even if it is with reception. It will be diminished even if it is a trine or a sextile without reception, even if it will be somewhat less of a reduction than in the case of the square. If it is a square or an opposition without reception it signifies the destruction of the matter, and that there will be no good or durability in it.

But if the Lord of the Ascendant and the Lord of the quesited matter join some planet which is heavier than them, and this planet receives their disposition, and also aspects the Ascendant or any other planet aspecting the Ascendant (and if it has any dignity in the Ascendant), and if it's not impeded, it signifies the goodness and the effecting of the matter, along with its durability and stability.

If the receiver of disposition does not aspect the Ascendant, and isn't joined to a planet who aspects the Ascendant from its own place, it will be bad, for it signifies annulment and malice, and the destruction of the matter itself.

However if the Lord of the Ascendant is heavier than the Lord of the quesited matter, and the Lord of the quesited matter is joined to him from a good aspect, or from any aspect (apart from opposition) with perfect reception, it signifies the goodness and durability of the matter. Understand the same for a conjunction with the Lord of the quesited matter, if the Lord of the quesited matter is not joined with the Lord of the Ascendant. And always understand this - that the significators, as much the Lord of the Ascendant as the Lord of the quesited matter, as the receiver of disposition, as the Moon, should be free from malefics and their impediments.

To give an example, someone posed a question about a marriage -whether it would be perfected or not - and the Ascendant of this question was 20 degrees Leo, with Saturn here at 17 degrees, the Sun in Libra at 14 degree. This signified that the matter would come to be and be perfected free from all contradiction: since both of the significators received each other, and that the perfected matter would be good, durable, peaceful, and happy. Say the same for other questions so configured.

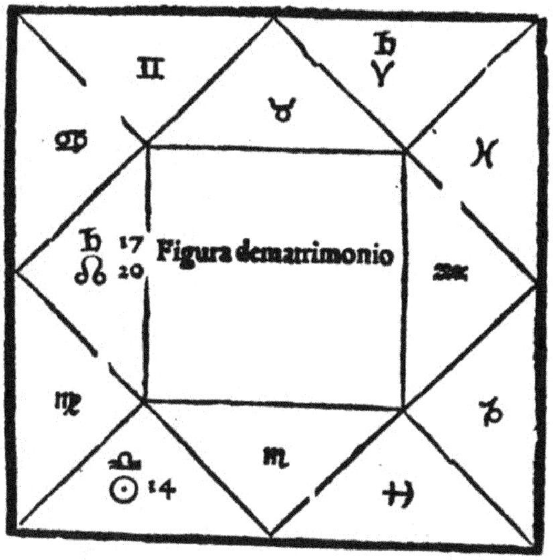

However, if the Sun was in Libra placed at 10 degrees, and Saturn was in Aries at 25 degrees, even if each significator receives the other, it still signifies the impediment of the matter, whatever the topic of the question was; and a diminution of the good which is signified by reception, and that it will hardly or never be perfected. And if it is perfected it will be with perseverance, and the greatest labour and anxiety; and even when it is perfected it will not be good or durable, in fact it appears that it will be destroyed after its perfection, and if it isn't destroyed it will endure in an evil and restless manner: since their aspect is from opposition and both of the significators are impeded.

Another Example Which Zael Placed In His Book Of Judgements

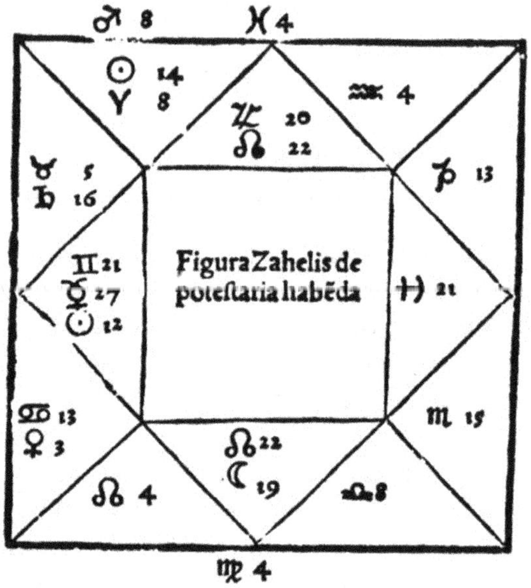

A certain soldier enquired as to whether he would get a position of authority in that year, and his question was absolute, since it did not specify which position, nevertheless he hoped to have a particular position. The Ascendant of his question was 21 degrees of Gemini, 13 degrees of Cancer was the 2nd house. 4 degrees Leo was the 3rd house. 4 degrees of Virgo was the 4th house. 8 degrees Libra was the 5th house. 15 degrees Scorpio was the 6th house. The remaining six houses were in opposition to the aforementioned. The places of the planets were as follows. Saturn was in 6 degrees of Gemini. Jupiter was stationary in 20 degrees of Pisces. Mars was in 8 degrees of Taurus. The Sun was in 12 degrees of Cancer. Venus in 3 degrees of Leo. Mercury in 27 degrees of Gemini. The Moon in 19 degrees of Virgo. The Caput Draconis in 22 degrees of Virgo. The Cauda in its opposition. The Part of Fortune was in 14 degrees of Aries.

Zael said, therefore I examined this question, namely the Ascendant and its Lord, and the Moon (which are the significators of the querent), and the Midheaven and its Lord, (which are the significators of the quesited matter). But Mercury, who is a significator of the querent, was in the 1st house, clearly in the Ascendant near the end of the sign, and was separating from Jupiter (who was a significator of the quesited matter). And this signified that he would not have a position of authority in that year.

Then I began to operate through the Moon, who was in opposition to Jupiter, a significator of the quesited matter. Whence as much as it is from this (that she joins him), it signifies that he would obtain a position of power in that year, but since the conjunction was from opposition it would only come with labour, inconvenience, perseverance, difficulties, and the greatest distress, which would not have been the case if the conjunction was from a trine or sextile aspect; in fact in this case he would have attained it easily, without labour, and with the greatest ease. Then I examined Jupiter, the significator of the quesited matter, and he was in the house signifying the quesited matter, which signified the effecting of the matter - if he happened to be in good condition and well disposeed that is; but he was in his first station, wanting to go retrograde. Whence, even if he received disposition from the Moon, nevertheless on account of his debility he could not uphold the matter, and this showed that he who is labouring at this so that the matter will be perfected, will not be able to lead it to effect. And so the bad disposition of Jupiter signified the destruction of the quesited matter and its annulment, and it appeared that he who had the position of authority at that time was the reason why this was not attained; and this was because Jupiter (who destroyed the matter) was the Lord of the 10th house, which signified the position of power. And if the Lord of the 11th house was the planet which was impeded, it would appear that the detriment and destruction of the matter ought to come from the side of some friend of the querent. And if it was the Lord of the twelfth it would have happened because of someone who pretends to be a friend of the querent, when he is in fact a hidden enemy. And if the Lord of the Ascendant was the receiver of disposition who impeded, and who was impeded, it would signify that the querent himself would be the cause of the destruction of the quesited matter; since he would commit to a course of action which would not cause the matter to be perfected. And since the Lord of the Ascendant moved from its own house into another, it signified that the querent would change his proposal quickly into another, and since it moved to the 2nd house, it appeared that this change was for the reason of acquiring substance which he didn't have. And it appeared that this change would be made to a certain place in which he was at another time on the occasion of acquiring money for himself. Besides this, Mars, who was the Lord of the 6th house, was harming the querent so that the matter would not come to be for him: since it appeared that the querent was to fall ill in the place to which he intended to travel, and this was signified by Mars receiving the Lord of the Ascendant, but nevertheless making him unfortunate. And if he did not fall ill, things would have befallen him and happened to him, and passed through his hands in such a way that the things he himself did would have been the reason why he did not obtain the quesited position of power. And a slave, or someone else under the querent's' power, would have risen up against him, and resist him so that he would not obtain the quesited position of power. Or perhaps it would have been the populace and others from the rabble who do not have any employment other than shouting and spreading rumours, not knowing what they are shouting about.

Similarly it was signified through Jupiter (the significator of the quesited matter), that some detriment would befall the querent, or some sorrow, on account of which he would not obtain the dignity in question. And even if he did not express the intention he had about this matter; nevertheless, Mercury (who was his significator) appeared to indicate that he had hope in it, since Mercury was at that time separating from Jupiter (the significator of the quesited matter). Whence it appeared that the question was posed as though from desperation, but not total desperation. And this was on account of Mercury, who, even if he was separating from Jupiter (the Lord of the 10th house), nevertheless he still aspected Jupiter. Whence you could say to the querent "even if you pretend to be ignorant of what you are enquiring about, I know very well that you had previously hoped for it, and that now you fear that you may not be able to perfect it." And just as I have discussed with you regarding the position of authority, you may understand similarly for any matter signified by any one of the twelve houses.

V

How to inspect planets impeding matters so that they do not come to pass

Allowing that it may appear more suitable to place this chapter somewhere else, nevertheless it appears to me that it should be placed here, since if it was deferred to the tractate on nativities, you might be in want of it in many other places; for it doesn't just have a place in nativities, but also in all questions, in all journeys, and in all beginnings of any matters which we want and intend to do. And the planet which impedes matters so that they do not come to be or are not perfected, is to be examined, and he can be called to be called strong, "killing", or "prohibiting" or "destroying" planet or the cutter, since he is the planet who cuts off the life of the native and destroys it, and does not permit the native to achieve a long life, namely to arrive at old age; and he is the one who corrupts matters and destroys them after they are thought to be arranged, and when they appear they ought to be perfected. And he is the one who our ancients called "the cutter" or "the abscisor", and you ought to examine him in nativities and in questions, so that you know whether a matter ought to be perfected or not, and whether it will arrive at the desired effect. And we will take this from the planet to whom the Lord of the Ascendant, or the significator of the quesited matter (or the Moon, if she herself is participating Lord of the Ascendant, or the significator of the quesited matter) is joined to.

For you ought to consider the planet to whom the significator of the querent, or the significator of the quesited matter, or the Moon is joined to and examine how this planet is disposeed, and the planet to whom this planet is conjoined. Because if the Lord of the Ascendant, or the Moon, or the significator of the quesited matter is joined to a malefic and badly disposeed planet, without reception - or if the malefic itself is not badly disposeed, but is joined to another badly disposeed malefic who doesn't receive him - it signifies the destruction of the quesited matter.

By a badly disposeed malefic planet I mean one that is peregrine, and retrograde, combust, cadent from the Ascendant or the house of the quesited matter (so it does not aspect the house in question, or at least its Lord, however the aspect of the house is stronger than the aspect of the house Lord in this case) - or a planet in its fall or descension. Indeed he is the one who is called the cutter or the destroyer.

Moreover if the significator of the querent or quesited matter, or the Moon, or a planet to which the Moon is joined, or if the Moon herself is the significator or participator with the Lord of the Ascendant, is joined to some unfortunate planet (unfortunate meaning retrograde, combust, or cadent), then examine if reception intervenes; since this will signify the perfection of the quesited matter, even if it will be burdensome and fatiguing to perfect. However if reception doesn't intervene, it signifies the corruption of the matter and its destruction, and that the matter will not be perfected after it is thought to be arranged. However if the planet who receives the Lord of the Ascendant or the Moon, or the Lord of the quesited matter, or a planet to whom one of them is joined, is not received and free, or received by an unfortunate planet, it signifies the perfection of the matter with ease.

And if the planet to whom the Lord of the Ascendant, or the Moon, or the Lord of the quesited matter is joined is free from malefics, but is joined to some benefic planet, which itself is joined to a malefic who is impeded, and doesn't receive him (and understand this for any one of the seven planets), the matter will not be perfected, nor will it arrive at a good end.

Always understand this: that if these conjunctions are made without reception: (since with reception it will be perfected, even if it will be with fatigue) the matter will perfect; nevertheless, with this having been considered and discerned first - that if some planet cuts off the light of one of the aforementioned planets when it wants to join with a malefic, that it takes away the harm, and then the malefic will not prohibit the perfection of the matter. But if the cutting-off of light does not intervene, the matter will be prohibited and it will not be perfected; and if it is perfected, it will be destroyed. And you will also consider this, that if reception intervenes, and not from opposition, or square aspect (since then if a planet is badly disposeed, it will not benefit from this reception, which is made by opposition or square aspect, and especially if the receiver is impeded) but from a trine or a sextile, then it will be efficacious, and it will be believed then that the matter ought to perfect. If the planet who receives is then well disposeed, regardless of what aspect this reception is made from, it will perfect the matter, and it will not be obstructed by a square or opposition. However if it is from a trine or a sextile, the matter will be perfected, because the planet to whom the significator is joined is well disposeed (whether it is with reception or not). Nevertheless, this must happen in such a way that the aspect or conjunction is not yet complete, and that it has not begun to separate in any way.

And if the significator is joined with a benefic which is not impeded, the matter will be perfected.

And if one of the planets transfers light or virtue between the significator and another planet; and the planet to whom the light is transferred is a malefic, and this malefic is also (as has been said) impeded, the matter will be corrupted, unless the impeding or receiving malefic is received itself. If indeed the significator of the querent (or the Moon), and the significator of the quesited matter are joined to any planet which collects the light of both of them, and this planet is unfortunate or malefic, it will destroy the matter and not permit it to be perfected, unless this planet receives both of the significators; for even if he receives one of them, the matter will nonetheless be destroyed.

Also consider whether the significator of the querent is found in the house of the quesited matter, or moving toward a conjunction with its Lord, since this signifies that the querent is moving towards the quesited matter. However if the significator of the quesited matter is found in the Ascendant, or moving towards a conjunction with the significator of the querent, it signifies that the quesited matter is coming to the querent: nevertheless, with the receptions and aspects and the Moon will remain in their own condition.

ON THE SECOND HOUSE

I

On The Substance Which The Querent Hopes To Get For Himself

If anyone inquires of you, whether they are going to get substance which they hope for, or not, find out from them of which kind of substance it is that they intend to get or acquire: and then examine the Ascendant and its Lord, and the Moon (which are the general significators of the querent). And do not let yourself be deceived in this - whatever kind of person he is who enquired about substance which he hoped to acquire, he will be given the 1st house, whether he is a king, or someone else, whether a cleric, or a layman, or the Pope, or any prelate, or a nobleman, or any other person .For nobody has the prerogative in this case, nor is any condition, order or sex preferred. All are equal in this matter, as long as they are asking for themselves. And you will give the second sign and its Lord to the substance, unless otherwise specified by the querent.

If the Lord of the Ascendant or the Moon is joined to the Lord of the house of substance, or the Lord of the house of substance is joined to the Lord of the Ascendant, or if the Lord of the house of substance is in the Ascendant; or if the Lord of the Ascendant or the Moon are in the house of substance; or if the Moon or some other planet is transferring light between the Lord of the Ascendant and the Lord of the house of substance (namely from one of them to the other), it signifies that the querent will obtain the substance which he enquired about. And if this is not the case for the Lord of the Ascendant, or the Moon, or the Lord of the house of substance, then examine if Jupiter, (who is the natural significator of substance) or Venus (who is naturally benefic), or the Caput Draconis (without the aspect of any malefic) is in the house of substance, for the querent will acquire and obtain the substance.

Understand the same if the question about substance is absolute, namely when the querent does not specify otherwise in his question, but only says: "will I acquire substance or not?". In this case you ought to examine as you did above. If you don't find anything about substance, tell him that he won't come find substance, but will remain in his current condition; unless a malefic (the malefics being Saturn, Mars, and the Cauda) is in the house of substance alone, without the aspect of any benefic; for this will cause the destruction of substance, unless perhaps the malefic is received by the Lord of the house of substance, or he himself is the Lord of this house, and otherwise in good condition (not retrograde, not combust, or impeded in any other way); since then his malice will be reduced.

And if the Cauda is with them in the house of substance it will increase their evil and make it worse. But if the Cauda is in the house of substance with benefics it will reduce much of their good, and will even take away one quarter of the substance after it is acquired, and sometimes more. And if you find one of the malefics in the house of substance in bad condition, and you find the Moon void-of-course, or joined to malefics impeding her, it signifies that he will not acquire substance at all over the whole course of his life, in fact it will appear that whatever he has will be reduced, and that he will always be indigent and mendicant.

II

From Where He Will Acquire Substance And From Where He Will Lose It, And From What Cause

If indeed you see that the querent is to acquire wealth, and you want to know from where he will acquire it, and from what cause - or if he is to lose it, in what circumstances will he will lose it; then examine the planets which I mentioned to you above, who participate in matters of substance. And consider the planet to whom another is joined; since the heavier planet of the two will signify by what means, and from where he will acquire substance.

Similarly examine which house the heavier planet of the two (the one to whom the other joins) is the Lord of, and see in what house the heavier planet who receives disposition is placed (namely the one to whom the other is joined).

For if he is in the Ascendant, or is the Lord of the Ascendant, the querent will acquire substance by the labour of his own hands and through his own person.

However if it is in the second, or is the Lord of the second, he will acquire it with his own substance, as through commerce and similar things, as do those working with their own things to acquire others which they don't have.

If it is in the third, or is the Lord of the third, he will acquire it from brothers, and if he doesn't have brothers, he will acquire it from his neighbours, or from fellow citizens, or from certain people known to him who make themselves appear to be his friends but are not perfect friends, or on the occasion of the aforementioned people.

If it is in the fourth, or is the Lord of the fourth, he will acquire it from his father, uncle, or father in law, or any of his older ancestors. If he does not have such parental figures, he will acquire it from land and estates or immovable things.

And if it is in the fifth, or is the Lord of the fifth, he will acquire it from his children, and if he doesn't have children, he will acquire it from certain people in whom he has confidence, who, even if they are not true friends, will still make him profit.

And if it is in the sixth, or is the Lord of the sixth, and the sixth is a human sign, he will acquire it from slaves and clients. If he doesn't have slaves or clients he will acquire it from small domestic animals, such as sheep, goats, pigs, and similar beasts (if the sixth is a quadrupedal sign). And if he doesn't have animals, he will acquire it from ill people, or at least from worthless people.

And if it is in the seventh, or is the Lord of the seventh, he will acquire it from women (if the seventh is a feminine sign); or he will acquire it from enemies; or perhaps in estates; or he will acquire it from associates; or from a contention with some people.

And if it is in the eighth, or is the Lord of the eighth, he will acquire it from his wife's goods; or from the inheritances of the dead; or he will acquire it in foreign lands which he travels to freely (not because he is forced).

And if it is in the 9th house, or is the Lord of the 9th house, he will acquire it from the religious; and if not from them, reckon it as coming from all consecrated clerics, or because of religion; or on the occasion of the teaching of divinity; or he will acquire it on the occasion of a long journey which he will make to places far from his own land, just as the Venetians do, and the Pisans, Genoans, Florentines, and all similar people who profit by long journeys.

And if it is in the tenth, or is the Lord of the tenth, he will acquire it from kings; and if not from kings, then from other magnates; or he will acquire it from offices or positions of power, if he is a person suitable to have such an office. If he were not suitable for this, he will acquire it from his own profession, with his own honour.

And if it is in the eleventh, or if it is the Lord of the eleventh, he will acquire it from friends, or from certain people in whom he has great hope; or he will acquire it from merchants that he does business with, as much in his own land as in foreign ones (yet this is stronger in his own land); or from things which come to him unexpectedly through his own good luck.

And if it is in the twelfth, or if it is the Lord of the twelfth, he will acquire it from hidden enemies, or people placed in confinement - if the twelfth is a human sign. If the twelfth is a quadrupedal sign, he will acquire it from large animals; if it is Taurus, from cattle; if it is Sagittarius, from horses or beasts of burden.

However, you should not forget this: that in whatever house you find the Cauda with a significator, it always reduces what is signified. And if you find the Caput there, it will increase what is signified. I maintain what was said above regarding their significations in the 2nd house.

III

On The Reason Why He Will Not Acquire Substance

If perhaps it does not appear that he will acquire substance, and you wish to know the reason why he will not acquire it, and what is the reason prohibiting him from acquiring substance, you should examine the receiver of disposition according to the method which I told you in the chapter above.

And if the planet who prohibits the acquisition of substance is the Lord of the Ascendant, the querent himself is the reason why he does not gain substance.

And if it is the Lord of the second, his substance will be the reason why he does not gain substance.

And if it is the Lord of the third, his brothers are the reason why he does not gain substance.

And understand this about the significators of all of the houses: that any one of them, by its own place and time, will be the reason why the querent does not gain substance, in accordance with what was said, that the reason that he will get it is by the same method, all the way up to the end of the twelve houses.

Those are the significations of the twelve houses. Whence, wherever you find the significator of substance, you ought to judge on the obtaining of substance through that house; and wherever you find the prohibitor of substance, you ought to judge on the prohibition of substance (so that it is not acquired by the querent) through that house. And so, look through all of the houses for the significations of all matters which pertain to you.

Moreover, the one who God willed to be a master said that since if the question is absolute, or not, it can be said whence he ought to have substance, we ought to determine the Ascendant and the house of substance (which is the second from the Ascendant just as was said elsewhere).

And we should examine the Lord of the house of life (which is the Lord of the Ascendant); and if we find him aspecting the Ascendant, or if he is joined to a planet which renders his light to the Ascendant, we ought to work with him.

If he does not aspect the Ascendant, nor some planet which aspected the Ascendant and rendered his light to the Ascendant, then we ought to examine the Moon; which if she aspects the Ascendant, or aspects some planet which aspects the Ascendant, and renders her light to the Ascendant, we ought to work with her.

If the Lord of the Ascendant and the Moon do not aspect the Ascendant, and neither of them were joined to a planet which aspects the Ascendant, then we ought to examine which of them (the Lord of the Ascendant and the Moon) is in more degrees in the sign in which it is in (which will leave the sign it is in and enter into another the fastest); and we ought to work with this planet. And the same philosopher said that it seems that if this planet, after it leaves the sign it is in, is immediately joined to the Lord of the house of substance, before another planet were joined to him, or before he is joined to another planet, it signifies that the querent will gain substance; regardless of whether the Lord of the Ascendant or the Moon (after it left the sign it was in) were received by the Lord of the house of substance.

And he does not relate whether the Lord of the house of substance should be a benefic or a malefic, since it is the conjunction of the Lord of the Ascendant or the Moon with the Lord of the house of substance that causes the obtaining of the matter (namely the substance which was sought).

Nevertheless, you ought to examine if the Lord of the house of substance is joined to some planet, or if some planet is joined to him, before the Lord of the Ascendant or the Moon is joined to the planet which the Lord of the house of substance commits his disposition to. And for this reason I said "immediately", lest some planet cut off the light or prohibit the conjunction of the Lord of the Ascendant or the Moon with the Lord of the house of substance.

If the question is about a determinate substance, see which house the quesited substance is signified; and examine if the Lord of the Ascendant and the Moon, or either of them, are joined with the Lord of the house signifying the matter: since the obtaining of the quesited matter will come to be through the conjunction of the Lord of the Ascendant (or the Moon) with the Lord of the house signifying the quesited matter. However, if the Lord of the Ascendant (or the Moon) were not joined with the Lord of the house signifying the quesited matter, then examine in all of the places, just as I said t you regarding the conjunction of the Lord of the house of substance in its change from one sign to another, and in the conjunction of the Lord of the quesited matter.

If indeed the Lord of the house of substance or the quesited matter commits his own disposition to another planet before he himself joins with the Lord of the Ascendant (or before the Lord of the Ascendant or the Moon is joined to him), examine who is the planet to whom the Lord of the house of substance or the quesited matter is joined, and say that this planet is the significator of the impediment making it so that the matter will not be perfected.

And examine which house he is the Lord of, since a person who is signified by that house is striving to make it so that the matter will not be perfected; especially if the planet t whom the Lord of the house of substance commits disposition is impeded - that is, if he is retrograde or combust, or in his fall, or in his descension, or cadent from the angles. If the receiver of disposition who joins the Lord of the house of substance or the quesited matter is impeded by any of the aforementioned impediments, and he is a benefic, he will not impede the quesited matter from being perfected, whether he receives the Lord of the Ascendant or not.

If he is a malefic, and he is not impeded by any of the aforementioned impediments, and receives the Lord of the Ascendant or the Moon, the matter will be perfected in a similar manner to the aspect by which the reception is made. If indeed this malefic does not receive the Lord of the Ascendant, and the conjunction is from a trine or sextile aspect, the matter will be perfected, even if it will happen with labour and delay. And if the conjunction is from a square aspect or from opposition, the quesited matter will hardly or never be perfected; and it is perfected it will be with such difficulties and such labour of the querent, that he will repeatedly say "*If only I had never gotten myself involved in this awful matter!*".

But if reception intervenes, the matter will be perfected. If it is a benefic that receives, the matter will come to be easily and in a short space of time. If it is a malefic who receives, the matter will come to be with burdens and delays. And there is no possibility that the matter will not be perfected, and there will be nothing that can prohibit it from happening, unless the querent wishes to give up on his proposal, so that the matter would not be perfected. But if the receiver of disposition is in an angle, it will hasten the effect of the matter; if it is in a succeedent it will delay it, and it will be less hastened; indeed if it is in a cadent it will be prolonged even more, even if it is received there. Indeed reception is of such fortitude, that it will not allow a matter to be annulled; for even if it is delayed, ultimately it will achieve the quesited effect, whether the question concerns substance or any other matter.

Besides this, if the Lord of the Ascendant and the Moon (or one of them) are joined to the Lord of the house of substance or of the quesited matter; or if they are joined to some benefic which is in the house of substance or of the quesited matter, the querent will obtain the thing or substance. And if one of them (namely the Lord of the Ascendant or the Moon) is joined to a benefic in the house of substance, but is joined to a malefic which is in the house of substance or of the quesited matter, and this malefic receives the Lord of the Ascendant or the Moon, the matter will come to be, and the Lord of the Ascendant or the querent will acquire it. And if this malefic does not receive the Lord of the Ascendant, nor the Moon: the if he himself has dignity in the house of substance or of the quesited matter: the querent will still acquire the substance or the quesited matter, even if it will be put off for a length time.

And if the Lord of the house of substance or of the quesited matter is lighter than the Lord of the Ascendant, and is joined to him (or some other planet which is in the house of substance or of the quesited matter, and is also lighter than the Lord of the Ascendant, and is joined to him) from a trine or sextile aspect, the substance will be acquired (or the quesited matter will come to be) with ease. If indeed the conjunction is from a square aspect, the matter will similarly come to be without great hardship if reception intervenes.

But if the Lord of the Ascendant is lighter, and is joined to the Lord of the 2nd house, or of the quesited matter, the matter will not come to be easily nor without the querent's effort. If the Lord of the quesited matter joins the Lord of the Ascendant (or of the querent), and receives him from a trine or sextile aspect, even more substance or more of the quesited matter will come to the querent than he had hoped for, and this will happen more easily. However if the Lord of the Ascendant or the Moon are not joined to the Lord of the house of substance or of the quesited matter, nor any planet which is in this house, you then ought to examine to which planet the Lord of the Ascendant or the Moon is joined to. Since if one of them is joined to a benefic, which itself is well disposeed and not impeded, or is in an angle, and this benefic is not joined to another planet, nor is another planet joined to the benefic who it receives it or commits its own disposition to it - the querent will acquire substance and the quesited matter will be perfected. But if this planet to whom the Lord of the Ascendant is joined receives another planet, and not the Lord of the Ascendant, or if the Moon joins him by a similar conjunction, and if he doesn't receive her, it is a different story; since the conjunction of the planet who receives, annuls the conjunction of the planet who does not receive. If the Lord of the Ascendant (or the Moon) is joined to a malefic which doesn't receive him, it signifies the destruction and annulation of the substance, or of the quesited matter, so that the querent will not acquire it, nor will the quesited matter be perfected for him, since the malefic planet insofar as it does not receive, will only strive towards the destruction of matters, just as benefics strive to perfect and obtain whether they receive or not; so do malefics strive to the contrary unless they receive, since then they refrain their own malice and perfect matters just like benefics do.

IV

Whether He Will Acquire The Substance Which He Seeks Or Which He Has Lent Or Entrusted To Someone

If there is a question from someone who enquires as to whether the person from whom he seeks money will give it to him; examine the Lord of the Ascendant and the Moon (which are the significators of the querent), and the second will be the house of his substance. The seventh and its Lord will be the significators of him from whom the money is sought, and the eighth and its Lord will be the significators of the substance of him from whom substance is sought.

Then examine if the Lord of the Ascendant or the Moon is joined to the Lord of the 8th house (who is the significator of the substance of the man from whom he seeks substance), or if one of them is joined to a planet placed in the 8th house; if the latte is a benefic, he will acquire the quesited substance: if he asks about getting something else, (namely from him from whom he seeks the substance), he will give it to him. If he seeks substance which he lent or entrusted to someone, he will similarly acquire it, whether the benefic is received (by the Lord of the Ascendant or the Moon) or not. If it is a malefic, and it receives the Lord of the Ascendant or Moon, he will similarly acquire the quesited substance. If it is not received, he will hardly or never recover it: and if he does get it, he will hardly or never get it in whole, and whatever he does get from it, he will only get with burdens, duress, and perseverance.

Similarly if the Lord of the eighth is in the first, or is in the second and the Lord of the second receives him, it signifies the attainment of the quesited matter. But if the Lord of the seventh or the Lord of the eighth is in the first or the second; and is not received by the Lord of the first, or the Moon, or the Lord of the second, it signifies that the querent will lose even more of his substance and it will increase the original injury. However if the Lord of the Ascendant or the Moon is joined to a benefic which has dignity in the Ascendant, the matter will come to be, or if any of them are joined to a malefic who has dignity in the Ascendant and receives the Lord of the Ascendant or the Moon, the matter which the querent asked about will come to be. And if the benefic to whom the Lord of the Ascendant or the Moon is joined is in a strong place, the matter will come to be, even without reception.

For all of these things said above, understand them to be referring to matters which are considered among lesser people and among those in communities, as are those living together in houses, states, castles, cities, and similar people, and not those which are not between persons of whom one greatly exceeds another in status. Understand people greatly exceeding others as kings, magnates, and those who are fit to be kings, as are the great dukes and the great marquises, for whom kingdoms are suitable, or even between religious people or between the lay and the religious, in matters which are not their own. And I will make mention of these things to you when they are considered in their own place and time, if it will please Our Lord Jesus Christ and True Man.

V

If He Will Obtain The Substance Of The King

Similarly, sometimes other questions on substance come into the hands of astrologers, such as when anyone enquires whether he will acquire the substance of any king, as soldiers of the king and other magnates sometimes do, such as when one of the aforementioned asks when will he get his soldiers pay from the king. and it is the same if he enquires about it when it is coming from the deputy of the king, or if it is someone who enquires about the substance which he believes he will have.

Then examine the Ascendant and its Lord, and the Moon (who are the significators of the querent), and the second from the Ascendant (which is the house of the querent's substance), and its Lord; and examine the tenth and its Lord, which are the significators of the king or his deputy, and of magnates who receive service; and examine the 11th house and its Lord, which are the significators of the substance of the king or magnate. If the Lord of the Ascendant or the Moon is joined with the Lord of the eleventh, or if one of them is joined to a planet placed in the eleventh (who is a benefic, and isn't impeded or badly disposeed), the querent will acquire that which he seeks from the kings substance, or from a magnates substance, whether he who enquired is a soldier, or anyone else, and whether the benefic receives the Lord of the Ascendant or the Moon, or not. If it is a malefic and he receives them, he will similarly obtain the quesited mater.. However if this malefic does not receive the Lord of the Ascendant or the Moon, the quesited matter will hardly or never be attained.

VI

On The Time Of The Aforementioned Things

If the querent also wanted to know when the quesited matter would come to be, examine then the planet to whom the Lord of the Ascendant or the Moon is joined, and who signified the effect of the matter; since if he aspects with the Lord of the Ascendant or the Moon by a trine or sextile aspect (whether it is a benefic that receives the Lord of the Ascendant or the Moon, or not) consider if he projects his light or rays upon the rays of the Lord of the Ascendant or the Moon. And see how many degrees are between them, namely from the degree in which one projects his rays upon the other, up to the perfection of the aspect degree for degree. And say that there will be that many days until the effecting of the matter if both are in cadents; if they are in succeedents it will be weeks; if they are in angles it will be months. And if it is a matter which appears that it could last longer, you can say that it will be years, and especially if the significators (namely the Lord of the Ascendant (or the Moon) and the planet to which it is joined), are in angles. If one of them is in an angle and the other is in a succeedent, then they signify months. If one is in a succeedent, and the other is in a cadent, then it signifies weeks. If one is in an angle and the other is in a cadent, it signifies months. And if it is the Sun, Venus, Mercury or the Moon, the degrees between them will similarly signify days, or the Sun and Venus might signify weeks or more.

Furthermore, Messala said that if this is not so, then it will be when the said planet corporeally joins with the Lord of the Ascendant, or with the Moon, degree for degree. If indeed at the hour of the question the planet who signified the effect of the matter with the Lord of the Ascendant in the same sign, the matter will come to be when they are corporeally conjunct in the same degree and minute - if the Lord of the Ascendant is heavier, (whether or not he is received by the planet who joins him). But if the Lord of the Ascendant is lighter, so that he moves toward the conjunction of the planet, signifying the effecting of the matter, and if he receives the Lord of the Ascendant, then the matter will come to be. If indeed he does not receive the Lord of the Ascendant, then the matter will not be perfected, unless the significator is in an angle when he makes the conjunction, or in a sign which is said to be his joy. If it is not like this, then it won't be perfected at that time; but it will be perfected when the planet to whom the Lord of the Ascendant or the Moon is joined (or who joins the Lord of the Ascendant) moves toward the Sun, or when the Sun moves towards him. And if he was combust, and exiting from combustion, then it will be when he begins to appear from under the rays of the Sun, whether he is before or after the Sun when he escapes from combustion, in such a way that he is seen outside of the Sun's rays. And if he is under the Sun's rays at the hour of the question, the matter will come to be when this planet begins to appear from under the rays.

ON THE THIRD HOUSE

I

On Brothers And Their Condition

If someone asks you about their brother, examine in what way he enquires, namely whether he enquires about a brother who is present, or about an absent brother, or a healthy brother, or an ill brother, or whatever state the querent's brother may be in.

Give the first to the querent, since the Ascendant signifies him, and then give the third to the brother. If an absent brother is quesited, then inspect the Lord of the 3rd house (who has the signification of the brother), and see where the Lord of the house of the brother is found. And you will see what his state and disposition ought to be like according to what is signified by the Lord of this house in which he is placed. And examine how the planets aspect him, whether he is in the aspect of benefics or malefics, and by what aspects they aspect him, and by what aspect he aspects them, or if they are corporeally conjunct.

For if the significator of the brother is in his own house, namely the third, and is not aspected by malefics from opposition or square aspect, you will then be able to say that his brother is well. If indeed he is aspected by malefics from opposition or square aspect, you will then be able to say that his brother lives, and is healthy, but is suffering distress, anxieties, and great worries. If indeed they aspect him from the mentioned aspects with reception, you will be able to say that his brother is suffering from the difficulties mentioned above, but will be well liberated, and will escape from them.

If indeed he is aspected by benefics from a trine or sextile aspect without reception, or from a square or opposition with reception, you will be able to say that his brother is well, and lives well in the land where he is. However if he is aspected by benefics by a trine or sextile aspect with reception, say that his brother is well, and is living well, and is prospering in all of his affairs, so that he lacks none of the necessities of life.

If indeed he is in the fourth without the aspects of malefics, he is striving to acquire money in the land which he is in.

If indeed he is in the fifth and is joined with the Lord of the fifth with reception (whether the Lord of the fifth is a benefic or not, as long as the he is not impeded in a bad way), it signifies that his brother finds himself well, and is happy, and rejoices with the people of that land in which he is. If indeed it is a benefic with whom the significator of the brother is joined, and the conjunction is by body, or a trine or sextile with reception, say that his brother is well, cheerful, happy, and rejoicing with the men and women of the place in which he is, and is enjoying food, drink, clothing, sex, and all things in which men delight - if he is a man suited to this, or who delights in such things (as are young men and those who are young at heart).

If indeed he is void-of-course in the fifth, or in corporeal conjunction with malefics, or in their square aspect or opposition without reception, and these malefics who impede him are similarly without reception, and themselves impeded, it signifies the brothers bad disposition, and his bad condition, and the poor temperament of his body, since the 5th house is the third from the house of the brother.

If indeed you find him in other houses (which won't be discussed here, as are the sixth, eighth, and twelfth, with the aforementioned significators, say the same, but it will be less good.

However if you find him in the eighth joined with a benefic by a trine or sextile aspect, say that his brother is not well, nor is he so ill that the querent ought to worry, nevertheless he has a bad temperament.

However if he is joined to malefics, and is in the sixth, or is joined to the Lord of the sixth, you will be able to say that his brother has fallen ill. And you can say the same if the Lord of the sixth is in the third, unless the Lord of the third is well disposeed, as said above. If you find the brother of the querent to be ill, then examine if the Lord of the third is joined to the Lord of the 8th house, or enters into combustion, for this signifies that he will die from this illness.

If indeed you find him in the seventh, say that he is in the land to which he has set out, he has not yet left from there, and stays in this land like a foreigner, and he is neither well disposed, nor very badly disposed, but finds himself between both.

If it is in the eighth, he should fear for himself, and especially if it is combust or joined to the Lord of the eighth in the eighth, or joined to malefics impeding him in the eighth, since then it signifies his death

If he is in the ninth it signifies that he is set out from the land where he was at first, and is going to another land further away; or perhaps he gave himself to some religion, or leads a clerical or religious life in some other way.

If indeed he is in the tenth and is joined to a benefic by trine or sextile aspect, and especially with reception, this signifies that he has acquired some office, or honour, or dignity in the land in which he is. If indeed it is joined to malefics by a square aspect or from opposition, or impeded in another way, or is combust in the tenth, his death will be feared.

If indeed he is in the eleventh joined to benefics by a good aspect, or is joined with the Lord of the eleventh, it signifies that he is with one of his friends with whom he is having a good time, rejoicing and delighting with him. If indeed malefics are aspecting him, it signifies that he is not happy with the things he has, nor does it appear to him that he is in good condition.

If indeed he is in the twelfth and is joined with benefics receiving him, and that benefic which receives him is not impeded, it signifies that he has some profession, or is dealing in horses and cattle, from which he is profiting, and he is leading his life in a laudable fashion. If indeed this benefic is impeded or is joined with malefics impeding it, it signifies his bad disposition, so that he is ill or badly disposed, and so that if he joins with the Lord of the eighth or is combust or entering into combustion, it is to be feared that the brother may die from this.

If it is in the first, he will rejoice and be made happy by those who love him, and he is well disposed.

If it is in the second, it signifies that whatever state he is in, he will not be rejoicing from it. It is possible that he is captured or detained in another way, so that he cannot leave the place which he is, when he wants.

If indeed it is retrograde, he will strive to return to his own place whenever he will be able.

And the present statements about brothers should suffice for you: since it would take a long time to discuss all of the accidents of brothers.

For if the querent asks about his ill brother, I will tell you about this below in the chapter on illness. If he enquires about a brother who is present and well, I will tell you those things which will be useful in the Tractate on Nativities in a discussion which will be as long as it needs to be.

Besides this it is fitting that I tell you certain other similar things which are possible to include in this chapter, which are as follows; namely if anyone enquires about the father, inspect the fourth for the father and say of him as you said on the brother in the 3rd house. And say of the fifth for the father as you said of the fourth for the brother. And say of the sixth for the father as you said for the fifth for the brother. And say of the seventh for the father as you said of the sixth for the brother. And say of the eighth for the father as you said of the seventh for the brother. And of the ninth for the father, say as you said of the eighth for the brother. And of the tenth say for the father, just as you said of the ninth for the brother. And of the eleventh for the father, say as you said of the tenth for the brother. And of the twelfth for the father, say as you said of the eleventh for the brother. And of the first for the father, say as you said of the twelfth for the brother. And of the second for the father, say as you said of the first for the brother. And of the third for the father as you said of the second for the brother.

If he enquires about his uncle, namely his father's brother, give him the fifth and say of the fifth for the uncle as you said of the third for the brother: and of the sixth for the uncle, as you said of the fourth for the brother, and so understand for all the houses.

If he enquires about a slave or a client, give the sixth to the slave, and say of the sixth for the slave, as you said of the third for the brother: and say of the seventh for the slave as you said of the fourth for the brother, and say of the eighth for the slave as you said of the fifth for the brother, and so on for them all.

For this is not something to be overlooked, since even if any house has its own sixth and its own eighth and its own twelfth, nevertheless in any question, the sixth of the question at its Lord signify its illness. The eighth of a question and its Lord signify its death. The twelfth and its Lord signify its capture. Still, they are diversified in this.

ON THE FOURTH HOUSE

I

On The House Or Inheritance Which Someone Intends To Buy, Or Get In Some Other Way, Whether The Querent Will Get It Or Not

If someone is concerned about some house, or about any piece of land, or a vineyard, or a meadow, or olive grove, or a forest, or some inheritance which he wants to buy, or otherwise hopes to get, and his question is absolute (so that he doesn't speak about the land or the house or the inheritance of such-and-such a person), examine the Ascendant and its Lord, and the Moon (which signify the querent), and examine the fourth sign and its Lord (which are the significators of the quesited matter)

If the Lord of the Ascendant (or the Moon) is in the fourth, or the fourth Lord is in the first, or one of them is corporeally conjunct with the other, or joined from a trine or sextile aspect with reception, he will attain the quesited matter easily and without any complications or impediment. If indeed it is without reception, or they are joined together by a square aspect or opposition with perfect reception, the querent will attain the quesited matter.

If they are not joined together either by body or aspect, but the Moon or another planet transfers light between them, the querent will attain the thing through someone who interposes themselves and leads the matter to effect by his sagacity and industry.

If indeed the planet who is lighter and who joins the other goes retrograde before their conjunction is perfected degree for degree, the matter will be destroyed after the querent thought it was completed, and it will be annulled. However if the matter is to be completed by the person who interposes himself to perfect the matter, and if it is the Moon who transfers light: see what house she is in, since the matter will be completed through that person who is signified by the house in which the Moon is. However if it is another planet which transfers light between the Lord of the Ascendant and the Lord signifying the quesited matter, examine what house it is the Lord of, since the matter will be perfected by the person signified by that house; so that if it is the Lord of the 3rd house, the matter will be completed by the querent's brother. If he doesn't have a brother, it will be perfected by one of his younger relatives. And if this is not so, it will be perfected by one of his neighbours. If it is the Lord of the fifth, the matter will be perfected by his son, or by any of the persons signified by the 5th house. If it is the Lord of the sixth, it will be perfected by slaves or clients or by someone who is signified by the 6th house.

And if it is the Lord of the seventh, it will be perfected by the wife, or a lover, or an associate. And if he does not have a wife, it will be perfected by one of those people signified by the 7th house. And if it is the Lord of the ninth, through some religious person. And if it is the Lord of the tenth, it will be perfected by some magnate or leader.

And if it is the Lord of the eleventh, it will be perfected by some friend of the querent.

And if it is the Lord of the twelfth it will be perfected by someone who makes himself out to be a friend of the querent, when he is actually not. And if it is the Lord of the second or the eighth, it will be perfected by an unexpected person who was not mentioned in the discussion of the matter.

If indeed the Lord of the fourth was not joined to the Lord of the Ascendant, nor the Lord of the Ascendant with the Lord of the fourth, nor the Moon; and if there wasn't any planet which transferred light between them; or if there was any planet who prohibited their conjunction, the matter will not be perfected.

However, if you want to know who it will be that does not permit the matter to be perfected: examine the planet who prohibits the conjunction between the Lord of the Ascendant or the Moon, and see which house he is the Lord of - since the annulation of the matter will come to be through a person who is signified by that house.

II

On The Kinds Of Things Bought, And Their Nature

If indeed the querent's asks, as often happens, "See what kind of thing is that I intend to buy or attain, whether it is fruitful or sterile land, or whether the foundation of the house is solid or cracked, or otherwise flawed; and whether are its labourers good and loyal, or not". Examine this similarly from the Ascendant and its Lord; since the Ascendant and its Lord signify the labourers of the land or vineyard, and the wood labourers, and the inhabitants of the house; and the fourth sign signifies the land, house or inheritance, and what kind it is, and what is in it; and the seventh signifies that which is in the land itself, namely the grain and barley, and other useful grains, domesticated plants which usually grow in gardens, such as cabbage, fenugreek, parsley, borrago, silverbeet, and similar things. And if it is the season when grains and domestic plants are in the fields and gardens: indeed it will be possible to signify vines such as vine-arbours and similar things.

If Jupiter is in the seventh, well disposeed, and in good condition, it signifies that there is grain in the land, and plants from which yield useful seeds, and which are more suited to eating and the utility of men. If Venus is here, or Mercury, or the Sun, or the Moon, well disposeed and in good condition, it signifies that in this land there are plants in which men delight, such as roses and others producing fragrant fruits, and flowers from which garlands are made, and similar things. However if Jupiter or Venus or the others are impeded here, there will be some of the things mentioned, but not much.

But if Saturn is here, there will be stones and heavy things in that land, troublesome things and serpents under the ground impeding the fruits of this land.

If indeed Mars is here and is well disposeed and in good condition without impediments, there will be wild rose gardens there and lambruscae, (namely woodland vines making fruits in hedgerows); or there might also be vines there which produce such wines that inebriate men. If indeed he is badly disposeed, there will be bramble there, salvincae and other kinds of poisonous thorny bushes which wound men.

The tenth from the Ascendant signifies the trees which are there. If Jupiter is in the tenth, free from impediments and well disposeed, it signifies that there will be an abundance of trees and that these trees produce good fruits, and fruits from which men derive utility and profit, such as pears, apples, olives, cherries, figs and similar things. However if Venus is there well disposeed, it signifies fragrant and delightful fruits, which youths, and indeed others, eagerly carry in their hands, as are fragrant apples, juniper berries, oranges, and similar things (and especially in warm regions). If indeed the Sun is here, free from impediments and otherwise well disposeed, it signifies good fruits of great trees, as are nuts, pine nuts, and indeed apples and cherries and similar things. However if Mars is here, free and well disposeed, it signifies fruits of trees which are picked from their trees with labour; and have spines in their rinds or other coverings. And it is possible for the Sun and Mars to signify domestic vines, or other fruits, such as chestnuts, medlar fruit, cornels, and similar things. However if Saturn is there, free and well disposeed, it signifies that there will not be a great quantity of trees there, and there will be trees which bear fruits having a bitter taste, such as pears, especially wild ones, and indeed sometimes sorb-apples, acorns, nuts and similar things. However if Mercury or the Moon are here, and in such a condition as was said of the others, it signifies fruits of many kinds, and of diverse tastes and diverse colours, and they signify them according to those signified by planets that they apply to.

If indeed Jupiter is badly disposeed, there will be trees there of little utility and trees of very little fruit, and trees who easily lose their fruits. Likewise of Venus if she is badly disposeed; but it will still be possible that there will be those trees of the sort mentioned above. However if Saturn is badly disposeed here, there will be a small number of wild trees whose fruits will hardly or never be edible by men. The same is to be understood for Mars and the Sun for the fruits and trees they signify, and similarly for those which Mercury and the Moon signify. They will signify similarly to the planets they apply to.

However, if any of the aforementioned planets are retrograde, he who buys the land will sell the fruits of these trees and keep very little of them for himself, nor will he want to have a share of them, except it Venus is the significator, since then he will save a share of the fruits for himself, especially the more delicious ones.

III

On The Quality Of The Labourers

However if you wish to know the condition of the labourers of the land or vineyard, or the custodians of a meadow or forest, or what kind of tenants are there, examine the Ascendant and see if Jupiter is there, direct and in good condition. For if he is, the labourers will be good and loyal; and they will be middle aged men. And if he is oriental, they will be youths of good spirit. And if he is occidental they will be beginning to grow old, or they might be old men; nevertheless they all will be of good spirit And if Jupiter is direct, the labourers will remain in their labour, and will be useful to the querent. And if he is retrograde they will leave their labour and the querent will lease the land to worse labourers.

And if Venus is in the place of Jupiter, the labourers will be good and loyal; and almost in everything they will be like those which are signified by Jupiter; except that Venus signifies them to be younger, and more delightful in the aforementioned qualities.

And if Saturn is in the place of Jupiter these labourers or tendons will be liars and thieves, even if they are old or decrepit men.

And if Mars is in his place, the labourers will be thieves and liars, and will more openly steal than those signified by Saturn, and they will be bandits and greater evil-doers than if they were only thieves.

And if Mars or Saturn is direct, they will remain in their labour: if they are not direct, they will leave from it, and he will locate better labourers, or at least better tenants.

IV

On The Oldness And Newness Of Things

However if you want to know about these trees or about the buildings, whether the trees are old or newly planted, or if the buildings were made recently; examine if any planet is in the tenth, for then the building will not be very old, nor newly made, and likewise of trees, which won't be very old or very new. If indeed there is no planet there, see where the Lord of the 10th house is placed, and if it aspects the 10th house from the place where it is (or if he doesn't aspect it, but aspects a planet who aspects the 10th from its own place); if so, the trees will be young, and the building recently constructed, (so that it is not old); and especially if the Lord of the tenth is oriental. However, if it is occidental, the trees will be old and the buildings will be old.

However if it doesn't aspect the tenth, and is not joined to any planets which aspect the tenth, or who render his light to the tenth, and he is occidental, these trees will be old and the building will be old. Then, if you want to know what will come of these trees or the building; examine the Lord of the 10th house, and see if he is direct, - for if so the trees and building will remain in their own condition, regardless of whether he is a benefic or a malefic. If indeed he is retrograde, the trees will be torn down from that land, and likewise the building.

If indeed the Lord of the tenth doesn't aspect the 10th house, and is not in the eleventh, third, fifth, or ninth from the Ascendant, the land will be without trees and without buildings: and it will not be cultivated; and if it is, it will be badly cultivated.

Additionally, to know whether there are seeds in it (wheat namely, or other grains), if it is a season suited to this, then examine the Lord of the 7th house - if he aspects the seventh, there will be seeds in this land which the owner of the land may hope to harvest for his own utility. If indeed the seventh Lord doesn't aspect the 7th house, there will not be useful seeds there.

V

On The Position Of The Land

However if you want to know what kind of site the land is, examine the 4th house and see whose triplicity the sign is. If it is the triplicity of Aries, the land will be mountainous, or there will be stones in it: and it will be badly disposed to tilling; and the land will be poor, and in need of cultivation and fertilising, and will require great effort to get any fruits out of it.

However if the fourth sign is of the triplicity of Taurus, the land will be flat, and suitable for tilling, and it will be fruitful.

And if the fourth sign is of the triplicity of Gemini, part of the land will be flat, and part will be mountainous, and it will neither be very fruitful nor very sterile.

Similarly if the 4th house is a bicorporeal sign, whatever triplicity it is, it will signify the land to be mountainous and flat, not truly one, or not truly the other.

If the 4th house is the triplicity of Cancer, the land will be marshy or covered in water, or watery in another way, or placed next to a body of water.

And if you want, examine the fourth and its partaking sign; since if they are fire signs, it signifies a dry, rocky and mountainous place.

And a certain man said that the 4th house and its Lord always signify the buying of immovable things, as are houses, land, and similar things. And he said that the fifth and its Lord signify profit from these things. And he said that if it is a moveable thing, and something which changes quickly and is passes from one person's hands to another's, that the seventh and its Lord signify this, and the eighth and its Lord signify profit from this thing.

VI

If It Will Be Useful To Rent The Land Or House

And if someone enquiries wishing to rent land or a house, whether he is a labourer who takes the land in the capacity of a labourer, or for a fixed lease on the land for a given year (as often happens), or a house to live in it - and he wants to know if it will be good for him to hire it out;; give the first and its Lord to him who rents the thing, and the seventh and its Lord to him who leases it. And give the tenth to the utility which can follow from the matter, and give the fourth to the end which will follow from it.

If the Lord of the Ascendant is in the Ascendant, or aspects it from a trine or sextile aspect: or there is a benefic in the Ascendant (whether it has dignity there or not), or the Part of Fortune (unimpeded), it signifies that the renter will rent the thing, hoping for good from it: and he won't regret renting it, and he will delight and rejoice in renting it.

If indeed there is a malefic in the Ascendant, one of these things will happen: either he will rent it, and regret renting it: or he won't rent it: or he will want to rent it so that he may deceive the lessor.

Next examine the seventh for him who leases the thing; if the Lord of the seventh is there, or aspects it from a trine or sextile aspect, or if there is a benefic there which is not impeded in a bad way, the lessor will perfect the matter so that it is agreeable to the renter, and he will keep his promise to him, and will be useful for him. However if there is a malefic there (who is not the Lord of the seventh), the lessor will not keep his promise to the renter, and will strive to deceive him, and will act fraudulently against him.

Next examine the tenth. If there is a benefic there, or a benefic is aspecting it by a trine or sextile aspect, the matter will be arranged and perfected.

If indeed there is a malefic there (who is not the Lord of the tenth), or if a malefic aspects the house by square or opposition, the renting will not be perfected, and it will be possible that a disagreement may arise regarding trees or buildings located on that land.

Next aspect the fourth and give it to the end of the matter. If a benefic is there, or the Lord of the 4th house, or if either of these aspects the house from a trine or sextile aspect, the end of the matter will be good, useful, and praiseworthy. If indeed a malefic is there (who is not the Lord of the fourth), the end will be bad, and the renter will derive loss and inconvenience from it

ON THE FIFTH HOUSE

I

Whether A Man Will Have Children By His Wife Or By Another Woman Who He Mentions, Or Likewise If She Should Ask About Children In A Similar Way

When you are asked by some man, whether he will have children by his wife (or by another women); or a woman enquires as to whether she will have children by her husband (or by someone else), take the shadow without delay, and order the figure according to the Ascendant and the remaining houses; and examine the Ascendant and its Lord, and the Moon, and if you see that the Lord of the Ascendant and the Moon (or one of them), are joined with the Lord of the fifth (which is the house of children), say that he will have children; likewise if the Lord of the fifth is joined to the Lord of the Ascendant.

And if they are not joined together, see if any planet transfers light between the Lord of the Ascendant and the Lord of the fifth, since this signifies children, even if they will come after a delay. If it is not like so, see if the Lord of the Ascendant or the Moon are in the 5th house; if so, say that he will have children. Similarly if the Lord of the fifth is in the Ascendant, say that he will have children. If this is not so, see if the Lord of the Ascendant, or the Moon, and the Lord of the fifth are both joined to some other planet who is heavier than them, since he will collect the light of both of them, and will be the receiver of disposition, and will be the significator of children, whether they ought to live or not. And see if he is free from the impediments which I told you about in the chapter on the impediments of the planets (namely that he is not retrograde or combust or cadent, etc.); then say that his children will live. If indeed this heavier planet who is the receiver of disposition is impeded - namely retrograde or combust or cadent (whether from the angles or the Ascendant), or besieged by malefics - his children won't live long, nor will their mother and father be blessed by them.

Next examine Jupiter, who naturally signifies children. If you find him in the Ascendant, or the third, or the fifth, or the ninth, or the eleventh, free from all the impediments mentioned above; say that the woman has either conceived or will conceive shortly, possibly in the first attempt or shortly after, so that it will be like a matter that appears to be done, or in the process of being done.

And if Venus is unimpeded in the fifth, and there is another unimpeded benefic there besides Jupiter or Venus, it signifies that the woman will be made pregnant soon.

If indeed Jupiter is impeded in the aforementioned places, say that either the conception won't happen, or if it does, it won't be perfected, but it will be a miscarriage or the woman will abort the baby. Similarly if Venus is joined to Saturn or Mars, or is under the beams of the Sun moving toward a bodily conjunction with the Sun, the woman will not get pregnant, unless a benefic is in the fifth, since then she will be better able to get pregnant, or will be soon, but the delivery of the baby will hardly be good.

If Saturn or Mars are in the fifth (or another malefic, chiefly the Cauda Draconis, which has the signification of emptying), or if they aspect the fifth from opposition, it signifies that the woman will not get pregnant. And even if the malefics aspect the fifth from square it appears that they will frustrate the conception.

II

When A Question About Children Is Absolute

If indeed a question is absolute, so that a man or woman says "*will he (or she) have children?*", not specifying whether it concerns a specific woman or a specific man; then examine the Ascendant and its Lord: and see if the Lord of the Ascendant is in the Ascendant, or if a benefic is there well disposeed, or in the tenth, or eleventh, or the fifth, and Jupiter (as was said) is in the third, fifth, ninth, or eleventh - he will have children, but there will be some delay in this, yet not a great delay.

However if the Lord of the Ascendant isn't in the fifth (which is the house of children), but is in the fourth or the seventh, and is not impeded by combustion or retrogradation, or is besieged by two malefics, or corporeally conjunct with one of the malefics who would impede him (namely Saturn or Mars), or is with the Cauda; and Jupiter is in any of the aforementioned places (the third, fifth, ninth, or eleventh); this man or woman will have children, but there will be a longer delay than the one mentioned above.

If indeed one of the malefics (namely Saturn, Mars, or the Cauda Draconis) is in the Ascendant, or aspecting it from square aspect, or from opposition; and the Lord of the Ascendant is impeded by retrogradation, or combustion, or fall, or is in the second, or the sixth, or the eighth, or the twelfth; and Jupiter is in a bad place (and especially in the eighth), or is impeded in a bad way by retrogradation, combustion, or fall - it signifies that the querent will either have no or few children: nor will he rejoice from them (which is to be blessed by them); and he will see their death. And see where the Moon is at that time, since if she is impeded, or the Lord of the fifth is impeded, and one of them is impeded in the sixth, he will be saddened on account of their illnesses. If in the eighth, on account of their death. If in the twelfth, on account of their capture.

And then see what sign is in any of the aforementioned houses, since the reason why the querent will be saddened on account of his children will be from the part of the body ruled by that sign. If it is Aries, it will be due to the head. If it is Taurus, it will be due to the neck. If it is Gemini it will be due to the lungs or the hands. If Cancer, the chest. If Leo, the stomach or the spine (or back). If Virgo, the belly and the parts adjacent to the navel. If Libra, the hips. If Scorpio, the private parts. If Sagittarius, the thighs. If Capricorn, the knees. If Aquarius, the legs. If Pisces, the feet.

And always take this into consideration; that if you find Jupiter, or Venus, or the Sun, or the Moon, or Mercury, or the Caput Draconis in the fifth not impeded by evil impediments, do not give up home of seeking children, since they all signify that he will have children. And if there is no benefic in the fifth, and you find some malefic there which has testimony, and if the chart of the question is not bad apart from this, it signifies that he will have children, but they will not inherit the goods of their mother and father, in fact it appears that the parents will see their death.

Furthermore examine Jupiter and see if he is in an angle, which has the signification of children, allowing not many of them. If he is oriental in an angle, it signifies speed in having children. If he is occidental in an angle, it signifies slowness in having them; and there will be some delay in this.

III

Whether A Woman Is Pregnant

Furthermore, if someone is concerned as to whether a woman has conceived and is carrying the conception (the baby) in her womb or not: examine the Lord of the Ascendant and the Moon (which signify the woman), or one of them; and examine the fifth and its Lord (who are the significators of the conception). If you find the Moon in the fifth, or if you find the Lord of the fifth in the Ascendant free from malefics and the other aforementioned impediments, it signifies that the woman has conceived and has the conception in her womb. Likewise, if the Lord of the Ascendant commits his disposition to some planet in an angle. And this will be more secure and more certain if that planet to whom the Lord of the Ascendant commits his disposition to is received, or he himself receives the Lord of the Ascendant. Since then it will signify conception.

If indeed the planet to whom the Lord of the Ascendant is joined, and whom the Lord of the Ascendant commits disposition, is in a cadent, it signifies that the woman has gotten an affliction, and that which appears to be pregnancy, will more likely be an illness than a conception. And if it is a conception, it will not come to a good end; especially if the Ascendant is Aries, Cancer, Libra, or Capricorn, or if one of the malefics in any of the angles; and this more strongly if the Cauda is there (since she has signifies abortion more so than the other malefics).

If indeed a heavier planet to which the Lord of the Ascendant commits disposition is in a good place from the Ascendant, and is not in conjunction with malefics, but is free from impediments; and the Moon is similarly safe, it signifies that the conception will come to a good end; and that the birth will not be frustrated. Similarly if the Lord of the fifth (who is the significator of children) is in the Ascendant free from the impediments mentioned above (namely that it is not retrograde, nor combust, nor joined to malefics: and especially the Cauda by bodily conjunction, or the other malefics by opposition or square aspect) it signifies conception. If indeed it is impeded by any of the above mentioned impediments, there will not be a conception, and if there is, it will be frustrated and terminated.

IV

Whether A Woman Is Pregnant Or Not

Women sometimes tend to doubt whether they are pregnant or not: and indeed their husbands, striving to have children, do not know whether she is pregnant or not: and they are in the habit of enquiring about this from an astrologer in order to be made certain of it. Whence if a question is made to you by a woman about herself, as to whether she is pregnant or not, and if she is not asking about anyone else; examine the Ascendant and its Lord, and see where the Lord of the Ascendant is, who, if he is in an angle free from malefics and from other impediments, signifies that the woman is pregnant. Similarly if the Lord of the Ascendant is in a succeedent, or even in a cadent - as long as he is received by a planet placed in an angle. If indeed he is in a house cadent from an angle, joined to a planet who does not receive him; or if he is received, and the receiver is retrograde, combust or cadent - this signifies that the woman is not pregnant. Similarly if the Moon is impeded; but if the Moon is received by a planet who is free from the aforementioned impediments, then she will be pregnant. If indeed the Moon is not received, and the Lord of the Ascendant is impeded, she will not be pregnant. And if the Lord of the Ascendant is in a good place, and aspects the Ascendant by a praiseworthy aspect, she will be pregnant.

If a certain man asks about a woman at her request, the judgement will be the same. However if a man asks of his own will and for himself, but the woman is ignorant of this, you will consider the conditions above according to the seventh and its Lord, and judge according to the Lord of the seventh just as you did for the Lord of the Ascendant, without overlooking the Moon.

V

If A Woman Who Has Conceived Carries One Or More Children In Her Womb

And if you are asked by a pregnant woman, or if you are asked by someone else, as to whether she carries one or more babies, examine this from the Ascendant; and see if the Ascendant is Gemini, Virgo, Sagittarius or Pisces; or if the Ascendant is any of the other signs and there are two benefic planets in it, or if there are two of them in the fifth, then she conceived two children. However if the Caput Draconis is with them there, say that she carries more than two in her womb, and it is possible that she carries four. And if there isn't a planet in the Ascendant or in the fifth see if any planet aspects the Ascendant or the fifth degree for degree, so that the aspect is not more than one degree in ahead of the line of the Ascendant or the fifth, or more than two degrees behind. Because however many planets aspect these degrees in this way, that is how many children have been conceived in the womb: even if all of the seventh planets aspect these degrees. And see how many there are and how many aspect from a trine or sextile aspect, for this many of them will make it to birth. Indeed however many aspect from square or opposition, that many of the conceived will suffer detriment.

And if you find the Sun and the Moon in one sign, yet in such a way that the Moon moves towards the Sun, and is not more than 5 degrees behind him, or two degrees in front of him, then you know that the woman carries one child, and no more. You will judge the same if the Sun or the Moon is in Gemini, Virgo, Sagittarius, and Pisces. You will also judge the same if the Ascendant is one of the fixed signs, or the mobile signs, and the fifth is also one of these signs; and the Sun and Moon are in fixed or mobile signs, and there are not more planets (or their aspects) in the Ascendant or the fifth as was said.

VI

If A Woman Carries A Male Or A Female

And if someone enquires as to whether a woman carries a male of a female, then inspect the Ascendant and its Lord, and the fifth and its Lord, and see if they are in Aries, or Gemini, or Leo, or Libra, or Sagittarius, or Aquarius. If so, then it signifies that she carries a male. If indeed they are not here, it appears that she carries a female. If indeed the Lord of the Ascendant is in a masculine sign, and the Lord of the fifth is in a feminine sign, or the Lord of the fifth is in a masculine sign and the Lord of the Ascendant is in a feminine sign, then revert to the Moon (who is the participator in all matters), and see if she is in a masculine sign and is joined to a planet which is in a masculine sign; for then she will attest to the planet in the masculine sign: or if she is in a feminine sign she will attest to the planet who is in a feminine sign (whether the Lord of the Ascendant is in a masculine sign, or the Lord of the fifth, or vice-versa).

Similarly if the Moon joins a masculine planet she will attest to the planet who is in a masculine sign: and if she is joined to a feminine planet she will attest to the planet who is in a feminine sign. Similarly if the Lord of the Ascendant or the Lord of the fifth is a masculine or feminine planet, the Moon will attest to that planet to whom her location is likened

And you should know that Saturn, Jupiter, Mars and the Sun are always masculine, except sometimes in certain cases where they are not. And Venus is always feminine, except sometimes in cases where she is not. Mercury, when he is oriental in the world, so that he rises in the morning before the Sun, is said to be masculine; when he is occidental in the world, so that he sets after the Sun in the evening, is said to be feminine. And similarly when he joins masculine planets he is masculine, and when he joins feminine planets he is feminine.

ON THE SIXTH HOUSE

I

Whether An Ill Person Will Be Freed From The Illness Which Hinders Him, Or Not

If there is a question made to you about some sick person, as to whether or not he will be freed from the illness which hinders him; first examine who it is that enquires, namely whether it the sick person himself, or another person who enquires on behalf of the sick person; and if it is his business to ask, or not; and if he enquires at the request of the sick person, or of his own accord. Since if he enquires at the request of the sick person, or with his permission, give the first to him and the sick person. However if he enquires from his own concern, give the first to him; but give the sick person the house by which his person is signified; so that if the querent enquires for his brother, give the first to the querent, and the third to the sick person. If for his father, give the first to the querent; the fourth to the sick person. And understand this for the significations of all the houses according to what is said above in the tractate on the twelve houses.

Also consider what social condition the sick person is of, namely whether he is a lay person or a cleric, or another kind of religious person; and whether he is someone who is put in front of a doctor, or someone in front of whom a doctor is put. Indeed there are many diverse opinions on this.

You must also examine what kind of illness it is, and of what nature it is; for a new illness is examined differently than an old one. And I will tell you about the conditions of infirmities and sick people: and which sick people a doctor should and shouldn't take charge of, and in which cases: and which sick are to be put in charge of a doctor, and which aren't, and in which cases, and how, and when, according to the diverse opinions for judging sick people, if Our Lord Jesus Christ presents me with His grace at this juncture.

For certain men give the Ascendant to the doctor, the tenth to the sick person, the seventh to the illness, and the fourth to the art of medicine; and Zael and his followers were of this opinion. And so according to this the doctor was placed before the sick person, and the seventh (the infirmity) before the tenth (the art of medicine). And they similarly placed the doctor before the sick person, so that if a question arose on a sick person (with the sick person and the doctor being ignorant) then the doctor would be placed before him. Since if another person asks for him, from his request, (whatever the condition of the sick person was) then the first would be given to the sick person, the tenth to the doctor, the seventh to the illness, the fourth to the art of medicine; and in this case the sick person would be placed before the doctor.

But if anyone from his own concern enquires about an ill king, with the king being ignorant of this, give the first to the doctor, the tenth to the sick person, the seventh to the illness, the fourth to the art of medicine. However if he enquires in the same way about the Pope, or some other cleric, give the first to the doctor, the ninth to the sick person, the seventh to the illness, and indeed the third to the art of medicine.

Now however I will tell you the circumstances of illness: for if you were to know the circumstances of illnesses, you would be able to judge better and more securely regarding them. And even if the art of medicine is said to have been invented for the wealthy and magnates, nevertheless the common country folk have now embraced remedies; and not surprisingly, since both themselves and magnates are taken ill and strive to be freed of it.

An illness is said to be of many years or old, I consider it as long-lived and long-standing, on account of it being a year old. Because year-old illnesses are never easily cured, in fact they are only cured with extreme difficulty. However I consider those illnesses which are not yet a year old, to be not old. Whence if an illness is old (which is more than a year), regardless of the circumstances of the sick person, you ought to give the twelfth to the illness. If it is a new illness (which is not yet a year old) you ought to give it the seventh - if you give the first to the doctor; since the doctor is the enemy of the illness. And if you give the tenth to the sick person, you ought to give the fourth to the art of medicine; since even if the art of medicine cures the sick person, it is still opposed to him; and the opposition indicates enmity. Whence the art of medicine is said to be the enemy of infirmity: since those things which are contrary to nature and do not nourish it, but rather sometimes exterminate it, are studied in the art of medicine. If you give the ninth to the sick person, the third is given to the art of medicine. If you give the third to the sick person, as sometimes happens, give the ninth to the medicine.

And it will be necessary for you to consider whether an illness is general or particular; since if it is general, you ought to judge generally of the whole body. If indeed it is particular, you ought to judge according to the body part in which the illness thrives. But if you enquire as to how the houses are diversified signifying infirmities, doctors, sick people, and the art of medicine, since these houses ought to be the same, in fact almost the same; I strongly believe that reasons could be given to you, but it would be long drawn out to explain them in detail, nor would it be possible to dispute everything everywhere: whence it is necessary for us to stick to the sayings of the philosophers, and know that they did not say this without a reason; so it is fitting for us to learn from them and believe them. I will lay-out to you the method of judging on the sick person as to whether he will be freed or not, however first I want you to know what Zael said on this matter, and what his followers said regarding how he is to be understood.

For when he said that the Ascendant signifies the doctor, he gave this as his reason; since the illness is signified by the seventh, and the doctor is the enemy of the illness; whence with the first being the enemy of the seventh, (which signifies the illness), the first is rightly given to the doctor since he is the enemy of the illness; and in this way the doctor is signified by the first. Wherefore insofar as the 1st house is fortunate, so the care of the doctor will benefit the sick person, and insofar as it is unfortunate, he will be harmed by the care of the doctor.

And from this Zael said that the first is given to the doctor, and he said that this was so since the tenth is given to the sick person, for no other reason than that the tenth signifies whether the sick person is obedient to the doctor, since if he obeys well, the treatment would be of some help to him. And this is known through the planet who is found in the tenth; since if he is a benefic, the sick person will be obedient, and for this reason he will be better able to be cured.

He gave the seventh to the infirmity; since though the seventh it is known whether the illness will be short or long; for if a benefic is there, he will be quickly freed, and especially if the benefic has dignity there. And if there is a malefic there who is not well disposeed, the illness will strengthen in the sick person.

He gave the fourth to the medical art; since by the fourth it is known whether the medical art will strengthen the ill person or not, according to whether the fourth is well or badly disposeed; for if there is a benefic there, the medical art will be good for the sick person. If indeed there is a malefic there, who doesn't have dignity there (namely house or exaltation or two of the other lesser dignities), the medical art will be more harmful to the sick person than useful to him.

But there is another way, and a straightforward one at that, to know whether an ill person will be freed or not. And this is to give the first and its Lord and the Moon to the sick person; and the sixth to the infirmity, if it is a new infirmity (which has not lasted longer than a year). If indeed it is an old illness which has lasted longer than one year, give it the twelfth, as has been said. You also ought to see whether the significator of the sick person is one of the planets which have friendship with the significator of the doctor (or of medical art, or of the illness) by whatever house, the doctor, or the sick person, or the medical art, or the illness is signified. Since if the significator of the doctor is one of those planets who love the significator of the sick person, the doctor will be useful to the sick person. And if the significator of the medical art is one of those planets, the treatment of the doctor will be useful to him. Similarly if the significator of the illness is one of those planets, the illness will harm him less. But if the significator of the doctor was one of the planets inimical that of the sick person, the doctor would not benefit him, nor would his medical art, but rather he would harm the sick person and things would go to the contrary for the sick person. And a planet who is friendly to the significator of the querent will benefit him; and a planet who is an enemy of the significator of the querent will harm him, etc. And if all of the significators were friends, all will benefit: and if all are enemies, all will be harmed.

And if the significator of the doctor, or the Moon, is joined with the Lord of the seventh, the illness will become more aggressive. And if it is joined with the Lord of the sixth, it will be prolonged more than it appears it ought to be; but in this case the sick person will ultimately escape, and be liberated.

Also consider whether the significator of the illness is in one of the azmena degrees, and is in the twelfth, or in the eighth, and is aspected by one of the malefics; since this signifies that the ill person won't be freed from this illness without some impediment lingering in that body part assigned to that sign in which the azmena degree is in. And it is to be inquired here from the sick person (or from anyone else who will be able to judge for you), as to the length of the illness; since if the illness has lasted many years, the ill person will not be liberated quickly.

II

On Whether The Sick Person Will Escape

If some sick person inquires of you as to whether he will be freed from an illness or not; examine the Ascendant and its Lord, and the Moon (which are the significators of the querent), and see if the Lord of the Ascendant is in the angle of the Ascendant, or in the angle of the Midheaven - for this signifies his liberation; unless it is impeded by malefics from a square aspect or from opposition, or is combust, or is with the Cauda Draconis in the same minute, or moving towards her, and there is less than 15 minutes between him and the Cauda without the aspect of a benefic; since the aspect of a benefic shatters the evil of the Cauda - it will help the Lord of the Ascendant: even if the aspect is a square (whether it has reception or not). But if it is from opposition with reception, it will likewise shatter the malice, except if this planet is the Lord of the 8th house; since then it won't help, but will harm, whether it is a benefic or a malefic who joins the Lord of the Ascendant, or to whom the Lord of the Ascendant is joined. However if the Lord of the Ascendant is impeded, then inspect the Moon, for if she is free from malefics, and is in an angle, and aspects the Ascendant, and is not aspected by, or corporeally joined to, the Lord of the eighth, she signifies his escape from the illness.

Also see if the Lord of the Ascendant or the Moon (namely the one by whom you operate, and who is stronger in signification), is above the earth; for this is a sign of escape, and especially if it aspects the Ascendant, or is joined to a planet who aspects the Ascendant, and renders the light of the Lord of the Ascendant to the Moon, or to the Ascendant, and if neither the Lord of the Ascendant or the Moon are joined to any planet placed below the earth, then it signifies liberation, unless a bad cure or bad care operates to the contrary. Since by no means would a sane sick person be able to treat himself poorly if he wished, saying "I will do what the astrologer says" by doing the opposite of what he ought to. Nevertheless, since you have discharged your duty, let him who thinks this assign the harm to himself through his own fault.

However if the Lord of the Ascendant or the Moon is below the earth, namely in the second, or third, or fourth, or fifth, or sixth, and is not joined to any planet placed above the earth, it signifies his death. However if a benefic planet (to which the Lord of the Ascendant or the Moon is joined) who signifies the escape of the sick person is retrograde, it signifies the prolongation of the illness. And this more strongly and for a longer duration, if the planet is cadent from an angle, nevertheless he will ultimately be freed.

However if that planet to whom the Lord of the Ascendant or the Moon is joined, and to whom they commit disposition, has entered into combustion, it signifies the death of the sick person. Besides this, if the Lord of the Ascendant is the significator (namely that he is so strong that the signification is attributed to him rather than the Moon), and is joined to any malefic planet placed below the earth, it signifies his death.

However if the Lord of the Ascendant is impeded, as was said, so that he cannot be the significator of the sick person, but the signification went to the Moon; see if she is joined to a malefic planet placed below the earth. For if so, even if she herself is above the earth, it signifies the death of the sick person.

Similarly if the Moon is joined to the Lord of the Ascendant, and he is fast-of-course, and descending from his auge up to the middle of his eccentric, or from his further longitude to his first station (which happens to him, when his argument is from fifteen degrees to two signs and fifteen degrees); then it signifies that the sick person will be freed quickly, and strength will quickly return to his body. And if you find the Moon, or the Lord of the Ascendant joined with Saturn, it signifies the prolongation of the illness, even if it is a new illness. If indeed it is an old illness, it signifies the lengthening of its already long duration. And if the Lord of the Ascendant is below the earth, and the Moon is joined to a planet in the third, sixth, ninth, or twelfth (which is cadent from the angles), it signifies the death of the sick person. Similarly if the Lord of the Ascendant is joined to the Lord of the 8th house, and the Moon is otherwise impeded, or if the Moon is joined to the Lord of the 8th house, and the Lord of the Ascendant is impeded, it signifies the death of the sick person. Still, this is to be paid attention to; that if the Lord of the Ascendant is received by the Lord of the 8th house, and the Lord of the Ascendant does not receive the Lord of the eighth - since it does not signify death, but signifies a very fearful illness, but the sick person will not be endangered, unless by error. However if the Lord of the Ascendant or the Moon receives the Lord of the 8th house, it signifies death.

Also examine whether the significator of the sick person or the Moon, is found in the ninth from the Ascendant of the question, since then it will return fear to him that a trivial error will be able to put him in danger, since it appears that he is going to the grave. However if you find the planet in question in the ninth from the house through which he himself is signified, it will cause even more fear for him. And if the Moon or another planet transfers light from the Lord of the Ascendant to the Lord of the eighth, it signifies the ultimate fear of the sick person, and that the slightest error in eating or diet could lead the ill person into danger, and he will hardly escape from it. Still it is possible that he escapes by way of the best cure, the best care, as much by those standing as for the sick person, and even the doctor, and by the sick person obeying the doctor.

However if the Lord of the Ascendant is in the eighth, and is received by the Lord of the eighth, and does not receive him, it signifies the liberation of the sick person after he has lost all hope. But if the Lord of the Ascendant receives the Lord of the eighth, it signifies death. However if the Lord of the eighth is heavier than the Lord of the Ascendant, and the Lord of the Ascendant is joined to him with reception (so that the Lord of the Ascendant receives the Lord of the eighth), it signifies death. However if the Lord of the Ascendant is conjoined with the Lord of the eighth, and this conjoining is by a trine or sextile aspect, it signifies death (whether the Lord of the Ascendant receives the Lord of the eighth or not). If the Lord of the Ascendant is in any of the angles, it signifies death, but not immediately; but when the Lord of the eighth arrives at the degree of the Ascendant. If it is not then, it will be when the Lord of the eighth arrives at the degree in which the Lord of the Ascendant was as the hour of the question: or if the Lord of the Ascendant was joined to the Lord of the eighth in an angle, it will be when it reaches the degree in which the Lord of the eighth was at the hour of the question.

Similarly if the Moon, or any other planet transfers virtue or light between the Lord of the Ascendant and the Lord of the house of death, and the Lord of the house of death himself is strong, or is in an angle, and the Lord of the Ascendant is cadent from an angle; or is in disposition of its own house, or its own exaltation, it signifies death. But if he is not cadent from an angle, even if he is in opposition to his own house or exaltation, it doesn't signify death (if he is received).

And if the Lord of the 8th house is in the Ascendant, and the Lord of the Ascendant and the Moon are impeded, it signifies that the illness will be greatly increased, and that the sick person will be in danger of death; nevertheless he will escape, though barely, and with good care and precautions, just as was said. Similarly if the Lord of the Ascendant and the Moon are impeded, and the planet to whom the Lord of the Ascendant (or the Moon) commits disposition to is impeded, it signifies death.

If indeed the sole receiver of the disposition, (who is the heavier planet that joins the Lord of the Ascendant or the Moon) is impeded, it signifies the prolongation of the illness, and this will happen because the sick person will relapse; moreover because he will not be cured, nor will he follow the prescribed diet, and he will adhere to the advice of fools, and those who counsel him badly. Similarly if the Lord of the Ascendant is below the earth, and is joined to the Lord of the eighth in the fourth; or is above the earth, and is joined to the Lord of the eighth in the eighth, or from the eighth, it signifies death; if the Lord of the Ascendant receives the

Lord of the eighth that is. However if he doesn't receive him, even if the Lord of the eighth receives the Lord of the Ascendant, the illness will get much more severe, and he will be in danger of death; nevertheless he will be liberated with the help shown to him. Similarly if the Lord of the Ascendant did not aspect the Lord of the eight, nor him the Lord of the Ascendant; but another planet transfers light between them, and the Lord of the Ascendant is cadent from the Ascendant; and the Lord of the eighth is in one of the angles (since his strength in the angles is very evil), it signifies that the sick person will die from this illness.

And Zael said that if the Lord of the Ascendant is combust, or is one of the superiors, and is in front of the Sun by thirteen degrees or less, or after the Sun by four degrees or less; or if he is one of the inferiors and is in front of the Sun by three degrees or less, or is after the Sun by fourteen degrees or less, it signifies the death of the sick person, unless the Lord of the Ascendant is received; since then it will signify escape after losing all hope; and perhaps he will appear to have died, when he has not; and it is possible that he will be believed to be dead and then be buried alive.

However if the heavier planet to which the Lord of the Ascendant commits its disposition or virtue is free from impediments, and is not cadent from an angle, nor from the Ascendant, nor commits the disposition which he received from the Lord of the Ascendant to another planet, and the Moon is similarly free from impediments, it signifies that the ill person will be freed, even without a great cure by doctors.

And a certain Cretan said that when the Part of Illness is between the beginning of the Ascendant up to the end of the 4th house, it signifies that the cause of the illness is something in the past. When it is placed from the beginning of the fifth up to the end of the eighth, it signifies the cause of the illness is something in the present. When it is placed from the beginning of the ninth up to the end of the twelfth, it signifies it is from a future cause.

To determine the nature of a certain illness, whether it is long lasting or not, examine the 6th house, which is the house of infirmities, and see if it is a fixed sign, for if so, the illness will be fixed and will remain in its current condition, and will not change to something else. If indeed it is a mobile sign, this illness will easily change to another. If indeed it is a common sign, the illness will be alleviated at one time and aggravated at another

To know whether an illness is old or new, examine the Moon and see from which planet she is separating from. If she is separating from an oriental planet it will be a new illness. If she is separating from an occidental planet it will be an old illness. If you find by the aforementioned conditions that an illness is old, consider the 12th house, and judge the condition of the illness through it, as you judged above through the 6th house for the new illness. Similarly examine regarding the liberation from illnesses if the Moon is joined to an oriental planet, since this signifies that the illness can be cured quickly. If indeed she is joined to an occidental planet, the illness will be cured slowly and with much difficulty. If she is not joined to any planets, move her from the sign she is in to the next; and see which planet she first joins after exiting from the sign in which she is placed, whether she joins an oriental planet or an occidental planet, and according to the planet she joins, judge on the swiftness or slowness of the liberation from illness.

And all of this will come to be better and faster if a benefic aspects the Lord of the Ascendant and the Lord of the Ascendant itself is not cadent from the Ascendant or the angles. Similarly examine if one of the malefics is joined to the Lord of the Ascendant (or if he is joined to a malefic), by body, or from opposition, or from square aspect - since it will make him unfortunate, and hardly or never permits escape from the illness. If the malefic is received by the Lord of the Ascendant, the sick person will just about escape; however, if it is not received, it is then to be feared that he does not escape, and that he will not be liberated.

Also consider the Moon, for if she is joined to a planet which is fast-of-course, and she herself is fast-of-course, it signifies that the sick person will be quickly liberated. If she is joined to a retrograde planet it signifies the prolongation of the illness, and its long duration. However if she is joined to a planet that is slow-of-course, it signifies the prolongation and aggravation of the illness, so that the sick person hardly escapes it, and it appears more likely that he will die from it than escape from it.

III

On The Critical Days, And Good Or Bad Crises In Illnesses

Besides this you ought to examine the place of the Moon at the hour of a question, or at the onset of an illness if you have its time, and examine where the Moon will be on the seventh day from the onset of an illness or question, and similarly where she will be on the fourteenth day, and where she will be on the twenty-first day, and where she will be on the twenty-eighth day. Since if she is well disposeed on any of these days, the sick person will then be alleviated, and it will seem to be better for him, and the crisis will happen for good, unless impeded by malefics in corporeal conjunction, or from opposition, or from square aspect without reception. And if the Moon is impeded on any of these days, and badly disposeed, it signifies that then the sick person will be made worse, and that it will go worse for him; and especially if she is then in conjunction with the Lord of the 6th house; since then the sick person will be feared for. If indeed that malefic which impedes her is the Lord of the eighth, then the sick person will die.

Besides this examine in which of the other days (besides the ones mentioned above) the Moon is joined to any benefic planets, for on that day the sick person will be alleviated, and will rest, and things will be better for him. And from this it happens that sometimes the crisis overcomes the sick person for the better, on a day which was not believed, and where it did not appear like it ought to happen. And examine on which days (besides the aforementioned) the Moon moves towards the corporeal conjunction of the malefics, or their opposition, or square aspect; since on that day the sick person will be made worse, and especially if the Moon is joined to the Lord of the 6th house. And if the crisis comes, it will be more likely to harm than to heal; and this especially if she happens to join with the Lord of the 8th house; since then the crisis may be more likely to lead to death than to life. And in this doctors are sometimes deceived, since when they have predicted the crisis to be on the critical day according to the medical arts, the crisis happens otherwise than they predicted: which happens on account of the conjunction of the Moon with the planets on those days: from which doctors are scorned by the laymen (since they are mistaken in their prognostications), but they are not to be censured.

However you will have to find the aforementioned days in this way; that if you want to know about the seventh day from the day of the illness, or from the day of the question, it is necessary that you consider in what degree the Moon was at the hour of the question, or the beginning of the illness; and add on another 90 degrees, and then you will have the seventh day. Then project those 90 degrees from the degree of the Moon and in whatever sign the number ends, the Moon will be there in that degree. Or you will be able to calculate it according to the tables and the same place will be found.

Then see how, and by whom, she is aspected and according to the aspects of benefic or malefic planets to the Moon, make your judgement good or bad for the sick person.

To find the fourteenth day from the day of the question or the beginning of the illness; add 180 degrees on to the first position of the Moon; and project those from the degree in which she was, and where the number falls, that is where the Moon will be on the fourteenth day from the day of the question or the beginning of the illness; and then judge of the fourteenth day as you judged above of the seventh.

To find the twenty-first day, add on 270 degrees to the place of the Moon, and project from the aforementioned place of the Moon, and where the number falls, that will be the place of the Moon on the twenty-first day from the day of the question or the beginning of the illness. Then examine the aspects of the planets to the Moon, and judge according to how you judged for the seventh day.

To find the twenty-eighth day, add 360 degrees to the place of the Moon 360, and you have the place of the Moon at the hour of the question or illness, and then judge as said above of the seventh day.

And know that always on these days, whenever the Moon comes to benefic planets, then the illness will be alleviated and whenever she comes to malefics, then it will become more severe.

IV

Whether Some Absent Person Will Become Ill

And if someone is vexed about some absent person, as to whether they are ill or not, examine the condition of the querent, and of the quesited person; and judge according to this - namely whether he enquires about his brother, his father, his son, or his servant, or his wife, or an associate, or an enemy, or a bishop, or any other religious person, or a king, or his master, or a friend, or a hidden enemy. Since it will be necessary for you to give the first to the querent, and the house through which the quesited person is signified to the quesited. Then examine the Ascendant and its Lord, and give it to the querent, and give the Lord of the house by which the quesited is signified (and the Moon) to the quesited.

If the Lord of the house of the quesited, or the Moon, is in an angle, and not impeded by malefics, it signifies that the quesited is well. The same if any of them are in a succeedent free from malefics and the other impediments mentioned above. However, if the Lord of the quesited is in the sixth, or is joined to its Lord by body, or in its opposition or square aspect, it signifies that he is ill, whether it is in the 6th house of the question, or the 6th house from its own house, or joined with its Lord. If indeed these above mentioned impediments are not present, say that he is not ill.

And the Master said that if the Lord of the Ascendant and the Moon are void-of-course, you ought to see which of them has travelled through more degrees in the sign which it is in, and move him to the succeeding sign; and examine who he joins first as to whether it is a benefic or a malefic. For if he joins a benefic who receives him, it signifies liberation, unless that benefic is impeded by the impediments mentioned above, or if the Lord of the 8th house is with him; since then the death of the sick person will be feared; and especially if the Lord of the Ascendant, or the Moon, receive the Lord of the 8th house. But if they do not receive him, then it signifies escape from illness, almost after losing all hope. Nevertheless it appears that he ought to escape, except if the error of a doctor or the sick person or someone attending acts to the contrary. And below is such an example.

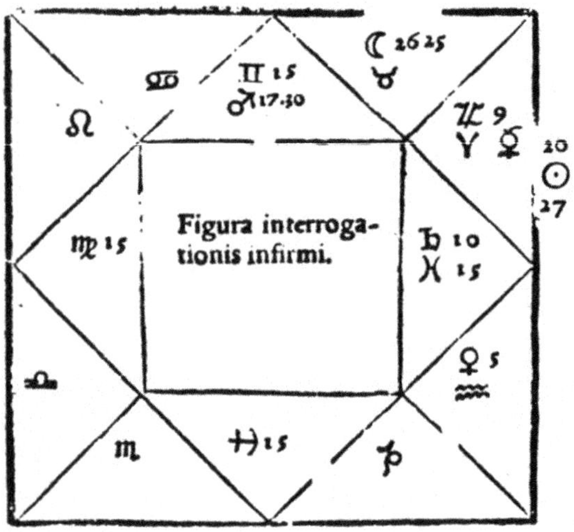

The question of a certain sick person had the Ascendant at 15 degrees Virgo, and the 10th house at 15 degrees Gemini, and Mars in Gemini at 17 degrees and 30 minutes. And the Moon in Taurus at 26 degrees 25 minutes. Jupiter in Taurus 9 degrees and 15 minutes. The Sun in Aries 17 degrees and 30 minutes. Saturn in Aries 10 degrees and 15 minutes. Mercury in Aries 20 degrees 50 minutes. Venus in Pisces 5 degrees 37 minutes.

And he said that he examined the Ascendant and its Lord, and the Moon, and the other planets and angles and the other houses. And Mercury (who was the Lord of the Ascendant) was void-of-course (joined to nobody), and the Moon was similarly void-of-course (joined to nobody). Therefore the Lord of the Ascendant, and the Moon, through being void-of-course signified the prolongation of his infirmity, and its severity. Whence he moved the Moon from the sign in which she was (namely from Taurus to Gemini). And he changed the Moon and not the Lord of the Ascendant for the reason that she had travelled through more degrees of the sign in which she was placed than the Lord of the Ascendant (namely Mercury) had in his sign. And after she had entered Gemini she was first joined to Venus (who was in Pisces) before any other planet, and committed her disposition to Venus. And Venus was joined to Jupiter, and received him from her own house (namely from Taurus), and Jupiter similarly received Venus from his own house (namely from Pisces). And neither did Jupiter commit disposition to anyone else, since he was not joined to Saturn - for he cannot join to any other planets, except for Saturn, who is heavier than him, indeed all the others join to him, since they are lighter than him.

And the conjoining which Venus makes with Jupiter by mutual reception signifies that the sick person ought to be liberated from this illness; nevertheless the infirmity would be on the increase until Venus perfects the conjunction with Jupiter degree for degree, and she transits him by one minute. And it appeared that the illness was to be on the increase for two days and fifteen hours, almost giving each degree one day, and every 5 minutes two hours, since there were 2 degrees and 38 minutes between their perfect conjunction, from which time onwards the sick person was to be alleviated. And he said that this sick person himself was one who enquired about his own condition, and his infirmity did not cease to increase until the conjunction of Venus with Jupiter was complete degree for degree, and immediately when Venus was separated from Jupiter by one minute, the sick person began to be relieved, and he got some rest, and his pain began to diminish.

And the same philosopher said that if Venus was joined to Mars and not Jupiter, that the sick person would have died, unless Mars (who was the Lord of the 8th house), received Venus, and she did not receive him: since if she received Mars, it would appear that the sick person would have received death, and would have died; since Mars signified the quesited matter, namely death. For when the Lord of the Ascendant or the Moon are both joined to the Lord of the quesited matter (or even one of them), the quesited matter is always perfected, especially if reception intervenes. For the judgement of death is not entirely the same as the judgement of other things, since if the Lord of the Ascendant or the Moon, is joined to the Lord of the 8th house without reception, it signifies death, unless the Lord of the 8th house receives the Lord of the Ascendant, or the Moon; and if the Lord of the Ascendant (or the Moon) does not receive him. But if the Lord of the Ascendant or the Moon receives the Lord of the eighth, it signifies death, regardless of whether or not the Lord of the eighth receives the Lord of the Ascendant or the Moon. For death is not like other matters, since when death is signified, one does not examine whether or not things will change after it occurs; for none of the significators can change or destroy death, after it has arrived in actuality. But other things are changed and destroyed, sometimes even after they are perfected.

For we see that when the Lord of the Ascendant, or the Moon, is joined to the Lord of the quesited matter, or the Lord of the quesited matter is joined to the Lord of the Ascendant, it signifies the effecting of that matter - but even if it sometimes perfects as I said to you above; after the Lord of the quesited matter is joined to a malefic impeding him, (who he commits disposition to), the matter will be destroyed after it is perfected. But with death this cannot happen (that the matter is destroyed after it is perfected): since it resolves all questions: and its sentence is of such a sort that it cannot be appealed. On health however, or liberation, this is not so; since if some planet signifies the liberation of the sick person, and afterwards it is joined to a malefic planet who impedes him, and who he commits his disposition to, the matter will be destroyed after it will appear to be arranged that it ought to be perfected (it being the liberation of the sick person). Whence the person who appears that he ought to be liberated, might die after it appears that he ought to be able to escape, but the person who is about to die will not be able to be revived after death, whatever the receiver of disposition appears to signify afterwards.

Also consider the Lord of the house signifying the sick person, and in what part of the figure you find him; namely whether he is in the first quarter, or in the second, or in the third, or in the fourth, and operate through him. Who, if you find him in the first quarter of the figure, signifies the querent is asking about an illness which is in the past. If he is in the second quarter, it signifies the querent is asking about an illness which is present. If indeed he is in the third quarter, it signifies he is enquiring about a future illness, or about a return of an illness: since it signifies that it is about to return. But if it is found in the final quarter, it signifies he is enquiring about a chronic illness, namely which was, and is, and will be, or one that is long lasting; and this is more certain if it is joined with any of the Lords of the signs of any of these quarters in its own quarter.

V

Whether A Slave Will Be Liberated From Slavery Or Not

In the preceding chapter we spoke about a sick person, as to whether he would be liberated from an illness or not. What remains to be discussed in this chapter is about a slave, as to whether he will be liberated from slavery or not. Nor is this by chance, since slavery can be compared to a most vicious illness; for there is not an illness which could possibly be said to be worse than slavery, which afflicts always, everywhere, indifferently and continually. For there is no illness which doesn't have some intermission or repose in its affliction - except for slavery; for in slavery intermission or repose does not intervene.

Whence if a question is posed to you by a slave; so that a slave says absolutely. "See if I will be liberated from slavery or not"; then give the first to the slave, and similarly the Lord of the Ascendant and the Moon; give the tenth to the master, whatever kind of master he is - even if he is another low-class person. Then examine the Lord of the Ascendant for the slave, and see if he is joined to the Lord of the 10th house, and making a perfect conjunction (whether it is made by body or aspect, whatever kind of aspect it is, whether with reception or without reception), and if the conjunction is complete degree for degree and minute for minute; say that he will be liberated from this slavery, easily and in a short space of time. If indeed the Lord of the Ascendant is separated from the Lord of the 10th house by one minute or by more, it signifies that he is already free from slavery. If indeed the Lord of the Ascendant is not as I said to you, then examine the significatrix (namely the Moon), and judge according to that which I told you about the Lord of the Ascendant. If indeed neither the Lord of the Ascendant or the Moon were as I said to you, namely that neither of them were separating from the Lord of the 10th house: inspect them again, and if you find them (or one of them) joined with the Sun (as was said for the Lord of the tenth) or separating from him by the aforementioned conditions, judge the same of them with the Sun as you judged with the Lord of the tenth.

If indeed his question was determinate and not absolute, such as if he said "Will I be liberated from the service of my master which I am in, or go out from his own power, or not"; then examine the Lord of the Ascendant, and see if he is cadent from an angle, and not aspecting the Ascendant (and not joined to a planet in an angle or aspecting the Ascendant) or if he is in the third or the ninth, or is joined to planets in them. If he is, say that he will be liberated from slavery, and escape the power of his master. If this is not true of the Lord of the Ascendant, but is true of the Moon; you can judge the same.

If indeed the Lord of the Ascendant or the Moon is in the Ascendant or in the tenth, or the fourth or the seventh, or if one of them is joined to a planet in these houses, he will not be liberated from slavery if that planet to whom the Lord of the Ascendant or the Moon is joined to is direct. If indeed it is retrograde, it signifies liberation, but with slowness and the greatest labour, complications, and delays.

However, if the Lord of the Ascendant is impeded in the Ascendant or in the tenth, or in the seventh, or in the fourth by the corporeal conjunction of any malefic planet, or by its opposition or square aspect; or if he is entering into combustion, he will not be liberated from his slavery, unless by death, which will provide a most wicked solution to all of his problems.

VI

Whether A Master Will Sell A Slave

If a certain slave sometimes hopes, or perhaps fears, lest his master sell him or give him away in another manner, enquires saying "Is my current master good for me, or will the other one to whom I am about to go to, be better to me?". Examine then the Lord of the 1st house, who, if he is joined to any planet who receives him from the sign in which he is in (by house or exaltation or by two of the other lesser dignities), and the Lord of the seventh is not received; then the slave will be better off with the master who he is with, and who has power over him. If indeed the Lord of the seventh is received, he to whom the slave wishes to go to is better for him.

Besides this, consider the Lord of the Ascendant, and the Moon, and see from whom one of them separates; and to whom one of them is joined. If it separates from a benefic and joins a malefic, he whom the slave is with is better for him. If indeed he separates from a malefic and joins a benefic, he to whom the slave intends to go to is better for him.

However, if one of them (namely the Lord of the Ascendant, or the Moon) separates from a benefic and is joined a benefic, both of them will be good to him; but if the condition of one benefic is better than the condition of the other, judge according to this. If indeed he separates from a malefic and is joined to a malefic, both of them will be bad to him, in accordance with how each of them is disposeed.

And if you do not find that the Lord of the Ascendant (or the Moon) is joined to any planets, and if one of them is void-of-course; see if this planet (namely the Lord of the Ascendant, or even the Moon) has greater dignity in the sign it is in, than it does in the seventh or the second (namely house or exaltation or term or triplicity or face); if so, the master he is currently with is better. If indeed he would have greater dignity in the second or in the seventh than in the sign of the Ascendant, the other master will be better for him than the first.

VII

On The Buying Of Slaves, Or Of Any Small Animals, Or A Slave-Girl

We have already discussed whether a slave shall be freed from slavery or not. The buying of slaves remains to be discussed in this chapter; and when I speak of a slave, you can understand the same of any small animal which cannot be ridden and is signified by the 6th house. Whence if anyone is interested in a slave and wishes to buy him, and poses a question to you as to whether or not he will complete the purchase of this slave whom he intends to buy; you will examine the Lord of the Ascendant and the significatrix (which is the Moon), who are the significators of the querent; and see if both of them are joined to, or one of them is joined to, the Lord of the 6th house, or if the Lord of the 6th house is joined to the Lord of the Ascendant; or if you find any planet which transfers light between the Lord of the Ascendant and the Lord of the sixth. If so, tell him that he will acquire the slave which he enquired about (or the animal which he enquired about, since it is signified by the 6th house). If indeed you do not find the Lord of the Ascendant (or the Moon) joined to the Lord of the sixth, or vice versa; and if you do not find a planet which transfers light between them, then he will not acquire the quesited slave or animal.

However, if the question was about buying a slave-girl, Sarcinator said that you then ought to give the twelfth to the slave-girl. Arastellus indeed gave the sixth to the slave-girl as much as the slave. Arastellus' view concerned when mention was made of a slave girl simply, just as there was in the chapter on slaves. Sarcinators view was according to the slave-girl being the wife of the slave who someone intended to buy, since if the sixth signifies his slave, the opposite (which is the twelfth) signifies the slave's wife - and so both of them spoke well. Whence if a question is made on the slave-girl in the sense of her being a type of slave, you can give her the sixth, just as you would with a slave. If indeed she is enquired about in the sense of her being the wife of the slave of who is quesited, you can give her the twelfth. Indeed you can give someone the twelfth for another reason, namely when someone seeks a slave-girl from someone, give the first to the querent, and the seventh to the person from whom he seeks the slave-girl: and the sixth from the seventh (which is the twelfth from the first) will be given to the slave-girl belonging to the person from whom she is sought. And indeed by this same manner you can also give the twelfth to a slave.

Whence if a question is posed to you on a slave-girl, and it is an absolute question, just like I said to you above on the liberation of a slave, then give her the sixth. If indeed there is a question on a slave girl in the sense of her being the wife of a slave, then you will give her the twelfth. And if you find in the first situation (an absolute question) that the Lord of the Ascendant (or the Moon) is joined with the Lord of the sixth, or the Lord of the sixth with the Lord of the Ascendant; say that he will obtain the quesited slave-girl. If indeed you find in the second situation that the Lord of the Ascendant (or the Moon) is joined with the Lord of the twelfth, or the Lord of the twelfth with them - judge the same. Similarly if any planets transfer light between them, it signifies the obtainment of the matter, as I said to you on the slave.

VIII

Whether A Master Will Obtain The Substance Of His Slave Or Slave-Girl

It remains to be discussed in this chapter as to whether the substance of a slave is to arrive into the hands of his master or not. Just as when there is a certain slave of a certain man who was discharged from his service, and he who owns the slave enquires as whether he is to obtain the leftover substance of this slave. And if such a question is posed to you, then you ought to examine the Lord of the Ascendant (and the Moon) and see if they both (or only one of them) are joined to the Lord of the 7th house (which has the signification of the substance of the slave, since it is the second from the sixth, which signifies slaves, and so the seventh signifies their substance). If this is so, say that this master will acquire the quesited substance (namely that which belonged to his slave). And say the same if the Lord of the seventh is joined to the Lord of the 1st house. Similarly if the Lord of the Ascendant or the Moon is in the seventh, or if the Lord of the seventh is in the Ascendant, or even in the second; but this is not as secure - since if the Lord of the second is impeded or is received by the Lord of the seventh, while not receiving the Lord of the seventh, the master may suffer detriment to his substance, by reason of recovering the substance of the slave. Similarly if any planet transfers light between the Lord of the Ascendant and the Lord of the seventh, the master will obtain the substance of the slave, but through the hands of someone who interposes himself in the matter.

ON THE SEVENTH HOUSE

I

On Whether A Marriage Will Be Perfected Or Not. And If It Is Perfected, How Will It Turn Out, And If It Is Not Perfected What Will Impede It That It Will Not Be Perfected

If a question is made to you on a marriage, as to whether it will be perfected or no; and if it ought to be perfected, and you want to know how it will be perfected: or if it ought not to happen, and you wish to know the cause which impedes it so that it is not perfected; then examine the Ascendant and its Lord, and the Moon (which are the significators of the querent), and the seventh and its Lord (which are the significators of the quesited). Since a woman can just as well enquire about a man, as a man can enquire about a woman. And examine how, and in what way, they aspect each other. If indeed the Lord of the Ascendant (or the Moon) is corporeally joined to the Lord of the seventh, if it is a man who enquires, he will obtain the woman; if it is a woman who enquires she will obtain the man; and the marriage will be perfected.

If indeed they aspect by a trine or sextile aspect, the marriage will similarly be perfected, whether this aspect or corporeally conjunction is made with reception or without reception. If indeed the aspect is from opposition, it will not be perfected unless reception intervenes; nor will there be any hope for it. If indeed it is a square aspect with reception, it will be perfected, even if it will come to be with some delay. However, if it is without reception, there will be hope for it to be perfected and it will be firmly believed that it will be perfected: yet it won't be perfected, unless perhaps (as sometimes happens) there are people who have it in their power to make the union happen (such as the friends of the querent), then the matter might be perfected, but only just about. It will be the same if the Lord of the seventh is joined to the Lord of the Ascendant by the aforementioned conditions.

Likewise if the Lord of the seventh is in the Ascendant, the marriage will be completed with ease, and without any trouble, and the woman's' desire for it shall be greater than the mans (if a man inquires). If a woman inquires, the man's desire for it shall be greater than the woman's.

However, if the significators don't aspect each other, but there is another planet which transfers light between them, the matter will be done by way of someone who introduces himself to the matter. And examine which house the planet who transfers light between them is the Lord of; since the matter will come to be by a person who is signified by that house. And if it is a masculine planet it will be a man; if it is a feminine planet it will be a woman. Next examinee the planet who transfers light or disposition between the Lord of the Ascendant and the Lord of the seventh, or to whom they (namely the Lord of the Ascendant, or the Moon, or the Lord of the seventh) commit disposition; if it is free from impediments, so that it is not retrograde, nor combust, nor cadent from the angles, nor from the Ascendant, nor is besieged by malefics, nor in their opposition, nor their square aspect without reception. For if this is the case, say that the matter will be perfected and will endure.

Similarly if a benefic is the receiver of disposition or the transferor of light, and is free from the impediments mentioned above, the marriage will endure in a good, tranquil, useful, and benign state. If indeed it is a malefic, even if it is found free of the above impediments, then it signifies the perfection of the marriage and its durability; nevertheless there will be many contentions, many altercations and many quarrels between them, allowing not all of the time. And there will be whisperings, with these coming more so from the side of the person whose significator is a malefic, (whether it is the man or the woman signified by this malefic): and they might divorce on account of these whisperings. If indeed this receiver of disposition or transferor of light is an unfortunate malefic, the matter will be destroyed after it is thought and believed to be arranged; and it will be destroyed by an evil destruction, so that ill-will, contentions and enmity will rise up from it. If indeed it is a benefic, and is impeded by the impediments mentioned above (or by one of them), understand that in any event the matter will not be perfected, even after it is thought to be arranged; but neither enmity nor contentions will arise from it. And if there are whisperings, they will not be long lasting, and both parties might even withdraw from the proposal from shared and complete consent.

II

What It Will Be That Impedes The Marriage

If you want to know the reason by which the destruction of the marriage happened after it was thought to be arranged, then examine who is the malefic who impedes the receiving of the disposition of the significators of the man and the woman.

If it is the Lord of the 2nd house, it will be by reason of the querent's substance, since the other party might say that he is a pauper.

If it is the Lord of the 3rd house, it will be by reason of the brothers of the querent; and if he doesn't have brothers: it will be by one of those things which are signified through the 3rd house.

And if it is the Lord of the fourth, it will be by reason of the father, or by one of those things which are signified by the 4th house.

And if it is the Lord of the fifth, it will be by reason of children: since perhaps it will be said that the querent has children, and this will continue to be the reason; and if he does not have children, it will be since he is not able to have children. Just as there are sometimes men who cannot beget children, and women who cannot conceive children, or who have passed the age of conceiving. Or it will be by reason of that the woman had another man, or it will be one of those things which are signified through the 5th house.

And if it is the Lord of the sixth, it will be by reason of the illness of the querent: and if he doesn't have an illness, it will be by one of those things which are signified through the 6th house.

And if it is the 8th house it will be by reason of the separation of the woman's dowry; or perhaps that the querent dies before the marriage is perfected; which you will be able to judge if the Lord of the Ascendant is impeded by the Lord of the 8th house, or is joined to him, or if the Lord of the eighth is joined to him, and they receive each other, as will be discussed in the chapter when death is considered. Or it will be through one of those things which are signified by the 8th house.

And if it is the Lord of the ninth, it will be by reason of some religious person, or perhaps that at some time the querent was a religious person, or that he took up the habit of some religion; or it will be through one of those things which are signified by the 9th house.

And if it is the Lord of the tenth, it will be by reason of a king or a powerful person, or some great nobleman, or some lay office which will have come to the querent, or by any of those things which are signified through the 10th house.

And if it is the Lord of the eleventh, it will be by reason of some friend who will disturb the matter, or through one of those things which are signified by the 11th house.

And if it is the Lord of the twelfth it will be by reason of an illness of the quesited, or that she is of low birth, or it will be through one of those things which are signified by the 12th house.

And if this planet which transfers light between the Lord of the Ascendant and the Lord of the seventh is naturally malefic, there will be detriment and destruction from the side of those who introduce themselves to the matter, and who appear to want to perfect it.

III

How Will They Act Together

Allowing that I touched a bit on it above, regarding how the man and wife will behave with each other, if the marriage was perfected: I will tell you something more on this matter; nor is it a matter which appears to me to be downplayed. And it is to check and see if the Lord of the Ascendant is joined to the Lord of the seventh, or the Lord of the seventh to the Lord of the Ascendant, by a trine aspect with reception; for then they will always live together while they endure, and in good and peaceful condition, and in harmony, which will not be disturbed by any means; and one will always want what the other wants.

If they are conjunct by a trine aspect without reception, or a sextile with reception, things will be almost the same; yet there will sometimes be some trivial contentions or altercations between them.

But neither of them will worry about these, nor will they hold them in their hearts.

If indeed they are conjunct by a sextile aspect without reception, or a square with reception, it signifies concord and a good condition between them: but there will be more discord and contentions between them, but they will not be long lasting. And if the Moon is joined to a planet in whose house or exaltation she is placed in, it will be the same.

Indeed, if they are joined from opposition, it signifies a multitude of discords and contentions between them, happening often and more often, and long lasting, and they will rarely act well together. And similarly if they are corporeally joined in one sign, so that there are less degrees between them than the quantity of one of their orbs (namely the planet with the smaller orb).

After this examine the Lord of the Ascendant and the Lord of the seventh, and see which of them is heavier or which is in an angle - since the person signified by that planet will rule. Just as if the significator of the husband was in an angle, or was heavier, and the significator of the wife was cadent from an angle and lighter, the husband would rule the wife, and especially if the significator of the wife was joined to the significator of the husband. If indeed the significator of the husband was cadent, and was lighter, and joined the significator of the wife; the wife would rule the man and be in charge of him. If indeed neither of them are in an angle, and neither is joined to the other, that person will rule whose significator is heavier; and whichever one of them is seeking a conjunction of the other, or is cadent, and the other is in an angle or a succeedent, that one will be subject to the other, whether it is the significator of the husband, or the significator of the wife, and this will be weaker unless one of the planets cuts off their light, or prohibits their conjunction, just as was said in the chapter on the prohibition of conjunctions or light.

Similarly if the Sun is impeded it will deteriorate the condition of the husband. If indeed Venus is impeded, the condition of the wife will be impeded and deteriorated. However, if the Moon is impeded it will signify the impediment and deterioration of the condition of the husband and the wife; even if they jointly wish to happily rejoice and treat each other well, they won't be able, and both will be made quite unfortunate. Similarly if the Moon is impeded and aspects the Ascendant, or if any of the malefics are on the Ascendant, there will be contentions and discord between them which will befall them from the side of the querent. If indeed there is a malefic in the seventh, they will befall them from the side of the quesited, and the occasion of these contentions and discords will be the significations of that house which that malefic (in the first or the seventh) is the Lord of. So that if it is the Lord of the second it will be by reason of substance: if it is the Lord of the third it will be by reason of brothers: and understand this for all of the other houses, each one according to the particular content of each one.

IV

On The Woman, Whether She Is Corrupted Or A Virgin, Or If She Has A Lover, Or Someone Else Whom She Loves Apart From Her Husband (If She Is Married), Or Apart From Her Lover (If She Has One)

If anyone might want to contract a marriage with some woman and suspects that she is not a virgin; since perhaps some people spoke ill of her, as many are in the habit of doing, sometimes due to jealousy: sometimes for the reason of disturbing the marriage so that it isn't completed, or perhaps someone who is seeking some sinful deed from her which she does not want to do, and the querent wishes to be made certain of this, and came to you to pose the question; whether this woman is a virgin or not.

Then consider the Ascendant and its Lord, and the significatrix (which is the Moon) - since in this case the querent doesn't have a house which signifies him, nor a planet as a significator - and examine if both are in angles and in fixed signs; if so, tell him that the woman is a virgin, and that indeed there is no blemish of corruption in her. And that if anyone speaks ill of her, do not believe what they say, since they are all lying, and nothing impure can be found out about her, not even if she was tempted by someone.

If indeed the Lord of the Ascendant and the Moon are in fixed signs, and the angles are mobile signs, she was tempted, but did not yield to the words of the suitor. However, if the Moon was joined with

Saturn, Jupiter, Mars, or the Sun by body or by aspect, so that there are 5 degrees or less between them, she was tempted by someone who bears the image of that planet to whom the Moon is joined. Indeed, if the Moon is joined to Venus or Mercury she was tempted by some woman on behalf of some man, yet she didn't care, nor yielded herself to their words, but derided this tempter. If indeed the Moon was separating from the above planets by three minutes, the woman was angry with the tempters, and they desisted from their tempting.

If indeed the angles were fixed signs, and the Lord of the Ascendant and the Moon were in mobile or common signs (but common signs introduce less than the mobile signs) she was tempted and is tempted still; and sometimes endured what was said to her by these tempting women: nevertheless she did not occupy herself with them, but remained in her virginity.

However if the Lord of the Ascendant or the Moon are in mobile signs, or both are in common signs and the Moon is joined with any of the aforementioned masculine planets, then she has been embraced and kissed by a certain man who bears the image of that planet to whom the Moon is joined, and he touched the woman's private parts, and indeed placed his member up against them: and the situation was such that he believed himself to have had carnal knowledge of her, and she herself was deceived that she lost her virginity. Nevertheless, she does not believe that she lost it, for the shameful act was not completed on her part; and so what happened was the reason for her bad reputation. And this type of thing often happens when men have many dealings with women, or often frequent them, or sometimes at great feasts, or travelling to arboretums, or when women travel to far off festivities or far from cities, and so on.

However, if the Moon is at that time with the Caput Draconis, the matter was in progress, but was not consummated, nor did she lose her virginity by this means. If indeed the Cauda Draconis is in the place of the Caput, neither in the past, the present, or the future, will she will be judged to be free of reproach. And the same can be said of Mars if he is in the place of the Caput, except that Mars does not impose as much malice in women as does the Cauda.If indeed the Moon is joined to Venus by the above conditions regarding the signs and angles, it does not appear that she completed the deed; nor did she persevere in it. But it appears that things are otherwise with her - since it appears that she loves girls, and rubs herself up against them, and sodomises them, and completes her shameful acts contrary to nature.

But if the Moon is impeded in the last face of Gemini, then the woman corrupted herself with her own hands and deflowered herself. However, if she is impeded in the last terms of this sign, it signifies that the woman persists in this evil. And if the ascending sign is a mobile sign or a common sign, or the Lord of the Ascendant and the Moon are in mobile or common signs, then the woman's virginity was taken earnestly and by her will; and even if she didn't want to, she was still deflowered. And if the Ascendant was a fixed sign and the Lord of the Ascendant was in a fixed sign (even if the Moon was in a mobile or common sign), or if the Moon was in a fixed sign (even if the Lord of the Ascendant was in a mobile sign, or the Ascendant was a mobile or common sign); then the woman did not lose her virginity. But it is possible that someone may have brought his member close to the woman’s private parts by force and ejaculated there, nevertheless she was not corrupted. And if the Lord of the Ascendant or the Moon are combust in a mobile sign, the woman was oppressed and her virginity was taken by force. And if they are combust in a fixed sign she was oppressed and someone wanted to corrupt her, yet she didn't allow herself to be corrupted. And if the Moon is in the Ascendant with Saturn, and the Ascendant is a fixed or common sign, she was not deflowered, but someone abused her by a wicked sodomitical deed. And if you find the Lord of the Ascendant or the Moon in the fifth, or the Lord of the fifth in the Ascendant, or if you find them corporeally conjunct in one sign, it appears that the woman has already conceived. And if they are separating from each other by 3 degrees or less, it appears that the woman has already given birth.

If indeed the Moon is impeded by Mars, and Mars is in square aspect with Venus, so that the aspect is now completed, (so that Venus is now separated from Mars by one minute or more); and Venus is in Cancer, or Scorpio, or Pisces, or Mars is in Aries or his triplicity and in square aspect to Venus (as long as she is separating from him as I said); say that she is a virgin and not corrupted. Indeed you can excuse the woman in this manner if you wish, even if you may have found her deflowered by any of the ways mentioned above - for she does not believe herself to be deflowered. Since if you find her to be a true virgin, say that nothing bad can be said about her. But if you find her deceived, as was said, so that her virginity was taken by hand or by another way (since sometimes women are corrupted and lose their virginity solely by the touch of their own hands, or those of another, or the touch of a finger - as long as she has an orgasm), and for this reason you can say that even if she fooled around with someone, nevertheless no man has carnal knowledge of her; regardless of whatever was said about her. And so the woman will remain excused from guilt in the eyes of the querent: since if you tell him the whole truth, it is possible that he will have her for corrupt and if she had gone with a man.

V

If A Woman Is Carrying On With Someone Besides Her Husband

If someone is affected with jealousy of their wife, worrying if she is doing something bad with someone else, and comes to you with a question; in this case examine the Ascendant and its Lord, and the Moon and the planet which she separates from (which are the significators of the querent), and the seventh and its Lord, and the planet to whom the Moon is joined (which are the woman's significators): and see to whom the Moon or the Lord of the seventh is joined to. Since if the Lord of the seventh and the Moon are joined to the Lord of the Ascendant, whether with reception or without reception (as long as they are not more closely joined to another planet by aspect or conjunction); say that regardless of what is said about her, the woman is not to be blamed.

If indeed the Lord of the seventh and the Moon (or either of them) are joined to the first, second or third triplicity Lord of the Ascendant, or one of them is joined to the Lord of the seventh, and the Lord of the seventh or the Moon is separated from the Lord of the Ascendant, it will appear that the woman has another man who she loves besides her husband. However, if the Lord of the seventh is void-of-course, the woman does not have a lover; nor is she to be blamed. However, if you find the Lord of the seventh or the Moon (or both of them), separating from another planet besides the Lord of the Ascendant, and they are not separated by more than 3 degrees, the woman loved someone besides the querent, but sent him away afterwards. If indeed the Lord of the seventh is with the Caput Draconis without the conjunction of another planet, say that the woman is not to be blamed. If indeed it is with the Cauda without the conjunction of another, it appears that she is blameworthy, and that she could be blamed in the past, present and future.

Next examine if the Lord of the Ascendant or the Moon is joined with Mars, and if the Caput Draconis is there; for if so, it appears that the woman has a lover who she loves, and who is intimate with her. And if the Cauda is joined with Mars and with the Lord of the seventh or the Moon (as I said), it will reduce the malice: and even if the woman may love someone who carries the image of Mars, nevertheless he hasn't locked her down. And if Mars is conjunct with the Lord of the seventh (or with the Moon) in one sign without the Cauda, the woman will have a lover in an area not far from her own house. And if they are in the same degree, it appears then that the lover is in the house, or is a member of the man's family. And if the Moon (or the Lord of the seventh) is separating from Mars, or Mars from them; the woman has a lover, and she may have had him before she had her husband: but now one has dismissed the other, nor have they a way of carrying on together.

If indeed Mars is the Lord of the seventh: or if the Moon is the Lord of the seventh and is in Aries, or Scorpio: and Mars aspects one of them with reception, namely that Mars receives ones of them, she loved someone a long time ago: but not enough to have carried on with him. If indeed Mars is not received by the Lord of the seventh or the Moon (even if they are in the aforementioned signs and received by Mars), the woman loves someone else, and he loves her too, but he is not carrying on with her; and if the opportunity arises, she would well consent to it.

However, if the Moon or the Lord of the seventh is joined to Jupiter without reception, the woman loves some nobleman, greater and nobler than her husband (whether he is a bishop or another prelate, or perhaps a judge) and even though she loves him, he does not love her. If indeed there is mutual reception between them, she loves him and he loves her: nor will anything else make it so that the matter will not be perfected, except if the opportunity is not there. However, if the Lord of the seventh or the Moon is conjoined with Mercury, it appears that the woman loves a literary youth, or a money-changer, or merchant who appears to be younger, more handsome, and more elegant than her husband. If indeed the Lord of the seventh or the Moon is joined to Venus with reception, from whatever aspect, even a trine or sextile, whether with reception or without reception, the woman doesn't care for men: but mixes with women and uses them improperly. However if the Lord of the ninth or Jupiter aspects Venus, or Venus and the Lord of the seventh commit their disposition to one of these planets, she will regret performing such foul acts with women, and will dismiss them: and she might adopt a religious life for this reason, and on account of her shame. However, if Saturn is in the place of Venus, the woman loves some man who carries the image of Saturn, or some old man, or some religious person clothed in black or dull vestments; and especially if Saturn is the Lord of the ninth, or is in the ninth, or is under the rays of the Sun. However, if the Sun is in the place of Venus (namely aspecting the Lord of the seventh or the Moon), the woman loves and has loved, some magnate from among those men who are almost fit for kingship; if there is reception he has been carrying on with her: if it is without reception, he doesn't care for her. However if multiple planets aspect the Lord of the seventh at once, especially if Saturn and Mercury are involved, she has slept with more than one person, and she has not been chastened by this up until now.

However if someone enquires by the above conditions about a woman who is not their wife, or their lover; give the woman the Ascendant, just as you gave her the seventh, unless it is a woman who has a determined house, such as a sister or a daughter or someone else who has a determined house; for you will give these women the houses attributed to them.

Nevertheless you ought to pay attention to this; that in the matters above which are not completed, reception signifies completion in the future, without reception indeed not.

VI

If The Conceived Is The Child Of Who It Is Said To Be

That if he (or perhaps someone else) doubts of his wife - as often happens when merchants go travelling, or when someone travels to the region of a city, or on a military campaign, or to similar places, and sometimes these men find their wives (or their lovers) pregnant when they return, and doubt if their wives are pregnant from them. And if one of them were to enquire of you as to whether the conceived child is legitimate or illegitimate; examine the Lord of the Ascendant and the Moon (which are the significators of the querent), and the fifth sign and its Lord (which are the significators of the child), and see if they are aspecting each other by a trine or sextile aspect (whether with reception or without reception); if so, the child will be legitimate. Indeed, if they are aspecting each other from square aspect or opposition with mutual and perfect reception: or if the Lord of the Ascendant or the Moon are in the house of children: or if the Lord of the 5th house is in the Ascendant without the aspect of malefics: or if benefics are aspecting the house of children or its Lord, the child will be legitimate. If this is not so, see if malefics (whether Saturn or Mercury or Mars) aspect the house of children, or its Lord, for then the child or conception will be from disgrace, and it will be exposed.

VII

If Someone Wants To Take A Corrupted Woman As A Wife

And if someone wishes to take a corrupted woman as a wife, and perhaps that it is said of her that she has children, as sometimes happens that widows or other corrupted women lie with someone secretly and conceive and give birth, and secretly nurse the child, and then give him up to an orphanage or some other religious place, and there are sometimes whispers of this being the case; whence if someone fears to take such wives on account of infamy: or perhaps for some other reason, and they come to you asking if this woman has a child, Zael said that you ought to examine Venus, and see if she is in Aquarius or Leo, and Mercury is with her. If so, then the woman never gave birth, nor conceived. Indeed, if

Venus and Mercury are both in Taurus or in Scorpio, he said that the woman has a child. Similarly if Mars along with Venus and the Moon (or only one of them) are in Gemini, Virgo, or Pisces, the woman has a child. If indeed the aforementioned planets are in Sagittarius, it signifies the barrenness of the woman in the past, present, and future; and if you find that she had given birth before now, that child will die, and will not outlive her. And if Saturn and Mars are in Aries, Cancer, Libra or Capricorn, the woman will be saddened from this child, and it will be born from a lover, not from her own husband, nor will she remain faithful to her husband. But if Jupiter and Venus are in the aforementioned signs, namely Aries, Cancer, Libra or Capricorn, this child or this conception will be that of her own husband without the blemish of wickedness.

VIII

Whether A Woman Departed Or Expelled From The House Will Return Or Not

This particular chapter is subordinated to the one above, so that it can be rightly comprehended under it; and just as it most frequently happens that husbands expel wives from the house, sometimes with cause, sometimes without cause, or wives withdraw from the houses of their husbands by their own will, or indeed with cause, or from fear of their husbands beating them, or for whatever other reason. And perchance a woman comes to you who has exited from the house in which she lives with her husband (or perhaps with her lover), and comes to you with a question to you as to whether she is to return to the house or not: then you should examine the Lord of the seventh (which is the Ascendant of the woman in this case, since the seventh is given to the expelled person); and see if it aspects the Ascendant, so that no other planets aspects the Ascendant as well as it does. If so, say that the woman will return to the house of which she spoke. Understand the same of the Moon.

If the Lord of the seventh doesn't aspect the Ascendant: but aspects another planet, who is not impeded, and who aspects the Ascendant, the woman will return into the house with the intervention of some person, who involves themselves in the matter, and brings her into harmony with her husband. If none of these were the case, then examine the Sun (who is the natural significator of the husband, and Venus (who is the natural significatrix of the wife). And if the Sun is above the earth, and Venus aspects the Ascendant by a laudable aspect (namely a trine or sextile); the woman will return into the quesited house with ease, and without any major clamour or rumours. And if the Sun is under the earth and Venus is above the earth, and similarly aspecting the Ascendant by a laudable aspect, the woman will return into the house, but with perseverance, delay, complications, and with duress and rumours, and it will be known by many people before she returns.

Similarly examine if the Moon is increasing in her light, that is, from her first appearance from under the rays of the Sun up to the completion of her second quarter: For if she is, the woman will return into the house, but with slowness and duress. If indeed the Moon is decreasing in light, so that she was already in her third quarter and had transited the combust degrees, up until she approached the rays of the Sun (yet in such a way that she is not so close to the rays of the Sun that she does not appear), the woman will return into the quesited house shortly, and without much duress or complications, and without rumours.

Similarly examine Venus, and see if she is occidental and retrograde, returning toward the Sun: for then the woman will return to her husband's house of her own accord, and by her own will, fearing that her husband may harass her and punish her for having left. If indeed Venus is retrograde, and is already appearing from under the rays of the Sun, the husband will regret expelling the woman from the house, and will rejoice at her return; but he will not regret beating her, nor doing her wrong; however the woman will return angrily just as she left angrily; and she will regret returning to the house, just as she regretted leaving, and even more so; nor will she have good will towards her husband.

IX

On A Lawsuit Or Dispute Which Exists Between Some People: Who Will Win, Or Who Will Lose; Or If They Will Settle Before The Lawsuit Or Not

If there is a lawsuit or a dispute which exists between some people, or which is being prepared by one of the parties, and someone who ought to win the case wishes to be made certain of this from you, and poses a question to you about this; examine the Ascendant at the hour which he asked you the question, and its Lord, and the significatrix (namely the Moon) for the querent; and the seventh and its Lord for the adversary; and see if the Lord of the Ascendant or the Moon is joined with the Lord of the seventh (or the Lord of the seventh with one of them), by a trine or sextile aspect with mutual reception. If so, then they will come to a clear agreement without anyone's interference. Indeed, if one receives the other, and the one received does not receive the receiver, they will come to an agreement without litigation, but not without the involvement of someone else; and those who involve themselves will come from the party whose significator receives the other planet. And if they are joined by square aspect or from opposition with reception, or by trine or sextile without reception, they will reach an agreement, but first they will go to court; and the agreement will always come from the party whose significator is less heavy, and who commits his disposition to the other planet. And this will be better if both of the significators receive the other. If the lighter planet is joined to the heavier one and doesn't receive him, and the heavier planet receives the lighter one; it signifies that the receiver wants to reach an agreement; even if the lighter one doesn't (nor will he stand with him); and this will be all the more so if the aspect is a trine or sextile, or if they are corporeally joined in one sign, so that their conjunction is not impeded by another planet, whether it is with reception or without reception; they will reach an agreement, even without the involvement of another.

After this examine the significator of the king, authority, or judge (which is the Lord of the 10th house), and see if he aspects one of the significators (namely the Lord of the Ascendant or the Lord of the seventh), or if he is corporeally joined to one of them; or if the Lord of the Ascendant wants to join with the Lord of the seventh (or the Lord of the seventh with him), and the Lord of the 10th house cuts off their conjunction. For then they will not reach an agreement, unless they first go to court and bring the matter before a judge: and this will happen from the side of the judge or authority; who will not allow them to settle, and will force them to go to court, possibly to extort something out of it.

Next examine the Moon, and see if she transfers light between the Lord of the Ascendant and the Lord of the seventh; and if the Moon doesn't transfer light between them, see if another planet does: since if this is so, someone will interpose himself and reconcile them, even if they have already begun litigation.

After this examine the Lord of the Ascendant (who signifies the querent), and the Lord of the seventh (who signifies the adversary): and see which of them is stronger, as the party whose significator is stronger ought to win. Indeed the stronger significator will be the one in an angle; and especially if he is in any of his own dignities, and in a dignity of greater quantity; and the greater number of fortitudes one of them has, that party will be stronger by that much, and especially if the planet is received in the place where he is (since he will be stronger in himself, and will have allies who will help him). And if they ought to reconcile (as was said); the beginning of the reconciliation will be initiated from the side of the lighter planet who commits disposition to the other: for if the Lord of the Ascendant is lighter, and the Lord of the seventh heavier, it will come from the side of the querent. If indeed the Lord of the Ascendant is heavier, and the Lord of the seventh is lighter, the reconciliation will be initiated by the adversary. And the planet which is cadent from an angle is said to be weaker, unless another planet (who is in a strong place and receives him) supports him.

It is also necessary that you look and examine whether the Lord of the seventh is in the Ascendant - since then it signifies that the Lord of the Ascendant (namely the querent), will win totally, and the adversary will lose.

And it is also necessary to examine if the Lord of the Ascendant is in the seventh, for this signifies that the adversary will win, and that the querent will succumb. For whichever of the significators is found in the house of the other will signify the person it signifies to be conquered. And this doesn't only happen in litigations or financial matters: indeed it also happens in battles and wars: since always whichever significator is found in the house of the other, is said to be conquered, and is similar to a conquered person.

After this it is necessary that you examine whether the Lord of the Ascendant or the Lord of the seventh is retrograde; since if the Lord of the Ascendant is retrograde, it signifies the weakness of the querent, and that he will not be firm in his standing in the lawsuit: and that he will refuse to speak the truth to the adversary, and will not confess it, nor will he believe he has the right. If indeed the Lord of the seventh is retrograde, it signifies weakness on the part of the adversary, and that he will flee the case insofar as he can, and will refuse to speak the truth, nor will he believe himself to have a good case. Also examine the significator of the judge (whether the person who ought to judge between the parties is a king, or a powerful person, or a judge), who will be the Lord of the 10th house; and see whether he aspects the significators of the lawsuit or not, which if he aspects them, and is direct, the judge will proceed according to the rule of law in this case, and that he will strive to make it short and to resolve it quickly. However if it is retrograde, it signifies that the judge, or king, or powerful person will not proceed according to the rule of law in this case, nor will he care to resolve it; indeed he will prolong it more than it ought to be prolonged by law. The same will be said on the prolongation of the case if the Lord of the Ascendant is separated from the Lord of the seventh, or if the Lord of the seventh is separated from the Lord of the Ascendant.

Besides this, see if the Lord of the Ascendant is joined with the Sun or with the Moon, or if either of them are joined with him, so that another planet does not impede their conjunction (as long as the Sun is not corporeally conjunct with him, since this signifies his impediment; unless a planet is in the Zamini of the Sun, since then it is made strong), or if the Lord of the Ascendant is in the domicile of one of the luminaries; or if the Sun, or the Moon is in the Ascendant; since if this is so, it signifies the strength of the querent. If indeed the Lord of the seventh is so disposeed (as was said of the Lord of the Ascendant) it signifies the strength of the adversary.

And examine if the Lord of the Ascendant is joined with the Lord of the 10th house; for then the querent will seek assistance from the judge, or from him who ought to know about the case: and it is possible that he will strive to corrupt him to pass sentence in his favour. And if the Lord of the 10th house receives the Lord of the second from the Ascendant, the judge will seek the querent's money. And if the Lord of the tenth receives the Lord of the Ascendant, the judge will acquiesce in the pleas of the querent: otherwise he will not. And similarly examine if the Lord of the 10th house is lighter than the Lord of the Ascendant and is joined to him for if so the judge or powerful person will do what the querent wants, even if he himself doesn't request it. However if the Lord of the seventh is joined with the Lord of the 10th house, the adversary will seek assistance from the judge or powerful person. If the Lord of the tenth receives the Lord of the seventh, the judge will acquiesce in the pleas of the adversary, and will allow himself to be corrupted, and will offer his support; otherwise he won't. But if the Lord of the tenth receives the Lord of the eighth, he will accept the adversaries' money. But if the significator of the judge (namely the Lord of the 10th house) is lighter than the Lord of the seventh, and is joined to him, then the judge or powerful person will strive to make the matter good for the adversary, even if he doesn't request it.

After you inspect the disposition and condition of both significators (namely the Lord of the Ascendant and the Lord of the seventh); and you see that they don't want to reconcile, nor does it appear to you that they will be reconciled, but rather that they seem to want to litigate; then examine if the Lord of the 10th house is joined to one of the significators (namely the Lord of the Ascendant or the Lord of the seventh), or if either of them are joined to him, in such a way that another planet does not impede their conjunction. Since then the judge or sentencer will be favourable to the party whose significator he is joined to. That is, if he is joined with the significator of the first, he will be favourable to the querent; if he is joined with the significator of the seventh, he will be favourable to the adversary; if he is joined with none of them, he will be favourable to none of them, but will proceed solely along the path of the law. If indeed he is joined to both of them with reception (as sometimes happens), the judge will settle between them and reconcile them together, whether they want to or not.

Next examine the 10th house (which is the sentencers), and see if any planets are in it; for if its Lord is there, the judge will judge the case as cautiously and quickly as he can, and in an honourable fashion, unless if it is Saturn. If indeed the term Lord, triplicity Lord, or face Lord is there, he will judge it, but will not be so painstaking in sentencing. However, if there is a planet in the 10th house which doesn't have dignity there, and is not received by the Lord of the 10th house, it signifies that the parties will not remain content with the judge or sentencer; for both will fear him, and they will agree on another judge, and will stand by his judgement. And also examine if Saturn is the significator of the judge, and is in the tenth; for that judge will not judge according to the law, nor according to how he ought to. If Jupiter, or Sun, or Mercury, or Venus, or the Moon, are then joined to him from any aspect (except for opposition) or if he is void-of-course, bad things will be said about the judge, but what is said will be quickly suppressed, and the judge will not be defamed from this. If indeed one of those planets is joined to him from opposition, bad things will be said of the judge on account of an unjust judgement, and it will endure for a long time. If indeed Mars then aspects Saturn from opposition or square aspect, whatever condition Mars is then in, the judge or powerful person will be defamed from the matter. However, if Mars is in bad condition, he will be defamed by a scandalous event, unless Saturn is then in Capricorn (since then Mars will refrain from his malice somewhat, especially if he is in good condition).

If you find that the parties do not remain content with the earlier judgement, but establish good faith, as it was said; examine if any planets are in the tenth; for through this planet you will be able to know the condition of the judge who will decide between the parties.

For if Jupiter is here, the judge who they get will be good, benevolent, just and benign, and will not allow himself to be corrupted by any means, neither by bribes nor by pleas, but will proceed solely by the way of truth.

If Mars is there, the judge will be false, irritable, unfaithful, not loving justice, and one who quickly moves and changes from proposal to proposal in such a way that his latest error is worse than the previous, and they will regret having chosen such a judge.

If it is the Sun, the judge will be a good soul, yet he will allow himself to be influenced by the pleas of friends, and will turn himself towards them, and lend them his ear, and give them the hope of him doing what they want; nevertheless in the end he will judge rightly.

And if Venus is there, the judge will be just and of good opinions, but will not be very profound in law; nevertheless he will judge in good faith.

And if Mercury is in the tenth, the judge will be of good intelligence and sharp, and will quickly see the cause of the matter. But he will judge according to the planets which Mercury applies to; if benefics, justly; if malefics, unjustly. If Mercury does not apply to anyone, he will judge according to the evidence he finds.

And in all of the above mentioned situations, the things to be considered are; the Lord of the Ascendant, the Lord of the seventh, and the other aforementioned significators, without the participation of the Moon, even if by her nature she participates in all things, some things are still taken away from her.

However, if the Moon is in the tenth, the judge will be fickle and unstable, and one who will judge in accordance as things appear to him, not giving much consideration to the law, nor caring about what he will judge, nor what will be said about his judgements, good or bad.

You should also consider a certain secret, which I do not remember finding in the sayings of the ancients; yet I still tested it and found it to be true. Namely, to consider the place of the Lord of the Ascendant and the place of the Lord of the second, and subtract the lesser from the greater; and that which is left over will be the remainder of the Lord of the first and the Lord of the second. Next consider the place of the Lord of the seventh and the place of the Lord of the eighth, and subtract the lesser from the greater: and that which is left over will be the remainder of the Lord of the seventh and the Lord of the eighth. And take those two remainders and subtract the lesser from the greater, and keep that as the third remainder. Next take the place of the Lord of the ninth and the place of the Lord of the twelfth, and subtract the lesser from the greater, and this will be the remainder of the Lord of the ninth and the Lord of the twelfth; and then take this and the third remainder, and subtract the lesser from the greater: and that which is left over will be the Part signifying assistance and fortitude of the querent or quesited. Add on, from above, the degree of the ascending sign, and project from the Ascendant as you do with the Part of Fortune - if it is in the day; however it is at night, project from the nadir.

And see in whose house, or exaltation, or terms, or triplicity the number finishes. For the planet who is the Lord of this place (or who is stronger and more powerful there) will be the one sought, namely the assistant of him whose significator more greatly and better aspects it minute for minute: or who is closer to this place (provided that they have some dignity in this place), and who renders him more strongly; and this will be all the more so if it is with reception. If both of these remainders are equal, the significator will be on the Ascendant in the day, and on its nadir at night. And when you do this, always prefer the house Lord; and if he is impeded, operate through the exaltation Lord. But if he is impeded, operate through the term Lord. If he is impeded, operate finally through the triplicity Lord. And the planet in whose dignities the Part falls; or who more greatly aspects it, or who (having dignity there) the Part is closer to - will signify the reason why and how the things said came to be, and from where they happen.

But if the Lord of the first and the Lord of the second are the same planet, its place will be just as the remainder of the Lord of the first and the Lord of the second. If indeed the Lord of the seventh and the Lord of the eighth are the same, the place will be just as the remainder of the Lord of the seventh and the Lord of the eighth. Then subtract the lesser from the greater and do as was said regarding the remainder of the Lord of the first and the second, and regarding the remainder of the Lord of the seventh and the Lord of the eighth. What is said on lawsuits, you may understand the same in battles and wars and in all controversies.

X

On Buying And Selling

If someone wants to buy something, and poses a question to you on the matter, as to whether he will obtain the thing or not: then examine the (Lord of the Ascendant), who is the significator of the querent, and similarly the Moon (who is not to be omitted); and examine the Lord of the seventh - who is the significator of the person selling, and the thing to be sold in an absolute sense, unless it is a determinate thing being sold.

And see if the Lord of the Ascendant or the Moon joins with the Lord of the seventh, or the Lord of the seventh with the Lord of the Ascendant: for then the querent will obtain the quesited item, and without great delay or complications; and the perfection of the purchase or sale will come from the side of the person whose significator is lighter. So if the Lord of the Ascendant is lighter, it will come from the side of the querent; if the Lord of the seventh is lighter, it will come from the side of the seller.

If indeed the aforementioned significators are not joined by any conjunction or aspect, see if the Moon or some other planet transfers their light between them: since if this is so, it signifies that some person will involve himself in the matter, and the matter will be perfected in this way. Even if the transfer of light is made from one planet to the other seven planets, as long as the light is led back to the Lord of the Ascendant, or at least to the Ascendant, the quesited matter will be perfected.

However, if a determinate thing was quesited, examine what the querent asked about; since if he enquired about buying a slave, or about one of those things which are signified through the house of slaves: you will give the first to the querent, and the sixth to the quesited matter. If he enquired about a horse, a cow, or one of those things which are signified by the 12th house: give the first to the querent, and the twelfth to the quesited matter. If he enquired about buying a city, a house, or a castle: give the first to thee querent, and the fourth to the quesited matter. And so you can understand about anything for sale through the house by which it is signified.

Next examine if the Lord of the seventh is in the first: for the seller will accost the buyer to buy the thing, and the desire of the seller will be greater than that of the buyer. Similarly examine if any benefic planet (namely Jupiter or Venus) is in the 1st house; for then the purchase will be completed without labour, without complications, and without delay, nor will the buyer strive to deceive the seller. If indeed the Sun is there, and he is not corporeally conjunct with any planet, it will be the same. And if Mercury or the Moon are there, and neither of them are in the aspect of any malefic, it signifies the same as the Sun. However, if Saturn or Mars (or the Sun joined to either of them by body, or Mercury or the Moon with the aspect of any malefics) are there, it signifies that the matter will hardly be able to be perfected; and if it is perfected, it will come to be with difficulty, complications and slowness, and the buyer will strive to deceive the seller, and commit fraud if he can, nor will he remain firm in the deal. If indeed if one of the aforementioned benefics is in the seventh in the manner I described, it signifies goodness on the part of the seller, just as I said to you for the first on the part of the buyer. If indeed there is one of the aforementioned malefics there, it signifies malice on the part of the seller, just as I told you about the buyer.

Next examine if the Moon is separated from some planet, and if she is joined to another immediately, and without any distance, namely when she is separated from one and immediately joins another degree for degree, (or 5 degrees or less falls between her and the planet which she is joined to): for then it appears that he who sells the thing didn't buy it, but got it from an inheritance, or in some other manner without buying it. And Zahel said that if it is a thing that the seller had bought, he has not yet paid the price to the person who sold it to him. And he said that if the Moon is separated from someone, and is not yet joined to another, that there will be delay, slowness, complications, and lawsuits or litigation. And he said that if the planet from which the Moon separates is entering into combustion, that he who sells the thing will never get it back, but will die before he gets it. Furthermore, you will see that if the planet from which the Moon is separating is free from impediments, and it aspects the Lord of the sign through which the item being sold is signified by a trine or a sextile aspect: that this signifies that the seller will repurchase the item, or get it back in another manner.

XI

Whether A Thief Or Someone Else Who Has Fled Will Be Found Or Not, Or If They Will Return Of Their Own Volition

If someone ever flees from someone, just as when a slave or a slave-girl or another servant does; or if perhaps there was someone who was a guest and he stole something and fled, or perhaps if someone's wife similarly fled, and the querent wanted to find the person in question, and he posed a question to you as to whether he would find them again or not, and in what direction the person fled: examine the Ascendant and its Lord, and the Sun, and give those to the querent, and give the seventh and its Lord to the fugitive, and also the Moon (who naturally has the signification of all fugitive things on account of her swift movement). Then examine if the Lord of the first is joined in any way with the Lord of the seventh, or if the Lord of the first is in the seventh; for this signifies that the querent will find them, if he wants to pursue him, and applies himself well to searching for him. And if the Lord of the seventh is joined with the Lord of the first, or if the Lord of the seventh is in the first, or is joined with a retrograde planet, it does not appear that it will be necessary for the querent to put much effort into searching for the fugitive: for it will be one of two things: for he will either return of his own volition, and free movement; or if the querent looks for him, he will find him before he gets too far from the house in which he was staying.

And similarly examine the Moon (which signifies the fugitive); since if she is then separated from the Lord of the first, and joined immediately to the Lord of the seventh, it signifies that someone who has news of the fugitive will come to the querent and tell him where the fugitive is. And if the Moon is separated from the Lord of the seventh and joined to the Lord of the first, the fugitive will regret his flight, but will fear returning, whence he will send someone to the querent in order to guarantee his own safety, and thus he will return without any other inquiries from the querent.

Next examine if the Lord of the seventh is joined to any malefic planet in an angle: or if a malefic is joined to him: for this signifies that the fugitive will be caught, if the querent wishes to pursue him well. And indeed if both of them (the Lord of the seventh and the malefics who impedes him) are not in an angle, but only one of them is in an angle: it signifies that the fugitive will not be caught in such a way that he would be put in prison, but will be found and detained without imprisonment. If indeed the Lord of the first aspects the malefic who impedes the Lord of the seventh, the querent will find the fugitive detained in the custody of such people that demand that the querent gives them money before they give the fugitive to him. Similarly if a malefic is in the ninth it signifies the impediment of the fugitive on his journey, and that he will be captured. But if a benefic is in the ninth the fugitive won't be caught, nor will it be possible to catch him, unless this benefic is heavily impeded.

Next examine if the Sun and Moon (or at least one of them) are joined to the Lord of the seventh or aspect him from any aspect: since then the fugitive will not be able to hide himself in such a way that he is not found. Indeed similarly if the Lord of the seventh is entering into combustion or is now combust, this signifies that the fugitive will be found, even if he hides himself. And if the Lord of the seventh is then aspected by the Lord of the first or one of malefics, the fugitive will be captured and led away as if he were conquered. Indeed, if the Lord of the seventh is joined with some benefic by body or aspect (whether he is under the rays or not), the fugitive will not be caught, even if he is found, except in one case: namely if that benefic is retrograde, combust, or entering under the rays of the Sun; for then it cannot defend him from being caught.

Next examine if the Lord of the seventh is joined with a stationary planet (in whatever station it is in, namely the first or the second), and is in an angle or in what succeeds an angle: for this signifies that the fugitive doesn't know how to flee, and will not know what course of action to follow, namely whether to flee or not to flee; and so he will stay where he is until he is found or caught.

Nevertheless, the captures which are made when the planet is stationary differ from those made when it is in its first station. For in the first station the querent will catch the fugitive, or someone else will catch him and give him to the querent. However if the planet is in its second station, the fugitive will be caught, and will perhaps be caught while in flight, and he will be imprisoned and bound, but he will flee again from this prison or from these chains: yet it hardly seems that he will escape so he will not be captured again.

And Zael said that if this planet who joins the Lord of the seventh is direct, the fugitive will be caught, but he will not be sent back to prison: however he will be returned to the querent or the person who seeks him, and they will not imprison him over this.

Moreover, if the Moon is increasing in light and number, the fugitive will be pursued for a long time before he is caught, and his capture or discovery will be greatly prolonged. If indeed the Moon is reducing in light and in number, he will be found quickly and with little labour.

To know which direction the fugitive is going, examine the significatrix of the fugitive (which is the Moon), and see where she is then: since if she is in the Ascendant, or between the Ascendant and the fourth, it signifies that the fugitive fled eastwards. If she is in the first, exactly to the east. If she is in the second, to the east declining somewhat to the north. If she is in the third, declining even more to the north. However, if the Moon is in the tenth, it signifies he fled to the south. If in the eleventh, to the south declining to the east: if in the twelfth, declining even more to the east. If she is in the seventh, it signifies that the fugitive travelled to the west. If she is in the eighth he travelled to the west declining to the south. If she is in the ninth, declining even more to the south. And if she is in the fourth, it signifies that the fugitive fled to the north. And if she is in the fifth he fled to north, declining to the west. And if she is in the sixth, even more greatly declining to the west. And you will be able to add or subtract something from this by your own industry, according as you see the Moon or the Lord of the seventh to be in a direction or sign that is eastern, southern, western, or northern.

If indeed the fugitive is a thief, and the querent, follower, or pursuer wants to get him, to the extent that he is a thief, it will be the same judgement in all cases and all matters as for other fugitives; and by that much worse if the planet with which the Lord of the seventh is joined to had entered into combustion: for this signifies that the thief will die by reason of his capture (if he is captured). And if the planet with whom the Lord of the seventh is joined to when it enters into combustion is joined with a malefic, it signifies that the thief will be found in such a manner that will not be useful to his discoverer. For he will find him hanged, decapitated, burned, or perhaps with his body mutilated. If indeed Mars is in the seventh and the Lord of the seventh is impeded in the tenth, he will be hanged. If indeed the Moon is under the rays of the Sun, and is otherwise impeded by Mars, he will be burned. And if Mars is in the Ascendant while impeding the Lord of the seventh or the Moon, he will be decapitated. However, if it is Saturn who impedes the Lord of the seventh or the Moon, and is under the earth, he will be submerged and suffocated in water; while if he is above the earth, he will be beaten and hit with sticks in such a way that this is the cause of his death, or that he almost dies, or that he is so broken by the beating that he cannot escape. And if the Moon is then joined with the Lord of the sign in which she is placed, or with the Lord of the 8th house, the querent will obtain the goods of the thief, even if the thief is dead.

It was said regarding a fugitive or a thief, and those who will follow them, and it is to be seen in this place regarding if (as sometimes happens) a fugitive enquires of you "Is it good for me to return to the place from which I fled, or not". In this case you then ought to examine the Moon, and see if she is separated from a benefic and joined to a malefic. If so, then it will be better for him to return to the place from where he fled. However, if she is separated from a malefic and joined to a benefic, it will be worse for him to return, and better for him to flee. However, if she is separated from a benefic and joined to a benefic, if the benefic from which she separates from is better disposeed, even if both are good, it will be better for him to return (and vice versa). Indeed, if she is separated from a malefic and joined to a malefic, both of them will be bad for him. But if the malefic from which she separates is more badly disposeed, to return would be worse for him (and vice versa).

XII

On Stolen Goods, Whether The Querent Will Recover Them Or Not

If someone approaches you about a theft that has been committed, and they pose a question to you on whether they will recover the stolen substance or not, and you wish to examine the matter: inspect the first hour of the question and its Lord, and the significatrix (namely the Moon), who are the significators of the querent; and examine the seventh and its Lord for the thief (since the thief is signified by the seventh Lord). If you find him in the seventh, it signifies that the querent will be able to find the thief, if he wants to search for him, and labours and strives at this (namely to find him).

If you want to know whether he will recover the stolen item, examine if the second from the Ascendant is joined with the Lord of the eighth and receives him. And since the Lord of the eighth signifies the substance of the thief, the querent will obtain the stolen item (or the goods of the thief, in such a way that he is suitably compensated for the theft committed. Say the same for the Lord of the first if he is joined with the Lord of the eighth and receives him. However if the Lord of the second from the Ascendant (which has the signification of the substance of the querent, and indeed the stolen item itself) is combust, it signifies that the thief has broken the item to bits, and consumed, dissipated, and destroyed it. Whence, even if the querent finds the thief, he will not find the stolen item. If the Lord of the second is exiting from combustion, the querent will find part of the stolen items, but won't find all of them, and he will hardly or never find more than half of the stolen items.

Then examine if the Lord of the seventh is in the first, or is joined to the Lord of the first: for then the thief will regret stealing the item and will return it to its owner. Then examine if the Lord of the first is joined to some planet placed in the tenth or the first, or at least in the seventh: for if this is so, the querent will find the thief even without extensive investigation. And if the Lord of the first is joined to a planet cadent from an angle who doesn't aspect the Ascendant, it signifies that the thief has already departed from that land, and has distanced himself so much that there isn't a hope of finding him. But if this cadent planet (to whom the Lord of the Ascendant is joined) aspects the Ascendant, it signifies the finding of the thief, almost after losing all hope, even if it will be with much watching and extensive investigation.

Besides this, if you find the Lord of the seventh combust, and the Lord of the first aspecting him, it signifies the discovery of the thief when he does not believe he will be found. Similarly if the Moon transfers light between the Lord of the first and the Lord of the seventh, it signifies the discovery of the thief. And if the Lord of the first doesn't aspect the Lord of the seventh, and he (the significator of the thief) is under the rays of the Sun, he will still be found, but not as easily. However, if the Lord of the first and the Lord of the second are both joined to the Lord of the tenth, the authorities or governor will compel the thief to return the stolen item to the querent (or whoever owns the item), or the thief will return it out of fear, lest he be led in front of the authorities or governor of the land in which he is detained. However if only the Lord of the first is joined to the Lord of the tenth, the querent will threaten the thief through the authorities, and will strive to scare him into return his goods, but the thief will not be frightened much by these threats; nevertheless the authorities or governor, will help the owner of the thing against the thief.

If indeed the Lord of the seventh is joined with the Lord of the tenth, even without the conjunction of the Lord of the first, the authorities or governor will not exercise their office well against the thief to make him return what was stolen, but on the contrary they will assist the thief. And if the Lord of the eighth (who signifies the substance of the thief) is joined with the Lord of the eleventh (who signifies the substance of the authorities), this signifies that the authority in question will accept money from the thief and help him. However, if the Lord of the second is joined to the Lord of the eleventh, it signifies that the authorities will accept money from the querent in order to proceed against the thief, and it will proceed for this reason. If indeed the Lord of the seventh is joined to the Lord of the third or the ninth, or if he is in the third or in the ninth, it signifies that the thief has departed from the region; or if it is in the third, then he is on a journey to exit the region, and is now approaching the borders of the region. If he is joined to the Lord of the third, then he has completely exited the region. If he is in the ninth, or joined with the Lord of the ninth, he has already greatly distanced himself from the region, in the direction which I said to you above when investigating the fugitive. However if the Lord of the seventh is in any of the angles, the thief has not yet left that land or region. And if you find that the thief has left the land or region, see whether benefic or malefic planets are joined the Lord of the seventh: since if a malefic is joined to him, or if he is joined to a malefic, things will go badly for him on the journey of his flight. Since if it is Mars, he will meet with highwaymen who will take away whatever he is carrying, and strike him, and possibly spill his blood. If it is Saturn he will meet with thieves who will steal what he is carrying. And if the significator of the thief is combust in any of the aforementioned houses (namely in the third or the ninth), and it is one of the superior planets and is before the Sun; or is one of the inferiors and is after the Sun; or if it is one of the inferiors and is retrograde before the Sun: it signifies that he will meet with labour, sorrow, difficulties and illness on the road, which will be the occasion for the taking away and loss of what he carries. Similarly if the Moon is joined to malefics, it signifies the loss of substance. If the Lord of the seventh is joined to a benefics and it is free of impediments, it signifies that things will go well for him in his flight, and on his journey, unless the benefic which joins the Lord of the seventh is impeded by retrogradation, fall, or combustion (which signifies the loss of that which the fugitive carries with him). Nevertheless, if that impeded benefic is then joined to another benefic which is in the first or the tenth, and is unimpeded, it signifies that he who pursues the thief will take away the substance of the thief: since the thief will cast aside his substance when he sees someone coming behind him, but this will not promise him to be caught.

And similarly if the Sun or Moon then aspect the significator of the thief or the significator of his substance by a trine or sextile aspect, it signifies that the querent will recover the stolen item. The same can be said if the Sun or Moon are in the first or tenth. Likewise if the Sun and Moon aspect each other from a trine or sextile aspect.

However if they aspect each other from opposition or from square aspect, it signifies the discovery of the lost item, but not until the querent has lost all hope of ever finding it again. And the discovery of the lost or stolen goods will happen after the Sun and Moon are separated from the Part of Fortune; or when they are both (or one of them is) corporeally conjunct with it. And examine the number of degrees between the Part of Fortune and the luminary closer to the Part of Fortune: for if the Part of Fortune is in an angle, the discovery will be within as many days as there are degrees between the luminary in question and the Part of Fortune, or within as many weeks. And if it is in a succeedent, it will be within as many weeks or months. And if it is in a cadent it will be within as many months or years. And the discovery made by the signification of the Sun will happen faster than that which is made by the signification of the Moon; and that which is made by the signification of the Moon will be delayed more than that which is made by the signification of the Sun. If you do not find that the Sun or the Moon aspects the first, nor aspect each other by any aspect; and neither of them aspects the Part of Fortune: this signifies that the thief won't be found, nor will he ever be exposed, nor will the stolen or lost goods be recovered through any means, nor through any labour, nor through any investigation which can be made by the querent or by anyone else on his behalf.

XIII

Whether A Lost Item Will Be Found

And if anyone ever enquires of you in an absolute sense regarding a missing or stolen item, and perhaps they made mention of it in terms of a theft, and perhaps they didn't; but said, "Examine over a certain item of mine which is lost, as to whether I will recover it or not", and you wish to examine for him, (whether it is a stolen item, or otherwise missing): you ought now to examine the Lord of the first, and the significatrix (namely the Moon). And if both of them are joined to the Lord of the second from the Ascendant (who is the significator of substance) it signifies the discovery of the lost item, quickly and with little labour. However if only one of them (namely either the Lord of the first or the Moon) is joined to the Lord of the second, it signifies the finding of the item that was taken, but not as easily as when both of them aspect it. If neither of them are joined to the Lord of the second, nor him to them: then examine then if any planet transfers the light of one of them to the other, which similarly signifies that the quesited item will be found. And if there is not a planet which transfers light between them, but there is a planet who is heavier than the Lord of the first and the Lord of the second, who both of them are joined to, and who receives the light of both of them, it signifies the finding of the quesited item. Similarly, if the Lord of the second (who takes care of substance) is in the second, or aspects it from a trine or sextile aspect, it signifies the finding of the missing item, but with delay and complications, and the concern and agitation of the querent. And if you do not find the Lord of the second in the second, but there is another planet in the second, and the Lord of the second is joined to him, or he is joined to the Lord of the second: it signifies the finding of the quesited item, whether the conjunction is by body or by aspect. However, if the Lord of the second is not in the second, and there is not a planet there which he aspects, and the planet doesn't aspect him by a trine or sextile aspect, it signifies the loss of the quesited item, and that it won't be recovered.

Besides this, if you find the Lord of the eighth from the Ascendant joined to the Lord of the 7th, the querent won't recover the lost item: since it signifies that he who has the item, whether he is a thief or someone else to whom the item has come, has appropriated it for himself. And say the same if the Lord of the seventh is joined to the Lord of the second, or if the Lord of the second is joined to him, without the conjunction of the Lord of the Ascendant or the Moon: for if the Lord of the first or the Moon aspects them when they are joined to each other in this way, it signifies the recovery of the quesited item, even if it will be with litigation and controversy. And if the Lord of the eighth is joined to the Lord of the second, it signifies that the querent will recover the missing item: since the conjunction of the eighth Lord signifies that the substance of the thief or of the person who has the quesited item, will go over into the substance of the querent, and will come to be his own just like it had been up until this point. And if there is litigation from this matter, the querent will win and recover the item. And if he does not recover the same item, he will get as much of the thief's goods, or the goods of the other adversary, as his own item is worth, and he will be compensated for the lost item, and maximally and most assuredly if the Lord of the first then aspects the Lord of the eighth or the second. And the Lord of the 10th house then aspects it, this signifies that the authorities, or the judge, or the governor will take the item, and it will end up in his hands, and there will be hope from this that he will do what ought to be done. However if the Lord of the 8th house is then joined to the

Lord of the 10th house, it signifies that the thief or adversary will give the authorities or governor money, so that they won't harm him, but rather that they will be of assistance to him. Next examine and see if the Lord of the second is not joined to the Lord of the first, nor to the Lord of the eighth: for this signifies that the quesited item is totally lost: and that the rest of it will not be recovered, and that it will almost come to nothing.

Next examine if the Lord of the second is joined with the Lord of the third, or with the Lord of the ninth, or with any planet placed in these houses, or if the planet itself is in these houses: for this signifies that he who stole the item, or the substance, or he to whom it arrived, has carried it out of that land and into another

Next examine if the Sun and Moon are both under the earth at the hour of the question, or at the hour when the item was taken away: for this signifies that the item will not be recovered by any means, nor will it be possible to recover it; nor will the thief be known, nor will the lost item be known, nor will it be known who has the item. Next examine if the Lord of the Ascendant and the Moon are both in the Ascendant, and the Sun aspects them from a trine or sextile aspect: for this signifies that the quesited item will be recovered on the same day that it was taken away or lost. If indeed the Sun aspects them from a square aspect, it will be found in that week. However, if he aspects them from opposition, the item will be found in that month, and it will be returned to its rightful owner. Understand the same for any item which is lost or taken in any manner whatsoever.

XIV

If The Thief Or The Person Who Has The Item Is A Family Member, Or What Condition He Is In

If the querent is suspicious as to whether the thief who has the quesited item is a family member, or curious as to of what type of person he is, and wants to know this from you: examine if the Sun and Moon are both aspecting the Ascendant at the same time, or if the Lord of the Ascendant is in the Ascendant, or if any of them are corporeally conjunct, or joined with the Lord of the seventh, or if the Sun and Moon are in their own domiciles, or if they are in the domiciles of the Lord of the Ascendant, and they aspect the Ascendant or its Lord; or the Lord of the Ascendant is remote from the degree of the cusp of the Ascendant, and another planet is with him in the same sign (so that this planet is closer to the degree of the Ascendant): for this signifies that the thief or the person who has the lost item is a family member. If indeed both of the luminaries are not as described, but only one of them is, he will not be a family member, but is a member of the household and born in that house in which the lost or stolen item was. And if the Sun and Moon are in their own triplicities, the thief will be of those people who have relation to the owner of the item by some kinship, but do not live in the house with him. However, if the luminaries are in their own terms or faces, the thief will not be an inhabitant of the house: but a familiar of an inhabitant of the house, and more familiar to the others than he is to the master of the house, yet he is known to him. And he is in their company frequently, in such a way that he is believed to be a relation of the family. However, if the luminaries aspect the Ascendant, and they don't aspect the seventh: the thief didn't enter the house at any other time, but first entered the house when he stole the quesited item. But if one of the luminaries is in a common sign, it signifies that the thief had entered the house at another time, but not for the purpose of stealing: and those in the house were aware of him having entered the house at another time.

Indeed, if the significator of the thief, (which is the Lord of the seventh from the Ascendant) is in the third from the first (which is the ninth from the seventh), it signifies that the thief is not from that land, but from another far away from it. If indeed the significator of the thief is in the twelfth from the Ascendant (which is the sixth from his own house), the thief will be a slave. And if it is in the ninth from the seventh (which is the third from the Ascendant), the thief will be a religious person. And if it is in the fourth from the Ascendant (which is the tenth from the seventh), he is someone who has duties related to the king. And if it is in the eleventh (which is the fifth from the seventh), he is a familiar of the king, or of a powerful person, or another magnate namely of one of those people who are fit for kingship.

And if it is in any of its own houses, it will be a man who usually has his own things, but is now indigent, and is ashamed to work to earn money.

And if it is in its own exaltation, it signifies that the thief is a nobleman: but on account of poverty he is forced to steal, since he is ashamed to beg or work in some other way to acquire money. And if it is in any of the lesser dignities (namely term, triplicity, or face), he will not be very well known in that city, but will be known in the area or neighbourhood where he lives.

Afterwards, to know which member of the querent's family, or which one of the inhabitants of his house the thief is; Zael said that if the Sun is the significator of the thief, that it is the father of the querent. If indeed the Moon is the significatrix, it will be the mother of the querent. And if it is Venus, it will be his wife. And if it is Saturn it will be his slave, or a foreigner. And if it is Jupiter, it will be the most noble of all the people in the house, and someone of whom there is no suspicion of him being the thief. And if it is Mars, it will be his son, or his daughter, or his brother. And if it is Mercury it will be a close friend.

Next, Zael said that if the significator of the thief is peregrine, to examine the Part of Fortune. If it is free from malefics, the thief had not stolen anything prior to this. Likewise if the Lord of the Ascendant is free from malefics. And if Mars is separated from the Lord of the seventh, they knew that he was a thief. Then he said that if Saturn aspects the Moon or the Ascendant, the thief stole the item with slyness and ingenuity. And if Jupiter is the significator of the thief, he did not enter the house to steal: but entered for the reason of some other business and he came upon the item in question and stole it. And he said that if Mars is the significator of the thief, he did not reach the item until he bored through the house, or dug under the wall of the part house in which the item was, or broke the bars on the doors, or the gate, or found a key. And if Venus is the significatrix, it signifies friendship, security, and his audacity around the family when he entered to converse with them, taking on the image and likeness of a visiting friend; and thus he stole from them. And if Mercury was the significator, the thief entered the house with ingenuity, slyness, or by some form of art. And he said that if the Sun and Moon aspect the Ascendant the thief will be one of the inhabitants of the house.

And if the significator of the thief is a benefic, he will be free; and if it is a malefic, he will be a slave.

On The Age Of The Thief

And he said that if Venus is the significatrix of the thief, it will be a youth or a girl, and if Mercury, they will be of a younger age than with Venus. And if Mars is the significator of the thief, he will be a young man, fully grown from the completion of youth, more than [the lesser years of] Saturn (that is more than a youth). And if it is Saturn he will be a decrepit old man. However, if he is oriental, he will be of mature age. And if the Moon is the significator, and is in the beginning of the month, he will be a youth. And if she is in the middle of the month, he will be middle aged (that is, the completion of manhood). And if she is in the end of the month, he will be an old man. If the Sun is the significator, and is between the Ascendant and the Midheaven, the thief will be in the age of youth; and you will not cease increasing the age in this manner until the Sun arrives at the angle of the earth, since this place is the end of life.

XV

On The Location Of The Stolen Goods

And if you are asked (or wish to know for yourself) where the stolen goods are deposited or hidden: then consider the 4th house (which has the signification of all hidden things) and see what sign is in the 4th house. Since if it is Aries, Leo, or Sagittarius, the stolen goods are hidden in a stable or in another place where animals live. If it is Aries, it will be in a place of small domesticated animals which are eaten, such as sheep, pigs, and the like. If it is Leo it will be in a place of domestic animals that bite, but are not eaten, such as dogs: or ones living in forests as if they were houses, such as wolves, lions and so on. If it is Sagittarius, it will be in a place of animals which are ridden, such as in the stables of horses.

And if it is in Taurus, Virgo, or Capricorn, it will be in the stables of horses or in another place where large animals which are eaten, and slaughtered (such as cows and the like) are kept. And if it is Virgo or Capricorn, it will be in a place where horses, asses, mules, or camels, and similar animals which are not slaughtered or eaten are kept. And Virgo signifies granaries, and especially those which are under the earth, as are pits; or those close to the earth, as are vegetable storage places, and similar things in which grains are stored. And similarly Capricorn signifies places where goats or sheep stay together, and similar things.

And if it is Gemini, or Libra, or Aquarius, it will be in the house. If it is Gemini it will be in a partition or wall of the house. And if the sign of the 4th house is Libra, the stolen goods will be near the roof of the house. And if it is Aquarius it will be next to the entrance, or above the door of the house, or above the gate in a high place.

And if it is Cancer, Scorpio, or Pisces, the location of the stolen goods will be near water. If it is Cancer, it will be close to a well, or stagnant water, or a cistern. If it is Scorpio it will be close to the place in which dirty water is kept or drained off. If it is Pisces it will be a place where it almost always remains damp.

Moreover, Zael said that if you find that the stolen goods are in the house and you want to know their location in the house: examine the Lord of the fourth and the planets which are in the 4th. If Saturn is there, they will be in the latrine of the house and in a remote and deep place. And if it is Jupiter, it signifies a place in a forest, or a place of prayer. And Mars signifies the kitchen, or a place of fire. And the Sun signifies the cloister of the house, and the place where the master of the house relaxes. Venus signifies the place where the woman of the house relaxes. And Mercury signifies a part of the building with paintings, and the library, or (especially in Virgo) the granary. And if it is the Moon they will be within a pit, or cistern, or bathroom. And he said, know that when a benefic is in the fourth from the Ascendant, the stolen goods will be in a place which is clean and beautiful, and they will have already been entrusted to some noble person. And if a malefic is there, they will be in a horrible and foul place, and they will have been given to some ignoble person.

On the number of stolen items, whether there are one or many

And if you wish to know, whether there are one or many items stolen, Zael said that you ought to look at the signs which are between the Moon and Mercury, and see whether there are an even or uneven number of them: since if there is an even number of them, the booty consists of many items, which are joined together or which are separate. If there is an uneven number of signs between them, there will be one item.

XVI

If He Who Is Suspected Of Being A Thief Is One Or Not

And if there is ever a man accused of being a thief (as often happens, or if he is captured, or otherwise detained on such an occasion that someone says he is a thief, and you want to know whether he is guilty or not (whether there is a question made to you on this, or you take the hour up for yourself): examine the Ascendant and its Lord, and the Moon (which has much to do in this), and consider the Moon first. If she is joined to a benefic (whether she is received or not) he will not be a thief. However if she is joined to a malefic, he is a thief (whether she is received or not).

If indeed the Lord of the Ascendant is in an angle, and is not joined to a planet cadent from an angle, it signifies that what is said of him is true. If indeed the Lord of the Ascendant is in an angle, and is joined to a planet cadent from an angle (who doesn't receive him), there was something bad said of him at some time, but this is not true. And if the Lord of the Ascendant (since in this case the Ascendant is given to the thief) is in a cadent, and is not joined to a planet in an angle who receives him, what is said about this detained person is false. However, if the Ascendant is a mobile sign, what is said about him will be false, and this much more strongly so if any malefic planet aspects the Ascendant, and this more strongly again if the Cauda Draconis is there.

And if you find the Moon void-of-course, announce that he is totally without blame. Likewise if the Moon is joined to a cadent planet, whether she is received by this cadent planet or not. If the four angles are fixed signs, what is said about him is true, and he is a thief. And if the Moon is joined to a planet in an angle, similarly it signifies that what is said about the detained person is true; and especially if she (or the planet to whom she is joined) is in the 10th house; and even if she is in an angle and is impeded, it signifies the falsity of how he presents himself.

And if you want to know whether he ever stole anything else besides that incident which he was accused of: see which of the significators (namely the Lord of the Ascendant or the Moon) is stronger. Since in such a case the first and its Lord and the Moon, are given to him who is suspected of evil. And having seen which of them is stronger, examine if it is separated from a malefic. If so, regardless of whether it is joined to a benefic or a malefic, it signifies that he has stolen something before this. And if it is not separated from a malefic, but is separated from the Lord of the second (which is the house of substance), regardless of whether it is a benefic or a malefic, it signifies that he has stolen something before. And if the Lord of the second is a benefic, he did not go through with the theft; but if it is a malefic he did go through with the theft. Indeed it is separating from a malefic he went through with the theft. If indeed it is separating from a benefic, whether it joins a benefic or not, nothing was stolen up until now, unless this benefic is the Lord of the 2nd house from the Ascendant: since then it signifies that he has stolen something at some time: and this more strongly if the Lord of the Ascendant joins any malefic after separating from the Lord of the second.

XVII

What Kind Of Things Are Those Which Were Stolen

If you want to know what kind of things are those which were stolen: examine the Ascendant and the Moon. And see where she is, namely in what sign and in what degree of this sign, and see in which planets terms this degree falls.

If it is in the terms of Saturn, and he is in the Ascendant, or in the tenth in an earth sign, the things will be of those which pertain to the preparation of the earth which are made of iron, as are ploughshares, hoes, tillers, and similar things. If Saturn is in the seventh or the fourth, they will be other iron implements, namely those with which heavy operations are performed, such as cutting stones, and similar tasks; or it will be an iron bar, or one of the aforementioned things except made out of lead; or it will be lead or copper itself, and similar things, and similarly if it is cadent from the Ascendant, and from the other angles. And if the Sun or Moon aspect him, then they will be iron weapons, heavy, shiny, polished, with some rust, and similar things. If indeed Saturn is not placed like this, but is cadent from the Ascendant so that he doesn't aspect it, and if he is not aspected by the Sun or the Moon (and especially if he is in Aries): this signifies that the stolen item is of little worth, and is one of those things with a view to abbots; or they are low quality arms, and of little worth, as are old knives, and swords, and similar things tend to shed blood. However if Saturn is in Gemini the things will be of diverse types and materials; still, the things will not appear to be expensive, unless another planet aspects Saturn. For if Jupiter aspects him from the first or the 10th house, it signifies that part of the stolen goods are gold, while the rest are things of low value. And if Jupiter aspects Saturn, and is in the seventh or the fourth, part of the stolen items will be silver, and the rest will be cheap things and of little worth.

If indeed the degree in which the Moon is placed, is in the terms of Jupiter, it should be examined who aspects her, and in what manner. Since if she is in Aries or in another fire sign, and she is aspected by Jupiter from the 1st house or from the tenth, it will be a gilded work, or one made from gold. If the Sun aspects her, it will be raw gold (that is, unworked). If she is aspected by one of them from the seventh or fourth, it will be silver or things made from silver. If Venus aspects Jupiter by any aspect, and Jupiter is in his own terms, they will be very expensive items, as are pearls and other precious stones.

If Jupiter is in Taurus, or in any earth sign, it signifies that the stolen items are expensive and noble garments.

However, if he is in Gemini or in any air sign, the items will be an animal, such as a horse, mule, cow, or something similar.

However, if Jupiter is in Cancer or in any water sign, it will be something which is taken from the water, as are pearls and similar things.

And Zael said that if the Moon is in the terms of Mars, then the thing will have passed through fire, or fire will have touched it in some manner.

If the Moon aspects Venus, then it has been dyed. And if the Moon is in the terms of Venus, in Aries or its triplicity, it will be gold or silver. And if she is in Taurus or its triplicity, or in Cancer or its triplicity, it will be ornate or abonasim garments (abonasim being a type of precious silk garment, of various colours and woven with various pictures). And he said that you will know about the goodness and beauty of the thing from the placement of Venus in the signs. If she is in Gemini and its triplicity, the items will not be made from animals. And he said that if Venus is emerging from the beams of the Sun, the items will be new. If indeed she is retrograde or in the end of her course, or diminished in number, the items will be old and hardened.

And he said that if she is in the terms of Mercury, they will be books. And if she is in Aries and its triplicity, they will be coins taken from a purse, or another container which is covered in red leather. And he said that if she is in Gemini and its triplicity, they will be coins.

Examine similarly in what sign the Moon is in; for if she is in Aries, it signifies that the stolen items are of the things which are carried on people's heads. And so if they are arms, they will be helmets made of steel or painted leather. And if they are not arms, and are of the things which pertain to women, they will be tiaras, hair bands, and other head ornaments which pertain to the adornment of women.

And if she is in Taurus, they will be precious things, namely necklaces and other ornaments with which the neck is adorned.

And if she is in Gemini, they will be arm and hand ornaments, or rings and similar things. And if Mercury then aspects her, they will be coins or other painted treasures which the figures of men are sculpted into. And if Mercury doesn't aspect her, they will be painted leather items, on which similar figures are depicted.

And if the Moon is then in Cancer, they will be things taken from the water; or they will be things which are naturally moist.

And if she is in Leo, they will be items worked with gold, or it will be yellow copper ore or burnished iron. And if the Sun aspects her, they will be gold things without pictures.

However if she is in Virgo, they will be garments worked on with intaglios. And if Mercury aspects her, it will be money in which a human figure will be sculpted.

And if she is in Libra, they will be scales. And if Venus aspects her, it will be things which are made for the ornamentation of women, and scented things of the kind which are sent to women.

And if the Moon is in Scorpio, it will be copper or a work of brass, or of gilded copper, and it is burnished and splendid. And if Mars aspects her it signifies that it is raw gold or silver.

And if she is in Sagittarius it will be various things, or of various colours, or diverse substances joined in one, which are of greater appearance than value. However if Jupiter aspects the Moon, it will be various things (as was said) but they will be precious.

And if she is in Capricorn they will be worthless things, and found in a vile place. And if Saturn then aspects the Moon, they will be things of little worth, almost similar to earth, or made of earth, and it may be copper or bronze.

And if the Moon is in Aquarius, they will be things which are extracted from an animal, such as certain stones which are called grapaldina, which are said to be extracted from the heads of old frogs. And if Jupiter aspects her, it will be gold or silver which has been worked on, or recently extracted from a mine. However, if the Sun aspects the Moon, it will be raw gold. And if Mercury or Venus aspect her, it will be silver. If indeed the Sun and Mercury aspect her at the same time, it will be coins wrapped up in a leather purse, or money bag, and similar things.

And if she is in Pisces, it will be silk, or haircloth, or works of silk or things made of silk. If indeed Jupiter aspects her they will be precious things taken from the water, as are pearls, amber, and similar things.

From Which Houses The Stolen Items Are To Be Sought

A certain one of the moderns said to consider what manor the stolen or missing items are in, since they are not all sought from one house, but from diverse houses, according to the diversity of the things. For there are, as he said, certain people who want to say that any stolen item will be sought from the 10th house - but this is not so, since things are to be sought according to what is signified by the houses. Indeed he said if the stolen things belong to anyone in the family, they will be sought from the second. And if they belong to the querent's' brother, or sister, or any of his relatives, they will be sought from the third. And if they belong to the querent's father, grandfather, or father in law, they will be sought from the fourth. And if they are his son's things, or if they are other pleasing things, as are women's belts or girdles, or anything similar, they will be sought from the fifth. And if they are arms, or a cuirass, or similar things, or any small animals, they will be sought from the sixth. And if they belong to the wife or a lover, they will be sought from the seventh. And if they are items of a dowry, or the money of a dowry, or items deposited for safe-keeping, they will be sought from the eighth. And if they belong to a cleric or a religious person, they will be sought from the ninth. And if they are the tax revenue of the king or of some community, they will be sought from the eleventh. And if they are large animals, or a prisoner, they will be sought from the twelfth. However, if they are coins, books, grain, oil, or similar things, they will be sought from the tenth. And this is according to the peculiarities of the aforementioned houses and their Lords. However on a similar note, whatever kind of thing it is, if it is of the querent's goods, it will be possible to be sought from the second and its Lord.

XVIII

The Figure Of The Thief

Albumasar gave a long discussion on what is said above, on the qualities of stolen items, but I do not put great energy into this, since enough has been said above through Zael; and I added on what I thought needed to be added on in order for it to suffice for you. Since there is not great utility in it: but rather some fame, for someone to appear that they know something. From which, to avoid too much prolixity, it appeared better to me to discuss that which can be said regarding the form of the thief, and his quality. And it is to examine the 7th house, since through this house it is possible to know the form or quality of the thief.

For if the house signifying the thief is the first face of Aries, it signifies that the thief is a brown coloured man, and when he stole the item he was wearing garments pertaining more to the colour white, than to any other colour. And if it is the second face of Aries, it signifies that the thief is a woman who was wearing garments pertaining more to the colour red than to any other colour at the time. And if it is the third face of Aries, it signifies that the thief had a pale colour, and had red hair, or almost red.

And if it is the first face of Taurus it signifies two men, one with a narrow face, and having promptitude; and another badly dressed. And if it is the second face of Taurus, it likewise signifies a badly and cheaply dressed man, but with a key in his hand. And if it is the third face of Taurus, it signifies that there are three thieves, one of which knows how to drive out serpents and similar things, and another who is an archer.

And if it is the first face of Gemini it signifies that the thief is accustomed to carry a stick or cane in his hand, and he has one companion with him. And if it is in the second face of Gemini, it signifies that the thief knows the flute and how to play musical instruments, and has one person with him who is stooped. And if it is the third face of Gemini, it signifies that the thief is one of those people who eagerly carry arms, indeed not urged by necessity, but to appear armed.

And if it is the first face of Cancer, it signifies that the thief is a well-dressed man, with beautiful and ornate garments, and a young girl is with him. And if it is the second face of Cancer it signifies that it is a young girl who eagerly carries a wreath of flowers and who is not a maiden, and she has with her another young girl who is a maiden. And if it is the third face of Cancer it signifies that there is one man and one woman who stole the item.

And if it is the first face of Leo it signifies that it is a man who wears courtly garments, and who eagerly keeps wild animals, such as wolves, hawks, and similar creatures. And if it is the second face of Leo it signifies that there are two thieves, one of whom eagerly carries a deer on his head, and another who carries and holds his hands higher up than other men do. And if it is the third face it signifies that it is a man who often carries a stick in his hand, and has an ugly face, and always looks as though he is sad.

And if it is the first face of Virgo it signifies that the thief is a certain girl who appears to be good, and of whom nobody would suspect anything bad of. And if it is the second face of Virgo it signifies that the thief is a brown man who is wearing leather clothing, or that there is leather stitched into his clothing, and he has long hair, or even is accustomed to having his hair long. And if it was the third face of Virgo it signifies that the thief is a certain white woman who does not hear well.

And if it was the first face of Libra it signifies that the thief is a man who knows about musical instruments, especially the flute, and appears as though he is always angry. And if it is the second face of Libra it signifies that there are two thieves who live with others, having no house of their own. And both of them travel around angrily. And if it is the third face it signifies that there are two men, one of whom is an archer and the other who is a man who only knows how to serve poorly, as though he is lazy; and who is badly dressed.

And if it is the first face of Scorpio it signifies that the thief is a woman of beautiful stature with a beautiful face. And if it is the second face of Scorpio it signifies that there is one man and one woman, who are indigent and badly dressed. And if it is the third face of Scorpio it signifies that it is one man who moves around stooped above his knees, and doesn't stand well on them.

And if it is the first face of Sagittarius it signifies that the thief is an ugly, deformed, and stinking man. And if it is the second face of Sagittarius it signifies that the thief is a certain woman who is well dressed. And if it is the third face it signifies a jaundiced man with a greyish face.

And if it is the first face of Capricorn it signifies that the thief is a black man or has a brown colour, and a woman of full age. And if it is the second face of Capricorn it signifies that the thief is two women of full age. And if it is the third face of Capricorn it signifies that it was one very shrewd brown woman.

And if it is the first face of Aquarius it signifies that the thief is of completed youth. And if it is the second face of Aquarius, it signifies that it is a man having a long chin or a beard. And if it is the third face of Aquarius it signifies that it is a brown coloured man who often goes about angrily.

And if it is the first face of Pisces it signifies that the thief is a man who wears beautiful and good garments. And if it was the second face of Pisces it signifies that the thief is a woman of good stature and with a beautiful face. And if it was the third face it signifies that the thief is a poor man who is badly dressed.

On The Figure Of The Thief Through The Signs Of The Seventh House

Besides this you will be able to say something more about the figure of the thief:

Since if the 7th house (which has the signification of the thief), is Capricorn or Aquarius it signifies that the thief is a black man, or brown as we might say: and he might have a mixture of some saffron with this blackness; and that he is heavy in his step, and rubs one foot off the other (or comes close to it) when he walks, and sinks his eyes to the earth when he walks; and that he is thin, or not very fleshy, and stooped, heaving small eyes, and rough skin; and prominent veins; and having a thin beard; his lips are not very thick, nor very slender; and having much hair on his body and also a unibrow.

However, if the 7th house is Sagittarius or Pisces, it signifies that the thief is a white man having eyes not completely black, yet big, and with large pupils; short and unequal nostrils; and he is bald, and has blackness in one tooth, having a fine stature, good manners and a good spirit (besides disappointing in this matter); and he has a thin beard and curly blonde hair.

However, if the 7th house is Aries or Scorpio, it signifies that the thief is a red man, having red hair, orange eyes, a horrible and sharp gaze, a round face, bold, having a sign or mole on his foot.

However, if the 7th house is Leo it signifies that the thief is a man having a colour which is not truly black, nor truly orange, nor truly red: but his colour is a certain whitishness, not far removed from black, with a certain touch of red: and he is a man of fine stature: and has somewhat curly hair, and blonde eyes, somewhat orange.

And if the 7th house is Cancer it signifies that the thief is a man having a white colour mixed with red, a unibrow, eyes not truly black, but almost black, a round face and a fine stature.

And if the 7th house is Taurus or Libra, it signifies that the thief is a man having a white colour, yet not truly white, leaning towards black in a certain way; having a beautiful form, beautiful hair, a face that isn't round, a chin that isn't very long, beautiful eyes, black eyes, a little too big, although not so large that they are unbecoming; displaying benevolence to almost everyone.

If indeed the 7th house is Gemini or Virgo it signifies that the thief is a man having a colour that is almost black: that is, neither truly white, nor truly dark, having a high forehead, a long nose, a long face, a thin beard, thin or little hair, beautiful eyes which are not wholly black, and long fingers on his hands.

And these statements on the figure of the thief should be sufficient for you.

XIX

On The Contracting Of A Partnership Between Two People, And Their Participation

If someone wishing to contract a partnership were to take it upon himself to ask you whether it would be useful to him or not, and poses a question to you about this, and you wish to satisfy yourself of the hour of the question: give the 1st house to the querent, and the seventh to him who the querent is striving to contract a partnership with (the Moon will also be a participator for both of them). Indeed from the 10th house you will be able to know what will happen to him from that partnership which he intends to contract. As to what end the partnership will arrive at, you will know this from the 4th house and the planet to whom the Moon is joined: yet even if the Moon does more for the side of the querent than for the side of the quesited, nevertheless the planet which she joins will signify for both parties, but less for the querent than for him who he wants to contract the partnership with. Indeed the planet from whom she is separating, or is separated from, does more for the querent than she does for the quesited.

And consider then if the he Lord of the first (who is the significator of the querent) and the Moon, are in Aries, Cancer, Libra, or Capricorn without perfect reception (namely from house or exaltation, or from two of the lesser dignities at the same time): for this signifies that in this partnership there will be discord and disturbance; and afterwards it will be rectified and the partnership will endure, but it will not really be of good stability, nor will it be of great utility, nor of much profit.

However if they are in Taurus, Leo, Scorpio, or Aquarius, the partnership will be durable and stable; yet it won't be very profitable, and when they buy anything it won't sell quickly, in fact it will stay with them longer than it usually ought to.

If they are in Gemini, Virgo, Sagittarius, or Pisces, it signifies that the partnership will be useful, good, and profitable, and that they will often repeat their buying and their selling, and that they will easily and quickly sell their merchandise, and things will be secure and legal between them, and there will be good feeling and good faith between them, nor will there be any fraud between them.

And if one significator (namely the Lord of the first or the Moon) is in a mobile sign; and the other is in a fixed or common sign, or vice versa: they will be as I said to you above, but not in whole, but less so.

And if malefics aspect the significators (namely the Lord of the first and the Lord of the seventh), their partnership will be bad, and one will use falsity and deception against the other, and one will not behave well towards the other. Whence examine the placement of the malefics impeding the significators (the Lord of the first and the Lord of the seventh), since discord will come between the partners for the reason of the things indicated by the houses in which the impeding malefics are placed. As to what will be signified by each of the houses - it has been repeated enough times to you already that you will be well able to know this yourself. And see if any malefics are in the first (whether they impede the Lord of the first or the Lord of the seventh or not): for this signifies that discord and fraud or deception, and indeed injury and malice will come from the side of the querent. If any of the malefics are in the seventh, then it signifies that this will come from the side of that person who the querent intends to contract a partnership with, or with whom the partnership is contracted with, if it has already been made.

And a question may be posed of what the future is of a partnership already contracted.

Moreover, examine if the Moon is separating from one benefic and joining to another: for then the partnership will begin well, and it will end with esteem, whether they make a profit or not. If indeed she separates from a benefic and joins a malefic, it will begin well and eagerly, but it will end badly, and with litigation and discord (unless this malefic is well disposeed, and receives the Moon from perfect reception, as I said to you above). If indeed she is separated from any malefic and joined to a benefic, it will eagerly begin, but finish well, and with esteem. However if the Moon is besieged (namely that she is separated from one malefic and joined to another malefic), it signifies that it will begin badly, persevere in this badness, and finish badly, with quarrels and discord. And understand all of these things to be true regardless of whether they profit or not.

Having inspected this, see if the Moon is joined to the Lord of the house in which she is placed in: since if he receives her from his own house, then the matter will not be impeded. And always consider this, since if the Moon is joined to the Lord of the house in which she is placed, the partnership will finish well, and clearly, and with the esteem of both the partners, and profit, so that each of them will remain content and will believe themselves to have done well in that partnership. However, if she is not joined to the Lord of her own house, nor any of the benefics from a good aspect, one of the partners will suspect evil of the other, and the other of him; and so they will be separated for this reason. And if malefic planets are under the earth, Zael said, they will separate on account of the bad opinions they have about each other.

Next examine the 10th house, and see which planet is in it: since if there are benefics in it (since it is the significator of the partnership), say that it signifies good things and profit from which they will rejoice and say that they did well. However, if there are malefics there, they will reduce their profit, in fact they will make almost no profit from the partnership; but an event will intervene which will break up all connections - namely death, which dissolves all ties. And this can be known through the following: namely if the Moon is joined to the Lord of the house in which she is placed, and both of them are joined again to a malefic planet, or joined to the Lord of the house of death - then they won't be separated unless through death.

XX

When Someone Travels To Some Man, Whether They Will Find Him Or Not

If someone sets out to meet someone, and asks you whether they will find him or not, and you wish to look over such a question for them: see what kind of person it is to whom they intend to travel, namely whether he is a king or prelate, or another religious figure, or whatever other individual.

If it is a king, see if the Lord of the 10th house is in the tenth, or the first, or the seventh, or the fourth, which signifies that the king is in the place where the querent intends to find him. If indeed the Lord of the 10th house is in the third, and the journey is of one day (which is called a short journey); or if it is in the ninth and the journey is one of multiple days (which is called a long journey), it signifies that he will find him on the road - if the Lord of the Ascendant and the Lord of the 10th house are joined together. However if it is in the eleventh, second, fifth, or the eighth, it signifies that he is not in the place in which the querent intended, but will not be so far away from that place that the querent won't be able to find him with his own investigation. However, if the Lord of the 10th house is in the sixth or the twelfth, he will not find him; nor will he find him if the tenth Lord is in the third or the ninth without a conjunction or aspect.

However, if the quesited is a cleric, and he is in the aforementioned places, he will be found as was said of the king.

However, if it was another individual lay person, then examine the Lord of the seventh: which if he is in the seventh, or the tenth, or the first, or the fourth, the person will be found in the place he was believed to be in; unless the seventh Lord is joined to a planet cadent from an angle, since then he will not be found immediately, unless the querent first asks about finding him. However, if the Lord of the seventh is in the eighth, or the eleventh, or the second, or the fifth, he will not be found in that place, but he will be close to it, not far from the assumed location. However if it is in the ninth, twelfth, third, or sixth, he will not be found in the place where he was believed to be, nor close to it, and especially if the Lord of the seventh is in the sixth or the twelfth. If he is in the third or the ninth, and the Lord of the seventh and the Lord of the ninth or third were joined together by body or by a known aspect: this signifies that he will be found or met on the road.

XXI

On Anyone Wanting To Travel In A Military Exercise, Or To War, Or To Begin A Battle, Whether A Duke, Or Another Person, Whoever He Is, Whether He Will Conquer Or Not

When there is a war between anyone, or it is hoped that there will be one in the future (as often happens), and someone from either side comes to you, and wants to be certified by you as to what could happen to them from this, whether it is a king or an emperor or a marquis, or a duke, or a count, or a powerful person, or any other lay person (or a cleric who also carries out lay duties) and who ought to preside over an army - whether they are noble, a commoner, or one of the country folk; as long as they are the conductor of the war or of one of the parts of a battle - they are called the leader of this army, or war, whether it was established for this purpose for himself, or for another.. And if anyone wishes to begin any war, or travel in an army against anyone; and they pose a question to you about these things, whether they pose it for themselves, or for someone who is very concerned about it, and he who they ask for is not the emperor or king: give the first and its Lord to him, and see from which planet the Moon is separating, and also give this planet to the querent. And give the seventh and its Lord, and the planet to whom the Moon is then joining, to the adversary.

However if it is an emperor, or an authority, or regent, and they enquire about the matters of the empire, or kingdom, or city which he rules: you will give him the tenth, and give his enemy the fourth. If indeed he enquires on his own affairs, and a specific one which is not a matter of the empire, or kingdom, or city: give him the first, and his enemy the seventh. And in all other matters you will judge for him just as you would for any other individual person.

If indeed the Moon is not separating from anyone, nor is joined to anyone, Zael said that the Moon is not to be used in that work. Therefore see if the Lord of the first is joined to the Lord of the seventh, or the Lord of the seventh to him, by a trine or sextile aspect with perfect reception (namely that one of them receives the other): for this signifies that peace will be made between them before the contention. If they are joined by a square aspect or from opposition, even if they receive each other, or if they are joined from a trine or sextile aspect without reception, they will not be pacified unless they first engage in battle and fight each other. But after they fight or battle they will reconcile with each other and the beginning of the peace or truce will come from the side of him whose significator is lighter.

And you ought to know that the superior planets (namely Saturn, Jupiter, and Mars) are stronger in battles and wars than the inferiors (namely the Sun, Venus, Mercury and the Moon), and more stable and more constant on account of the slowness of their motion. And because the inferiors apply to them, while they don't apply to the inferiors.

Whence if you are able, always make it so that in your inceptions for wars or battles that you have one of the superior planets as a significator (as will be said elsewhere). However if you cannot have a superior planet, take the best one of the inferiors that you can get: since it is better for you to have an inferior planet in good condition than an unfortunate or impeded superior planet.

Afterwards consider from what you saw, of the peacemakers themselves: if either of the significators (namely the Lord of the Ascendant and the Lord of the seventh) are direct, as then there will be peace or harmony which will make together will be good and firm, and especially if they aspect each other by trine or sextile. If either of them are retrograde, it will be a false peace and will not be good or durable, but rather it will be with cunning, evil, and slyness, and each party will strive to deceive the other. If one is direct and one is retrograde, the party which has the retrograde significator will strive to deceive the other, and will advance against the other with evil intentions and slyness.

And examine in which place the other planet is from the significator of him who he tries to deceive: since if he is in the second from the first, after they have reconciled with each other, and when one has confidence in the other, he will take his substance.

And if it is in the third, the first will deceive him on account of his brother, since he will take his brother from him and hold him to extort something from the deceived, or perhaps make an agreement with his brother that he will do something to harm him, or he will send him out of the land in exile. If he doesn't have a brother, he will be deceived from another matter signified by the 3rd house.

If it is in the fourth, he will be captured, and held in an underground and hidden prison until the deceiver takes what he intended to from him: or he will take away his kingdom, city, castle, villa, house, or other estate, in proportion to the discord between them.

If it is in the fifth, he will do the same with his child, or because of his child, as was said with his brother or because of his brother.

If it is in the sixth he will hold and incarcerate him to take away his slaves or any small animals (such as livestock, pigs, goats, dogs, hawks, and similar things).

If it is in the eighth (since the seventh doesn't come into this work, except in the manner of the first) he will place him in prison and will make him die there, or he will kill him in another way.

And if it is in the ninth, he will send him on a long journey, and make him suffer punishments there.

And if it is in the tenth, he will place him in the hands of the authorities or another magnate in order to hurt him, or perhaps he will imprison him in some castle or in some tower or in another elevated place.

And if he is in the eleventh, he will hand him to some soldier or close associate of the king or a powerful person or some other magnate, to extort something from him, or he will hand him over to one of his friends for the same reason, or to guard him.

And if it is in the twelfth, he will hold him and detain him in a remote prison, and having said good words to him, will treat him as bad as he possibly can in detention, and will hold him there for a long time, for so long that he loses all hope, nor will he believe that he will ever be able to escape, or he will take away his horses, bulls, camels and other large animals.

And know that the fourth signifies the prison. The seventh signifies incarceration or incarcerating. The eighth signifies the act of incarceration. The tenth signifies him who is already incarcerated.

Next examinee the Lord of the seventh (who signifies him who is imprisoned).If it is retrograde, it signifies that he will flee from the prison. Then examine which planet it first joins in its retrogradation: since if it joins a benefic, it signifies good for him in his flight. Next examine if you do not see that they will reconcile or be pacified. And see if the Lord of the first is separating from the Lord of the seventh, or vice versa: for this signifies that this battle, litigation, contention, or discord will be of a long duration, nor will it appear that it will be completed in a short time. And if the Lord of the first is one of the three superior planets, and is in the first, or the tenth, or possibly in the fourth with reception, (unless the planet who receives him is the Lord of the seventh or the eighth) - indeed the fourth is much below the tenth, and below the first - it signifies that the querent will conquer and win against his enemy, unless the planet is combust or is then entering into combustion. If the Lord of the seventh is one of the three superior planets, and is in the seventh, the fourth, or with reception in the tenth (but the tenth will be below the fourth); unless the planet who receives him is the Lord of the first, or the second, it signifies that the enemy will conquer and win against the querent, unless it is combust, or then entering into combustion: since then he will be debilitated and there will be no strength in him.

Consider this also over these significators, (namely over the Lord of the first and over the Lord of the seventh): since even if the Lord of the Ascendant being cadent from the Ascendant is greatly debilitated, nevertheless if he is one of the superior planets, he will be strong against the enemies on account of his superiority: and the adversary will be weakened on account of inferiority - since the Lord of the seventh will be one of the inferiors, which are not as strong in matters of war as the superiors are. Whence, due to this, you ought not to say to the querent that he will succumb; but not before you see the first planet to whom the Lord of the seventh is joined. Since even if the Lord of the first (who is one of the superiors) is cadent from an angle, and the Lord of the seventh (who is one of the inferiors) is in an angle: nevertheless the Lord of the first is not less strong than the Lord of the seventh because of this, unless the Lord of the seventh is joined to any planet who fortifies him. For if the Lord of the seventh is joined with some planet who is in a strong place (namely in an angle), and who receives him, then the Lord of the seventh will be fortified; and you can say to the querent that he will succumb and be conquered by his adversary or enemy. If indeed the Lord of the seventh is joined to a planet who doesn't receive him, he will not be fortified by this to the extent that the querent will succumb for this reason.

And vice versa, say of the Lord of the seventh (if he is one of the superiors), what I said of the Lord of the first. Since if the Lord of the seventh is one of the superiors, and is cadent from his own angle (namely from the seventh), you will not judge the victory of the querent over his enemy, even if the Lord of the first (who is one of the inferiors) is in an angle - unless he is joined to another planet in an angle who receives him. For if he is so received, he will be fortified to the extent that you will be able to judge for the victory of the querent over his enemy, if the Lord of the seventh is cadent from an angle and is one of the superiors.

For example, if you find the Lord of the first strong in an angle, even if he is joined to some planet cadent from an angle (which signifies his impediment); nevertheless he will still be strong then, since the strength which he has from an angle is greater than the weakness which is brought to him by the planet cadent from an angle. And this will endure for him as long as he is in that place and degree which was the angle at that time, or until he is elongated from it by fifteen degrees, unless the conjunction between him and the planet cadent from an angle who impedes him is completed first. But whenever the conjunction between him and the cadent planet is completed degree for degree, he will be immediately weakened, and after that it will be feared lest the querent succumb, even if things were proceeding well at the beginning: and the enemy will become strong, even if things were going badly for him at the beginning.

Judge the same way for the Lord of the seventh as you judged for the Lord of the first: namely if you find the Lord of the Ascendant strong in an angle, even he is joined to a planet cadent from an angle which signifies his impediment, nevertheless he still will be strong then, since the strength he has from his placement in an angle is greater than the weakness which he has from the conjunction of the planet cadent from an angle who impedes him, until he is in that place and that degree which was the angle at that time, or until he is elongated from it by fifteen degrees, unless the conjunction between him and the cadent planet who impedes him competes first degree for degree. But whenever this conjunction is completed, immediately he will be weakened, and it will appear that the enemy ought to succumb to the querent, even if from the beginning it appeared it would turn out well for him, and the querent will be strengthened, even if it appeared that it would go badly for him from the beginning.

And Zael said the same of this: say regarding the Lord of the first and the Lord of the seventh if they enter into combustion, just as you said on the occasion of the perfection of the conjunction of any of them with a malefic planet cadent from an angle that impeded them. However if the Lord of the first or the Lord of seventh is not joined with any planet in the sign in which he is in, see who he joins first when he enters the next sign, after his exit from the sign in which he is in: since if he joins to one of the superior planets from a trine or sextile aspect with reception, and this planet is in a strong place (namely in an angle or a succeedent from an angle), or is joined to a benefic by a trine or sextile aspect, and without reception, or from a square or opposition aspect with reception, it signifies that he whose significator this is will conquer and win everything just as he wished: and everything will turn out favourably for him (whether it is the Lord of the first, or the Lord of the seventh). If indeed this conjunction is from a square aspect or opposition with reception, and the receiver is in a strong place (as I said); or from a trine or sextile aspect without reception, it will turn out semi-favourably for him, but not perfectly. However, if the conjunction is from square or opposition without reception, and this malefic is cadent or combust, or entering into combustion, it signifies that everything will turn out adversely for him in the finish of things, regardless of how the beginning might have went.

And Zael said that when you change the significator to the following sign, you shouldn't judge through the strength of the inferior planets, unless through the goodness of their place from the Ascendant, and through their freedom from impeding planets, and through the assistance of other planets towards them. Moreover, you ought to know that the significators (namely the Lord of the first and the Lord of the seventh) can have strengths and weaknesses relative to their position in a place. And these are: that if the Lord of the seventh is in the first, it is the greatest weakness, and the Lord of the first is maximally strong, because it signifies that the querent will conquer the enemy, and the enemy will not have a defence against the querent. It seems that the same thing can be said in elections, just as happened to us when we rode against Valbona: for the Ascendant was Taurus, and Mars was in the Ascendant, and we conquered all those who wanted to resist us.

However, if the Lord of the first was in the seventh (which is the greatest weakness for the querent, and the enemies greatest strength), it would have signified the enemy conquering the querent. And Zael said, "And those things which I told you will come to be more strongly if one of the significators aspects that planet who is in his own house; that is, if the Lord of the first aspects the Lord of the seventh in the first, the querent will obtain over the enemy and conquer him. And if the Lord of the seventh aspects the Lord of the first in the seventh, the enemy will obtain over the querent and conquer him.

Similarly look to see lest the Lord of the first falls in the eighth: since if this is so, or if the Lord of the first is conjoined to the Lord of the eighth, it causes fear in the querent; or if the Lord of the eighth is joined to the Lord of the first, then it signifies the death of the querent. And if the Lord of the seventh is in the second from the first, or is joined to its Lord, or its Lord is joined to him, it causes fear in the enemy, and signifies his death; and maximally if the Lord of the second is impeded by any of the aforementioned impediments by which a planet is impeded; since the second from the first is the eighth from the seventh, just as the second from the seventh is the eighth from the first. And say the same about the Lord of the eighth if he is impeded; since then it signifies death, in such a way that he will hardly or never escape it, unless that planet which is the lighter of the two is received by the heavier, and this lighter planet doesn't receive the heavier one, or vice versa: since if both receive and are received, it signifies death. If indeed one receives and the other does not receive, it does not impose such a necessity of death, even if it still threatens death.

Next consider if the Lord of the first is joined to the Lord of the tenth, or it to him, and along with this the Lord of the first is in the tenth: for this signifies that if that war or battle is in the district or kingdom of the querent, he will be strong, in fact stronger than all who come against him; and that he will conquer them all (unless perhaps there is an innumerable multitude), and he will capture the adversary or enemy whom he is contending with; and this will be better and stronger if he who is heavier (namely out the Lord of the first and the Lord of the tenth) is in an angle (namely the first or the tenth), or in a succeedent from an angle (namely the second, or the eleventh): because this will signify that it will not be possible to conquer him, nor will anyone be so strong that they will be able to have power against him in his district or kingdom.

However, if it was in the district of another, he will conquer the enemy by the aforementioned conditions, but still he will not be so strong, that he will be able to do it without losing his substance, and even his men: however, the common belief and rumour will be that he won: but he will not be able to win against such numbers as he would be in his own district: yet he will be able to against an equal number, or against those greater than him by one fourth, or one third.

However if the Lord of the seventh is in the fourth (which is his tenth), or is joined to the Lord of the fourth, or the Lord of the fourth is joined to him, and the heavier one of them is in an angle (the seventh namely, or the fourth), or in a succeedent of an angle (the fifth namely or the eighth), it signifies that the enemy will not be conquered, and that nothing can be done against him if the battle is in the district of the enemy. However, if the battle is in the district of the querent, it is to be feared lest the querent lose his district or kingdom.

And Zael said that if one of the significators are joined to some planet in an angle, or the Lord of an angle, and this will be better again if the significator is in an angle, since then it signifies the fortitude of the same significator. And he said that if one of the significators is in an angle, free from malefics, and is in a mobile sign, it signifies death soon after he obtains victory. Similarly look to see if the Lord of the seventh in the first, not aspecting the Lord of the first, or if he is in the twelfth: for this signifies the flight of the enemy. If indeed the Lord of the first aspects him, the querent will conquer the enemy. And if one of them is retrograde, it signifies his flight and total defeat and the breaking up of his side. If indeed the Lord of the first is in the seventh, and the Lord of the seventh doesn't aspect him, or if the Lord of the first is in the sixth, it signifies the flight of the querent. However, if he is retrograde it signifies his flight, and breaking up, and the total defeat of his side.

Next examine if you see the Lord of the tenth in the first: for it appears that the king is going to assist the querent. If indeed the Lord of the tenth is in the seventh, it appears that he will assist the enemy. Say the same if the Sun or the Moon (or one of them) are joined to one of the significators (namely the Lord of the first or the Lord of the seventh): for whichever one of them is joined with the luminaries, he will be assisted by the king.

Moreover, examine the significatrix (which is the Moon), and see if she is separating from one of the significators and joining to the other: since this signifies the strength of the planet which she joins and the debility of that planet from which she separates. Since if she separates from the Lord of the seventh and joins to the Lord of the first, it signifies victory on the part of the querent against the enemy. And if she is separated from the Lord of the first and joined to the Lord of the seventh, it signifies victory on the part of the enemy against the querent.

Next examine the place of Saturn in matters of war: since his presence in an angle is malefic in the case of battles, since he signifies the strength and savageness of the war. Whence if you see him in any angle at the hour of a question or at the inception of a battle, announce the strength, cruelty, and long duration of the war. And if he is retrograde, he will impede more and act worse, whether he has dignity or power in the angle, or not. If he is in the first it will be a great and strong war on the part of the querent. If he is in the fourth, it will be less than this on account of his placement here. If he is in the seventh it will be great and durable, and maximally on the part of the enemy. However, if it is in the tenth, it will be a great, strong, cruel and famous war.

Say the same as this if Mars is in Capricorn or Aries at the hour of the question or the hour of the inception of the battle, but the battle will not be wholly terrible. Moreover, see if Mars is the significator of one of the parties: since if he is he significator of the querent, or the inceptor, or his assistant, and he is direct, it signifies that those on the side of the querent will be good warriors, and will not think to flee in their hearts. And if Mars is then stationary in his second station, they would rather be killed before they flee or fall back. However if Mars is then retrograde, the warriors will be unstable, and will not persevere well in war, unless they are those who rise up against others in the manner of bandits and highwaymen. And it will be to the contrary if he is the significator of the enemy or his assistants: for he will signify the same for the enemy as was said for the querent. If indeed he is not the significator of either of them, it signifies the strength or weakness of both according to his condition, and in his station he signifies the ultimate strength in war.

And the retrogradation of Saturn signifies the prolongation of the war and its repetition. Indeed the retrogradation of Mars does not prolong the war as much as the retrogradation of Saturn. And if Mars is in the tenth at that time (namely at the hour of the question or the inception of the war) it will be a famous war; and will last so long that it will become known through many diverse and far off regions. And if he is placed between the 10th house and the occidental angle it will be a long lasting war and it will grow and be multiplied, but the captain or commander of one army will strive to deceive the other, and whatever either of them does will be done with slyness, ingenuity and shrewdness.

Indeed consider if Mars is in an angle, (namely himself or a planet who aspects him) since this signifies the strength of the war, even without the interference of Saturn in this war, but not the ultimate strength. However, if Mars is in a succeedent from an angle, and the planet who aspects him is in an angle, or vice versa, it signifies greater strength of the war than if both of them were in angles. And if both are in succeedents it signifies even greater strength of the war than was said above. And if one is in an angle, or in a succeedent, and the other is in a cadent, it signifies even greater strength of the war again. If both of them are in cadents, it signifies a strong, terrible war of many conflicts, beyond what Mars signifies in the tenth: since at this time Mars debilitates the war. And if one of the malefics is in fourth aspect to the other, and one of them is with the Cauda, it signifies the strength of the war. And if Mars is in Aries, Virgo, or Scorpio, and it is a diurnal war (or a diurnal question); or if it is nocturnal and Mars is in Cancer or Pisces, it signifies a middling war. And if he is in Taurus or Libra, regardless of whether the battle or the question is diurnal or nocturnal, it will be a light war in respect of other wars, and won't last long, but will break apart in a short time.

Besides this you ought to examine the Moon, and see if she is corporeally joined with Mars in any house, and especially in the eighth: since then the killing of the querent, or the inceptor of the battle, is signified, unless a benefic aspects her then. Since if a benefic aspects her then, however horrible a danger oppresses the querent, it will still free him from death, even if it only barely saves him.

Similarly see if the Moon is in the first and Mars is in the seventh, or vice versa. If so, counsel him who wants to go to, or begin a war that he should not go, nor begin the battle - since it signifies his killing. And if Mars is in the fourth, or the sixth, or the tenth, he will be captured, and wounded by a frightful injury, unless perhaps (as was said) he is aspected by a benefic. For if he is aspected by a benefic, it will mitigate his malice, and perhaps he won't be killed, nevertheless it always brings fear for him. However, if the Moon is then separated from Mars by body, and is corporeally joined to Saturn, or by opposition, without perfect reception (and this more strongly if she is in the second), it signifies the killing of the enemy, unless a benefic were to then aspect her (namely when she is joined to Saturn) as was said when she is joined to Mars. And this will happen more strongly, if Mars or Saturn are then with the Caput or Cauda Draconis, and it will happen much more strongly if it is like this at the hour of the inception of the battle.

Next examine the Sun, who similarly, if he is found with the Caput or Cauda Draconis at the hour of the question (but more strongly in the hour of the inception of the battle), signifies the greatest killing on both sides. But it will be greater on the part of those who hold their backs against the south, or against the west; nor will they be pacified from this conflict. If the Lord of the first is then in this conjunction (namely that of the Sun with the Caput or Cauda Draconis), it signifies that this killing will be so strong, and so terrible, and so great, that almost all parties will be killed, so that almost nobody will remain in comparison to those who are killed. However it will be worse with the Cauda than with the Caput, and their bodies will be lost.

And you ought to know that just as Mars (and the planet to whom he is joined, or who is joined to him) signifies the strength or weakness of a war, so the Moon signifies its greatness or smallness. Since if she is in an angle, it signifies the smallness of the war, and especially if she is aspected by the Lord of the house which she is in, and if he is likewise in an angle. However, if she is in a succeedent, it signifies a middling war, and especially if the Lord of the house she is placed in aspects her, or is in an angle or a succeedent, or is in Taurus or Cancer. However, if the Moon is in a cadent and is joined to the Lord of the house she is placed in, and he is in a cadent, it signifies the great size of the battles and the war. You can say the same if she is in Scorpio, Capricorn, or in the final half of Libra.

And always be careful that you never give an impeded Lord of the first, or Moon, or Mars, or the planet from which the Moon separates, to him who wishes to begin a war. And if you cannot avoid this completely, avoid what you can; at the least avoid the impediment of the Lord of the first, lest the inceptor succumb. And beware in the inception of a war, or a journey to war, lest the Lord of the first is joined to, or moving towards a conjunction with the Lord of the seventh: and the greater his desire is to leave for battle, the greater will the worry for him; and it will be worse for him, if the Lord of the seventh receives the Lord of the first.

XXII

Which Side Has More Assistants

If anyone wishes to know which of the significators has more men, or is supported by more assistants, examine which of the significators (namely the Lord of the first or the Lord of the seventh) is greater in dignity, and who better aspects their own house, and who is aspected by more planets, and who has more planets on its side (namely on the side the Ascendant or the side of the seventh): since whoever is so placed, has more soldiers or more assistants. And just as the first signifies the querent or the inceptor, so the second signifies his soldiers, assistants, or agents. And just as the seventh signifies the enemy, so the eighth signifies his assistants. And just as the tenth signifies the king, so will the eleventh signify his soldiers, assistants, or agents.

And Zael said that if there is a benefic in the second, or aspecting it, and the Lord of the second is in a good place, it signifies the strength of the assistants of the querent, and their loyalty and assistance. And through the eighth and its Lord judge the assistants of the enemy, just as you judged through the second and its Lord on the assistants of the querent. And if the benefic which is in the second is in a common sign, or if it is in Cancer, Scorpio, Pisces, Aries, Libra, or Capricorn, announce a multitude of soldiers or assistants for the querent. And say the same for the enemy when there is a benefic in the eighth; and the same for the king and his deputy.

And Zael said that the fifth signifies the city and all who live in it.

And he said that if there is an oriental planet in its own house, or if the Lord of the second is direct and oriental, the soldiers or assistants of the querent will pursue the truth, if indeed he is retrograde they will not obey him.

For the king's soldiers, or his assistants, or deputies, examine the eleventh, and see if there are any malefic planets there: for if there is, they will not be obedient. If indeed this malefic is retrograde, not only will the soldiers of the king be disobedient, but they will also be traitors. And this more strongly if Mercury and the Cauda Draconis are 13 degrees or less away from the Sun: or if there is some malefic in the 8th house from the sign in which the Sun is placed in at that time. If this malefic is retrograde, not only will the assistants of the king be evil-doers or traitors, indeed the king himself or the deputy will also be evil and unjust. You will understand this to be the case if the armies are not to make peace.

If indeed you find that they ought to make peace, examine which planet the significator of the commander or the leader of the army commits his disposition to: for this planet has the signification of the person who interposes himself to reconcile or make peace between the two sides. If you wish to see what kind of person he is, see if the planet is in any of his own dignities. For if the receiver of disposition (and the one who interposes himself to bring them into agreement) is in its own house, it will be one of those people from the leader's own army. And if it is in its exaltation, it will be a powerful person representing the people of the land where this army is. If indeed the planet is in its own terms, he will be of those people who have relatives in the army, or someone in either army who they don't want any bad things to happen to. And if the planet is in its own triplicity, he will be of those people who the commander has as his friends or assistants, who will come into the army at his request. And if the planet is in its own face, it will be a man who does work for the army in his profession. And if the planet is not in any of its own dignities, he will be another person who arrives from somewhere, either a member of the public, or a traveller. And you will be able to know about him more attentively through his significator, and perhaps even his appearance through the same planet.

For if it is Saturn, it will seem that he is an ignoble old man, and maximally if Saturn is occidental. However if he is oriental, he will be less old.

And if it is Jupter, it will appear that he is of mature age, and is noble, and it is also possible that he will be a bishop, or a judge, or someone similar to this.

However, if the planet is Mars, it will be a man who habitually, or who used to lead out armies, and he will be a deceitful man, and who at some time was a highwayman or another kind of evil-doer.

And if it is the Sun, it will be a man of great nobility, namely one of those men who are fit to rule; or perhaps it will be a king or someone in charge of many peoples.

And if it is Venus it will be someone in their youth, who is of little wisdom or learning: but who will still do it, and operate in good faith, without any kind of slyness.

And if it is Mercury, it will be a wise and learned man, as much in a natural sense as acquired wisdom, or a literary man.

And if it is the Moon it will be a man who involves himself in the matter, from just motives and good will.

And if you see Mercury under the rays of the Sun, and the Lord of the first and the Lord of the seventh are impeding him, it signifies that one side strives to deceive and destroy the other. And if you then find Mars with Mercury, this treachery will be propagated, so that it is known openly by everyone. And if both of the planets at the extremities (which are Saturn and Moon) aspect the Ascendant, or are in the Ascendant, or with the Lord of the Ascendant, it signifies that this treachery will be carried out by one party against the other. And if neither Mercury nor the Moon are not in the Ascendant, but one or both of them aspect it from a square aspect or from opposition, it signifies that the person who interposes himself to make peace if not faithful or lawful. And if then his significator is under the rays of the Sun, it signifies that he will be discovered to be part of the army opposed to them. And if the Moon is then corporeally conjunct with Mars, or the planet from which Mars is separating from (or who is separating from him), he will be captured. And if in addition to this Mercury is oriental, he will be placed in prison but nevertheless will ultimately escape. And if Mercury is then corporeally conjunct with another malefic, and this malefic is northern from him, he will be beaten in jail , and will suffer detriment there. And if he is joined to a benefic, and this benefic is southerly from him, he will escape from this detriment. And if Mars is the significator of him, who impedes the significator of the peace-maker, the person who beats him will be a bellicose soldier. And if it is the Sun, it will be a leader of the army, and especially one of those who are greater and more excellent than him. And if Mercury is then in Gemini or Virgo, or Sagittarius or Pisces, there will be many people who interpose themselves to make peace between the armies. However if Jupiter then aspects the Ascendant or the Moon, everything will be done with lawfulness and goodness, and no deception or betrayal will fall in this group of people.

XXIII

On The Knowledge Of The Victory Of The War, And Who Will Win

Indeed to examine for the knowledge of victory of war, and which of the combatants ought to be the victor, you will see if the Sun and Moon are placed from the line of the 10th house up to the line of the 4th house on the side of the Ascendant; or from the line of the 4th house up to the line of the Midheaven on the occidental side, and they are free and clean (namely fortunate and strong): since they will signify the victory of the war for the side in which they are on. So that if they are on the side of the Ascendant, they signify victory for the querent or inceptor. However, if they are on the occidental side they will signify victory for the adversary. If indeed they are malefic and debilitated, they signify the contrary: since he who has them in his part will succumb.

XXIV

What Was The Reason Why This War Arose, And Whether It Was Just Or Unjust

If anyone ever enquires (as often happens) as to what was the reason a war arose, or if you otherwise wish to tell this to someone else: Zael said that you ought to examine Mars, since he is the natural significator of war, and all wars are attributed to him (as is said elsewhere). And see what planet he is separating from, or what planet is separating from him, since through this planet you will perceive him who begins the war, and from the planet to whom Mars is joined, or who is joined to him, you will perceive the enemy or adversary. If he separates from a benefic, or a benefic separates from him, and he joins a malefic or a malefic joins him, it signifies that the querent or inceptor was moved by a just cause to begin that war, and that he uses justice and truth, and that the adversary uses the contrary. If indeed he is separating from a malefic, or a malefic is separating from him, and he is joined to a benefic, it signifies that the querent was moved unjustly, and that he doesn't use truth, and that the adversary defends justice and truth. And if Mars is separated from a benefic and joined to a benefic, it signifies that both parties have a just cause - which rarely happens. If indeed he separates from a malefic and joins to a malefic, it signifies that both strive contrary to justice and contrary to truth.

Next examine if any malefics are in the first, and especially if Mars is there, since this signifies that the war arose by reason of envy which one had towards the other: or perhaps that one wanted to take away some of the others provisions.

And if Mars is in the second, the war arose for the reason that one wanted to take the others goods, substance, or money for himself.

And if he is in the third, it appears that one injured the brother of the other, and the war arose for this reason: or perhaps that one said the other wasn't a Catholic.

And if he was in the fourth it will appear that it was for a reason of a city or a castle that one stole from the other, or wished to take from the other: or perhaps he wanted to take his house, land, field, inheritance, or vineyard from him, or that he injured his father.

And if he was in the fifth it signifies that it was done by reason of the child of one party who was injured by the other: or by reason of a woman or some luxurious item; or by reason of parental goods, especially immoveable ones. And if you then see the Moon joined to Mercury from a trine or sextile aspect, it appears that the cause of the war was a city or castle that one of them wanted to occupy for himself.

And if he was in the sixth it will happen because of a slave or slave-girl, or by reason of a small animal taken from one party by the other; or it will be almost for nothing or for a matter which shouldn't be grounds for war

And if it is in the seventh, it will be by reason of a woman being taken away or offended or injured, and especially the wife or lover of one of the parties; or it will happen on account of avenging some evil deed.

And if it is in the eighth it will happen because of some old thing on account of which blood was spilled; or it will happen because of the inheritance of some dead person, who did not pertain much to either of them.

And if it was in the ninth, it will be by reason of religion or some religious person: or that one wants to convert the other so that he will follow what he follows, and revere what he reveres.

And if he is in the tenth, it will be for the cause of the king and his honour, and the cause of growing his dominion. And if the Moon is then in the tenth and is corporeally joined to Mars, or aspects him from square aspect or from opposition, the war will be made greater and there will be much killing from it.

And if Mars is in the eleventh, it will happen because of friends, or it will be to defend the substance of the king or his assistants.

And if it is in the twelfth it will be for the cause of old enmity, and ill-will which exists between the parties, or between the leaders of the armies: but nevertheless, even if there will be war for this reason, the parties will not fight at once by a general battle: and they will easily reconcile, if there is anyone who wishes to interpose himself to settle between them.

XXV

The Greatness Or Smallness Of The Armies

If at any time the leader of some army was in doubt about the army of his enemy, and wishes to know from you whether it is great or small, and you wish to examine for him: what you should examine for this matter is the place of the Moon by sign and degree, and Mercury similarly; and subtract the place of the Moon from the place of Mercury, and see how many signs you have remaining. If there is an even number of them, it is a great army; and the more signs remain after the subtraction, the greater the army will be. And if there are an odd number it will be a small army; and the fewer signs there are, the smaller the army will be. If indeed the place of Mercury is not enough for you to subtract the place of the Moon from it, add on twelve signs to it, and afterwards subtract the place of the Moon from this, and do as was said.

And also examine if there is a greater number of planets on the occidental side (which is from the angle of the earth up to the tenth on the western side), than there is on the oriental side (which is from the angle of the tenth up to the fourth on the eastern side). This will signify a greater number of men on the side of the adversary. If indeed there is a greater quantity of planets on the oriental side than there is on the occidental, it signifies a decreased number of men on the side of the adversary, even if by the aforementioned reason his army was signified to be large; and vice versa on the part of the querent.

XXVI

To Know All Of The Instruments And Other Things Which Pertain To War

To know the general instruments which pertain to war, Zael said that the Ascendant signifies the one beginning the war and his reasons, and what happened to excite the war, and whether it began with truth or falsehoods.

The first signifies the one beginning of war: since the first thing which comes in a war is the one beginning it.

The second from the Ascendant signifies whether there will be a war or not: and whether it will be to the benefit or harm of the one beginning it: since the second thing which comes in war after the beginning is the effecting of the warriors.

And he said that the third from the first signifies the arms and with what kind of arms will the victory or obtaining happen : and what types of arms will not be necessary in this war; since the third thing which comes in war is arms, since without these it is not possible for anyone to wage war well.

And he said that the fourth from the first signifies the place in which the war will be - namely whether it will be in the fields or the mountains, or whether it will be on the seashore or next to a river, or if there are fruitful trees or groves. Since the location is a thing so necessary for war that without it war cannot be made.

And that the fifth signifies the probity, marching, valour, and laziness of the combatants; since probity is a thing without which the combatants cannot wage war well.

And he said that the sixth signifies the military animals, which are horses, asses, mules, or camels: since the horses or other animals which carry them are of great utility to soldiers.

And he said that the seventh signifies the catapults, and whether war will be made with slyness or not; since these things are truly useful for war, after the other aforementioned instruments.

And he said that the eighth signifies plagues, capture, death, and the breaking-up and flight of the conquered: since these are the completed acts of war and are those things in which wars tend to ultimately come down to.

And he said that the ninth signifies the work of scouts and the knowledge of the enemies affairs, and their reputation and skilfulness; since these are things which a commander ought to pay great attention to in war, namely to know the actions of the enemy and the new things which are at his disposal, and how apprehensive he is about the affairs of the war, and how clever or ingenious he is.

And he said that the tenth signifies the habits or acts of the commander who is greater than the rest of the leaders which are under his command. Since either you or someone else ought to try to see whether the king or commander is painstaking and attentive around those matters which have a view to war, or not; and whether he is cautious or astute in those things which pertain to it.

And he said that the eleventh signifies their battle lines and the order that they march against the enemy. Since this is something for a commander to serve very well, in order to know the order of his own lines, and his fighters, and to instruct them how to conduct themselves in matters of war: and from this alone many have conquered their enemies.

And he said that the twelfth signifies the city and those who are besieged and assaulted in it, since these are things which combatants ought to know, and from which they can depend on to know what they have to do and how they can be strengthened against their enemy.

XXVII

How You Ought To Examine The Significations Of The Twelve Houses

Allowing that much has been said above in this same chapter on those things which pertain to matters of war or contentions; I will still say certain useful things which I think should not be omitted. Nor should you believe that I wish to contradict the above opinions; since if you inspect what was said closely and understand it well, you will find no contradiction here. Whence if you distinguish the times correctly, the things that ought to agree, will agree.

Therefore when you have examined all of the houses well (as was said) and you want to know the significations of any of them: examine all houses for the querent or the inceptor in the order written below, beginning from the first: indeed for the enemy examine from the seventh and make it the first of the enemy, and make the eighth his second, make the ninth his third, make the tenth his fourth, make the eleventh his fifth, make the twelfth his sixth, make the first his seventh, make the second his eighth, make the third his ninth, make the fourth his tenth, make the fifth his eleventh, and make the sixth his twelfth.

Next examine if there is a malefic in the first, or aspecting it from a square aspect or from opposition: for this signifies that the querent will not perform those acts which have to be performed in war well, nor will he be painstaking around them: and this could be the reason why things do not turn out well for him in the war, unless this malefic is the Lord of the Ascendant, or at least its exaltation Lord. And it also signifies that the querent or inceptor of the war is not in the right, but it is more likely that he is in the wrong. However, if there is a benefic here, or aspecting the aforementioned place (instead of the malefic) from a trine aspect, it signifies good: a malefic signifies the contrary.

If there is a malefic in the second, or aspecting it from square or opposition, who is not the Lord of the second or its exaltation, it signifies that there will not be a war; and if there is, it will be to the harm of the querent, and will not be useful for him. However, if a benefic is here, or a benefics aspect, as was said in the first, it signifies that there will be a war; and if there is, it will be of utility to the querent.

If indeed there is a malefic in the third and it is Mars, and he is in good condition, [specific] military arms will be necessary in this war, and the querent will have to use them if he wants to win. You can say the same for Jupiter here. And if Mars is in bad condition, it signifies that the arms used on the querent's side will be those of bandits, highwaymen, and unreliable men; and they will not be useful to him.

However, if there is a malefic in the fourth, or its aforementioned aspects, it signifies that the location of the war, if it is a field, will be disagreeable and unsuitable for the side of the querent. If it is mountains, the mountains will be rough and inhabitable, and wooded. If indeed it is near water, it will be marshy and muddy and badly suited to combat.

However, if there is a benefic in the fifth, or its aforementioned aspects, or Mars is there, and he is in good condition, it signifies that the soldiers and assistants of the querent will be upright, courageous, and will advance easily, and are well suited to combat. And if a malefic is here, or its aforementioned aspects, or Mars himself is there in bad condition, it signifies that they are low quality, lazy and only advancing with difficulty, and tardy, and badly suited to combat.

If there is a benefic or its aforementioned aspects in the 6th house, or the Caput Draconis, the animals which are used for this war will be expensive horses; likewise if Mars is here and he is in good condition, these horses will be fierce, firm, and impatient. And if a malefic is here, and especially Saturn, these horses will be of low quality, as are rowneys and other old horses, and for the most part of little worth; and there will be asses and camels (if it is a region where there are camels). And if the Cauda is here they will be mules, and other animals not well accustomed to war.

However if there is a benefic in the seventh, or the aforementioned aspect of a benefic, it signifies that the instruments with which stones are hurled will be useful and will do what they are supposed to do, and do it well. And it even signifies the goodness of the enemy. And if a malefic or its aforementioned aspect is here, it signifies the utility of the aforementioned instruments and that he will strive greatly to fight with slyness, deception and treachery: and indeed it signifies the low quality of the enemy.

If there is a benefic in the eighth, it signifies that few plagues will follow from this war, and little mortality: and that not many of the injuries will be dangerous, nor will many captures follow from it, nor will there be great capitulations, nor great flights. However, if a malefic is here (and especially a retrograde Saturn) it signifies many plagues and dangers and great killing and captures and ruptures.

However if there is a benefic in the ninth, or its aspect, it signifies that his enemy is well disposeed, and that he has hope from certain rumours he heard, and these rumours are useful to him; and that he is a shrewd man, and that he will strive to deceive the querent if he can.

However if there is a benefic or its aspect in the tenth, it signifies that the querent or he who is the major or captain of his army is sagacious, and learned in such things which pertain to war - and it will be the same for others to whom any of those things which pertain to war have been entrusted. However if a malefic is here it signifies regarding the querent or his leader or major of his army, and other leaders of the army to whom matters of war are entrusted, that all of them, or the greater part of them are unfit to exercise such matters.

If there is a benefic in the eleventh it signifies that the querent or leaders of the army are discerning men who know how to order their lines well, and how to lead them out to war well, and that they know how to advance against enemies or adversaries well, and how to do all things which pertain to this. However, if there is a malefic or its aforementioned aspects here, it signifies that the leader of the army is ignorant and undistinguished, and he does not know how to order his lines, nor how to lead them out to battle, nor how to do those things pertain to the leading of an army, even if he might otherwise be of good will.

If there is a benefic in the twelfth it signifies that those who are in the city or other land which is besieged, are well disposed and suitable for defending, and are unanimous, and that they will strengthen in response to the siege, and that they will appear to be afraid of nothing. If indeed there is a malefic or its aspect here, it signifies that they are badly disposed and that they are not suitable for defending, and that they are not unanimous, and that they are timid people and shaking with fear.

Nor will you forget this one thing which I will say to you now: since even if I did not find it in any of the sayings of the philosophers, I still found it proven through experience; that always whenever Mars is in the twelfth, betrayal is always to be feared, and you could nearly say the same for Cauda.

And just as you examine all the houses beginning from the first and finishing at the twelfth for the side of the querent: so examine all of the houses beginning from the seventh and ending at the sixth for the enemy when you are judging for him. Just as you judged for the first of the querent or inceptor: so judge for the seventh of the enemy. And as you judged for the second of the querent, judge for the eighth of the enemy. And as you judged for the third of the querent, judge for the ninth of the enemy. And as you judged for the fourth of the querent, judge for the tenth of the enemy. And as you judged for the fifth of the querent, judge for the eleventh of the enemy. And as you judged for the sixth of the querent, judge for the twelfth of the enemy. And as you judged for the seventh of the querent, judge for the first of the enemy. And as you judged for the eighth of the querent, judge for the second of the enemy. And as you judged for the ninth of the querent, judge for the third of the enemy. And as you judged for the tenth of the querent, judge for the fourth of the enemy. And as you judged for the eleventh of the querent, judge for the fifth of the enemy. And as you judged for the twelfth of the querent, judge for the sixth of the enemy.

But you ought to know this: that if you find the significators of the armies (namely the Lord of the first and the Lord of the seventh) equally strong and well disposeed in all matters, or equally debilitated and badly disposeed: then it signifies victory on the part of the person who started the battle, unless the aforementioned combust hours operate against this. And if one is well disposeed and the other badly disposeed: and he who has his significator well disposeed begins the battle, he will win. However if he who has the badly disposeed significator begins, he will succumb, even if they were equal in all other matters.

XXVIII

Whether There Will Be A Battle Between The Armies Or Not

If someone asks you whether there will be a battle between the armies or not, examine the first and its Lord, and the Moon, and the seventh and its Lord: and see if they are corporeally joined in any of the angles: since this signifies that there will be a battle between them. However, if they are not corporeally joined, see if they join from opposition or square aspect, since this similarly signifies that there will be a battle between them. And if none of the significators are placed in these manners, see if any planet transfers light between them from opposition or square aspect: since this signifies that there will be a battle - if it is without reception that is. However, if the heavier planet out of them receives the planet who transfers light between them, this signifies that there will not be a battle: and if there is, they will make peace either in that engagement or shortly after that engagement. And if it is otherwise, namely that the significators of the armies, (the Lord of the first and the Lord of the seventh) are not joined anywhere, and they do not hinder each other, and if there is no one who transfers light between them (as was said), it signifies that there will not be a battle.

An example of such a thing is this:

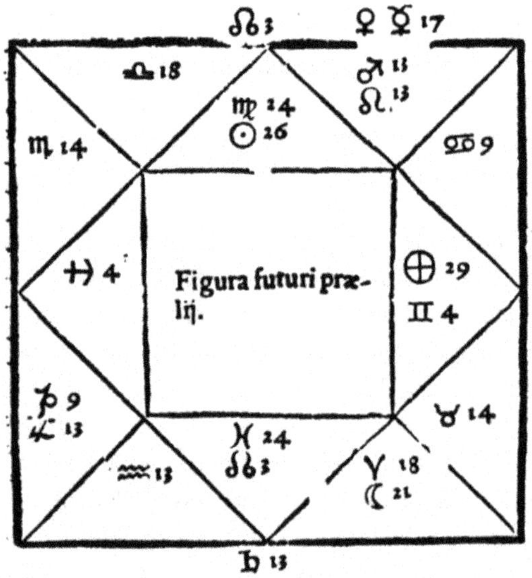

When Count Guido Novello held power in Florence, and we were with the army over the district of the Luccans, and the Luccans were stationed in their district with their army of close to one thousand soldiers, or slightly less, he enquired as to whether there will be a battle between the armies or not.

I examined this question, whose Ascendant was 4 degrees of Sagittarius, and the Midheaven was 24 degrees of Virgo. With Mars there at 13 degrees 30 minutes and Venus at 17 degrees 6 minutes. Mercury at 17 degrees 13 minutes in the ninth, cadent from an angle, and the Sun in the same at 26 degrees and 4 minutes, in the angle of the 10th house. 18 degrees Libra was the 11th house, with the Cauda there at 3 degrees. 14 degrees of Scorpio was the 12th house. 9 degrees of Capricorn was the 2nd house. Jupiter was there at 13 degrees. 13 degrees of Aquarius was the 3rd house. 24 degrees of Pisces was the 4th house. 18 degrees of Aries was the 5th house, with the Caput there at 3 degrees, and Saturn there retrograde at 13 degrees. The Moon was in it at 21 degrees. 14 degrees Taurus was the 6th house. 4 degrees of Gemini was the 7th house, with the Part of Fortune there at 29 degrees. 9 degrees of Cancer was the 8th house. 13 degrees of Leo was the 9th house. This was the era of the Arabs, 658 years, 9 months, and about 16 days. The altitude of the Sun was 48 degrees before the meridiem. It was Monday the 12th September.

I examined the Ascendant of this question and its Lord (who was Jupiter), and the seventh and its Lord (who was Mercury). The first of which was in the second in Capricorn, namely in his fall: which appeared to signify the low quality of the querent's side, in such a way that he would not seek battle; but since he was in the second, it signified some strength for him.

Next I examined the Moon, which was void-of-course in Aries, which similarly signified the weakness and low quality of the querent's side.

Next I examined Mercury for the adversary, who was in Virgo, combust and cadent from an angle; who, even if he was in his own house (which is similar to him who is in his own land), still signified their weakness, indeed so that they would not seek battle.

Whence I judged the question for him, and he came back since they did not position themselves at the location of the battle; and both parties departed afterwards, just as will be said in the chapter below on the besieged castle.

XXIX

Whether A Besieged, Or Soon To Be Besieged City Or Castle Will Be Captured Or Not

The ancient astrologers did not care much for this matter, which is amazing to me, since it is something which so often comes into one's hands; but it is possible that they might have done this, as they regarded it as a simple matter: and they assumed that anyone could know this; and therefore they did not care to speak of it. Nevertheless I will append something on this here for you.

However Zodyal said something on this, whose intention I do not understand very well. Whence if there was a question made to you on any city, or any besieged castle, or one about to be besieged, as to whether it would be captured or not from that siege: examine the first, which is the querent; and the fourth, which has the signification of the city or castle under siege; even if some of the moderns may have said that the tenth signifies the city: and were moved by this reason: that the fourth signifies the land of the querent - so by the same logic the tenth should signify the land of the enemy, not differentiating between land or inheritance of estates and cities or castles. However it seems to me that we ought not to give the fourth to the city or the castle, since the fourth signifies the inheritance of the querent, and his land and houses, and the tenth signifies his honour: and no honour is greater than rulership (and no shame greater than being deposed from rulership). Whence if the tenth signifies the honour of the querent, (which is signified more through the city or castle than through other riches), it is fitting that the fourth signifies the honour of the adversary, which is opposite to the honour of the querent: and so it appears that the fourth signifies the enemy's city or castle.

Nevertheless do not believe this is contrary to what Zael said: indeed he appeared to want to say that the twelfth signifies the besieged castle or city; but his intention was not the city besieged by an army who were encamped around them, but one besieged by the enemy entering into their jurisdiction by force, and he spoke concerning the defenders of the castle or city themselves.

Whence if you find the Lord of the first fortunate and strong, or you find him joined with the Lord of the fourth (or the Moon) in the first, or in the tenth, or even in the eleventh or in any place besides the unfortunate ones (which are the twelfth, eighth or sixth), so that the Lord of the first receives the Lord of the fourth, or even if the Moon receives him (even if she is not received by him), it signifies the taking of the city and its capture. Similarly if the Lord of the fourth is in a malignant place, not aspecting its own house - unless the Lord of the seventh is in the fourth, since this signifies its protection. Similarly if the Lord of the fourth is impeded with a malefic, it signifies its capture; or if there is a malefic in the fourth without any benefic or the laudable aspect of a benefic, it signifies its capture. Say the same if the Cauda Draconis is there, since she has the signification of loss and evacuation.

However, if there are not any of these configurations which I said to you, see if the Lord of the fourth is strong or fortunate in the fourth, so that it is not retrograde, nor combust, nor besieged by malefics; or if the Lord of the seventh is there, free from malefics and from other impediments; or if Jupiter is there, or Venus, or the Sun, or the Caput Draconis, and the Lord of the first is neither receiving nor impeding the Lord of the fourth: for this signifies that the castle or city will not be captured by that army; especially if the Lord of the first is impeded while not having dignity there, even if one of the malefics are in the fourth, as long as there is a benefic there which goes to the line of the 4th angle first, before the malefic does, especially if the Lord of the first is debilitated, (as was said). If indeed there is a benefic there, and the Lord of the first is strong and fortunate and aspects the fourth (or the Moon), it signifies capture. If indeed it doesn't aspect it, or is impeded, it signifies that on account of uselessness and laziness the querent's side desisted from doing those things by which a besieged castle is captured: and so from the negligence and low quality of the attackers, the besieged castle will remain unconquered, when it could have been captured.

Zodyal indeed said that the Ascendant and its Lord are to be examined for the querent; the seventh and its Lord for the city or castle. And he said that whichever one of them was badly disposeed, or retrograde, or in its fall, its signified party would be overcome. And if the Lord of the Ascendant entered the 7th house, and the seventh Lord gives force to him, the city or castle would be captured. If the angles are joined to benefic and malefic planets, support would arrive for both of them (namely the city and the attackers). And it is always to be considered whether the Moon is fortunate or malefic: since if she is placed anywhere between the 10th house and the beginning of the fourth on the oriental side, help will arrive to the querent: if she is in the remainder, to the center of the city.

This is an example of such a matter.

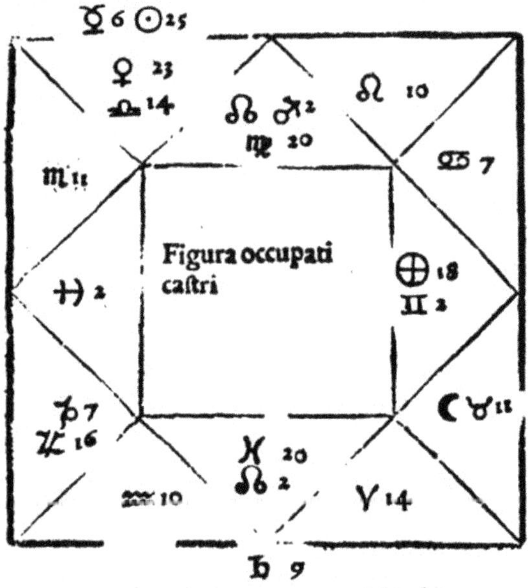

When Count Novello was besieging a certain castle of a company of the Luccans, he asked a question regarding whether he was going to occupy the castle. The Ascendant of this question was 2 degrees Sagittarius. The 2nd house was 7 degrees Capricorn, Jupiter was in it at 16 degrees. The 3rd house was 10 degrees Aquarius. The 4th house was 20 degrees Pisces. The 5th house was 14 degrees Aries. The Caput Draconis was in it at 2 degrees, and Saturn retrograde at 9 degrees. The 6th house was 11 degrees Taurus. The Moon was here at 11 degrees. The 7th house was 2 degrees Gemini. The Part of Fortune here at 18 degrees. 7 degrees Cancer was the 8th house. 10 degrees Leo was the 9th house. 20 degrees Virgo was the 10th house. 14 degrees Libra was the 11th house. Mars here at 2 degrees. The Cauda here at 2 degrees. Venus here combust at 23 degrees. The Sun here at 25 degrees. 11 degrees Scorpio was the 12th house. Mercury was here at 6 degrees.

And so Jupiter, who was in 16 degrees Capricorn aspecting the fourth, signified the capture of the castle; and maximally with him being the Lord of the first, and the Lord of the fourth. And since one and the same planet was the Lord of the first and the fourth, it appeared that he ought to have in harmony - as long as the things which had to be done to ensure its capture came to pass first.. And the Moon (who was in her exaltation in Taurus) signified honour on the side of the querent. And Mercury (who was close to the 12th house, yet not inside it) signified the weakness of the querent's enemies, but even if Jupiter appeared to signify the capture of the camp, nevertheless since he was in his descension and aspecting the fourth and not the first, and even if the Moon was in her exaltation, she was still in the sixth in a cadent from an angle and from the Ascendant: this signified that their uselessness, laziness, tardiness, and weakness was so great that they did not apply themselves to those things by which the castle could have, and ought to have been taken. And for this reason they did not capture that castle which they ought to have captured. Since even though the Caput was in the fourth, nevertheless Saturn was close to it, so that he was placed at the entrance to the 4th house.

Whence I responded to him under these circumstances, and I said to him that it appeared to me that their quality was so poor that the castle would more likely stand than to be captured. Ultimately they were so worthless and so weak, that they in no way performed any of those things which are done to capture a castle; and so it remained almost unharmed, and the army left the field. And the army stood so great that they would have been well able to storm the castle if they were willing to do what had to be done in such a situation. Finally he consulted me about the change of the air before they withdrew from the camp, and I found that there would be a big change three days from the day of the question, and it was such a change that they were happy when they returned home, for it had been four months since it had rained.

XXX

Whether Someone Has Public Or Hidden Enemies

Benefics are more numerous than malefics, nevertheless unfortunate events appear more numerous than fortunate ones: not because they are greater in number, but because they are felt more strongly. Whence some men are fortunate, and it is not known why (unless perhaps by experienced men). Similarly there are certain unfortunate men not knowing why this happened to them: indeed they serve everyone indifferently, allowing perhaps one more so than another, they are devoted to nobody, and still some people are inimical to them (and sometimes many people), not knowing what cause to assign as to why they hate them, except that they may be moved by jealousy, since they see they are good and not evil. Whence they sometimes ponder over these things and consult an astrologer, asking whether they have enemies because of which contrary things happen to them, or not.

Whence if anyone poses a question to you on whether they have enemies or not: you should know if they enquire about anyone by name, whether so and so is inimical to them or not, or if they enquire absolutely "Have I enemies or not?"

If indeed they named someone to you, seek him from the 7th house, if the Lord of the 7th aspects the Lord of the first (or the Moon) by a square aspect or from opposition, you know that he is inimical to the querent and speaks ill of him and causes the querent's troubles. Similarly if the seventh Lord is in the 12th from the Ascendant, or in the 12th from the Lord of the first, or from the Moon, or is joined with any planet who is in opposition to the Lord of the first or the Moon, or in their square aspect without reception. If indeed this is not so, he will not be an enemy of the querent.

However, if he enquires absolutely as to whether he has enemies or not, seek this from the 12th house, and see if the Lord of the 12th is in opposition to it, or in opposition to the Moon (whether with reception or without reception), or in square aspect without reception. If so, then he has enemies who plot evil things for him, and do evil when they can do so without rumours (so that it is not known publicly), and make themselves appear to be his friend to his face. Next examine in which house the Lord of the 12th is so disposeed, and say that the people signified through that house are those who are inimical to the querent. And examine if any of the planets are in opposition to the Lord of the first or the Moon, or in their square aspect without reception: since the people signified by the house which this planet rules, will be inimical to the querent. Understand the same of those who are signified through the house in which the planet is when it opposes the Lord of the first or the Moon: and all of these people will be moved more by jealousy than any other cause.

Whether or Not Someone Will Avenge An Injury Inflicted On Him

If there is an injury inflicted on someone, just as often happens that if someone's father, grandfather, or brother, or son, or anyone was killed, or someone was beaten, or there was an injury inflicted on the querent of such a kind that he wished to take revenge: and he posed a question to you as to whether he would get his revenge or not: it is necessary in this case for you to examine the first and its Lord, and the Moon, and also the fourth. And see if the first and the fourth are both mobile signs -namely Aries, or Cancer, or Libra, or Capricorn, and if the Moon is in any of these four signs: for this signifies that he will not get the quesited revenge, unless the Lord of the first is in the first or aspects it from a trine or sextile aspect, and the Lord of the sign in which the Moon is placed in aspects her likewise; or that the first and the fourth are both fixed signs: since if it is like this, without a doubt the quesited revenge will come to be, unless it is stopped by the querent not wanting to do it - but he will have the aptitude to do it, if he wants, and to do it in a short time after the question was made. And if the Lord of the 4th house aspects the Lord of the 7th house from any aspect, or its Lord from square or opposition, the querent get revenge if he wants it, and he will get it by his own hands, and by spilling the blood of him who inflicted the injury on him and done an injustice to him.

But if in addition to what I said, the Moon is joined to a benefic, it signifies that he will not be able to get revenge, unless by means of betrayal: and this will be because they will make peace, and afterwards, under the security of peace, the querent will kill him who done an injury to him; and this more strongly if that benefic to whom the Moon is joined, is joined with some malefic from opposition or square aspect: since then it signifies open betrayal. However, if the aspect is a trine or sextile, it signifies that the evil-doer will be captured and placed in shackles or on a stake because of it. And if the significator of the evil-doer, or the benefic planet to which the Moon is joined, or the malefic joined by that benefic to whom the Moon is joined, is in Aries, or Cancer, or Libra, or Capricorn, and the Lord of the sign in which any of the aforementioned planets are in (according to the method I told you) and is fast-of-course and aspecting the significator of the evil-doer (namely the Lord of the seventh), he will be released from that prison in a short space of time. However, if it is a common sign or that malefic to which the benefic is joined is of equal-course, he will remain in prison for longer than he believes. However, if he is in a fixed sign or the planet mentioned above is slower-of-course or stationary, he will be held captive for a longer time and will be held in chains. If indeed that benefic to whom the Moon is joined is in a mobile sign, and the Lord of this sign aspect him from a trine or sextile aspect, he will be freed from prison: since he who has power over that captive, or over the confinement, will release him without impediment: and if he aspects them from a square aspect or from opposition he will do less.

XXXI

On Hunting Birds And Wild Animals On Land And Water

There are two ways of hunting, one is on land and by means of land: the other is in water and by means of water. The hunting which is done on land is twofold: for it is either for wild animals or it is for birds. And it is subdivided again insofar as it is for wild animals as for birds, since it is either in mountains or on flat land.

If a question is made to you on hunting (and on the determination of the hunt) by land, and it is for wild animals, and the Ascendant is an earth sign: then examine the Ascendant and its Lord, and also examine the Lord of the hour, since the Lord of the hour has much to do in matters of hunting, (whether it is by land or water). Also examine if it is one of the quadrupedal signs: since they almost work the same as earth signs in hunting for wild animals on land. Also examine if your hunt is in the mountains: for if the Ascendant is one of the fire signs, it will be good. If it is on flat land, and the Ascendant is any of the fire signs it will also be good. If it is on flat land and the Ascendant is an earth sign or a quadrupedal sign, it signifies similar goodness, as much as it pertains to this.

In hunting birds however, whether they are aerial birds, terrestrial birds, or swamp birds, air signs should be adapted. Next examine the seventh (which has the signification of the hunt) and its Lord. And see where it is; and see if it aspects the seventh from a trine or sextile aspect: for this signifies the catching of the quarry without great labour, and without much searching, and this will be better if the Lord of the first receives the Lord of the seventh: since then it signifies the catch will be made with ease and pleasantness. And if they are joined from opposition or square aspect, it signifies that whatever is caught on the hunt will be caught with much labour and much fatigue, almost after losing all hope.

However, if they are not joined by any aspect, nor by body, and there is another planet who transfers the disposition or virtue of one of them to the other - namely from the Lord of the seventh to the Lord of the first; and the Lord of the first doesn't commit disposition to another planet, it also signifies the catch of the quarry, even if it won't be much, but rather a small amount. If the Lord of the first does commit disposition to another planet, or another planet transfers its disposition to the Lord of the seventh, it signifies that he will come close to catching the quarry, however he won't make the catch. But they will still rejoice from what they will see on the hunt, such as the chase and similar things. If indeed they are not joined together by conjunction or from aspect, or from transfer of light, it signifies that nothing will be caught on the hunt.

However, if you find that they are to catch something on the hunt, and the seventh sign is Aries or Taurus, or the last half of Sagittarius, or Capricorn, and the question is in the hour of Jupiter, and the Lord of the hour is in the first or the tenth: the hunter will catch a fast running quadruped of the forest, as are stags, deer, hares and similar animals. However, if it is Leo, his quarry will be one of the quadrupeds of the forest which inflict wounds, as are bears, wolves, foxes, hogs, and similar animals. However, if the 7th house is one of the houses of the malefics, and signifies the catching of the quarry: see if a benefic is there, or aspects it; since this signifies the catch happening with the safety of the hunter. However, if a benefic is not there, nor aspecting it, this signifies great fatigue on this hunt, and in the catch, and that very little will be obtained from it, and that it is to be feared lest anything bad happen to this hunter on account of the hunt, or to his own person from the quarry itself.

And if Saturn is the Lord of the seventh, or has any dignity there, and the question (or the inception of the hunt) signifies the catch of the quarry - not much will be caught on the hunt. But it is to be feared lest someone on the hunt strikes the hunter, believing that he is striking the wild animal, and other forms of harm. Nevertheless it will not be a big wound, but if he wounds himself, it might be serious for him: since this spilling of blood pertains to Mars, whence Saturn will impede less, since all blood which is spilled in hunting naturally pertains to Mars: and therefore Saturn's malice will be reduced in this case, and he will harm less. But if Jupiter (who is the natural dissolver of all maleficence) then aspects Mars, the hunter will not be impeded, and maximally if Jupiter is the Lord of the hour, or if the Ascendant is Sagittarius or Pisces: for then he will hunt with the safety of his body, and will catch much quarry, and will do this easily and quickly, with little labour, and little fatigue.

If indeed the seventh is an earth sign or an air sign, and there is a benefic in it, even if the Lord of the seventh is a malefic, and the Lord of the hour is similarly a malefic, he will still be safe and unharmed on the hunt, but he won’t catch all that he intended and believed he would catch on the hunt: and the wild animals and birds which he intended to hunt will sense him and his dogs (or his leopards, or any other animals with which he hunts) from afar, and they will flee in terror from them, so that he won't catch them, and he will boldly and laboriously search for them; yet nothing useful will come of it this; and he will do so safely.

And if Jupiter (the breaker of malice) or Mercury, are with the Lord of the seventh, or with the malefic who is the Lord of the hour, the hunter will not stop until he has his prize. For then Mercury takes over in the place of Mars in matters of hunting in such a case.

XXXII

On The Greatness Or Smallness Of The Catch

If however you wish to know the quantity of the catch, whether the hunter will obtain much or little: first examine the hour of the question or when he set out to hunt. And examine the tenth sign of this figure, and see if it is Aries or Scorpio, or you find Mars in it, and if Jupiter or Mercury aspect him, and the Ascendant is one of the domiciles of either of these two planets, and Mars is in the tenth; and if the Ascendant is not one of their domiciles, but either of these planets are the Lord of the hour, and along with this they aspect Mars. For this signifies that a lot of quarry will be caught, and it will be found in great quantity, so that not only will he catch it by instruments, but indeed he will catch it by his own hands, and without great labour: unless Saturn then aspects Mars. For if he aspects Mars without the aspect of Jupiter, and this aspect is a square, or from any of the angles, or if Saturn is in the tenth, or if Capricorn or Aquarius are the 10th house, he will not catch anything, only perhaps a small amount (since in this case Saturn diminishes the catch, and he will introduce labour, sorrow, and difficulty into the hunt). For if Jupiter does not aspect Mars, and Saturn is in any of the places signifying the hunt, and especially in an angle, impediment to the person of the hunter or the master of the hunt is to be feared; and the quarry will vanish before his eyes, and there will be difficulty in going to the hunt: and if they catch anything it will be a small amount, and he will not be happy with it; and it is possible that he will lose the quarry after he catches it, and especially if it is a hunt on land (regardless of whether it is on flat land or in the mountains).

XXXIII

On Hunting By Water

And if your intention (or that of the one setting out) to hunt fish, which is called sea hunting, and likewise understand under this heading all fishing spots, whatever type of water it is, whether it is a river, or a lake, or a marsh, or whatever other place it is, as long as it is a fishing spot: since all of these hunts fall under sea hunting: examine if the Ascendant is a water sign, of which the most useful is Pisces: then Cancer, and Scorpio is below Cancer. Mars is not useful at this time, since he impedes hunting by water. Whence if the Moon or the Lord of the hour is joined to Mars, nothing will be caught unless Venus is then in conjunction with the Moon: for in this case Venus shatters the malice of Mars.

For if the Moon, which has great virtue in hunting is joined with Mars in a hunt by water, it signifies little utility in fishing, or almost none: and whatever is caught, will only be caught with difficulty and burdens; and similarly with the impediment of the fisherman. It is different with Saturn, for he does not impede the Moon in hunting by water, just as Mars does not impede in hunting by land. In fact if the Moon is joined with Saturn in a hunt by water, it will multiply the catch, unless Mars aspects her.

And if Saturn and Venus are joined from any aspect (unless she is in Libra, or Capricorn, or Aquarius) it is to be feared lest the hunter or the fisherman suffers a shipwreck, or drowns in some other manner. If indeed she is in Capricorn or Aquarius, it is to be feared lest he falls in the water, but he won't drown. However, if she is in Libra, it signifies he will get wet through rain or trees or plants moistened by dew; and this will happen since Mars and Saturn are enemies of Venus.

In the tractate on elections I will say other things to you (from the sayings of the ancients) which pertain to the matter of hunting, whether it is on water, plains, or mountains.

ON THE EIGHTH HOUSE

I

On Someone Who Is Absent, Or Who Has Set Out Somewhere, Whether He Is Dead Or Alive

Sometimes certain people are in the habit of making themselves absent from their own home or their own land, and this happens for many and diverse reasons: indeed certain men set out to go on pilgrimages, other men because of commerce, others because of delights, others due to some governance, others to take up arms: and men travel far away from their children or family for many other reasons, indeed so that among their own there is no news of them, nor is the truth of their condition known. And perhaps someone concerned about one of these people wishes to know from you whether that person whom they are concerned about is alive or not, and they pose a question to you on him, and you wish to respond to them over it.

If so, then examine who the querent is, and see who he is asking about, whether for his father, or his brother, or his son, or his slave, or his wife, or a wife for her husband, or for a religious person, or for a master, or for a friend, or for someone who does not like him, but who makes himself appear to be his friend sometimes, and similar people. Then give the first to the querent, and as for the quesited, give him whatever house he is signified by, (and also the Moon). And see if you find the significator of the quesited in the fourth or the eighth from his own domicile, or the 4th and the 8th of the question: for this signifies his death. Likewise if it is in the twelfth from its own domicile with any malefics, or is aspected by any malefics from square aspect or from opposition: and if the Sun or Moon were then impeded, this similarly signifies his death.

However Zael said that the Lord of the Ascendant and the Moon are to be examined to see if they are in the fourth from the Ascendant, or in the house of death (which is the eighth from the Ascendant), or if they are combust, or in their descension, or with the Lord of the house of death: for this signifies death. And he said that if you do not find either of them disposeed as said, examine the aspects of the malefics and benefics to them. If the Lord of the Ascendant is retrograde in the fourth, or retrograde in the house of death, or separating from the Lord of the house of death by retrogradation, examine if he returns to the degree of combustion - for then he will be dead. Similarly he said that if the Moon is joined to a planet below the earth, he will be dead; and if she is joined to a planet above the earth, he will live. Similarly he said that if you find the Lord of the Ascendant in the twelfth with malefics, or with malefics aspecting him: and one of the luminaries are impeded, judge that he is dead. And he said, that if there are also malefics with the luminaries (which are the Sun and the Moon), in the one sign (corporeally joined that is) without the aspect of benefics, it signifies death. And similarly if the Moon is in the fourth with Mars and benefics do not aspect him. And he said that the same is signified if the Part of Fortune is in the fourth with malefics, or the seventh, eighth, or twelfth from the Ascendant without the aspect of benefics. And he said, know that what is above the earth signifies life, and what is below the earth signifies death. And he said, therefore you find him combust under the rays with no benefics aspecting him, and the Moon is under the earth, cadent from the Ascendant (in the third or the sixth), know that the quesited person is dead; maximally if the Moon happens to be in Scorpio, and in the third degree of the same sign, impeded by Saturn (who naturally signifies death). Then you will guarantee the death of the quesited person.

To which I (being familiar enough with the topic) assent to, apart from his assignment of houses: since he appears to wish to give the first to the absent person regardless of whom it is who asks the question; while to me it appears that he should be given the house which signifies him. Nevertheless it may have been a flaw in the translation or transcription. Use whichever method you wish, since when you experience it frequently, you will see which of these are more correct. Since it is not my intention to take anything away from good men, but to recommend and approve whatever they said, and to believe that they said it in good conscience.

However, if the significator of the absent person is in the sixth from his own domicile, or in the sixth from the Ascendant, or anywhere joined with the Lord of the sixth, or in his square aspect or opposition without reception, and is without the aspect of an unimpeded benefic: it signifies him to be ill. If f he is seeking the conjunction of the Lord of the sixth by the above conditions, it signifies that he will fall ill. However if it is moving away from a conjunction with a malefic by body or any of the aforementioned aspects, in such a way that it is separated from them, or if it is escaping combustion: this signifies his escape from illness or from other impediments similar to illnesses. You will judge the severity or levity of an illness according to the completed conjunction, from which the significator has escaped.

Nevertheless, you should remember not to judge him to be infirm, unless you first see whether he is sleeping at that time; nor to judge him to be dead unless you first see if he is drunk; nor to judge him injured unless you first see if he is letting blood; and you will be able to have knowledge of these things. Consider if the significator of the absent person is in the sixth, and not joined to the Lord of the sixth, nor with any malefic impeding him: and if he is joined to any free, strong, and unimpeded benefic; or to a fortunate, unimpeded, and strong planet who is friendly towards him: for this signifies he is not ill, but rather sleeping: and not injured, rather letting blood. Understand the same if he is in the eighth by the aforementioned conditions, since this signifies he is drunk, and not dead.

II

Whether An Exile, Expelled Person, Or Banished Person Will Return To His Homeland Or Not

Sometimes someone expelled from their home or city in which they live, or who has withdrawn from it in another manner, may wish to know whether they will return to the house or land where they usually live, and they consult an astrologer over this.

It is fitting therefore that you know what circumstances such a querent is in, since it is possible for a person to be outside of his own house or his own land in many different ways and for many reasons: for he could be expelled, an exile, a pilgrim, a fugitive, banished, or a missing person, or deported .

Therefore if you are asked about one of the aforementioned things, see who it is that is that asked the question: whether it is the same person or another asking for him. If it is someone who is concerned about the exiles affairs, see how he relates to the exile, and through which manner he wishes to enquire, (namely whether as a father, mother, brother or son, etc.).

Give the first to the querent, give the quesited the house through which he is signified, and judge according to this. Since if the Lord of the house through which the quesited is signified aspects the first, or is in the first, or is joined to a planet who is in the first, or is joined to another planet who does not aspect the first, but who is joined to a planet that does aspect the first and who raises up his virtue and light to the first - it signifies his return. Understand the same of the Moon. And also that if there is a question on brothers and the Lord of the third aspects the first, or the Lord of the fourth in the case of the father, and if the son, the Lord of the fifth; and understand this for the significations of all houses.

If indeed the querent enquires for himself, namely that he himself is the absent person who enquires: see whether he is an absent person who left of his own will, and has hope and intention of returning - as sometimes merchants do, or those who travel for important offices and other governances, or indeed through another manner for the reason of profit, or for the reason of fun, or by whatever means, as long as it is of their own free will (and he is not a pilgrim), always give the eighth to the querent for his own person. And give the first to the land from which he withdrew (even if it is suspected that something bad might have happened to him, on account of which he would have been expelled): however he is said to be an absent person and not an expelled person, unless after he withdrew something happened to him that he does not dare to return. Whence if the Lord of the 8th house aspects the first or the Moon by any aspect, it signifies his return: but if it aspects from an angle or from a trine aspect, it will hasten his return; if from a succeedent or a sextile a sextile aspect, it will delay his return somewhat. However if it is from a cadent or a square aspect, it will be much delayed. However, if from opposition it will be delayed even more, and his return will be postponed.

A pilgrim is given the twelfth on account of the anger, sorrow and tribulation which befall him on his pilgrimage. And certain men give him the seventh: nevertheless you will be able to choose which one seems more suitable to signify what you intend.

However, if this absent person was violently expelled from his land, or fled, or was exiled, or made himself absent due to some fear, or was banished, or deported, or was a pilgrim (for pilgrims are in a certain sense compelled to go on pilgrimages, in such a way that they cannot withdraw from that which they proposed to do on their pilgrimage without offending God), you will examine this in another way. Since if the querent is expelled, or banished, or deported, or who left on account of fearing the authorities, or an enemy, or someone else: you will give him the seventh and its Lord, and the Moon for his person, and give the first to his own land from which he was expelled. Whence if the Lord of the seventh or the Moon is in the first, it signifies his return. However, if neither of them are in the first and the seventh Lord or the Moon aspects the first, or are joined to the Lord of the first (if the Lord of the first aspects the first), it signifies his return. However, if neither of them aspect the Lord of the first, but one of them aspects another planet, and this other planet aspects the first, but also joins another who doesn't aspect the first, and this planet is joined to yet another planet who aspects the first, even if the conjunction comes to be from one planet to all seven planets (just as it seemed to Messala), one will raise his light to the other and renders its light to the first and perfect the quesited matter: even if it will be done with the interjection of many persons, and these people will be those who are signified by those houses ruled by the planets which interpose themselves. If indeed you find none of the things mentioned above, it signifies that he will not return.

But if the absent person enquires about his own affairs, give the first to his person; the fourth to his city or land, and also to any of his immovable things, and for his other concerns, give them their appropriate houses which are assigned to them.

III

The Arrival Of An Absent Person

Astrologers most frequently meet with questions on absent people, regarding whether they will return or not, and when they will return - which is difficult, even if those people who enquire do not believe that it takes more labour to respond than it does to ask.

Whence if you are asked a question about someone who is absent, as to whether they will return or not, and when - examine the Lord of the house by which the absent person is signified (as was said to you above in the preceding chapter), and see if his significator is in the Ascendant (whatever type of journey it is), or if it is in the ninth (if it is a long journey), or if it is in the twelfth (if it is a very long journey), or in the fifth (if it is a moderate journey), or in the third (if it is a short journey): for this signifies his return. Indeed a short journey is of one day; I say a moderate one is from one day up to three; a long journey from three up to sixty; and a very long journey from sixty to as long as a journey can be. Or see if it is joined to some planet in these houses, to whom the significator commits his disposition to: for this also signifies that the absent person will return.

And if it is in the seventh it signifies his return, but not quickly, but rather his return will be deferred: and it signifies that he is in the land to which he set out for, and has not exited it yet for the reason of returning, nevertheless he is concerned about his return. However if it is in the fourth it signifies a greater prolongation of his return than what was signified by the seventh, nevertheless his he intends to head back when he will be able to do it; and he will return, unless the significator is impeded by some malefic in his own domicile. And if it is in the third or the ninth, and is joined to a planet in the Ascendant, it signifies that the absent person is prepared, or will prepare himself immediately for returning. And if you find it in the second, and it is joined to a planet in the 9th house, or in the 10th house, it signifies that he is preparing himself to return: nor will there be much of a delay in his arrival.

However, if you find him cadent from the Ascendant, so that he does not aspect it, even if he is not otherwise impeded, it signifies his slowness, harshness and prolongation in returning, and that he will not care about returning; and if he does care, he will not be able to do it. If indeed he is cadent from the Ascendant and otherwise impeded, and is not joined to a planet which raises him, and who aspects the Ascendant, and renders his light to the Ascendant, it will remove his hope of returning, and it will appear that he will not return. If indeed the significator of the absent person is retrograde, or himself or the Moon are joined to a retrograde planet, and aspecting the Ascendant, it signifies his swift return. And if he is impeded by some planet, see who it is that impedes him. For if it is the Lord of the fourth, it appears that he is detained; if it is the Lord of the sixth, it appears that he is ill; if it is the Lord of the eighth, his death is to be feared; if it is the Lord of the twelfth, it appears that he is shut up in jail. These appear to be the things which impede his return. However if the Lord of the eighth impedes him, and he does not receive the Lord of the eighth, even if the Lord of the eighth receives the significator of the absent person, it won't signify death.

And if the significator of the absent person is not impeded, as said, then revert the judgement to the significatrix (which is the Moon). Who signifies his quick arrival if she is joined with the significator of the absent person, and commits her disposition to him in the Ascendant, or three degrees above the line of the Ascendant, or twelve degrees below. However, if she commits disposition above the line of the Ascendant from three degrees up to five, or below the line from 12 degrees up to the completion of the house, it signifies the delay of his return, albeit not by much.

However, if the significator of the absent person is impeded outside of the aforementioned houses, it does not signify great impediment, perhaps allowing for some. However, if the significator of the absent person is in the eighth, and is not otherwise impeded, his arrival will be prolonged further, and there will be a delay in it. If indeed it is impeded, it will cast doubt on him, and it will be feared that he might not return, as was said above. If indeed the Moon is separated from the Lord of the fourth or from the Lord of the seventh, or from the Lord of the ninth, or from the Lord of the third, or from any planet who is under the earth (which is said to be left of the Ascendant), and joined to the Lord of the Ascendant, or a planet which is above the earth (which is said to be right the Ascendant): it signifies the return of the absent person; and even if the Moon is cadent from the Ascendant, and joined to the Lord of the Ascendant, it nonetheless signifies his arrival. And if the Moon is joined from to a planet to right of the Ascendant placed in the tenth, it signifies his return, albeit with delay, since the Moon is then to the right of the Ascendant. But if she is to the left of the Ascendant, and joined to a planet in the tenth, will signify impediment, duress, and delay in his return.

However Zael, as I said to you in another chapter, gave the absent person the first.

Moreover, it is fitting for you to consider something else about the absent person: since there are many and diverse types of absence, as was said in the preceding chapter. For there are absent people who are exiles, pilgrims, expelled, banished, deported, and there are fugitives - whence the absent person is a certain kind of general matter; however an absent person is specifically said to be someone who of his own accord and free will made himself absent, whether he went to a fixed or determinate location, or not, just as long as he left with the proposal and intention; as said elsewhere.

An exile is said to be him who left his own land not knowing why; unless perhaps led by some folly; or perhaps went of wandering or searching to see if he could find a land more suited to him than the one he was in: and perhaps the place to which he was going was not premeditated, nor did he depart with a mind return, or not to return, but left as if he was roaming.

A pilgrim is said to be him who makes himself absent of his own accord and free will, to go to some place in the manner of kings, or in the service of God, such as if he wishes to cross the sea to visit Saint Jacob's, or Saint Peter's, or similar places.

An expelled person is said to be a person who is expelled from the land in which he used to live against his own will, by some enemy of his, or more likely by some party, just as sometimes happens between factions in cities, castles, or other lands, when one faction expels another.

A banished person is said to be him who on account of some wrongdoing, or for some other reason was expelled, such as the authorities or community of the land in which he lived expelled him from that land and banished him, and he does not dare to return there, even if he wishes to.

A deported person is said to be him who the people of his land send under custody for some reason to a specific location, and who cannot leave without the permission of the guards or those who preside over him.

A fugitive is said to be someone who for fear of something bad happening to him, fled from the land in which he lived, and fears to return to it: yet he is not banished; however there may be some people who would be eager to harm him if he returns.

Whence, all such people in whichever one of these cases are absent people. And if a question is posed on any of them, as to whether they will return to their own land, whether it is posed by themselves, or by another, always give the eighth to the person of he who made himself absent of his own free will without the intention of returning (as said) and give the first to his homeland, (unless he is a pilgrim): as for all the others, as much absent people as expelled people, as the banished and the fugitives and pilgrims, you will give them the seventh for their person, and the first for their homeland, just as to the expelled person, as was said in another chapter.

On The Time Of The Absent Persons Arrival

To know the time of the absent persons arrival, see how many degrees his significator is from the line of the cusp of the house in which it is placed, if he is in any of the houses mentioned above; and if he is not in any of them, see how many degrees he is from the planet in one of these houses to whom he commits his disposition (degree for degree). Since if it is a short journey, it signifies that he will arrive within as many days: if it is a moderate journey it signifies that he will arrive within as many weeks: if it is a long journey it signifies that he will arrive within as many months: and if it is a very long journey it signifies that he will arrive within as many years.

IV

On The Death Of The Querent

Some people sometimes worry about the arrival of death, and they fear lest it overtakes them before the time when it appears naturally fitting, and that they won't be able to get their affairs in order; and they consult an astrologer over this, so they can be made certain of it. Whence if someone poses a question to you on their own death, whether they make it absolutely or determinately; look at the hour of his question and establish a figure for the question over it - namely the first and the tenth and the rest of the houses, and the positions of the planets by their degrees and minutes, and by their direct motion, and retrogradation, and according to their longitude and latitude.

If someone asks a determinate question, saying “See if I will die in one or two or three years from now, or more or less”, according to how it seems fitting to them to enquire: you should examine the Lord of the first and the Moon, and utilise them in this matter, and see where they are: whether in angles, or in succeedents, or in cadents; or if they are in their own dignities, or if they are peregrine; or void-of-course, or joined to some other planets. For if the Lord of the first is joined with one of the benefic planets, and commits his disposition to it, and this planet is strong, (so that it does not commit its disposition to another): then examine if that good and benefic planet is the Lord of the 8th house. Since if it is not the Lord of the eighth, and is disposeed as I said, it signifies that he will not die within the quesited time. If indeed it is the Lord of the 8th house, (that is, the planet who the Lord of the first joins and commits disposition to), whether it is benefic or malefic it will kill, and the querent will die within the quesited time; and this will be predicted more strongly if the Moon is then impeded, unless another planet is joined to the Lord of the first who receives him (or at least the Moon): for this signifies that he will not die within the quesited time, regardless of whether it is a benefic or malefic who receives the Lord of the first or the Moon, provided that it is not the Lord of the 8th house.

Also examine if the Lord of the first is joined to some malefic planet who doesn’t receive him from house or exaltation or two of the lesser dignities and the Moon is then impeded: for this signifies his death. Say the same if the Lord of the first is joined to the Lord of the eighth, unless the Lord of the eighth receives him without the Lord of the first receiving the Lord of the eighth. Since if the Lord of the eighth receives the Lord of the first, and the Lord of the first receives the Lord of the eighth, death is to be feared, regardless of whether the Lord of the eighth is a benefic or a malefic. But if the Lord of the eighth receives the Lord of the first, and the Lord of the first does not receive the Lord of the eighth, he won't impede him, whether he is a benefic or a malefic.

However, if you see that he is not to die within the quesited time, examine when the Lord of the first is joined to the planet who receives him by a complete conjunction: since from that time of year he will be safe, and it will bring certainty to him that he will not die. However, if you see that he is to die, examine when the Lord of the first joins the Lord of the eighth, or when it joins the malefic planet mentioned above who does not receive him, but impedes him: since when their conjunction is complete, whether by body or by aspect, then his death is signified. However, if the Lord of the first is disposeed in such a way that you do not believe you are able to judge through him on the death, or the evasion of death, then examine the Moon, according to what Messala said, and judge through her, just as you ought to judge through the Lord of the first, by the conditions mentioned above on death, or its evasion. However, if, as I said to you above, the Lord of the eighth and the Lord of the first are joined together and each receives the other; or at least if the Lord of the first receives the Lord of the eighth, it signifies his death within the aforementioned time period, that is when the one arrives to the degree in which the other was at the time of the aspect. Understand the same if it suffers the misfortune of combustion within the quesited time.

On The Time Of Death In An Absolute Question On Death

However, if the question was absolute, so that he did not make his question determinate to you, but said "See when I will die": then you should examine the Lord of the first and the Moon, and the Lord of the eighth, and the planet who to whom the Lord of the first or the Moon are joined, and judge for his death according to the distance of the degrees between the Lord of the first and the Lord of the eighth or a planet to whom he or the Moon is joined; since he will die within as many months. If the Lord of the first is in an angle he will die within that many years. If it is in a succeedent, within that many months. If it is in a cadent, it will be within that many weeks. However if it does not signify death, it signifies that he will live for that many years, or for as many months, or for as many weeks as there are degrees in their distance: that is, by how many degrees the Lord of the first and the Lord of the eighth or the impeding malefic planet are apart from each other, this will be how many of these years, months, or weeks there are.

And you should know this, since in this case you ought to observe the Lord of the 1st house more than the Moon: since he is stronger in this matter than the Moon. Whence the conjunction of the Lord of the first with the Lord of the eighth (or with any other impeding malefic) is to be more greatly feared than that of the Moon with these planets: since the Lord of the first signifies the life and body of the native through its own nature, not accidentally. However, if the Lord of the first was separating from the Lord of the eighth, or the Lord of the eighth from him, or if the first Lord was separating from a malefic planet who impedes him, it will not kill him, nor will he be killed up until as many years as were signified for him, or months if months were signified for him, or weeks if they were signified for him, just as was said above: how many degrees fall between the separated planet and the conjunction which they made together. And the conjunction of the Moon with the Lord of the eighth will not kill, unless the Lord of the first is joined to him and is otherwise strong and free from impediments - which does not happen from the Moon. Because even if the Moon is strong and free, nevertheless if the Lord of the first is joined with the Lord of the eighth or in to a malefic by the conditions mentioned above, the goodness of the Moon will not be enough for the native or querent to escape even if she has the greatest signification with the Lord of the first in other matters.

V

Whether The Husband Or Wife Will Die First

And if a husband or wife asks you which one of them will die first, examine the Lord of the first and the Lord of the seventh, and see which of them falls into the misfortune of combustion first, or which of them will be the first to suffer one of the aforementioned impediments and conditions: this signifies that the first to die will be the person whose significator is so disposeed.

VI

What Kind Of Death Will The Querent Die From

And if someone says to you "See what kind of death I will die of", examine the Ascendant and its Lord. Which if you find it in the eighth, and the 8th house is Leo, and its Lord is unfortunate or impeded, he will be lacerated by the teeth or claws of some beast, or it signifies that he will be killed by beasts in another manner. But if Saturn is joined with the Lord of the eighth, and if he impedes Saturn from Scorpio or Pisces, it will be feared that he will die from a snake bite or from another poisonous animal. If he escapes this, it will be feared that he will die by drowning in water. If Mars is with the Lord of the eighth in the eighth, or the sixth, the fourth, or the twelfth, without perfect reception, with the Lord of the first impeded by Mars, announce he will die by a sword or fire: yet a sword will be more likely. However other places will not predict this as securely.

ON THE NINTH HOUSE

I

On A Journey Or Pilgrimage Whether It Will Happen Or Not. And If It Will, Whether It Be Useful Or Not

Sometimes some people will propose to make a journey and they will agree amongst themselves to make it; or perhaps only one person will propose a journey, and he will pose a question, as to whether he will make this journey, or not; and if he doesn't, what will it be that impedes it. Then you will examine the Lord of the first and the significatrix (which is the Moon) who are both the significators of the querent; and examine the ninth and its Lord, who have the signification of long journeys or pilgrimages (the third having short journeys, the fifth having journeys of moderate length, and the twelfth having very long journeys),

Since if you find the Lord of the first in the ninth, or the Moon, or if either of them are joined with the Lord of the ninth, and this more strongly if they are in the 3rd, 5th, 7th, or 11th, then the journey or pilgrimage will happen, and the querent himself will be the reason why the journey takes places: nor will anything external or extraneous befall him, which will move him to travel, he will only be moved to travel on his own account and from his own will.

Next examine the Lord of the 9th and see where he is. For if he is in the first, it signifies that news will come to him regarding the place to which he intends to travel, which will move him to go to the place, and to go quicker than he had intended to go. However, if in addition to this the Lord of the first (or the significatrix, which is the Moon) is in the 9th, such news will arrive that it will hardly or never happen that he won't travel. However, if it was the case that the Lord of the 9th is in the first, and he is joined with the Lord of the first, he will be overcome with such things, that in no way will it happen otherwise than he travels, unless perhaps the querent wishes to make a force of a nature out of his own will.

If the Lord of the 9th is not in the first joined with the Lord of the first, see if one of the planets will render the light of one of them to the other: for this signifies that the journey will be made. However, if there is not a planet who transfers the light of the Lord of the first, or the Lord of the ninth (namely from one to the other) then examine if the Lord of the first and the Lord of the ninth are both joined to some planet who is heavier than them, and this heavier planet aspects the 9th house: for this also signifies that the journey will be made. However, if the Lord of the 9th is not joined with the Lord of the 1st, and if there is no planet which transfers light between them, and they are not joined to a heavier planet who aspects the 9th house - judge that the querent will not make the quesited journey.

Similarly if the Lord of the first is in an angle and is joined to some planet in the 3rd, this signifies that the journey will be made - if he is free from malefics, as certain men said, with whom Zael appears to agree. If it is joined to a planet who is in the 2nd, it will signify a journey just like it would in the 3rd, as long as it is free from the aspects or conjunctions of malefics. If indeed the Lord of the first and the Moon are joined to some planet in an angle, and are not in any of the places mentioned above which signify journeys, as was said, it signifies that the journey will not be made.

You still ought to consider this also: that if the Lord of the 1st is joined with the Lord of the 9th, and it appears by their conjunction that the journey ought to be made, and you find one of the malefics in the first who does not have dignity there, and he impedes both of them (or one of them), the signification of the journey will be annulled and it won't be made; and the destroying cause will be something which befalls the querent which impedes his journey so that it doesn't happen, even if he begins it.

However, if that malefic is in the second, something will happen to his substance that will disturb the journey, or it will be a member of his household who holds him back.

If it is in the third it will happen because of brothers; and if he doesn't have brothers, it will be by reason of one of the things which are signified by the 3rd house.

And if it is in the fourth it will happen because of his father, and if he doesn't have a father, it will happen because of one of the things which are signified by the 4th house, such as land.

And if it is in the fifth, it will happen because of children, and if he doesn't have children, it will happen because of one of the things which are signified by the 5th house.

And if it is in the sixth it will happen because of illness, or because of a slave or the servants of his house, or one of the things which are signified by the 6th house.

And if it is in the seventh, it will happen because of rumours which come to him from that land to which he wishes to travel, or because of something he intends to get, or because of his wife, or because of enemies or bandits. And Zael said that if it aspects from the Ascendant he will fear murder or one of the things which are signified through the 7th house.

And if he is in the eighth, it will happen to him because of death, or one of those things which are signified by the 8th house.

And if it is in the ninth, it will happen to him because of rumours which he will hear regarding his journey; or perhaps that the road is not safe, or due to one of the other things which are signified by the 9th house.

And if it is in the tenth it will happen to him due to someone who rules over him, who does not permit him to make the journey, such as someone with a position of authority and the like, or one of the things signified through the 10th house.

And if it is in the eleventh it will happen to him because of friends, or one of the things which are signified through the 11th house.

And if it is in the twelfth it will happen to him because of someone who makes themselves appear to be his friend when they are actually not, but rather they are secretly inimical to him, or one of the things which are signified by the 12th house.

If indeed the Lord of the first is joined to the Lord of the ninth, and afterwards joins a malefic by conjunction or from opposition or square aspect, and he peregrine it signifies destruction which will occur after he leaves. And Zael said that this destruction will be according to the quality of the enmity of this malefic: that is, if he is the Lord of the sixth, it will be illness. If he is the Lord of the fourth, it will be imprisonment or another sorrow. And if he is the Lord of the eighth it will be death. And if he is the Lord of the seventh or the twelfth, it signifies destruction by bandits and enemies. And if he aspects from the Ascendant, murder will be feared. If from the second, it signifies the detriment of substance. Similarly the square aspect from the Ascendant signifies detriment to the body: and the other second square aspect, namely that of the seventh and tenth, signify the detriment of substance. And he said that if you find the Lord of the Ascendant in the seventh or the eighth, it signifies labour on the pilgrimage, and especially if it is a malefic.

However if the Lord of the Ascendant is in the eighth, and is not a malefic, and receives the Lord of the eighth, and is not received by him, it signifies that the traveller will obtain another's goods in the place where he intends to travel.

Next examine if the Lord of the first is free from impediments, namely retrogradation, fall, combustion, conjunction of malefics, or their square aspect or opposition: for this signifies that the journey will be safe and easy, not difficult and not laborious. Say the same if the Moon is received by perfect reception from house or exaltation, or from two of the lesser dignities, for then the journey will be light, free of impediments and labour: and especially if she is received by the Lord of the ninth or its exaltation: even if this receiver is a malefic who is not impeded by terrible impediments. However if the Moon is not received, it signifies the difficulty of the journey, and slowness, delay, and complications on it; and that the journey will not be useful or profitable: and it seems that those to whom he travels, or the people of the land to which he intends to travel, will not receive him well: and will also be hateful towards him.

And Zael said that if you find the Lord of the Ascendant in the Ascendant or in its other domicile joined with the Lord of the ninth, it signifies he will go on a pilgrimage, even if it is a fixed sign. And he said that a fixed sign does not destroy a journey. He also said to know that the Ascendant signifies the pilgrim and the Midheaven signifies his affairs, and the seventh from the Ascendant the land to which he travels, and the fourth from the Ascendant signifies the end of the matter. However if you find a benefic in the first after you see that the journey will be made or that it will not be prohibited, it signifies that the journey will be good and useful and with the health of body and soul. If a benefic is in the tenth, it signifies that the merchandise or things which he carries will be conspicuous if he carries merchandise with him. However if there is a benefic in the seventh, the land to which he intends to travel will be good and useful for him, and he will be happy and rejoice in those things which he finds there: for he will find which he wanted to find there. If there is a benefic in the fourth it signifies that his journey will finish in such a way that will please him what happens to him on that journey will be practically the same as he wished.

If you find one of the malefics in the aforementioned places, not having any dignity in them, the journey will not go according to his wishes, but rather to the contrary: since if the malefic is in the first, something terrible will befall him on the road. If it is in the seventh, a horrible illness or something similar will befall him in the land to which he intends to travel. If it is in the tenth, the things which he carries will suffer deterioration and damage. If it is in the fourth, distress will befall him, and a decrease of his goods, and the labour which he endures will be in vain and useless.

II

What Did The Traveller Set Out For, Or For What Purpose Was The Journey Made

Sometimes certain men tend to hide the intention of their question from the astrologer: and at other times what reason they ask it for: since they do not wish to disclose to someone what they have in mind: as often happens with journeys lest anyone may ambush them or perhaps for another reason, in accordance with how it appears to them. If after they pose the question, you see that the journey is going to happen, and you wish to know what the traveller intends to travel for: examine the significatrix (which is the Moon) and see to whom she is joined. Since the planet to whom the Moon joins signifies those to whom the traveller intends to travel, or for what reason he intends to travel.

If the Moon is joined to Saturn he travels to lower class and ignoble people, or to monks or other religious people wearing black vestments, or too old or decrepit men, or to Jews.

And if she joins Jupiter it appears that his journey is made to citizens or bishops or the secular religious, or to judges or lawyers.

And if she is joined to Mars it signifies that he travels to warriors or to bellicose soldiers or pirates or highwaymen.

And if she is joined to the Sun it signifies that he travels to kings or some noble, wealthy, and honourable magnate.

And if she is joined to Venus, it signifies that he travels to women or else players who carry out womanly duties.

And if she is joined to Mercury it signifies that he travels to philosophers or writers or other wise literary men, or to merchants or masters of works.

If indeed the Moon is then void of course, his journey is for this: to find a certain absent person who is known to him.

If in addition to this (being void-of-course) she is then separating from Saturn, it signifies that his journey is to escape trouble from creditors on account of a helping hand he lent to someone, or even on account of his own debt, since he is not fit to satisfy his creditors.

If she is separating from Jupiter, it signifies that his journey is made for the reason of separating from (or wanting to separate himself from) some bishop, or prelate or judge, or some other noble citizen

And if she is separating from Mars, it signifies that he made his journey for the reason that he intended to separate himself from someone who usually leads an army, or who presides over some army at that time, or from some bellicose soldier, in accordance with how you see Mars in his own dignity. Since if he is then in his exaltation, he fled or intends to flee from a king. If he is in his domicile, from a duke. If in one of his lesser dignities, from a bellicose soldier. If he is peregrine, he fled (or wants to flee) from thieves or highwaymen.

If indeed she is separating from the Sun it signifies that he is separating from some king or very noble magnate, or intends to separate from them, perhaps fearing them.

And if she is separating from Venus it signifies that his journey is made for the reason of separating from some woman, or he intends to separate himself from her; or perhaps that he deceived her, or betrayed her.

However if she is separating from Mercury, it signifies that the journey or flight was made for the reason that he fled from (or intends to flee from, or separate himself from) some writer, or another literary man, or from some merchant.

Similarly examine to which planet the Moon is joined to first (if she is void of course): who, if he is in his own domicile, the person to whom the traveller goes to will be from that region; and if the planet is in his own exaltation the person will be from outside of the region, but will hold some lay dignity there, such as a position of authority, and similar things. And if he is in his own triplicity, it signifies that it is a man from outside of the region, but staying in it as if he was a citizen or this region or this land. And if he is in his own terms, it will be a man who stays in that region, and whose parents live there. And if he is in his own face it will be a foreigner, but one who now stays in this land or region, and is considered as a citizen.

And if the Lord of the house in which the planet to whom the Moon joins to is placed in aspects it, he whom the traveller seeks will be well known in that region where he stays. If indeed he does not aspect the house, the person is not publicly known in that region or land in which he stays at that time. And if he does aspect, see whether the aspect he aspects it from is good or bad: since if he aspects it by trine aspect, he will be a man who all of his neighbours esteem and honour, and who is very pleasing to them. If he aspects it from a sextile aspect, he will be esteemed and honoured in that land, but this will be somewhat less than the case of a trine. If indeed the aspect is a square, he will not be greatly esteemed, nor will he be greatly hated; and certain men will speak good of him; yet more will speak ill of him than will commend him. If the aspect is an opposition, he will be a man of whom men communally and unanimously say bad things about, and almost all who have dealings with him hate him, and he is considered as being contentious and whisperer. If it is a corporeal conjunction, it signifies that he is a verbose man, and one who interjects himself into much of his own, and others dealings, and from this interjection he tries to get money from men; nor does he seek to involve himself in anything, unless he can acquire something from it, and he will do so by all means, lawful and unlawful, soliciting and extorting money from everyone.

Examine similarly if you see that the querent made a proposal, and see if the Lord of the Ascendant or the Moon is impeded by one of the malefics, and see who is the malefic who impedes it, and examine in what sign he is in. Since the impediment will come according to the nature of the sign in which the impeding malefic is placed, and according to the significations of the house in which he is. You ought to know the significations of the houses well, so it is not necessary that I repeat them here.

And if it is in Gemini, Libra, Aquarius, or the first half of Sagittarius, the impediment will come from men, whence you ought to warn him, to beware of thieves, bandits, robbers and highwaymen.

However, if it is in Cancer or Scorpio of Pisces, and the malefic is Saturn, tell him to guard himself against shipwrecks, submersion, or drowning. If it is Mars, tell him to beware of pirates sailing the sea, and thieves of the sea and land.

However, if it is in Aries, Taurus, the last half of Sagittarius, or Capricorn, he should beware of falling afoul of beasts, and their kicking or attacks.

If it is in Leo, say that he should beware of lions, wolves, bears, dogs, scorpions, and spines and spiders and similar things.

And if it is in Pisces, tell him to beware of aquatic serpents and other poisonous animals that come out of the water.

And if it is in Virgo, tell him to beware lest some tree (or some branch) falls on him, or impedes him in some other way: and also to beware of rivers or falls from high places, and even to beware of poison.

And Zael said that Mars impedes more on land, and Saturn impedes more on water.

III

How Things Will Go For The Traveller In The City Which He Enters

If some traveller or pilgrim wishes to know what will happen to him when he enters into any city or foreign land, or if you want to know this for yourself: examine the 1st house when he enters this land or when the querent asks the question. And see if the Lord of the 2nd house (which signifies the substance of this city) is direct: for then he will return in no great length of time and will perfect what he intended quickly enough. If he is stationary in his second station there will be a delay in his return, but he will nevertheless perfect the matter for which he travelled: however he will meet with many impediments contrary to his business, so that he will not believe that he will be able to perfect it. If it is stationary in its first station he will believe that he will be able to perfect what he intended, however ultimately it won't be perfected, and he will return angrily after some delay, since it will bring no profit - but rather he will spend more than he makes. However if it is retrograde he will return quickly from that land and will not perfect the matter for which he travelled, nor will he make any profit from it, nor will anything good come to him from it.

If the Lord of the second is in the first, or the tenth, or the eleventh, this journey or entry into that land will be useful, good, and profitable; and he will be happy and rejoice for this reason.

However, if the Lord of the second is in the seventh, many contrary and horrible things will befall him: and it will be necessary for him to enter into litigation for this reason, since the person with whom he had business with will not tell him the truth, and especially if their significators (namely the Lords of the seventh) are malefics, and he will meet with contentions and discord, and many other things which will disturb him and bring grief and sorrow to him.

If indeed the Lord of the second is in the third or ninth from the Ascendant it signifies the instability of the querent, and of his movement in the land in which he entered or another that he had arrived in; and he will not stay there unless it is a very short stay, or almost not at all, and if he does stay, it will not be of his own will, but rather against his wishes, and it will likely that he will be forced to stay there.

If indeed it is in the fourth, and is aspected by any malefics from square aspect or from opposition, unless it is received with good reception he will not easily travel further. And if it is corporeally joined to him it does not appear that he will return to his own home again; and it appears that he will die there. If indeed Mars is the malefic who impedes the Lord of the second, and the Moon is joined to the Lord of the second, or is joined to Mercury from a square aspect or opposition, or by body, and then Mars aspects the Moon, horrible things will happen to him, and he will fall into contention with some bad people, and those who use those things which pertain to Mars. And it is signified through the aspect that they will strike him and injure him causing frightful wounds, so that if the Moon is in the fourth and Mars aspects her from any aspect, the querent or traveller will die from this. But if he is wounded, scars will appear in the locations of the wounds. And if he is tortured the imprints of this torture will remain in the locations constrained by the torture device. If indeed the Moon is in the aspect of Mars and Jupiter, or the Sun, or Venus, or Mercury did not aspect him, and if he himself is then in good condition, something horrible will happen to the querent or the traveller from the significations of the sign or house in which Mars is in. If indeed one of the aforementioned benefics then aspected the Moon, it is possible that the horrible things which were mentioned will not happen to him; nevertheless if they do happen, the querent or traveller will be liberated from them, and will escape and find relief for all of these things, and will escape them. If indeed one of the benefics mentioned above do not aspect the Moon, it is then to be feared that these horrible things are very bad, and that they will adhere to the traveller or querent in such a way that he dies from them.

IV

How Things Will Go For The Traveller On His Journey, Or Regarding The Reason For Which He Travels, Whether He Is A King Or Some Other Person

When men travel on some journey or pilgrimage or any such thing, they sometimes tend to ask how things ought to turn out or go for them in that journey or for their objective on that journey. Or perhaps that you want to know for yourself how things ought to turn out for them. If so, then examine the Ascendant at the hour of the question if he enquires, or of his departure if he didn't enquire, and verify all of the houses from the first up to the twelfth, and examine the disposition of the significators of all houses, and their condition: and judge good things for those which you find well disposeed; and judge bad things for those which you find badly disposeed.

Besides this you will judge the travellers' condition according to another less particular method: namely that you ought to examine the planets who are between the first and the fourth, and especially those which are in the second. And if a malefic planet is there, who does not have domicile there, or exaltation, or term, or triplicity, or face, it will signify that damage will happen to those things which he leaves behind. If he is a king or another great nobleman, the damage or detriment will be in his kingdom, duchy, or retinue, or those who pertain to him from his relatives. However if it does not have any of the aforementioned dignities, nor has face or haym there, it signifies damage to the travellers goods, whether he is a magnate or lower class; and especially if it is a lower class person who does not have a kingdom, city, or castle, it signifies damage to what they possess, and in the items of their house, as much for moveable items as for others; and for anyone it signifies detriment of those close to them, and their relatives who love them. If this malefic who is in the second is Mars, the detriment will happen to him on account of war or another contention, or through burning by fire or the spilling of blood, or through highwaymen, or the death of small animals, or slaves, or slave-girls, insofar as Mars is then disposeed to signify any of the aforementioned things. However if it is Saturn, this horrible thing or detriment will be from a shipwreck or submersion, or a building collapsing, or thieves, or the death of large animals, or illness. If the Cauda is there, it will be on occasion of each of the significations of some house, since the damage will occur from those things which are signified by the house whose Lord is impeded. However if this malefic has dignity in the 2nd house, and is direct, or is received, its malice will be destroyed, nor will it impede by very perceptible impediments. If it is retrograde it will not destroy its malice in whole, however it will harm very little, provided that it is received; but if it is retrograde and is not received, nor in its own dignity, its malice will be increased and it will do great harm. Say the same if it is in its fall or descension.

However, if there are benefics in the place of malefics (namely in the second): say that this journey should not make him fearful of his goods which he leaves behind him, nor will they be diminished for this reason, but rather they will be improved and grow.

And Zael said that if the Lord of the Ascendant or the Moon are impeded, it signifies difficulty and sorrow on the road. Whence when you see that some journey or pilgrimage threatens harm to the querent, you ought to see which planet is impeding, who causes the fear, and who is the cause of the detriment which appears like it is going to befall the traveller, and where this planet is. For if it is between the first and the tenth, as Zael said, this detriment or damage will come on his return. If it is between the seventh and the tenth: on his departure. And if it is between the first and the fourth, below the earth: in those things which he acquires on his departure. If indeed it is between the fourth and the seventh, on his return.

Yet it appears to me that this translator did not know the Arabic language very well. From which he may have been mistaken in his translation: since it appears fitting that if the impeding malefic was between the first and the fourth the impediments ought to happen in his departure from the land in which he was, going to the other one up to the middle of his journey. If it was between the fourth and the seventh they ought to happen from the middle of his journey up to the land which the traveller intended to go. And if it was between the seventh and the tenth it would happen to him in his return up to the middle of his return journey, especially in those things which he acquired. And if it was between the tenth and the first, it would happen after the middle of his return journey to his own house or his own land.

The accidents according to each house and each planet will be put down here; and so that you may know the particulars of it - examine the helping benefics and the impeding malefics, and see in which houses they are: since in those portions of the journey their significations will happen, insofar as they are benefic or malefic. For if they are in the first, they will happen in the beginning of the journey, a little outside of the gates of the land from which he withdrew, or perhaps within the gates. If they are in the second, they will happen within a fifth part of the journey. If they are in the third, they will happen within a third part of the journey. If they are in the fourth they will happen in the middle of the journey. If they are in the fifth they will happen within a third part of the journey remaining after the first half. If they are in the sixth they will happen after two parts remaining of the journey after the first half. If they are in the seventh they will happen in the place to which the traveller is going. If they are in the eighth they will happen in the separation from that place, or close to a fifth part of the return journey from the place from which he returns. If they are in the ninth, they will happen in the third part of the return journey. If in the tenth, they will happen in the middle of the return journey. If they are in the eleventh they will happen after the second part of the return journey. If they are in the twelfth they will happen close to the land which the traveller returns to.

Next examine in which of the aforementioned houses you find a benefic, since that is where the traveller will rejoice and good things will happen to him, so if it is Jupiter it signifies the acquiring of money: if it is Venus he will rejoice with women and food, and similar things. However, if you find a malefic there, the contrary will happen to him: so that if it is Saturn, harm will come to him from the cause of thieves, fire, hidden and shadowy affairs, or because of a shipwreck. However if Mars is there, they will happen from the cause of fire or highwaymen, or bloodshed, or similar things.

V

Against What Direction It Would be Better To Go

And if a traveller or anyone else comes to you with a question, saying "In what direction is it better for me to travel?": then examine the figure which you erected, and see in which quarter the benefics are, and which are fitter and in better condition, and according to this you will say to him where it is better to travel. If they are in the east, toward the east; if in the south, toward the south; if in the west, toward the west; if in the north, toward the north. And in whichever quarter there are more (and better disposeed) benefics, it is better to travel in that direction.

And say the same for malefics, since in whatever quarter there are more malefics, it is worse to travel in that direction. And if it seems that the traveller ought to meet someone, and if the Lord of the first is joined with one of the significators of the question, he will meet them on the road. If it is the Lord of the third, he will meet his brother. If it is the Lord of the fourth he will meet his father. If it is the Lord of the fifth he will meet children. That is if he has a brother or father etc. And understand the same for all the significations of the houses. And if the significator of the brother is in the first, his brother will come to him. And if the Lord of the first is in the third the traveller will go to his brother. And say the same of all the significators of the houses, if the querent or traveller has a brother or father, etc. And always take care to examine the second and the eighth in journeys. As Ptolemy says:

"Beware of malefics in the eighth and their aspects going out on a journey, and in the second returning from a journey: since a malefic or unfortunate planet in the eighth signifies detriment to profit in the land to which the traveller intends to go, and in the second in the land to which the traveller intends to return".

Whence you ought to place benefics in the eighth in any given journey, or make it so that one of them aspects it, and if you place the Caput with them it will be better. And beware then of the Cauda, and if it happens that you cannot avoid having a malefic there, place the Cauda with him, and then beware of the Caput. Understand the same of the second when he returns from the journey, as I said to you of the eighth when he leaves - that there is not a malefic there, nor aspecting it; and if you cannot avoid that a malefic aspects it, make the aspect a trine or at least a sextile, and always place a benefic there, or make it so that a benefic aspects it.

VI

Which Of Two Lands, Or Houses, Or Whatever Things, Or Which Of Two Or More Business Deals Or Journeys, And Similar Things, Will Be Better For The Querent

Certain men sometimes have many business deals on their hands, and don't know which of them is of more utility to them: and they consult an astrologer to choose which of the business deals is better for them. Whence if someone comes to you who has some business deals on their hands whether they are journeys, or purchases, or sales, of if he has offices, or marriages, or changes from land to land, or from one house to another, or something similar to these things, and he wanted to satisfy himself of the matter: it appeared that there were diverse opinions on this among our ancient sages. But if one rightly considers it, it does not appear to me that there were diverse opinions: but rather that one said more than another, just as it seemed to him, not to contradict the sayings of another, nor to break with the opinions of such men as Messala and Albumasar (who appeared to speak subtly, even perhaps secretly). Those however who are in my time such as Hugo Abalugant, Benduardinus Davidbam, Johannes Papiensis, Dominicus Hispanus, Michael Scot, Stephanus Francigena, Gerard of Cremona, and many others used the first and the seventh in all of the aforementioned things, yet extended their judgements in these two ways. Bellonos Pisanus used all 4 angles for the aforementioned. Grandeus, (the son of David mentioned above) used his own hidden method which he showed to nobody, and it worked out well in his judgments. I however, not contradicting any of these men(neither the ancients nor the moderns), and with the help of Our Lord, Son of The Blessed Virgin, have made good and authentic judgements using the following method: and I will advise you as to how to use it. Namely if a question was made to me by anyone on any of the aforementioned matters which contain more than one of the same thing, I securely took three things under one Ascendant, and I judged over them just as if over one thing: and used the triplicity Lords of the house signifying the quesited matter, and I judged over these.

To give an example: someone wanted to take a wife, and had many women on his hands, and made a question and formed it like so: "I have a verbal agreement to take Mariam as a wife, and Bertam, and Inveldam, see which of them is better or more useful to me: and if the marriage between me and one of them will be completed, and with whom will the marriage be completed". And posit that the Ascendant was Aries, which signified the querent; and Libra was given to the women. From which I examined the triplicity Lords of Libra, namely Saturn (who is the first), Mercury (who is the second), and Jupiter (who is the third). And whichever one of them I found in conjunction with Mars (who was the significator of the querent), I said that the marriage would be perfected with that woman. And if Mars was joined with two of them, or with all of them, I said that it would be perfected with her whose significator is closer to being joined with Mars. And if all of them are equally joined to him (whether by body or by aspect), I said that he could perfect it with whoever he liked. But if one was joined to Mars by aspect and the other by body, the one who is conjunct is more deserving, and the marriage will be perfected with her. Understand the same of all other such things: that you will judge the better and more useful through that planet who is better, and best disposeed and more fortunate.

However, if it is a question of one thing only, judge through the Lord of the 7th house or through whatever house it is signified by.

And if he enquires about more than three things, then you will change the judgement. If there are four things you will give the Lord of the house as the significator of the first thing; the first triplicity Lord to the second thing; the second triplicity Lord to the third thing; and the third triplicity Lord to the fourth thing. And if you are asked about five things in the same way you will change the judgement again, and you will give the Lord of the house to the first thing; the Lord of the exaltation to the second thing; the first triplicity Lord to the third thing; the second triplicity Lord to the fourth thing; and the third triplicity Lord to the fifth thing. And if it is not the exaltation of any planet, you will give the Lord of the house to the first thing as was said; the first triplicity Lord to the second thing; the second triplicity Lord to the third thing; the third triplicity Lord to the fourth thing; and you will give the Lord of the terms of the significator of the quesited matter to the fifth thing.

Examine in all matters and in all questions according to this method which I gave to you: so that if you are asked by someone who is in any land and things are not turning out well for him there; or if he wants to change from it to another for any reason; or from one house to another; or from one office to another; or from one art to another; or of any similar things. And he said to you: "See which of these is better for me, is it this, or that?": examine what the condition of the first Lord and the seventh Lord is like. For if the Lord of the first is in better condition than the Lord of the seventh, he should remain in that land, or that house in which he is, or hold that art which he practices; or exercise those duties which he exercises. If indeed the Lord of the seventh is in better condition than the Lord of the first, he should travel to that land which he wishes to go to; or move to another house; or take up another art; for these things will be better and more useful for him.

Similarly examine if in addition to this the Moon is separating from some benefic, whether she is received when she is conjunct with him or not; or separating from some malefic who isn't impeded and who received her when she was joined to him; or if she was joined to some malefic without perfect reception, so that from this reception her condition would be improved. If so, then say that the land in which he is, or the house in which he stays: or the art which he exercises, is better for him. If indeed she is separating from a malefic and is joined to one of the malefics: tell him that he should beware of this move. Say the same about the Part of Fortune benefics are separated from it and malefics are joined to it: say it will be bad. If malefics are separated and benefics are joined: say it will be good. If both are benefics, either option will be good for him; whether he wants to do what he intended or not; but whichever of these significators is in better condition will be better for him. If indeed both are malefics, both conditions will be bad for him: but whichever significator is in less bad condition, will be less bad for him. Say the same of the Moon and of the Part of Fortune.

However the Lord of the first is good and the Moon is separating from benefics, and benefics aspect the Part of Fortune, say that the thing which he does, or the house, or the land in which he stays, is most useful to him, in such a way that it cannot be made better. If indeed any of them is missing, it will be below this in accordance with what is missing from any of the aforementioned good things. However, if the condition of the Lord of the seventh is bad, and the Moon is joined to malefics, and malefics aspect the Part of Fortune, it signifies that the thing which he wants to do, or the house or land to which he wants to travel or move to, will be so bad for him that things could not get any worse. If indeed any of them are missing, it will be less bad than this, according to the quantity of what is lacking the malefic.

VII

Whether That Land Is Better For Him

And Zael said that when you are asked by anyone "Is the land I am in better for me, or is the one to which I wish to travel better?": then examine if the Moon is separated from a malefic: for then leaving will be better for him. If indeed she is separating from a benefic, remaining will be better for him. He also said, and if you are asked a question saying "Is it good for me if I depart to this business, or to do this business": then examine the Lord of the Ascendant and the Moon, and see if they are separating from malefics and joined to benefics. If so, then advise him to do what he wishes. If indeed they are separating from benefics and joining malefics, advise him not to approach the work. If indeed the Lord of the Ascendant is in good condition, remaining will be better for him. However, if the condition of the Lord of the seventh is better, travelling will be more useful to him. And if the Moon is separated from an oriental, direct, and strong malefic who receives her from trine or sextile aspect, and she is joined to an impeded benefic who doesn't receive her, it signifies that it is worse to do the quesited matter, than it is to dismiss it, even if it is good to do. And if she is separated from an impeded and badly disposeed benefic, not receiving her from square aspect or from opposition, and is joined to a malefic who is direct, oriental, strong and well disposeed, receiving her from a trine or sextile aspect, it signifies that it is worse to dismiss the matter than to do it, even if it is not good to do it. Say the same if she is separating from them, as said, and is void of course, and is not separating from or joining to a benefic. However it appears to me that I have satisfied you on all of these things.

However if the significators of the quesited matter are equal in strength or debility, so that you cannot discern the truth from any of them, nor similarly through the Moon, then subtract the place of one significator from the place of the other significator and add the degrees of the ascending sign to the remainder, and project from the Ascendant, and see where the number falls: since you will be able to judge on the matter according to this place, and according to the Lord of this sign, and according to its condition. So that if it is well disposeed, you will be able to say good things; however if it is badly disposeed, you will judge the contrary. But if their places are equal, the significator will remain in the degree of the Ascendant.

VIII

On Someone Placed In Prison Or Chains, What Will Happen To Him Regarding His Incarceration, Namely Whether He Will Be Freed From The Prison Or Not, And If So, When

When some prisoner asks you (or if someone asks on his behalf using the prisoners own words) whether he will be liberated from that prison or not, and if so, when, not fixing any terms on the time of his liberation: then examine the Lord of the Ascendant and the Moon, and see if they are both in angles. For this signifies the holding of this captive, and the prolongation of his imprisonment. Similarly if the Lord of the first and the Lord of the tenth, and the seventh, and the Lord of the fourth are in angles, this signifies him being held for the whole of that year.

And if all four of the Lords of the mentioned houses are not in angles, and three of them are, or only two, it similarly signifies his holding for the whole of that year. Besides this, if only the Lord of the first is in an angle, even if the Moon is not in an angle, it signifies his holding and the prolongation of his imprisonment. Similarly if the Lord of the first or the Moon is in a fixed sign, it signifies the prolongation of imprisonment. If indeed the Lord of the first is in the first, it will also be so - namely the imprisonment will be prolonged. If it is in the tenth, his stay in prison will be longer, since what is signified in the first in days, in the tenth is signified as weeks: what is signified as weeks in the first, is signified as months in the tenth: what is signified as months in the first, is years in the tenth. And if it is in the seventh, what is signified as days in the first, in the seventh is signified as weeks: and what is signified as weeks in the first, in the seventh is signified as months: what is signified as months in the first, in the seventh is years. If it is in the fourth, what is signified as hours in the first, is signified as days in the fourth: what is signified as days in the first, is signified as weeks in the fourth: what is signified as weeks in the first, is signified as months in the fourth: what is signified as months in the first, is signified as years in the fourth.

And see if the Lord of the twelfth then aspects the Lord of the first, namely with the Lord of the first or the Moon being in the fourth: if so, evil and difficulties will happen to him in prison, so that due to that prison, and due to those difficulties, the death of the prisoner is to be feared.

And Zael said that if the Lord of the Ascendant is cadent from the Ascendant, and is joined to a planet in an angle, it signifies that his imprisonment will be prolonged after he had hoped to escape. If indeed the Lord of the first is in an angle, and is joined to a planet who is cadent from an angle, it signifies that the prisoner will lose all hope in prison: nevertheless he will escape afterwards. Next examine if the Lord of the first is joined to some malefic planet placed in the fourth, or if the Lord of the eighth is in the first: for then the prisoner will die in that prison. And understand the same of the significatrix (which is the Moon) as what was said of the Lord of the first.

If indeed the Lord of the first and the Moon (or only one of them) is joined with the Lord of the third or the Lord of the ninth, it signifies that the prisoner will be liberated. But if the Lord of the third or the Lord of the 9th house were the Lord of some angle (namely the tenth, or the seventh, or the fourth), his exit from prison will be delayed: however afterwards he will escape, nor will there be anyone who extracts him from prison: but he himself will shatter the bolts of the door, or his chains and flee; or he will operate in another manner so that he escapes from prison. However, if the Lord of the third or the Lord of the ninth is lighter than the Lord of the first, so that one of them joins him, it signifies that someone, even without the seeking of the prisoner, will work on his behalf, and make it so that he is liberated. However, if the Lord of the first is joined to the Lord of the twelfth, or the Lord of the twelfth is joined to him; or the Lord of the third, or the Lord of the ninth, is corporeally joined with the Lord of the twelfth, it signifies that the prisoner will flee from prison, and will be liberated in this manner.

But if the Lord of the first, and the Lord of the third or the Lord of the ninth, when they are joined together, were then joined to some planet heavier than them who receives their disposition, and this heavier planet is in an angle, they will signify that the prisoner will not exit from captivity, until that heavier planet who receives the disposition of the aforementioned significators leaves from the sign in which he is in; or until he transits as many degrees in the sign he is in, as there are who made up the house up to five degrees away from the line succeeding the angle.

To give an example: the line of the angle was the fourth degree of Aries: and the line of the succeedent was the seventh degree of Taurus, and the heavier planet who received disposition was in 25 degrees of Aries. By this method the prisoner will not leave until the receiver of disposition transits all of Aries, and there were 5 degrees remaining to transit of Aries, and two degrees of Taurus: since the other five are of the succeedent, as you know, up to 17 degrees of Taurus.

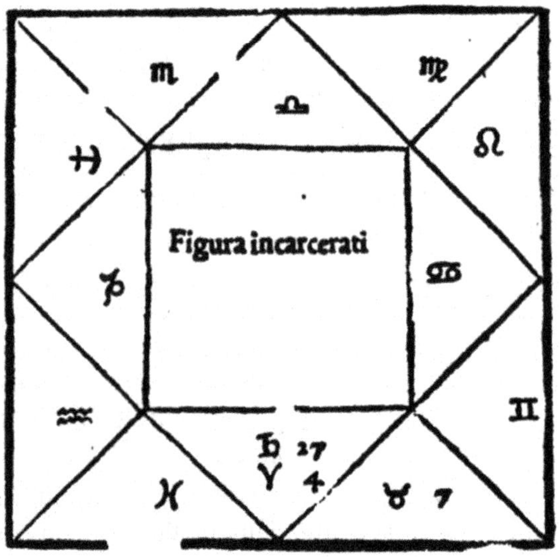

And also examine the planet who is the Lord of the house in which the Moon is in, and see whether he joins the Lord of the first or not: since if he is joined with him it signifies the prolongation of the imprisonment, and the delay of the prisoners exit from prison.

And Zael said, after you have finished examining the Lord of the Ascendant, and the conjunction of stars with him, examine the place of the significatrix, which is the Moon. Since if she is in a mobile sign, it signifies the swiftness of his liberation (besides Cancer, which is slow since it is her domicile). And Aries and Libra are faster in liberation than Capricorn. And he said that he will not be delayed in prison, and he will find many assistants there. And he said, indeed Capricorn signifies slowness, solicitude, and sorrow, and enemies labouring to keep him in chains. And he said, that if she is in a fixed sign, it signifies the slowness of his exit, and the slowest of them all is Aquarius. And he said that if the Moon is in a common sign, and he is not liberated before she leaves this sign, his imprisonment will be prolonged, and this all the more strongly if she is in a domicile of Jupiter and he does not aspect her. And he said, if indeed she is in the house of Mercury he will find goodness and joy in this prison. And he said, then examine the conjunction, and if it is in an angle, and is joined to a planet to the left of the Ascendant, and the Lord of the Ascendant gives testimony, it likewise signifies liberation. And he said, if the Moon is cadent and is joined to some planet in an angle, it signifies the prolongation of imprisonment, unless this planet is the Lord of the third or the ninth: for then he will be liberated when this planet changes sign. And if the Moon is cadent from an angle, and is joined to some planet who is the Lord of any angle, the prisoner will hope, and firmly believe he will exit from prison: nor will he believe that it is possible for anything to prevent him from leaving; and this hope will endure for him, and will be in him until that planet to whom the Moon is joined moves from the place in which it is, to the sign that was then an angle when the question was made (or when he was placed in prison), and again transits all of those degrees which then made the angle to which he was closer to; and then he will despair and afterwards will not believe that he will be able to leave the prison. But even if he will lose hope, nevertheless if the Lord of the angle to whom the Moon is joined, is itself joined to another planet who is in the third or the ninth he will still exit from prison after losing hope, and better than he believed. And always have this in mind since when the Moon is joined to the Lord of any angle, unless something else assists (as was said), it indicates a delay in exiting from prison.

Afterwards consider if you see that the prisoner is to exit from prison, if there is a malefic planet in the fourth who does not have domicile there, or exaltation, or two of his lesser dignities, and is direct in addition this: for this signifies misfortune which will befall him after his exit from prison. If it is Mars, he will be killed; if it is Saturn, he will be submerged in water, and perhaps he will suffocate from this submersion, or get badly beaten with sticks, or fall from a high place in such a way that he might die from this fall, or break a part of his body. And this will befall him following the significations of the sign in which this malefic is placed.

If the Lord of the first is then entering into combustion, so that he is already touched by the rays of the Sun, it signifies that the quesited prisoner is dead, or sick with a fatal illness. I say that this will happen if the aforementioned malefic is in the fourth, and doesn't have any dignity there, as was said. If indeed the Lord of the first transits combustion by one minute up to one degree, it signifies that he is ill, or about to fall ill with a dangerous illness; yet there is hope of liberation from this illness. If indeed he transits combustion, that is that he is separated from the body of the Sun by more than one degree up to five complete degrees, it signifies that he is ill, or about to be ill, with an extremely strong illness, but he will be liberated. If indeed he is separated from the degree of the Sun up until he is elongated from it by 12 complete degrees, it signifies that he is ill, or might become ill, with an illness that is not very strong or dangerous. If indeed he is separated from him by more than twelve degrees up to his apparition from under the rays of the Sun it signifies that he was ill, but has now escaped from that illness, and is free. And understand the same as this for any absent person whose condition is unknown: since if you find his significator like this, you can judge the same for him.

And Zael said that the further away you see this malefic in an angle from the degree of the Sun, the lighter his illness will be, and the more quickly he will be liberated from it. However, if the Lord of the first is then so disposeed (namely joined with the Lord of the eighth or with the Lord of the fourth), the prisoner, or the absent person will die from this illness. However, if you do not find him to be ill, but only imprisoned, and he is corporeally joined to Saturn, or aspecting him from opposition or square aspect without perfect reception, it signifies the impediment of the body of the body of the prisoner, and the diminution and detriment of his substance. If indeed Saturn is then impeded, even if he receives the significator of the prisoner, he will still impede him, but not as gravely as he would impede without reception. However, if Mars is in the place of Saturn, it signifies that he will be afflicted by a strong affliction; and that his prison will oppress him more than usual, and it will be stronger than usual.

And examine the significatrix (which is the Moon), who if you find impeded, disagreeable things and impediments will befall him in prison, which will come from unknown causes, and for reasons not discovered; and certain ones by nature, others by accident, even without any actions of the guards or those who hold him in prison, unless the Lord of the house in which the Moon is in then aspects her. Since if the Lord of her own house aspects her, it will reduce this malice and alleviate it.

Also examine if Mars is in the twelfth: for this signifies the death of the prisoner before he leaves that prison, and the master of the prison will be the cause of his death. The same is to be said of the Cauda. Similarly if Mars is the Lord of the twelfth, and is joined with the significator of the prisoner; and this more strongly if their conjunction is in the eighth. However, if Saturn is in the place of Mars, it signifies his death due to illness.

On Those Who Are Against Him In Prison

However, if you wish to know if there are any people who strive against the prisoner, to have him kept in prison and not released from it, whether he Is incarcerated or not: see if the Lord of the first and the Lord of the seventh aspect each other by a friendly aspect (namely a trine or a sextile): since if this is so, someone who is moved by a just cause will work against him so that he is not freed from prison, and will make him be held in chains, lest he escapes and is harmed because of this. And fearing this, he works against him so that he does not escape, unless he first reconciles with him, and is not found in a bad way against him. If they aspect each other from opposition or square aspect, it will not appear that the person who prevents him from escaping captivity will use justice, but rather he will harass him with insolence and injustice, and will strive with the greatest perseverance, to get the prisoner to concede his fortune to him, believing himself to be extorted of something from this, asserting that he has the right, and that he ought to hand it over to him.

And to examine the house of prison: look at the fourth if the prison is not very harsh, and if it is tolerable: but if it is intolerable and unusually bad (that is, very harsh) it will be signified by the 12th. If you find the Cauda Draconis there, it signifies the evacuation of the prison, and that the prisoner in question has left the prison: unless the Lord of the first or the Moon is found there: since the Cauda always signifies the evacuation and diminution of things.

IX

Whether Those Things Which Appear In Dreams Have Any Signification Or Not; And When They Signify Something; And When They Do Not Signify Something

Sometimes things tend to appear in dreams which terrify men, and other things which make them rejoice; and sometimes horrible things appear to them which are supernatural; and sometimes certain things appear which are natural; sometimes certain things appear which happen afterwards, just as they were seen in dreams, or almost like they were seen in dreams; sometimes nothing happens from any of the things which were see; sometimes they have some effect; sometimes none; sometimes men remember the things which they saw while dreaming; sometimes they forget them and don't remember at all. Whence men, not knowing the difficulty of judging of dreams, and those who are unable to know what is signified by them in terms of what will happen afterwards, often ask of an astrologer to tell them the truth about what their dream signifies. Whence, even if we cannot respond to them in accordance with what they want; it is fitting to tell them whatever can be said about their dreams.

If someone comes to you and poses a question on that which they dreamt, or narrates a dream to you, and you wish to know whether it signified anything or not; and if it did signify something, what did it signify: examine the Ascendant at the hour of the question or recounting, and all other houses, and verify their twelve cusps, just as best you can.

Next, since this chapter is under the heading of the 9th house, and since in a certain way this signifies religion, it is fitting that it begins from the 9th house, and that whatever can be discovered of it, be discovered from the 9th house. Therefore examine the 9th house, and give it to the dream. If you find one of the seven planets there, then this planet will have signification over the dream. If it is Saturn, it signifies that the dreamer, or querent dreamt that he saw something which terrified him, and which caused fear, and it was some extraordinary thing which is not truly natural, but seemed to him as if it were. However if the Cauda is in the place of Saturn, or if the Cauda is there with him, he saw an even more horrible and more fearful thing, and if he saw anything which made him flee, and he feared that it might kill him: or something similar to this, and it hardly appeared possible for him to escape, and so on.

Afterwards see in which house Capricorn falls, and in which house Aquarius falls: since that fear or horror will befall him from the things signified by these houses, that is. So that if Capricorn or Aquarius is the 1st house, the dreamer or querent himself will be the reason why that fear or horror came to him. And if it is the 2nd house, his substance is the reason why that horrible thing came to him If it is the 3rd house that horrible thing will come to him because of brothers, and if he does not have brothers, the cause of the fear will be from one of the other things which are signified by the 3rd house. And if it is the 4th house, this fear will come to him because of his father or grandfather: and if he does not have a father or grandfather, it will be one of the other things which are signified by the 4th house. And if it is the 5th house, the fear will befall him because of children; if he does not have children, it will happen to him from one of the things which are signified by the 5th house. And if it is the 6th house the fear will be because of his slave, slavegirl, or client: and if he doesn't have slaves, it will be one of the other things which are signified by the 6th house. And if it is the 7th house, the cause of the fear is an enemy, a wife, or an associate, or one of the things which are signified by the 7th house. And if it is the 8th house, it is death which terrifies him, or capture, or dead person, or one of those things which are signified by the 8th house. And if it is the 9th house, some journey is the cause of this fear, or flight, or one of those other things which are signified by the 9th house. And if it is the 10th house it signifies that it is a powerful person or king, or hanging, or one of those things which are signified by the 10th house. And if it is the 11th house, it signifies that it is a friend, or the substance of the king, or one of those things which are signified bẏ the 11th house. And if it is the 12th house, it signifies that it is an enemy or imprisonment, or one of those other things which are signified by the 12th house.

If you do not find any planet in the ninth, consider the tenth, and see if any of the planets are there, and judge according to this just as you judged by the 9th house: since whatever kind of planet is in the tenth, will be the significator of the dreamers dream, as to whether he dreamt something good or bad. However if there is not a planet in the tenth, then examine the first, and if one of the planets is there, he will be the significator of the dream. If you do not fin one of the planets there, then consider the seventh: which if there is any planet placed there, he will be the significator of the dream. If you do not find any planets there, then consider the fourth, and if there is any planet there, he will be the significator of the dream. If you do not find one of the planets there, then you will consider the third; if you do not find any planets there, then it is necessary that it is in the 2nd, 5th, 6th, 8th, 11th, or 12th - all of these six houses being ones which have the signification of the falsity of dreams; and that the dream which happened at that time will have no effect. And it will be possible that the dreamer forgot his dream, and so his dream disappeared and came to nothing.

However if Jupiter is in the ninth at the hour of the question, or at the hour of the recounting of the dream, then the dreamer saw a delightful thing, namely one of those things which are of the nature of Jupiter, as are the dignities of magnates; or he saw the magnates, nobles, or kings themselves or those who are fit to rule, or those who are placed in dignities and prelatures, and things of which men take pleasure in and are elevated by. Whence it is then to be seen where Jupiter is placed, and in which house Sagittarius or Pisces falls: because if either of them, and especially Sagittarius, is the 1st house, it appears that the dreamer himself will be the cause of the delightful thing which happened to him. If it is the 2nd house, his wealth will be the cause of that delightful thing which occurred for him. If it is the 3rd house, its cause will be a brother, or any of his relatives, or any of those things which are signified by the 3rd house. And understand in this way for all the other houses, as was said above in the significations of Saturn: in whichever one of the aforementioned six houses he is found (namely the ninth, tenth, first, seventh, fourth, or third), he will be the significator of the dream. However if he is not found in any of them, he will not have any signification over dreams, but he who was found in one of them (namely the first of them) will be the significator. Since if one planet is in the ninth, and another in the tenth, he who is in the ninth will be placed first, and will be the significator of the dream: and understand the same of the others.

And if Mars is the significator, the vision which that dreamer saw in his sleep, was a horrible thing, namely one of those things which are of the nature of Mars, as is bloodshed, or he will see mutilated men. If he does not see this, he will see burnings or battles, or an armed conflict, or the laceration of quarry: or perhaps the hunt itself, or the eating of raw or putrid meat; or he might have seen the instruments with which stones are hurled to destroy the enemies things, or any of those other things which are signified by Mars.

And if the Sun is the significator, it signifies that he saw a king. And if the Caput is with him, he dreamt that he saw God, or heavenly matters; or he saw luminaries, namely several Suns, or several Moons; or gold: or he saw himself flying, or another person flying; or anything which is of the nature of the Sun, and similar things.

And if Venus is then the significatrix, it signifies that he dreamt of sleeping with women. And if she then aspects Saturn, he dreamed that he misused them, or abused boys in an inhuman way (namely sodomy): or that he is with prostitutes or other women, and delighted with them; or saw games, singing, drinking, and fragrant things, and necklaces, and beautiful garments, especially those in which he delights; precious stones, and other things which are of the nature of Venus.

And if Mercury is then the significator, it signifies that he saw pictures or writings, and coins and commerce, or houses of prayer, and people praying in them; or something else which is signified by Mercury.

And if the Moon is then the significatrix, it signifies that he will see sailors, or sailing of the sea, or that he himself will board a ship, or see floods of water, or waters in which he swam; or he saw his mother or other women, and these women will be old rather than young.

And if the Caput is in any of the aforementioned places, whether he is alone, or with other planets, then it signifies that he saw gold, fragrant things, and delightful pleasure gardens, and things in which he delights, and the like.

And if the Cauda is the significatrix, it signifies that he saw dark smoke, or perhaps he saw someone consumed by fire, or saw mist, or ill people, or illnesses or weeping, or heard murmuring, or saw death, or the burial of the dead, or tombs, and he was terrified for this reason, or he saw verbal disputes between some people, or a beheading, and similar things.

And Zael said, and if the significator of dreams is in a masculine sign, it signifies that he saw a sunken place or it was almost as if he appeared to ascend from a sunken place to a high place, and he could not complete his ascent; or he dreamed of crossing over a place failing under his feet, and that he could not cross over it without great labour and great entanglement, and he appeared to go through a narrow place. And if it is a feminine sign in which the signifying planet is placed, it signifies fear, and that this dreamer saw a great elevated shore, from which he appeared to fall, or another high place, namely a cliff, or something similar from which he feared he would fall: and he saw himself sunken in a fearful place; or perhaps he saw a storm at sea, or a very great wind, which frightened him.

And if the significator of dreams (or the planet inducing fear)in Aries, Leo, or the first half of Sagittarius, it signifies that he saw a dark mist, a black, or someone hanged, or decapitated, or burned or grazed. And if the significator of dreams (or the planet inducing fear) is in Taurus, Virgo, or Capricorn, or the latter half of Sagittarius, it signifies that this dreamer or querent saw himself being cut, or stoned, or saw himself in a place where he was besieged, and from this he feared, lest he be oppressed; or it appeared to him that he fell from a bank or from another elevated place; or he fell into a place in which he was hidden and compressed, and it did not appear that he would be able to escape from it; or he travelled by a compressed and narrow road or place. And if Saturn is the significator, or if the Cauda is there, it signifies that he saw a demon, or a dead person causing him fear. And if it is in Gemini, Libra, or Aquarius, it signifies that he saw birds, winds, or the climbing of trees; or saw himself flying, or another person flying; or he fled from someone, and fled in such a way that he could be caught. And if it is in Cancer, Scorpio, or Pisces, it signifies that he saw himself board a ship, and this ship appeared to sink, or he saw another shipwreck or endangering of a ship, or submersion, or an overflowing of waters, and sometimes in places where there is not usually water; or he may see a flood or the sea.

And then examine if the Moon is in a fixed sign: since this dream will then appear to have an effect, whether for good or for bad. If she is in a common sign, something from it will appear. If she is in a mobile sign, it will wholly disappear, and there will be no signification for him.

Next examine the significator of the vision, and the Lord of the Ascendant and the Moon: and see if all of them (or two of them) are joined together; if at least one or two of them are joined with good planets, it signifies that utility and good will follow from this dream: and especially from the things which are signified by that house whose Lord is the planet who is the significator of the dream, as was said. If it is the Lord of the first, the utility will follow from his own person. If it is the Lord of the second, it will be an improvement in his wealth. If it is the Lord of the third, it will be in brothers, and because of brothers, or one of the things which are signified by the 3rd house. If it is the Lord of the fourth, it will be in the father, or because of the father, or grandfather, or one of the things which are signified by the 4th house. If it is the Lord of the fifth, it will be in children or one of those things which are signified by the 5th house. And if it is the Lord of the sixth, it will be in slaves, or because of slaves or small animals, or one of those things which are signified by the 6th house. If it is the Lord of the seventh, it will be in wives, or because of them, or one of those things which are signified by the 7th house. If it is the Lord of the eighth, it will be because of someone's death or imprisonment, or one of those things which are signified by the 8th house. If it is the Lord of the ninth, it will be because of journeys, religions, or religious people, or one of those things which are signified by the 9th house. If it is the Lord of the tenth, it will be because of kings, or the kingdom, or his office, or one of those things which are signified by the 10th house. If it is the Lord of the eleventh, it will be because of friends, or because of something that comes to him from an unexpected matter, or one of those things which are signified by the 11th house. If it is the Lord of the twelfth, it will be because of horses or cows, or one of those people who do not esteem him, and make themselves out to be his friends, or one of those things which are signified by the 12th house.

However if the planet to which the Lord of the first is joined is the significator of the vision, or either of them (whether with the conjunction of the Moon or without) were malefic: say that this evil will come to him according to the signification of the house ruled by this malefic, just as I said of the assistance: and judge according to this same method for the succession of the twelve houses or cusps.

X

On Bishoprics, Abbacies, Cardinalships, Or Any Other Kind Of Clerical Dignity, Whether In An Order Or A Religion: The Querent's Intention Being Whether He Will Obtain It Or Not

Even if it appears dishonourable to desire religious dignities, (when they should be expected to come as a divine gift from above): nevertheless there are many today who indifferently strive for clerical dignities, such as the Papacy, Cardinalships, Archbishoprics, Abbacies, Priorships, and other clerical dignities, and orders, (as much Brothers as others who are called secular clerics). Whence if anyone desiring to arrive at one of the aforementioned dignities arrives to you to pose a question over this, as to whether they are to be promoted to the dignity or office which they desire: you will first consider the sign on the oriental line, and see if its Lord or the Moon (both of them namely, or one of them, namely the stronger one) is joined with the Lord of the 9th (who has the signification of the quesited matter). And if the Lord of the ninth is in the ninth, or aspects it, it signifies the obtaining of the questioned matter, nevertheless with his own labour, seeking or striving. If none of them are joined with the Lord of the ninth, nor the Lord of the ninth with them, then examine if one of them (namely the Lord of the first or the Moon), is in the 9th: since this signifies the obtaining of that which the querent intended, provided that the planet which is in the ninth is not impeded, that is, that he is not retrograde or combust, and that no malefics aspect him from square aspect or from opposition without perfect reception: since this signifies the dissolution of the matter, even after it appears that it ought to be perfected. However if the Lord of the ninth is in the first, whether the Lord of the first or the Moon aspects him or not, whatever condition the Lord of the first and the Moon are in: or if the Lord of the ninth is joined to the Lord of the first (that is that he is lighter than him, and joins to him): it signifies the obtaining of the quesited matter without a doubt, without the striving of the querent. However if the Lord of the ninth is not in the first, and is not joined to the Lord of the first, but was joined to Jupiter, or even the Sun, by a trine or sextile aspect, and Jupiter or the Sun were then in the first: it signifies the obtaining of the matter with a little labour. If this conjunction is with reception and the aspects mentioned above, the quesited will arrive to him unexpectedly, namely gratuitously, while he is sitting in his own home. However if it is a square, it will not come to him so easily, even if it is with reception: and it will come because reception intervenes, even if the receiver who is in the first does not have any power there, and even more so, if the Lord of the ninth receives the Lord of the first or the Moon, regardless of what place they received from, even if it is from a cadent, it signifies the perfection of the quesited matter. If none of the things I said to you are so, examine if one of the planets transfers light between the Lord of the first and the Lord of the ninth, since this signifies the obtaining of the quesited matter by the hands of a legate running between the two parties, unless the planet who is heavier, (to whom the transferor gives light, which he receives from the lighter planet) commits his disposition to the other planet: since this signifies detriment, even after it is believed that the matter is perfected. However if the Lord of the first is not joined with the Lord of the ninth, but seeks his conjunction, and is joined to him before another planet cuts off their light, it signifies the perfection of the matter, but with perseverance and inconvenience. And if none of these things I said to you are so, but there is a transfer of light made by several planets from one to another, it is possible that the matter will be perfected: but not without great complications, and many words, entanglements, and threats from both side, and with a lot of racket and discord. If the Lord of the first is joined to a malefic who does not receive him, and this malefic is not the Lord of the ninth, nor commits his disposition to any of the planets who receive the Lord of the first or the Moon, the quesited matter will not be perfected. But if this malefic commits his disposition to any one of the benefics who is in a strong place from the Ascendant, it will perfect the matter: for the conjunction of malefics does not perfect matters unless they are received: but if they are received, it will perfect it, even if it won't be done easily.

And you should know this: that whenever a planet signifies the effecting of any matter, and he is in an angle, it will hasten the matter. If he is in a succeedent it will slow it. However if he is in a cadent, it will postpone it, even if it will be perfected afterwards: except in certain cases, of which nothing will be said at present, But you should understand these things, and similar things which are said here.

Also see if any malefic aspects the Lord of the first or the Moon from a square aspect or from opposition without reception: for unless he then commits his disposition, he will impede the Lord of the first or the Moon, and the querent will be angered and disturbed with him who interposes himself to deal with this matter, and the querent will be inimical to him, and will say that he is not acting faithfully. However if the aspect is a trine or sextile, he will not get angry with him, even if he does not perfect the matter.

If the Lord of the first and the Lord of the ninth both commit disposition from any aspect to a planet who is not impeded and not made retrograde before he leaves the sign in which he is placed, it signifies the effecting of the matter. Similarly if the Moon is received in the place in which she is, and is free from malefics and from all other impediments, it signifies the obtaining of the quesited matter, and that he will have many assistants striving to perfect what he intended. However if the Lord of the first and the Lord of the ninth are joined together anywhere, and neither of them are impeded, and the Moon commits her disposition to either of them, it signifies that the matter will be completely perfected. However if the Moon does not commit disposition to either of them, but is received by one of the planets, and they are joined together as was said, it still signifies the perfection of the matter, even if it will be slower.

You will say the same if the Lord of the ninth is joined to the Lord of the fourth, and the Lord of the fourth is joined to the Lord of the first: for this signifies that the quesited matter will be perfected, and without great labour. If the Lord of the first is joined with the Lord of the fourth, and the Lord of the fourth is joined with the Lord of the ninth, it also signifies the perfection of the quesited matter, yet with the greatest labour, duress, delay, and complications, in such a way that the querent will lose all hope of the quesited matter being perfected, even if it will still be perfected afterwards.

And after you know that he is going to obtain the quesited matter, and if you wish to know something else about his accidents: you will judge on them through the 9th house according to what you will find indicated below for the king by the 10th house, namely if he is to obtain it or not, and what ought to happen to him out of it. And you will follow these steps for everything: since all of these things will be discussed more widely there.

XI

On When A Letter Or Rumour Will Arrive, And Whether What It Is In A Letter Is Good Or Not

Sometimes certain business deals are done in some places of which the truth is not known by certain people, and from this they desire to know something. And they might enquire of an astrologer saying "When will we hear news of such a business deal?", or they might be expecting that some letter will arrive from somewhere, saying "When will such a letter arrive?"

If so, then you will examine the first and the second, and see if Mercury is in the first or in the second and so close to the end of the second that he seeks to go into the first, namely that he is one or two degrees below the second, going into the first; or if the Moon is joined to the Lord of the first, or if the Lord of the first is joined to the Lord of the Moon, or vice versa: or if Mercury is the Lord of the first according to how it appeared to Sarcinator: it signifies the arrival of the letter or rumour about the quesited matter.

And Sarcinator said, if Mercury is not in the first, then the letter or rumour will arrive at the hour in which Mercury enters the Ascendant. And if the Moon joins Mercury, it will come in the hour when they join together, or in the hour when the Moon comes to the Ascendant. And if this is not so, observe the significatrix (which is the Moon): for if she receives light or nature from Mercury in the degree of the Ascendant, or from its Lord, the time of the arrival of the letter or rumour will be when the Moon comes to the Lord of the Ascendant, or to the Ascendant, according to what the same sage said.

When The Letter Was Made

And if you wish to know how long ago the letter was made, or when the messenger who was supposed to carry the rumour began his journey, you will examine from which planet the Moon is separating, and see how many degrees away she is from this planet, and see if she is in an angle, and similarly if the planet from which she separates is in an angle: for this signifies that there are this many months. If they are in succeedents, it signifies weeks. If they are in cadents, it signifies how many days. And if you wish to know when it will arrive, see to whom the Moon is joined, and how many degrees are between her and the planet to which she is joined, or to whom she will join first, and according to this number place months, weeks, or days, by the aforementioned conditions.

XII

If Someone Is Ever Ignorant As To Whom A Letter Was Sent, And Wishes To Know Of What Nature The Recipient Is

If it is ever unknown to whom a letter or rumour was sent, and there is someone fearful of the letter or epistle being opened: examine the Ascendant of the hour of this questions, and see to which planet the Moon is joined to: since by her conjunction with the planets, you will be able to know the nature of the person to whom the letter was sent. If the Moon joins Saturn, it was sent to an old man, or a Jew, or a religious person wearing black, or off-black, vestments, or a commoner of base condition, as are farmers and the like. However if she is joined to Jupiter, it was sent to a nobleman or great religious figure, as are bishops and the like; or to a judge, or to a great, rich, and famous merchant. And if she is joined to Mars, it was sent to some leader of an army, or some bellicose soldier. And if she is joined to the Sun, it was sent to some king, or some magnate who is fit to rule, or another famous man. And if she is joined to Venus, it was sent to some famous, beautiful, or lascivious woman. And if she is joined to Mercury, it was sent to someone excellent at writing and Scripture, or a not very famous judge, or a merchant, or to a young man.

You will also be able to know the rank of the persons by the place of the Moon: since by how much she is in a greater and stronger place, by that much it signifies the greater status of the people. So that if she is in exaltation, and in an angle, it signifies the greater status of the people mentioned above. If she is in her exaltation and not in an angle, it will be something below this. If she is in her domicile and an angle, it will be something even more below this, even if it is only slightly less. If she is in her domicile and not in an angle, it will be something even more below this again. And triplicity is much below domicile, and term is something below triplicity, and face is below term. And if she is not in any of her own dignities, it will be a low class person.

XIII

What Is Contained In The Letter, Whether It Is Good Or Bad

Sometimes certain magnates and noblemen tend to want to redress people, but to avoid infamy, they send another person to them who will redress them. And the nobles give these men their letters or their epistles, saying to them, to go to such a place, and to such men, to redress them for their services, and sometimes for other reasons. And sometimes remuneration for services provided is sometimes contained in these letters that they carry; sometimes news of punishments for the evil deeds carried out: such as hanging, or decapitation, or mutilation, and similar things.

Whence some of them sometimes fear that something sinister might be contained in the letter, and seek certification from an astrologer on that which is contained in the letter. Whence, if someone were to ask you what is contained in such a letter, first examine the hour of the question, and see where Mercury (who is the general significator of all writings) is placed, and see who he is separating from. Since this planet alone has the signification of the letter, and the Moon does not participate with him, (which very rarely happens for her): but since she is the significator of rumours, and maximally those without writing, writings are given to Mercury. And if Mercury is separated from benefics, something good is contained in the letter: and that he will be remunerated for the services which he provided. If he is separating from a malefic, the letter contains something bad.

Then examine if Mercury, or the malefic from which he separates, is in the Ascendant: for this signifies evil in the person of the querent. If he is in the second it signifies detriment to his substance. If he is in the third, it signifies harm to the brothers, or to those things signified by the 3rd house, and so on for the rest. And if it is in the fourth, it signifies harm to an older relative, etc. And if it is in the fifth, it signifies harm to children, etc. And if it is in the sixth, it signifies harm to slaves, etc. And if it is in the seventh if signifies harm to the wife, etc. And if it is in the eighth, it does not have a certain signification, (except that sometimes it can signify the substance of the dead), nor does it in the 9th, or the 10th. But if it is in the 11th, it signifies harm to friends, etc. And if it is in the 12th, it signifies the loss of horses and cattle.

And if the Moon is then impeded, and she is in Aries, it signifies his decapitation or dismemberment. And if she is in Taurus, it signifies his beheading, especially if she is joined to Mars. And if she is in Gemini, it signifies the severing of his hands. And if she is in Cancer, Leo, Virgo, or Libra, it signifies a beating for him. If she is in Scorpio, it signifies detriment to his genitals. And if she is in Sagittarius, Capricorn or Aquarius, it signifies his imprisonment. And if she is in Pisces, it signifies the severing of his foot. If the Moon is free and safe from impediments, it will mean the safety of the significations of that house in which she is placed.

What Will Be The Response To A Letter

And if there is a letter sent to the aforementioned people, or anyone else, to which a response is expected to be made, and you wish to know whether the response will be pleasing to the sender: then you will examine if Mercury or the Moon, (since the Moon has a place here) are both joined to benefics: for then the response to the letter will be pleasing to the sender. If one of them is joined to a benefic, and the other isn't, the response will be partly pleasing, but not entirely in accordance with his wishes. However if both are void-of-course, there will be no response.

It appeared to Zael that you ought to judge the response to a letter by the second conjunction of the second more so than the first.

Whether A Letter Is Sealed Or Not

And if you do not know the truth of any letter which you desire to know about: and you wish to know something about whether it was written or not, examine the Moon: who, if she is in conjunction with Mercury, so that there is one degree or less between them, it signifies that the letter has been written, but is not sealed; nevertheless it will be sealed. However if the Moon is then separated from Mercury by 59 minutes or less, it signifies that the letter is already sealed. But if the Moon has transited him by 3 degrees, it will not be sealed, and it has not been written. If you find Mercury joined to the Sun, or separating from him up to the end of three degrees or less, it signifies that it is now written, and that it will be sealed.

From Whom A Letter Came, Or To Whom It Was Sent

And if you wish to know from whom a letter came, or to whom it was sent: examine Mercury, who if you find having transited the Sun, or the Lord of the tenth, or the tenth itself, by 15 minutes or less, signifies that the letter came from a king, or from a great nobleman, namely from those who are fit to rule. However if Mercury is joined to any of the aforementioned, it signifies that the letter was sent to the king or great nobleman mentioned above.

XIV

On Rumours - Whether They Are True Or Not, And When They Are Completely True, And When They Are Completely False, And When They Are Partially True And Partially False

It seemed to certain men that the chapter on rumours ought to be placed among the chapters of the 12th house, and they had this by the logic that rumours, as they are mostly found, are otherwise than they are made out to be; and when it is believed that there is truth in them, they are more likely to be found to contain lies, even if they are sometimes true. However it appears to me that the chapter on rumours ought to be placed under the 9th house, since many of them come from far off regions, and it is not known immediately when they are heard whether they actually are as they are made out to be or not. And this signifies that yet another occurrence was expected again, which will be brought from a far off region, which is in a certain way similar to journeys and places far removed. However you can take whichever one of them you want.

Whence, when you are asked about some rumour, whether it is true or false, or you heard the rumour itself, and you want to investigate its truth for yourself: examine the Ascendant of the hour of the question (or the announcement of this rumour) and the Moon. And see which one of them is stronger, and operate through him. Indeed the stronger one is that which is in an angle free from malefics. However if neither of them are in an angle, see if the Ascendant is a fixed sign, and if the rest of the angles are fixed signs also: for if so, it signifies the truth of the rumour, unless the Lord of the first and the Moon (or one of them) are joined with Saturn or Mars without reception, or if they are with the Cauda.

Then consider what the Ascendant is like, for if Jupiter, or the Sun, or Venus, or the Caput Draconis is there, it signifies the truth of the rumour. However if none of these are in the first, consider the third. And if you do not find any of them in the third, consider the 5th. And if you do not find any of them in the 5th, consider the 9th. And if you find any of the aforementioned planets (which are truth-speaking) in any of these places, it signifies the truth of the rumour; even if it is alone there, as long as it is not impeded. However the Sun, on account of his clarity, does not have as much signification over rumours as the other benefics have, for it is characteristic of the Sun to show certitude, something which is not easily found in rumours. If you do not find any of the mentioned planets in any of the aforementioned places, it is uncertain whether the rumour is true or not.

Examine if you find Saturn, Mars, or the Cauda in any of the aforementioned places, for this signifies the falsity of the rumour, even if they are alone there. Besides this consider (as I said) if the Lord of the first is in an angle free from malefics, and is not joined to a planet who is cadent from an angle: for this signifies the truth of the rumour. And if the Lord of the first is not as I said to you, then you should consider the Moon by the following conditions, who if you find free in an angle, and not joined to a planet cadent from an angle, signifies the truth of the rumour; and this more strongly if she is received. It is the same if the Lord of the first is in a succeedent of an angle, or even if he is in a cadent and joined to a planet who is in an angle, and if it is a benefic; for then the rumours will be true. If the planet to whom the Lord of the first is joined is a malefic, and it is not retrograde or combust, and receives him: the rumours are true. However if he doesn't receive the Lord of the first, the rumours will be partially true, but not entirely.

You will say the same of the significatrix as about the Lord of the first. Which if she is cadent from an angle, and is joined to the planet in an angle mentioned above, then these rumours will be true. However if this malefic does not receive the Lord of the first or the Moon, the rumours will be false. If it is a benefic planet in the angle to whom the Lord of the first joins, or who joins the Lord of the first, and it receives him, and it is not impeded, you will know that the rumours are wholly true, nor will it be necessary for you to consider anything else, only this thing alone: and this chiefly and maximally, if this planet to whom the Lord of the first joins, is in the tenth, since then they will be true in every way with all of their parts, without any diminution; in fact it is possible that there is more of these rumours than has been said at that time. You will understand the same of the Moon, as what I said to you on the Lord of the first.

You will also examine if the Lord of the first or the Moon is joined to any planet who is in an angle, and if they commit their disposition to this planet: for this signifies the truth of the rumour. And see if this planet to whom the Lord of the first or the Moon commits their disposition to is in the first: if so, the rumours have already been heard, and something was said about them in that land before you heard of them, or before the question was made to you regarding whether they are true or not. And if it is in the 4th, not a word has been heard about these rumours in that land, in fact they were secret up until now.. And if it is in the 7th, those rumours have already been made known, almost being announced publicly. And if it is in the tenth, even if these rumours may be new to you, nevertheless they have already been publicly divulged; and their truth is known among the men of that area.

If The Rumours Are Not True

If the Lord of the first or the Moon is in an angle, and is joined to a planet who is cadent from an angle, the rumours will be false, unless this cadent planet is a benefic, and receives the Lord of the Ascendant or the Moon, but something was said about them, so that they appeared to be so. If it is a benefic, and it receives the Lord of the Ascendant or the Moon, it signifies the truth of the rumours, even if they are not completely true, as was said. And if this cadent planet does not receive the Lord of the first or the Moon, or if it is a malefic (whether it receives the Lord of the first or the Moon or not): the rumours will be false, even if something was said of them; and nothing of them will arrive into action. However if the Lord of the first, or the Moon, is joined to the malefic planet itself who is impeded, it signifies that the rumours are false, and that these rumours will be quickly suppressed. But if this malefic is not impeded, and it receives the Lord of the first or the Moon, it signifies some truth to the rumours, even if they are not entirely true.

For Zael said that you ought to examine the Lord of the Ascendant and the Moon, and see which of them is stronger, and you ought to judge on the matter of rumours through him. From which, his intention was only to give force to one of them. Yet it appears to me that if we can use both of them (namely the Lord of the first and the Moon), that we should: however it does not seem to me that we ought to dismiss his steps.

You also ought to examine whether the angles are mobile signs: since insofar as it pertains to this, it signifies that the rumours are false. For just as when the angles are fixed signs, it signifies the truth of the rumours, in like manner when the angles are mobile signs, it signifies the falsity of the rumours. And the falsity of the rumours will be more strongly signified if the Lord of the first or the Moon is joined with any of the malefics by conjunction or by aspect, unless perhaps they are received by perfect reception, from domicile namely, or exaltation; but even with this, there will be little truth in these rumours. But if this malefic is retrograde, they will be false rumours, regardless of whether the malefic, or the Moon, or the Lord of the Ascendant, is in an angle or outside of an angle, and regardless of which planet is joined with it, and regardless of whether the angles are fixed signs, or not, or whether he is received or not - the rumours will still be false.

And Zael said that if the Moon is impeded in an angle, and is joined to a malefic planet who does not receive her, the rumours will be false. And examine if the Lord of the first and the Moon (or one of them) are joined to any impeded planet, specifically a retrograde or combust one, or one that is not retrograde, and does not receive him: for this signifies the falsity of the rumours, even if it is said indifferently by everyone, that these rumours are true, and they are believed to be true by everybody.

Nevertheless, you should consider as to what nature of these rumours which you heard, or of which a question was made to you about. For if they are about the matters which are signified and come to be through fire and iron, and bloodshed, and highwaymen and the like, and Mars is there, it will be said that he signifies them (to be true). And if it is about the tearing down of a house, or a castle, or a city, or similar things, and the Cauda is there, it signifies that there is something in the rumours. And if it is about a submersion, or a fall from a high place, and Saturn is there, or the Cauda herself, it signifies the same. And you can understand the same for the significations of every planet; and this more strongly if their houses are signs agreeing with their nature.

ON THE TENTH HOUSE

I

On A Kingdom Or Empire, Or Generalship, Or A Retinue Position , Or Any Other Lay Dignity Which The Querent Has Hope Or Faith Of Attaining, Whether He Will Attain What He Intends, Or Not

Men sometimes tend to desire dignities: namely kingships, generalships, or retinue positions, or other lay dignities or offices or a stewardship of an estate. Whence they enquire of an astrologer as to whether they will attain what they intend to, or not. And if someone poses a question to you on any of the aforementioned things, whether it is an empire, or kingdom, or generalship, or authority position, or judgeship, or a senatorship, or whatever other office, or whatever other dignity, whether it is great or small: even if it is the guard of some castle, or of some gate of a city or castle, as long as it arrives by way of an office or stewardship: the first is given to the querent, the tenth is given to the kingship, or office, or dignity, or stewardship.

Then examine the Lord of the first and the Moon, and see if both (or one) are joined to the Sun or to the Lord of the tenth (who signify the dignity or office); and that planet, (namely the Lord of the tenth) aspects the tenth or is in the tenth: for this signifies that the querent will get what he intended, but not gratuitously; but rather it will be necessary for him to struggle, strive, and seek in every way he can to be able to obtain the quesited matter. However if none of them are joined to the Lord of the tenth, examine if the Lord of the first or the Moon is in the tenth: for if so, he will obtain what he intended, provided that neither the Lord of the first or the Moon are impeded (namely that they are not combust, retrograde, or aspected by a malefic planet from opposition, or a square aspect without reception): since then it signifies the dissolution of the matter, even if it appeared to be arranged, and that it ought to be perfected. However if the Lord of the tenth is in the first, whether the Lord of the first or the Moon aspects him or not (whatever way the Lord of the first is at that time); or if the Lord of the 10th house is joined with the Lord of the first, so that he moves towards the conjunction, (that is, that the Lord of the tenth is lighter): without a doubt it signifies the obtaining of the empire, or kingship, or magistracy, or lay dignity, or office, or stewardship, without any of his own striving, labour, or inconvenience. And if the Lord of the tenth is not in the first, nor joined to the Lord of the first; but is joined to Jupiter, or Venus, or the Sun by aspect, (apart from the opposition of the Sun, since with the others the opposition does not impede as it does with the Sun), and the planet to whom the Lord of the tenth is joined is in the first: he will obtain the quesited matter with ease. If it is joined to Mars or Saturn, and this planet (Mars or Saturn) is in the first, and the Ascendant is one of their domiciles or exaltations, and the planet is oriental or direct, and one of them is not in opposition to the other: it signifies the obtaining of the quesited matter, even if it will be with complications, striving, or inconvenience; nevertheless it will be little or no inconvenience.

However it appeared to Messala, that whether the malefic was received or not, that the matter would be perfected, and that if the aspect was a trine or sextile, and the planet who was in the first was a benefic, the quesited matter would arrive to the querent in his own home, without any striving. If it was a square or opposition, or it was a malefic with a trine or sextile, it would also come to him with ease. If it was an opposition, and it was a malefic, it would come to him, even if it would come with harshness and delay: and all of these things are true whether the planet in the first joined to the Lord of the tenth has testimony in the first or not.

And Messala also said, that if the Lord of the tenth receives the Lord of the first or the Moon, from whatever place this reception is: the matter would be perfected with goodness, stability, utility, and profit.

And if there are not any of those configurations which I said to you, see if there is any planet who transfers light between the Lord of the first and the Lord of the tenth: since if this is so, it signifies the obtaining of the quesited matter, but not by the querent himself, for it will be necessary that another person interposes himself by way of managing the matter so that it is perfected; and it will be perfected unless he who receives the disposition of the other planet is then joined to yet another planet to whom he commits disposition: since this signifies the dissolution of the matter, after it will be thought to be arranged. But if he does not commit disposition to anyone, and is not retrograde or combust, it signifies the obtaining of the quesited matter. Similarly if the Lord of the tenth does not seek the conjunction or the Lord of the first, but the Lord of the first seeks the conjunction of the Lord of the tenth, and joins to him before another planet cuts off their conjunction: the matter will come to be, but not without the striving of the querent, and perseverance and inconvenience. Similarly if the Lord of the tenth is not joined to the Lord of the first, nor the Lord of the first to him, and if neither of them are joined to any of the benefics; but are joined to one of the malefics, and this malefic is joined to another malefic, and this other malefic is joined to one of the benefics, and this benefic is joined to the Lord of the tenth, if the conjunction of the first malefic is with the Lord of the first, or if this last planet joins with the Lord of the first (if the first was conjunct with the Lord of the tenth): it signifies the obtaining of the questied matter, allowing with many interjections, and a diversity of diverse persons. You will be able to recognise the significations of the above persons by the houses which are ruled by those planets by whom the conjunction is made from conjunction to conjunction, until the conjunction arrives at the significator of the questied matter, or to the Lord of the first or the tenth, as was said, even if this conjunction comes to be from the planet through all the seven planets.

And Messala said that the same thing will happen with conjunctions by body.

And he said that if there is not a conjunction between the Lord of the Midheaven and the Lord of the Ascendant or the Moon, and there is not a planet transferring light between them, then you ought to examine who is stronger out of the Lord of the Ascendant and the Moon, and operate through the stronger one of them. And if it is not joined to the Lord of the Midheaven, but is joined to another (provided that the stronger one is in an angle, or in a strong place): it will perfect the quesited matter, whether it receives the Lord of the Ascendant or the Moon, or not. And he said, that if the planet whom the Lord of the Ascendant or the Moon is joined to is a malefic, and it receives him, the matter will be perfected. However if it is a malefic, and it is not the Lord of the Midheaven, nor receiving the Lord of the Ascendant, and if this malefic does not commit its disposition to another planet, then the matter will not be perfected: since the malefic will destroy the matter. But if this malefic commits his disposition to another malefic, and this other malefic receives the Lord of the Ascendant or the Moon, the quesited matter will be perfected. And if this malefic commits disposition to a benefic who is in a strong place, the matter will be perfected.

Similarly examine if any of the aforementioned planets are in the first, or in the tenth, and if this planet is a benefic: for then it signifies the perfection of the matter, whether it is received or not, and that the querent will gain profit and will acquire substance for this reason. However if it is a malefic, and it receives the Lord of the first or the Moon, the matter will be perfected: however if it is not received, it will not be perfected. However if the 10th house is the domicile or exaltation of this malefic planet, and the malefic himself is in there, the matter will also be perfected, whether this malefic receives the Lord of the first or the Moon, or not: just as when a benefic is in the tenth, and the Lord of the first or the Moon aspects it: since then the matter will be perfected, whether this benefic receives the Lord of the first or the Moon, or not; regardless of whether or not it has dignity in the tenth.

And you ought to know this: that whenever a planet who is the significator of any matter is in an angle, it will quicken the effecting of the matter; in a succeedent it will slow it; and in a cadent it will postpone it, even if the matter will ultimately be perfected.

And examine if a malefic aspects the Lord of the Ascendant or the Moon from opposition or from a square aspect without reception: since unless it then commits its disposition to another, it will impede him, and the querent will be disturbed by the person who interposes himself to handle the matter, and the querent will not believe him to act faithfully; and it is possible that they will be made enemies due of this. And if it aspects from a trine or a sextile aspect, he will not get angry with him, nor will he charge him with anything, even if he will not perfect the matter. And if the Lord of the first and the Lord of the tenth commit their disposition to another planet from whatever aspect, whether it is with reception or without reception, whether it is a benefic or a malefic; and provided that is not retrograde, combust, or cadent, and does not exit from the sign in which it is in before the conjunction of those two Lords (the first and the tenth) is perfected with him; and if the Moon is joined to the Lord of the first or the Lord of the tenth: the querent will obtain the quesited item. But if there is a collection of the light or disposition of the Lord of the first and the Lord of the tenth as I said, and the Moon does not aspect either of these two planets; but aspects another planet who receives her from house or exaltation, or from two other dignities, and is not otherwise impeded (that is, that she is free from fall and combustion, and is not besieged by malefics, or in their opposition, or square aspect without reception): it signifies the obtainment of the quesited matter: and that many men will assist the querent so that the matter he seeks is perfected.

However it appeared that almost all those wise in the judgements of the stars agree that when the Lord of the first and the Lord of the questied matter are joined together, and the Moon commits disposition to one of them, that the quesited matter will be wholly perfected. However if she does not commit disposition to any of them, but the Moon is joined to a planet not receiving her, and this planet aspects the house of the quesited matter, or aspects the 1st house: it signifies that the querent will obtain a part of those things which he seeks, even if he will not obtain them in whole (if it is a divisible thing).

And Zael said that when the Lord of the Ascendant receives disposition from the Moon, the seeking of a kingship will be easier, that is, it will be gotten more easily. However if the planet to whom the Moon or the Lord of the first commits disposition is impeded, namely that he is retrograde, or combust, or cadent, or besieged by two malefics, or in their opposition, or square aspect without reception: it signifies that the matter will not be perfected. Next examine if the Lord of the 1st house is joined to the Lord of the 4th house, and the Lord of the 4th house is joined to the Lord of the 1st house: for if so, the quesited matter will be perfected for the querent, and without great labour. However if the Lord of the 1st house is joined to the Lord of the 4th house, and again the Lord of the 4th house is joined to the Lord of the 10th house, the quesited matter will be perfected for the querent: but not unless it is with such great labour, and such great duress, complications, and delay, and with the querent losing all hope of being able to perfect what he intended: nevertheless ultimately the matter will be perfected.

Where His Magistracy Will Be

After you have seen that the querent is to obtain the dignity, or office, or magistracy which he intended to obtain: examine the Lord of the first, and see if he is in his own domicile: for if so, you will know that he will obtain this magistracy or dignity, in the land in which he lives. And if it is in its exaltation, he will obtain a magistracy to which other magistracies and other offices are subordinated: and other dignities will be contained within it or below it: and as to whether he is to obtain this in his own land, or in a foreign one, it will not appear that it ought not to be very far from his own land. However if it is in its own triplicity, it appears that he will obtain a great office or magistracy outside of the land in which he lives, and more than 20 miliaria away from it. And if it is in its own terms, he will not acquire a great office, but rather it will be below the aforementioned: and it is possible that this will come to him because the person who is in charge of assigning this office is a relative of his: and for this reason he will be chosen and placed over this kingship or office: or it may be that one of his relatives is chosen for some office, and will commit it to the querent. And if it is in its own face, it will come to him on account of his own magistracy or his own wisdom: and this office will be lower than what was written above. However if it does not have dignity in the place in which it is, dignity will be given to the querent in a land where almost nobody knows him; and this office or this dignity or stewardship will be much below what is written above.

And if the Lord of the first and the Lord of the tenth are the same planet (which can happen with Jupiter and Mercury), and it is received anywhere by any planet, and the Moon is joined to him from any of the angles: it signifies the attainment of the quesited matter. However if the Moon is not joined with the Lord of the first, but is joined to another planet who receives her, and the Lord of the first is also received himself, and both of them are not cadent from an angle, nor from the Ascendant: the querent will obtain part of that thing which he seeks (if it is a divisible thing), but will not obtain it in whole.

If The Quesited Matter Is Not Obtained

If the Moon is impeded, and the Lord of the first is not received, and neither of them are in the house of the quesited matter: the querent will not obtain what he seeks. And it will appear that the reason why he will not obtain it, is because he seeks a thing which is not suited to him. However if the Lord of the first or the Moon does not aspect the Lord of the tenth, and the Lord of the tenth does not aspect either of them, and the angles are fixed signs, and there are none of the aspects mentioned above signifying the effecting of the matter: then examine where the Sun is, and where Venus is, and see if both of them aspect the tenth, and if both are received: since if so, it signifies the effecting of the matter, and that the querent will acquire the kingship or magistracy in which he has confidence in getting; and it will be useful and profitable to him, and he will acquire a great deal of money from it. However if both of them are not received, but only one of them is, see if the Moon then aspects him who is not received: for if so the quesited matter will be perfected since the Moon commits her disposition and strength to the planet who she joins. Also examine if the Moon aspects the degree of the 10th house; or even if the Lord of the first himself aspects the degree of the 10th house; or if one of them are in the tenth; or if the Lord of the 10th house is in the degree of the Ascendant: for this signifies that he has already been selected for the position, and news of his selection will quickly arrive to him.

And Messala and Zael said, that if the Moon is joined to the light of the Lord of the Midheaven or has transited above him, namely that she is north of him while she transits through his rays, or is joined to his body, and aspects the Midheaven, the querent will obtain it: and if she is received by the Lord of the house in which the Moon is placed, and both aspect the tenth, he will obtain the quesited matter. And if the Moon is in any sign in which the light of any planet is in, but it does not join her body before she leaves the sign she is in, the matter will not be perfected, unless the Lord of the first and the Lord of the tenth (or the Lord of another quesited matter), are both in places in which they have dignity, and they aspect the tenth or the place of the quesited matter.

And Zael said that a defect of the Moons condition and that of the Lord of the Midheaven, signify diminution in the matter of work; and this will be worse if the receiver of the Moons disposition is impeded: since then it signifies the detriment of the work. And he said if the Moon is joined with the Lord of the Ascendant or the Lord of the Midheaven, it will assist its effect And if the receiver and the Lord of the Midheaven push their strength and disposition to the planet who receives them, and the planet who receives them has strength in its own place and the place of the quesited matter, and it does not aspect the Midheaven: the matter will not be perfected in the same manner in which it was sought. And he said that when the significator is inimical to its own house, it signifies duress and complications in the seeking of the matter. And to be inimical to its house is to be cadent from it in the twelfth, second, or sixth; or to be in the eighth from its own house. And if it (namely the Lord of the quesited matter) aspects its house from the seventh, it signifies that the quesited matter will not be obtained, but it will not totally prohibit it from coming to be, but rather it is possible that the quesited matter will not be perfected, but if it is perfected, it will be with lawsuits, controversies and contentions.

II

Whether He Will Be Praised Or Censured On The Occasion Of His Kingship, Or Office, Or Magistracy

After you have ascertained that the querent is to obtain the kingship, or the other thing which he intends to obtain, and you wish to know what is to happen to him in this kingship, or office, or magistracy: examine the Lord of the first and his place, and see how he is disposeed: since he has the signification of what will happen to the querent from his kingship or magistracy.

However if you find the Lord of the first in the tenth, not remote from the degree of the 10th house by more than three degrees ahead of it, or at most 12 degrees behind; or if a benefic is there which is not impeded; or if a benefic aspects this place (namely the tenth), 3 degrees ahead, or five (or at most 7) behind; understand the same if there is a benefic not impeded, or aspects it (as said regarding the tenth): and also understand this for the eleventh - it signifies that he will acquire honour and praise from this office or kingship (provided that it is not impeded in a bad way from the impediments mentioned above) especially if the Caput Draconis is there. But if the Cauda is there, it will diminish a third part of this honour. However if it is in the 11th, it will be below this, nevertheless his kingship will end well, and good things will be said about him. However if it is in the first, he will be praised and good things will be said about him: yet certain men will strive to slander him: but their malice will not be made public. If it is well disposeed in other places, he will withdraw from his kingship or office, and will do so with neither great honour, nor censure, but in the way that leaders commonly withdraw from their governances, provided that there are not badly disposeed malefics in the aforementioned places.

However if a badly disposeed malefic is in the first or the tenth, who does not have dignity there: or aspects as was said earlier concerning the tenth and the first, and especially if it is retrograde or in its fall (and this will be stronger if the Caput Draconis is there): it signifies that the querent will be condemned because of it. And if the Lord of the fourth is a malefic and aspects him from a square aspect, or from opposition, it signifies that he will be captured and detained for this reason, yet without being put in prison. And if the Lord of the twelfth aspects him by the above conditions, he will be incarcerated. And also if the Lord of the eighth aspects him in the aforementioned manner, he will be confined in prison, and it is to be feared that he may die for this reason. And if the Cauda Draconis is there, it will reduce a third part of this condemnation.

And if there is a free benefic in the second, it signifies that he will acquire wealth for this reason, and benefits and good things will follow from it; or if benefics aspect it as was said of the other houses, and this will be better if the Part of Fortune is there: and if it is in other places it similarly signifies good and profit, and it will increase it); however if it is badly disposeed, it signifies evil and impediment. And if there is a malefic here, or aspecting from a square aspect or from opposition, it signifies the dispersion of wealth and its diminution.

And you should always keep this in mind: that whenever the Caput is in any house which signifies good, it always increases it for a third part. And whenever the Cauda is in any house which signifies good, it always diminishes a third part of this good. And whenever she is in any house which signifies evil, she will always reduce a third part of this evil, just as whenever the Caput is in any house which signifies evil, he will increase it for a third part.

And if there is a benefic free in the third (or aspecting it), it signifies good things for the querent's brothers, and for the querent from his brothers (if he has brothers). And if there is a malefic here, or aspecting the third from a square or opposition, it signifies evil and detriment.

And if there is a free benefic in the fourth, or aspecting it, it signifies that the end of this governorship will be good and praiseworthy. And if there is a malefic there, or aspecting it, it signifies that its end will be bad and disgraceful.

And if there is a benefic in the fifth, or aspects it as was said, it signifies good things and fortune from children or because of children, and that if he has children, good things will happen to them. And if there is a malefic there, or aspecting it, it signifies the contrary, as was said of the others.

And if there is a benefic in the sixth, it signifies that things will turn out well for him from slaves and servants, and that things will go well for his slaves and servants. However if a malefic is there, or aspecting it, it signifies the contrary.

However if a benefic is in the seventh, or aspecting it, it signifies that things will go well for those who are subject to him in that kingdom, and that things will go well for his scribes: and that his enemies will have good opinions of him. And if there is a malefic there, or aspecting it, it signifies the contrary of what I said.

And if there is a benefic in the eighth, or aspecting it, it signifies that the goods of those who he has to rule will be increased, and they will grow and be amplified. And if there is a malefic there, or aspecting it, it signifies that they will suffer detriment and diminution.

And if there is a benefic in the ninth, or aspecting it, it signifies that the ruler who was before him was honoured and revered, and that his governorship ended well for him. And if there is a malefic there, or aspecting it, it signifies the contrary of what I said.

And if there is a benefic in the tenth: or if there is a malefic there, it will be as said above on the 10th house.

And if there is a benefic in the eleventh, or aspecting it, it signifies that things will go well for him in the governorship or magistracy, and that things will go well for him in his kingship or office, and that he will be honoured and revered, and that things will go well for him in it. And if there is a malefic there, or aspecting it, it signifies the contrary of what I said.

And if there is a benefic in the twelfth, it signifies that things will go well for him from horses, mules, cattle, asses, and camels; and that nobody will plot to his detriment. And if there is a malefic there, it signifies that things will turn out to the contrary in these matters which I said: and especially if Mars is there (since then betrayal is signified).

And you should always understand that when I say "if a malefic is in such a place it signifies evil": I mean unless it has dignity there: namely house, exaltation, or two of the other dignities.

III

Again On The Same, And Its End

Similarly consider if you find the Lord of the first well disposeed in a good place: namely if it is in the 10th, the 11th, the 1st, or the 5th, not impeded, whether it is received or not, or whether it is with the Part of Fortune or not: for it signifies a good end. However if it is in the second, the third, the ninth, the seventh, or even in the fourth (but in the 4th is more weakly placed than in any of the above mentioned places), and is well disposeed, and in impeded in no other way: its end will be below this, but it will not be blameworthy or abhorrent. If it is impeded in any of the aforementioned five places, it signifies evil and impediments. However if it is in the 6th, the 8th, or the 12th, it signifies that he will be disgracefully deposed from his kingship or magistracy, and with opprobrium and shame: but more severe shame in the 6th and the 12th than in the 8th, unless it is received: since then it signifies that his second in command will impede him, and rise up against him in his condemnation, and this more strongly if the Caput is there. And if the Cauda is there it will be weaker: however if the Lord of the first is received he will not be impeded: and if he is impeded he will be freed from this impediment without great perseverance or complications. And if it is not received, and is in the aforementioned three places, and is otherwise impeded, something will happen to him after he is deposed, which will be more harmful to him, and more blameworthy than being deposed from his magistracy.

And if the Lord of the 12th house is joined to the Lord of the first, and it does not receive the Lord of the first, it signifies that he who is deposed will be bound in chains, and shamed, and his shame and condemnation will be signified much more strongly if this conjunction is in one of the four angles, and the 10th house is more blameworthy than all of them. For just as it signifies greater honour than the rest of the houses, so too if it is turned to the contrary, it signifies greater condemnation: since it signifies that he will be held in chains publicly for everyone wanting to see him, and everyone who wants to will be able to deride him. However if the conjunction is in the first, it signifies that he will be placed in chains, and there will be a rumour from this: but not as great as when it is in the tenth. However if the conjunction is in the seventh, it will be his own subjects (of whom he is the leader or governor) will be those who put him in prison or chains. However if the conjunction is in the fourth, he will be put in chains or prison, but there will not be much defamation from it. However if in addition to this the Lord of the 1st house is in the cadents from the angles, and is above the earth, even if he is joined with the Lord of the twelfth, he will not be captured in that land in which he was the governor, leader, steward, or official, but rather he will be led to another place, and he will be held captive there. However if it is below the earth he will be chained on the road when he is being led to the place of his detention. However if the Lord of the first, when it is separated from the Lord of the twelfth, makes his first conjunction with the Lord of the eighth, it signifies that he will die in that prison. However if the Lord of the first joins with the Lord of the tenth after he has separated from the Lord of the twelfth, and before he joins another planet, it signifies that after he is captured, he will be freed from prison, and another kingship or office will be given to him.

And you should understand the same if the Lord of the first is joined to Mars, since this signifies that the same signified things will happen to him as when it was joined to the Lord of the twelfth, and even stronger ones: since Mars signifies beatings and blows of weapons, and bloodshed, and also sometimes death, which the Lord of the twelfth does not do. And if Mars is not corporeally joined with the Lord of the first, but is joined by opposition or square aspect, and he is the Lord of the second or the eighth, it signifies the same as what was said above.

And also examine if the Lord of the first is impeded by any of the malefics: since the affliction which he will suffer will be according to the nature and significations of this malefic who impedes the Lord of the first. If it is Mars as I said, this impediment will be from shackles that bind the arms or legs (or both of them) and injure them with grazes: and he will suffer from iron instruments, and will be bound with iron bands, and perhaps he will be pierced by a sword or iron rods. However if it is Saturn, he will be imprisoned in a dark or subterranean jail, and will be beaten by canes: and he might be stoned or cut by rocks.

IV

When He Enters The Kingship Or Office, And Begins To Command Or Rule: What Will Happen To Him In The Office

And if you wish to know what will happen to him in that kingship or office, see when he enters into that office or his kingship or empire. And the hour of his entry is when he is placed on his throne, or begins to command or order, or manage the matters of the kingdom or office by way of assigning duties.

If this beginning is in the day, examine the Lord of the first and the Sun. And if the Lord of the first is badly disposeed, and the Sun is joined with Saturn anywhere, or malefics aspect him from square aspect or opposition without perfect reception: it signifies his deposition, and this will be his deposition from that kingship or office. However if you find the Lord of the first and the Sun in the aspect or conjunction of benefics, and they are in the first, or the tenth, or the eleventh, or the fifth, and in addition with this they are in a fixed sign: it signifies that his kingship or office will last and be prolonged, and he will delight in it: and the things which he wished for, and will delight in, will happen to him in it, and he will rejoice from this. However if the Lord of the first and the Sun are in corporeal conjunction, or even in the aspect of Mars without perfect reception, as I said, and he is north of the Sun, or Mars is in the tenth, and the Sun is in the first, and the Ascendant is a mobile sign: it signifies that a certain man of those who he has to rule over will rise up against him, and will strive to resist him in his kingship or office: and the king or official will fear lest he succeeds in deposing them from their office, and it is to be feared lest he will be killed, or die in another way before he completes his office. However if any of the aforementioned things are lacking, that is, that Mars is not in the tenth, or the Sun is not in the first, or the Ascendant is not a mobile sign: it signifies that this person will not rise up against him, and if he does rise up, he will not be able to succeed against him, and will succumb If the Lord of the first and the Sun (or at least the Sun), is corporeally joined with Jupiter, or in his aspect from trine or sextile, whether it is with reception or without reception, or in square or opposition with reception, or if Jupiter is in the tenth and is free from the above mentioned impediments, (namely that he is not retrograde, or combust, or cadent), and the Sun is in the first, or the eleventh, or the fifth, and if the Sun is in a fixed sign along with this: it signifies that his kingship or office will be very praiseworthy, and it will be a great honour, and will always increase in goodness, and that it will endure long in praise and fame, and that it will be useful and profitable to the querent, and that it will be said for a long time that "*such a man ruled us well and his reign was very useful for us*".

You should also examine if you see that the Sun in the sixth or the eighth, and the Lord of the first is in the first or the tenth, and the Lord of the first is Jupiter, or the Sun, or Venus: for if so, his office or kingship will be well disposed, and have a good end; except that it seems that he will become sorrowful during it, since it signifies the death of the person who promoted him to that office or kingship.

And if the entry to this kingship or office (namely when he begins to exercise his office or rulership) was at night: examine the Moon as you examined the Sun in the diurnal entry, and see if she is free from the impediments mentioned above, and that she is not combust, or cadent, or in the conjunction of malefics. If so, then it signifies that he will complete his rulership with the health and integrity of his body, and that he will remain healthy and will not be sick during this rulership.

And if the Moon is corporeally joined with any of the malefics mentioned above, or is in their square aspect, or in their opposition, or even in their trine or sextile aspect without reception, it signifies his deposition from his rulership, and that he will be deposed in a short space of time. And if the Moon, or the Lord of the house in which she is placed, is in a bad place: he will come upon bad things in that land, and in that rulership, and there will be many who will complain of him for reason of not doing or handling his rulership well.

And if this malefic who impedes the Moon is the Lord of the tenth, he will be accused of having ruled them badly.

And if it is the Lord of the eleventh, he will be charged that he took away in an evil manner, or wasted the goods of the community or king.

And if it is the Lord of the second he will be charged that he took away or wasted the money of the citizens who he had to govern.

And if it is the Lord of the fifth he will be charged with that disgraceful vice of abusing boys.

And if it is the Lord of the seventh he will be charged with using the citizens wives.

And if it is the Lord of the eighth he will be accused that he judged some people unjustly.

And if it is the Lord of any of the other houses, it does not signify a certain or a special charge, except for the rumours of the people and the foolish.

And if the Moon is then 4 degrees of less away from the Caput Draconis, or the Cauda, it signifies that this office or rulership will not be useful to him, nor will he acquire wealth or fame in it. If she is distant from the Caput or Cauda by more than 4 degrees up to the completion of the 12th degree, and the significator of this governor is impeded or detained, and the Moon is in a mobile sign at that time: it signifies that his detention and impediment will endure as many days as there are degrees between the Moon and the perfection of her separation from the Caput or Cauda, until she is elongated from it by a distance of 12 full degrees. And if she is in a common sign, it will last for as many months. And if she is in a fixed sign, it will last for as many years. And if there is a fraction of a degree there, and it signifies detention in days: one hour is signified for every signified for every two and a half minutes. And it signifies months, it will signify a week for every 15 minutes. And if it signifies years, it will signify a month for every 5 minutes. And if he is not detained or otherwise impeded, but if it is feared that something sinister might befall him, it will be feared until the Moon is elongated from the Caput or Cauda by those 12 degrees, just as was said.

And similarly examine if when he begins to govern or when he takes his oath, if the Ascendant is any of the degrees which are in the terms or Mars or Saturn, and if either of them aspect this degree: for this signifies that he will not do a good job of governing in this office or rulership, and that he will conduct himself disgracefully in it, and men will say disgraceful things about him. Even if the ruler is otherwise good there, it will detract from his goodness, and he will act weakly in it. You could almost say the same if the Moon is impeded in the 4th at the hour of his entry into that rulership. If the degree of the Ascendant is in the terms of any of these three planets: namely Jupiter, Venus, or Mercury, and this planet is fortunate and aspects the degree of the Ascendant: he will complete his rulership with honour and good praise, and all manner of good things will be said about him, and the sound of his name will be magnified for this reason, and all profit which is made on the occasion of this rulership will be said to be good by those who he has to rule.

Just as he will be praised from good works when there is a benefic in the first at the hour of his entry into the rulership or office, so too will he be condemned when there is one of the malefics there, just as was said: and it will be so much worse that he might die for this reason.

V

Will The Beginning Of His Rulership Be Good Or Bad, And What Will Its End Be Like

And also examine in the beginning of his rulership if there is a benefic in the first: for if so, its beginning will be very good and laudable - if that benefic is not impeded. However if it is impeded, or if there is an oriental and direct malefic there in its own domicile or exaltation, and who is not otherwise impeded: it signifies that the beginning of his rulership will be laudable, but not very much so.

And if in addition to this there is a malefic is in the 4th, it signifies that whatever kind of beginning it has, its end will be bad. And if there is a malefic in the first which does not have testimony there, as I said, it signifies that the beginning of his rulership will be evil. However if there is a well disposeed benefic in the 4th, the end will be laudable, and whoever said bad things about him at the beginning will speak well of him later, and will honour him, and will say good things about him. And if there is an impeded benefic there, or an oriental, direct malefic in its own domicile or exaltation, and not otherwise impeded, it signifies that its end will be laudable, but not very much so. And if such a planet is in both the first and the fourth, its beginning and end will be similarly deserving of praise. However if there is a malefic in both of them, both will be blameworthy.

Similarly if the Cauda Draconis is in the first, and the Lord of the first is in the 2nd, 6th, 7th, 8th, the 9th (unless it is the Sun), or the 12th, and this more strongly if it is in the conjunction or aspect of any malefic planet without reception, and if a malefic is in the first, 10th, 7th, or 4th; and in addition to this the Moon is impeded by one of the malefic planets: it signifies that his familiars will be unfaithful, and his ministers will be base persons, and his deputies and officials will be evil doers and will cause him to be sorrowful and trembling, and their actions will be such that they make him blameworthy in his kingship or rulership; and these evil deeds which they perpetrate will be the cause of the destruction of his rulership or kingship, and they will sadden him; and he will always fear that he may be maligned in his rulership or office as long as he remains in it.

And you should always have this in mind: that whenever any malefic threatens deposition from any rulership or office, and you find Jupiter in the tenth or the first, and he is oriental: either he will cancel the deposition entirely, or he will alleviate and delay it. And if deposition is not signified, and you find him in the tenth, he will acquire praise in that rulership or office: so that for this reason he will attain a greater rulership or office. However if a malefic is there, he will be detained and fettered, and will meet with the anger of the king or magnate who presides over him, and everything which arrived into his hands of wealth and profit will be taken away.

However if you find a benefic in the first, and a malefic in the 10th, and a benefic in the fourth, the beginning and the end will be good, however the middle will be bad. If you find a benefic in every one of them, the beginning, middle, and end will be good. If you find a malefic in the first, a benefic in the tenth, and a malefic in the fourth, the beginning and end will be bad, but the middle will be good. If you find a malefic in each of them, the beginning, middle, and end will be bad.

However if benefics and malefics are in the aforementioned places together, the significations will be according to the nature of the planet who has more degrees in that sign, but nevertheless the other planet will diminish something of the significations of the other: so that if a benefic obtained signification, namely that it had more degrees than the malefic, the malefic would reduce something of the good signified by the benefic; and if a malefic obtained signification, the benefic would diminish the evil signified by the malefic.

And if Mercury is joined to Jupiter in the tenth at the hour of his entry into the kingship or office, it signifies that he will complete his rulership wisely, and with discretion and reason, and he will increase the jurisdiction of those who he has to rule, and he will be increased. The same thing will happen to him if the Moon is joined to Jupiter in the 10th, and Venus is there also, or in the 11th, or the 1st, or the 5th.

And you should know this: that whenever you find Mars in the seventh in the hour of an entrance into a rulership or kingship, it always threatens death: unless a benefic is in the first. However if a benefic is there, and he is deposed from that rulership: the cause of his deposition will be fine and honourable, and he will rejoice from it, and he will not be sorrowful from it; nor will any harm or shame follow from it, nor will it be considered as being injurious to him.

And if the Lord of the 9th is joined to the Lord of the 1st, he himself will seek to be removed from this office. And when the Lord of the 4th is well disposeed it will always signify a good end to this rulership, whether this is in the entry of a king, or in a question.

And you should also take this as a given: that whenever you find Jupiter in any of the places or aspecting any of the places of the circle, and he is well disposeed, and is not retrograde, combust, or cadent from an angle; nor in Gemini, Virgo, or Capricorn: that no evil will be able to work any malice in that place which Jupiter will not shatter. Even if two malefics are in this place, and he is there, and is disposeed as I said, even if he cannot perform the good which someone would want, nevertheless he will remove all the malice of the malefics.

VI

If He Will Remain In That Kingship Or Office, Or If He Will Be Removed From It

And if someone placed in an office or kingship were to ever enquire of you saying, "See if I will remain in this kingship or rulership or not": consider the Lord of the first and the Lord of the tenth, and see if they are joined together from a corporeal conjunction or any aspect. And examine if the heavier one of them (who is called the receiver of disposition) is in an angle other than the fourth: if so say to him that he will not be removed from that office or rulership before the time that he ought to be. However if this receiver of disposition is under the earth, which is said to be "left of the Ascendant", it signifies that he will exit from this office or rulership, but he will return to it a second time; and this more surely if the receiver is received in the place where it is, since then it signifies that his return will be quick and honourable.

You will be able to say the same as this if the Lord of the first is joined to the Lord of the third or the ninth, or to a planet placed in these houses, and if after his separation from them he is joined to a planet in an angle other than the fourth, and by that much more will his exit from the kingship be good, secure, and useful. If they are separating from each other, so that their conjunction has already completed, and one has transited over the other: it signifies his departure from this kingship. And if one of them, or the significatrix (which is the Moon) commits their disposition to a planet in any of the angles except for the fourth, and this planet is slow-of-course: he will not be removed from this kingship or rulership until the receiver is made retrograde, or enters under the rays of the Sun, or leaves the sign in which it is placed: since that will be the time of his removal from his governorship.

If the Lord of the first is joined to some planet which is in the sign opposite to the house of its exaltation (namely opposite to the exaltation of that planet to whom the Lord of the first is joined): he will conduct himself in a bad way during this governorship; in such a way that his death will be feared for this reason. However if the Lord of the domicile opposite to the exaltation of the Lord of the first is joined to him, the men of this kingdom will bring false testimony against him, and this falsity will be believed by those ignorant of the truth, and this belief will remain in their hearts for a long time.

However if the Lord of the 10th house is joined to the Lord of the domicile opposite its exaltation, his kingship or the land which he has to rule will suffer great detriment and depression.

Besides this, if the Moon is joined to the Lord of the tenth, and the Lord of the tenth is in the tenth: this king or governor will not be deposed from his rulership. And if the Lord of the first or the Moon (or one of them) are joined to the Lord of the tenth, and the Lord of the tenth is heavier than them, and is in a good place from the Ascendant (namely in the 10th, the 11th, or the 5th), free from impediments; even if he does not aspect the tenth, nevertheless if he is in any rulership, he will be established over another kingship or governorship. But if this planet aspects the tenth, he will remain firmly in that kingship or governorship.

However if the Lord of the first and the Moon are in angles, and the angles are mobile signs, and the Moon is not joined to the Lord of the domicile, or the exaltation, in which she is placed: it signifies that he will depart from his rulership. Similarly if the Moon is joined to a planet who is not in any of its own dignities, even if it is received, unless perhaps the reception is from a benefic from a trine or sextile aspect, and this benefic is in the third or the ninth: he will depart from the kingship or governorship. This will also befall him if the Moon or the Lord of the first is in the 4th, and the 4th is Aries, Cancer, Libra, or Capricorn; and this more strongly if the Moon is then joined to the Lord of the fourth, and this planet is peregrine. And this will occur even more strongly if the Moon is joined to a planet who is in the sign opposite to its own domicile or exaltation, or if the Moon is in Capricorn. This will befall him likewise if the Moon is void-of-course.

VII

What Will The King Or Governor Do With The Wealth Which Is Acquired On The Occasion Of His Rulership

It happens sometimes to those to whom substance or wealth comes into their hands on the occasion of their kingship, or rulership, or office, that it is necessary for them to spend it, sometimes willingly, sometimes unwillingly. Whence if you (or another person whose interest it is in) wish to know on what he is to spend the wealth, and he poses a question to you on this, it will be necessary for you to examine in a different manner than in other questions. Since in this case the Lord of the 2nd house is to be examined, whom you will examine to see whether he is a benefic or a malefic.

If he is a benefic, and this benefic is Jupiter, he will expend it in good works, and things pleasing to God and men, such as building churches, treaties, hospitals, monasteries, helping the needy with alms, and the like.

However if it is the Sun, he will expend it on matters of kings, magnates, and noblemen, and on those things which pertain to temporal lay honours, or the building of houses, castles, or towers, and on those kinds of things which pertain to lay ostentation; and also in giving things to others by way of vain-glory, and similar things.

If it is Venus, he will spend it on sex, gifts to women, actors, garments, in feasts, food, drink, and by wasting it, and in exercising luxury. And if Venus is elevated over Saturn at this time (that is, if she is north of him), it signifies that he will spend part of his money in a blameworthy manner: on the use of that disgraceful and horrendous vice of sodomy.

And if it is Mercury he will spend it on things of which he expects profit, such as merchandise to sell, and in the manner of sales and purchases which are quickly repeated; and the whole of his intention will be in profiting, and most of his expenses will be by way of commerce.

And if it is the Moon, and she is in her own light, or void-of-course, this wealth will not be spent in his utility, and he will dissipate it, not knowing how, or on what, all the while consuming it in a wasteful manner. And if she is not void-of-course, he will spend it in the manner in which it would be expended if the significator was the planet to whom the Moon is joined.

However if it is Saturn, he will expend it in an unjust manner, and he will always fear that the manner of spending it may be harmful to him, and he will be worried around this, and will strive to spend it on the harming of others, almost by way of veneration, and things will go badly for those with whom he has dealings with, and with those who he gets involved with.

And if it is Mars, he will spend it on all things unjust, criminal, and evil; such as war, whispers, in perpetrating burnings, bloodshed, fornication, serving friends by arming them for war, and similar things.

VIII

On Someone Who Was Removed From His Kingship Or Office, Or On The Absent King, Whether He Will Return To His Kingship Or Office, Or Not

If someone was removed from their kingship, or from their governorship or lay office, just as sometimes tends to happen; or if some king or leader removes himself from his kingship or rulership, just as sometimes these type of men tend to set out for a distant place, and a question is made to you on whether or not the absent king will return to his kingdom, or the leader to his leadership, or the person removed from his rulership to his rulership, or the official to his office: examine as I will tell you in this chapter.

Since if someone enquires on behalf a king, as to whether he will return to his kingdom, or on behalf of a leader, as to whether he will return to his leadership (namely when the king or leader is absent); or if someone enquires who removed themselves from their office or kingship: always give the first to him, namely as much for the king as for the leader, as for the removed person.

From which you ought to consider if the Lord of the first is anywhere joined with the Lord of the tenth, and see if the heavier one of them (who receives the disposition of the lighter one) aspects the tenth: for if he does, the king will return and reign in his kingdom, and the leader will return to his leadership, and the person removed will return to the quesited rulership or office. However if this receiver of disposition does not aspect the tenth, then examine the significatrix (which is the Moon), and see if she is joined to any planet who is in the tenth or the first: for if she is, this signifies his return.

And similarly examine if the Moon is in Aries, Cancer, Libra, or Capricorn, for if this is so, he will return more quickly. If it is the Lord of the tenth there, it signifies the return of the absent king to his kingdom, and the person who was removed from their office or rulership to their office or rulership.

And if the Lord of the tenth is lighter than the Lord of the fourth, and is separated from him: it signifies the return of the king to the kingdom, and the removed person to the office (and likewise with the Lord of the first). And if the Lord of the fourth is lighter than the Lord of the 10th, and is joined to him, he will return and persevere in it.

Similarly if the Moon is joined to the Lord of the tenth, and she aspects the tenth, he will also return, unless she commits her disposition to a planet placed below the earth who is peregrine.

Similarly if the Lord of the first is received by an unimpeded planet; however if it is not received, he will not return.

Similarly if the Moon is joined to a planet who is in the 9th, it signifies that the quesited king will depart from his kingship (unless it is a benefic). However if the Planet to whom the Moon joins is a benefic, and it is in Aries, Taurus, Cancer, Leo, Libra, Scorpio, Capricorn, or Aquarius: it signifies the return of the king or removed person. And if she is in Gemini, Virgo, Sagittarius or Pisces: it signifies that the king is to acquire another kingdom, or the leader another leadership, or the removed person another office.

And Zael said that the king will rule this kingdom for three years, because the receiver of the Moon's disposition would not fall until it comes to the 12th place from the Ascendant. And he will be in better condition in the second year, and will be held in greater respect, and his desires will be more satisfied than they were in the first year. And it will be better if the Moon is joined with benefics; unless one of the malefics comes and enters the tenth before the receiver of the Moon's disposition comes to the 12th from the Ascendant at the hour of the question. Since if any of the malefics come to the 10th house of the question (which signifies kingship) before the receiver arrives to the mentioned house, it will impede the kingship that the king was going to obtain, and will not permit him to obtain it; and this more strongly if this malefic goes retrograde in the sign which was the 10th house at that time. And if he gets it, and the Moon is joined to malefics, he will acquire condemnation for this reason. However if she is joined to a planet in the 10th, he will acquire praise from this, and will endure in it for two years. This will likewise occur if she is joined to a planet in the fifth, since then he will reign in the kingdom or rulership for 2 years. And if she is joined to a planet in the 11th (and this more strongly if it receives her) he will remain in the kingship or rulership for one year, provided that none of the malefics enter into the 10th, and go retrograde in it. Similarly if the Moon is joined to a planet in the first, he will remain in the rulership for one year.

And if the Moon is joined with the Lord of the tenth, or if they are not joined, and both of them are well disposeed in their own places, and they are in Gemini, Virgo, Sagittarius, or Pisces, he will return to his kingship or office. However if he is presently in the office, he will persevere in it; and he will remain more strongly in it than he usually has up until this point, and another kingdom or office will be added on top of it. However if you find the Lord of the 10th and the Moon impeded in any of the angles from the corporeal conjunction of some malefic: it signifies that the absent king will never return to his kingdom, nor the removed person to his office; and if he is in it, he will be removed, and will remain removed forever.

IX

Whether Or Not A Kingship Or Rulership Is Going To Last, And For How Long

It was said in the preceding chapters whether someone is to obtain a kingship or not, and whether an absent king is to return to his kingdom or not, and the same of other rulers or officials removed from their offices, (whether they were to return to them or not). However now it is to be discussed if a kingship or another similar thing is going to last, and for how long.

Since if you saw the hour of his entry into the kingship, or when he received it, or when he was confirmed in it, or the hour of his question: you will be able to know the duration of his time in that kingship or office, and what ought to happen to him in it, and how his subjects will revere him, and how he will be honoured by them, and how the memories of him will be regarding those things which he managed in his rulership, and how things will go for him against his enemies, or those of his kingdom, and what kind of victory he will have over them, and how he will maintain the goods of his kingdom, and what he will acquire from the goods of the enemy, and similar things.

Whence the Lord of the first and the Lord of the tenth are to be examined to see if they are both suffering the misfortune of combustion in the sign which was the Ascendant (or the 10th, 7th, or 4th) at the hour of the entry or confirmation, or of his question over these matters, 3 degrees before the line of any of the aforementioned houses, or 5 degrees behind: for this signifies that he will be deposed from his kingdom or rulership.

You will understand the same for the planet who was in the first at the aforementioned hour, if he has any signification in the kingship or office, as was said in another chapter before this one. However, if what was said is not so regarding the Lord of the first, nor of the planet placed in the first, nor of the Lord of the 10th, and it is not joined to a planet in the first who has any signification over kingship in the hour of his confirmation or entry into the kingship: then examine if any planet is in the 10th, who has any signification over kingship, namely a planet who has some dignity in the 10th: if there is, you will be able to judge the same.

Likewise when Mars or Saturn arrive to the degree, or to the minute, in which the aforementioned planet was at that time, since then it signifies his removal without a doubt; and more strongly if they go retrograde in the same degree.

You could say the same if the planet who was the Lord of the 4th house of his entry to the kingdom or his confirmation is retrograde, combust, or is in the 10th house of his entry to the kingship, if the 10th house was the exaltation of any planet. However if the 10th house was not the exaltation of any planet, but was the descension of any planet, you will judge the same according to the planet who was its Lord, if the planet who was the significator of the king when his reign began aspects the planet whose descension was the 10th house at the hour of his entry to the kingship.

If you do not find a planet in any of the aforementioned places (namely the 1st, 10th, 7th, or 4th), or a planet disposeed as I said, and his entry to the kingship or the office was diurnal: examine if the Sun is joined to one of the malefic planets (namely Saturn or Mars), and see the degree in which they were joined at the hour of his entrance to the kingship. Since when the Sun arrives to that minute in which their conjunction was completed, minute for minute, and this minute is found in the angle of the tenth or the first (and certain men wished to say similarly for the 7th or the 4th, but I have not had as much experience of the 7th or the 4th working as of the 1st and the 10th), right on the line of the angle (or one degree ahead, or two after), it signifies that the king or governor will then be deposed. You will be able to say the same of his conjunction with Mars, as you said of his conjunction with Saturn. If the Sun is joined to Jupiter, it signifies his deposition when Saturn arrives to the degree and minute in which the Sun was placed at that time. And if it is not then, it will be when Saturn arrives to the degree and minute of his square aspect or his opposition. And if it is not then, it will be when he arrives corporeally to the degree and minute in which the Sun was at that time, unless the aspect or opposition happens before his arrival to that place. If his arrival to that place is preceded by an aspect or opposition, his deposition will be then. However if the Sun is not joined to Jupiter, but if Venus is joined to him, and she is then (namely at his entry to the kingship) in the 9th, or the 11th, and she has dignity there, then when Saturn or Mars reach the minute in which Venus was at that time, or to her opposition or square aspect (or their own opposition), just as was said in the consideration of the Sun, the deposition of this king will be at this time.

However if his entry to the kingship was nocturnal: then examine the Moon (who is the luminary of the night), and see if she is joined to Mars or Saturn: since this signifies that when the planet to whom she is joined arrives to the degree and minute of any of the angles, or to the degree and minute in which the Moon was at that time, or to her opposition, or to her square aspect, the promoted king will be deposed from his rulership. Also see if the Moon is joined to the Sun: since the Sun signifies what the Moon ought to signify. If she is not joined to him, but were separated from him, see if she joins Mars or Saturn: for then the signification will similarly remain which the Moon herself (or the Sun) ought to signify. If the Moon is not joined to the Sun, nor separated from him, or if she is joined to Mars, or Saturn (or Mercury while he is not placed fortunately): it signifies that the king or official will not complete his reign, whether this reign or office is long, or not; and whatever it is like, he will not persevere in it for one full year. If indeed the Lord of the first and the Lord of the 10th are suffering the misfortune of combustion in the first, the 10th, or the 7th: or if Mars is impeded: it signifies that the removal of the receiver from his honour or magistracy is quickly being prepared, nor will he be able to cheat this so that he is not removed in a short space of time or at least before a year of his kingship or office is completed.

And if you wish to know when he will be deposed from it before a year is completed: see when the Lord of the first or the Lord of the tenth suffer combustion, and in what place the combustion of whichever one of them will be: and when Mars or Saturn will arrive to this place, and when any of the aforementioned malefics arrive to this degree, that will be the time of the deposition of the promoted from his office or rulership. And if Mars or Saturn do not reach that degree in that year, his deposition will be when one of them arrives to its opposition or square aspect (namely of the place in which the combustion mentioned above took place).

Examine afterwards if the Moon joins Mercury, and if their conjunction is in Taurus, Leo, Scorpio, Aquarius, Gemini, Virgo, or Sagittarius, and it is a rulership of a year: if so, he will be deposed within five months. However if it exceeds a year, he will be deposed within 8 months after one year. If their conjunction is in Aries, Cancer, Libra, or Capricorn, and it is an office or rulership of a year, he will be deposed within five months. However if it is exceeding a year, he will be deposed within 10 months. If the Moon is joined to another planet which is impeded (whatever way it is impeded, whether by malefics or combustion): examine how many degrees are between him and the planet who impedes him, or between him and the degree in which he completes his combustion (namely the degree in which he unites with the Sun): since he will be deposed within as many months, if it is a rulership of one year. However if it is a reign which is believed to be forever, or for a long time, he will be deposed within as many years. However if the Moon is received in the place in which she is, it signifies that he will remain in rulership for one year. And if she is not received, but she is in the exaltation of one of the planets, and the planet whose exaltation she is in is received in the place he is in: it likewise signifies that he will stay in the rulership or kingship for one year. And if the Moon is not received, nor the exaltation Lord of the place she is in, it signifies his removal or deposition from the kingship or office.

If He Will Reign For A Second Year

And when you find that he is to remain in power for one year, examine when he completes this year: and its completion will be when the Sun will return to the same point in which it was when that king or governor ascended: that is, when he entered that rulership, and assumed that Lordship or magistracy. For the year will then be completed when the Sun travels around a full 360 degrees; and then the second year will begin, when he begins to enter that same minute that he was in when his reign or that rulership began.

To give an example: in the beginning the Sun was in the first minute of 5 degrees of Taurus: and he had passed 4 seconds of this minute when the Sun had travelled around the whole zodiac: and when he arrives again to 4 seconds of the first minute of five degrees Taurus, then the year will be complete; and when he will touch 5 seconds 5 degrees of Taurus, another year will begin, and this will be the second year after the first. Therefore calculate the planets to that hour, and to that minute of the hour, and verify the 12 cusps, (namely the first and the tenth and the rest of the houses): and then you will be able to know whether he is to remain in that kingship in the second year or not, and what ought to happen to him in that second year. And do this for the rest of the years if you see that he is to remain longer in his kingship.

On The Third Year

And similarly see where the Lord of this hour is, namely the Lord of Ascendant of the revolution of the year: since by him it will be known if the mentioned promoted person will remain in his rulership again for another year or not. For if he is well disposeed and free from the impediments of malefics, it signifies that he will remain on again for another year. And understand this for every revolution: since when the Lord of the Ascendant of the revolution is free from the impediments of malefics, it always signifies that he will remain on another year again in that rulership. However if the Moon is joined to a planet who receives her, see if this receiver is free from malefics: since if he is free, it signifies that he is going to stay in power for longer than was believed at the beginning when he was elected to the position. If this planet is not free, examine how many degrees he is away from the degree of the malefic impeding him, or from their aspect degree for degree, and take this number and use it, and take the number of the lesser years of the Lord of the Ascendant of the elevation of the kingship. Also examine if the Ascendant of the elevation of the kingship is one of the domiciles of Saturn: if so, add on 30 to the number of degrees which are between the planet who receives the Moon and the degree of the malefic impeding him. If the Ascendant is one of the domiciles of Jupiter, add 12. If it is one of the domiciles of Mars, add 15. And add the degrees of distance mentioned above, and the years of whichever planets lesser years together, and revolve the year for that many years past the year in which the elevation to kingship took place; and see if in that year if the Lord of the Ascendant of that revolution is combust in the 1st, the 10th, or the 7th, or even the 4th; or if the malefic mentioned above is joined with the Lord of the 10th in the 10th: since this signifies the destruction of the kingship, or of the land that he had to rule or to lead; and similarly if it signifies months, within as many months. If it signifies weeks, it will be within as many weeks. And if this malefic is in the 1st in that revolution, it signifies the destruction of his deputies and officials. And if the Lord of the first is combust in the 10th, it signifies that this promoted man will die in his kingship or rulership. And if this malefic is in the second in the revolution, it signifies destruction of the substance of the promoted man and his subjects in that year. And if it is in the 10th it signifies his depression and the loss of his rulership. And if it is in the 11th it signifies the loss and destruction of the tributes or tax revenue of his kingdom.

Whence you should examine which of the aforementioned superior planets will have authority in the elevation or entry of this rulership: who, if he is strong in the first, and some other planet commits its disposition to him, then it will signify that this rulership is to endure for as many years as there are degrees of distance between this planet and a malefic, plus its lesser years. However if it is weak (that is, if none of the planets commit their disposition to him), it will signify months in place of years. And if he is weaker again (that is, that he is not in the first, nor in any of his dignities, and no planet commits its disposition to him) it will signify weeks in place of months. And if he is weaker again, (namely that he is outside of his own dignities, and no planet commits its disposition to him, and in addition to this he is retrograde or combust) it will signify days in place of weeks.

On His Infamy After His Fall

Indeed after you have seen the wasting or destruction of his rulership, see if the Lord of the Ascendant of his elevation to kingship, (or the Lord of the tenth of the same), is retrograde or combust in the revolution of the year which is threatening this detriment. Since if it is next to the line of any of the angles of the Ascendant of this revolution, (that is 3 degrees ahead or 12 after), this detriment will be predicted by the mob for a long time, and it will be in the voice of the people; and it will be openly said by the men of this region that "this will happen to us", nevertheless they will not know what they are saying, but they will speak in an almost prophetic manner. If it is distant from the line of the angle by 4 ahead, or 15 degrees behind, this evil or destruction will occur somewhat faster, and it will be predicted and foreknown by certain men of that region, but not as openly as before. And if it is distant from the line of the angle by more than 4 degrees up to the completion of 5 degrees ahead, or behind from 15 degrees up to the completion of this angle, this evil and destruction will occur suddenly, and unexpectedly and secretly, and it will be hastened so that it is unforeseen.

However if you find Jupiter in the 1st or the 10th of the elevation of the kingship, or leadership, or another rulership, and he has any dignity there, or if a planet commits disposition to him: this will signify that the reign or rulership will endure for as many years as there are degrees of distance between the planet receiving the Moon at the hour of the elevation to kingship or rulership and the malefic just as was said, adding on the number of the lesser years of Jupiter, which is 12. If he is weak, it signifies months in place of years, etc., just as was said of Saturn.

However if Mars is in the place of Jupiter, and is strong and fortunate, or if one of the planets commits its strength to him, it likewise signifies years according to the number mentioned above. And if he is weak it signifies months in place of years, etc., as was said of Saturn, and it will be that much worse, and all the more so. Wherefore if Mars is in the first or the tenth, and the Moon is in the fourth or the seventh, or if the Moon is in the first or the tenth, and Mars is in the fourth or the seventh (unless Jupiter, the Sun, or Venus aspects Mars or the Moon): it signifies the destruction of the kingdom or region in which he was elevated to rule, by vigorous killing, and much decapitations and bloodshed.

However if the Ascendant is Leo, and the Sun is strong in the first or the tenth, or if a planet commits its disposition to him: it signifies that the kingship is to last for 19 years. However if the Sun is debilitated, it signifies months in place of years. And if he is more greatly debilitated, he will signify weeks (or possibly days) in place of months.

However if the Ascendant of the elevation or entry to kingship is any of the domiciles of Venus, and she is in the first or the tenth, strong in any of her own dignities, or if one of the planets commits its disposition to her, it will signify that this kingship or rulership will endure for as many years as there are degrees between the aforementioned planet receiving the Moon and the degree of the impeding malefic, with the lesser years of Venus added on (which are eight). And if she is debilitated, it signifies months in the place of years. And if she is even more debilitated, it signifies weeks in the place of months. Therefore revolve the year for as many years as were added on to the year of the elevation to the kingship or rulership, and then see if one of the malefics falls in the first or the tenth of the elevation or revolution: since then it signifies the destruction of this kingship: and also returns the same fear for the king himself, and it will be a great thing if he escapes destruction.

And if Mercury is then in the place of Venus (namely that the Ascendant is one of his domiciles, and he is placed as was said of Venus), it will signify that the kingship will last for as many years as the distance between the aforementioned degrees; and with as many months added on, as are Mercury's lesser years (which are 20). Since on account of his repeated misfortune of combustion he cannot give years. And if he is debilitated, he will add weeks (or possibly days) instead of months, to the number to the number of years from the distance. Revolve the year to this time, and judge the same as you judged in the case of Venus. Moreover, if Mercury is combust in any of the angles of this revolution, and the Lord of the tenth is found in the opposition or square aspect of Saturn or Mars, or if he is corporeally joined to one of them: it signifies the destruction of this kingdom, or at least the deposition of this king.

Moreover, see if Mars is then in the first or tenth of that revolution. And if the misfortune of combustion were to befall him, then it signifies the destruction of the kingdom or this Lord within as many months as there are years of his lesser years (which are 15), and if he completes his combustion degree for degree in one of the angles of the revolution of the elevation of this kingship: it signifies the destruction of the kingdom or rulership, and it is possible that it will signify his own destruction (namely that of the promoted king).

If the Ascendant is Cancer, and the Moon is free from the impediments of malefics, and is joined to the Lord of the domicile or exaltation of the sign she is in: it signifies that this kingship will endure for 25 years, with the number of the distance added on. And if the Moon is debilitated, it signifies months in place of years, etc.as was said on Venus. Similarly examine if the Moon is joined to any planet to whom she commits her disposition: which planet, if it is combust in any of the angles, will signify the destruction of the kingdom or rulership. And if the planet to whom the Moon commits disposition is received by any of the seven planets, it signifies that his kingship will endure for as many years as are the lesser years of this planet. And if then this receiver is debilitated, it signifies months in place of years, etc. as was said in the case of Venus. You will judge likewise when Mars or Saturn reaches the degree in which the Moon was, or to the degree of the planet to whom she commits her disposition, or to the opposition or to the square aspect of these degrees: since then it signifies the destruction of the kingship, or at least his deposition from it.

You also ought to know that when any of the aforementioned planets signify some time which shows the duration of some rulership to be a certain amount of years: and if in some revolution of a year it was going to receive an impediment in one of the signs which were angles in the hour of elevation or entrance to the rulership - you ought not to despair of his deposition from rulership in this year until you first examine the revolution of the following year. Having done this, you will see if the aforementioned planet is free from malefics, and from combustion and retrogradation: since if this is so, he will still complete his rulership. And if it is impeded by one of the aforementioned impediments: it will signify his deposition from that kingship or rulership.

Then look in the revolutions of the years for the rays of the planet who is the Lord of the revolution (or Lord of the profection, giving one year to each and every sign): and according to this you will be able to see what will happen to him in that year which you have revolved. And see what is the distance between his rays and the malefics, or the rays of the malefics from him: and you will judge according to the lesser distance. Which if they are in angles, you will give each degree of distance a month. If they are in succeedents, you will give each degree a week. If they are in cadents, you will give each degree a day. Whence, for as many degrees are there are between the rays of this planet who is the Lord of the revolution and the body of the malefics, or between his body and the rays of the malefic who impedes him, there will be as many months, or weeks, or days, until the arrival of that impediment which is going to come in that year.

And you will always make the Lord of the Ascendant of the revolution participate with him, and the Lord of the Ascendant of the elevation of entry to kingship or rulership, and the Moon, so that if he is well disposeed, and the Lord of the Ascendant of the revolution and the Lord of the Ascendant of the entry are well disposeed, and the Moon likewise: it signifies that the malice of the impeding malefic will be taken away and removed, in such a way that it will only harm slightly. And if he is badly disposeed, and the others likewise, it will increase the malice of the malefic, and it will impede more greatly and rapidly. However if he is well disposeed, and the others are badly disposeed, his goodness will be of little benefit. However if he is badly disposeed, and the others are well disposeed, his bad disposition will only harm slightly. However if he is badly or well disposeed, and one of the others is well disposeed, and the other is badly disposeed: the one who is well disposeed will assist his goodness, and the badly disposeed one will increase his malice and diminish the goodness.

And even if I said "the Lord of the revolution" to you, you will not understand that he is the Lord of the Ascendant of the revolution: for he is often different from this. Since he is the Lord of the profection for every year according to one sign. To give an example, the Ascendant of the elevation or entrance was 10 degrees Pisces. Jupiter was then the Lord of the elevation of this rulership. In the following year Mars was the Lord of the revolution or profection - Mars being the Lord of the second sign from the Ascendant of the elevation (namely Aries). In the third year the Lord of the profection was Venus, who is the Lord of the third sign from the Ascendant of the elevation (namely Taurus, which is the third from Pisces). In the fourth year the Lord of the revolution or profection was Mercury, who is the Lord of the fourth sign from Pisces, (namely Gemini). And so you will understand for the succession of the Lords of all the signs up until their end.

Also examine if benefics aspect the Lord of the profection, since this will signify the good condition of the king in the year of that revolution, if the Lord of the Ascendant of the revolution is in good condition (however if it is not in good condition, the condition of the king or ruler will be below what I said).

And see from where those benefics are aspecting him (or the Lord of the Ascendant of the revolution or elevation; or the Lord of the tenth of either of them; or the Moon). Since the good and the fortune will come from the significations of the house that this benefic is placed in, and from those of the house that this benefic is the Lord of. However if malefics aspect him and impede him, see from which houses the impede, and of which houses they are the Lords of: since the impediment will come from there, and the cause of his deposition will come from there: just as the cause of his confirmation and stability will come from the benefics and their places. And the salvation of the Moon is very effective in this: and her impediment harms greatly.

Furthermore, this is always to be placed in your work, and you should always fear this: that whenever the Lord of the tenth of the revolution is impeded by retrogradation, or combustion, or besiegement by two malefics, it always signifies a shameful and horrible deposition in that year. However if he is free, it signifies his strength and stability. And if he is oriental from the Sun, and he is fortunate, and he is one of the superiors, it signifies that he will be renewed in that kingship or office. And if he is one of the inferiors, and is occidental and fortunate, it will be similar. And if he is one of the superiors, and is occidental, it signifies detriment and deposition: and this more strongly if the Sun is cadent from the angles, and the Moon is in the 7th or the 12th. And if it is one of the inferiors, and it is oriental, it signifies the same. Likewise if the Lord of the 10th is joined with the Lord of the 4th: since this signifies deposition and evil. However it will be different if the Lord of the fourth is joined to the Lord of the tenth: since then it signifies stability. And examine if the Lord of the Ascendant of the revolution of the year is joined with benefics or with malefics, or if he is found in places in which they were at the hour of the elevation, and judge according to this, and according to the luminary who has authority.

If you diligently inspect each and every one of these things, and consider them well, you will be able to know about the durability, end, and deposition of any person promoted to a kingship, rulership, or office.

ON THE ELEVENTH HOUSE

I

On The Faith Or Hope Which Someone Has In Some Matter

Since hope is one of those things in which all men rejoice and which delights them, it is not surprising if men have hope of getting things which they desire; and from this men sometimes hope of getting things which are possible to get, sometimes of things which are impossible to get - and they clearly see that it is impossible to get these things, yet they still they desire them.

Whence if someone poses a question to you about some matter which they have hope in, see if it is impossible: if so, do not involve yourself with that judgement. However if it is one of the possible things, examine the sign of the Ascendant at the hour of the question (which is called the 1st house) and its Lord, and the Moon, and the Lord of the eleventh: and see if the Lord of the first or the Moon are joined to the Lord of the eleventh, or if the Lord of the eleventh is corporeally joined to the Lord of the first. For this signifies that he is to obtain the matter of which he has faith in. If it is joined by aspect, examine what kind of aspect it is: since if it is a trine or sexile without reception, he will obtain it easily. However if it is with reception, he will obtain it extremely easily. If the aspect is a square with reception, he will obtain it, but not very easily, even if it won't be difficult. And if it is without reception, or if it is an opposition with reception, he will obtain it with difficulty. And if it is an opposition without reception, he will obtain it with severe difficulty, almost after losing all hope.

If the Lord of the eleventh is in the first, or the tenth, or the seventh, or the fourth, and the Moon is joined to him by a noted aspect, or is joined to a planet who receives her: he will obtain the thing in which he has faith, in accordance with his prayers; unless the Moon commits her disposition to another planet who is badly disposeed. For if the Moon then commits her disposition to a planet, and this planet is in Gemini, Virgo, Sagittarius, or Pisces: it signifies that the querent will obtain something of the matter which he hoped for, but not so much that his mind will be content with it; nevertheless he will obtain it with little labour. However if it is in Aries, Cancer, Libra, or Capricorn, he will obtain it; but what is obtained will be very little, and will only be obtained with the greatest labour and difficulty. However if it is in Taurus, Leo, or Aquarius, he will obtain the whole of what he intended, and without great labour. However if it is in Scorpio, he will obtain it, but not entirely, and it will be obtained with labour, unless it is then received by Mars: since if it is received, he will obtain it in the same way as the other fixed signs. And if the planet to whom the Moon commits her disposition to is impeded, it signifies that the matter will almost arrive into effect, and it will be in progress, and will be fully believed to be coming, and it is even possible that he will obtain it: however it will be destroyed after being obtained, or after it is thought to be arranged. And if it is not impeded, but is in conjunction with some planet who receives it: it signifies the obtaining of the matter, and also that it will be more perfect than the querent believed. The same will happen to him if the Lord of the first is joined to some planet who receives him.

II

Whether A Person Spoken Of By The Querent Is A Friend Or Not, Or If He Will Become A Friend Or Not

There are some men who sometimes make themselves out to be friends of someone, or wish to say that they want to become their friend; however those wishing to be more certain of these things consult an astrologer, to see whether it will be so or not.

Whence if anyone comes to you to pose a question to you about this: examine the first and its Lord, and the Moon and the Lord of the eleventh, according to what was said in the preceding chapter; and see if the Lord of the first or the Moon is joined to the Lord of the eleventh by body or from a trine or sextile aspect; or if the Lord of the eleventh is joined with the Lord of the first. For this signifies that he is a friend, and that who said he wants to become a friend, will become one, and they will join together in a true and stable friendship. And if this is with reception, their friendship will endure forever; even being passed down to their successors. And if the Lord of the fifth then aspects any of the aforementioned planets from a friendly aspect, their friendship will even endure with their children, and other descendants. And if it is without reception, or from a square aspect with reception: that friendship will last for a long time, but will not be extended to the next generation. And if it is from opposition (whether it is with reception or without reception), or from a square without reception: that friendship will be whisperous, contentious, and will have many contrarieties: and each one will be contrary to the other, nor will they be very friendly, nor will their friendship be durable. And the opposition will devastate the friendship more than the square aspect.

On A Matter Which The Querent Does Not Wish To Disclose To You

However if someone enquires about some matter which they do not wish to disclose to you, but say to you "See if I will obtain the thing which I hope to obtain, or not": then you ought to consider the Lord of the first, and the significatrix (which is the Moon). And see if both of them are joined to benefics, and benefics to them, and the benefics are in angles (or one is in an angle, and the other is in a succeedent, or if both are in succeedents): if so, say that he will obtain the thing which he hopes for. If one is in an angle and the other in a cadent, provided that they are joined together from noted aspects, and it is a divisible thing, he will obtain part of the thing which he hoped for. If one is in a succeedent and the other in a cadent, he will obtain less than this. And if they are joined from cadents, he will obtain very little or nothing. And if they do not aspect each other, he will not obtain the thing for which he hopes.

And similarly see what planet the Lord of the first or the Moon is joined to, and what house it is the Lord of: since the thing will be of the nature of the significations of that house. And if it is the Lord of two houses, it will be of the nature of that house which is more greatly aspected or which he is going to aspect first, or the one which he will enter first.

ON THE TWELFTH HOUSE

I

On A Race Held In Any Place, Which One Of The Horses Or Other Animals (Whether Rational Or Irrational), Will Come In First

If anyone ever comes to you with a question on a race, whether a horse or another animal will win it, or who will come first in it: it will be necessary for you to examine this differently than other matters. Since the 12th is given to the animals running in the race, and the hour is given to the race, and the Lord of the hour is given to the animals.

Whence you should examine where the Lord of the hour of the question is at that time: who, if he is in the first, the querent's animal will come first. And if the animal is not the querent's, but another person's, and he wants to be certified of this, the judgement will be the same, and he will come before all the other animals: and this more strongly and surely if the Lord of the first and the Lord of the hour are the same planet: for if so, he will greatly precede the other animals. If it is in the 10th, he will come second; and if it is in the 11th, he will come third; and if it is in the seventh; he will come fourth; and if it is in the fifth, he will be fifth; and if it is in the ninth, he will be sixth; and if it is in the third, he will be seventh; and if it is in the second, he will be eighth; and if it is in the eighth, he will be ninth; and if it is in the sixth he will be tenth; and if it is in the 4th he will be 11th, or the equivalent of last; and if it is in the 12th, he will be last or the equivalent of it. However if there are more than twelve (which rarely happens): judge for them according to the aspect which the significators of the running animals will have to the fourth, or the twelfth of the house.

Indeed for the salvation of the person riding the horse, or the other animal, similarly examine the same Lord of the hour: who, if he is in his own domicile or exaltation, will save the riders body from impediments, unless the Lord of the eighth aspects him: since then it signifies impediment without the breaking of limbs. And if he is in term, triplicity, or face, and free from malefics, he will similarly be saved. And if he is in his fall, it signifies the fall of the rider from the horse, and he will be impeded in a bad way. And if he is in his descension, it signifies his fall, and it is possible that the horse will fall with him. And if one of the malefics then aspect him from opposition or square aspect, or is corporeally joined with him: he will break one of the parts of his body. And if this malefic who impedes him does so from Aries, he will injure his head; if from Taurus, he will injure his neck; if from Gemini, his upper arm, lower arm, or hands; if from Cancer, he will be injured around his chest; if from Leo, he will be injured around his back; if from Virgo, he will be injured around his navel; if from Libra, he will be injured around his hips; if from Scorpio, he will be injured around his privates; if from Sagittarius, he will be injured around his upper thighs; if from Capricorn, he will be injured around his knees; if from Aquarius, he will be injured around his legs; if from Pisces, he will be injured around his feet. However if the Lord of the first is in the eighth with a malefic, or otherwise impeded, or if in addition to this the Lord of the eighth is impeded, or if the Moon is impeded: it signifies his death from that fall.

II

If Someone Does Not Have An Animal Amongst Those Running In The Race Asks: Which Animal Will Win

And if someone who doesn't have a horse or an animal amongst the animals or horses running in the race, was concerned about the result, and he said "Which of the horses or other animals running in that race will win it?": by this question you will be able to see what animal will win, and his colour, his age, and his goodness, and fame. Whence you ought to examine the Lord of the house with a most truthful instrument that will not deceive you: which if you find in the first, or in the 10th, or the 11th, or if you find another planet in any of the aforementioned places, you will be able to say to him that the horse (or the other animal) which will win the race will be of that colour which is signified by that planet; and do not prefer the 11th to the 10th, nor the 10th to the 1st, but do prefer the 1st to the 10th, and the 10th to the 11th.

Whence, by knowing the colour of the animal, the winner will be known. Next, once you have seen which animal ought to win, examine if his significator is in its own house: if so, this animal will be noble, just as it is more dexterous among the other horses, and he will be renowned. And if it is in its own exaltation, he will be of greater fame, and greater renown, and of good stock, and he will be well accustomed to beating other animals. And if it is in its own triplicity, he will be much below this, and will not be an animal of great renown, nor of good stock. And if it is in its own terms, he will be below this again, and will be of hardly any renown. And if it is in its own face, he will be a relatively unknown animal, or he will be foreign, from another land, almost unknown in that land. However if he is not in these places, it is a completely unknown animal, and not of great worth, as is a rowney or something similar. And if the animal's significator is in its fall, he will be flawed and defective; even if his flaws may not be well known. However if it is in its descension, he will be more flawed and his flaws will be known.

Whether The Animal Who Wins The Race Is Old Or Not

If you wish to know whether the winning animal is old or not: examine the planet by which this animal is signified: who, if he is oriental, signifies a young animal; and if he is occidental, signifies an old animal. And if it is before the Sun or after him by five signs or more, he will be middle aged.

III

Of What Quality Is The Animals Master

And if you wish to know the quality of the animal's master, Zael said that if the Ascendant is the house of the Sun, he will be a king, but to me it appears that he will be greater than all the other men whose animals are running. And if it is one of the houses of Saturn, it will be an old man, not of good stock; unless Saturn is then in an angle, or in an optimal place from the Ascendant. And if it is one of the houses of Jupiter, it will be some famous and noble man, who has domesticity with nobles and magnates, or perhaps he will be a bishop or great judge. And if it is one of the houses of Mars, it will be some bellicose soldier, or bearer of arms, or perhaps some general. And the same philosopher said, that if it is one of the houses of Venus or Mercury, it will be some magnate or nobleman, or a woman, or a writer, or a sage or literary man. And if it is the house of the Moon, it will be some sailor, or some merchant who ran the animal in order for it to ascend to fame so that he could sell it better.

IV

On Things Which People Sometimes Fear: Whether What They Fear Will Befall Them Or Not

It sometimes happens that someone on account of a threat which someone made to him, or on account of an act he committed, or for whatever other reason falls into fear, and from this he comes to you to ask whether he ought to fear that thing which he fears, or not. And if you wish to examine this for him, you should examine the first and its Lord: and if he is in the first, or the tenth, or even the seventh or the fourth, free from malefics and their impediments: say that the threats are false, and the fear which he has is empty, and that he will not fall into any danger from those things which he fears.

However if the Lord of the first is in the houses cadent from the Ascendant (which are the second, sixth, eighth, and twelfth), these threats were made to him openly, and are common knowledge, and he fears threats made to him. And if they ought to befall him and be perfected: then examine the Lord of the first: if he is placed in any of the aforementioned weak places, and if one of the malefics aspect him from opposition or square aspect, or if they are joined to him by body: announce to him that unless he guards himself well, that which he fears and which was threatened might befall him. And if the malefics aspect from trine or sextile aspect without perfect reception, he will fall into great difficulty and great horrors, and will suffer detriment; however in the end he will escape. However if they receive him, they will impede very little or not at all. If he is free from malefics, and from their impediments, the fear has already increased in him in such a way that it cannot be increased any more, but instead it will be reduced, and he will escape from these threats, and from this fear. And if he is impeded by malefics (whether he is in a cadent, or a succeedent, or an angle) - and this will be worse if he is in an angle, and the malefic who impedes him is also in an angle: for this will similarly signify that the greatest impediment and detriment will befall him from this fear.

And examine if the impeding malefic who is the Lord of the second from the Ascendant: for then his substance will be taken away for this reason. And if it is the Lord of the third, his brother will harm him, if he has a brother, and if not, it will be one of the persons signified by the 3rd house. And if it is the Lord of the fourth, one of the things signified by the 4th house. And if it is the Lord of the fifth, it will be a child or one of the things signified by the 5th house. And if it is the Lord of the sixth, it will be a slave or something signified by the 6th house. And if it is the Lord of the seventh, it will be a wife or lover, or something signified by the 7th house. And if it is the Lord of the 8th, it signifies his death for this reason. And if it is the Lord of the ninth it will be a religious person or something signified by the 9th house. And if it is the Lord of the tenth, it will be some powerful nobleman, etc. And if it is the Lord of the 11th it will be some member of a magnate's household, etc. And if it is the Lord of the 12th, it will be the punishment of prison.

And if this is not so, but the Lord of the first is in the twelfth, and the Lord of the 12th aspects him from opposition or square aspect, or if the Lord of the seventh is joined to him from any aspect, or if it is corporeally joined to him: it signifies detriment and difficulty, and that an enemy, or the person who the querent fears, will conquer him and do harm to him. And if none of them aspect him, he will be liberated, and will escape from all of these dangers, and his enemy will not have power over him, and even if he is caught by the enemy, he will flee from him. And if the Moon is joined to a malefic who does not receive her, or who is not the Lord of the house in which the Lord of the first is placed: if the querent flees, he will meet with detriment and difficulty in that flight. And if this malefic receives the Moon, or is the Lord of the house in which the Lord of the first is placed, he will be liberated from all the things mentioned above.

You will understand the same about anything which is feared.

V

On A Diverse Multitude Of Things Which Are Asked About At The Same Time

Many times certain men have come to an astrologer indiscriminately asking him about many and diverse matters. And they believe that it is as easy to respond as it is to enquire. And it is easy to respond to them about a number of things at once as it is to respond on a single topic, although it is second best.

Whence since you do not have a determinate Ascendant for this, it is necessary that you give a more general thing to the querent, and this is the Moon; and the rest of the planets will signify the quesited things. Whence it is necessary for you to consider the number of quesited things: and if these things are six or less, you will be able to judge on them according to the conjunctions which the Moon makes with the six planets.

For you will be able to know the nature of the first thing by the nature of the planet to whom the Moon first joins after the question is made; and examine the disposition of this planet, and you will judge on the effect of this matter according to how he is disposeed. For if he is well disposeed in a strong place (such as the angles, or the succeedents of the angles), and in his own dignities, and free from the impediments which I have named to you many times, the effecting of this matter will be good. If his disposition is the contrary of what I said, its effect will be to the contrary.

Next examine to which planet the Moon is joined to after she is separated from the first planet; and examine what his disposition is like, and judge on the second thing according to that. Afterwards examine to whom the Moon is joined after her separation from the second planet, and judge on the third thing according to the disposition of this third planet to whom she joins. Next examine the fourth planet (the one to whom she will join after her separation from the third), and judge on the fourth thing according to his disposition. Next examine to whom she will be joined after her separation from the fourth, and judge on the fifth thing according to the disposition of this planet. Next examine to whom she will be joined after her separation from the fifth, and judge on the sixth thing according to his disposition. And you will understand the same of an aspect as of a corporeal conjunction.

And if these things, or questions, are more than six, judge afterwards by the triplicity Lords of the houses in which the planets are in when the Moon is joined to them (whether by body or aspect).

To give an example, the Moon was joined to Mars in the first conjunction which she made after the question was made, and Mars was in Virgo: then, using the method which you completed the number of the 6 planets, you will judge of the 7th thing according to the first triplicity Lord of Virgo, which is Venus. The Moon (after she was separated from Mars) made her second conjunction with Saturn, who was in Cancer: and so you ought to judge on the 8th thing according to the first triplicity Lord of Cancer, which is likewise Venus. In her third conjunction (after she separated from Saturn), the Moon joined to Mercury, who was in Libra: and so you ought to judge on the 9th thing according to the first triplicity Lord of Libra, who is Saturn. And after separating from Mercury, the Moon joined Jupiter, who was in Sagittarius: and so you ought to judge on the tenth thing according to the disposition of the Sun (who is the first triplicity Lord of Sagittarius).

After you have completed the primary Lords of the four triplicities, and there are more than 10 things, judge again by the secondary triplicity Lords, just as you judged by the primary ones.

And if there is a greater abundance of things, judge by the tertiary triplicity Lords, just as you judged by the primary and the secondary ones.

And if there is an even greater abundance of things (which never happened to me) judge according to the triplicity Lords of the angles.

Similarly if you are asked about some item, as to whether it is true or not: examine the Lord of the first, and the Moon. If they are well disposeed that thing will be genuine in its nature. And if this thing is gold, see if the Sun is well disposeed: if so, then it is genuine; if not, it is false. If it is silver, examine the Moon: for if she is well disposeed, it will be genuine silver; if she is badly disposeed, it will be false. If they are pearls, examine Venus: for if she is well disposeed, they are genuine; if she is badly disposeed, they are false. Understand the same as this for all precious stones, and for all expensive and fragrant things, as are musk, amber, balm, and similar things. If they are denaris other things sculpted in metals, use Mercury in their testimony. If they are religious ornaments, use the testimony of Jupiter.

And if someone enquires about multiple things (namely 2 or 3), asking which one of them is better or more useful (or more truthful, if they were rumours), or something else: such as which of two (or more) things he will obtain: examine the Lord of the first and the Moon, and see which one of them is stronger, and operate by that one. If the stronger one of them is in an angle free from impediments, and is received, it signifies that the thing which was named first will be more true, and better, and will be obtained by the querent. If it (the Lord of the first or the Moon) is impeded as was said, it will be the first named thing, but afterwards it will come to nothing; and if the quesited thing is obtained, it will be destroyed after it is obtained. However if the Lord of the first aspects the first or the Moon, and is received in a succeedent, or free from impediments: it signifies that the second of the quesited things will be true, and will be obtained. And if it is in a cadent, free from other impediments, and with reception: the third thing that was named will be obtained, or will be more deserving or true. However if it (the Lord of the Ascendant or the Moon) is impeded, and in a cadent, nothing will come of those things which were named to you.

VI

If Someone Is Invited To A Banquet, Whether They Should Go Or Not, And What Food Will Be There

Sometimes banquets are held in certain places, and in certain regions more so than others, with the Italians tending to hold them most often, and especially the Romanioli, and the Ravenna soldiers above all others. And many people are invited to these banquets (which they cannot willingly avoid) and also to weddings, and other great feasts. Whence sometimes they want to be made certain by an astrologer as to whether or not they should go to that banquet, or to that feast, and they pose a question to you about this. Or perhaps you yourself are invited to that meal, and you want to know whether you should go or not. In either case, examine the sign which was ascending at that time.

And see if the Moon is there alone, joined to nobody, since then it signifies that you will be able to travel to the meal, and you (or the querent) will neither be revered there, nor held in low esteem there. And if she is in the 10th, almost the same thing will happen, except that you (or the other person who enquires) will be held in greater reverence there. In the seventh her significations will be below the first. In the fourth they will be below the seventh, and all other places will be below this; and in accordance with how the house is weaker than the rest, so will he who travels to that feast be held in less esteem

If the Moon is in the first and is joined to another planet, see who it is that she is joined to: since if she is joined to Saturn, it signifies that there will be unfit, unclean and badly prepared food at the meal, and it will not be well displayed or ordered, and the peppers and delicacies there will not taste as they ought to, nor will the travellers to the meal rejoice from this food, nor from these delicacies, and they will regret going to it: whence it is better that you do not go to it, than to go to it.

However if she is joined to Jupiter, you will be able to travel to the banquet with confidence, since you will dine well there, and there will be good and sweet tasting food there, and there will be delicacies, and there will be foods there made with laughter and similar things, and you will be honoured there, in such a way that few people will be honoured more than you, or perhaps nobody will be honoured more than you.

If she is joined with Mars, you should not go to that wedding or that banquet: since there will not be tasty food there, and the food will taste bitter, and it is to be feared lest there be disputes and discord between the guests.

However if she is joined with the Sun, you would be able to go if you wished: for there will be good tasting food there, made with rocket or mustard; or country food and similar tasty things, and received and placed with foresight.

If she is joined with Venus, travel confidently, since it signifies that there will be delicious good tasting food there, and there will similarly be joy, games, and many delights, and there will be many diverse dishes, and diverse drinks, and there will be things there which are pleasing to you (or whoever else travels to the banquet), and in which you will delight: or the greater part of the food will be rich and oily.

And if she is joined to Mercury, it signifies that you will be well able to travel, since there will be many types and diverse kinds of food and drinks, and they will be appetising and sharp tasting. And good words will be said there, namely words of wisdom, and they will also narrate the deeds of the ancients there, and many new things will also be said, and they will recite heard and unheard things, believable and unbelievable: and it will also be a gathering of many men.

And Zael said that if the Moon is joined to Saturn from a water sign, from a trine or sextile aspect, they will eat trout. And if he aspects her from square or opposition, it signifies that they will eat cold meat, such as sulz and similar things. And if the Moon is in Libra, it signifies eating legumes. And if she is in Gemini or Aquarius, it signifies eating poultry. And if Jupiter aspects her, it signifies the consumption of delicacies. And if Mars aspects her it signifies the consumption of hot and roasted food. And if the Sun then aspects Mars, it signifies that part of the meat will be burnt. Other planets will not impede her.

However if the Moon is outside of the Ascendant, and is in the tenth, the meal will be similar to the one when she is in the first, but more renowned. If she is in the 7th, it will be less than this. However if she is in the 4th, it will be even less than this again. Indeed in the rest of the houses it will be less than this in proportion to the strength of each house.

VII

Whether The Banquet Will Be Held Over One Course Or Many

To truly know whether one course of food will be served at the meal, or many, examine what sign is then found on the oriental line: if it is a fixed sign, and its Lord is in a fixed sign, and the Moon similarly, they will contently dine on one type of food. However if the Lord of the first is in a common sign, they will have other food, (namely a second course), but it will be something less the first. However if it is with this the Moon is in a common sign, the second course will be bigger than the first, or it will be double it. However if the Ascendant is a common sign, and its Lord and the Moon are in a fixed sign, they will have two courses. If the Lord of the first and the Moon are in common signs, they will have three courses. If the Ascendant is a mobile sign, and the Lord of the first and the Moon are in fixed or common signs, they will have three courses, and something else after the third. And if the Lord of the first is in a mobile sign, they will have four diverse courses, with every kind of food, and something after this fourth one. And if in addition to this, the Part of Fortune and its Lord are in mobile signs, they will have many kinds of courses, perhaps six or more, without taking into account the fruits of trees and similar things, which are not counted among the courses at a banquet.

VIII

The Reason Why The Banquet Is Held

The worthless and the jealous, and those whom their hearts will not allow them to do good, are sometimes in the habit of saying, almost in the manner of a condemnation: "Why does he do that?" whenever someone from the nobility of his heart, or perhaps for another reason holds a banquet. And if you, or someone else who asks you about it, wishes to know the reason why they do it: examine the Ascendant at the hour of the inception of the banquet, or the question, or when you are called to this banquet, and examine from which of the planets the Moon is separated, and to which of them she is joined. Since if she is separated from one of the malefics, and is not joined to another planet, but is void-of-course : he is not holding this banquet for any manifestly apparent reason, but he was almost led by a certain insipidity to do it. However if she is joined to a benefic from opposition or square aspect, he is holding this banquet for such a reason that he cannot avoid it, such as for the reason of a wedding, or that such a thing is coming to his house, that he couldn't have it that he didn't have a banquet without blame, and similar situations. However if the aspect is from trine or sextile, he is holding the banquet in his own honour, and to rejoice and be happy with his guests; or perhaps that someone invited him to a banquet and he wants to return the favour, and similar things.

`How Long The Banquet Will Last

If you want to know how long a banquet will last, examine the planet to whom the Moon is joined at that time: which if it is in an angle and in a fixed sign: that banquet will finish in one course. If it is in a common sign, there will be two courses. And if it is in a succeedent and a common sign, it will not finish in two courses. And if it is in a cadent and a mobile sign, or even a common sign, the banquet will last two days or more.

If The Guests Will Fight

And if the planet to whom the Moon is joined is the Lord of her house, some people in that meal will have a dispute with each other, yet they will not leave the banquet without eating.

When The Food Will Be Served At The Banquet

To know how the food will be brought out at the banquet: you should examine the Lord of the hour of the inception of the banquet, or the question, or the beginning of the journey when someone travels there, to see whether the Lord of the hour is found in the first or the tenth. For then everything will be obtained and prepared well and orderly, safe from the conditions mentioned above; and the things to be served will be on the served before they are seated. And if it is in the 4th or the 7th they will be seated first, and the place will be full of guests before the food is served.

When To Beware Of The Food At A Banquet

And if you (or another person travelling to the banquet) fears that the food there will have to be to be avoided, examine if the Moon is then in Cancer, Libra, or Capricorn in the conjunction or aspect of any malefics, (unless she is aspected by Saturn or Mars in Capricorn): since then the plants, whether cooked or raw, are not to be eaten; and when she is in Libra, and aspected by any of the malefics, or corporeally joined to them, not even are legumes to be eaten; likewise if she is in Virgo.

And Zael said that if the Moon is in Scorpio with the Cauda, fatty things are not to be eaten. And if she is in Leo or Sagittarius, the flesh of wild animals is not to be eaten. And if she is in Pisces, trout, or other salty fish are not to be eaten. And understand the same for all of these things when the Moon is in the aforementioned signs in the square or opposition aspects of malefics without reception.

IX

Which House Signifies Meals, The Reason, And Similar Things Of It

And Zael said that the Ascendant signifies the reason for the banquet. And he said, that if the Ascendant of the meal is any of the domiciles of Venus, that it will be held because of a wedding. And if it is one of the domiciles of Mercury it will be held because of children. And if it is one of the domiciles of Jupiter it will be held because of a friend.

And the second from the Ascendant signifies the drinking vessels, and the furniture of the house. Whence if the 2nd house is a common sign, the vessels will be coloured. And if Mars is then in the second, the vessel will be made with bronze. And if Venus is there, it will be made with silver. And if Jupiter is there, it will be made with silver and gold. And if Saturn is there it will be wood or earthenware. And if there is a benefic in the second, it will signify the beauty of the ornaments of the house. And if that benefic has dignity in the second, those ornaments will be their own. However if it is peregrine, they will be borrowed.

The third signifies the guests. If there is a benefic there, they will be men of good condition. If Saturn is there, they will be low class. However if Mars is there, they will be whisperers, or they will be bellicose men, or highwaymen, and the like.

The fourth signifies the place of the banquet. If there is a benefic there, it will be a beautiful, fitting, and decent place. However if there is a malefic there, it will be an unsuitable, shameful, or foul place. And Zael said that if it is a common sign, the place of the banquet will be in a porch. And if the Sun or Jupiter is there, it will be in an enclosed space in the house, or at midday.

And the fifth signifies their drinks. If the fifth is a fixed sign, they will have one kind of drink. If it is a common sign, there will be diverse drinks. And if Jupiter or Mercury are in the fifth, their drinks will be sweet and tasty. If Mars is there, the drinks will taste bitter. And if Mars is there impeded by Saturn, the drinks will taste acrid. And if the Sun is there, they will be harsh with some sharpness. And if Venus is there, it will be honeyed-wine, or something else sweet and good-tasting. However if the Moon is there, they will be weak drinks.

The sixth signifies the servants at the banquet. If there is a benefic here, the servants will be fitting and decent. If there is a malefic here, they will be inept and dirty, not knowing how to serve.

The seventh signifies the cooks and bartenders. If there is a benefic there, they will be apt; if there is a malefic there, they will be inept.

The eighth signifies stewards.

The ninth signifies those placing and carrying the courses on dishes. If there is a benefic here, they will be fit for this, and will know how to do it well. However if there is a malefic here, they will not be good at it.

The tenth signifies the general goodness of the banquet, and the merriment which the guests will have together. And if there is a benefic there, it will be a decent and laudable banquet, and the guests will rejoice and be happy together. And if there is a malefic there, it will be an indecent meal, in such a way that the guests will be hateful towards their fellow guests.

The eleventh signifies if the host and the guests are friends.

The twelfth signifies the host of the banquet or the head of the household. If there is a benefic there, it will show the joy and happiness which he will have from the banquet. However if there is a malefic there, he will be sorrowful within himself, and will regret holding the banquet.

And whenever you find a benefic in any of the aforementioned places, and it is fortunate, it signifies the increase of the good. And if a malefic is unfortunate in any of the aforementioned places, it signifies the increase of the malice.

FINIS

www.ingramcontent.com/pod-product-compliance
Lightning Source LLC
Chambersburg PA
CBHW062000090426
42811CB00006B/998
* 9 7 8 1 5 2 7 2 9 4 7 6 9 *